The Unity of Public Law

The Unity of Public Law

Edited by
DAVID DYZENHAUS
University of Toronto

OXFORD AND PORTLAND OREGON
2004

Published in North America (US and Canada) by
Hart Publishing
c/o International Specialized Book Services
5804 NE Hassalo Street
Portland, Oregon
97213-3644
USA

© The editor and contributors 2004

The contributors have asserted their right under the Copyright,
Designs and Patents Act 1988,
to be identified as the authors of this work.

Hart Publishing is a specialist legal publisher based in Oxford, England.
To order further copies of this book or to request a list of
other publications please write to:

Hart Publishing, Salters Boatyard, Folly Bridge,
Abingdon Rd, Oxford, OX1 4LB
Telephone: +44 (0)1865 245533 Fax: +44 (0) 1865 794882
email: mail@hartpub.co.uk
WEBSITE: http//:www.hartpub.co.uk

British Library Cataloguing in Publication Data
Data Available

ISBN 1-84113-434-1 (hardback)

Typeset by Olympus Infotech Pvt. Ltd., India, in Sabon 10/12 pt.
Printed and bound in Great Britain by
Biddles Ltd, *www.biddles.co.uk*

Preface and Acknowledgments

This book is the product of a conference held at the Faculty of Law of the University of Toronto in January 2003. Its focus might seem narrow, the decision of the Supreme Court of Canada in 1999 in *Baker v Canada (Minister of Citizenship and Immigration)* [1999] 2 SCR 817. But it will be quickly apparent to the reader that the decision unites themes and opens up questions of universal significance for the common law world, as lawyers and judges grapple with their role in public law in an era of experiments in constitutionalism and in domestic implementation of human rights. Indeed, those themes and questions have a new urgency in the wake of the legislative, executive and judicial reactions to the events of 11 September 2001.

In particular, *Baker* seems to presuppose the unity of public law, where by unity I mean a public law based in fundamental constitutional values. Such values include human rights and they are expressed in the materials of administrative law, constitutional law and public international law.

All the contributions to this book were prepared and circulated before the conference, and then revised in its light, with several exceptions. My chapter was written after the conference and Mike Taggart's was first delivered, more or less *ex tempore*, in the final wrap up session of the conference and so written in full for the first time after the conference. In addition, in order to promote discussion at the conference, those who contributed papers did not present them. Instead, at each panel all the papers for that panel were presented by a presenter/commentator, who then had the opportunity after the conference to work up his or her presentation into an independent contribution.

The idea for the conference was first proposed by Mike Taggart, after he, Murray Hunt and I had together taught an intensive course on the internationalisation of administrative law at the University of Toronto in 2001. That course focused on *Baker* and the decision has continued to fascinate us. While I was in the early throes of organising that conference, I learned that my colleague Mayo Moran was organising a conference similarly inspired by *Baker*. Mayo was at the time an Associate Dean of the Law Faculty, but she had to postpone her conference because of an urgent administrative matter which occupied her for some months. We decided to combine forces and were able to persuade the Social Sciences and Humanities Council of Canada and also the Connaught Fund of the University of Toronto to permit us to combine budgets as well. These funds, as well as an additional generous budget provided by Ron Daniels, Dean of the Law Faculty, allowed me to invite contributors from Australia,

New Zealand and the United Kingdom, as well as Canadians from outside of Toronto, and to provide hospitality to all those who attended the conference over its two days.

I want to thank Mike and Mayo for all their help and all those who provided funding. In addition, I thank Colin Grey for helping with the practicalities of the two days of the conference and Jennifer Tam, Special Events Coordinator of the Law Faculty, who made sure that the conference ran like clockwork. Erika Eineigel and Umut Ozsu took on the job of assisting with editing the manuscript at a busy time and I am very grateful to them. Richard Hart, as always, proved a dedicated publisher and friend to the world of academic inquiry.

The *sine qua non* of the conference was of course the majority judgment in *Baker*, given by Madame Justice Claire L'Heureux-Dubé. The conference occurred just days after her final stint as a judge of Canada's Supreme Court and it seemed appropriate to hold the conference in honour of her career and to dedicate this collection to her. (Unfortunately, a last minute flu prevented her from attending the conference.) Not all the chapters take an uncritical or even admiring view of her jurisprudence, but, as a dedicated dissenter, she welcomes criticism.

More important than praise or critique is that one can trace a direct line from her reasoning in *Baker* to 1609, to a case which also sought to articulate the deepest assumptions of the common law tradition: *Dr Bonham's Case*. Her assertion that 'discretion must be exercised in accordance with the boundaries imposed in the statute, the principles of the rule of law, the principles of administrative law, the fundamental values of Canadian society, and the principles of the *Charter*' both echoes and takes forward Coke CJ's equally profound and enigmatic dictum that 'the common law will controul Acts of Parliament, and sometimes adjudge them to be utterly void: for when an Act of Parliament is against common right and reason, or repugnant, or impossible to be performed, the common law will controul it, and adjudge such Act to be void' ((1609) 8 Co Rep 107, at 118a.)

So the dedication is to a great judge in the common law tradition.

Table of Contents

Preface and Acknowledgments   v
List of Contributors   ix
Table of Cases   xi

1. *Baker*: The Unity of Public Law?   1
   David Dyzenhaus

2. Deference from *Baker* to *Suresh* and Beyond—Interpreting the Conflicting Signals   21
   David Mullan

3. The *Baker* Effect: A New Interface Between the *Canadian Charter of Rights and Freedoms* and Administrative Law—The Case of Discretion   61
   Geneviève Cartier

4. The Rule of Policy: *Baker* and the Impact of Judicial Review on Administrative Discretion   87
   Lorne Sossin

5. 'Alert, alive and sensitive': *Baker*, the Duty to Give Reasons, and the Ethos of Justification in Canadian Public Law   113
   Mary Liston

6. The Internal Morality of Administration: The Form and Structure of Reasonableness   143
   Evan Fox-Decent

7. The State of Law's Borders and the Law of States' Borders   173
   Audrey Macklin

8. Refugees, Asylum Seekers, the Rule of Law and Human Rights   201
   Colin Harvey

9. Judicial Review of Expulsion Decisions: Reflections on the UK Experience   225
   Nicholas Blake QC

10. Rights in the Balance: Non-Citizens and State Sovereignty Under the Charter   253
    Ninette Kelley

11. Common Law Reason and the Limits of Judicial Deference 289
    Trevor Allan

12. Of Cocoons and Small 'c' Constitutionalism: The Principle
    of Legality and an Australian Perspective on *Baker* 307
    Margaret Allars

13. Judicial Review, Intensity and Deference in EU Law 335
    Paul Craig

14. A Hesitant Embrace: *Baker* and the Application of
    International Law by Canadian Courts 357
    Jutta Brunnée & Stephen J Toope

15. Authority, Influence and Persuasion: *Baker*, Charter
    Values and the Puzzle of Method 389
    Mayo Moran

16. The Common Law Constitution and Legal Cosmopolitanism 431
    Mark D Walters

17. The Tub of Public Law 455
    Michael Taggart

Bibliography 481

List of Contributors

TREVOR ALLAN is Reader in Legal and Constitutional Theory, University of Cambridge.
MARGARET ALLARS is Professor of Law, University of Sydney and barrister at Wentworth Chambers, Sydney.
NICHOLAS BLAKE QC is a barrister at Matrix Chambers, London.
JUTTA BRUNNÉE is Professor of Law & Metcalf Chair in Environmental Law, University of Toronto.
GENEVIÈVE CARTIER is Professor of Law, Sherbrooke University.
PAUL CRAIG is Professor of English Law, St. John's College, Oxford.
DAVID DYZENHAUS is Professor of Law and Philosophy, University of Toronto.
EVAN FOX-DECENT is Post-doctoral Research Fellow at McGill University, Faculty of Law.
COLIN HARVEY is Professor of Constitutional and Human Rights Law, University of Leeds.
NINETTE KELLEY is a Canadian lawyer, currently legal and policy consultant in the Office of the United Nations High Commissioner for Refugees.
MARY LISTON is a graduate of the Faculty of Law, University of Toronto, and is working on a doctorate in Political Science at the same University.
AUDREY MACKLIN is Associate Professor of Law, University of Toronto.
MAYO MORAN is Associate Professor of Law, University of Toronto.
DAVID MULLAN is Osler, Hoskin & Harcourt Professor of Constitutional and Administrative Law, Queen's University, Kingston, Ontario.
LORNE SOSSIN is Associate Professor of Law, University of Toronto.
MICHAEL TAGGART is Professor of Law, University of Auckland.
STEPHEN J TOOPE is President, Pierre Elliott Trudeau Foundation and Professor of Law, McGill University (on leave).
MARK WALTERS is Associate Professor of Law, Queen's University, Kingston, Ontario.

Table of Cases

114957 Canada Ltee (Spraytech, Societe d'arrosage) *v* Hudson (Town) [2001]
2 SCR 241 ....41, 377, 378, 436
A and others *v* Secretary of State for the Home Department [2002] EWCA Civ
1502 ....219, 220, 221
Abdulaziz (1985) 7 EHRR 471 234
Adams *v* Yung (1998) 51 ALD 584 317
Agee *v* UK Commission (1976) 7 D and R 164 236
Ahani *v* Canada [1995] 3 FC 669 (TD) aff [1996] FCJ No 937 (CA) 271
Ahani *v* Canada (Attorney General) (2002) 58 OR (3d) 107 ....13, 46,
173, 181, 363, 399, 403, 404, 406, 407, 409, 411
Ahani *v* Canada (Minister of Citizenship and Immigration)
2002 SCC 2 ....50, 56, 174, 280, 364, 365, 399
Ainsley Financial Corporation *v* Ontario Securities Commission (1995)
21 OR (3d) 104 (CA)..93, 94
Ainsworth *v* Criminal Justice Commission (1992) 175 CLR 564....................327
AIUFFASS *v* Commission [1996] ECR II–2169 Case T–380/94.........................345
Al Sagban *v* Canada (Minister of Citizenship and Immigration)
2002 SCC 4 ....50, 51, 57, 287
Amrollahi *v* Denmark 11/07/2002 App No 00056811/00 235
Andrews *v* Law Society of British Columbia [1989] 1 SCR 143 174
Anisminic Ltd *v* Foreign Compensation Commission [1969] 2 AC 147..............320
Annetts *v* McCann (1990) 170 CLR 596...327
Annibaldi *v* Sindaco del Commune di Guidonia and Presidente Regione Lazio
[1997] ECR I–7493 Case C–309/96 349
Antillean Rice Mills NV *v* Commission [1999] ECR I–769 Case C–390/95P 345
Argentina *v* Mellino [1987] 1 SCR 536 261
Asif Khan *v* IAT [1985] 1 All ER 40; [1984] 1 WLR 1337 233
Associated Provincial Picture Houses Ltd *v.* Wednesbury Corporation [1948]
1 KB 44 (CA) 8, 27, 36, 65, 67, 155, 228, 229, 297, 472, 473, 474
Attorney General of Canada *v* Cain [1906] AC 542 253
Attorney-General (NSW) *v* Quin (1990) 170 CLR 1 328
Australian National University *v* Burns (1982) 43 ALR 25 318
B (A Minor) *v* DPP [2000] 2 AC 428 (HL) 433
B *v* Secretary of State for the Home Department [2000] Imm AR 478................232
Babcock *v* Canada, 2002 SCC 57 57
Baker *v* Canada (Minister of Citizenship and Immigration) [1999] 2 SCR 817;
(1999) 174 DLR (4th) 193 ....1–20, 21–60, 61,
63, 67, 70, 71–83, 85–6, 87, 90, 91, 94, 96–107, 109, 110–12, 113–41,
143–71, 173, 176, 177, 183, 188, 189–93, 232, 271–6, 279–83, 287, 288,
295–7, 307, 308, 312, 314–16, 321, 324–5, 327–8, 330, 332–34, 357–60,
362–3, 365, 368, 370–80, 383–4, 386, 389–97, 399–402, 405–9, 412,
422, 425, 428–9, 435–38, 451–2, 454–5, 460–70, 474, 478

xii *Table of Cases*

Balog *v* Independent Commission Against Corruption
  (1990) 169 CLR 625 311
Barbuit's Case (1735) Cases t Talb 28 443
Bela-Mühle Josef Bergman KG *v* Grows-Farm GmbH & Co KG [1977]
  ECR 1211 Case 114/76 344
Bell *v* The Queen [1979] SCR 212...64
Bellinger *v* Bellinger [2001] EWCA Civ 1140 (2002) 1 All ER 311 251
Bezaire *v* Windsor Roman Catholic Separate
  School Board (1992) 9 OR (3d) 737 (Div Ct) 94
Bibeault *v* McCaffrey [1984] 1 SCR 176 27
Blencoe *v* British Columbia (Human Rights Commission)
  [2000] 2 SCR 307...62, 74, 186, 187, 190, 466
Blundell *v* Catterall (1821) 5 Barn & Ald 268 ....443, 444
Board of Education of the Indian Head School Division
  No 19 of Saskatchewan *v* Knight [1990] 1 SCR 653 26
Bocchi Food Trade International GmbH *v* Commission [2001]
  ECR II–943 Case T–30/99 345
Bonsignore (Angelo), Cologne *v* Oberstadtdirektor of the City of Cologne
  [1975] ECR 297 232
Boultif *v* Switzerland [2001] 33 EHRR 50...235
Bouzari *v* Iran (1 May 2002), Toronto 00–CV–201372
  (Ont Sup Ct) 361, 375, 380, 381
Briggs *v* Baptiste [2000] AC 40 (PC (Trin)) 403
Brown *v* Stott (Procurator Fiscal, Dunfermline) [2001] 2 WLR 817 290
Brunner *v* European Union Treaty [1994] 1 CMLR 57 349
Burns *v* Australian National University (1982) 40 ALR 707 318
Calvin's Case (The Case of the Posnati) (1608) 2 St Tr 559 442
CAIMAW *v* Paccar of Canada Ltd [1989] 2 RCS 983 66
Canada *v* Schmidt [1987] 1 SCR 500 ....43, 261
Canada (A G) *v* Ontario (A G) [1937] A C 326 (PC)..364
Canada (Attorney General) *v* Ward [1993] 2 SCR 689 ....287, 363
Canada (Commissioner of Competition) *v* Superior Propane Inc
  [2001] 3 FC 185 (CA)..49
Canada (Deputy Minister of National Revenue) *v* Mattel Canada Inc
  [2001] 2 SCR 100..48
Canada (Director of Investigation and Research) *v* Southam Inc·
  [1997] 1 SCR 748...9, 17, 35, 36, 49, 71, 137, 151, 154, 293
Canada (Minister of Employment and Immigration) *v* Chiarelli [1992]
  1 SCR 711 ....5, 174, 264, 265, 266, 269, 270, 274, 285
Canadian Magen David Adom for Israel *v* Canada (Minister of National
  Revenue–M N R), 2002 FCA 323..102
Canadian Union of Public Employees, Local 963 *v* New Brunswick Liquor
  Corporation [1979] 2 SCR 227 ....8, 17, 24, 63, 64, 65, 67, 69, 121, 155
Canal Satelite Digital SL *v* Aministacion General del Estado and Distribuidora de
  Television Gigital SA (DTS), January 22 2002. Case C–390/99 346
Capital Cities Communications Inc *v* Canadian Radio-Television
  Commission [1978] 2 SCR 141 ....93, 96, 363

Carpenter v Secretary of State for Work and Pensions
  [2003] EWCA Civ 33 ....232, 234
Carpenter v Secretary of State for the Home Department
  Case C–60/00 [2003] 2 WLR 267..234
Carter v Downish (1690) 1 Shower KB 127 443
CAS v Alberta (Director of Child Welfare)
  [2002] AJ No 895, 2002 ABQB 631..139
Chahal v UK [2000] 3 WLR 1240 (CA) 217, 236
Chahal v United Kingdom (1996) 23 EHRR 413 ....217, 225, 303
Chahal v Secretary of State for the Home
  Department [1995] 20 EHRR CD 19 ....233, 237
Chamberlain v Surrey School District No 36, 2002 SCC 86 ....23, 25, 36, 37, 53
Chaudhary v Minister for Immigration and
  Ethnic Affairs (1994) 121 ALR 315 321
Chen v Canada (Minister of Employment and Immigration)
  [1995] 1 SCR..287
Chevron USA Inc v NRDC 467 US 837 (1984) 339
Chiarelli v Canada (Minister of Employment and Immigration)
  [1992] 1 SCR 283 (SCC) 182, 189, 467
Chieu v Canada (Minister of Citizenship and Immigration
  2002 SCC 3 ....50, 51, 57, 129, 148, 287
CNTA SA v Commission [1975] ECR 533 Case 74/74 341
Coco v R (1994) 179 CLR 427 311
Coenen v Social Economische Raad [1975] ECR 1547 Case 39/75 346
Comalco New Zealand Ltd v Broadcasting Standards Authority [1995]
  3 NZLR 469 (HC), upheld on appeal: (1995) 9 PRNZ 153 (CA)..................478
Commissioner of Police v Tanos (1958) 98 CLR 383 327
Committee for Equal Treatment of Asbestos Minority
  Shareholders v Ontario (Securities Commission) [2001] 2 SCR 132 48
Compagnie Nationale Air France v Commission [1996]
  ECR II–2109 Case T–358/94 345
Congo v Venne [1971] SCR 997 376
Conka v Belgium 05/02/2002 App No 0051564/99...227
Corporation of the City of Enfield v Development
  Assessment Commission (2000) 199 CLR 135 314
Coope v Iuliano (1996) 65 SASR 405 316
Cooper v Canada (Human Rights Commission) [1996]
  3 SCR 854 ....44, 95, 185, 186
Council v Hautala, December 6 2001 [1993]
  OJ L340/43 Case C–353/99P 343
Council of Civil Service Unions v
  Minister for the Civil Service (1985) AC 374 (HL Eng) 410 65
Craig v South Australia (1995) 184 CLR 163 320
Crevier v Quebec (AG) [1981] 2 SCR 220..54
Criminal Proceedings against X [1996] ECR I–6609
  Cases C–74/95 and 129/95 349
Cuddy Chicks Ltd v Ontario
  (Labour Relations Board) [1991] 2 SCR 5 ....42, 185

Dagenais v Société Radio-Canada [1994] 3 SCR 835 70
Daly v Secretary of State for the
  Home Department [2001] 2 WLR 1622 (HL) 27
Daniels v R. [1968] SCR 517 362
Darling Casino Ltd v New South Wales
  Casino Control Authority (1997) 191 CLR 602 .... 322, 324
Dayco (Canada) Ltd v CAW-Canada [1993] 2 SCR 230 66
Defrenne v Sabena [1978] ECR 1365 Case 149/77 348
Dehghani v Canada (Minister of Employment
  and Immigration) [1993] 1 SCR 1053 .... 174, 268, 269, 270, 274
Deuka, Deutsche Kraftfutter GmbH, B J Stolp v Einfuhr-und
  Vorratsstelle für Getreide und Futtermittel [1975]
  ECR 421, 432. Case 78/74 .... 341, 342
Dietrich v R (1992) 177 CLR 292 311
Douglas Aircraft Co of Canada v McConnell [1980] 1 SCR 245 .... 185, 463
Douglas/Kwantlen Faculty Assn v Douglas College [1990] 3 SCR 570 185
DPP v Bhagwan [1972] AC 60 228
East African Asians v UK 3 EHRR 76 227
East India v Sandys (1683–85) 10 St Tr 371 444
Elliniki Radiophonia Tileorassi AE v Dimotiki Etairia
  Pliroforissis and Sotirios Kouvelas [1991]
  ECR I–2925 Case C–260/89 .... 349, 354
Emperor of Austria v Day (1861) 2 Giff 628 445
Executif Régional Wallon and Glaverbel SA v Commission
  [1988] ECR 1573 Cases 62 and 72/87 341
Ex parte Wurth; Re Tully (1954) 55 SR (NSW) 47 320
Firma A Racke v Hauptzollamt Mainz [1979] ECR 69 Case 98/78 341
Fitzpatrick v Sterling Housing [1999] 3 WLR 1113 251
Francis v R [1956] SCR 618 364
Friends of Oldman River Society v Canada (Minister of Transport)
  [1992] 1 SCR 3 93
Fuduche v Minister for Immigration, Local
  Government and Ethnic Affairs (1993) 117 ALR 418 321
Gallant v Canada (Deputy Commissioner,
  Correctional Services) [1989] 3 FC 329 (CA) 55
Gana v MMI [1970] SCR 699 256
Geitling v High Authority [1960] ECR 423 Cases 36, 37, 38, 40/59 348
George v Secretary of State for the Environment (1979) 38 P & CR 609 478
Goodwin v United Kingdom (2002) 35 EHRR 447 251
Goss v Withers (1758) 2 Keny 325 443
Gough v Chief Constable of Derbyshire [2002] EWCA Civ 351 247
Gray v Ontario (Disability Support Program,
  Director) [2002] OJ No 1531 (CA) 35, 162
Hammond v Assn of British Columbia
  Profession Foresters (1991) 47 Admin LR 20 (BCSC) 94
Hauer v Land Rheinland-Pfalz [1979] ECR 3727 Case 44/79 .... 343, 348
Hawthorne v Canada (Minister of Citizenship
  and Immigration) 2002 FCA 475 .... 39, 130, 149, 158, 160, 161

Heathfield v Chilton (1767) 4 Burr 2015 443
Hervey v Aston (1738) West t Hard 350 .... 443, 444
Higgs v Minister of National Security [2000] 2 AC 228 (PC) 434, 435
Hilal v UK (2001) 33 EHRR 2 241
Hill v Church of Scientology [1995] 2 SCR 1130 ...... 416, 417, 419, 420, 421, 424
Hockey v Yelland (1984) 157 CLR 124 319
Holder v Canada (Minister of Citizenship and Immigration) [2001]
 FCJ No 267 147
Hofer v Wollman [1992] 3 SCR 165 139
Hopedale Developments Ltd. v Oakville (town) [1965] 1 OR 259 93
Horvath v Secretary of State for the
 Home Department [2000] 1 AC 489 (HL) 210, 233
Hot Holdings Pty Ltd v Creasy [2002] HCA 51 333
Houssein v Under Secretary Department of
 Industrial Relations and Technology (1982) 148 CLR 88 319
Housen v Nikolaisen, 2002 SCC 33 49
In the Matter of a Reference re Public Service
 Employee Relations Act (Alta) [1987] 1 SCR 313 .... 179, 465
In re Racal Communications Ltd [1981] AC 374 470
Internationale Handelsgesellschaft v Einfuhr-und Vorratstelle
 für Getreide und Futtermittel [1970] ECR 1125 348
International Transport Roth GMBH v Secretary of State
 for the Home Department [2002] EWCA Civ 158 247
Irwin Toy v AG Quebec [1989] 1SCR 927 261
Ivanhoe Inc v UFCW, Local 500 [2001] 2 SCR 565 48
Jany v Staatssecretaris van Justitie [2001] ECR I-8615; [2003] All ER
 (EC) 193; Case No 268/99 249
Johnston v Chief Constable of the Royal Ulster Constabulary
 [1986] ECR 1651 Case 222/84 349
Kioa v West (1985) 159 CLR 550 .... 323, 332
Kindler v Canada (Minister of Justice) [1991]
 2 SCR 779 .... 259, 263, 264, 270, 274
Kirkwood v United Kingdom [1984] DR 37, p 158 263
Knight v Indian Head School Division No 19 [1990] 1 SCR 653 159
Kremzow v Austria [1997] ECR I-2629 Case C-299/95 349
Lalonde v Ontario (2002) 56 OR (3d) 505 (CA) 40, 134, 135, 433, 434
Langner v Canada (Minister of Employment
 and Immigration) [1995] FCJ No 469 (FCA) 147, 465
Lavoie v Canada 2002 SCC 23 174
Le Case del Union d'Escose ove Angleterre (1606) Moore 790 442
Legault v Canada (Minister of Citizenship and Immigration (2002)
 212 DLR (4th) 139 (FCA), rev'g [2001] 3 FC 277 (TD) 11, 38, 39, 105,
                                                                  106, 129, 130, 143, 146, 147, 148, 149
Leiba v MMI (1972) 23 DLR (3d) 476 (SCC) 256
Lewis v Attorney General of Jamaica [2001] 2 AC 50 245
Little Sisters Book and Art Emporium v Canada
 (Minister of Justice) [2000] 2 SCR 1120 .... 91, 92
Liversidge v Anderson [1942] AC 206 229

Lobo v Minister for Immigration and
  Multicultural and Indigenous Affairs [2003] FCA 144 ....144, 325
M v Home Office [1994] 1 AC 377..230
Mabo v Queensland (No 2) (1992) 175 CLR 1 (HC) 311, 434, 459
Macdonell v Quebec (Commission d'accès à l'information) 2002 SCC 71......48, 85
Mack v Canada (AG) OJ No 3488 (CA)(QL) 376, 381
Maouia v France 5/10/2000 App No 00039652/98 234
Maurin [1996] ECR I–2909 Case C–144/95 349
Maple Lodge Farms Ltd. v Canada [1982] 2 SCR 2 93
Martineau v Matsqui Institution [1978] 1 SCR 118 91
McKinney v University of Guelph [1990] 3 SCR 229 261
Meggadow v Holt (1692) 12 Mod 15 443
Mendoza v Ghaidam [2002] EWCA Civ 1533 251
Minister for Aboriginal Affairs v Peko-Wallsend (1986) 162 CLR 24 463
Minister of Energy v Petrocorp
  Exploration Ltd [1989] 1 NZLR 348 (CA)..478
Minister for Immigration and Ethnic Affairs v
  Wu Shan Liang (1996) 185 CLR 259 318
Minister for Immigration and Multicultural Affairs v
  Eshetu (1999) 197 CLR 611 463
Minister for Immigration and Multicultural Affairs v
  Jia (2001) 178 CLR 42 313
Minister for Immigration and Multicultural Affairs v
  Yusuf (2001) 180 ALR 1..321, 323
Minister for Immigration, Local Government and
  Ethnic Affairs v Taveli (1990) 23 FCR 162 318
Ministry of State for Immigration and Ethnic Affairs v Teoh (1995)
  183 CLR 273 (HC) 10, 233, 311, 312, 328, 329, 330, 331, 332,
                                                             401, 402, 408, 410, 435, 462, 469
Ministry of Transport v Noort [1992] 3 NZLR 260 476
Moonen v Film & Literature Board of Review [2000] 2 NZLR 9 (CA)..............476
Morris v CW Martin & Sons Ltd [1966] 1 QB 716 (CA) 466
Mount Sinai Hospital Center v Quebec (Minister of Health and Social
  Services) [2001] SCJ No 43, 2001 SCC 41 ....131, 137
NAAV v Minister for Immigration and Multicultural Affairs [2002]
  FCAFC 228 ....323, 324, 325
Nanaimo (City) v Rascal Trucking Ltd [2000] 1 SCR 342...................................25
Naredo v Canada (Minister of Employment and
  Immigration) (1995) 184 NR 352..465
National Corn Growers Assn v Canada
  (Import Tribunal) [1990] 2 SCR 1324 ....66, 363
Nazli v Stadt [2000] 1– ECR p 957 232
New Brunswick Broadcasting Co v
  Nova Scotia (Speaker of the House of Assembly) [1993] 1 SCR 319 59
New South Wales v Osmond (1986) 159 CLR 656 ....315, 478
New York Times v Sullivan 376 US 254 (1964)..417
New Zealand Fishing Industry Association Inc v Minister of Agriculture &
  Fisheries [1988] 1 NZLR 544 (CA) 463, 478

Nicholson *v* Haldimand-Norfolk Regional Board of Commissioners of
 Police [1979] 1 SCR 311 .... 26, 83, 121, 168
Nold *v* Commission [1974] ECR 491 .... 232, 348
Norberg *v* Wynrib [1992] 2 SCR 226 122
Northern Telecom Ltd *v* Communications Workers of Canada
 [1980] 1 SCR 115 43
Northwestern Utilities Ltd *v* City of Edmonton [1979] 1 SCR 684 166
Northwood Inc *v* British Columbia (Forest Products Board)
 (2001) 86 BCLR (3d) 215 (BCCA) 23
NSH *v* SSHD [1988] Imm AR 389 236
Operation Dismantle Inc *v* The Queen [1985] 1 SCR 441 58
Opinion 2/94 on Accession by the Community
 to the ECHR [1996] ECR I–1759 349
O'Reilly *v* Mackman [1983] 2 AC 237 (HL) 478
O'Toole *v* Charles David Pty Ltd (1990) 171 CLR 232 322
Pezim *v* British Columbia
 (Superintendent of Brokers) [1994] 2 SCR 577 .... 42, 93
Philip Morris Holland BV *v*
 Commission [1980] ECR 2671 Case 730/79 340
Piandiong et al *v* The Philippines Co No 869/1999 194
Pinder *v* The Queen (PC (Bah)) [2002] 3 WLR 1443 245
Plaintiff S157/2002 *v* Commonwealth of Australia
 ('Plaintiff S157/2002') [2003] HCA 2 .... 325, 326, 327, 333, 334
Podlaszecka *v* MMI (1972) 23 DLR 3d 331 (SCC) 256
Polyukovich *v* Commonwealth (1991) 172 CLR 501 309
Powell *v* Evreniades (1989) 21 FCR 252 318
Public Service Board of New South Wales *v* Osmond (1985–86)
 159 CLR 656 (HCA) 315, 478
Puli'uvea *v* Removal Review Authority (1996) 2 HRNZ 510 464
Pushpanathan *v* Canada (Minister of Employment and Immigration)
 [1998] 1 SCR 982 .... 30, 49, 51, 70, 153, 287, 293, 294,
 298, 362, 363
R *v* Bernard [1988] 2 SCR 833 76
R *v* Big M Drug Mart Ltd [1985] 1 SCR 295 70
R *v* Bouchereau [1978] QB 732 232
R *v* Braich [2002] SCJ No 29, 2002 SCC 27 127
R *v* Butler [1992] 1 SCR 452 .... 92, 420
R *v* Civil Service Appeal Board; *ex parte*
 Cunningham [1991] 4 All ER 310 315
R *v* Cook [1998] 2 SCR 597 .... 368, 369
R *v* DPP *ex parte* Kibilene [2000] 2 AC 326 (HL) 434, 435
R *v* Edwards Books [1986] 2 SCR 713 261
R *v* Esau [1997] 2 SCR 777 121
R *v* Governor of Brixton Prison *ex parte*
 Guerin (1907) 51 Sol Journal 571 228
R *v* Governor of Brixton prison *ex parte* Soblen [1963] 2 QB 243 231
R *v* Hickman; *ex parte* Fox and Clinton (1945) 70 CLR 598 322

R v Immigration Appeal Tribunal ex parte Shah; Islam and others v Secretary
of State for the Home Department [1999] 2 All ER 545 (HL)..................211, 219
R v Immigration Appeal Tribunal *ex parte* Secretary of State and
Surinder Singh [1992] Imm AR 565 ECJ Case C 370/90.....................234
R v Intervention Board for Agricultural Produce, *ex parte* E D & F Man (Sugar)
Ltd [1985] ECR 2889 Case 181/84..337, 344
R v IRC *ex parte* Federation of Self-Employed &
Small Businesses Ltd [1982] AC 617...473
R v Keegstra [1990] 3 SCR 697..368, 420
R v Lord Chancellor, *ex parte* Witham [1997] 2 All ER 779 (QB).....................433
R v Medical Appeal Tribunal; *ex parte* Gilmore [1957] 1 QB 574......................326
R v Minister for Agriculture, Fisheries, and Food
ex parte Fedesa [1990] ECR 4023 Case C–331/88 ....344, 345
R v Minister of Defence *ex parte* Smith [1995] 4
All ER 427; [1996] 1 All ER 257 (CA), [1996] 2 WLR 305 ....242, 299, 433
R v Murray; *ex parte* Proctor (1949) 77 CLR 387................................323
R v Nat Bell Liquors Ltd [1922] 2 AC 128 (PC) 476
R v Oakes [1986]1 SCR 103 ....70, 151, 164, 260
R v Palacios (1984) 45 OR (2d) 269 (CA) 363
R v Pieck [1981] QB 571..231
R v RDS [1997] 23 SCR 484 123
R v Salituro [1991] 3 SCR 654 ....416, 417, 418, 423
R v Schwartz [1988] 2 SCR 443 261
R v Secretary of State for Education and
Employment *ex parte* Begbie [2000] 1 WLR 1115 ....94, 298
R v Secretary of State for the Environment
ex parte Hammersmith & Fulham LBC [1991] 1 AC 521..............................298
R v Secretary of State for Foreign and Commonwealth Affairs
ex parte Abassi [2002] EWCA Civ 1598........................228, 229, 431
R v Secretary for the Home Department
ex parte Adan [2001] 2 AC 477 (HL).....................................208, 209
R v Secretary for the Home Department *ex parte*
Ahmed and Patel [1998] INLR 570 ....435, 233, 235
R v Secretary of State for the Home Department *ex parte*
Amankwah [1994] Imm AR 233, 240
R v Secretary of State for the Home Department *ex parte*
Bugdacay and Mususi [1987] AC 514 ....214, 215, 230, 242
R v Secretary of State for the Home Department *ex parte*
Brind [1991] 1 AC 696 (HL) 299, 435, 470
R v Secretary of State for the Home Department *ex parte*
Cheblak [1991] 2 All ER 319 236
R v Secretary of State for the Home Department *ex parte*
Daly [2001] 3 All ER 433 (HL) 250, 445, 471, 475
R v Secretary of State for the Home Department *ex parte*
Doody [1994] 1 AC 531 ....315, 316
R v Secretary of State for the Home Department *ex parte*
Farrakhan [2002] 3 WLR 481 (CA) 222, 227, 303, 304

R v Secretary of State for the Home Department *ex parte*
   Fire Brigades Union [1995] 2 AC 513 (HL) 433
R v Secretary of State for the Home Department *ex parte*
   Hosenball [1977] 1 WLR 766..236
R v Secretary of State for the Home Department *ex parte*
   Javed and Ahmed (2001) 3 WLR 323: (2002) QB 12 228
R v Secretary for the Home Department *ex parte*
   Joint Council for the Welfare of Immigrants [1997] 1 WLR 275 (CA) 212
R v Secretary of State for the Home Department *ex parte*
   Khawaja [1984] AC 74; [1983] 2 WLR 321; [1982] Imm AR 139 228
R v Secretary of State for the Home Department *ex parte*
   Launder [1997] 1 WLR 839 (HL)..435
R v Secretary of State for the Home Department *ex parte*
   Leech [1994] QB 198 434
R v Secretary of State for the Home Department, *ex parte*
   McQuillan [1995] 4 All ER 400 303
R v Secretary of State for the Home Department *ex parte*
   Muboyayi [1992] QB 244..230
R v Secretary of State for the Home Department, *ex parte*
   Pierson [1998] AC 539 (HL).. 433, 434, 471
R v Secretary of State for the Home Department *ex parte*
   Phull [1996] Imm AR 72 234
R v Secretary of State for the Home Department *ex parte*
   Ravichandran [1996] Imm AR 418..233
R v Secretary of State for the Home Department *ex parte*
   Saadi [2002] UKHL 41 ....212, 226
R v Secretary of State for the Home Department *ex parte*
   Samaroo [2001] INLR 55 232
R v Secretary of State for the Home Department *ex parte*
   Shingara [1997] 3 CMLR 703 240
R v Secretary of State for the Home Department, *ex parte*
   Simms [2000] 2 AC 115 (HL)..445, 471
R v Secretary of State for the Home Department *ex parte*
   Sivakumaran [1988] 1 AC 958 (HL)..207
R v Secretary of State for the Home Department *ex parte*
   Turgut [2001] 1 All ER 719 242
R v Secretary of State for the Home Department, *ex parte*
   Venables [1998] AC 407 (HL) 435, 436
R v Sheppard [2002] SCJ No 30, 2002 SCC 26 ....124, 126, 127, 128, 478
R v Swain [1991] 1 SCR 933..419
R v Zinck [2003] SCJ No 5, 2003 SCC 6 125
Re Arrow River & Tributaries Slide & Boom Co.
   [1931] 2 DLR 216 at 217 (Ont SC (App Div)) 363
Re Ashby et al [1934] OR 421 156
Re Bolton *ex parte* Beane (1987) 162 CLR 514..311
Re Gooliah and Minister of Citizenship and
   Immigration 91967), 63 DLR (2d) 224 (Man CA) 256

xx Table of Cases

Re Hopedale Developments Ltd v
  Town of Oakville (1964) 47 DLR (2d) 482 96
Re Minister for Immigration and Multicultural
  and Indigenous Affairs; *ex parte* Applicants
  S134/2002 Prosecutors [2003] HCA 1 326
Re Munshi Singh (1914) 20 BCR 243 (CA) 255
Reference re Secession of Quebec [1998] 2 SCR 217 .... 30, 40, 140, 376
Reference Re Amendment of Constitution of Canada
  [1981] 1 SCR 753 386
Reference Re Mining and Other Natural Resources
  of the Continental Shelf (1983) 41 Nfld & PEIR 271 (Nfld CA) 376
Reference re Powers of Ottawa (City) & Rockcliffe Park
  (Village) to Levy Rates on Foreign Legations and
  High Commissioners Residences [1943] SCR 208 363
Reference re Public Service Employee Relations Act
  (Alberta) [1987] 1 SCR 313 .... 368, 369, 383
Reference re Secession of Quebec [1998] 2 SCR 217 .... 376, 386, 387
Regina v Thurborn (1848) 1 Den 387 .... 443, 444
Retail, Wholesale and Department Store Union,
  Local 580 v Dolphin Delivery Ltd [1986] 2 SCR 573 .... 261, 415, 416
Rewe Zentrale v Bundesmonopolverwaltung für
  Branntwein [1979] ECR 649 Case 120/78 347
Rex v Lord Yarborough (1828) 2 Bligh NS PC 147 .... 443, 444
Ridge v Baldwin [1964] AC 40 323
Romans v Canada (Minister of Citizenship and
  Immigration) [2001] FCJ No 740 (FCTD) 286
Roncarelli v Duplesis 1959] SCR 121 R 24, 34, 118, 155, 156, 159
Roberts v Hopwood [1925] AC 578 229
Ross v New Brunswick School District
  No 15 [1996] 1 SCR 825 .... 62, 67, 68, 69, 71, 75, 183, 184, 189, 466
Roth International v Secretary of State
  [2002] EWCA Civ 158 (22nd February 2002) 247
Rowe v Young (1820) 2 Bligh PC 391 443
R (Q and others) v Secretary of State for the Home Department [2003]
  EWHC 195 (Admin) 212
Rutili v Ministre de l'Intérieur [1975] ECR 1219 Case 36/75 346
RWDSU v Pepsi-Cola 2002 SCC 8 .... 416, 417, 421, 424
Saint John (City) v Fraser-Brace Overseas Corp [1958] SCR 263 376
Schavernoch v Canada (Foreign Claims Commission) [1982] 1 SCR 1092 363
Schier v Removal Review Authority [1999] 1 NZLR 703 (CA) 465
Schmidt v Secretary of State For Home Affairs [1969] 2 Ch 149 231
Schreiber v Canada (Attorney General) 2002 SCC 62 .... 362, 376, 381
Scrimshire v Scrimshire (1752) 2 Hag Con 395 443
Secretary of State for the Home Department *ex parte*
  Adan [2001] 2 AC 477 (HL) 208-09, 219
Secretary of State for the Home Department v
  Rehman [2001] 3 WLR 877 (HL) 5, 11, 43, 217, 218, 219, 281, 301, 302
Sen v Netherlands [2003] 36 EHRR 7 235

Sept-Îles (City) *v* Quebec (Labour Court) [2001] 2 SCR 670 48
Service Employees' International Union *v* Nipawin Union Hospital [1975]
    1 SCR 382 24
Sgarlata and others *v* Commission [1965] ECR 215 Case 40/64 348
Shah *v* Canada (Minister of Employment and
    Immigration (1990), 170 NR 238 (FCA) 28, 462
Sharpe *v* AG Canada [2001] 1 SCR 45 397
Sheehan *v* Ontario (Criminal Injuries
    Compensation Board) (1974) 52 DLR (3d) 728 (Ont CA) 24
Shell Canada Products Ltd *v* Vancouver (City) [1994] 1 SCR 231 ....25, 53
Singh *v* Canada (Minister of Employment and
    Immigration [1985] 1 SCR 177 ....174, 182, 257, 258, 259, 262, 279, 280
Slaight Communications Inc *v* Davidson [1989]
    1 SCR 1038 ....62, 67, 68, 71, 75, 180, 183, 189, 368, 369, 437, 466
Smith and Brady *v* United Kingdom (2000) 29 EHRR 493 ....241, 300
SOCAN *v* Canadian Association of Internet
    Providers (2002) 215 DLR (4th) 118 (FCA) 49
Soering *v* United Kingdom (1989) 11 EHRR 439 ....238, 263
States *v* Burns [2001] 1 SCR 283 263
Stauder *v* City of Ulm [1969] ECR 419 348
Stoffman *v* Vancouver General Hospital [1990] 3 SCR 483.................................261
Stork *v* High Authority [1959] ECR 17 Case 1/58...348
Suresh *v* Canada (Minister of Citizenship
    and Immigration) [2002] SCC 1 ....11, 21, 22, 26, 38, 41, 42, 43, 44, 45,
                            46, 47, 56, 57, 58, 59, 60, 94, 129, 147, 148, 149,
                    173, 218, 276, 280, 281, 304, 359, 364, 368, 379, 380, 437, 467
T *v* Secretary of State for the Home Department [1996] AC 742 (HL) 216, 233
Tan Te Lam *v* Superintendent of Tai Chau Detention Centre [1997] AC 97 228
Tangiora *v* Wellington District Legal Services
    Committee [2000] 1 NZLR 17 (PC, New Zealand) 460
Tavita *v* Minister of Immigration, [1994] 2 NZLR 257...............331, 402, 403, 470
Tetreault-Gadoury *v* Canada (Employment and
    Immigration Commission) [1991] 2 SCR 22..185, 186
Thai Bicycle Industry Co Ltd *v* Council [1998] ECR II–2991
    Case T–118/96 345
The 'Fama' (1804) 5 C Rob 106 443
The King *v* Guerchy (1765) 1 Bl W 545 443
The 'Snipe' (1812) Edw 381 443
Thomas *v* Baptiste [2000] 2 AC 1 PC 398, 409, 410, 435, 437
Tiller *v* Atlantic Coast Railroad Co, 318 US 54 (1943) 474
Tremblay *v* Daigle [1989] 2 SCR 530 261
Trinity Western University *v* British Columbia
    College of Teachers [2001] 1 SCR 722 ....50, 51, 57
UES Local 298 *v* Bibeault [1988] 2 SCR 1048..121
United Brotherhood of Carpenters and Joiners of America,
    Local 579 *v* Bradco Construction Ltd, [1993] 2 SCR 316..............................66
United States *v* Allard [1987] 1 SCR 564...261
United States *v* Burns [2001] 1 SCR 283 ....174, 195, 263, 368, 391

United States v Morgan 313 US 409 (1941) 478
United States of America v Cotroni [1989] 1 SCR 1469 261
Union des employés de service, Local 298 v
  Bibeault, [1988] 2 SCR 1048 ....48, 64
Van Binsbergen v Bestuur van de Bedrijfsvereniging
  Metaalnijverheid [1974] ECR 1299 Case 33/74 346
Van Duyn v Home Office [1975] 3 All ER 190;
  [1974] ECR 1337 231
Vereinigte Familiapress Zeitungsverlags-und
  vertriebs GmbH v Heinrich Bauer Verlag [1997]
  ECR I–3689 Case C–368/95 ....349, 354
Via Rail Canada Inc v Canada (National Transportation Agency)
  [2001] 2 FC 25 (FCA)...136, 161
Vincenzo Zardi v Consorzio Agrario Provinciale di
  Ferrara [1990] ECR I–2515, 2532–3 Case C–8/89 345
Wachauf v Germany [1989] ECR 2609;
  Cases C–74/95 and 129/95 349
Waldner v Ponderosa Hutterian Brethren
  [2003] AJ No 7, 2003 ABQB 139
Westzucker GmbH v Einfuhr-und Vorratsstelle
  für Zucker [1973] ECR 321 Case 57/72 341
Yiadom v SSHD [1998] EWCA Civ 660 240
Yung v Adams (1997) 150 ALR 436 316

1

Baker: *The Unity of Public Law?*

DAVID DYZENHAUS

INTRODUCTION

THIS COLLECTION OF essays was produced for a conference at the Faculty of Law at the University of Toronto in early 2003. Contributors were asked to reflect on the Supreme Court of Canada's decision in *Baker v Canada (Minister of Citizenship and Immigration)*,[1] a case which brings together the major developments in Canadian administrative law over the past 30 years. But *Baker's* significance for a conference of lawyers from the common law world lies in its potential to help in constructing a basis for the legal relationship between individual and state over the next couple of decades. Madame Justice Claire L'Heureux-Dubé's judgment for the majority both fits with and takes forward an international judicial debate about the relationship between international rights documents and domestic legal regimes. It establishes for the first time in the common law world a general duty for administrative decision-makers to give reasons for their decisions and it imposes a reasonableness standard as the criterion for evaluating the legality of exercises of official discretion. Finally, it suggests that the rule of law is the rule of the fundamental legal values of a society, values which are located in various sources, written and unwritten, international and domestic.

The title of the conference was 'The Authority of Reasons: A New Understanding of the Rule of Law?' Once the papers had arrived, it became clear that while the topics of reason-giving and reasonableness (and the link which *Baker* establishes between them) were dealt with by several of the contributors, the principal theme was the unity of public law. *Baker* seems best understood as a decision which conceives of public law as based in a set of fundamental values, which are expressed—sometimes in different ways—in administrative law, in constitutional law and in international law, especially in international human rights instruments.[2] Its vision is clearly

---

[1] [1999] 2 SCR 817.
[2] And as Paul Craig shows, the same jurisprudential issues arise in the European Union case law dealing with review of both Community and Member State action.

reminiscent of the common law tradition's understanding of positive law as serving a kind of evidentiary function for the values of the common law, values which have been articulated by judges from time immemorial. Indeed, its vision is of a common public law. But its aspiration is rather different from the older understandings of the common law tradition because of its future-looking aspect—its orientation towards updating the fundamental values of the common public law in the light of the international law of human rights. Hence the change in title from conference to book.

Baker concerned the kind of judicial review appropriate for deportation and many of the other cases discussed by the contributors have to do with review of immigration and refugee determinations. This area of judicial review raises the theme of the unity of public law in a particularly stark fashion because of the traditional assumption that when it comes to non-citizens, the question of who gets into a country and who is to be deported is a matter for the unfettered discretion of the executive. When that discretion is overlaid, as we have been reminded by events after 11 September 2001, with an assumed, unfettered discretion to deal with matters pertaining to national security, things become even starker. The assumptions here have much to do with the fact that the discretionary powers are direct descendants of what were once considered to be unreviewable or unjusticiable executive prerogatives. As Gerhart Anschütz, Weimar's most distinguished constitutional lawyer, said, it might seem that in these areas, 'Here public law stops short'.[3] Put differently, there are some highly political areas of official decision-making where the writ of the rule of law does not run, even though very important interests of the individual are affected by the decisions.

The idea that some areas of official decision-making can be sealed off from the rule of law is in tension with the idea that there is a unity of public law. We know from Dicey that the political point of the idea of unity is supposed to be that all those who are subject to the law should be dealt with by public officials in accordance with the rule of law, and hence, in accordance with the values that underpin the rule of law. Much depends then on whether one adopts a more political and substantive or a more formal account of the rule of law. But the idea of the unity of public law presupposes a substantive account of the rule of law and that idea and that account is the point of departure for most of the contributors to the volume.[4]

---

[3] Quoted by Carl Schmitt, in his 1933 Preface to the second edition of *Politische Theologie* (Berlin, Duncker & Humblot, 1990).
[4] Here I agree with Trevor Allan's view that Dicey provided a substantive account of the rule of law, and hence with his critique of Paul Craig's account. TRS Allan, *Constitutional Justice: A Liberal Theory of the Rule of Law* (Oxford, Oxford University Press, 2001), 18–19, commenting on P Craig, 'Formal and Substantive Conceptions of the Rule of Law', [1997] *Public Law* 467.

Judges divide deeply on this issue. As Michael Taggart pointed out, one can tell almost everything about a judge in an immigration case by the way he or she starts the judgment: 'the executive has traditionally ...' as opposed to 'in this case, we are concerned with the fate of an individual who has lived in Canada for ten years, has three children ...'. The second judge is well on the path to being what we might think of as a human rights judge, one who believes (as depicted both in Mark Walter's chapter and his oral interventions) that individuals possess inherent *legal* rights because of their common humanity, rights which are expressed in the values of international human rights law, which in turn expresses the ideals of Kant's *ius cosmopoliticum*. Indeed, it is an international debate between judges about human rights law, and in particular, international human rights law, that has provided much of the basis for the claim that there is a unity to public law, organised around fundamental human rights.

For the sake of a contrast, and in line with the usage of several of the contributors, I will call the judges who do not share this claim 'positivists'.[5] While positivist judges might uphold the idea of universal human rights, they do not think that the moral status or importance of these rights translates without more into legal status within the domestic legal order. They view the only legitimate source of fundamental legal values as a legislative body or constituent assembly, so that they and other actors in the legal order, for example the executive, have no business articulating such values. Only when such values have been explicitly posited in a bill of rights by the body with authority to do so, or legislatively ordained to apply to a particular administrative regime or regimes, should other actors apply those values within the appropriate domains.

In a common law legal order, positivist judges are well aware that in private law they are constantly in the business of interpreting a body of law replete with values for whose presence the judges themselves are responsible. Further, they know that, in so far as the common law of judicial review is about the value of fairness—the right to a fair hearing and to an impartial adjudication—that value is one for whose presence judges are responsible. But in public law they attempt to iron out any tensions between their role as bearers of the common law tradition and their positivism by making the application of the value depend on tests which, in their view, are signals by the legislature that it wishes the value to apply to its administrative delegate. The value is not then a fundamental legal value, since its application is contingent on explicit legislative invitation. And their emphasis on the requirement of legislative invitation means that they adopt a dualism when it comes to domestic law which is much more thoroughgoing than was perhaps understood when the term dualism was coined to describe

---

[5] I do not claim all contributors would follow this usage.

a particular understanding of the relationship between 'soft' international law and domestic law.

Dualism described the attitude that international law which has not achieved the 'hard' status of customary international law is 'soft', more or less irrelevant to the domestic legal obligations of government, until its softness has been transformed by legislative incorporation. So the dualism exists between, say, a government's international legal obligations incurred by its ratification of a human rights convention and the complete lack of domestic effect of those obligations until they are transformed by implementation through legislation. *Baker* challenges that dualism, but whether its challenge is effective or not is contentious. This issue is explored in this volume in the exchange between Jutta Brunnée and Stephen Toope, on the one side, arguing that *Baker* is ineffective, and Mayo Moran and Mark Walters, on the other, where Moran argues explicitly and Walters assumes that one needs an anti-positivist understanding of the nature of legal authority to explain *Baker*. But as one can see from some of the contributions which confine themselves to the domestic legal order, in particular, Trevor Allan, Geneviève Cartier, Mary Liston and Evan Fox-Decent, what they want to challenge is precisely the idea that there is a dualism between administrative law and certain fundamental moral values, whether these are located in the written constitution or in the common law. On their view, administrative law is also constitutional law; the difference is only that its fundamental values are unwritten. Here they can point to L'Heureux-Dubé J's assertion in *Baker* that 'discretion must be exercised in accordance with the boundaries imposed in the statute, the principles of the rule of law, the principles of administrative law, the fundamental values of Canadian society, and the principles of the *Charter*'.[6]

For the moment, I want to stick with the point that for positivist judges there is no intrinsic unity to public law and no tension arises when constitutionally or legislatively ordained values apply to one group, say citizens, but not to another, say, non-citizens. Human rights judges differ, then, from such positivists in at least four related respects. They will think of public law as a unity, so that the same fundamental values underpin the whole enterprise of public law. They will think that constitutional law in the sense of written law is an explicit articulation of that set of values rather than their source. Correspondingly, they will be alert to the impact of fundamental values as unwritten constitutional values, even when, perhaps especially when, the written texts of the constitution do not cover an exercise of public power.[7] And they will think that other actors, besides legislatures and constituent assemblies, have a legitimate role in articulating what these

---

[6] *Baker*, para 56.
[7] The important question of when an exercise of power is public is not covered in this collection.

values are. This other set will include at least judges. It might, as we will see, also include the executive both in its role in signing and ratifying international treaties and in its role in making and implementing domestic policy in the cause of serving such values, the actors on the international stage from whose interaction emerge explicit articulations of human rights, and, last but not least, the individuals, lawyers and organisations who raise human rights challenges to both domestic and international bodies.

In this volume, Colin Harvey traces the ever growing reach of the substantive rule of law into the immigration/refugee area in the United Kingdom, while Margaret Allars sketches the retreat, even demise,[8] of the substantive rule of law in the same area in Australia. But other countries in the common law world should not be complacent, as Trevor Allan's and Nick Blake's account of *Rehman*[9] and other recent post-11 September decisions in the United Kingdom tells us, and as several of the analyses of Canadian jurisprudence warn—Brunnée and Toope, Ninette Kelley, Audrey Macklin, David Mullan.

Together these chapters raise the question whether the immigration area, particularly the overlap between refugee and security determinations, can be quarantined from the reach of the rule of law without, as it were the virus of judicial abdication of supervision of administrative decision-making spreading to other areas.[10] Indeed, this virus is no respecter of national boundaries. While at one time human rights enthusiasts welcomed a kind of international dialogue between appellate judges about the ways in which international developments in human rights law should influence domestic law, they now have to pause to consider the way in which the same judges are engaged in a dialogue about how to disengage from that first hesitant embrace in *Baker*, to borrow from Brunnée's and Toope's title. And the progressive, human rights-friendly articulation in *Baker* of the idea of a unity of public law can be properly appreciated only when one takes into account the context set out by Ninette Kelley. As she shows, in *Chiarelli*[11] the late Mr Justice Sopinka successfully deflected the Supreme Court from a course which would have accorded non-citizens the same rights as citizens.

Thus even if one welcomes *Baker* as a progressive decision, one has to take into account Mullan's argument that individuals who are protected by

---

[8] Allars discusses some resurrectionary possibilities, which arose in a High Court decision after the conference.
[9] *Secretary of State for the Home Department v Rehman* [2001] 3 WLR 877 (HL).
[10] Paul Craig, who provided the metaphor of virus, suggested that in the United Kingdom there was little or no danger of the virus spreading. Audrey Macklin thought that its spread might alert citizens to inroads on human rights which they would not feel if only the alien 'others' were affected. Mary Eberts was pessimistic about the possibility of citizens responding even if they were directly affected.
[11] *Canada (Minister of Employment and Immigration) v Chiarelli* [1992] 1 SCR 711.

written constitutional values are likely entitled to a more intense scrutiny of the official decision, to greater procedural protections and to a wider array of remedies than they would get through the common law. However, one then has to balance against that argument Allan's and Cartier's challenge to the assumption that when judges are enforcing unwritten fundamental values judicial review is necessarily less intense than when they are enforcing a bill of rights. And Allan can be understood as also challenging any assumption about the more limited array of remedies available to judges enforcing the unwritten constitution. In order to show how these themes arise in *Baker* and, further, in order to set the stage properly for the debate between the contributors, I will now turn to an account of the decision.

THE UNITY OF *BAKER*?

Baker arose because the delegates of the Minister of Immigration declined to find that their statutory discretion to stay an order of deportation against Mavis Baker on 'humanitarian and compassionate' grounds should be exercised in her favour. They could rely on the fact that the Court which had jurisdiction to review their decisions, the Federal Court Trial Division and Court of Appeal, has a long tradition of executive-mindedness when it comes to review of immigration and refugee matters. Most of the judges of that Court seem disposed to start with the presumption that the issue is the unfettered discretion (or prerogative power) of the minister to admit or expel non-citizens and that, in so far as a statute might provide any grounds for staying an exercise of such power, it is for the minister to decide whether those grounds exist. In *Baker,* the Federal Court did not disappoint the delegates and made scant mention of the notes which the junior immigration official had drafted as a basis for the senior official's decision, which were given to Baker's lawyers on their request, although there was no statutory duty to do so. These notes disclosed such hostility towards Baker that the Supreme Court would find that their decision was manifestly biased and should be invalidated for that reason alone. As it recognised, the Supreme Court could have confined itself to that issue and there would have been no occasion for the conference and book. However, it elaborated the structure implicit in the finding of bias and it is that complex structure which provided the occasion.

It is important at the outset to see why it might distort the structure of the Court's reasoning in *Baker*, or at least of Madame Justice Claire L'Heureux-Dubé's judgment for the majority, to suppose that the finding about bias is the *ratio* of the decision, so that all the rest is obiter.

As I have mentioned, there was no statutory duty to give reasons for humanitarian and compassionate decisions, and no general duty to give reasons had been established in the common law world. In addition, the traditional grounds for review of abuse of discretion are 'improper purpose', 'bad faith', and reliance on 'irrelevant considerations' and the onus is on the applicant to show that there is evidence that the discretion was abused in this way. So it was lucky for Baker that the immigration officials acceded to the request for the notes on which the decision was based. Further, because the notes disclosed that prejudice and stereotypes drove the decision rather than attention to what humanity and compassion demanded, it was foolish to disclose these particular notes, even though the officials could count on the Federal Court to uphold their decision. Had the Supreme Court overturned the decision solely on the ground of bias, the message it would have sent to the executive was not to be foolish in the future. Thus, if the Court wanted to face up to the arbitrariness that had been brought to its attention, it was necessary that it took the extra step and articulated a general duty to give reasons when an official decision affects an important interest of the individual. One way, then, of understanding L'Heureux-Dubé J's judgment is that she wishes to remove the element of luck or arbitrariness which made it improbable that most applicants for review of discretion would be successful even when the facts cried out for review, just because the facts would hardly ever be disclosed.

However, there is a deeper issue about luck or arbitrariness at stake. The language which L'Heureux-Dubé J used to describe the basis of the duty to give reasons makes it clear that one of the values—perhaps the main value—which the duty serves is the dignity of the individual. It would be an affront to the dignity of the individual if her fate (literally meant) depends on the luck of the draw of executive officials.[12] It is not enough that the officials who make decisions affecting important or fate-affecting interests of the individual disclose their reasons, in case they are acting in bad faith, in a biased fashion etc. For a duty to give reasons is rather ineffective if the message heard by the executive is that officials should in the future be very careful not to disclose reasons which provide evidence of bias etc, even if these are the real reasons. And it would not be very difficult to recraft the notes in *Baker* so as to reach the same result without the stink of prejudice and stereotype. So a general duty to give reasons does not remove sufficiently the element of luck, which is why yet another step is necessary.

This step is the link L'Heureux-Dubé J established between the reasons for the decision and the review of those reasons and she held that these reasons should be reviewed on a reasonableness standard—they had to display a reasonable justification for the decision. This extra step might not look like a big deal in most common law jurisdictions. After all, *Wednesbury* unreasonableness as a ground for judicial review of discretion has been around since 1948, when Lord Greene MR said that, besides the traditional grounds for finding that there had been an abuse of discretion, an act of

---

[12] *Baker*, para 43.

discretion is also unreasonable and thus invalid when it is 'so absurd that no sensible person could ever dream that it lay within the powers of the authority'.[13]

Wednesbury unreasonableness has not, however, played much of a role in Canadian jurisprudence on review of discretion and this standard was not what L'Heureux-Dubé J had in mind in *Baker*. *Wednesbury* unreasonableness is very difficult to demonstrate and may even not add anything to the traditional grounds of review of discretion, since it might be the case that it is demonstrated only if there is evidence that the decision-maker abused his authority in ways that the traditional grounds would in any case condemn. Moreover, L'Heureux-Dubé J drew the standard from the array which Canadian courts had developed not for review of discretion, but for review of executive interpretations of the law that governed particular administrative regimes.

Since the 1979 Supreme Court decision in *CUPE*,[14] Canadian courts had understood that a privative or ouster provision in a statute directed them to review interpretations of the law which fell within the jurisdiction of the tribunal on a standard of patent unreasonableness, while all other interpretations—especially of the limits of the tribunal's authority—would be reviewed on a correctness standard. The metaphor developed to describe what happened when a court reasoned both that a decision was within jurisdiction and met the appropriate standard was that of deference. The court should defer to the determination of the tribunal, thus loosening its grip on a formal conception of the separation of powers in which judges have a monopoly on interpretation of the law.

As the Supreme Court soon recognised, the distinction between jurisdictional issues and others is a very slippery one, and so it tried to articulate a number of criteria that would go into a 'pragmatic and functional' test for determining both whether an issue is jurisdictional and also when a determination made within jurisdiction fails to meet the patent unreasonableness standard. Since these criteria included the presence of a privative clause and the expertise of the tribunal, it was only a matter of time before the Court had to confront three related issues. The first is how to understand the patent unreasonableness standard. Some judges wanted to understand it as akin to *Wednesbury* unreasonableness, as a standard which required no substantive evaluation of the reasons for decision, precisely because they feared that any such evaluation put judges on a slippery slope to a correctness standard under the guise of patent unreasonableness. However, as other judges pointed out, it was difficult to understand how they

---

[13] *Associated Provincial Picture Houses Ltd v Wednesbury Corporation*. [1948] 1 KB 223, 228–9.
[14] *Canadian Union of Public Employees, Local 963 v New Brunswick Liquor Corporation* [1979] 2 SCR 227.

could make a determination that the reasons justified the decision without evaluating the reasons.

The second issue came about because it seemed that the presence of a privative clause was not a necessary condition for deference, if courts should be taking seriously the expertise of the particular tribunal—its superior ability to justify its interpretations of the law because of its expertise. So, again under the direction of the Supreme Court, Canadian courts have to consider whether there are reasons for deference, even if there is no privative clause, indeed, even if there is a statutory right of appeal. But it became simultaneously apparent that while the correctness standard seemed too exacting for review of this class of decisions, it was also the case that with others, especially those which affected important individual interests, patent unreasonableness would not be exacting enough. So the Court announced a new standard, 'reasonableness *simpliciter*', one which is not as intensive or 'probing' as correctness, but is more intensive than patent unreasonableness.[15]

In *Baker*, L'Heureux-Dubé J was clear that reasonableness *simpliciter* was the appropriate standard. The Immigration Minister had, she recognised, been given a very wide discretion when it came to deportation and the question of humanitarian and compassionate considerations, and this militated in favour of more deference. But the importance of the interest affected by the decision militated in favour of a closer scrutiny. Moreover, since Baker had four Canadian-born children, a decision that was both humanitarian and compassionate has to take into account the children's interests. In making this claim, L'Heureux-Dubé J could rely on the fact that the Immigration Act had the promotion of family unity as an objective and that departmental guidelines required officials to attend to the interests of children when making their decisions. But she also adverted to the *International Convention on the Rights of the Child*, which Canada had ratified but not incorporated, and which directed in Article 3 that administrative decisions that affected children should make the 'best interests of the child' 'a primary consideration'.[16]

It was her reliance on the *Convention* that attracted a partial dissent from two judges, Iacobucci and Cory JJ on the basis that to give any domestic effect to an unratified treaty was to offend against the separation of powers. Such effect, they argued, amounted to backdoor incorporation since it accorded a law-making authority to the executive which the separation of powers required be reserved to Parliament. Here they rely on a different part of the formal conception of the separation of powers, Parliament's monopoly on legislation or the creation of legal rights and duties.

---

[15] *Canada (Director of Investigation and Research) v Southam Inc.* [1997] 1 SCR 748.
[16] *Convention on the Rights of the Child*, 20 November 1989, Can. T.S. 1992 No 3.

L'Heureux-Dubé J's judgment attempts to draw the teeth from this charge by not relying on the claim advanced by the High Court of Australia in *Teoh*[17] that executive ratification of the *Convention* created legitimate expectations that officials would observe Article 3; indeed, both the majority and the dissent in *Baker* observed a remarkable taboo on mentioning *Teoh*. She was also at pains to emphasise that the *Convention* was only one of a number of sources for the Court's understanding of the content of the reasonableness standard in this context. However, it is also clear that what the *Convention* added to the other sources was weight, or at the least, inspiration for the claim that a special weight had to be given to the interests of the children. The children's interests could not be merely taken account of, they had to be taken into account appropriately. In this regard, L'Heureux-Dubé J avoided the particular phrase used in the *Convention* with almost the same fervour as she avoided mention of *Teoh*. She substituted several alternatives for 'a primary consideration', most notably the claim that the officer had 'to be alert, alive and sensitive' to the interests of the children,[18] a phrase that provides the impulse for Liston's contribution to this volume.

It is at this stage of L'Heureux-Dubé J's judgment that she takes the third and final step which is required in order to go as far as judges can on review to deal with arbitrariness or the element of luck. That this step is as necessary as the others to the structure of the judgment is demonstrated by the fact that to the extent that the notes were mentioned by the judges of the Federal Court, they were taken as evidence that the officials had taken the children's interests into account. However, the notes in fact show that the children had been taken account of in that that Baker had produced four children in Canada was regarded as an additional reason to get rid of her. So the distinction I want to draw between taking into account and taking account of is one which does not equate mere mention of the children as a factor in the decision with taking their interests into account. A mere tick in the box is not enough.

The problem here—one explored in detail by Fox-Decent—is whether a court engaged in review of a decision to see whether the official was alert, alive and sensitive to the children's interests can avoid reweighing the interests in a fashion that makes an illegitimate judgment about the substantive merits of the decision. In his judgment for the Federal Court of Appeal in *Baker*, Strayer JA had given a lucid warning that any attempt by courts to attach weight to factors that had to be taken into account by administrative decision-makers would put judges into the business of second-guessing the decision-makers on the merits.[19] And in two decisions subsequent to *Baker*, the Federal Court has sought to challenge the integrity of its structure by

---

[17] *Minister for Immigration and Ethnic Affairs v Teoh* (1995) 183 CLR 273 (HCA).
[18] *Baker*, paras 74–5.
[19] *Baker v Canada* 142 DLR (4th) 554 (FCA), para 12.

asserting that a purely 'procedural' interpretation of the judgment, one that reserves the issue of weight for the administration, is the only way for the courts to avoid full substantive review.[20]

Since the Supreme Court has denied leave to appeal in one of these cases and in the other—*Suresh*[21]—affirmed that the Federal Court of Appeal's 'procedural' or box ticking interpretation of the situation in administrative law is the correct one, it might seem that the Court has peered into the abyss of merits review and stepped back to a more traditional understanding of administrative law, where judges stay firmly on the process side of a distinction between process and substance.

One way to understand the Court's retreat in *Suresh* from *Baker* is as a reaction to the events of 11 September 2001. Suresh had refugee status in Canada, had applied for landed immigrant status or permanent residence, but the minister wanted to deport him to his native Sri Lanka on the basis that he was a 'danger to the security of Canada'. Suresh challenged that determination and argued that he faced a substantial risk of torture if he were deported, so that deportation would both threaten his constitutionally protected right to 'life, liberty and security of the person' and Canada's obligations under international law. Argument had concluded well before 11 September. It became clear that the government was concerned that the spirit of *Baker* might get in the way of its ability to make unconstrained determinations about national security and the Minister of Justice urged the Court to reconvene to hear argument about the need for courts after 11 September to reconceive their role. The Court did not accede to this request but it did reconceive its role. It adopted a very troubling dictum by Lord Hoffmann in his speech for the House of Lords in *Rehman*[22] and apparently his formal view of the separation of powers with all the consequences that that view underwrites for administrative law. However, it is important to keep in mind that the dissent in *Baker*, like Strayer JA's decision for the Federal Court of Appeal in the same case, were not driven by panic but by tradition. So another way of understanding the conjuncture of *Suresh* or *Rehman* and 11 September is that 11 September served as a wake up call to the judiciary about the dangers of departing from traditional assumptions.[23]

---

[20] See *Suresh v Canada (Minister of Citizenship and Immigration)* (2000), 183 DLR (4th) 629 (FCA) and *Legault v Canada (Minister of Citizenship and Immigration)*. (2002) 212 DLR (4th) 139 (FCA).
[21] *Suresh v Canada (Minister of Citizenship and Immigration)*, 2002 SCC 1.
[22] *Ibid*, para 33, quoting from *Rehman*, para 62.
[23] This more charitable interpretation of *Suresh* is difficult to square with the fact that the Court also imposed a fairly stiff hearing requirement on the officials who made the determination that someone faces the risk of torture. That is, on the traditional or formal understanding of the separation of powers, to impose the hearing requirement is to trench on Parliament's authority to legislate.

If that is right, then the structure of L'Heureux-Dubé J's judgment in *Baker* might begin to unravel, leaving the dissenting judgment as the official view of the Court, which then goes to show that the dissent was not in fact confined to the issue of giving any domestic effect to an unincorporated convention.[24] Indeed, the formal view of the separation of powers articulated in that dissent underwrites in principle much more than a stance on this issue. It also underwrites an objection to any attempt by judges to complicate the process/substance distinction or to articulate a role for themselves as guardians of unwritten fundamental values, values which do not have their source in legislative pronouncement. The objection is, that is, not only to backdoor incorporation of the *Convention*, but also to what would be deemed from the traditional perspective an illegitimate judicial introduction of the kind of proportionality test mandated by the *European Convention* or by the Canadian *Charter* into the common law.

As already noted, Mullan wants to support the traditional view in so far as it underwrites the claim that courts should not second-guess administrative officials on how to weigh the reasons that are in the balance. If courts are able to do this, then, in his opinion, they abandon deference for they are using a correctness standard under the guise of reasonableness. Indeed, Mullan and Allars are the two contributors to this volume who would most want to insert a question mark after its title. For Mullan, at least, seems to prefer the public law world envisioned by the dissent in *Baker*, one in which written constitutional values are given full effect within their scope while in administrative law, judges refrain from imposing their values on the administration. Allars's view might be the same in that she seems to suggest that in Australia, because of the absence of a constitution which protects fundamental values, the legislature may legitimately shield an area of administrative decision-making from judicial scrutiny, thus introducing an area where the writ of the substantive rule of law does not run. But, we must keep in mind, it is not that they want the interests of the Bakers, Sureshes and Teohs of this worlds to go unprotected, only that they think that the best way to protect them is through the equivalent of a bill of rights which judges interpret generously.

It is not clear to me whether Mullan and Allars would also want to question the legitimacy of judicial reliance, as in *Baker* and *Teoh*, on unincorporated conventions, since that reliance is, as I understand it, designed to bring about the unity of public law. Perhaps they would not object, as long as the reliance does not give such 'soft' international law the kind of weight that would turn the conventions into a binding source of authority. For precisely this reason, Brunnée and Toope want to inscribe a distinction between binding and persuasive authority into the courts' understanding of

---

[24] The judgment in *Suresh* was a judgment of the Court, of which L'Heureux-Dubé J was a member.

international law, but to expand the category of binding authority.[25] Only if international law, generously understood, is regarded as binding will the courts' hesitant embrace become a consummated union. An analogy here is with judicial control of discretion and the distinctions between relevant factors, mandatory relevant factors, and weighted mandatory relevant factors. If factors are considered relevant, an official cannot be faulted for not taking them into account. If they are mandatory, then they have to be taken into account but the official might do so, as I suggested above, by merely ticking the box without according the factor any weight. Such an exercise is what Brunnée and Toope deem according something persuasive authority—one opens oneself up to the possibility of persuasion but can refuse to be persuaded, exactly the procedural requirement the High Court of Australia imposed on immigration officials in *Teoh*. So Brunnée and Toope seem to be advocating that courts should treat international law as a weighted mandatory relevant factor in their own reasoning. It is binding, in that the courts have to take it into account and take it into account seriously. But it is not binding in the sense that it will dictate solutions, as it will be up to the judges to decide how, say, making the best interests of the children a primary consideration applies in the immigration context.

If this is the right interpretation of their argument, then the difference between them and Moran seems mostly terminological, as Moran's identification of a distinct kind of authority—influential authority—might seem to accord exactly the same force to international law as Brunnée and Toope: something in between dictation of a particular result and apparent openness to persuasion. And Brunnée and Toope were clear at the conference that they thought that there were important instrumental reasons for drawing the distinction between binding and persuasive authority. The category of influential authority is hard to distinguish from persuasive authority, and so risks losing any power over judges, while the idea of bindingness is something that judges understand and will have to take seriously.

But as Macklin argues, it might be exactly when judges think that the outcome of their decision is going to be dictated by a force outside the borders of the nation state, the alien other of international law, that they are likely to move international law into a category where they can decide ultimately to ignore it. In her view, the difference between *Baker* and *Ahani*[26]—a decision of the Ontario Court of Appeal discussed by several contributors—is that in *Baker* the reliance on international law could be diffused or dissipated, because there were domestic sources for the Court's emphasis on the obligations attached to the best interests of the children,

---

[25] And here there is an analogy with Mullan, who wants to expand the scope of which interests are constitutionally protected and then give these fuller protection than they would get at common law.
[26] *Ahani v Canada (Attorney General)* (2002) 58 OR (3d) 107.

while in *Ahani*, 'soft' international law was the only possible source and thus had ultimately to be ignored.

In addition, when one reads Moran, Macklin and Walters together, the issues at stake seem more fundamentally methodological than instrumental. Macklin argues that as soon as the Supreme Court makes what looks like an advance in one area of administrative law, the demarcations or borders of other areas, which might at first seem not implicated by the decision, start to disintegrate. However, her argument is not designed to reveal a normative basis to *Baker*, one that can then be put to work to redesign the whole. Rather, she presents a kind of archeology of *Baker*—an inquiry into what is revealed as one digs ever deeper into its structure, finding the sedimented and mixed together remains of other structures, which in turn require excavation. But one never strikes rock bottom.

In contrast, Moran and Walters might be understood to argue that what is revealed is the methodology of the common law, one in which judges are continually rearticulating the values of the tradition which seeks to expose the reason of the law. Such reason legitimately controls the exercise of public power, since public power is legitimate only when it serves the fundamental, constitutional values of a society, values which are now best understood as including the aspiration to live up to the human rights which have crystalised in international treaties and conventions. This view of the reason of the common law also animates Allan's account of a constitutional basis for adjudication, whether or not there is an entrenched bill of rights. And it underlies both the analysis and the positive prescriptions in Cartier's careful untying of one of the hardest knots in Canadian public law, one which will likely occur in any common law legal order that takes the step of adopting a bill of rights—the question of the relationship between the common law of judicial review and constitutional review in the wake of the adoption of the bill of rights. Cartier argues that what we get is not an infusion of value from the constitutional domain into the administrative domain. Rather, we get a rediscovery of the value basis of the common law of judicial review, a discovery which should lead to a role for administrative law in nurturing constitutional law, just as much as we might think that constitutional law will nurture administrative law. On Cartier's account of the relationship between constitutional and administrative law, it would be a mistake to think of judges as imposing a proportionality test on the common law of judicial review. Rather, the development by courts of a proportionality test for the *Charter* for dealing with *Charter*-protected values helped judges to better understand how to go about value-based review at common law, which was their task all along.

Such deliberately romantic and optimistic accounts of the common law tradition, suitably updated for an era of constitutionalism and human rights, were challenged not only by the chapters by Allars, Blake, Kelley, Macklin and Mullan, who chart the judicial retreat from constitutionalism and human rights, but also in oral interventions at the conference by two of Canada's most distinguished human rights lawyers, Mary Eberts and Barbara Jackman. The impression from their interventions of the fabric of constitutionalism and human rights protection in Canada was far from optimistic. They wished to draw attention not only to a retreat from constitutionalism on the part of the Canadian judiciary, but also to the way in which the federal government is placing ever more procedural obstacles in the path of judicial review, thus making it ever harder to get one's claim into a court and then, if one gets into court, to challenge the basis of the executive's decision.[27] Indeed, one might conclude that judges, prompted by the legislature and by government, have dealt with the relationship between bills of rights and the common law of judicial review by seeking to push matters into the administrative law realm, precisely because there scrutiny is less intense and the available remedies are fewer and less effective.[28] At most, as Mary Eberts put it, the common law of judicial review can be like the canary in the coal mine, warning of impending disaster but unable to deal with it. And if, as she suggested, the jurisdiction's bill of rights has been marginalised and the politicians and their supporters don't care, the disaster will take place.

Blake, however, who has the same kind of record of advocacy in the United Kingdom as Eberts and Jackman, seemed more optimistic. While his chapter describes a one step forward, two steps back approach by the English courts, the first step, on his account, is a stride taken with a ten league boot that far outstrips the two steps back in decisions such as *Rehman*. And in one of his oral interventions he brought Walter's necessarily abstract sketch of Kant's *ius cosmopoliticum* in which the individual must be seen as bearer of rights, whether or not she is a citizen, into sharp relief. Blake depicted the human rights advocate's role as an attempt to get the judge to see that the individual whose fate turns on his decision is not an abstraction, but a human being, who might be killed, disappeared, or tortured, if the judge gets the decision wrong. And at this point one might connect Blake's arguments about the decisions in his chapter, many of

---

[27] One should also take into account that the judges are no less capable of this kind of procedural move. At the conference, Cheryl Milne reminded us that there is a sense in which *Baker* might be understood to have marginalised the interests of the children, as the Court refused to grant standing to the children of Mavis Baker at the Federal Court trial and appeal levels, and therefore, avoided addressing directly the children's constitutional rights.

[28] On this view, one might have a rather less sanguine interpretation than the one offered by Allan in his chapter and by Paul Craig in his oral interventions of the rediscovery by English judges of the value basis of the common law in the period leading up to the enactment of the *Human Rights Act* (1998). That is, the judges would say that there was no need to have regard to the European Convention since the common law could do all the work but they then would find that the common law did not give any relief to the applicant in cases where the European Convention would have required more; see Hunt, *Using Human Rights Law in English Courts* (Oxford, Hart Publishing, 1997).

which are cases in which he has appeared, with Allan's emphasis on the need for more intensive judicial review, the more the fate of a particular individual turns on an administrative decision. Both Allan and Blake, perhaps in contrast to Mullan, seem to be warning against any attempt to design a set of formal criteria on which judges should base their decisions about when it is appropriate to defer to the executive.

There is another perspective that has to be taken into account, which also goes some way to mitigate the pessimism. The conference was forcefully reminded by Susan Davis and Milly Morton, lawyers who have worked with or for government in the area of immigration policy, that one should not underestimate the good faith or efforts of governments to implement their immigration policies in a humane and compassionate way. Government is not always the big bad other. It might be the principal agent for putting in place human rights criteria and then attempting to follow through on them, though necessarily in a way that takes account of competing policy considerations, etc. The contrast here, between the stance of the Canadian government and that depicted by Allars of the Australian government could not be starker.

And, as both chapters in this book and much of the discussion of the conference made clear, this issue has profound theoretical implications. As we have seen from *Baker*, there were two levels at which we could understand the executive as an implementer of human rights. First, there was the fact that the executive had ratified the *Convention*, even though L'Heureux-Dubé J tried to steer well clear of placing any significance on this fact. Second, and here she placed a great deal of significance, there was the fact of statutory language—'humanitarian and compassionate' grounds—and the departmental policies that were standing directives about how officials should implement that language. As Lorne Sossin argues, if we are to take seriously the issue of the impact of judicial decisions like *Baker* on the administration, we also have to consider the status of the policy crafted by the administrators in order to implement the Court's understanding of legality or the rule of law. One might indeed have to understand such policy as 'soft law', as having legal force in much the same way as 'soft' international law should have legal force domestically; indeed, the administrative soft law is a way of implementing the international soft law.

This argument introduces several fruitful tensions into the already complex picture. As we have seen, the dissent in *Baker* is based on a formal conception of the separation of powers which underwrites an objection to the executive being permitted by judges to become a source of legal duties. The romantic view of the common law does not, however, operate with this formal conception. Rather, it urges an understanding of the relationship between legislature and judiciary, in which both are involved in a common project whose purpose is to articulate the fundamental values of the society. Judges should interpret legislation in light of these values unless the legislature very explicitly disabuses judges of its intention to be part of the project. Sossin's account of the impact of soft administrative law invites us to consider the executive as part of this same common project. But if the executive is to be part of this project, then the formal conception of the role of the executive will have to be revised in two fundamental respects. Neither the formal conception's allocation of a legislative monopoly to parliament, nor its allocation of a monopoly on interpretation of the law to the judiciary can be maintained, since the soft law of the executive is the product both of executive law creation and executive interpretation of the law.

One way to salvage the formal conception is to insist that judges will always review executive interpretation of the law on a correctness standard and to deny any legal force to acts like executive ratification of human rights conventions or to executive policy which might try to put those conventions into practice when there is no statutory requirement to do so. This, as suggested, is more or less the stance of the dissent in *Baker*.[29] But, Sossin points out, there is a rule of law cost to this formal stance since, at least at the level of policy,[30] it seems to consider policy to be arbitrary, unlawlike, the product of executive whim. Indeed, it might be that this understanding of policy leads to metaphors like 'abuse of discretion', where the controlling idea is that the executive can do what it likes until it does something egregious. In contrast, Liston, Fox-Decent, Sossin, Cartier and others want to rethink the concept of discretion along lines prompted by L'Heureux-Dubé J's requirement that decision makers be 'alert, alive and sensitive'; here Cartier suggests a different metaphor for understanding discretion, discretion as a 'dialogue' between decision-maker and individual. But it follows that if we want the executive to be controlled by the rule of law, we have to take its policy seriously as law. And this requires not only that judges have to consider deferring to the more interpretative exercises of executive judgment, but that we should consider how to make the more legislative exercises more responsive to mechanisms for ensuring accountability and transparency.

As Mullan reminds us, even if one has concerns that *Baker* might endanger the distinction between review and appeal on the merits, these have to take into account that L'Heureux-Dubé J purported to be following the Supreme

---

[29] 'Less' if one takes into account that the two judges did not disapprove of the Canadian jurisprudence on deference developed since *CUPE* and that one of the two dissenters, Cory J, was one of the main proponents of a strong theory of deference. However, 'more' if one takes into account that Iacobucci J's development of the standard of reasonableness in *Southam* might be best understood as opening the door to correctness review of precisely the kind of interpretation of general and abstract propositions of law that *CUPE* said required the patent unreasonableness standard. If this is the correct understanding of *Southam*, then Allan's account of deference offers the opposite analysis of when deference is appropriate.

[30] I say at least, because there was some discussion at the conference of the possibility that the executive should be considered (contrary to the dominant view) to be under a duty to make policy which attempts to implement ratified human rights treaties. This discussion then raised the question whether such a duty would not chill executive ratification.

Court of Canada's jurisprudence on deference and indeed takes that jurisprudence a step forward in her recognition that courts should consider deferring to executive determinations of the content of fairness. And since Cartier thinks that the nurturing relationship between *Charter* and administrative law is two-way, one might infer that she would think that courts should be open to the possibility that different degrees of intensity of judicial review should be available even when the issue is the impact of an administrative decision on a *Charter*-protected value.

There is a potentially fruitful link here between Sossin's account of soft law and Allan's analysis of deference. For on Allan's analysis, it is much more likely that judges should defer when the executive is making highly abstract general policy decisions about how to interpret the law, even if these are to be accorded legal force, so that we think of it as acting in a quasi-legislative capacity, than when it acts in a more judicial capacity and interprets that policy so as to apply it to a particular individual. This is not to say that judges should refrain from review when it comes to the quasi-legislative role, for there, as Sossin might be suggesting, they should have a role in ensuring that mechanisms for accountability and transparency are in place. One might then avoid the danger, against which Allan warns, of permitting accounts of deference to serve the role occupied hitherto by justiciability—providing masks for judges to evade a responsibility to enforce the rule of law in highly charged political matters.

INSTRUMENTALISM AND METHODOLOGY

The chapters ahead might seem to offer a simple choice when it comes to the question of the unity of public law. We should conceive of public law as a unity or as compartmentalised in more traditional ways, depending on what will serve us best. The choice will then be determined on instrumental grounds with the criteria for choice being the set of values one argues public law should seek to advance.

However, I doubt that such instrumentalism can assist in clarifying the issues, in part because methodological issues intrude. These issues have to do with how best to understand law, in particular the common law tradition and its relationship with parliament, the executive and the international legal order. As Michael Taggart argues in the closing chapter, his sustained reflection on the conference as a whole, the lesson of *Baker* is that when we try to make sense of the common law of public law we find ourselves in a tub of values and sources which perpetually rub and dub.[31] As I understand this rich metaphor, that we are in a tub tells us that no neat compartmentalisation is possible; at best we can make tentative efforts to reduce the

[31] According to my *Oxford English Dictionary*, dubbing has to do with the beat of a drum.

friction and harmonise the noise. But those efforts must be made because on them often turns the fate of individuals who may rightly demand that they are treated in accordance with the rule of law.

And, at this point, I want to assert the prerogative of the editor, writing the introductory chapter, and leave it to the others to provide enlightenment.

2

Deference from Baker[1] *to* Suresh[2] *and Beyond—Interpreting the Conflicting Signals*

DAVID MULLAN[3]

There should really be no doubt in any reader's mind that the application of the functional and pragmatic approach to the discretionary decisions at stake in *Baker* marks not an extension of deference but a retreat from it.

JLH Sprague, 'Another View of *Baker*'.[4]

INTRODUCTION

ON 21 DECEMBER 2001, over 20 years after she arrived in Canada as a visitor from Jamaica, Mavis Baker achieved her ambition: permanent resident status in this country.[5] In the course of her struggles to this end, Mavis Baker had a massive collateral impact. The judgment on her appeal to the Supreme Court of Canada involved a consideration and re-evaluation of several concerns that are central to the ways in which statutory and prerogative authorities take decisions and particularly exercise discretionary powers. The consequences of *Baker* for Canadian judicial review theory was one of the main reasons for the conference which provided the basis for this collection.

---

[1] *Baker v Canada (Minister of Citizenship and Immigration)* [1999] 2 SCR 817.
[2] *Suresh v Canada (Minister of Citizenship and Immigration)* [2002] 1 SCR 3.
[3] This chapter owes a great deal to comments that I received on the conference version from both David Dyzenhaus and Evan Fox-Decent. It also benefited from Evan's presentation of my paper at the conference and the questions he raised in that presentation, as well as many further insights that I gained from reading the other conference papers and listening to the various presentations and interventions. I am also very grateful to Allison Kuntz of Law '03 (Queen's) for her diligent unearthing and analysis of all Canadian judgments in which *Baker* had been cited until the end of 2001.
[4] (1999) 7 *Reid's Administrative Law* 163 at 163.
[5] C Gillis, 'Mother in battle over deportation legally a resident', *National Post*, 22 December 2001.

The starting point for this chapter is *Baker*'s impact on the standard of review that the courts apply in reviewing exercises of public power; the degree of deference, if any they pay to the judgment of the designated decision-maker. One of the keenest debates about the impact of *Baker* has focused on whether the principles for review of discretionary decision-making set out in the majority judgment of L'Heureux-Dubé J presaged an era of greater, the same, or less deference in the conduct of judicial review. What I will do first is to evaluate that question simply on the basis of *Baker* itself and its place in the development of Canadian judicial review of administrative action.

I will then consider how deference theory has fared subsequently mainly in the Supreme Court of Canada in the domains of both executive or discretionary decision-making and tribunal adjudications. Does the subsequent jurisprudence provide any answers or clues to the issue of whether *Baker* heralded renewed judicial interventionism in the administrative process? My answer to that question, as with my analysis of *Baker* on its own terms, is that the message is mixed. In some areas of judicial review, there are clear signs of a lessening of judicial deference or respect for statutory decision-making, though, in most instances, I believe it is difficult to attribute that to *Baker*. In the particular context of discretionary or executive decision-making, the opposite has been true or, perhaps more accurately, the Court has actually deployed *Baker* or concepts underpinning *Baker* to confirm and even increase traditional patterns of considerable deference to the highest levels of that form of decision-making. Here, the principal 'villain' is the Court's judgment in *Suresh v Canada (Minister of Citizenship and Immigration)*[6] in which a highly deferential approach was taken to the exercise of discretion in a case involving national security issues but which also, because of the possibility of a substantial risk of torture at the hands of another government, implicated rights protected under section 7 of the *Canadian Charter of Rights and Freedoms*.

In the final section of my chapter, I will step back from the detailed evaluation of case law and attempt, by reference to an evaluation of what 'deference' as a concept is actually addressing, to suggest that the Supreme Court is beginning to get it all backwards. In other words, I will argue that, while I continue to applaud *Baker* itself, the Court has subsequently been lessening deference in domains where it is most justified and increasing deference in relation to decision-making where there is frequently strong justification for judicial scrutiny of the grounds on which those mainly discretionary decisions are taken. More specifically, I will argue that, where, as in *Suresh*, discretionary decision-making engaging *Charter* rights is at issue, without a fully articulated justification under section 1 of the *Charter*,

---

[6] Above n 2.

it is perverse to adopt a standard of review, that of patent unreasonableness, which is less searching than that adopted in *Baker*. This is so irrespective of the way in which the Court's posture towards discretionary decision-making in *Baker* is interpreted.

BAKER AND DEFERENCE

Heightened Deference Indicators

One of *Baker*'s principal contributions to Canadian judicial review is its extension of the 'pragmatic and functional' approach to delineating the appropriate standard of review. To that point, this approach had been associated primarily with the determination of the appropriate standard of review for questions of law, mixed law and fact, and fact addressed by tribunals charged with resolving issues arising under what were often detailed statutory schemes. It had not been associated all that often with the review of grants of broad discretionary power to governmental officials. In *Baker*, L'Heureux-Dubé J noted the difficulty at the margins in drawing distinctions between the determination of issues of law and fact and the exercise of discretionary power. If that is so, why would standard of review analysis apply in one domain and not the other? More generally, was there any reason to believe that the bases on which the courts paid more deference to some tribunals than others were not also bases that would be useful in determining the extent to which the exercise of broader discretionary decision-making powers should be subjected to review? The Court, therefore, pronounced that henceforth all forms of decision-making would be subjected to a threshold standard of review analysis. On the basis of a pragmatic and functional analysis, which of the three commonly accepted standards applied: incorrectness, unreasonableness, or patent unreasonableness?[7]

This extension of standard of review analysis to territory where it had not generally been a factor raises the obvious question: would there now be more or less room to review discretionary decision-making? My early position was that, for the most part, it would in fact impose an even more

---

[7] For the purposes of this chapter, I am assuming that 'reasonableness' and 'reasonableness *simpliciter*' are the same beast and am ignoring other possible refinements such as British Columbia authority that suggests that, even within the correctness standard, there is room for deference: eg *Northwood Inc v British Columbia (Forest Products Board)* (2001) 86 BCLR (3d) 215 (BCCA) at para 36 (*per* Lambert JA). Indeed, this issue seems settled by the dogmatic statement of McLachlin CJ for the majority in *Chamberlain v Surrey School District No 36*, 2002 SCC 86 (20 December 2002) at para 5: 'The pragmatic and functional approach applicable to judicial review allows for three standards of review: correctness, patent unreasonableness and an intermediate standard of reasonableness'. [Now affirmed in *Law Society of New Brunswick v Ryan*, 2003 SCC 20 at para 20].

deferential standard of review in such cases.[8] My basis for this was the manner in which the existing grounds for judicial intervention in discretionary decision-making were framed in the language of 'correctness'. Taking account of irrelevant factors, failing to take account of relevant factors, acting for a wrongful purpose or one not contemplated by the empowering legislation all spoke to the reviewing court determining on a correctness basis whether the decision-maker had erred in law in the interpretation of what factors were relevant and what were appropriate purposes in terms of the governing statute.[9] The vocabulary, if not the practice[10] of this area of judicial review law, did not seem to concede to the decision-maker any room for manoeuvre in determining any of these questions save in situations where the relevant statutory provision conferred on the authority a subjective discretion as to relevance.[11]

What the judgment of L'Heureux-Dubé J suggested at various points was that the application of standard of review analysis to challenges based on these grounds[12] would involve the potential for much more deference to decision-making in which there was a high level of discretion. Only in rare

---

[8] See *'Baker v Canada (Minister of Citizenship and Immigration)*—A Defining Moment in Canadian Administrative Law' (1999) 7 *Reid's Administrative Law* 145.

[9] Indeed, one of the problematic aspects of the foundational cases in modern Canadian administrative law on the need for deference to decisions taken by administrative tribunals within their home territory or expected area of expertise was that Dickson J (as he then was) left open the possibility that 'patent unreasonableness' would exist whenever a statutory authority was 'basing the decision on extraneous matters, [or] failing to take relevant factors into account': *Canadian Union of Public Employees, Local 963 v New Brunswick Liquor Corporation* [1979] 2 SCR 227 at 237, by reference back to his judgment in *Service Employees' International Union v Nipawin Union Hospital* [1975] 1 SCR 382 at 389. What this suggested is that the Court should determine, on a correctness basis, whether the decision-maker had taken into account irrelevant factors or failed to take account of relevant factors. If this had in fact happened, there was patent unreasonableness. Such an approach seems to leave little room for deference or respect for decision-maker appreciation of those factors or considerations that were relevant to the interpretation of a particular statutory provision or the exercise of a particular statutory power. In other words, there was a built-in contradiction in the theory developed by Dickson J and espoused by the Court.

[10] In fact, particularly in the domain of judicial review of executive decision-making, this rhetoric or theory was not one that led to many instances of judicial review. Deference to the higher levels of discretionary powers conferred on the executive branch (as opposed to tribunals) remained the practice with few examples of wrongful purpose, irrelevant consideration and failure to take account of relevant considerations review. I have developed this theme in 'The Role of the Judiciary in the Review of Administrative Policy Decisions: Issues of Legality' in *The Judiciary as Third Branch of Government: Manifestations and Challenges to Legitimacy,* Mossman and Otis, eds, (Montréal, Les Éditions Thémis, 2000). Among the exceptions is, of course, *Roncarelli v Duplessis* [1959] SCR 121, which is cited in *Baker* at para 53 and may provide some indication of one way to resolve the apparent inconsistencies in L'Heureux-Dubé J's judgment on review for abuse of discretion. I return to this matter below.

[11] See, eg, *Sheehan v Ontario (Criminal Injuries Compensation Board)* (1974) 52 DLR (3d) 728 (Ont CA).

[12] Obviously, the whole standard of review analysis has no application to a number of the other accepted bases for challenging exercises of discretion: bad faith, acting under dictation, wrongful delegation and also (probably) wrongful fettering.

cases would the inquiry still be a correctness one: was the decision-maker correct in treating or failing to treat this as a relevant factor? Rather, in the vast majority of cases, the inquiry would become: was the decision-maker unreasonable or patently unreasonable in treating or failing to treat this as a relevant factor? If so, this was going to make it harder for those challenging on these grounds to succeed.

This sense emerges most clearly in the following extract from the judgment:

> Incorporating judicial review of decisions that involve considerable discretion into the pragmatic and functional analysis for errors of law should not be seen as reducing the level of deference given to decisions of a highly discretionary nature. In fact, deferential standards of review may give substantial leeway to the discretionary decision-maker in determining the 'proper purpose' or 'relevant considerations' involved in making a given determination. The pragmatic and functional approach can take into account the fact that the more discretion is left to a decision-maker, the more reluctant the courts should be to interfere with the manner in which decision-makers have made choices among various options.[13]

Indeed, it is significant that in this statement L'Heureux-Dubé J extends the reach of deference to the decision-maker's discernment of the purpose of the relevant statutory provisions. Taken at face value, this is quite surprising since it amounts to a concession that, at least in certain contexts, the Court is accepting that the legislature's delegate will have a better sense of the legislative purpose than the reviewing court.[14] In other words, it suggests that the Court will not always be the best interpreter of the underlying purposes of the statute in general and the relevant provisions in particular. Rather, those involved in the day to day administration of the statute have claims to deference and respect from the reviewing court in their articulation of the underlying purposes in the context of giving meaning to particular terms or discerning the boundaries of broad discretions.

---

[13] At para 56.
[14] In this context, compare the judgment of Sopinka J for the majority in *Shell Canada Products Ltd v Vancouver (City)* [1994] 1 SCR 231. There, he applied a correctness standard automatically in the context of a challenge to the City's decision not to trade with Shell Canada as long as its parent and a related company were still engaged in trade with apartheid South Africa. Despite the municipality's broad discretionary powers over governance of the City, the majority was clear that its assessment of what was a proper municipal purpose was entitled to no deference from the Court. In contrast, McLachlin J, speaking for a minority of four, would have accorded the municipality considerable deference in its assessment of what was appropriate for 'the good rule and government of the city' and 'for the health, welfare, safety and good government of the city'. In this context, the decisions of elected municipal officials has as strong a claim to deference as those taken by 'non-elected statutory boards and agencies' (at 246–47). In fact, in the light of *Baker*, it is questionable whether *Shell Canada* remains good law. In this regard, see *Chamberlain v Surrey School District, No 36*, above n 7 and *Nanaimo (City) v Rascal Trucking Ltd* [2000] 1 SCR 342.

What also seemed clear on the facts of *Baker* was that, to the extent that the Court adopted the 'unreasonableness' standard for review of the Minister's humanitarian and compassionate discretion conferred by the relevant regulation, it was relying upon some very particular considerations: the extent of the impact of the decision on Baker and her children, the absence of any polycentric dimensions in the regular exercise of this discretion, and, at least implicitly, the fact that low level officials were exercising the power on behalf of the Minister. The clear implication of all of this was that, in the domain of decision-making where the individual interests at stake were less valued and the determination not a stand alone one dependent on facts peculiar to a particular person, the standard of review for discretionary decision-making would be that of patent unreasonableness. Indeed, given the strength of the factors in *Baker* pointing towards more intrusive review, it is difficult to conceive of many instances where the Court would have taken the next step and moved to correctness as the standard save perhaps where *Charter* or other constitutional rights and freedoms were at stake,[15] an argument never reached by the Court in *Baker*. In so far as the focus remains on the determination of what constitutes relevant factors and permissible purposes (as opposed to any assessment of the way in which those factors and purposes were applied to the facts of the particular case), this speaks to the extent of the movement away from intrusive correctness review in cases concerning the boundaries of the relevant discretion.

It is also worth recollecting that *Baker* was the first instance[16] in which, in the domain of general procedural fairness requirements, the Court clearly articulated that, in assessing the level of procedures that the common law required in the face of legislative silence or a gap, the procedural choices of

---

[15] Indeed, as will be seen below, even that did not prove to be the case in *Suresh v Canada (Minister of Citizenship and Immigration)*, above n 2.

[16] There were, however, earlier judgments of the Court which seemed to acknowledge that administrative authorities were entitled to a certain leeway in their procedural choices. Thus, in the foundation case of *Nicholson v Haldimand-Norfolk Regional Board of Commissioners of Police* [1979] 1 SCR 311, Laskin CJ (at 328), in referring the question of Nicholson's status back to the Board to be dealt with in accordance with the principles of procedural fairness allowed the Board discretion to reconsider the question of Nicholson's future as a police officer 'whether orally or in writing as the Board might determine'. In similar vein, in *Board of Education of the Indian Head School Division No 19 of Saskatchewan v Knight* [1990] 1 SCR 653 at 685, L'Heureux-Dubé J made the following statement:

> It must not be forgotten that every administrative body is the master of its own procedure and need not assume the trappings of a court. The object is not to import into administrative proceedings the rigidity of the requirements of natural justice that must be observed by a court, but rather to allow **administrative bodies to work out a system** that is flexible, adapted to their needs and fair [emphasis added].

Such statements clearly foreshadowed the more explicit recognition of the need on occasion for deference to procedural rules and rulings. (*Quaere*, however, whether it is ever appropriate to go even further as suggested by *Knight* and to allow for contracting out of the procedural protections that the common law would normally require.)

the decision-maker were at least on occasion entitled to deference or respect. This was to be the case both where

> the statute leaves to the decision-maker the ability to choose its own procedures, **or** when the agency has expertise in determining what procedures are appropriate in the circumstances [emphasis added].[17]

While there had been some recognition of the need for deference to the exercise of explicit statutory conferrals of discretion over procedures,[18] the operating assumption in all other situations had been one of straight correctness review. Procedural issues were the domain *par excellence* of the superior courts.

On the basis of this, I assumed that *Baker* was in fact adding further dimensions to the application of principles of deference, and this despite the fact that the Court did intervene and review the decision on both procedural and substantive grounds.

Heightened Intervention Indicators

For those, such as Sprague, who feared that *Baker* was ushering in an era of much greater judicial intervention in discretionary decision-making, the principal concern was that the judgment invited either straight incorrectness review or unreasonableness review of the substance of discretionary exercises of power. Indeed, his view was shared by some who rather than regretting such an innovation largely rejoiced in it.[19]

Their contention was that this altered dramatically the previously accepted law. That law was to the effect that, provided the decision-maker did not commit any of the very specific sins in discretionary decision-making (taking account of irrelevant factors, and so on), the decision-maker was almost completely immune from review. Only where the decision was, under the famous *Wednesbury* standard,[20] so unreasonable that no reasonable

---

[17] At para 27.
[18] See *Bibeault v McCaffrey* [1984] 1 SCR 176.
[19] See D Dyzenhaus and E Fox-Decent, 'Rethinking the Process/Substance Distinction: *Baker v Canada*' (2001) 51 *University of Toronto Law Journal* 193, as well as aspects of D Dyzenhaus, M Taggart and M Hunt, 'The Principle of Legality in Administrative Law: Internationalization as Constitutionalization' (2001) 1 *Oxford University Commonwealth Law Journal* 5 and D Dyzenhaus, 'Constituting the Rule of Law: Fundamental Values in Administrative Law' (2002) 27 *Queen's Law Journal* 445. See also L Sossin, 'Developments in Administrative Law: The 1997–98 and 1998–99 Terms' (2000) 11 *Supreme Court Law Review* (2d) 37.
[20] *Associated Provincial Picture Houses Ltd v Wednesbury Corporation* [1948] 1 KB 44 (CA). In fact, the *Wednesbury* test has in effect been replaced in English law by a more intrusive proportionality test. Eg *Daly v Secretary of State for the Home Department*, [2001] 2 WLR 1622 (HL) and the discussion by M Hunt, 'Sovereignty's Blight: Why Contemporary Public Law Needs the Concept of "Due Deference"', in N Leyland and P Bamforth (eds) *Public Law in a Multi-Layered Constitution* (Oxford, Hart Publishing, forthcoming).

authority could ever have come to it, would there be intervention. This was a very high standard for challengers to meet as exemplified by the almost complete absence of Canadian case law where *Wednesbury* unreasonableness had been pleaded successfully.[21] Now, it was asserted, for many tribunals, it would be a case of open-ended unreasonableness or incorrectness review of the merits for a broad range of decision-making. This was seen as a significant derogation from deference.

Support for that argument took two forms. First, there was the Court's repudiation of the earlier 'governing' Federal Court of Appeal judgment in *Shah v Canada (Minister of Employment and Immigration)*.[22] There, the Court of Appeal had stated that the exercise of the humanitarian and compassionate authority was in effect substantively unreviewable in that it was 'wholly a matter of judgment and discretion'.[23] Even more pertinently, there was the heading to the merits portion of the judgment in *Baker* ('Was this Decision Unreasonable?') and the application of the standard to the facts that followed under that heading. Not only did this suggest at large unreasonableness review but, in this context, also considerable room for judicial reweighing of the various factors that the ministerial officials had taken into account. The question to be asked was not just whether the decision-maker had given any consideration to the interests of Baker's children but also whether the officials had given those interests 'serious weight',[24] 'close attention',[25] or 'alive, attentive, or sensitive' consideration.[26] Then, in terms of the consequences to Baker herself, the Court's view was that the decision-makers had 'failed to give sufficient weight or consideration'[27] to the potential hardship involved in a return to Jamaica.

All of this seemed to leave great latitude for a reviewing court to assess whether the decision-maker had weighed all the relevant considerations properly. Indeed, even though this was all to be done under the umbrella of unreasonableness review, it bespoke a version of unreasonableness that comes close to a straight reassessment of the merits of Baker's claim. Instead of asking whether it was unreasonable not to take account of the interests of Baker's children (a finding that the Court in effect actually made here), the reviewing court could, indeed should also inquire whether it was unreasonable not to give that consideration considerable weight in making the assessment that the exercise of the discretion requires. While this does not speak to the precise weight to be accorded to the children's interests, it obviously allows more room for intervention in the balancing of interests or

---

[21] See DJ Mullan, *Administrative Law* (Toronto, Irwin Law, 2001) at 121–22.
[22] (1990) 170 NR 238 (F.C.A.).
[23] *Ibid*, at 239.
[24] At para 65.
[25] At para 67.
[26] At para 73.
[27] *Ibid*.

considerations by the decision-maker. Also, to the extent that this formulation became part of patent unreasonableness review in situations where that was the appropriate standard, it would have the same tendency to expand the granting of relief even under that most deferential of tests.

There was also another way in which many saw *Baker* as expansive. That was in the sense of its extension of the factors to which decision-makers would have to be attentive in making a decision. In *Baker*, the Court relied upon three primary indicators in reaching the conclusion that the interests of Baker's children was a relevant factor deserving of serious consideration: the purposes of the relevant legislation, the internal guidelines provided to immigration officials by the Minister, and the international Convention on the Rights of the Child.[28] Of these, the first was standard and uncontroversial. The second was novel but in its own way deferential in the sense that the Court was taking account of the views of those who were primarily responsible for giving effect to the exercise of discretion by developing policy guidelines for line officers. Presumably, their view as to relevance should count for more than that of the line officers themselves. It was, however, the third factor that attracted the most attention from commentators as well as the concurring judgment of Iacobucci and Cory JJ which demurred from the majority's use of a ratified but unincorporated treaty as an instrument to guide the assessment of what constituted relevant factors under domestic legislation.

According to the minority,[29] by requiring discretionary decision-makers to take account of ratified but unincorporated treaties, the majority was challenging the doctrine of legislative supremacy on which was based the rule that such treaties are not part of the domestic law of Canada.[30] More

---

[28] Can TS 1992 No 3.
[29] Above n 1 at paras 79–81.
[30] In fact, L'Heureux-Dubé J tried to take a middle ground on this matter. While explicitly accepting that such ratified but unincorporated treaties could have 'no direct application in Canadian law', she did regard Canada's ratification of the Convention on the Rights of the Child as an 'indicator of the importance of considering the interests of children': *ibid*, at para 69. Reconciling these two statements is not all that easy. However, it might be that all she is saying in this paragraph is that, just as the ministerial guidelines provide good evidence of how a discretion must be exercised, so too must other executive acts (such as ratification) provide evidence of what constitutes relevant considerations to the exercise of an open-ended discretion. However, thereafter (at paras 70–71), she goes on to speak more generally of the relevance of international law to the exercise of domestic discretionary powers. In this context, she seems to treat the Convention as part of a more general principle of international human rights law mandating the giving of serious consideration in all circumstances to the interests of children. In this domain, presumably, she is talking in terms of a peremptory norm of international law or customary international law, which do have force domestically irrespective of legislative implementation absent, according to parliamentary supremacists, legislative abrogation. I have no problem with either of these conceptions in the sense that they both have strong claims for recognition as legitimate sources for constraining or empowering the exercise of broad discretionary powers and, indeed, the giving of meaning to legislative provisions. Statutes, and particularly those conferring powers on public officials, do not exist in a vacuum and must be parsed within the context of the entire legal and political

generally, it was seen by some as adding a new (and for the critics) problematic dimension to the exercise of statutory power—the requirement that line decision-makers know of and actually attribute appropriate weight to all ratified but unincorporated treaties.[31] Given this, there would obviously be more opportunities for judicial review. Moreover, to the extent that the Court had earlier in *Pushpanathan v Canada (Minister of Employment and Immigration)*[32] refused to accord the Immigration and Refugee Board any deference when deciding a question of international law, when that issue was raised, there would be correctness, not deferential review.

More generally, L'Heureux-Dubé J stated that:

> discretion must be exercised in accordance with the boundaries imposed in the statute, the principles of the rule of law, the principles of administrative law, the fundamental values of Canadian society, and the principles of the *Charter*.[33]

At least three of these factors are uncontroversial (the statute, the *Charter*, and the principles of administrative law) A fourth, the rule of law is arguably a concept of such generality as not to have any free-standing force as a specific ground of review of exercises of discretion. However, to the extent that it is conceived of more expansively than in a formal Diceyan sense and is imbued with a substantive content, it may well have scope for providing 'new' limits on the exercise of discretionary power. Also, requiring the decision-maker to be attuned to the 'fundamental values of Canadian society' not only invites debate as to what precisely those values are or where they are to be found but also suggests room for judicial intervention if the court and the person exercising discretion are not in accord on what is fundamental.

Lurking in the background more generally and perhaps as part of the fundamental values of Canadian society are also the four underlying principles of the Canadian constitution identified in *Reference re Secession of Quebec*[34]: federalism, democracy, constitutionalism and the rule of law and the protection of minorities.[35] These 'substantive limitations upon

---

environment. Indeed, there is also a case to be made for the direct application of certain ratified but not specifically incorporated treaties. Some treaty obligations can be seen as not needing direct legislative implementation because of the capacities of existing statutory regimes to absorb them by reason of the breadth of the discretion or terms of the statutory provision to which they are clearly relevant. For fuller analysis, see J Brunnée and SJ Toope's chapter: 'A Hesitant Embrace: *Baker* and the Application of International Law by Canadian Courts'.

[31] This is not necessarily an insuperable problem as L Sossin argues in his chapter, 'The Rule of Policy: *Baker* and the Impact of Judicial Review on Administrative Discretion'.
[32] [1998] 1 SCR 982.
[33] At para 56.
[34] Hereinafter '*Secession Reference*'.
[35] [1998] 2 SCR 217.

government action'[36] also presaged an era of greater scope for judicial review of administrative action.

Reconciling the Two Polarities

Given these two very different readings of *Baker*, the question that naturally arises is whether this part of L'Heureux-Dubé J's judgment is internally inconsistent. Can the theory she develops[37] fit coherently with the application of that theory to the particular facts[38] of *Baker*?

One way of reconciling the two parts of the judgment that has the merit of simplicity is to see the application of the theory to the facts as amounting to a judgment by the Court that the line officers did not (other than negatively) take the children's interests into account in reaching their decision and that, under the appropriate standard, this was unreasonable. Moreover, to the extent that the Court spoke at least twice in terms of the obligation of the line officers to be 'alive, attentive, or sensitive' to the interests of the children, the Court was simply making a statement of what taking a factor into account, as opposed to not giving it any weight, actually involves. Tokenism will not suffice. Seen in this light, the Court is doing no more than saying that it was unreasonable for the line officers not to take the interests of the children into account. As such, it is consistent with the theory developed earlier in this part of the judgment.

However, this stands the danger of being branded as facile and disingenuous. After all, in other parts of the theory/fact application section, L'Heureux-Dubé J used language that clearly indicated that the Court was concerned with weight. As already noted, she spoke of the need to treat the best interests of the children 'as an important factor', and to give them 'substantial weight'. The same is true of Mavis Baker's own interests. The officials did not 'give sufficient weight or consideration' to the possible hardship she would suffer. Each of these statements goes beyond an evaluation of whether it was reasonable for the officials not to take particular factors into account. Rather they amount to assertions that reasonable officials were not only obliged to take them into account but to give them a certain weight. That clearly calls for another explanation of how the two relevant parts of the judgment are in agreement.

One other way of looking at it may be to focus on the characterisation or description of the consideration or factor that the applicant for relief is claiming is relevant. If that characterisation or description legitimately incorporates elements of weight or degree, then there may be a way out of

---

[36] At para 54.
[37] At paras 49–56.
[38] At paras 63–75 particularly.

the apparent dilemma of the judgment. Thus, in *Baker*, the question might be stated as whether or not it was unreasonable for the officials to value less than significantly the interests of the children and the hardship to Baker herself. Seen in these terms, the consideration for which the claim is being made is not just the interests of the children and the hardship to Baker herself but the seriousness of those interests and that hardship.

While that too may provide a neat way of reconciling the apparent contradiction or internal inconsistency in the judgment, there are some obvious objections to such a theory. The first is that it complicates even further the task of judicial review of discretionary decision-making. Not only does the reviewing court have to make a decision as to which of three standards applies to the actual decision but also it has to apply that standard to one of a number of possible variations on how the consideration is to be defined: permissibly relevant or mandatorily relevant and, if mandatorily relevant, entitled to just some weight, moderate weight, a lot of weight or decisive weight.[39] Thereafter, the next stage in the analysis will involve assessing whether the requisite attention has been paid to the consideration as defined. Thus, if on a patent unreasonableness standard, it would be patently unreasonable for the decision-maker not to give a lot of weight to a certain factor, the reviewing court will have to ask whether that considerable weight has in fact been given.

That leads into a second objection: the more gradations or variations that are recognised within this framework, the closer the ultimate stage becomes one of actually reweighing the manner in which the decision-maker exercised his or her discretion. Under some of the variations of this analysis (and in particular moderate weight and a lot of weight), it is virtually impossible to deal with the particular factor in isolation; it is only in relation to the other factors or considerations that were properly taken into account that a judgment can be made as to whether that particular factor was appropriately evaluated. At this stage, the task of the court is indeed one of reweighing albeit that the process of reweighing has been reached under the umbrella of an initial standard of review analysis.

Can this be justified either generally or on the particular facts of *Baker*? My belief is that, if there is a justification for a court going down this complex and ultimately interventionist path, it has to be based on strong reasons for that court accepting an applicant's argument that what counts as a consideration should be defined in terms of its importance or significance and not just its subject matter. If that indeed represents a substantial onus, then the general principles of deference are not necessarily compromised inappropriately. However, much will depend on what constitute the criteria that have to be addressed in meeting that onus.

---

[39] Other classifications are also possible representing either synonyms or more refined variations: primary consideration; serious consideration, to take two variants from *Baker* itself.

In terms of this latter concern, *Baker* is in fact instructive. It is in the context of the three critical indicators that L'Heureux-Dubé J moves to asserting that the interests at stake require not just some attention but close or serious consideration. The Act's intention that the discretion be exercised in light of a general policy of keeping family members together, the reiteration of that policy in the ministerial guidelines, and the protection accorded to the interests of children under the Convention on the Rights of the Child and more general international law provide the backdrop against which the Court moves to defining the considerations that reasonably have to be taken into account in terms of both subject matter (the interests of Baker's children and the hardship to her) and weight.

Seen in this light, the Court is not in fact asserting a general competence to review the weight to be attributed to all factors that might bear upon the exercise of the humanitarian and compassionate discretion or, indeed, dictating that all such permissive considerations are mandatory ones. Rather, the Court is isolating particular factors that it sees on a reasonableness standard of review as having particular significance, thereby justifying the attribution of weight as a component of them as considerations which have to be taken into account. In general terms, that seems to me to be legitimate.

It is also worth noting in this context that, at least in terms of the way the judgment is crafted, it is not possible to accuse the Court of double counting. The initial analysis that produced unreasonableness as the appropriate standard of review proceeds at a far higher level of generality. Thus, in describing the nature of the question to be asked, the Court at this point confines itself to talking of it in terms of one that 'relates directly to the rights and interests of an individual in relation to government, rather than balancing the interests of various constituencies or mediating between them'.[40] It does not refer to the more specific interests of Baker and her children which will be affected by the ultimate decision. They only emerge once the standard of review is established and the Court has moved to a consideration of whether the line officers failed the relevance test within that standard. However, the fact that that is so does beg at least one question and that is why, if in general standard of review determinations are so context-sensitive, these factors were not actually accounted for in the initial determination of what constituted the standard of review. Why did the Court in this case proceed at such a level of generality? Will that always be appropriate when standard of review analysis is being conducted in the context of broad discretionary powers?

In fact, the route just described is not the only way of reconciling the possible inconsistencies in L'Heureux-Dubé J's judgment. There is at least one other account or, at the very least, a variation on or addition to the argument just outlined. In the very paragraph in which she accepts

---

[40] *Ibid*, at para 60.

that deferential standards of review 'may give substantial leeway' to a discretionary decision-maker's assessment of what are proper purposes or relevant factors, she goes on to in effect qualify that by reference to the list which in a more general sense constitutes the boundaries within which discretion has to be exercised, including, as seen already, the rule of law and 'the fundamental values of Canadian society'. When the interests at stake come within the realm of these boundary-defining principles, either closer judicial scrutiny is required or the standard becomes a correctness one. Thus, it could be argued that when the Court later, by reference to the three indicators, becomes involved in the weight to be attributed to the interests of the children and the possible hardship suffered by Baker by a return to Jamaica, the Court is implicitly recognising that these are factors that implicate the boundaries—principles of international law (as part of a substantive conception of the rule of law) in the case of the interests of the children and the fundamental values of Canadian society in the case of the hardship to Mavis Baker.

It is in this context that there are the strongest echoes of *Roncarelli v Duplessis*.[41] There, the Court, in reviewing what was a broad discretion over liquor licenses, applied underlying conceptions of the Canadian constitution to conclude that the regulatory authority acting under the dictates of the Premier had proceeded on the basis of irrelevant considerations or for impermissible purposes in cancelling Roncarelli's liquor license: taking religious affiliations into account and punishing someone for exercising a recognised civil liberty, that of posting bail for those charged with criminal offences. In *Baker*, underlying principles surface to impose on the discretionary decision-maker the obligation to attribute a particular weight to factors which arise out of those underlying principles. Once again, under this theory, it is not every potentially relevant factor that will justify this treatment but only those which arise out of the underlying principles listed in the judgment. In general, it is once again hard to take issue with this.

There is, however, one aspect of the application of both this theory and the earlier one to the facts of *Baker* that is highly problematic. The way I have constructed each of these theories makes them out to be exceptions to the normal process of reviewing for abuse of discretion under an unreasonableness or patent unreasonableness standard. They each assert that, even in the exercise of broad discretions attracting a generally deferential posture on the part of the courts, considerations may become relevant and which, because of their significance, demand closer scrutiny in the context of judicial review. They may have to be not just taken into account but also given appropriate weight. They may even dictate that the discretionary decision-maker correctly define their content and accurately or precisely calibrate their relevance to the particular facts.

---

[41] Above n 10.

Even though the interests of children is likely to be a recurring issue in the exercise of the humanitarian and compassionate discretion, in the light of the Convention, general international law and, indeed, the fundamental values of Canadian society, it is a factor or consideration that presents strong claims for special treatment. Moreover, to the extent that it will not be a factor in every case, according it special status does not undercut the more general policy of being deferential to the 'Minister's' discretionary determinations and the reflection of that in the adoption of an unreasonableness standard. However, the same cannot be said of the issue of the hardship to Ms Baker herself. The potential hardship caused to the applicant by deportation will always be a factor in any claim to a favourable exercise of the Minister's discretion. To therefore decide at one level that the Minister's discretion deserves deference but then to assert, in the name of hardship to the applicant, a more intrusive level of scrutiny and one which concerns itself with the weight to be attributed to hardship, is to undercut the initial determination of the standard of review. Going back to a point made earlier in the context of the first theory, to the extent that the plight of applicants is a matter that will be relevant in every exercise of the discretion, it is a factor that should have been taken into account specifically in the determining of the initial standard of review and not postponed to emerge as a consideration dictating more intrusive scrutiny within that standard. This was a general factor; it was not one peculiar to Ms Baker or a subset of applicants for the favourable exercise of this discretion.

Indeed, if the initial issue of the standard of review was to be addressed appropriately, it probably did demand that the Court take seriously and not ignore the applicant's contention that her *Charter* rights were at stake here. To define the general standard of review in terms of an intermediate standard of deference without considering whether her *Charter* rights were implicated was to short change the applicant. Of course, it could be said that this omission was more than compensated for by the reality that the applicant was successful. However, as argued, the way in which that outcome was accomplished was troubling at least in so far as it depended on the ranking of hardship as a special consideration in the specific exercise of the discretion. It also postponed for another day the issues of whether the rights at stake here did engage the *Charter* rights of the applicant and, more generally, of how review of this kind of discretion was to be conducted when *Charter* rights were in issue.

None of what has been said to this point, however, accounts for the fact that the Court headed the relevant portion of the judgment: 'was this decision unreasonable?'[42] Indeed, the Court[43] by reference to the judgment of Iacobucci J in *Canada (Director of Investigation and Research)*

---

[42] Between paras 62 and 63.
[43] At para 63.

v Southam Inc,⁴⁴ then went on to describe an unreasonable decision as 'one that, in the main, is not supported by any reasons that can stand up to a somewhat proving examination'. That suggests that the Court is accepting that, in the context of review for abuse of discretion, the test of unreasonableness is one that addresses the overall conclusions of the decision-maker as well as the various component parts of the relevant decision. In other words, it invites a stepping back from the detail of the reasons provided and asking whether, in the light of all the circumstances, the decision itself is unreasonable on the facts.

In such an exercise, the reviewing court will of necessity have to assess the way in which the discretionary authority balanced all considerations. Indeed, in terms of the claims made above, this exercise is legitimised by the Court not in terms of special considerations relating to the rule of law and the values of Canadian society but 'by reference to the boundaries set out by the words of the statute and the values of administrative law'.⁴⁵ The process of overall assessment is one that must take place generally and not just when more underlying interests are at stake. When the standard of review is unreasonableness, the residual or catchall category of review exemplified by the *Wednesbury* standard shifts from a decision so unreasonable that no reasonable authority could ever have reached it (a type of patent unreasonableness standard) to one of straight unreasonableness. This obviously does have the potential for more intrusive review at least to the extent the courts become more inclined to treat discretionary decisions as subject to reasonableness rather than patent unreasonableness review.

However, it is worthwhile noting that, in the very context of this discussion, L'Heureux-Dubé J does not engage in any overall balancing exercise but focuses very specifically on the way in which one factor, the interests of the children was treated by the line officers.⁴⁶ The unreasonableness is related to a more specific ground of judicial review—failure to take account of relevant considerations. It does not depend on a global assessment. It is also worthy of reiteration that, in Canadian law, the *Wednesbury* standard has seldom been invoked successfully, and part of the reason for this may well be that, in any case approaching the *Wednesbury* standard, there will almost inevitably be present one of the more specific bases for intervention rendering any overall assessment of the merits redundant. There is at least a hint in L'Heureux-Dubé J's judgment at this point that she is more inclined to see unreasonableness in the context of the more specific grounds of judicial review for abuse of discretion than in terms of a global assessment.⁴⁷ Also,

---

⁴⁴ [1997] 1 SCR 748 at para 56.
⁴⁵ At para 66.
⁴⁶ At paras 64–65.
⁴⁷ Further evidence that the Supreme Court sees it this way is provided by the judgment of the majority (delivered by McLachlin CJ) in *Chamberlain v Surrey School District No 36*, above n 7. There the Court adopted a reasonableness standard with respect to a school board decision

in her reference to the work of Dyzenhaus and the concept of deference as respect,[48] she implies that one of the major concerns of the Court under the reasonableness standard is to ensure that the discretionary decision-maker both recognised the relevant considerations and justified the conclusion reached by reference to those considerations. Reasonableness in this sense becomes more a matter of adhering to a modality of decision-making.

In sum, there are many currents at play in *Baker* on the standard of review issue and how it plays out in the context of discretionary decision-making generally and the specific grounds of abuse of discretion review in particular. To the extent that the judgment does not explicitly tie many of these strands together, the judgment's message is unclear and it is not surprising that this has generated debate on whether, in applying the pragmatic and functional approach to discretionary decision-making, it opens up the door for more intrusive review of that form of decision-making thereby lessening the deference or respect that officials exercising such authority have commonly received from Canadian courts.

This undoubtedly left the lower courts with some dilemmas and, most notably, in cases where the applicant was urging that a decision was unreasonable in the sense that the decision-maker, while not ignoring a mandatory relevant factor, had none the less acted unreasonably in the weight attributed to it or in balancing it against other relevant considerations emerging from the facts of the case. To what extent did *Baker* mandate or authorise the reviewing court to deal with such an argument?

DEFERENCE IN THE POST-*BAKER* ERA

General

In the immediate aftermath of *Baker*, there is no doubt that first instance courts, sometimes quite reluctantly, saw the Supreme Court as having established the principle that, in the review of exercises of statutory power, including broad discretions, the courts' task now involved an assessment of whether proper weight had been given to those factors identified as relevant. Perhaps not surprisingly, this was particularly so in the case of the Federal

---

prohibiting the use of certain books for classroom instruction. Once again, however, the finding that the decision did not meet those standards is for the most part related to very specific failure to take account of a number of factors made relevant by primary and subordinate legislation as well as other failings that the Court in effect classified as errors of law.

[48] At para 65. See D Dyzenhaus, 'The Politics of Deference: Judicial Review and Democracy' in M Taggart (ed), *The Province of Administrative Law* (Oxford, Hart Publishing, 1997) at 279.

Court, Trial Division in immigration matters.[49] Lawyers also began to plead the underlying principles of constitutional law from the *Secession Reference* as grounds for setting aside exercises of statutory and prerogative power. As well, the invocation of international law both conventional and customary became more common.

However, in the past 12 months, there has been a sea change at least in the domain of immigration discretions, and a more restrictive interpretation of *Baker* has begun to emerge. Primary responsibility for this rests with the Supreme Court's revisiting of *Baker* in *Suresh v Canada (Minister of Citizenship and Immigration)*,[50] to which I will return in more detail below. Thus, shortly after *Suresh* was handed down, the Federal Court of Appeal reversed a Trial Division judgment which had featured prominently in the case of those who asserted that *Baker* had increased dramatically the room for reviewing courts to reweigh the factors or considerations relevant to the taking of a decision. This was in *Legault v Canada (Minister of Citizenship and Immigration)*.[51] Here, the Court accepts what it describes as the 'process'[52] interpretation of the relevant aspect of *Baker*. It is the court's task to ask whether the decision-maker took a relevant factor into account and that requires being 'alert, alive and sensitive to it', as opposed presumably to mere tokenism. However, once the reviewing court concludes that requirement has been met,

> it is up to the immigration officer to determine the appropriate weight to be accorded to this factor in the circumstances of the case. It is not the role of the courts to reexamine the weight given to different factors by the officers.[53]

Leave to appeal was denied in this case[54] and presumably, at least for the present, this represents the Court of Appeal's riding instructions to the Trial Division. This should lead to less intrusive scrutiny of the various discretions created in the immigration and other federal legislation.

None the less, it does not resolve all issues arising out of *Baker*. Left dangling still is the question of the relationship between the standard of review and the prescription that the decision-maker be 'alert, alive and sensitive' to the best interests of the child. Is that formula descriptive of a reasonableness standard? Beyond this, however, there remains the problem of what

---

[49] See H Janisch and E Smith, *Administrative Law Supplement*, a supplement to JM Evans, HN Janisch, DJ Mullan and RCB Risk, *Administrative Law—Cases, Text and Materials*, 4th edn (Toronto, Emond Montgomery Publications, 1995) at 156–58. This includes reference to a statistical study conducted in June, 2001 by B Ellis and E Smith, then students at the Faculty of Law, University of Toronto.
[50] Above n 2.
[51] (2002) 212 DLR (4th) 139 (FCA), rev'g [2001] 3 FC 277 (TD).
[52] *Ibid*, at para 5.
[53] *Ibid*, at para 11.
[54] On 21 November 2002. See [2002] SCCA No 220 (QL).

precisely constitutes the difference between a court engaging in 'illegitimate' reweighing and being assured that the decision-maker has been 'alert, alive and sensitive' to a relevant factor. This is well exemplified by a later Federal Court of Appeal judgment on review of the humanitarian and compassionate discretion: *Hawthorne v Canada (Minister of Citizenship and Immigration)*.[55]

In *Hawthorne*, all three members of the Court held that the immigration official had not been 'alert, alive and sensitive' to the interests of the child of the female applicant. While acknowledging the authority of *Legault*, the majority held that the immigration official had ignored various components of what went into making up the child's best interests and, in particular, the child's own concerns and the financial implications for the child of her mother's removal.[56] This looks like review based on a failure to take account of facts that were relevant to the consideration of the child's best interests. In a somewhat different vein but to the same ultimate effect, the concurring judgment, that of Evans JA, held that the official had erred by viewing the best interests of the child from the negative perspective of whether demonstrable harm would result to her if her mother was forced to leave Canada, as opposed to considering her interests from the positive perspective of the benefits that would likely accrue to her were her mother not removed. As opposed to the majority, this is more like a judgment to the effect that the official had erred legally in the test she set up for determining the child's bests interests.

While neither approach might be said to involve a reweighing of the various factors, both judgments clearly involve close attention to the way in which the officer purported to deal with the critical factor of the child's best interests. This was not something that was demanded of the Supreme Court by the facts in *Baker*. Here, as opposed to *Baker*, there was no sense in which the officer had been completely dismissive of the child's best interests. The problem lay in how those best interests were characterised as a matter of fact or of law. Seen in this way, the judgments raise the interesting question of whether they represent an appropriate compromise between the two different interpretations of *Baker*: on the one hand, the interpretation that all *Baker* mandates is that the interests of the child be taken into account, and, on the other, the reading of *Baker* that posits the Supreme Court as having opened up the exercise of discretion to overall unreasonableness review in which the judge asks whether the officer had achieved a reasonable balance in light of all of the competing factors.[57]

---

[55] [2003] 2 FC 555.
[56] *Ibid*, at para 10 (Décary JA (Rothstein JA concurring)).
[57] In this regard, it is worthy of note that Evans JA in his concurring judgment (at para 76) left for another day the question of whether the *Suresh/Legault* prohibition on assessing the weight attributed to a particular factor precluded, absent a nominate ground for intervention, overall unreasonableness review in the English sense of a result which was disproportionate. There is, of course, also the more general question of how both *Baker* and the *Suresh/Legault* prohibition

As for the underlying principles of the Canadian constitution, frequent evocation has not led to frequent success. In fact, the only notable occasion on which a court has invoked an underlying principle as the basis for intervention in a discretionary decision is *Lalonde v Ontario (Commission de restructuration des services de santé)*.[58] There, in reviewing the exercise of a broad discretion, the Court held that the Commission had failed to take account of the fourth underlying principle from the *Secession Reference*, the protection of minorities. The Commission's order which involved a substantial change to and downgrading of the role of the Montfort Hospital in Ottawa, the City's only francophone hospital, had 'failed to give serious weight and consideration to the linguistic and cultural significance of Montfort to the survival of the Franco-Ontarian minority'.[59]

As well as the *Secession Reference*, the Ontario Court of Appeal relies on *Baker* to support its conclusions on this point. In that context, without ever ruling on what the appropriate standard of judicial review should be in this case, the Court expressed the view that,

> where constitutional and quasi-constitutional rights or values are concerned, correctness or reasonableness will often be the appropriate standard.[60]

This was also a case which was decided on the basis of the failure, indeed refusal of the Commission 'to take into account or give any weight to Montfort's broader institutional role'.[61] The Court was therefore not called upon to address the question of whether, in a case such as this, the Court should have any concern with the weight accorded to constitutional or quasi-constitutional factors in the exercise of discretion. The use of the term 'serious weight and consideration' must therefore be read in that context and not as necessarily accepting the proposition that, when underlying constitutional principles are at play in the exercise of broad discretionary powers, the reviewing court's role extends to reassessing the weight given to such factors. Whether that should be the case and, indeed, whether the court's review should proceed on a correctness basis when constitutional

---

on assessing weight relate to review for error of fact. In the domain of error of fact, does it too follow the standard of review produced by the pragmatic and functional approach or does it still stand apart subject in all cases (save where the statute makes it otherwise abundantly clear) to review only in the traditional instance of 'no evidence' or in cases where the findings of fact are patently unreasonable? This is an issue of peculiar significance for the Federal Court given that the *Federal Court Act*, RSC 1985, c F–7 (as amended by SC 1990, c 8), s 18.1(4)(d) contains a codification of review for error of fact that looks a lot like a patent unreasonableness standard: 'based its decision or order on an erroneous finding of fact that it made in a perverse or capricious manner or without regard for the material before it'.

[58] (2001) 56 OR (3d) 505 (CA), aff'g. (1999) 48 OR (3d) 50 (Div Ct).
[59] *Ibid*, at para 187.
[60] *Ibid*, at para 186.
[61] *Ibid*.

values are at stake is a question to which I return in the concluding section of this chapter.

As perhaps might have been expected, questions about the role of international law in the exercise of statutory powers have arisen somewhat more frequently than ones involving the underlying principles. After all, Canada has a constitution which includes a *Charter of Rights and Freedoms* in which many of the issues arising out of the underlying principles are dealt with directly or explicitly. While the constitution also incorporates aspects of international law (and particularly international human rights law), it is in no sense comprehensive in its coverage of international law nor, as *Baker* makes clear, are all of Canada's international obligations explicitly incorporated into domestic legislation.

Thus, in the wake of *Baker*, it was not surprising to see a majority of the Supreme Court of Canada in *114957 Canada Ltée (Spraytech, Société d'arrosage) v Hudson (Town)*[62] look to international sources as part of its justification for upholding a municipal by-law prohibiting the recreational use of pesticides. In interpreting the scope of the by-law making power, L'Heureux-Dubé J held that it was permissible for the Court to look at the 'precautionary principle' of sustainable development which she appeared to accept as part of customary international law. This helped inform the decision that a broad power to make by-laws included authority not only to regulate the use of pesticides but also to ban their use entirely for certain purposes.[63]

The use of international law was to surface yet again in *Suresh* to which I will now turn.

Suresh v Canada (Minister of Citizenship and Immigration)

Suresh involved a revisiting of a number of the issues raised in *Baker* and coming within the scope of this chapter. It involved the exercise of a ministerial discretion to declare a landed immigrant or someone applying for landed immigrant status to be a 'danger to the security of Canada' and to deport that person even when that person's life or freedom would be threatened by a return to her or his homeland in the extreme form of a substantial risk of torture.

In terms of the first part of this process, the Court held that the Minister was not affecting *Charter* rights and freedoms in making the declaration. As a consequence, judicial review of that determination depended on straight administrative law principles. The Court then proceeded to engage

---

[62] [2001] 2 SCR 241.
[63] At paras 30–32. As in *Baker*, the concurring judgment of LeBel J (supported by Iacobucci and Major JJ) vigorously protested the insinuation of international law: para 48.

in a pragmatic and functional analysis, the outcome of which was a finding that, despite the impact of such a determination on affected individuals and the subject specific nature of the factual inquiry, it should intervene only if the ministerial decision was patently unreasonable.

The Court also, by way of dealing with the uncertainties that had arisen as to the meaning of the judgment in *Baker*, made it abundantly clear that it was no part of the patent unreasonableness inquiry to reweigh the factors that went into the Minister's determination. The reviewing court was restricted to inquiring whether the declaration was made 'arbitrarily or in bad faith, ... cannot be supported on the evidence, or [resulted from a failure] to consider the appropriate factors'.[64] At another point, this was expressed in terms of the court not intervening unless the Minister has 'made some error in principle in exercising its discretion or has exercised its discretion in a capricious or vexatious manner'.[65] The Court then went on to state that:

> *Baker* does not authorize courts reviewing decisions on the discretionary end of the spectrum to engage in a new weighing process, but draws on an established line of cases concerning the failure of ministerial delegates to consider and weigh implied limitations and/or patently relevant factors.[66]

In other words, the role of the courts was to ensure that the relevant factors were weighed and no others but that the court had no business in inquiring further into the relative weight assigned to the various relevant factors or the balancing of them one against the other.

The Court then dealt with the standard of review applicable to the second part of the Minister's decision-making task: the discretion to deport someone who was a danger to the security of Canada even if deportation might involve a substantial risk of danger to life and liberty (including torture). Here, the refugee section 7 *Charter* rights were engaged and, at this point, there was reason to believe that the Court would move to a correctness standard of review in recognition of previous authority that had suggested that, in determining constitutional questions, the decision-maker had to get it right.[67] However, the Court rejected the applicability of such an all-embracing theory to all aspects or stages of this decision affecting the refugee's *Charter* rights.

On the factual aspects of the inquiry as to whether Suresh faced a 'substantial risk of torture' on deportation, it involved issues 'largely outside

---

[64] Above, n 2 at para 29.
[65] *Ibid*, at para 34, quoting the judgment of Iacobucci J in *Pezim v British Columbia (Superintendent of Brokers)* [1994] 2 SCR 577 at 607.
[66] *Ibid*, at para 37.
[67] Eg *Cuddy Chicks Ltd v Ontario (Labour Relations Board)* [1991] 2 SCR 5 at 17 where LaForest J, in the course of holding that the Board could consider constitutional (including *Charter*) questions, stated that 'it can expect no deference with respect to constitutional determinations'.

the realm of expertise of reviewing courts'.⁶⁸ As such, this threshold determination was entitled to deference in the sense that the court could not reweigh the factors relied on by the Minister but only interfere if the determination was 'not supported by the evidence' or had resulted from a failure to consider the appropriate factors.⁶⁹

In fact, there is some warrant for this conclusion in the case law. On occasion, in both division of powers cases and *Charter* cases,⁷⁰ the courts have accorded a degree of deference to the relevant authorities' determination of facts on which constitutional questions hinge.⁷¹ However, what is problematic⁷² about *Suresh* is in the Court's seeming extension of deference to the next stage in the decision-making process, the decision on whether to deport on the basis of the facts as found. Without any real consideration of whether this second stage involved the same considerations which suggested deference to the factual findings of the Minister, the Court simply asserted that on the actual decision to deport in the light of the facts, there is also an entitlement to deference:

> If the Minister has considered the correct factors, the courts should not reweigh them. Provided the [decision to deport under this provision] is not

---

⁶⁸ *Ibid*, at para 39.
⁶⁹ *Ibid*.
⁷⁰ Eg *Northern Telecom Ltd v Communications Workers of Canada* [1980] 1 SCR 115.
⁷¹ In the course of its judgment in *Suresh*, the Supreme Court makes frequent reference to the judgment of the House of Lords in *Secretary of State for the Home Department v Rehman* [2001] 3 WLR 877 (HL) including the judgment of Lord Hoffmann. In dealing with the issue of deference to executive judgment in the domain of national security, Lord Hoffmann (at para 54) introduced the following qualification in the context of the provisions of the European Convention, the equivalent for these purposes of the *Charter*:

> Thirdly, an appeal to the Commission may turn upon issues which at no point lie within the exclusive province of the executive. A good example is the question ... as to whether deporting someone would infringe his rights under art 3 of the Convention because there was a substantial risk that he would suffer torture or inhuman or degrading treatment. The European jurisprudence makes it clear that whether deportation is in the interests of national security is irrelevant to rights under s 3. If there is a danger of torture, the Government must find some other way of dealing with a threat to national security. Whether a sufficient risk exists is a question of evaluation and prediction based on evidence. In answering such a question, the executive enjoys no constitutional prerogative.

The Supreme Court neither cited nor made reference to this portion of Lord Hoffmann's judgment, one which speaks to both a total prohibition on deportation to torture and little or no deference to executive judgment as to the likelihood of that risk.
⁷² Though probably not unique. Thus, in one of the early s 7 *Charter* challenges to an extradition order, *Canada v Schmidt* [1987] 1 SCR 500, LaForest J, delivering the judgment of the Court, stated (at 523) seemingly in relation to both executive appraisal of the requesting country's general system of criminal justice and its more particular salience to the precise factual situation before the Court:

> The courts have a duty to uphold the constitution. None the less, this is an area where the executive is likely to be far better informed than the courts, and where the courts must be extremely circumspect so as to avoid interfering unduly in decisions involving

> patently unreasonable—unreasonable on its face, unsupported by evidence, or vitiated by failure to consider the proper factors or apply appropriate procedures—it should be upheld. At the same time, the courts have an important role to play in ensuring that the Minister has considered the relevant factors and complied with the requirements of the Act and the Constitution.[73]

Without the last sentence, this seems to state unequivocally that, even in cases where the Minister has determined as a matter of fact that there is a 'substantial risk of torture', the courts are obliged to defer to the ministerial judgment that, as a danger to the security of Canada, the refugee should, none the less, be deported. In other words, the task of balancing between the refugee's *Charter* rights and the risks to Canada is primarily for the Minister and to be reviewed only if patently unreasonable. This seems to go a good way in the direction of abdicating responsibility for the protection of *Charter* rights in cases such as this.[74] As long as the Minister has taken the *Charter* rights into account seriously, the decision stands.

However, there is an ambiguity here. All the Court might be talking about in this context is the decision to deport in cases where the Minister has determined that as a matter of fact, there is *no risk* to *Charter* rights. Support for that interpretation comes from the last sentence quoted above and the Court's subsequent holding that 'barring extraordinary circumstances, deportation to torture will generally violate the principles of fundamental justice'[75] and that, in such cases, 'the Minister should generally decline to deport refugees where on the evidence there is a substantial risk of torture'.[76] In the next paragraph, the Court then speaks of the state justifying the deportation either as part of a section 7 balancing process or under section 1.[77]

As these are constitutional requirements in terms of the last sentence of the quote, it could be argued that the entitlement to deference disappears when that is the judgment to be made. Rather than simply asking whether

> the good faith and honour of this country in its relation with other states. In a word, judicial intervention must be limited to cases of real substance.

[73] *Ibid*, at para 41.
[74] As suggested on a number of occasions at the conference, it is also difficult to reconcile this aspect of the judgment with the Court's reluctance in other contexts and most notably in *Cooper v Canada (Human Rights Commission)* [1996] 3 SCR 854 to concede to statutory authorities the jurisdiction or competence to even determine constitutional issues tentatively. See in particular A Macklin's chapter: 'The State of Law's Borders and the Law of State Borders'. What, however, this may suggest is a narrow interpretation of *Cooper* which restricts its *ratio* to cases in which the challenge is to the constitutional validity of the relevant legislative provisions as opposed to the question of how a valid provision must be exercised to accord with the *Charter*. Frankly, that would be no bad thing. *Cooper* is almost certainly no longer good law: *Nova Scotia (Workers' Compensation Board) v Martin; Nova Scotia (Workers' Compensation Board) v Laseur*, 2003 SCC 54.
[75] *Ibid*, at para 76.
[76] *Ibid*, at para 77.
[77] *Ibid*, at para 78.

the Minister took the refugee's constitutional right into account, the Court should at least be able to ask whether the Minister has provided ample justification for deporting in the particular circumstances. In other words, the courts should have the last word in such cases over whether the facts demonstrate the 'extraordinary circumstances'[78] justifying this 'rare' exercise of discretion. To do any less would be to abdicate judicial responsibility for the upholding of constitutional rights. It is therefore to be hoped that subsequent courts see this as a faithful reading of this aspect of the judgment in *Suresh*.

The relevance of *Suresh* to the impact of *Baker* does not, however, stop there. In two other respects at least, *Suresh* has ramifications for future applications of *Baker* and, in each instance, it is a reading or application of *Baker* which favours deference.

First, the Court accepts that a prohibition on deportation to torture is almost certainly an emerging peremptory norm of international law.[79] Moreover, it also accepts that the Convention Against Torture, which Canada has ratified, is the predominant international treaty to which Canada is a party and that it and the emerging peremptory norm of international law reject deportation to torture even where national security interests are at stake.[80] However, that did not necessarily mean that the 'principles of fundamental justice' demand a complete ban on deportation to torture. The Convention and international law only 'inform',[81] but do not settle the content of the principles of fundamental justice. Thereafter, in three paragraphs,[82] the Court held that the principles of fundamental justice as informed by the treaty and the emerging norm did not require an absolute prohibition but only that the power to deport be exercised sparingly. Why that is so is justified only by the broadest of references to national security concerns. Though there is subsequently mention of a possible section 1 justification of such an action, the general principle that there is not an outright prohibition is rooted in section 7 and not in any sense of the government having to provide a detailed justification of the necessity for the qualified application of the Treaty and the peremptory norm.

What does this say about *Baker* and the questions that it leaves open about the use of unincorporated treaties specifically as well as more general principles of international law as reflected in peremptory norms and customary international law? First, it affirms the relevance of international law in both the assessment of the constitutional validity of statutes and the exercise of discretion under those statutes. However, even where *Charter* rights and freedoms are at stake, a treaty is not determinative but only influential

---

[78] *Ibid*, at para 76.
[79] *Ibid*, at para 65.
[80] *Ibid*, at para 75.
[81] *Ibid*, at para 46.
[82] *Ibid*, at paras 76–78.

or an important factor in giving effect to the constitutional right. There is also the very alarming suggestion that the same holds true for peremptory norms of international law. While never definitively ruling that a prohibition on deportation to torture was a peremptory norm of international law, the Court nevertheless, despite its reservation on this point, worded the balance of its judgment on this whole issue as though it were.[83]

The other aspects of *Suresh* that have relevance to *Baker* emerge from the procedural portion of the judgment. Here, the Court stated that the five factors[84] identified in *Baker* as relevant to the determination of the content of the duty of procedural fairness applied in the domain of section 7 of the *Charter* and the demands of the principles of fundamental justice in its procedural sense. This did not mean that the common law and the *Charter* had merged for these purposes but that the higher level constitutional norms were to be evaluated by reference to the same considerations as governed at common law but with the overlay that a constitutionally protected right was at stake. That seems appropriate as a general principle. However, what it does do is insinuate into the inquiry two countervailing factors from the *Baker* list. The first is the fifth *Baker* factor requiring, in certain circumstances, deference to agency choice of procedures. And the second is the consideration that is given to state interests in evaluating the nature of the decision that has to be made, or the first *Baker* factor. A more concrete aspect is given to this by the reservation entered later in the judgment on this issue that the refugee's access to the contrary material as a component of fundamental justice may have to give way to 'privilege or similar valid reasons for reduced disclosure, such as safeguarding confidential security documents'.[85]

In short, while the judgment is otherwise reasonably generous in its according of procedural protections to persons in Suresh's situation,[86] what

---

[83] See also in this regard, the split judgment of the Ontario Court of Appeal in *Ahani v Canada (Attorney General)* (2002) 58 OR (3d) 107. This was the follow up to the companion case to *Suresh*, which Ahani lost. The question that then arose was whether the Court should enjoin the government from deporting Ahani until such time as his communication to the United Nations Human Rights Committee under the Optional Protocol to the Covenant on Civil and Political Rights had been dealt with. While Canada was a signatory to the Optional Protocol, it had never been specifically incorporated into domestic law. Relying primarily on this consideration and the fact that the states parties had never agreed to give effect domestically to the Committee's final views nor to postpone enforcement of its domestic laws pending the completion of that process, the majority denied relief. This was over a very strong dissent by Rosenberg JA. Thereafter, the Supreme Court of Canada denied leave to appeal although in a highly unusual, if not unique move, L'Heureux-Dubé J indicated dissent (though without giving reasons) from the position of the other two judges on the leave to appeal panel: [2002] SCCA No 62 (QL). For criticism of the majority decisions, see A Macklin's chapter, above n 74. See also J Brunnée and SJ Toope's chapter, above n 30.
[84] *Ibid*, at paras 114–15.
[85] *Ibid*, at para 122.
[86] There might be concern as to the requirement that the refugee establish a *prima facie* case of risk of torture before being eligible for the kind of hearing prescribed by the Court. See para 127. The hearing contemplated is, as in *Baker*, a written one and that too raises problems particularly as issues of credibility are likely to be far more often critical in this kind of case.

the Court is accepting is a certain level of deference to procedural choices even when *Charter* rights are at stake. It is also indicating that the balancing of competing state interests in less than full disclosure should take place in the determination of the scope of the principles of fundamental justice and not as part of a section 1 justification where the state bears the primary onus. It does, of course, have to be acknowledged that there are precedents supporting this taking account of state interests in the delineation of the content of the principles of fundamental justice within section 7 leaving little work for section 1 to do or room to be applied when there has been a violation of the principles of fundamental justice. However, there is also a strong argument that, to the extent that the procedures afforded are less than ideal for providing notice and an adequate opportunity to respond, the state should have to justify them by reference to section 1 particularly when the justifications are ones based on arguments such as national security and other state reasons for the suppression of relevant information.[87]

In summary, *Suresh* makes it clear that even where *Charter* rights are at stake, deference will at least on occasion play a considerable role in the delineation of both substantive and procedural rights. Moreover, the fact that the Court affirms the relevance of deference even in *Charter* cases suggests that it must be taken as having, for the most part, endorsed the more restrictive, pro-deference interpretations of *Baker*. This is particularly the case in the disputed territory of review of the exercises of broad discretion and the extent to which the reviewing court can engage in reweighing. However, as the prior discussion of *Baker* suggests and the decision of the Federal Court of Appeal in *Hawthorne* makes clear, the point at which a court moves from appropriate determination of whether a relevant consideration or factor was taken into account to inappropriate weighing is by no means a bright line distinction. There are also grave questions raised about the extent to which any abnegation of weighing relevant factors as part of judicial review should carry over to situations where constitutional rights are in question. I will return to this theme in the last section of this chapter.

Deference More Generally

Since *Baker*, there have been a number of instances in which the Supreme Court has applied the 'pragmatic and functional' approach and reached what on the surface seem to be the appropriate conclusions about the standard of review: patent unreasonableness in the case of expert tribunals

---

[87] See E Goodman, 'Social Interest Justifications', a paper prepared for credit in the course in Advanced Constitutional Law at the Faculty of Law Queen's University, Winter Term 2002 and the winner of the 2002 Department of Justice/Canadian Bar Association Essay Contest marking the 20th Anniversary of the *Charter* [on file].

determination of questions of law or mixed law and fact which match their expertise and where there is no right of appeal but rather a privative clause,[88] and unreasonableness where the situation is the same but there is a right of appeal and no or a partial privative clause.[89] To the extent that *Baker* is a case in which the same kind of analysis was deployed in the case of a broad discretionary power, there might seem to be a unity of purpose and approach here. Deference based on a pragmatic and functional analysis also characterises the Court's judgment in *Suresh*. However, there are now serious signs that the Court's application of the pragmatic and functional approach is losing all claim to coherence with *Suresh* being a major but not the only contributor to that phenomenon.

On a number of occasions, the Court has gone to a correctness standard of review in the context of various forms of statutory appeal from administrative tribunals and, on at least one occasion, in the context of a judicial review application. The hardest of this group of judgments to justify is *Canada (Deputy Minister of National Revenue) v Mattel Canada Inc*.[90] There, the Court treated the determination of the meaning of the term 'sale [of goods] for export to Canada' as involving a question 'intrinsic to commercial law'[91] as opposed to one engaging the expertise of the Canadian International Trade Tribunal. It is, however, difficult to appreciate how, given the context, this constituted a question of general commercial law and one on which the reviewing court was as, if not more expert than the tribunal. What was at stake was the identification of the point at which there was a 'sale' for customs duty, not general commercial law purposes. This seems intrinsically a customs duty question dependent on the purposes and intricacies of that statute and the particular group of statutory provisions. None the less, the Court also described the relevant questions as 'pure questions of law that require the application of principles of statutory interpretation'.[92] If this suggests that pure questions of statutory interpretation attract correctness review, it is fraught with danger for the whole enterprise of deference to statutorily designated decision-makers when determining legal questions at the core of their jurisdiction. However, given that this

---

[88] *Ivanhoe Inc v UFCW, Local 500* [2001] 2 SCR 565 and *Sept-Îles (City) v Quebec (Labour Court)* [2001] 2 SCR 670, both involving labour tribunals and the former in effect reversing *UES, Local 298 v Bibeault* [1988] 2 SCR 1048, in which the Court had applied a correctness standard to the very issue that was at stake in *Ivanhoe*. There had been changes to the legislation in the meantime so as to now justify the most deferential standard. All of this was, however, without threat to the general approach to standard of review enunciated in *Bibeault* and in which Beetz J used the discourse of 'pragmatic and functional' for the first time.
[89] *Committee for Equal Treatment of Asbestos Minority Shareholders v Ontario (Securities Commission)* [2001] 2 SCR 132 (in the context of a statutory appeal from the Ontario Securities Commission) and *Macdonell v Quebec (Commission d'accès à l'information)*, [2002] 3 SCR 661 (involving an appeal from the Quebec Access to Information Commissioner).
[90] [2001] 2 SCR 100.
[91] *Ibid*, at para 33.
[92] *Ibid*.

proposition was linked to the Court's classification of the nature of the particular question, that was probably not the intention.

On the other hand, particularly in the context of statutory rights of appeal, there is a growing body of case law to the effect that if the interpretation of a statutory term is one that will produce a ruling of general application, the standard is that of correctness.[93] That too invites correctness intervention not by reference to the expertise of the tribunal and the relationship between that expertise and the particular question but in terms of the significance of the question to the overall operation of the statutory scheme. To do that may well be to overreach.

This willingness to intervene on a correctness basis in commercial matters of a highly technical kind where *Charter* rights and freedoms are not at stake stands in rather stark contrast to the levels of deference revealed in *Suresh*. Indeed, the contrast is even more dramatic when one looks at the recent Supreme Court case law involving other aspects of immigration legislation and also another prominent case in which *Charter* rights and freedoms were implicated in tribunal decision-making.

Pushpanathan v Canada (Minister of Citizenship and Immigration)[94] has been the critical judgment in much of recent Supreme Court standard of review assessments. There, as noted already, Bastarache J (delivering the judgment of the Court) was not prepared to concede to the Immigration and Refugee Board any deference in determining whether a convention refugee claimant had engaged in activities contrary to the principles and purposes of the United Nations. Albeit that this question arose in the context of a provision in the *Immigration Act* creating an exception to the normal right of convention refugees to remain in Canada, a provision itself derived from the Convention Refugee Treaty, its determination involved

---

[93] See especially the judgment of Evans JA in *Canada (Commissioner of Competition) v Superior Propane Inc* [2001] 3 FC 185 (CA) at paras 42–46, relying on a statement by Iacobucci J in *Canada (Director of Investigation and Research) v Southam Inc* [1997] 1 SCR 748 at para 45. See also his judgment for the Court in *SOCAN v Canadian Association of Internet Providers* (2002) 215 DLR (4th) 118 (FCA), where the context was judicial review rather than statutory appeal. He also relies upon *Housen v Nikolaisen*, 2002 SCC 33, a case that is assuming an increasing presence in judicial review and statutory appeals despite the fact that it involved the appellate standard of review of trial judge findings in a negligence action. In a lengthy analysis of the nature of questions of mixed law and fact, the Court held that any questions of legal principle 'readily extricable' (para 33) from the process of applying the law to the facts were subject to correctness review. However, that does not transfer automatically to the judicial review and statutory appeal context. In both cases, there is still the question of whether the extricated question of law is one intended primarily for the statutory authority or the reviewing court. This point emerges most clearly from the judgment of Bastarache J in *Pushpanathan v Canada (Minister of Citizenship and Immigration)*, above, n 32 at para 37, where, after referring to Iacobucci J's statement in *Southam* about the determination of questions of law which will be of general application, then makes it clear that this is but one and not a decisive factor in the pragmatic and functional analysis: para 37.
[94] Above n 32.

questions of general international law not within the expected area of expertise of members of the Refugee Division of the Board.

The very same day as *Suresh* and its companion case of *Ahani*[95] were released, the Court also rendered judgment in another linked pair of immigration cases, *Chieu v Canada (Minister of Citizenship and Immigration)*[96] and *Al Sagban v Canada (Minister of Citizenship and Immigration)*.[97] In each of these, the issue was whether the Immigration Appeal Division of the Immigration and Refugee Board was allowed to take into account foreign hardship in determining whether to order the removal of permanent residents from Canada for cause. The *Charter* does not feature in the judgments and the language of the empowering provision ('having regard to all of the circumstances of the case') suggested a legislative conferral of considerable latitude on the designated decision-makers. Nevertheless, the Court decided the issue as to the permissibility of taking this consideration into account on a correctness basis and went so far as to classify it as a 'true' jurisdictional question, a creature thought by many to have become extinct. Significantly, the Court also treated as an important factor in the 'pragmatic and functional' analysis the fact that the issue involved 'the rights of individuals vis-à-vis the state'. This 'weighs in favour of a less deferential standard of review'.[98]

My final point of reference is *Trinity Western University v British Columbia College of Teachers*.[99] Here, the Court applied a standard of correctness to the College's determination of whether Trinity Western University was engaged in discriminatory practices of a kind that should result in the denial of the University's application to have full responsibility for a teacher education programme. Those opposing registration pointed to the position of the University on same sex sexual relationships. The University asserted in part its right to freedom of religion and conscience. On this issue of accommodating competing *Charter* rights, the Court held:

> More importantly, the Council is not particularly well equipped to determine the scope of freedom of religion and conscience and to weigh those rights against the right to equality in the context of a pluralistic society. The public dimension of religious freedom and the right to determine one's moral conduct have been recognized long before the advent of the *Charter* ... and have been considered to be legal issues. The accommodation of beliefs is a legal question ....[100]

---

[95] *Ahani v Canada (Minister of Citizenship and Immigration)*, [2002] 1 SCR 72.
[96] [2002] 1 SCR 84.
[97] [2002] 1 SCR 133.
[98] Above n 96 at para 26.
[99] [2001] 1 SCR 722.
[100] *Ibid*, at para 19.

Indeed, the Court rejected reliance on the dissenting judgment of Rowles JA in the British Columbia Court of Appeal. She had segmented the decision-making process into two categories—on the one hand, the determination of whether the Council of the College of Teachers had jurisdiction to take discriminatory practices into account and the existence of discriminatory practices generally, and, on the other, the effects of the discriminatory practices generally and whether as a result registration would be contrary to the public interest. She classified the first as questions of law subject to correctness review and the second as questions of fact on which the standard should be unreasonableness.[101] The Court rejected this, holding that even the issues of 'fact' had 'very little to do, if anything, with the particular expertise of the members of the' College.[102]

In what state does all of this leave the issue of the standard of review? Despite protestations by the courts to the contrary, there clearly seems to be a weakening of the policy of deference in a number of areas. In the field of pure questions of law and the discernment of legal principles to be applied to particular facts, the courts are increasingly inclined to see themselves as having as much or greater expertise than the designated decision-maker and willing to classify questions as ones of general law subject to correctness review. In most instances, particularly where commercial interests in complex legislative regimes are at stake, this reassertion of judicial imperialism is to be regretted. Indeed, some (such as Sprague) would argue that the willingness of the Court to intervene on other than a patent unreasonableness basis even in the case of broad discretionary determinations which have a serious effect on individual rights is equally pernicious. Whether it be questions of law as in *Pushpanathan*, *Chieu* and *Al Sagban* or exercises of discretion as in *Baker*, they would contend that deference should be the order of the day even, for example, when one's status to remain in Canada is at stake. Legislative choice of tribunal or conferral of extensive discretion should still matter in these domains and the courts should be reluctant to assert correctness or merits unreasonableness review by classifying the matters in issue as being within the domain of expertise of the courts.

Undoubtedly, this is contentious territory and, indeed, one's position may depend on another form of pragmatism, that of whether the reviewing court's or administrative authority's interpretations and exercises of discretion provide the better reading of legislative text and purpose. After all, there is no particular point in having a high degree of judicial interventionism in human rights tribunal adjudications when the tribunals are more in tune with the underlying purposes of the relevant legislation than the reviewing or appellate court. However, irrespective of how one reacts to the issue of whether the courts should be more or less inclined to classify issues

---

[101] As recounted at para 16 of the Supreme Court's judgment.
[102] *Ibid*, at para 18.

as ones of general law requiring little or no deference, the judgment in *Suresh* remains a serious anomaly. It is to that issue that I will now turn.

THE ROLE OF DEFERENCE

On what principles do and should the Courts accord deference to statutory and prerogative decision-making? The answer most commonly provided is that of respect for legislative choice of instruments for the performance of certain tasks. That answer, predicated as it is on traditional notions of parliamentary sovereignty, concedes to the legislature the right or entitlement to put certain issues beyond the ken of the regular courts.[103] In terms of the pragmatic and functional analysis, it is reflected in the factors that focus the reviewing court's attention on the overall purposes of the legislation and more specific indicia of legislative intention such as privative clauses and the conferral of discretionary powers in broad or unstructured terms.

The issue can also be framed around issues of institutional competence. There are certain domains where the courts do not possess the expertise or the facilities to engage in a reassessment of matters already evaluated by a tribunal or a member of the executive branch. This is most obviously the case in the instance of politics and policy choice but, as reflected in the standard of review jurisprudence, can also be so in the more narrow confines of giving meaning to terms governing the operation of specialised administrative regimes and assessing facts that bear upon that exercise. Indeed, an open-ended or *de novo* re-evaluation of many questions would severely tax the institutional resources of the courts. Here, under the pragmatic and functional approach, the most relevant consideration is the expected competence of the designated decision-maker in relation to the specific issue or issues and the court's own expertise matched against that of the designated decision-maker.

These conceptions are ones that have by and large served Canadian judicial review law well since the late 1970s when the Supreme Court reversed an era of excessive interventionism in the affairs of expert administrative tribunals, interventionism that critics characterised as in many instances stemming from a covert hostility to the growth of the administrative state and the implementation of various government social reforms. The adoption of the pragmatic and functional approach to discerning the appropriate scope for judicial review of mainly tribunal decision-making gave many administrative tribunals the credit they deserved for their intimate knowledge of the regimes with which they worked regularly and at the

---

[103] For a rejection of this as the starting point for justifications of deference, see M Hunt, 'Sovereignty's Blight: Why Contemporary Public Law Needs the Concept of "Due Deference"', above n 20.

same time represented a degree of judicial self-awareness of the limits of curial expertise. Indeed, there is room for concern to the extent that, as argued above, there has been some weakening of this posture of deference in the name of competence over issues of statutory interpretation or matters having precedential value for the future workings of a particular tribunal.

In extending the 'pragmatic and functional' method of analysis to discretionary decision-making (and in a limited way to the review of procedural rules and rulings), *Baker* recognised that issues of the appropriate scope of judicial intervention were not confined to adjudicative-style tribunals interpreting their constitutive statute.[104] Similar tensions arose in the review of discretionary decision-making by the executive branch and public officials generally. Also, in the domain of complex administrative schemes, courts did not have a complete monopoly on wisdom as to the detailed components of a procedurally fair process.

As opposed, however, to the case of judicial review of adjudicative-style tribunals, *Baker*'s extension of the pragmatic and functional approach did not mean one way traffic in the direction of less intensive review. Its impact in fact has cut both ways. As exemplified by *Baker* itself as well as numerous of its progeny, previous conceptions of very restricted review of the discretionary power of Cabinet, Ministers and high government officials have been modified in the operation of a test that focuses rather less than total attention on the character of the decision-maker and rather more attention on the nature of the interest that is at stake and whether discretion was exercised on the basis of facts peculiar to the applicant. In contrast, there were areas of discretionary power where the courts were previously quite willing to intrude without embarrassment. Municipal decision-making was a prime example and, within that category, the judgment of the majority in *Shell Canada v Vancouver (City)*[105] provides a graphic illustration of judicial unwillingness to allow municipalities slack in their conception of what were appropriate municipal purposes under broad legislative grants of power. In emphasising that deference required that courts respect the judgment of statutory authorities as to what were proper purposes in the case of unstructured statutory discretions, *Baker* was also ushering in an era of greater respect for the capacities of municipalities and, indeed, administrative tribunals exercising broad discretion as part of their mandate.

However, there are certainly domains where the claims of the decision-maker to deference based on legislative choice and comparative institutional

---

[104] Note, however, the doubts expressed by LeBel J in *Chamberlain v Surrey School District No 36*, above n 7 at paras 188–205, as to whether there always is an appropriate fit between the 'pragmatic and functional' approach and the review of discretionary powers. More generally, see TRS Allan's chapter, 'Common Law Reason and the Limits of Judicial Deference' where he claims that a broad discretion applied to individuals should attract little or no judicial deference, while a discretion to formulate policy should attract deference. For Allan, it is the precisely the former area where the courts are needed.
[105] Above n 14.

competence and practical advantage run out. Under accepted Canadian constitutional law principles, they run out when the statutory decision-maker is dealing with questions as to the scope of its jurisdiction or behaves in such a way as to lose or exceed its jurisdiction. That limitation is explained most commonly in constitutional terms. Sections 96 to 100 of the *Constitution Act, 1867* entitle the superior courts to constitutionally guaranteed jurisdiction to engage in judicial review for jurisdictional error, a capacity that cannot be removed legislatively.[106] It is also a limitation that can, in many instances, be justified by reference to legislative intention—in setting up the administrative scheme, the legislature had certain limits in mind and, as an inference from this, the courts exist for the purpose of ensuring that legislative limits are respected. It also has pragmatic justifications—the delineation of the outer limits of power should not depend on the self-interested evaluations of those who stand to benefit from a particular outcome to the determination of that issue.

Others, such as Dyzenhaus,[107] would deploy a version of the rule of law as an underlying principle of Canadian constitutional law as a basis for placing normative constraints on the exercise of statutory power, constraints that transcend normal conceptions of parliamentary sovereignty and the positivist approach that it imposes on thinking about the limits of judicial review. It is also the case that the whole project of underlying constitutional principles depends ultimately as much, if not more on the normative recognition of fundamental or transcendent values as it does on a reading of Canadian and British constitutional history and the supposed promise of the preamble to the *Constitution Act, 1867*.

The limits of that theory are the subject of much contemporary debate. None the less, one does not have to travel down that road very far, if at all to start taking issue with important parts of the judgment of the Supreme Court of Canada in *Suresh*.

In *Baker*, the Court never reached the issue of whether the compassionate and humanitarian discretion either generally or in relation to Baker's specific case engaged any *Charter* right and, more particularly, section 7. However, even without that dimension, the Court was prepared to balance executive demands for deference and legislative indicators of that intention with a conception of Baker's entitlement to due consideration and respect from the law. That exercise produced, in my view, a legitimate compromise in which the Court accepted a reasonableness standard of review instead of the standard generally applied to ministerial exercises of broad discretionary powers.

---

[106] *Crevier v Quebec (AG)* [1981] 2 SCR 220.
[107] See *inter alia*, 'Humpty Dumpty Rules or the Rule of Law: Legal Theory and the Adjudication of National Security', *Australian Journal of Legal Philosophy*, forthcoming.

The extent of that compromise, in the sense of how the unreasonableness standard actually applies, has been a matter of considerable debate. That is a debate on which, for reasons of both text and principle, I tend to take a conservative position in the sense of not seeing *Baker* as authorising a complete re-evaluation of the overall decision on a reasonableness basis or a straight re-weighing by the reviewing court of all the various factors relevant to the exercise of the discretion. To go that far in relation to the discretion at issue in *Baker* (even within the framework of a statutory regime which requires leave to seek judicial review and then to appeal to the Federal Court of Appeal) would simply be to invite, admittedly within a framework of reasonableness rather than correctness review, a revisiting of every exercise of this frequently sought discretion. Absent a broad statutory right of appeal, I hesitate to see this on a pragmatic and functional analysis as an appropriate role for the Federal Court.

In large measure, that conservative reading of *Baker* has been accepted by the Court in *Suresh* and applied there in much the same manner. Why should I take objection to that? My principal problem with the Court's application of this version of the *Baker* principles is that it pays far too little regard to the fact that an explicit constitutional guarantee was at stake and acknowledged to be at stake.

That should not necessarily lead to a *de novo* or correctness re-evaluation of all the facts on which the relevant conclusions have been drawn and, in particular, the facts surrounding whether Suresh was a danger to the security of Canada and whether he was at serious risk of torture in the event of a return to Sri Lanka. However, that said or conceded, the application of a patent unreasonableness standard of review to the factual aspects of both of these decisions is surely not appropriate when important constitutional rights are at stake. At the very least, the reviewing court should be attentive to the executive's evidentiary justification of both of the relevant conclusions and inquire whether there is a reasonable foundation in the evidence advanced for the factual conclusions that have been reached. Indeed, particularly when information is being suppressed from the applicant in the name of national security, there is a strong argument that the government should have to justify its factual conclusions on the basis of providing the court with information as to the reliability of its sources of information and information-gathering techniques.[108]

Indeed, the Court misconceives its role as constitutional adjudicator right at the outset of its analysis when it characterises the first question, that of whether Suresh was a danger to the security of Canada, as not part of the constitutional matrix. On its very own terms, the Court goes on to accept that the principles of fundamental justice in this instance require a

---

[108] For a good illustration of this in operation, see the dissenting judgment of Desjardins JA in *Gallant v Canada (Deputy Commissioner, Correctional Services)* [1989] 3 FC 329 (CA).

balancing of the extent to which Suresh is such a danger against the prospects for his subjection to torture. It also attempts to characterise this aspect of the decision as almost completely contingent on the facts and devoid of issues of legal principle thus avoiding any possible argument that the Minster misconceived the legal dimensions of 'national security' or the factors which go into such a determination.

There is also a problem with the Court's automatic application of its interpretation of *Baker* to the judicial assessment of the relevance of factors in the determination of an issue which did engage section 7—the question of whether Suresh faced a substantial threat of torture. The Court never justifies applying the same deferential standard that it associated with *Baker* save once again by reference to the high factual content of that determination, facts that were beyond the Court's realm of expertise. Why that is so except in the sense of it being a potentially complicated inquiry is never made clear and there is certainly no discussion of why it should be the same in the domain of constitutional adjudication as it was in *Baker*.

Beyond that, the Court has left uncertain whether its general prescription of patent unreasonableness review for this kind of ministerial discretion includes the situation in which the Minister, having determined that there is a substantial risk of torture, is then balancing that against national security interests. If that turns out to be the case, then the Court has imposed a more deferential standard of review in a situation where *Charter* rights are at stake than in the case of *Baker* and all in the name of the Minister's authority over national security issues. This comes close to an abdication of its responsibility for ensuring the protection of constitutionally guaranteed rights.

Indeed, in even allowing that the 'principles of fundamental justice' permit such a balancing exercise, the Court has flown in the face of Canada's international obligations in a situation where parliamentary intention as reflected sometimes in a deliberate decision not to incorporate should count for little, if anything. Where *Charter* rights are at stake, legislative inaction whether deliberate or not is irrelevant. Rather, it is the weight that international law principles carry with them (whether or not specifically incorporated into domestic law) which should be the critical determinant in the discerning of the normative content of the 'principles of fundamental justice'.

Of course, Suresh did actually obtain judicial review albeit on procedural fairness grounds.[109] However, in delineating the content of fundamental justice, the Court makes it clear that state interests form part of the evaluation of the extent to which fundamental justice permits derogations

---

[109] In contrast, the Court found in the parallel case of *Ahani* that, despite the fact that the procedures followed did not accord precisely with the edict in *Suresh*, there had been sufficient compliance with the procedural requirements of the principles of fundamental justice: above n 95 at paras 25–26.

from an effective opportunity for the target of the proposed action to know and meet the case. Aside from the fact that the Court does little to justify particular derogations, such as the absence of an entitlement to an in-person hearing when credibility may well be critical, there remains the question as to why this whole question should not take place within a section 1 justification. It is also a corollary of this that the opportunities for substantive review are further weakened in that the reservation on access to security information means that the Court will have less than a full record on which to confidently conduct its judicial review of the exercise of discretion. Moreover, this is unlikely to be rectified in the course of whatever right exists to discovery on the subsequent judicial review application, particularly given the executive privilege provisions in the *Canada Evidence Act*.[110]

What is also problematic is the extent of the inconsistency between the Court's approach in this case and its stance in other more recent standard of review case law. Thus, in the immigration cases, *Chieu* and *Al Sagban*, decided the same day and not predicated on *Charter* rights, the Court elevates a question of the relevance of a particular factor to a jurisdictional question attracting correctness review. It also suggests that claims to deference in a purely administrative law setting diminish when the state and an individual are protagonists. Then, in the *Charter* setting of *Trinity Western University*, the Court refuses the invitation to embrace a limited amount of deference by segmenting the decision-making process into questions of law, mixed law and fact and fact. That was not appropriate where the College was attempting to balance potentially competing *Charter* rights and freedoms, a task at which it had no claim to expertise.

Applying this case law to *Suresh*, we see the state acting as the protagonist against an individual in a matter involving not just administrative law interests but also *Charter* rights. For the reasons identified above, segmenting the decision-making process into questions of law and fact with the heavier component by far that of fact was never appropriately justified in *Suresh* and, on the surface, just as problematic and inappropriate as it was in *Trinity Western University*. Finally, while the courts have always treated questions of national security as especially within the expert domain of the highest level of the federal executive, the lessons of history are that virtual

---

[110] RSC 1985, c.C–5, ss 37–39. National security is a specific category of protected information. Where an objection is made, it is determined under s 38 for the most part by way of *ex parte* hearing *in camera*. Also, if the information is certified as constituting 'a confidence of the Queen's Privy Council for Canada', disclosure must be refused under s 39. The constitutionality of this provision was recently sustained in *Babcock v Canada*, [2002] 3 SCR 3, though with the Court conceding some scope for judicial review when the information for which the protection was claimed did not on its face fit within the relevant category or where the person seeking disclosure was able to establish that the Clerk to the Privy Council had improperly exercised her or his discretion in issuing the certificate, presumably (though this is not said) by reference to a patent unreasonableness standard.

abnegation of judicial review authority in this domain has both hidden and provided an encouragement to excessive use of powers of detention, confiscation and deportation. To afford deference in the expectation the executive will be attentive to and good at balancing *Charter* rights and interests against the pressures generated not only within Canada but also by certain sectors of the international community is not realistic. It also runs the danger of making the assertion of *Charter* rights in this domain effectively non-justiciable.

To all of this, the pragmatist might simply react with the response that it is I who am being unrealistic in a post-September 11 world where national security concerns trump all. While Canadian law does not have a political questions doctrine at least where constitutional (including *Charter*) questions are in issue,[111] the Court should at least be entitled to deploy a close surrogate when national security interests are at stake, that surrogate being considerable deference to executive judgment. However, that is not what the constitution and the *Charter* say. In the case of the *Charter*, the trump should only apply in the event of legislative override or a properly founded section 1 justification.

More generally though, *Suresh* raises questions as to the way in which *Charter* rights will be dealt with when they are at stake in other high level executive decision-making. The history of Canadian law in this domain, *Baker* notwithstanding, exhibits and continues to exhibit a high level of deference to Cabinet, ministerial and other senior executive prerogatives.[112] For that to survive intact or by reference to a patent unreasonableness standard of review when *Charter* rights are in issue would be inexcusable. In short, at the very least it is to be hoped that the *Suresh* application of a highly deferential standard of review to decisions which involve *Charter* rights will at least be confined to the special category of case in which national security interests are clearly or obviously implicated.

I do acknowledge that we now function in an era where there is frequent reassertion of the notion that administrative law itself is a branch of constitutional law and/or that there should be cross- fertilisation in both directions as between these two components of our public law.[113] I also accept that this invites the criticism that the argument that I have just made puts far too much emphasis on the distinction between cases in which *Charter* or other 'true' constitutional rights are in issue and those where the interests at stake are justiciable only by reference to administrative law principles.

However, even accepting that there is merit in the contention that there should not be a wide gulf in the scope of judicial review on constitutional

---

[111] *Operation Dismantle Inc v The Queen* [1985] 1 SCR 441.
[112] Above n 10 at 313.
[113] See in particular G Cartier's chapter, 'The *Baker* Effect: A New Interface Between the *Charter* and Administrative Law—The Case of Discretion'. See also TRS Allan's chapter, above n 104 and M Hunt, 'Sovereignty's Blight', above n 20, in which the argument for a theory of deference conceived of in terms of 'justification' is rooted firmly in a conception of administrative law as part of constitutional law.

and non-constitutional grounds does not in any way affect my criticism of *Suresh*. Lessening the gulf may be one thing; it is another to go to the extreme of being more deferential in *Suresh*, a constitutional case than in *Baker*, a case where the Court found it unnecessary to reach the *Charter* arguments. That does not lessen the gulf. It reverses the entire order of things. Moreover, as indicated above, I do not accept that that reversal can be justified in the name of the pragmatic and functional approach. Even accepting that national security considerations weigh heavily in normal standard of review or deference calculus does not give them priority in that calculus over explicit constitutional rights particularly in a domain where the government does have the ability to justify its actions and decisions and trump the constitutional right in appropriate circumstances by reference to section 1 of the *Charter*. Indeed, I would make the same assertion even against an argument that the maintenance of national security is yet another underlying principle of the Canadian constitution.[114]

More generally, I would respond to the criticism that the argument makes too much of the difference between constitutional rights and other administrative law interests by suggesting that, as *Baker* itself indicates, there is presently a continuum of sorts. The nature of the interests at stake in *Baker* took the standard of review away from patent unreasonableness, the standard normally applicable to broadly-framed executive discretions, to that of straight unreasonableness. Convert the interests at stake in *Baker* to *Charter* rights and the standard becomes either that of overall correctness or correctness in relation to the critical elements of the decision.

Indeed, there may be more shades than that. As contended above, it may be a fair reading of *Baker* to allow for more intense scrutiny of the exercise of broad discretions when their exercise involves underlying constitutional principles or considerations emanating from a substantive conception of the rule of law (such as ratified but unimplemented treaties and the general principles of international law) and the fundamental values of Canadian society. If so, the line between constitutional and administrative law review becomes even less pronounced. This sense of a continuum also emerges in the constitutional domain at least to the extent that there is legitimacy in at least some level of deference to the factual findings of decision-makers when constitutional rights are at stake.

CONCLUSIONS

Despite the uncertainties surrounding *Baker* and what precisely it is saying about the conduct of review of the exercise of an administrative discretion under an unreasonableness standard, that part of the Court's judgment has

---

[114] In so doing, I am aware of the fact that in *New Brunswick Broadcasting Co v Nova Scotia (Speaker of the House of Assembly)* [1993] 1 SCR 319, the Supreme Court held that underlying principles of parliamentary privilege could trump a *Charter* right.

made an important contribution to the overall coherence of Canadian judicial review law. In holding that the pragmatic and functional approach to delineating the standard of review is applicable across the entire spectrum of statutory and prerogative decision-making, it has given Canadian judicial review law a unity in the domain of substantive review that it did not have previously. It is also understandable why, in such a clear case of an unreasonable failure to take a critical factor into account, the Court did not develop a detailed template for how unreasonableness review is to be conducted within the framework of broad discretionary powers.

However, it is equally understandable that the matters left unresolved by the judgment have led lower courts to disagree as to the extent to which the kind of unreasonableness review asserted in *Baker* allows for the re-weighing of factors relevant to the exercise of discretion. In that context, *Suresh*'s holding that *Baker* did not authorise a re-weighing of the various factors may seem a welcome clarification. However, it too suffers from a lack of detailed attention to the complexity of the issue. Moreover, its apparent use of the pragmatic and functional approach to justify a highly deferential approach to review of most, if not all aspects of a process in which *Charter* rights were at stake seems to be perversion of the whole thrust of *Baker* and its willingness to allow for unreasonableness as opposed to patent unreasonableness review of a broad ministerial discretion in a case involving highly valued individual interests. More generally, *Suresh* points to the great difficulties that common law courts have always had in dealing with rights-based claims in times of crisis or in the face of executive assertions of national security. It is to be hoped that there will be sufficient recognition of that highly contextual factor to dilute *Suresh*'s impact on the further necessary clarification and evolution of the law governing the principles of review of discretionary decision-making in the wake of *Baker*.

3

The Baker *Effect: A New Interface Between the* Canadian Charter of Rights and Freedoms *and Administrative Law—The Case of Discretion*

GENEVIÈVE CARTIER[1]

INTRODUCTION

UNTIL THE DECISION of the Supreme Court of Canada in *Baker v Canada (Minister of Citizenship and Immigration)*,[2] the Canadian judiciary had endorsed a dual approach to the review of administrative action. When called upon to review administrative interpretations of the law, courts were mandated to demonstrate 'deference', that is to refrain from reviewing decisions which were considered best left to the executive for decision, unless those decisions were unreasonable or patently unreasonable. When the conditions for deference were not met, courts would review administrative decisions on a correctness basis. By contrast, the control of administrative discretion was conceived as ensuring that legal limits were respected by the decision-makers, without allowing courts to get involved in the substance of those decisions. Exercises of discretion required policy choices, with which courts ought not to meddle. Courts therefore considered that interpretations of the law on the one hand, and discretion on the other, raised different issues which called for different types of control.

---

[1] This Chapter builds upon, and takes further, an argument that I first developed in G Cartier, 'Administrative Law Twenty Years After the *Charter*', forthcoming in the 2003 *Revue du Barreau du Québec Numéro Spécial 197*. I would like to thank David Dyzenhaus for inviting me to the conference and for invaluable comments on previous drafts of this chapter. I greatly benefited from the contributions of all the participants at the conference, especially Evan Fox-Decent who took the time to send me written comments and suggestions.
[2] [1999] 2 SCR 817 (hereafter *Baker*).

The decision of the Supreme Court in *Baker* shatters the foundation for this dual approach to judicial review. It indicates that nothing essentially differentiates administrative interpretations of the law from administrative exercises of discretionary power and that, consequently, the same approach should be used for the review of both kinds of decision. *Baker* in fact brings discretion into the realm of law, reuniting both sides of administrative law. I contend that this aspect of *Baker* has fundamental implications for the relationship between administrative law and the constitutionally entrenched *Canadian Charter of Rights and Freedoms*.[3]

In Canada, the adoption of the *Charter* raised the question of the relationship between judicial review under the *Charter* and judicial review under the common law of administrative law.[4] Among others, JM Evans expressed the view that constitutional litigation should only be used as a kind of last resort in administrative law situations. He urged courts not to abandon their role in the common law of administrative law whenever common law remedies existed, and warned that to resort to the *Charter* when the common law of administrative law offered solutions would lead the common law to atrophy.[5] Later on, Le Bel J also warned that systematic resort to the *Charter* 'would be a recipe for freezing and sterilizing the natural and necessary evolution of the common law and the civil law of this country'.[6]

As it turned out however, the Supreme Court gave reasons for concerns that the *Charter* would precisely have a sterilising effect on administrative law. Called upon to review administrative, discretionary decisions challenged on the basis of *Charter* arguments, the Court in two important cases[7] chose to resort to the constitutional standard of review provided for in the *Charter* rather than the administrative law standard for review of discretion. As we shall see, the rationale for this choice is the product of what I would call the '*Charter* effect', that is the tendency of courts to reduce administrative law to a purely formal role when there exist constitutional documents protecting fundamental values. However, I contend that *Baker* paves the way for the development of a new interface between the *Charter* and administrative law. More specifically, I argue that the

---

[3] Part I of the *Constitution Act 1982*, being Schedule B of the *Canada Act, 1982* (UK), 1982, ch 11 (hereafter *Charter*).
[4] As David Dyzenhaus rightly indicates in his introduction to this volume, this is a question that is likely to be raised in any common law jurisdiction that adopts a written instrument for the protection of fundamental rights.
[5] '[A] rich source of thought and experience about law and government will be overlooked or lost altogether, and will eventually atrophy': JM Evans, 'The Principles of Fundamental Justice: The Constitution and The Common Law' (1991) 29 *Osgoode Hall Law Journal* 51 at 73.
[6] *Blencoe v British Columbia (Human Rights Commission)* [2000] 2 SCR 307, at para 189 (hereafter *Blencoe*).
[7] *Slaight Communications Inc v Davidson*, [1989] 1 SCR 1038 (hereafter *Slaight*) and *Ross v New Brunswick School District No 15*, [1996] 1 SCR 825 (hereafter *Ross*).

'*Baker* effect' allows for administrative law and the *Charter* to co-exist in a way that is responsive to the preoccupations expressed by JM Evans and Le Bel J, at least in the domain of administrative discretion, and that this in turn favours the unity of public law.

My chapter has two parts. In Part I, I present a sketch of the first stage of the Canadian approach to the relationship between administrative law and the *Charter*. As we shall see, the decisions of the Supreme Court handed down during this stage were based on assumptions which expressed an impoverished version of administrative law. In Part II, I show how Canadian law has entered a new stage with *Baker*. On the one hand, *Baker* questioned the fundamental assumptions that formed the basis for the preceding phase. On the other hand, it opened up the way for re-conceiving the relationship between the *Charter* and administrative law. In my view, *Baker* proposes both a methodology and an understanding of the rule of law that lay down the foundations for the development of a relationship that is likely to ensure cross-fertilisation between the *Charter* and administrative law. More generally, underlying *Baker* is a vision of public law as a unity, capable of maintaining a substantive role for administrative law.

ADMINISTRATIVE LAW AND THE *CHARTER*: A DIFFICULT START

As I alluded to in the introduction, Canadian administrative law traditionally differentiated executive interpretations of the law from discretionary decisions for the purpose of judicial review.[8] The modern approach to the review of the former was first articulated in the decision of the Supreme Court in *Canadian Union of Public Employees Local 963 v New Brunswick Liquor Corporation*.[9] In that case, the Court made it clear that administrative interpretations of legal questions that fell 'within the jurisdiction' of the tribunal (termed 'non-jurisdictional' questions) and which were protected by a privative clause, would be reviewed only if they were 'patently unreasonable'. All other interpretations (that is, interpretations of legal questions which fell outside, or determined the limits of, the jurisdiction of the tribunal, termed 'jurisdictional' questions) would be reviewed on a standard of correctness. The Court justified resorting to a standard of patent unreasonableness in regard to non-jurisdictional questions, both on the necessity to take seriously clear legislative indications to limit judicial intervention, and on the substantive reasons for doing so, especially the expertise of administrative tribunals on the legal questions they were mandated to decide.

In the years that followed *CUPE*, courts have had to tackle the difficult question of how to determine if a question is jurisdictional or not.

---

[8] This is also a feature of British, Australian and New Zealand administrative law.
[9] [1979] 2 SCR 227 (hereafter *CUPE*).

In an attempt to avoid formal classification and with a view to being alive to the spirit of *CUPE* that there were substantive reasons for respecting administrative decisions, courts developed what was termed a 'pragmatic and functional approach' to the review of administrative determinations of legal questions. That approach purported to articulate a number of criteria which gave indications as to the intent of the legislature on the question whether the issue was to be left to the courts (jurisdictional questions) or to the tribunals (non-jurisdictional questions).[10]

The review of discretion proceeded differently. Since discretion dictated no specific outcome, it was conceived as conferring on the decision-maker the power to choose 'among possible courses of action or inaction'.[11] Courts thus understood their role as ensuring that, within legal limits, administrative agencies were left free to take any decision they saw fit. The review was therefore limited to sanctioning excesses of jurisdiction, that is, any decision which did not conform with the object of the delegating statute, which manifested bad faith or discrimination, made use of improper considerations or failed to consider relevant ones. 'Unreasonableness' was sometimes invoked as a ground of review, although usually to reinforce an argument already made on the basis of one of the specific heads of review just mentioned.[12]

At first glance, the dual approach to judicial review resulted in the same 'hands-off' approach to administrative decision-making: courts would refrain from reviewing either non-jurisdictional legal questions or discretionary decisions, unless there were serious reasons for intervention. But different reasons justified these apparently similar results. The hands-off approach to administrative interpretations of non-jurisdictional questions was justified on the basis that law-interpretation was not the monopoly of the courts and that in many cases, expert, administrative agencies were equally, and sometimes more qualified than courts to interpret a statutory provision. The endorsement of a standard of patent unreasonableness thus signalled a departure from a formal conception of the separation of powers and inaugurated a politics of judicial 'deference' to administrative agencies: the recognition of their legitimacy to participate in the task of law-interpretation and the necessity to allow them some margin of autonomy for doing so.[13]

---

[10] That approach was first articulated by Beetz J. in *Union des employés de service, Local 298 v Bibeault*, [1988] 2 SCR 1048.

[11] KC Davis, *Discretionary Justice—A Preliminary Inquiry* (Baton Rouge, Louisiana State University Press, 1969), 4 quoted in *Baker*, above n 2, at para 52.

[12] See especially DJ Mullan, *Administrative Law* (Toronto, Irwin Law, 2001), 121. *Bell v The Queen*, [1979] SCR 212 is a rare example of the use of unreasonableness as the main ground of review. By contrast, in the UK, unreasonableness played a major role in the control of discretion. See especially P Craig, *Administrative Law*, 4th ed (London, Sweet & Maxwell, 1999) 581ff.

[13] See especially D Dyzenhaus, 'The Politics of Deference: Judicial Review and Democracy', in M Taggart (ed), *The Province of Administrative Law* (Oxford, Hart Publishing, 1997) 279 (hereafter 'Politics of Deference').

By contrast, the hands-off approach to discretion was precisely dictated by the necessity to maintain the judiciary in a position which was compatible with a formal view of the separation of powers. Because discretion required choices that could be based on political or policy considerations, subjecting discretion to substantive legal scrutiny was viewed as bringing courts on to the slippery ground of politics. Therefore, the heads of review available limited the potential for intrusion into the substance of those decisions and maintained the judiciary in a position which was compatible with a formal view of the separation of powers. Thus, in the field of discretion, the justification for restraint was not based on a posture of judicial 'deference', that is, the recognition of a legitimate role for the executive in law-interpretation, but on judicial 'abstinence',[14] that is the necessity to keep the judiciary away from decisions which were viewed as taken outside the realm of the law.

In either case however, there were situations where deference or abstinence would have to give way to judicial review. Indeed, both review approaches recognised that 'unreasonable' decisions mandated intervention. Reasonableness was viewed as a kind of safety net, indicating that there had to remain a potential ground for intervention in cases which 'exceeded the limits'. The challenge for courts was to properly define and apply a standard of review based on reasonableness while at the same time being faithful to the rationale for deference or abstinence.

In the context of the review of discretion, the notion of unreasonableness was usually understood in the *Wednesbury*[15] sense of 'something so absurd that no sensible person could ever dream that it lay within the power of the authority',[16] later reformulated by the House of Lords as 'a decision which is so outrageous in its defiance of logic or of accepted moral standards that no sensible person who had applied his mind to the question to be decided could have arrived at it'.[17] *Wednesbury* did not seem to require any serious involvement with the merits of the decision since the defect it sanctioned was to clearly appear on its face. By contrast, in the context of the review of executive interpretations of the law, *CUPE* defined a patently unreasonable decision as one which could not be 'rationally supported by the relevant legislation'.[18] As appeared from post-*CUPE* jurisprudence however, it was not clear whether the determination of this rational support required an analysis of the substance, or merits of the decision.[19] Some judges thought that the standard of patent unreasonableness could not require

---

[14] The expression is from RA Macdonald, 'Judicial Review and Procedural Fairness in Administrative Law: I' (1980) *McGill Law Journal* 520, 534.
[15] Named after the famous dictum of Lord Greene in *Associated Provincial Picture Houses Ltd v Wednesbury Corporation*, (1948) 1 KB 223.
[16] *Ibid*, at 229.
[17] *Council of Civil Service Unions v Minister for the Civil Service*, (1985) AC 374 (HL Eng) 410.
[18] *CUPE*, above n 9, at 237.
[19] UK law faces the same difficulty: 'While all accept that it is not for courts to substitute judgment, it is also recognised that there should be some control over the rationality of the

any evaluation of the substance of the decision without running the risk of subverting itself into a correctness standard. Other judges expressed the view that the reasonableness of a decision, that is the existence of a rational support for the decision on the relevant legislation, required at least some attention to substance, without implying that courts take the decision in place of the administrative decision-maker.[20]

All this expressed a dual view of judicial review, based on a particular conception of the role of the judiciary towards law interpretation as well as discretion, and it also revealed tensions in regard to the definition and application of the relevant standards of review based on reasonableness. This legal background partly explains the initial attitude of the Supreme Court towards the question of the relationship between the *Charter* and administrative law, as the following analysis reveals.

In two important cases, *Slaight* and *Ross*, the Supreme Court of Canada was asked to determine the validity of a discretionary decision challenged on the basis that it limited a *Charter*-protected right. Given the picture that was sketched above, the review of those decisions should have been approached as any other instance of review of discretion. But the case was not so clear, since the argument that was put forward to challenge the decision was based on the *Charter*, and the *Charter* itself included a standard for review of decisions affecting *Charter*-protected rights. So the Court had to address the question of the relationship between judicial review under the *Charter* and judicial review under the common law of administrative law, to determine which standard of review should be used in the circumstances.

There were two options available. One was to rely on the administrative law standard of review of discretion, as articulated in the dual view of the common law of judicial review exposed above. This option implicitly relied on the idea that administrative law had the resources to deal with any question arising out of any exercise of discretionary power, and that the standards of review articulated under the common law applied irrespective of the kind of argument put forward to challenge the decisions of the executive. The other option was to use the constitutional standard of review specifically provided for in section 1 of the *Charter*. This standard provides that a governmental decision limiting a right protected by the *Charter* may

---

decisions made by the administration. The tension between these two ideas has shaped much of the jurisprudence in this area ... The theme which runs throughout this area is the desire to fashion a criterion which will allow judicial control, without thereby leading to substitution of judgment or too great an intrusion on the merits'.: PP Craig, above n 12, at 580.

[20] See especially *CAIMAW v Paccar of Canada Ltd*, [1989] 2 RCS 983, *National Corn Growers Assn v Canada (Import Tribunal)*, [1990] 2 SCR 1324, *Dayco (Canada) Ltd v CAW-Canada*, [1993] 2 SCR 230 and *United Brotherhood of Carpenters and Joiners of America, Local 579 v Bradco Construction Ltd*, [1993] 2 SCR 316. See also D Dyzenhaus' introduction to this volume, and his 'Constituting the Rule of Law: Fundamental Values in Administrative Law', (2002) 27 *Queen's Law Journal* 445, 493ff (hereafter 'Constituting the Rule of Law').

none the less be valid if it can be established that it sets 'reasonable limits prescribed by law as can be demonstrably justified in a free and democratic society'. The Court chose the latter option in both *Slaight* and *Ross*, for reasons which, I contend, express an impoverished conception of administrative law.[21]

In *Slaight*, a labour adjudicator found that Slaight Communications had unjustly dismissed Davidson. As a remedy, the adjudicator issued an order which purported, in what the Court termed its positive aspect, to constrain the employer to give Davidson a letter of recommendation whose content was fixed by the terms of the order. Furthermore, the negative aspect of the order required the employer and its staff strictly to limit their answers to inquiries about Davidson's employment by sending a copy of the said letter. A majority of the Supreme Court found that both aspects of the order placed a limit on the employer's freedom of expression guaranteed by the *Charter*, but concluded that the limit was justified under section 1.

Slaight was typical of the difficulties inherent in the pre-*Baker*, dual approach to judicial review of administrative action. It involved the review of a discretionary order (an adjudicator had discretion to issue the appropriate remedy in the circumstances), theoretically implying the administrative law approach to the review of discretion. But this order was made in the larger context of a decision involving the interpretation of rules of law (the adjudicator had to settle the question whether the dismissal had been made for sufficient and just cause), a kind of decision that implied the application of the pragmatic and functional approach. Thus, the decision in *Slaight* potentially appealed to both approaches to the review of administrative action and to both senses of the reasonableness standard: the *CUPE* sense and the *Wednesbury* sense. But since the argument put forward to challenge the adjudicator's order was based on the *Charter*, the Court also had to consider a third contender: the constitutional standard of section 1.

Both Lamer J and Dickson CJ concluded that the constitutional standard of section 1 was the sole standard which could be used when discretionary decisions were challenged on the basis of *Charter* arguments.[22] But they put forward different reasons for so concluding. Lamer J views his choice as between *Wednesbury* unreasonableness and section 1 of the *Charter*. In his opinion, *Charter*-types of inquiry call for an analysis of the substance of discretionary decisions, but since the administrative, *Wednesbury* standard of review of discretion does not allow for any substantive analysis, courts are compelled to resort to the constitutional standard of section 1.

---

[21] For a detailed analysis of *Slaight* and *Ross*, see G Cartier, 'Administrative Law Twenty Years After the *Charter*', forthcoming in 2003 *Revue du Barreau du Québec Numéro Spécial* 197.

[22] However, they held different positions on the question of the sequence in which the standards should be used. Lamer J submitted the decision to the *Charter* standard only after concluding that the decision could not be invalidated on a common law ground, while Dickson CJ went straight to the *Charter* standard.

In other words, administrative law does not have the appropriate tools to evaluate the legality of discretionary decisions challenged on the basis of *Charter* arguments because the administrative law standard does not allow a court to 'examine [the] appropriateness [of a discretionary decision] or [...] substitute its own opinion for that of the person making the order [...]'.[23] For Dickson CJ, the choice is between *CUPE* unreasonableness and section 1 of the *Charter*. In his opinion, the administrative law standard of patent unreasonableness is relevant only when the questions raised are 'untouched by the *Charter*', since this standard lacks the qualities required for the analysis of *Charter* arguments: it is less 'onerous' than section 1 and it 'rests to a large extent on unarticulated and undeveloped values and lacks the same degree of structure and sophistication of analysis'.[24] In the 'realm of value inquiry', courts must rely on the constitutional standard of section 1.

So while Lamer J thought the administrative law standard was ill-suited to *Charter* challenges because of its inability to inquire into the substance of discretionary decisions, Dickson CJ thought it was ill-suited because of its inability to properly unravel the value inquiries involved in any *Charter* litigation. The analysis required by *Charter* arguments could only be adequately analysed under the constitutional standard of section 1.

This expresses what I would call a 'hierarchical view' of the relationship between administrative law and the *Charter*. 'Hierarchy' conveys the idea that the very existence of the *Charter* tends to 'formalise' administrative law: its role is reduced to one of formal determination of jurisdiction on the basis of statutory interpretation, and it does not have the ability to deal with issues of fundamental values.

Lamer J's and Dickson CJ's opinions both inform the decision of the Supreme Court in *Ross*, a case which shares this hierarchical view. Over a number of years Ross, a school teacher, had publicly expressed during his off-duty time racist and discriminatory comments against Jews. A complaint was filed by Jewish parents and a human rights board of inquiry (HRBI) was established. The HRBI concluded that the School Board which employed Ross had acted in a discriminatory manner towards the parents and their children by failing to discipline him appropriately. The HRBI had the power to 'order any party found to have violated the *Act* to do certain things designed to rectify the violation'.[25] In its order, the HRBI mandated the School Board immediately to terminate any kind of employment Ross might have with the School Board if he returned to the behaviour that had led to the complaints. Ross applied for judicial review of the decision of the HRBI and attacked the order on both administrative law and *Charter* grounds.

---

[23] *Slaight*, above n 7, at 1074.
[24] *Ibid*.
[25] *Ross*, above n 7, at para 9.

On the administrative law side, one of the issues raised was whether the HRBI had exceeded its jurisdiction in making the order. On the *Charter* side, Ross contended that the order violated his freedom of religion and conscience as well as his freedom of expression.

Again, La Forest J, speaking for a unanimous Court, chose to analyse the *Charter* argument with the *Charter* standard. La Forest J's choice was seemingly between *CUPE* unreasonableness and section 1.[26] Two assumptions formed the basis for the choice of the latter. The first was that the *Charter* standard was always more severe than its administrative law analogue. That is, it is more difficult for the government to justify an infringement under the constitutional standard of section 1 than to show that its decision is reasonable in the *CUPE* sense. Thus, using section 1 always at the same time ensures that the exigencies of administrative law are met. The second assumption was that only the *Charter* standard possesses the required qualities to conduct 'value inquiries'. This clearly appears from his description of the administrative law review process. He said that administrative law was merely concerned with the determination of the statutory jurisdiction of the Board, an issue 'untouched by the *Charter*'. It was to be 'determined in accordance with the interpretation of the [relevant statutory] provisions'. Having so proceeded, he considered that it was 'enough to say that the Board's discretionary power is set forth [in the Act] in such broad terms that it cannot be said to fall outside its jurisdiction. [The Act] authorise[s] the Board to make any order to effect compliance with the Act or to rectify the harm caused by a violation of the Act', provided only that the order was based on a full consideration of the facts and 'apart from *Charter* issues'.[27]

Such a formal approach empties the control of discretion on administrative law grounds of any (explicit) reference to values, which form the core of *Charter* challenges, and contributes to presenting an impoverished picture of administrative law.

So overall, three elements might explain the choice of the constitutional standard by Lamer J, Dickson CJ and La Forest J in *Slaight* and *Ross*. The first is a restrictive view of the role of courts in the control of discretion: a formal, value-free exercise in statutory interpretation to determine the limits within which the decision-maker is authorised to act, and one which avoids any examination of the substance of the decision. The second is the consideration that the *CUPE* standard of patent unreasonableness fails to provide a sufficiently structured and value articulated analysis. And the third is the contention that the constitutional standard is always more severe than the *CUPE* standard.

---

[26] I say 'seemingly' since he does not expressly indicate that this is the case, but refers to Dickson J's opinion in *Slaight* and quotes a number of Supreme Court decisions associated with the *CUPE* sense of reasonableness.
[27] *Ross*, above n 7, at para 33.

The first consideration was built in the traditional, dual approach to judicial review which viewed discretion as 'non law', or as giving the executive 'free reign within legal limits'.[28] Courts were reluctant to proceed to any intrusive control of discretion for fear of being seen as interfering with policy decisions or value choices, which would be incompatible with their task under a formal conception of the separation of powers. Moreover, it was never clear to what extent *CUPE* allowed analyses of the substance or merits of the decisions, and because *Wednesbury* clearly did not, this created an interstice for the *Charter* standard to get in. Indeed, the *Charter* clearly authorised substantive review and therefore appeared as the sole appropriate contender for *Charter* challenges to exercises of discretion.

The second element accurately describes the nature of the *CUPE* standard at the time *Slaight* and *Ross* were handed down. Indeed, that the *CUPE* standard rests on less articulated and developed values than the *Charter* standard is not open to question. A number of Supreme Court decisions purported to elucidate, clarify and bring to the forefront the substantive elements which framed the questions at issue in *Charter* challenges of public action.[29] By contrast, the values at play when the administrative law standard is applied are seldom clearly articulated. To determine the appropriate level of deference to be given to a decision-maker, courts purport to give effect to legislative will, through the application of the pragmatic and functional approach discussed in numerous Supreme Court decisions.[30] However, the analysis does not, as in the case of the *Charter* standard of section 1, explicitly reach the level of the values at stake, even though such analyses exist in academic writings.[31] That the *CUPE* standard lacks the structure and sophistication of analysis found in section 1 is beyond doubt as well. *R v Big M Drug Mart Ltd*.[32] stands for the establishment

---

[28] D Dyzenhaus and E Fox-Decent, 'Rethinking the Process/Substance Distinction: *Baker v Canada*', (2001) 51 *University of Toronto Law Journal* 193, 204.

[29] This is clearly expressed in one of the first *Charter* cases, *R v Oakes*, [1986] 1 SCR 103, as the following excerpts show: '[s 1] states explicitly the exclusive justificatory criteria against which limitations on those rights and freedoms must be measured ... The underlying values and principles of a free and democratic society are the genesis of the rights and freedoms guaranteed by the *Charter* and the ultimate standard against which a limit on a right or freedom must be shown, despite its effect, to be reasonable and demonstrably justified ... [These underlying values and principles include] respect for the inherent dignity of the human person, commitment to social justice and equality, accommodation of a wide variety of beliefs, respect for cultural and group identity, and faith in social and political institutions which enhance the participation of individuals and groups in society'.: *Oakes*, at 135–36. See also *Dagenais v Société Radio-Canada*, [1994] 3 SCR 835.

[30] For a recent attempt to present a summary of the law on this highly complex issue, see *Pushpanathan v Canada (Minister of Citizenship and Immigration)*, [1998] 1 SCR 982.

[31] See especially Dyzenhaus, 'Politics of Deference', above n 13, where the author develops the theoretical underpinnings for endorsing a notion of deference as respect, related to democratic and egalitarian considerations.

[32] [1985] 1 SCR 295.

of the general structure of the analysis mandated by section 1 (establishing an objective of pressing and substantial concern in a free and democratic society and proportionality between the latter and the impugned measure), and numerous subsequent decisions refined the process. By contrast, the administrative law standard of reasonableness is applied much less stringently, mostly because the Court never clearly showed how a judge could reconcile the need to establish rational support for a decision with the need to demonstrate deference to the decision-makers. As already mentioned, it is far from clear whether the standard of patent unreasonableness requires, or even allows, analyses of the merits of the decisions.[33]

As to the third element, it is in fact based on a misinterpretation of Dickson CJ's opinion: he did not choose the *Charter* standard because it is more severe, but because it is 'more onerous', that is because it has the capacity to reach more accurate results. Given the importance of the values protected by the *Charter*, violations must be identified and sanctioned, but an insufficiently specific standard could lead to unwarranted, excessive or over-intrusive invalidation. In other words, the standard of review must be precise enough to ensure that the Court reaches its target. But even if the third element correctly expressed Dickson CJ's view in *Slaight*, authors have demonstrated that this proposition was debatable at the time *Ross* was handed down, since the application of the *Charter* standard of section 1 mandated a contextual analysis that sometimes resulted in a highly deferential stance.[34] At any rate, it seems now a very difficult position to sustain, because administrative law developed a third standard of review, termed 'reasonableness *simpliciter*', that is 'more deferential than correctness but less deferential than "not patently unreasonable"'.[35] This suggests that it is even more probable today that a situation will arise where the contextual analysis required by the constitutional standard of section 1 results in a posture of deference that is not significantly different from that which would be appropriate under the administrative law, pragmatic and functional approach.

As we shall see, *Baker* questions important aspects of these elements and paves the way for the development of a new kind of relationship between administrative law and the *Charter*.

---

[33] See n 19 and corresponding text, above.
[34] See P Blache and S Comtois, 'L'affaire *Ross* : Normes de contrôle judiciaire—Droits de la personne—Insuffisance de preuve. Rapport entre la norme de raisonnabilité de l'article 1 de la Charte et celle du droit administratif', [1997] *Revue du Barreau du Québec* 105, at 134 ff who demonstrate that the contextual analysis mandated under s 1 actually resulted in the application of a very deferential *Charter* standard in *Ross*. The substantial developments to which La Forest J proceeds in this regard appear in *Ross*, above n 7, at para 77ff.
[35] *Canada (Director of Investigation and Research) v Southam Inc*, [1997] 1 SCR 748, at para 54.

BAKER: FROM DUALISM AND HIERARCHY TO COORDINATION AND UNITY

Shattering the Foundations for Dualism and Hierarchy

The preceding analysis highlighted the considerations that led to the choice of the constitutional standard for the review of discretionary decisions challenged on the basis of *Charter* arguments. I contended that these considerations constituted the foundations for a hierarchical view of the relationship between administrative law and the *Charter*. I submit that *Baker* shatters these foundations.

Baker questions the traditional, dual approach to judicial review of administrative action, which paved the way for the restrictive view of the control of discretion under the common law, expressed in *Slaight* and *Ross*. Recall that the dual approach was based on the assumption that discretion and law-interpretation are inherently different and therefore call for a different kind of review. Now in *Baker*, L'Heureux-Dubé J said that there is 'no rigid dichotomy' between discretion and law-interpretation and therefore no justification for such a dual approach.[36] Moreover, she expressed the view that the 'pragmatic and functional approach' developed for the review of interpretations of the law is suitable for the review of discretion, since it reflects the two central ideas incorporated in the traditional approach to the review of that kind of power: that the decision-maker must be given substantial leeway, but that she must none the less act within certain limits. L'Heureux-Dubé J expressed herself as follows:

> The pragmatic and functional approach can take into account the fact that the more discretion that is left to a decision-maker, the more reluctant courts should be to interfere with the manner in which decision-makers have made choices among various options. However, though discretionary decisions will generally be given considerable respect, that discretion must be exercised in accordance with the boundaries imposed in the statute, the principles of the rule of law, the principles of administrative law, the fundamental values of Canadian society, and the principles of the *Charter*.[37]

Hence *Baker*, by applying the pragmatic and functional approach to the control of discretion, marks the end of the dual approach to judicial review in the common law of administrative law.

---

[36] 'It is ... inaccurate to speak of a rigid dichotomy of "discretionary" or "non-discretionary" decisions. Most administrative decisions involve the exercise of implicit discretion in relation to many aspects of decision making ... In addition, there is no easy distinction between interpretation and the exercise of discretion; interpreting legal rules involves considerable discretion to clarify, fill in gaps, and make choices among various options': *Baker*, above n 2, at para 54 (per L'Heureux-Dubé J).

[37] *Baker*, above n 2, at para 56.

But what makes *Baker* really significant for the traditional view of the control of discretion is the recognition that the administrative law standards based on reasonableness are not limited to sanctioning formal legal limits to the exercise of discretion. Indeed, *Baker* expressly conditions the reasonableness of a decision on the consistency of the reasons supporting the decision with the values underlying the grant of the power to decide. In the circumstances of *Baker*, L'Heureux-Dubé J concluded that the decision of the Minister failed to meet the required standard: it was unreasonable because it was 'inconsistent with the *values* underlying the grant of discretion' (emphasis added).[38] Indeed, the reasons which supported the decision showed that the officer failed to give 'serious weight and consideration to the interests of the children',[39] while a number of indications led to the conclusion that those were central values of the Canadian society. *Baker* therefore imports substance and values into the standards of reasonableness and moves away from the formal approach of *Slaight* and *Ross*.

More generally, *Baker* shifts the starting point for determining the legality of executive action, from the nature of the power to the consequences of the exercise of that power on the individual. The rationale put forward by the Court for imposing a duty to give reasons on decision-makers endowed with extensive discretionary powers, is evidence for this shift:

> The profound importance of an [humanitarian and compassionate] decision to those affected ... militates in favour of a requirement that reasons be provided. It would be unfair for a person subject to a decision such as this one which is so critical to their future not to be told why the result was reached.[40]

So the duty to give reasons does not depend on the kind of power that is exercised by the executive, but on the consideration that the dignity of the individual requires that she be told why a decision that is critical to her future was made. This shift is in tension with the dualism in the common law of administrative law, since the focus on the consequences of the decision weakens the justification for conditioning the approach to judicial review on distinctions between the types of decision.

By submitting public authorities endowed with wide discretionary powers to a duty to act reasonably and to give reasons when important individual interests are at stake, *Baker* moves closer to a conception of discretion as exercised in a 'space controlled by law'[41] as opposed to a conception of discretion as inherently political or giving the executive 'free reign within legal limits'.[42] This blurs the distinction between discretion and

---

[38] *Ibid.*
[39] *Baker*, above n 2, at para 65.
[40] *Baker*, above n 2, at para 42.
[41] Dyzenhaus and Fox-Decent, above n 28, at 218.
[42] Dyzenhaus and Fox-Decent, above n 28, at 204.

law-interpretation and it replaces judicial abstinence towards administrative discretion with judicial deference. But *Baker* not only brings dualism to an end, it also suggests a conception of the standard of review which bears clear similarities with the *Charter* standard. It establishes that in order to resist judicial intervention, the decision-maker must be able to justify her discretionary decision. And such a justification requires the demonstration that the reasons for the decision are compatible with the limits established at the close of a contextual approach to statutory interpretation, which involves the consideration of the values underlying the grant of the power. Such an approach is clearly in tension with the assumptions underlying *Slaight* and *Ross*.

Baker also suggests that the contention that the administrative law standard is based on unarticulated and undeveloped values is open to question. Indeed, since *Baker* conditions the reasonableness of any given exercise of discretion on its consistency with the values underlying the grant of the power, it clearly indicates that the values at play in administrative law are sufficiently articulated and developed to condition the legality of administrative discretion. As we shall see, the *Charter* should be viewed as creating an impulse for better developing and articulating such values, but not for concluding that judges have a monopoly on value determinations.

So *Baker* shatters the foundations for the hierarchical view of the relationship between the *Charter* and administrative law, but more importantly, it lays the foundations for a new conception of this relationship that is likely to provide a coherent, legitimating basis for administrative law.

Laying the Foundations for Coordination and Unity

I submit that *Baker* lays the foundations for the development of a new kind of relationship between the *Charter* and administrative law in matters of discretion, a kind of relationship which substitutes coordination and unity for hierarchy and dualism.

Le Bel J's statement in *Blencoe*[43] that the common law of administrative law will be sterilised if litigants assume that the *Charter* must solve every legal problem is in fact a call for administrative lawyers to identify and apply 'non-*Charter*' solutions to judicial review litigations. But as long as the review of administrative discretion based on non-*Charter* grounds is conceived as a mere exercise of formal statutory interpretation, as suggested in *Slaight* and *Ross*, the potential for such a development and application of administrative law solutions is severely restricted. From this perspective, *Baker*'s requirement of reasons and alternative conception of discretion open up the space for putting the common law of administrative law on

---

[43] See n 6 and corresponding text, above.

a substantive, that is, value basis, while at the same time indicating how the *Charter* can contribute to that task.

As we saw, *Slaight* and *Ross* established a duality between cases involving *Charter* issues and cases relying on administrative law arguments, resulting in the application of a particular standard of review to each category of cases. Now such a duality was, to a large extent, conditioned on an extremely restrictive conception of the control of discretion, reducing it to formal exercises of statutory interpretation, detrimental to an understanding of administrative law as based on values.[44] This is paradoxical, since the impulse of rights adjudication that was created by the advent of the *Charter* should have created a similar impulse in the common law of administrative law. But it appeared that the formal inclusion of values in a constitutional document had the effect of emptying, so to speak, the rest of the law of value, as if the entrenchment of the *Charter*, and the explicit delegation of the power to take into account fundamental values, conferred the monopoly on value-laden questions on courts called upon to decide *Charter* cases. In other words, courts developed a culture of rights under the authority of the constitutional document, but made significant efforts not to be seen as expanding the reach of the *Charter* in areas not formally covered by its provisions.[45] Courts thus seemed reluctant to invoke values in the sphere of administrative law, as exemplified in *Slaight* and *Ross*. From this perspective, the *Charter* had the paradoxical effect of seemingly diminishing the substantive role of administrative law in the protection of rights and consideration of values. *Baker* suggests a way out of the paradox.

Baker clearly indicates that there can be no strict separation between law and values. By imposing a requirement of justification through both the giving of reasons and the introduction of a standard of reasonableness involving value inquiries, *Baker* indicates that judicial review of discretionary decisions involves much more than formal exercises of statutory interpretation. So *Baker* moves away from the restrictive conception of the review of discretion endorsed in *Slaight* and *Ross*, and breaks with the assumptions which contributed to the emergence of an impoverished version of administrative law.

In addition, *Baker* suggests how the *Charter* nurtures administrative law. The *Charter* expressly articulates some of the most fundamental rights and freedoms of our society, but it does not confine the influence of those values

---

[44] See Part I, above.
[45] That idea was also expressed in D Dyzenhaus, M Hunt and M Taggart, 'The Principle of Legality in Administrative Law: Internationalisation as Constitutionalisation', [2001] 1 *Oxford University Commonwealth Law Journal* 5, at 16: '[O]n the one hand, one has the constitutional sphere in which values oblige in the sense of determining results, while, on the other hand, one has a non-constitutional public law sphere devoid of values unless these are explicitly incorporated by statute. Paradoxically, the stronger the protection given to values in the constitutional document, the more traditionalist judges might be inclined to maintain seals on the spheres'.

to the realm delimited by the strict ambit of its text. The *Charter* nurtures administrative law, not because it infuses administrative law with values, since administrative law was itself born out of careful articulation of fundamental values (fairness, for example). Rather, the *Charter* gives the common law of administrative law the impulse to better articulate its constitutive values. The *Charter* is one major source of inspiration for administrative law in its task of realising *Baker*'s agenda, that is to articulate better the values at play in the review of discretion under the common law. So *Baker* suggests how we can escape from the excessively restrictive view of discretion from which few legal remedies could emerge outside a *Charter* context, to reach a situation in which the *Charter* contributes to developing non-*Charter* solutions. The *Charter* plays this nurturing role together with other elements of the legal background (like international norms) which ensure the constant evolution of the values of the common law.[46]

Besides, since the common law and the *Charter* ultimately draw upon the same fundamental values, the nurturing relationship is two-way, that is, the common law also contributes to the definition of the norms of the *Charter*.[47] The fundamental values entrenched in the *Charter* are neither 'revealed' nor identifiable 'out there', but result from 'social consensus'.[48] The common law of administrative law, resulting from centuries of careful judicial crafting of rules and principles informed by values which evolved over time, is a crucial element in the search for this consensus. Indeed, judges called upon to define the norms of the *Charter* in the wake of its entrenchment naturally resorted to the common law for assistance in this task.[49] The fact that the common law of administrative law is a major source of inspiration for the interpretation and application of *Charter*-protected interests emphasises the need to prevent atrophy of administrative law.

From this perspective, administrative law is coordinated with, rather than subordinated to, the *Charter*, a form of relationship which ensures cross-fertilisation and avoids 'freezing and sterilizing the natural and necessary

---

[46] Dyzenhaus, Hunt and Taggart, above n 45, at 7. See also Evans, above n 5, at 82–83.
[47] Evans, above n 5, at 75. Evans suggests that it would be difficult to conclude that something not unfair at common law would be unfair under the *Charter*, since both draw upon the same values. See also *R v Bernard*, [1988] 2 SCR 833, 881–892: 'As a repository of our traditional values [common law rules] may, in fact, assist in defining [the] norms [of the *Charter*]'. (per La Forest J, quoted in Evans, at 85).
[48] See S Sedley, 'Human Rights: a Twenty-First Century Agenda', (1995) *Public Law* 386, at 399.
[49] For an early suggestion for doing so in the task of defining the notion of 'fundamental justice' provided for in the *Charter*, see LB Tremblay, 'S 7 of the *Charter*: Substantive Due Process?', [1984] 18 *University of British Columbia Law Review* 201, at 247 and 253: '[S]everal presumptions, because of their specific role and historical importance, must be referred to as safeguards of the principles of fundamental justice that the Constitution now requires ... [T]he presumptions found at common law are not the only means of identifying the principles of fundamental justice. Other principles of fundamental justice can exist elsewhere in jurisprudence. [And they are not] frozen at the date of the enactment of the *Charter* of Rights. Those principles have always evolved and will continue to do so. The courts are at liberty to find and create new principles of fundamental justice where it appears necessary'.

evolution of the common law' of administrative law. Moreover, by signalling that discretion must:

> be exercised in a manner that is within a reasonable interpretation of the margin of manoeuvre contemplated by the legislature, in accordance with the principles of the rule of law ... in line with general principles of administrative law governing the exercise of discretion, and consistent with the [*Charter*],[50]

the Court indicates that the ultimate objective consists in finding a justification for public power.

Coordination and articulation are possible since administrative law and the *Charter* are both equally dedicated to the protection of fundamental rights and are firmly embedded in a context of constitutionalism. The advent of the *Charter* required the courts to look for a justification for legislative enactments and governmental action under the methodology of section 1, a methodology which required the identification of values at play in the decision and in the standard of review. *Baker* suggests greater control of administrative discretion (the requirement of reasons and the adoption of a review standard of reasonableness) and constitutes a similar requirement of justification for administrative action generally, a requirement which should be seen as related to the question of the legitimacy of public power deriving from the rule of law, and which exists irrespective of the *Charter*. Hence, the main objective of both administrative law and the *Charter* is to identify and make effective the constraints which apply to governmental action generally. It matters little whether these constraints are in the written constitution or in ordinary statutes. Reaching for the values underlying the texts renders any differentiation based on the status of the text (constitutional or statutory) secondary. What is of importance is the values which they express. *Baker* suggests a general approach to the review of discretion which requires that the determination of the standard of review of discretion does not depend on the question whether *Charter* arguments are raised or not, but on the question whether the values at stake deserve more or less strict protection. The weight of the values at issue, more than the text which embodies them, becomes the centre of the analysis in administrative law as well as under the *Charter*.

From this perspective, far from introducing more ambiguity in the approach to the determination of the legality of administrative action, the emergence of a discourse on values moves away from formal conceptions of administrative law and rather paves the way for the development of a more principled and transparent approach to the control of discretion.

So the development and articulation of the values referred to in *Baker* take centre stage. But this will not be an easy task to perform. As a matter

---

[50] *Baker*, above n 2, at para 53.

of fact, L'Heureux-Dubé J's opinion on that point is somewhat ambiguous: the 'values underlying the grant of discretion',[51] the 'values of administrative law'[52] and the 'values in Canadian society'[53] all figure in her judgment without any precise indication as to their specific meaning and role. Stephen Sedley provides a useful starting point when he states that the question whether a right should rank as a human right is a question 'to be answered by social consensus from time to time, not by definition a priori and certainly not by derivation from some higher law'.[54] So to be true to the spirit of *Baker*, we must craft appropriate means for this consensus to emerge and be expressed. As David Dyzenhaus alluded to in the introduction to this volume, the unity of public law implies that the same fundamental values underpin the entirety of public law and that legislatures are not the only legitimate participants in the task of articulating what these values are.[55] Indeed, the three branches of the state have a legitimate role in the articulation of those values, together with the individual concerned.

The legislative branch—The legislative branch contributes to the articulation and development of values through formal enactments of statutes, and perhaps also when it decides not to legislate in a particular sphere of activity. Those actions (or inactions) are indications of the importance that the legislature attaches to particular values, and they form part of the legal background which courts must necessarily consider when determining the set of values at play in a case of judicial review of administrative discretion. In *Baker*, part of the analysis of L'Heureux-Dubé J is indeed aimed at elucidating the statement of the legislature. She examines the 'words' of the statute ('compassionate and humanitarian considerations') and looks for their 'meaning'.[56] This exercise is usually framed in terms of a search for 'parliamentary intent'. This concept was often reduced to the formal application of technical rules of interpretation, but L'Heureux-Dubé J's approach in contrast seeks to openly articulate the substantive considerations leading to her interpretation of the statute.

The legitimacy of the contribution of the legislative branch to the development and articulation of values is usually uncontentious. What has attracted considerable attention and criticism, and with particular vehemence in the wake of the entrenchment of the *Charter*, is the question whether the legislature (or constituent assembly) has the monopoly on this role. Hence, the fundamental difference between L'Heureux-Dubé J's position and that of La Forest J's, for example, is that the latter views the legislature as having the final word on the determination of the values or

---

[51] *Baker*, above n 2, at para 65.
[52] *Baker*, above n 2, at para 67.
[53] *Ibid*.
[54] Sedley, above n 48, at 399.
[55] See Introduction, above.
[56] *Baker*, above n 2, at para 66.

considerations which can be taken into account by the judiciary, while L'Heureux-Dubé J clearly indicates that the words of the statute *'and the values* of administrative law'[57] (emphasis added) are both part of the legal background. For L'Heureux-Dubé J, positive sources like statutory enactment influence the content of the values of the common law, but they do not exhaust it. The legislative branch therefore offers only one contribution to the social debate on the content of the values involved in the control of administrative action.

Baker is a reminder that, although one admits that discretion must be exercised within the bounds of the jurisdiction conferred by the statute, the statute is not the only element which determines the bounds of this jurisdiction. There are also fundamental values that must be taken into account. *Baker* integrates them in a contextual approach to interpretation, but for a judge or administrator to take into account these values does not depend upon legislative authorisation. L'Heureux-Dubé J does take into account the language of the statute, but she also takes account of fundamental values that she identifies through 'indications' such as administrative guidelines and international conventions. So *Baker* reminds us that the common law of administrative law inherently requires the consideration of values, and that this is not dependent upon legislative authorisation. And *Baker* also suggests a methodology for doing so, one that is highly influenced by the *Charter*.[58]

The judicial branch—In Canada, the legitimacy of the judiciary has been the subject of much debate and criticism since the adoption of the *Charter*.[59] When courts strike down statutes on the basis that they violate the *Charter*, accusations of judicial activism or 'judicial government' often lurk in the background. In recent years however, considerable attention was devoted to suggesting a different view of the role of the judiciary in matters involving fundamental values of the *Charter*. It was suggested that courts striking down legislation violating the *Charter* participated in a dialogue with the legislature, rather than claiming they had the final word.[60]

Now reflections on the role of the judiciary under the *Charter* contribute to a better understanding of its role under the common law. The *Charter* makes more evident, and in some cases more spectacular, the role of the

---

[57] *Baker*, above n 2, at para 67.
[58] '[T]he common law Constitution provides protection even when there is no explicit or positive source for such protection, at the same time as our understanding of its content is influenced by positive sources, most notably the *Charter*'.: Dyzenhaus, 'Constituting the Rule of Law', above n 20, at 503.
[59] See, eg, K Roach, *The Supreme Court on Trial: Judicial Activism and Democratic Dialogue* (Toronto, Irwin Law, 2001), esp Part I, ch I and the references indicated by the author (hereafter 'Judicial Activism').
[60] See especially K Roach, 'Constitutional and Common Law Dialogues Between the Supreme Court and Canadian Legislatures', (2001) 80 *Canadian Bar Review* 482 (hereafter 'Dialogues') and Roach, 'Judicial Activism', above n 59.

courts and their relationship with the legislature in the determination and adjudication of rights. However, the role of the courts and their relationship with the legislature is similar under the common law. Indeed, dialogue between courts and the legislature existed under the common law long before the entrenchment of the *Charter*. When courts refuse to give effect to a statute on the basis that it offends a fundamental value of the common law, such as fairness, courts contribute to the articulation and development of values, without necessarily having the final word either. Courts merely 'alert the legislature and the public to important values that they are liable to neglect or ignore'.[61] In my opinion, the effect of *Baker* is to use the *Charter* experience as an impetus to contribute even more significantly to the articulation of values under the common law. Discussion of the legitimacy of the role of courts under the *Charter* therefore benefits the common law. So *Baker* in fact indicates how the *Charter* stimulates the courts to exercise their role in alerting the legislature and the public to important values in the common law.

Viewing the role of the courts from this perspective suggests an answer to the preoccupation that allowing for common law judicial review on the basis of fundamental values might not be compatible with the politics of deference endorsed by the Supreme Court.[62] This is premised on the assumption that the determination of what those values are remain the monopoly of the courts, while I contend that all institutions in the state, and the individuals as well, have a say in this matter. In my opinion, there can be reconciliation between judicial review on the basis of value and judicial deference if one admits that the task of value articulation is shared between institutions and is not the monopoly of courts. So to control discretion on the basis of its compatibility with values would not necessarily reduce deference.

Indeed, *Baker* demonstrates that courts will apply a deferential standard even when a decision affects a fundamental value. This flows from the fact that the Court considers that in the field of procedural fairness, the executive has expertise which justifies courts in deferring to the particular framework crafted by the executive to make sure that the value of fairness is respected. So the Court recognised that tribunals were best equipped to evaluate the appropriateness of procedures under the duty of fairness and therefore concluded that courts had to express deference to administrative decisions affecting the fundamental value of fairness.

---

[61] Roach, 'Dialogues', above n 60, at 532.
[62] DJ Mullan, 'The Supreme Court of Canada and Tribunals—Deference to the Administrative Process: A Recent Phenomenon or a Return to Basics?', (2001) 80 *Canadian Bar Review* 399, at 431–32: '[T]he task of the Court over the next period will be to become more specific as to how precisely some of its more recent pronouncements on underlying constitutional values intersect with the accepted policy of deference to the expertise and statutory mandate of not only tribunals but also discretionary decision-makers of all stripes'.

This demonstrates a willingness to demonstrate deference towards administrative decision-makers even in situations where fundamental values are at stake.

The executive branch—The executive branch also contributes to value articulation and development. This contribution manifests itself in two main ways. On the one hand, contemporary legislatures widely delegate important regulatory powers to the executive, so that it is often called upon to conceive and enact norms of conduct. This law-making role is not necessarily confined to enacting matters of detail or technical points. When this is so, the justification for the delegation of the power to regulate lies in the expertise of the executive and in the recognition that it is often best placed to evaluate the means by which to tackle a particular question. But legislatures sometimes choose to enact statutes limited to providing a general framework and then delegate the task of substantial law-making to the executive. When this is so, formal enactments of regulations by the executive, and perhaps its decision not to adopt norms in some cases, constitute statements that express dedication, or not, to values. In some cases, the executive will itself take the time to establish a dialogue with the individual likely to be affected by regulating schemes, especially when the field that is the subject of regulation has never been formally regulated. The executive may then acquire gradual experience of a given field of activity. Its regulations would then be the result of a limited consensus between it and the actors concerned. In a sense, the executive then takes up the role of the legislature in value articulation. And this executive statement is then analysed by legislatures and courts who can refine such articulation.

On the other hand, the executive is usually on the front line either when the legislature issues statutes, or when the judiciary renders judgments, since it must ensure that all its constituents promptly and properly understand these official decisions and integrate them into their decision-making processes. This is done through the establishment of policies and guidelines, which then themselves become executive statements of values, or at the very least, executive understanding of the values as expressed by the legislature and courts. The issuance of directives is in fact an 'executive translation' of legislative and judicial statements, and this translation is in itself a contribution to value articulation and development.[63]

Recognising that the executive has a role to play in the articulation of the values underlying the grant of discretion does not square with the traditional, formal conception of the separation of powers. That conception viewed the executive as exercising purely instrumental functions, and as a transmission belt between the legislature and the citizens.

---

[63] Lorne Sossin's chapter in this collection is evidence of the importance of the role of the executive in the building of norms. See also F Houle, 'L'arrêt Baker: Le rôle des règles administratives dans la réception du droit international des droits de la personne en droit interne', (2002) 28 *Queen's Law Journal* 511.

By contrast, when the legislature confers discretionary powers on the executive and recognises its role in value articulation, it indicates that the government actively participates in the legal order.

This not only changes the conception of the role of the executive, but also the relationship between the three branches of the State. This is unavoidable, because if

> administrators at all levels of government ... participate to some decisive degree in ruling the republic [the] important issue that surfaces is that administrative agencies will be looked upon as institutions of government and *not simply as instruments to be controlled*.[64](emphasis added)

This does not mean that the executive gains more power, but rather that the control of this power must be structured so as to allow the executive to demonstrate that it lived up to the requirements of the rule of law. This role in fact confers additional responsibilities on the executive. The executive does not have the democratic legitimacy of the legislature, nor the constitutional legitimacy of the judiciary in crafting values of the common law, but as a participant in the building of the legal landscape, it must also establish justifications for its decisions and actions. It is in this search and preoccupation for justification that the executive must participate in value articulation and development.

The individuals—Individuals also participate in the development and articulation of values, and particularly so, I contend, in the field of discretion. This might have seemed paradoxical under the traditional conception of discretion, since it viewed the decision-maker as free to take any decision it wished to make, without even needing to hear the individual affected by the decision. However, the conception of discretion put forward in *Baker* clearly indicates that the decision-maker must be responsive to the particular situation of the individual concerned, and all the more so when the decision deals with issues that are crucial for the person's life. *Baker*'s requirement of reasons and reasonableness thus clearly points to the importance of the individual in the process of discretionary decision-making by this shift in emphasis from the freedom of the decision-maker to the consequences to the individual affected by the decision.

The background to endorsing this review approach is the recognition that discretion is exercised in a realm filled with legal principles,[65] a fundamental change from the previous conception of that kind of power. The traditional approach assumed that the only legitimate role for courts reviewing discretion was to police the boundaries within which it was exercised.

---

[64] CB Graham and SW Hays, 'Citizen Access and the Control of Administrative Discretion', in DH Shumavon and HK Hibbeln (ed), *Administrative Discretion and Public Policy Implementation* (New York, Praeger Publishing, 1986) 233 at 244.
[65] Dyzenhaus and Fox-Decent, above n 28, at 203.

Inside those legal limits, the administrative state was given freedom to act. *Nicholson v Haldimand-Norfolk Regional Board of Commissioners of Police*[66] marked the first attempt to alter this view of discretion, with the imposition of procedural obligations on decision-makers exercising 'non quasi-judicial' functions. *Baker* is in line with *Nicholson*'s agenda. It imposes substantive obligations on discretionary decision-makers, with a view to ensuring that they live up to the appropriate standard of reasonableness, the determination of which depends on the consistency of the decision with the values underlying the grant of discretion.

The decision of the Court in *Baker* is in fact a judicial statement of the value of human dignity. In that decision, the Court contributed to the articulation of this fundamental value, by establishing that administrative decisions which have important consequences for an individual can only be legally made at the close of a process that ensures responsiveness to the needs of that person. Responsiveness requires being alive and sensitive to the particular situation of the person concerned, and this cannot be done when the individual is not given the opportunity to communicate her real situation, nor when the decision-maker is not sensitive and responsive to this situation.

Now it is my contention that, particularly in the field of discretion where the decision-maker is given substantial leeway, the contribution of the individual to the decision-making process is not limited to establishing the particulars of his situation. In my opinion, precisely because the norms which govern the decision-maker are not determinate, the individual should also be allowed to have a say in the choice of the norms that will determine the outcome. Thus, he should be personally called upon to express not only his particular situation, but his conception of the values which should guide the decision-maker. Thus, the individual would contribute to the articulation of the values underlying the grant of discretion.

This view of the concrete role of the individual in value-articulation requires a re-conception of the notion of discretion, one that is suggested in *Baker*. The traditional conception of discretion espoused the perspective of the decision-maker. It could be expressed as 'discretion as power', where discretionary powers were seen as 'direct descendants of what were once considered to be unreviewable or unjusticiable executive prerogatives'.[67] By contrast, since it shifts the emphasis from the nature of the power to the consequences of the exercise of that power on the individual, *Baker* requires that discretion be conceived from a new perspective, one that is centred on the individual affected by the decision. I suggest that such a new conception of discretion should see discretion as a dialogue between the decision-maker and the individual, one in which the latter not only

---

[66] [1979] SCR 311.
[67] Dyzenhaus, Introduction, above.

establishes the particularities of her situation, but also one in which she is allowed to express her view of the norms and values which should govern the decision-maker. Discretion is then viewed as an invitation to communicate with the individual, so as to identify the solution which best fits her particular situation. It indicates that when the law does not establish in advance the norms which must govern a given situation, the margin of manoeuvre must benefit, not the decision-maker but the individual, to the extent that her particular situation must be seen as highly important in the choice of the final decision made by the agency. Discretion thus becomes one occasion for this deliberation to take place. It indicates that there is a space, a distance between the legislature's word and the execution of this word. And administrative agencies must view this space as requiring a dialogue with citizens.[68]

This does not mean that the agency cannot take into account considerations of public interest, but rather that these considerations must be balanced in the context of a process dedicated to the particular situation of the individual. Since the reasonableness of any discretionary decision is conditioned on its consistency with the values underlying the grant of discretion, and since the identification of these underlying values requires the contribution of the individual concerned, the justification for any executive discretionary decision is therefore closely linked to the establishment of a proper dialogue with this individual. If discretion is to be seen as a dialogue between subjects and the executive (or the holder of the power), then the control of discretion by courts must be informed by that vision.

This view of the role of the individual is likely to foster individual responsibility[69] and active citizenry.[70] And this view of dialogue is not antithetical to the legal system, since

> the determination of the content of the law is viewed in terms of a relationship of reciprocity between legislature and subject, so that interpretative authority is shared between the institutions of the legal order, including the subject who as citizen contests the law within the domain of its application to him.[71]

---

[68] See, for a general account of this argument, G Cartier, 'La discrétion administrative: une occasion de dialogue entre citoyens et tribunaux?' in SG Coughlan and D Russell (eds), *Citizenship and Citizen Participation in the Administration of Justice* (Montréal, Éditions Thémis, 2001) at 233.

[69] 'The law should encourage the exercise of individual responsibility, in preference to requiring conformity to collective judgments about controversial questions of value, because that approach is most consistent with the ideal of personal moral judgement that underlies the rule of law itself'.: TRS Allan, *Constitutional Justice—A Liberal Theory of the Rule of Law* (Oxford, Oxford University Press, 2001) at 311–12.

[70] 'The active citizen can require more than a legal warrant in positive law for official coercion, for he is equipped with resources to participate in the making of the law and to hold officials to account by principles of fair participation'.: D Dyzenhaus, 'Form and Substance in the Rule of Law: A Democratic Justification for Judicial Review?', in C Forsyth (ed), *Judicial Review and the Constitution* (Oxford, Hart Publishing, 2000) at 172.

[71] Dyzenhaus, 'Constituting the Rule of Law', above n 20, at 501.

The greatest challenge remains, I suggest, the development of a structured analysis within which to integrate and apply the values articulated through dialogue and conversation among the legislature, the judiciary, the executive and the individuals. If the reasonableness of any discretionary decision depends on its consistency with the values underlying the grant of the power, the task of identifying those values is not enough. One must still conceive a structure of analysis which allows courts to actually determine in concrete cases whether a decision lives up to those values. But the administrative law standards of patent unreasonableness and reasonableness *simpliciter* are not easy to apply concretely and this actually results in considerable room for variation in results. There is ample empirical evidence for that.[72] By contrast, the structure and sophistication of analysis developed under the constitutional standard, through numerous and complex Supreme Court decisions, provide courts with substantial support for their task of determining whether the values of the *Charter* have been violated or not. But if administrative law and the *Charter* are viewed as coordinated, here again administrative law should not be sterilised by the presence of the *Charter*, but should rather take advantage, and benefit from the impulse, of the *Charter* experience to refine its own structure of analysis.

Elucidating and structuring the values involved in the process of discretionary decision-making and in its control are the kinds of task that await administrative lawyers. This promises to be a very difficult mission indeed. But I contend that the coordination model suggested by the decision of the Supreme Court in *Baker* sets the stage for this mission to give significant impulse to the maintenance and evolution of a substantive role for administrative law in the articulation and protection of fundamental values.

In sum, *Baker* undermines *Slaight* and *Ross* and allows the *Charter* and administrative law to move away from the hierarchical view of their relationship suggested in those decisions. As such, this does not lead to concluding that there is no justification for using the constitutional standard of the *Charter* when discretionary decisions are challenged on the basis of *Charter* arguments. Rather, this indicates that the choice of the constitutional standard should not be based on assumptions which undermine and sterilise administrative law, especially in regard to the control of discretion, as *Slaight* and *Ross* tended to assume. From this perspective, the *Charter* might rather help administrative lawyers to face the challenges raised in *Baker* by acting as a source of inspiration on the question of value articulation and structure of analysis. This is hardly surprising since administrative law and the *Charter* draw upon the same fundamental values.

---

[72] Take as an example the recent decision of the Supreme Court of Canada in *Macdonell v Québec (Commission, d'accès à l'information)*, 2002 CSC 71, where the Court unanimously concluded that the applicable standard was 'reasonableness *simpliciter*', but divided 5 to 4 on the question whether the decision at issue did meet the required standard.

CONCLUSION

The first chapter in the story of the relationship between the *Charter* and administrative law offered no promising prospect for the latter. That relationship was informed by a restrictive vision of administrative discretion and of the role of the courts in its control, and undermined the idea that administrative law could play a substantive role in protecting individuals against state arbitrariness. This difficult start led to a paradox, that in which courts given the constitutional role of sanctioning fundamental values tended to resist recognising those values in contexts found to be outside the limits of the written, constitutional mandate. Such was the '*Charter* effect'.

Now the '*Baker* effect' resolves this paradox and suggests a new view of the relationship between the *Charter* and administrative law. *Baker* breaks down the dualism within administrative law itself, between discretion and law-interpretation. This leads the Court to include the review of discretion under the umbrella of the pragmatic and functional approach, thus leaning towards a unified approach to judicial review. This unified approach is intrinsically compatible with the requirement that all exercises of public power (law-interpretation as much as discretion) be justified. But *Baker* also recalls that this justification is to be found ultimately in the same fundamental values, so that courts are not merely allowed, they are required to analyse the legality of official action in the light of those values. And they are to do this in both *Charter* and non-*Charter* cases. That is not to say that the entrenchment of the *Charter* did not change anything in the legal landscape. Quite the contrary. The *Charter* is a reminder that some values are clearly fundamental and that they cannot be violated lightly. But this reminder is not only addressed to litigants covered by the ambit of the formal text of the *Charter*. It serves all the participants in the legal system, so that courts must use it for enriching other legal fields, as administrative law.

'At its root, a Charter of Rights is a statement about who we are as individuals, about the kind of society in which we live and about an ideal which we seek to maintain'.[73] This is certainly accurate, but *Baker* reminds us that this *Charter* statement must be added to, rather than take precedence over, the statements expressed by all the other participants to the legal order. From this perspective, *Baker* indicates how the *Charter* and administrative law cooperate in the task of articulating a unified set of fundamental values at the same time as the decision justifies the application of that very set. And those shared values form the heart of public law conceived as a unity.

---

[73] RE Hawkins, 'Making s 1 Work', in The Law Society of Upper Canada, *Charter of Rights and Administrative Law 1983–1984* (Toronto, Carswell, 1983) 123 at 124.

4

The Rule of Policy: Baker *and the Impact of Judicial Review on Administrative Discretion*

LORNE SOSSIN*

INTRODUCTION

MUCH OF THIS book investigates the *impact* of the Supreme Court's decision in *Baker v Canada (Minister of Citizenship and Immigration)*?[1] Implicitly or explicitly, most of us have an idea of what we mean by impact, whether this relates to a shift in the jurisprudence on reasons, or standard of review or a new approach to the role of international law norms in public law litigation. I consider the question from a different, and often neglected public law perspective. I attempt to assess the impact of the Supreme Court's decision in *Baker* on bureaucratic discretion. How did *Baker* alter the legal and administrative landscape of 'humanitarian and compassionate' grounds decision-making, if at all? How broadly and how deeply has *Baker* affected discretionary decision-making outside the immigration context? When assessing the impact of judicial review, whose point of view should we be adopting? Are long-term effects

---

* I wish to acknowledge the generous financial support for this research by the Social Science and Humanities Research Council of Canada, the Connaught Foundation and the University of Toronto, Faculty of Law. This paper was prepared for the Authority of Reasons: A New Understanding of the Rule of Law conference, held at the University of Toronto, in January of 2003. I am grateful to the many participants at that conference who shared their thoughts and offered suggestions on this research, and in particular to Evan Fox-Decent, who commented on my paper, and to David Dyzenhaus for his always thoughtful a'nd helpful input. An earlier version of this paper was presented to the Tilburg International Workshop on *Judicial Review and Bureaucratic Impact*, 8 November 2002. I am grateful to the participants of that workshop who shared their comments and insights on this research, including Peter Cane, Bradley Canon, Robin Creyke, Yoav Dotan, Malcolm Feeley, Simon Halliday, Marc Hertogh, John McMillan, Ginevra Richardson, Martin Shapiro and Maurice Sunkin. Aaron Delaney and Laura Pottie have provided superb research assistance throughout.
[1] [1999] 2 SCR 817 ['*Baker*'].

of judicial review more significant than short-term effects, and can either empirically be measured? Which norms or criteria allow us to distinguish desirable from undesirable impact? These questions raise a more fundamental one: what ought to be the role of courts in the administrative process?

There is remarkably little literature in Canada addressing the impact of judicial decisions on bureaucratic discretion. Since the enactment of Canada's *Charter of Rights and Freedoms* in 1982, scholarly interest has concerned primarily the influence of the *Charter* on the policy-making process (notably the rise in importance of the federal and provincial justice ministries),[2] and the legislative process,[3] rather than the impact of judicial decisions on the exercise of administrative discretion. For most observers, it is as if the Court's decision is the end of the story of a legal challenge to government action, rather than the beginning of a complex, new chapter.[4] I aim to shift the focus of the analysis to the process by which judicial decisions influence the exercise of discretionary authority by front-line decision-makers.

There is good cause to be suspicious of the assumption that once a court has issued a ruling, public officials simply comply with it, and if they do not, further litigation (or the threat of it) serves as an adequate regulatory remedy. Front-line discretionary decision-makers typically will not have the time, expertise or the inclination to read and digest case law, even when judicial orders or reasons directly relate to their decision-making. The remoteness of the judicial action, and the difficulty in accessing judicial reasoning, are accentuated when the decision at issue is general in nature,

---

[2] See E Shilton, '*Charter* Litigation and the Policy Processes of Government: A Public Interest Account' in P Monahan and M Finkelstein (eds), *The Impact of the Charter on the Public Policy Process* (North York, On, York University Centre for Public Law and Public Policy, 1993); and J Kelly, 'Bureaucratic Activism and the *Charter of Rights*: The Department of Justice and its entry into the centre of government' (1999) 42 *Canadian Public Administration*, 476.

[3] See P Hogg and A Bushell, 'The *Charter* Dialogue Between Courts and Legislatures (Or Perhaps the *Charter of Rights* Isn't Such a Bad Thing After All)' (1997) 35 *Osgoode Hall Law Journal* 75. See also K Roach, 'Constitutional and Common Law Dialogues Between the Supreme Court and Canadian Legislatures' (2001) 80 *Canadian Bar Review* 481. For an earlier approach, see J Hiebert, *Determining the Limits of Charter Rights: How Much Discretion do Governments Retain* (Toronto, PhD, Dissertation, 1991).

[4] There is a growing literature, however, in the United States, Europe and Australia on judicial impact on administrative decision-making on which this study builds. See, for example, S Halliday, 'The Influence of Judicial Review on Bureaucratic Decision-Making' [2000] *Public Law* 110; G Richardson and D Machin, 'Judicial Review and Tribunal Decision-Making: A Study of the Mental Health Review Tribunal' [2000] *Public Law* 494; M Sunkin and K Pick, 'The Changing Impact of Judicial Review' [2001] *Public Law* 736; R Creyke and J MacMillan, 'The External Review Project' (2002) 9 *Australian Journal of Administrative Law* 163; and B Canon and C Johnson, *Judicial Policies: Implementation and Impact*, 2nd edn (Washington, CQ Press, 1999).

dealing with broad principles of statutory interpretation rather than a particular factual circumstance. In such circumstances, it may be possible to construe a court's findings in broad or narrow terms, with significant or trivial consequences for administrative decision-makers. The task of interpreting judicial standards often resides with government lawyers, but the task of disseminating those standards usually falls to the policy-making apparatus of government. Neither of these groups, however, can guarantee how these standards ultimately will be received and applied by front-line decision-makers.

Principally, judicial standards are disseminated to front-line decision-makers through a variety of informal guidelines, circulars, operational memoranda, directives, codes and oral instructions which, collectively, may be characterised as 'soft law'.[5] Soft law is distinct and broader than the power afforded some administrative bodies to issue delegated legislation or quasi-legislation',[6] As employed here, the term encompasses the full range of influences over discretionary authority, including both formal instruments and ingrained administrative practices.[7] While soft law reflects a diverse set of legal and policy constraints operating on decision-makers, these constraints must be seen in a contextual light. Determining the impact of judicial decisions through soft law requires due attention to the dynamics of administrative culture, institutional relations as well as the predilections and convictions of individual decision-makers.[8]

---

[5] The term 'soft law' is one of several terms adopted to convey a range of non-legislative guidelines, rules and administrative policies. It was adopted in the context of codes of ethics in A Campbell and KC Glass, 'The Legal Status of Clinical and Ethics Policies, Codes, and Guidelines in Medical Practice and Research' (2001) 46 *McGill Law Journal* 473–89. I have examined dimensions of soft law in two other papers related to this research: L Sossin and C Smith, 'Hard Choices and Soft Law: Ethical Codes, Policy Guidelines and the Role of Law in Regulating Government' (2003) 40 *Alberta Law Review* 867; and L Sossin, 'Discretion Unbound: Reconciling Soft Law and the *Charter*' (2002) 45 *Canadian Public Administration* 465. Soft law should not be confused with binding guidelines or with binding rules. Occasionally, a statute will delegate to an administrative body the authority to issue guidelines or rules which may bind decision-makers (see for example, s 27(2) of the *Canadian Human Rights Act*, which confers this authority on the Canadian Human Rights Commission). On this distinction, see generally D Mullan, *Administrative Law* (Toronto, Irwin, 2001) 375–79; and F Houle, 'La zone fictive de l'infra-droit: l'integration des regles administratives dans la categorie des texts reglementaires' (2001) 47 *McGill Law Journal* 161.
[6] See G Ganz, *Quasi-Legislation: Recent Developments in Secondary Legislation* (London, Sweet & Maxwell, 1987) 16–22.
[7] For a discussion of the proper classification of various non-legislative instruments, see R Baldwin and J Houghton, 'Circular Arguments: The Status and Legitimacy of Administrative Rules' (1985) *Public Law* 239–84. See also Houle, above n 5, at 180–85.
[8] Simon Halliday refers to these as 'non-legal' influences which 'co-exist' with concerns of legality in the decision-making process and include, 'professional intuition, systemic suspicion, bureaucratic expediency, judgments about the moral deserts of applicants, inter-office relations, financial constraint and other values and pressures all played a part in how judicial review impacted upon decision-making...'. Halliday, above n 4 at 117.

The complexity and centrality of soft law in the administrative process is a key feature of the Supreme Court's decision in *Baker*[9] in two distinct but related ways. First, the Court looked to the immigration policy guidelines as a constraint on the reasonableness of the immigration officer's reasons. Given that non-legislative guidelines conventionally are understood as incapable of binding administrative decision-makers, this aspect of *Baker* highlights a tension in administrative law jurisprudence as to the legal status of soft law. Second, the judicially determined standards for a Humanitarian and Compassionate [H&C] decision in *Baker* were communicated to front line decision-makers through soft law instruments, principally an operational memorandum discussed below. In a very real sense, from the perspective of immigration decision-makers and those affected by their decisions, what the guidelines say about the Court's judgment in *Baker* becomes far more important than what the Court may have actually said or intended to say. Indeed, that the task of implementing the Court's decision is left to the losing party in judicial review litigation may well give rise to conflicts and tensions both within bureaucratic settings (for example, between Department of Justice litigators, immigration policy-makers and decision-makers, who each might view the case differently) as well as between courts and executive bodies more broadly.

While such concerns should not be lightly discarded, the process of policy-makers interpreting judicial reasons, like the process of courts educating themselves about bureaucratic contexts to determine standards of deference and reasonableness, also provides for unique opportunities both to exchange and refine judicial and executive perspectives on discretionary authority. Based on a consideration of these dimensions of *Baker*, I argue that soft law may serve as an important conduit for judicial-executive dialogue on discretionary authority. To fulfill this potential, however, the form and content of the soft law must reflect an authentic attempt to engage with the judicial reasons and rulings.[10] While it may be impossible fully to measure bureaucratic compliance with judicial standards, it is in my view desirable that the process of interpreting those standards be as transparent as possible, and that this process be capable of justification on normative as well as pragmatic grounds.[11] The rule of law, in other words, must extend to the rules of policy, and by so doing, the danger that broad statutory discretion

---

[9] Above n 1.
[10] For a discussion of 'authenticity' in the context of bureaucratic discourse, see Vining, *The Authoritative and the Authoritarian* (Chicago, University of Chicago Press, 1986). This is a theme also pursued in slightly different terms in J Mashaw, *Due Process in the Administrative State* (New Haven, Conn, Yale University Press, 1985), 87–93.
[11] This procedural emphasis is consistent with a broader movement in Canadian administrative law, and beyond, toward transparency in discretionary decision-making. For a discussion of this emerging 'culture of justification', see D Dyzenhaus, M Hunt, and M Taggart, 'The Principle of Legality in Administrative Law: Internationalization as Constitutionalization' in (2001) 1 *Oxford University Commonwealth Law Journal* 5.

will conceal unprincipled, inconsistent and unjust decision-making may be meaningfully diminished.

This analysis is divided into three sections. The first section outlines the role of soft law both in informing judicial standards regarding discretionary decision-making and in disseminating new or modified judicial standards to front-line decision-makers. The second section examines the role soft law played in the *Baker* decision, and its role in communicating the Court's reasons to front-line decision-makers. Finally, in the third section, I suggest a framework for better ascertaining and evaluating the impact of judicial review on bureaucratic decision-making. I conclude that the *form* of judicial review's impact on bureaucratic action may be as important as the content. In short, where judicial standards are communicated transparently through instruments of soft law, and the interpretation of those standards by policy-makers and front-line decision-makers is made equally transparent, greater coherence and accountability over discretionary decision-making may follow.

SOFT LAW AS EXECUTIVE-JUDICIAL DIALOGUE

Soft law is a particularly significant window into the relationship between judicial and bureaucratic decision-making. Non-legislative instruments embody the policy choices of decision-making bodies, including the interpretation and application of new judicial standards. Such discretionary standards and guidelines, in turn, are considered as part of the decision-maker's 'expertise', which attracts deference from the Court when discretionary decisions are challenged. While Courts have been willing to look to soft law as part of the administrative context of decision-making, they have been reluctant to see these instruments as part of the legal framework of decision-making.[12] The Court's dichotomous understanding of hard law and soft law has waxed and waned over the years. It has enjoyed a resurgence as a result of the Supreme Court's judgment in *Little Sisters Book and Art Emporium v Canada (Minister of Justice)*.[13] In *Little Sisters*, the Court

---

[12] The first Supreme Court case to consider the status of soft law was *Martineau v Matsqui Institution*, [1978] 1 SCR. 118, in which a narrow majority of the Court held that directives issued to guide a Parole Board were merely 'administrative' and thus could not bind the Board. Four dissenting Justices held that the directives were 'law' since they were authorised by the Act and affected the rights of an individual. Pidgeon J, writing for the majority, concluded that, 'In my opinion it is important to distinguish between duties imposed on public employees by statutes or regulations having the force of law and obligations prescribed by virtue of their condition of public employees. The members of a disciplinary board are not high public officers but ordinarily civil servants. The Commissioner's directives are no more than directions as to the manner of carrying out their duties in the administration of the institution where they are employed' (p 129).
[13] [2000] 2 SCR. 1120. The analysis of soft law in this case is discussed in more detail in L Sossin, 'The Politics of Soft Law: How Judicial Decisions Influence Bureaucratic Discretion in Canada' Paper presented to the Tilburg Workshop on *Judicial Review and Bureaucratic Impact*, 8 November 2002.

was asked to respond to the argument that a Customs Operational Manual (Memorandum D9–1–1), developed to guide Customs officers in exercising their statutory discretion to identify and seize obscene material being imported into Canada, was the source of discriminatory seizures targeting a bookstore featuring gay and lesbian oriented publications. The Court had already concluded that the impugned provision of the *Customs Act*, which simply afforded officials a discretion to seize material deemed to be 'obscene' was not unconstitutional.

Justice Binnie, writing for the majority, characterised the administration of this authority under the *Customs Act* as 'oppressive',[14] and concluded that its effect—whether intended or not—was to isolate and disparage Little Sisters on the basis of sexual orientation. Binnie J took note of the general bureaucratic culture as well. Officials were chosen to screen imported material for obscenity as a means of 'paying their dues' or as a form of informal punishment. The officials were overburdened and under-resourced which meant having too little time to judge the artistic merit of a work. Often this resulted in officials skipping to the allegedly obscene sections and comparing them to the examples of obscenity set out in the manual. The Court recognized that a source of the targeting of Little Sisters lay in Memorandum D9–1–1. To take but one example, the Manual suggested that all acts of anal penetration violated the obscenity standard in direct contradiction to the standard set out in the previous *Butler* decision, and affirmed by directives from the Department of Justice.[15] Notwithstanding the evidence that Customs officers followed the Manual in most if not all instances, however, Binnie J was unwilling to subject this non-legislative instrument to *Charter* scrutiny. He explained this conclusion in the following terms:

> The trial judge concluded that Customs' failure to make Memorandum D9–1–1 conform to the Justice Department opinion on the definition of obscenity violated the appellants' *Charter* rights. However, I agree with the British Columbia Court of Appeal that the trial judge put too much weight on the Memorandum, which was nothing more than an internal administrative aid to Customs inspectors. It was not law. It could never have been relied upon by Customs in court to defend a challenged prohibition. The failure of

---

[14] *Ibid*, at para 40.
[15] In *R v Butler*, [1992] 1 SCR 452, the Supreme Court had linked the concept of obscenity to the threat of harm to which depictions of sex and violence gives rise. Based on this standard, the mere depiction of acts of homosexual intercourse could not be considered obscene. Binnie J found that, 'The evidence established that for all practical purposes Memorandum D9–1–1, and especially the companion illustrated manual, governed Customs' view of obscenity. The Customs' view was occasionally intransigent. Reference has already been made to the opinion from the Department of Justice that depiction of anal intercourse was not as such obscene. That opinion was ignored for at least two years while imported materials depicting anal intercourse continued to be prohibited on the basis of the outdated D9–1–1 Memorandum' (*ibid* at para 85).

Customs to keep the document updated is deplorable public administration, because use of the defective guide led to erroneous decisions that imposed an unnecessary administrative burden and cost on importers and Customs officers alike. Where an importer could not have afforded to carry the fight to the courts a defective Memorandum D9–1–1 may have directly contributed to a denial of constitutional rights. *It is the statutory decision, however, not the manual, that constituted the denial. It is simply not feasible for the courts to review for Charter compliance the vast array of manuals and guides prepared by the public service for the internal guidance of officials. The courts are concerned with the legality of the decisions, not the quality of the guidebooks, although of course the fate of the two are not unrelated.*[16] (Emphasis added.)

The Court's distinction between statutes and guidebooks, of course, is not really one of feasibility (there is a similarly vast array of Regulations prepared by the public service but these are all subject to judicial scrutiny if impugned under the *Charter*) so much as one of legitimacy. Legislation and Regulations are subject to Parliamentary accountability and procedural formality (they must be enacted or issued in a particular fashion, subject to the *Statutory Instruments Act*,[17] published in a particular form, vetted for compliance with constitutional strictures, and are subject to Parliamentary debate). Soft law is subject to no such criteria, and can be modified or discarded at will by administrative units on any policy grounds, with or without express statutory authority to do so. The case law on non-legislative guidelines[18] leads to a circular rationale to justify why soft law is considered 'policy' and not 'law'. Because soft law is not subject to any internal oversight (eg vetting by Department of Justice for compliance with the Constitution), external review (eg by courts, boards or tribunals), or procedural standards in its development, modification or application, courts have treated soft law as inappropriate to bind decision-makers. Because courts have held soft law not to be binding, in turn, the development, modification and application of these instruments has been treated as beyond the reach of internal oversight, external review and procedural standards.

The distinction between hard law and soft law is formal rather than functional in origin. By this I mean the distinction is driven not by an empirical understanding of how soft law actually is utilised in a particular setting (ie does the instrument in question have a substantial role in shaping or

---

[16] *Ibid*, at para 85.
[17] See RSC 1985, c.S-22. For a discussion of this *Act* and its significance, see Houle, above n 5.
[18] See *Ainsley Financial Corporation v Ontario Securities Commission* (1995), 21 OR (3d) 104 (C.A.) at 108–09; *Hopedale Developments Ltd v Oakville (town)*, [1965] 1 OR 259 at 263 (Ont. C.A.); *Maple Lodge Farms Ltd v Canada*, [1982] 2 SCR 2 at 6–7; *Capital Cities*, [1978] 2 SCR 141; *Friends of Oldman River Society v Canada (Minister of Transport)*, [1992] 1 SCR 3 at 35; *Pezim v BC (Superintendent of Brokers)*, [1994] 2 SCR 557 at 596; Law Reform Commission of Canada Report 26, *Report on Independent Administrative Agencies: Framework for Decision Making* (1985) at 29–31.

constraining the exercise of discretion) but rather by a categorical approach rooted in the separation of powers (ie is the instrument in question a law or a policy). In other words, courts do not treat guidelines as 'law' because to do so would recognise that public administration is subject to laws of its own design rather than subordinate to the will of Parliament.[19] Thus, if guidelines or practices formally are treated as 'binding', this will be held to constitute an unlawful fettering of administrative discretion.[20] However, by the same token, given the clear reliance on soft law in a variety of decision-making settings, and the desirability of such reliance to ensure coherent and consistent exercises of discretion, courts have been unwilling to turn a blind eye to deviations from soft law standards. Courts often have reconciled this dilemma by recourse to familiar administrative law doctrines. If a decision-maker ignores a policy guideline without explanation, as in *Baker*, courts have held that this may be an indication that the administrative decision-maker acted unreasonably.[21] If a decision-maker departs from its own guidelines in circumstances where affected parties would have had a legitimate expectation that they be followed, this may be considered a breach of the duty of fairness.[22] Thus, while soft law may not be 'law', it does appear to give rise to important legal duties and obligations on the part of decision-makers.[23] Elsewhere, I have suggested that the solution to this

---

[19] For a review of the separation of powers doctrine in Canada, see L Sossin and M Bryant, *Public Law* (Toronto, Carswell, 2002) at pp 98–111. In the context of discretionary authority, the Supreme Court recently deployed the separation of powers doctrine to justify curial deference to ministerial decision-making. In *Suresh v Canada (Minister of Citizenship and Immigration)* 2002 SCC 1, which concerned the discretion to deport a suspected terrorist, the Court observed that (at para 38) 'Parliament's task is to establish the criteria and procedures governing deportation, within the limits of the Constitution. The Minister's task is to make a decision that conforms to Parliament's criteria and procedures as well as the Constitution. The court's task, if called upon to review the Minister's decision, is to determine whether the Minister has exercised her decision-making power within the constraints imposed by Parliament's legislation and the Constitution. If the Minister has considered the appropriate factors in conformity with these constraints, the court must uphold her decision. It cannot set it aside even if it would have weighed the factors differently and arrived at a different conclusion'.

[20] See *Ainsley*, above n 19, where the Ontario Court of Appeal referred to the 'Rubicon between a non-mandatory guideline and a mandatory pronouncement having the same effect of a statutory instrument'. (at 109)

[21] See the discussion of *Baker* below. This aspect of reasonableness may be seen as a Canadian variation on substantive legitimate expectations doctrine developed in the UK in cases such as *R v Secretary of State for Education and Employment, ex parte Begbie*, [2000] 1 WLR 1115. For a discussion of this doctrine in the context of *Baker*, see TRS Allan, 'Common Law Reason and the Limits of Judicial Deference' in this volume.

[22] See *Bezaire v Windsor Roman Catholic Separate School Board* (1992) 9 O.R. (3d) 737 (Div Ct) (in which a school board's decision to close nine schools was quashed because neither ministerial nor school board policy guidelines, which called for consultations with affected parties, were followed). See also *Hammond v Assn of British Columbia Profession Foresters* (1991), 47 Admin LR 20 (BCSC).

[23] Paradoxically, one of those duties may well be not to treat guidelines as binding. Often, guidelines, such as those discussed below in the context of the *Baker* case, will include a provision which prohibits a decision-maker from restricting herself to following the guidelines irrespective of other factors.

conundrum is to subject the development and application of soft law to minimal procedural and substantive standards.[24] However, this proposed solution is not without its risks. If the development, modification and application of soft law becomes more procedurally onerous, it may undermine the flexibility needed to adapt to rapidly changing policy environments, and add yet another layer of formalism to the judicial-executive dialogue over discretionary authority.[25] It would render the constitutional distinction between regulations and guidelines difficult to justify on principled grounds. Yet, to maintain the status quo, in my view, carries with it even more serious risks. To permit crucially important forms of public authority to be exercised according to internal and unaccountable principles and policies, not subject to meaningful forms of public review, undermines the integrity of public administration and the constitutional principle of the rule of law.[26]

Even in the midst of its uncertain legal status, or perhaps because of this, soft law represents a potentially flexible and effective mechanism for disseminating judicial standards to decision-makers. Soft law instruments can adapt diffuse or abstract judicial commentaries into usable, relevant decision-making criteria. Depending on the context, a judicial standard may be presented to decision-makers as a checklist of relevant factors, a commentary on what principles, rules or exceptions should guide a decision, or as a fact based illustration of how to apply a standard from which decision-makers may reason from analogy. A further, potential benefit to soft law as a means of disseminating judicial standards is that most guidelines and directives are now available to the public, or easily can be made public, either through ministry websites or by responses to freedom of information requests. Since decision-makers in high-volume discretionary settings rarely have the resources to issue detailed written reasons for their determinations, publicly available guidelines which incorporate relevant judicial standards may provide an important (and, often, the only) window to affected parties

---

[24] See L Sossin, 'Discretion Unbound: Reconciling the *Charter* and Soft Law', above n 5.
[25] See D Dyzenhaus, 'Constituting the Rule of Law: Fundamental Values in Administrative Law' (2002) 27 *Queen's Law Journal* 445 at 471–80.
[26] This concern dovetails with the caution raised by Lamer CJ (writing for himself in a concurring decision) in *Cooper v Canada (Human Rights Commission)*, [1996] 3 SCR 854 at para 13, in relation to administrative tribunals having the jurisdiction to apply the *Charter*. In arguing that only courts should have *Charter* jurisdiction, Lamer CJ stated, 'The reason is that only courts have the requisite *independence* to be entrusted with the constitutional scrutiny of legislation when that scrutiny leads a court to declare invalid an enactment of the legislature. Mere creatures of the legislature, whose very existence can be terminated at the stroke of a legislative pen, whose members, while the tribunal is in existence, usually serve at the pleasure of the government of the day, and whose decisions in some circumstances are properly governed by guidelines established by the executive branch of government, are not suited to this task'. (Emphasis in original) See also the discussion of the rule of law concept in this context, H Richardson, 'Administrative Policy-Making: Rule of Law or Bureaucracy?' in D Dyzenhaus (ed), *Recrafting the Rule of Law* (Oxford, Hart Publishing, 1999).

about how a particular discretionary decision was reached, and what basis may be available to challenge it.[27]

Whereas statutes and regulations are meant to define the boundaries and mandates of public authority, soft law is intended to ensure coherence and consistency in the implementation of those mandates. In his landmark study of administrative discretion, KC Davis advocated rule-making as an important tool both for confining discretionary power and for structuring it.[28] His main concern was countering the potential for arbitrary or oppressive uses of administrative discretion. For Davis, plans, rules, findings, reasons, precedents and a fair informal procedure were all variations on the same theme of greater transparency and accountability. This democratic justification for clear standard-setting has served as a touchstone for much administrative law scholarship on discretionary authority,[29] and has met with some judicial favour in Canada.[30]

The dilemma in using soft law instruments such as guidelines and manuals to convey judicial standards is that, as indicated above, such instruments, by definition, cannot purport to be legally binding. Judicially determined decision-making standards, by contrast, are binding, in the sense that once a judicial standard has been articulated, it is not open to an executive decision-maker to adopt a different standard. That inherently non-binding instruments are employed to convey inherently binding standards is clearly a dilemma. This dilemma is yet another reason to prefer forms of soft law which convey judicial standards in a clear and transparent fashion, so that judicial standards can be disaggregated from policy preferences expressed through soft law. This dilemma may be overcome if we abandon the binding/non-binding dichotomy and focus the analysis of soft law instead on the extent to which its *content* should influence decision-makers.[31] Of course, this distinction is not always so clear either. Because judicial standards themselves are subject to interpretation and may not apply in the same

---

[27] Of equal importance is the fact that guidelines may sometimes reflect input and negotiations between affected parties and decision-makers. For example, in *Capital Cities Communications Inc v Canadian Radio-Television Commission*, above n 19, the Supreme Court held that, while existing regulations would prevail against policy statements, absent any regulation, the CRTC was obliged to consider its policy statement in making the determination at issue. In reference to the policy guidelines under discussion, Laskin CJ, writing for the majority, referred approvingly to democratic input as a justification for giving weight to the guidelines, noting, that 'the guidelines on this matter were arrived at after extensive hearings at which interested parties were present and made submissions' (p 171).

[28] KC Davis, *Discretionary Justice: A Preliminary Inquiry* (Baton Rouge, Louisiana State University, 1969).

[29] See the discussion of Davis' influence in D Galligan, *Discretionary Powers: A Legal Study of Official Discretion* (Oxford, Clarendon Press, 1986), 170–77; and K Hawkins, 'The Uses of Legal Discretion: Perspectives from Law and Social Science' in K Hawkins (ed), *The Uses of Discretion* (Oxford, Clarendon Press, 1992), 16–17.

[30] See, eg: *Re Hopedale Developments Ltd v Town of Oakville* (1964) 47 DLR (2d) 482.

[31] Mayo Moran's contribution to this volume, 'Authority, Influence and Persuasion: *Baker*, *Charter* Values and the Puzzle of Method' explores 'influential authority' as a way of mediating and overcoming the traditional duality between binding authority on the one hand and

way to different legal and factual contexts, it may well be open to a decision-maker legitimately to disagree with the communication of a judicial standard in a guideline and to approach that standard unfettered by the guideline. In this sense, while the underlying judicial standard must be treated as governing, the manner in which policy-makers conclude that standard should affect decision-makers will be a matter for interpretation, just as the manner in which decision-makers apply that standard to individual cases and circumstances, will be a matter for its discretion. It is in this interpretive domain that reasons and justification emerge as a paramount concern. If judicial standards are disseminated by policy makers to decision-makers as a mere checklist, without explanation or elaboration, neither decision-makers nor affected parties will know the basis for the interpretive choices of the policy-makers, and whether such choices were reasonable and made in good faith. Similarly, if a denial of a discretionary benefit is not accompanied by reasons, affected parties will not know whether the discretion was based on relevant or irrelevant factors. At the end of the day, the form and content of soft law cannot be so easily disentangled. To express a principled preference for guidelines which elaborate both the relevant judicial standards, and the interpretation of those standards, reflects the importance both of form and content in the development and dissemination of soft law. This is analogous, in my view, to the relationship between the administrative law duty to provide reasons for a decision, and the correlative requirement that the decision be reasonable.[32]

To conclude, while soft law has the potential to serve as a conduit between the executive and judiciary for exchanging knowledge about legal and administrative aspects of discretionary authority, the ambiguity surrounding the legal status of soft law has impaired the fulfilment of this potential. It has also meant that the development and application of soft law is subject to little or no accountability, with little or no guarantee of consistency. Interviews with legal, policy and operational staff in several different ministry settings reveal that, while the importance of soft law to the discretionary process is universally recognised, standards for its use simply do not exist. Guidelines, manuals and directives may be designed in an ad hoc or well-planned manner, they may be disclosed to the public or kept

---

mere persuasive authority on the other in the context of international law (which, in terms of its domestic application, has been treated as a another form of soft law by Canadian courts). Moran's focus on justification strikes me as particularly crucial to this project. See also Houle, above n 5; and H Janisch, 'The Choice of Decision-Making Method: Adjudication, Policies and Rule-Making' in *Administrative Law: Principles, Practices and Pluralism*, Special Lectures of the Law Society of Upper Canada (Scarborough, Ont, Carswell, 1992).

[32] On this relationship between reasons and reasonableness in administrative law, see the discussion of *Baker* in D Dyzenhaus and E Fox-Decent, 'Rethinking the Process/Substance Distinction: *Baker v Canada*' (2001) 51 *University of Toronto Law Journal* 193. On the broader relationship between the rule of law and judicial scrutiny of administrative policies, see TRS Allan, 'Common Law Reason and the Limits of Judicial Deference' in this volume.

secret, they may be vetted by lawyers or not, and they may be based on the input of affected parties or drafted behind closed doors. To the extent soft law serves as a vehicle for communicating judicial decisions to front-line decision-makers, no supervisory process exists to ensure that this is done in an effective and expeditious fashion or to ensure that it captures the spirit as well as the letter of the judicial determination (except, of course, by way of further litigation).

In the following section, I explore the potential and limitations of soft law through a more detailed examination of the *Baker* decision and its aftermath. *Baker* suggests that the distinction between 'law' and 'policy' often is invoked strategically, by courts and administrative decision-makers, in order to support desired outcomes in particular cases. The result is that a courtroom victory, elusive as this often may be, can turn bittersweet as litigants witness administrative decision-makers respond to judicial orders with defiance, confusion or indifference. It remains to be seen, however, whether this instrumental approach to soft law can be supplanted by a transparent and constructive exchange of perspectives between courts, policy-makers and decision-makers. *Baker* provides both a basis for optimism and a measure of caution in addressing these possibilities.

SOFT LAW AND DISCRETION: *BAKER v CANADA*

It is difficult to think of a decision-making context in which discretion plays a larger role than the immigration and refugee process. As Bouchard and Carroll recently observed in their study of administrative discretion in the immigration selection process,

> In complex policy areas that are characterized by high and emotive content like immigration, politicians, policy analysts, and the general public are less inclined to engage in policy debates which might challenge the broader framework of accepted social values. As a result, decisions that may have major public policy implications can be made by default by bureaucrats exercising their powers of discretion. These decisions, or policy outcomes, can have serious unintended consequences for the broader society.[33]

Arguably, within immigration decision-making, the broadest statutory discretion afforded is the 'humanitarian and compassionate' exemption under

---

[33] G Bouchard and BW Carroll, 'Policy-Making and Administrative Discretion: The Case of Immigration in Canada' (2002) 45 *Canadian Public Administration* 239 at 239–40. On the problems of accountability in the context of discretionary decision-makers generally, see M Lipsky, *Street Level Bureaucracy: Dilemmas of the Individual in Public Services* (New York, Russell Sage Foundation, 1980).

the Canadian *Immigration Act*.[34] This statutory provision contained no criteria for the determination of humanitarian and compassionate grounds. The Regulation issued pursuant to this provision was similarly broad and undefined.[35] Guidelines were issued as part of the Inland Processing Manual No 5 ('IP5'). These guidelines were intended to structure the exercise of this broad discretion.[36] None the less, the essence of the determination of 'humanitarian and compassionate' grounds ultimately rests with the subjective conclusions of individual immigration officers as vividly illustrated in *Baker v Canada (Minister of Immigration and Citizenship)*.[37]

While the facts of this case are no doubt by now notorious, they are important to understanding the nature and scope of the discretion exercised in this case. Mavis Baker was an illegal immigrant who had had four Canadian-born children during the 11 years she had lived illegally in Canada. The question for the immigration officer was whether the prospect of separating Mrs Baker from her children constituted humanitarian and compassionate grounds for exempting her from being deported pursuant to the *Immigration Act*. The immigration officer denied her application, disclosing in his reasons a number of biases against Mrs Baker. The following passage from those reasons illustrates the complex mix of personal judgements, objective evidence and immigration policy which figured in the determination:

> PC is unemployed—on Welfare. No income shown—no assets. Has four Cdn.—born children—four other children in Jamaica—HAS A TOTAL OF EIGHT CHILDREN Says only two children are in her 'direct custody'. (No info on who has ghe [sic] other two). There is nothing for her in Jamaica—hasn't been there

---

[34] S 114(2) of the *Immigration Act* reads 'The Governor in Council may, by regulation, authorize the Minister to exempt any person from any regulation made under subsection (1) or otherwise facilitate the admission of any person where the Minister is satisfied that the person should be exempted from that regulation or that the person's admission should be facilitated owing to the existence of compassionate or humanitarian considerations'. This section was amended by the *Immigration and Refugee Protection Act*, 2002, in part as a consequence of the *Baker* decision and now reads: '25. (1) The Minister shall, upon request of a foreign national who is inadmissible or who does not meet the requirements of this Act, and may, on the Minister's own initiative, examine the circumstances concerning the foreign national and may grant the foreign national permanent resident status or an exemption from any applicable criteria or obligation of this Act if the Minister is of the opinion that it is justified by humanitarian and compassionate considerations relating to them, taking into account the best interests of a child directly affected, or by public policy considerations'.
[35] Immigration Regulations, 1978, SOR/78–172, as amended by SOR/93–44, 2.1 'The Minister is hereby authorized to exempt any person from any regulation made under subsection 114(1) of the Act or otherwise facilitate the admission to Canada of any person where the Minister is satisfied that the person should be exempted from that regulation or that the person's admission should be facilitated owing to the existence of compassionate or humanitarian considerations'.
[36] *Immigration Manual: Examination and Enforcement*, ch 9. Apart from integrating interpretive principles from case law, as discussed further below, this manual also served to transmit the decisions and interpretations of the immigration and refugee board, which unlike judicial decisions, are not binding apart from the particular case at issue before the board. For a discussion of this 'cohering' function of guidelines, see Houle, above n 5, at 183–85.
[37] Above n 1.

in a long time—no longer close to her children there—no jobs there—she has no skills other than as a domestic—children would suffer—can't take them with her and can't leave them with anyone here. ... Lawyer says PS [sic] is sole caregiver and single parent of two Cdn born children. Pc's mental condition would suffer a setback if she is deported etc. This case is a catastrophy [sic]. It is also an indictment of our 'system' that the client came as a visitor in August '81, was not ordered deported until December '92 and in APRIL '94 IS STILL HERE! The PC is a paranoid schizophrenic and on welfare. She has no qualifications other than as a domestic. She has FOUR CHILDREN IN JAMAICA AND ANOTHER FOUR BORN HERE. She will, of course, be a tremendous strain on our social welfare systems for (probably) the rest of her life. There are no H&C factors other than her FOUR CANADIAN-BORN CHILDREN. Do we let her stay because of that? I am of the opinion that Canada can no longer afford this kind of generosity. However, because of the circumstances involved, there is a potential for adverse publicity. I recommend refusal but you may wish to clear this with someone at Region. There is also a potential for violence—see charge of 'assault with a weapon' [Capitalization in original.] [38]

The decision of the officer was quashed by the Supreme Court on the basis of bias and on the grounds that it was an unreasonable exercise of discretion. In the second part of the decision, the Court considered the ministry guidelines which officers were supposed to rely upon. Guideline 9.05,[39] for example, directed officers to carefully consider all aspects of the case, using their best judgement and asking themselves what a reasonable person would do in such a situation. It also states that although officers are not expected to delve into areas which are not presented during examination or interviews, they should attempt to clarify possible humanitarian grounds and public policy considerations even if these are not well articulated. According to the Court, the guidelines also set out two bases upon which the discretion conferred by section 114(2) and the regulations should be exercised: public policy considerations and humanitarian and compassionate grounds. Public policy reasons included marriage to a Canadian resident, the fact that the person has lived in Canada, has become 'established', and has become an 'illegal de facto resident', or the fact that the person may be a long-term holder of employment authorisation or has worked as a foreign domestic. The guideline further provided that humanitarian and compassionate grounds included whether unusual, undeserved or disproportionate hardship would be caused to the person seeking consideration if he or she had to leave Canada. Finally, and most importantly for the Court, the guideline made specific reference to the consideration of familial issues in determining whether grounds for an H&C exemption were present.

L'Heureux-Dubé J, writing for the Court in *Baker*, characterised the Minister's guidelines as of 'great assistance to the Court in determining

---
[38] *Ibid*, at para 5.
[39] Above n 35.

whether the reasons ... are supportable .... They are a useful indicator of what constitutes a reasonable interpretation of the power conferred by the section'.[40] At another point in the judgment, she acknowledged that these guidelines 'constitute instructions to immigration officers about how to exercise the discretion delegated to them',[41] and set out the criteria on which discretion should be exercised. In general, the Court's approach in *Baker* suggests that soft law may serve to delineate the scope of what will be accepted by a court as a reasonable exercise of discretion.[42] That the decision taken in *Baker* was at odds with the guidelines was a primary ground cited by the Supreme Court for quashing the decision as an unreasonable exercise of discretion.[43] Can this finding be reconciled with the Court's earlier position that guidelines cannot be construed as binding? At first glance, L'Heureux-Dubé J appears to treat guidelines not as law but as a reflection of Canada's 'compassionate and humanitarian values'.[44] However, by linking the finding of unreasonableness directly to the inconsistency between the reasons of the immigration officer and the guidelines, L'Heureux-Dubé J appears to treat the guidelines themselves as part of the legally enforceable constraints on the exercise of the statutory discretion. L'Heureux-Dubé J's ambivalence, in my view, stems from a conflict between her desire for a functional, contextual approach to supervising discretionary authority, and her commitment to a rule of law based approach under which all legislative grants of discretion must contain legally cognisable limits—or to use Rand J's phrase from *Roncarelli v Duplesis*,[45] no discretion may be untrammelled.

The statutory discretion at issue in *Baker*, however, was entirely subjective. France Houle characterised it as sponge-like because it would absorb all the values, assumptions or policy preferences to which it is exposed.[46] While we may agree on what are relevant or irrelevant factors for the granting of a liquor licence, would we expect a similar consensus on the factors relevant to a determination of compassion?[47] Can the reasonableness of

---

[40] Above n 1, at para 72.
[41] *Ibid*, at para 16.
[42] *Ibid*, at para 67, 72.
[43] *Ibid*, at para 74–75.
[44] *Ibid*.
[45] [1959] SCR 121.
[46] F Houle, 'L'arrêt Baker: Le rôle des règles administratives dans la réception du droit international des droits de la personne en droit interne' (2002) 28 *Queen's Law Journal* 511 at 516.
[47] This point was demonstrated in an innovative ministry of citizenship and immigration initiative on administrative ethics, which involved consultations with all ministry staff, and led to the publication in December of 1998 of the 'Ethical Compass'. This publication was a compendium of complex, hypothetical case studies which engage the values and judgement of immigration and refugee officials in applying the statutory authority, rules and guidelines to particular circumstances. Each hypothetical scenario was presented to a focus group of immigration officers who were asked how they would resolve the ethical dilemma. A consensus emerged in all but one example, which dealt with the role of compassion in the exercise of ministerial powers. See Citizenship and Immigration Canada, *The Ethical Compass* (March 1998), at http://www.cic.gc.ca/english/pub/values%2De.html#case4 (Accessed 13 May 2002).

compassion truly be ascertained by a court? The policy guidelines in this statutory setting do not elaborate a legal standard; they are the legal standard. Or, more precisely, since the discretionary exercise of this authority by immigration officials is the only expression of law that matters, guidelines provide the only meaningful constraint on this statutory discretion. What L'Heureux-Dubé J appeared to recognise but was unwilling to address in *Baker* is that the rule of law in settings of broad discretion and minimal supervision becomes the rules of policy.

The guidelines in *Baker* served as more than a check on arbitrary state authority. They communicated political preferences and policy choices and incorporated legal sources other than the legislation. Specifically, as I outline below, they incorporated judicial standards for the application of discretionary authority. As Houle explores in her assessment of *Baker*, guidelines may also incorporate international law norms.[48] Indeed, revisions to the guidelines for H&C decisions in 1999 (which counsel for Baker and the interveners unsuccessfully attempted to introduce before the Supreme Court during the hearing of the appeal) made specific reference to the International Covenant on Rights of the Child. Houle concludes that soft law may prove a more hospitable forum for harmonising governmental action with Canada's international obligations than more cumbersome forms of legislative implementation.[49] Thus, when L'Heureux-Dubé J views reasonableness in *Baker* through the prism of policy guidelines, administrative and judicial considerations on the proper scope of 'humanitarian and compassionate' grounds merge and interact. The judicial reasons which resulted from this intermingling led to a variety of challenges for policy-makers and decision-makers in the Ministry. It is to the place of soft law in the aftermath of *Baker* that I now turn.

Soft Law and the Aftermath of *Baker*

The aftermath of *Baker* can be approached from different vantages in determining the judicial impact on bureaucratic discretion. For Mavis Baker, the impact of the judgment was clear and profound. While the remedy granted

---

[48] *Ibid*, at 538.

[49] On this point, however, courts have differed on the legality of guidelines which purport to impose international law norms on domestic decision-makers. In *Canadian Magen David Adom for Israel v Canada (Minister of National Revenue—M.N.R.)*, 2002 FCA 323, the Federal Court of Appeal held that it was not open to the Minister to exercise his discretion to revoke an organisation's charitable status based on an internal policy which stated that organisations operating to assist Israeli settlements in the West Bank could not hold charitable status because Canada supported UN resolutions which called on Israel to withdraw from the occupied territories. The Court concluded that only Parliament or the Governor in Council, not an internal policy directive, could direct that the discretion to revoke charitable status be circumscribed in this fashion. On the complexities which arise in the use of international law norms in the interpretation or application of domestic statutory duties, see J Brunnée and S Toope, 'A Hesitant Embrace: *Baker* and the Application of International Law by Canadian Courts' in this volume.

by the Court was a rehearing before a different immigration officer, the result of this process appeared a foregone conclusion given the tenor of the Court's treatment of her case. Finally, in December of 2001, after her application was granted, *Baker* received her official status as a permanent resident. The Court's judgment led to macro change as well. In the legislative amendments accompanying the new immigration statute, the humanitarian and compassionate grounds exemption was modified, inter alia, expressly to mandate consideration of the best interests of any children directly affected by an application.[50] The *Baker* judgment also set in motion a number of administrative and policy changes relating to the exercise of discretion under the Act.

Following the decision in *Baker*, H&C determinations (particularly those involving children) were left in a state of temporary limbo while policy-makers determined the impact of the Court's ruling and its reasons. This is telling because, in normal circumstances, policy staff would have begun working on contingency arrangements and policy options in the event of an adverse judicial ruling early on in the litigation process.[51] In this case, it took a year from the time of the Court's judgment before the Ministry published an 'operational memorandum' on *Baker* and its implications for future decision-making.[52] This memorandum was divided into separate sections on 'case details', 'court's reasons for deciding to return for redetermination', 'summary of issues and impact on CIC [the ministry]', and 'conclusion [which included a web link to the full text of the decision]'. The memorandum points out those policies and practices which the Court affirmed as legally sufficient (for example, the Court's finding that note-taking met the legal requirement for 'reasons') as well as those which the Court held to be legally deficient (for example, the failure to take proper consideration of the best interests of the children). The memorandum concludes with a passage on 'why the *Baker* decision was not upheld'. In this section, the memorandum details the basis for the Court's ruling that the decision-maker's exercise of discretion was both unreasonable and biased.[53] The memorandum employs a mixture of summary, paraphrasing, quoting and analysing of the Supreme Court reasons, in order to remain

---

[50] See the new statutory language, above n 33.
[51] Interview with CIC policy official, 16 July 2002. The cause of delay was characterised first as 'a breakdown in communications' and later, as 'bureaucratic drift'.
[52] See Operational Memorandum #8, www.cic.gc.ca/manuals-guides/english/om-web/2000/ip/ip00-08e.html (Issued 10 July 2000, OM #00-08) (Accessed 13 May 2002). Approximately three to four cases each year are the subject of operational memoranda. These are subsequently incorporated into revised Manuals. Most memoranda are issued following significant Supreme Court decisions but they may follow lower court rulings as well. Some are issued as 'one-time instruction only' while others are eventually incorporated into the text of the manual. Based on interviews with ministry staff, the decision when to issue a memorandum, and what content the memorandum should contain, are subject to no general standards, and appears to be policy judgments made collectively by the legal services and policy branches of the ministry, often but not always on the advice of the litigation team who argued the case.
[53] *Ibid*, at p 4.

faithful to the text but also to be clear about the broader relevance of the judgment for discretionary decision-making.

The memorandum, however, also engages in an interpretation of the Supreme Court's reasons. For example, under the heading 'Consideration of the Children's Interests', the memorandum states that the impact of *Baker* for decision-makers will be as follows:

> While the best interests of children must always be taken into account as an important factor that is given substantial weight, this does not mean that they will outweigh other factors of the case. There may be grounds for refusing an H&C application even after considering the best interests of children.[54]

This approach to disseminating a new judicial standard highlights the potential of soft law to facilitate judicial-executive dialogue. Of course, simply providing a useful summary of a case is not in and of itself likely to have a significant impact on bureaucratic action. After all, the 'biased and unreasonable' views at issue in *Baker* were not exceptional—they were drafted in a shorthand fashion between a junior and senior immigration official which suggested shared assumptions about the immigration system, an impression confirmed by the fact that the reasons were not only accepted by the senior immigration officer, but also deemed appropriate to provide to the applicant.[55] Rather than serve as a clarion call to immigration decision-makers, the judgment in *Baker* may just as easily serve as a 'roadmap' showing how decision-makers can phrase 'reasons' in order to avoid successful judicial review in the future.

Perhaps with such concerns in mind, the ministry undertook an unusual pilot project in February of 2001 in the Toronto region. With the assistance of York University's Centre for Practical Ethics, the ministry organised a day of workshops and lectures on the Supreme Court's judgment, entitled 'Baker and Beyond'. Approximately one-hundred front line decision-makers from the Toronto region attended the event, and heard from academics, lawyers and ministry staff on the significance of the decision. More importantly, those attending had an opportunity in workshops and 'breakout session' to discuss the case and hypothetical scenarios raising similar issues.[56]

---

[54] *Ibid*, at p 3. This 'impact' statement closely paraphrases para 75 of the *Baker* judgement, but with subtle modifications. For example, while the judgment states that it is not the position of the Court that the best interests of children 'must always' outweigh other factors, the memorandum states that it is not the position of the Court that the children's best interests 'will' outweigh other factors.

[55] This impression is further supported by Bouchard and Carroll's study which found the view that Canada's immigration system has become too lax and easy to manipulate is widely held both within and outside the ministry of citizenship and immigration. Above n 34, at 244–45.

[56] I should disclose that I participated in the 'Baker and Beyond' retreat, giving a lecture on the 'reasons' requirement arising out of the Supreme Court decision. A follow up training session, entitled 'Women and Children First: Gender and the Best Interests of the Child in Discretionary Decision-Making' was held in Toronto at Ryerson University in February of 2003.

The discussion at these small group meetings was revealing. Decision-makers disclosed that they sometimes viewed their own government lawyers as adversaries, and offered anecdotes about how judicial reviews of their decisions succeeded only because they were not permitted by government lawyers to put the 'real story' before the court. A number of decision-makers emphasised that the guidelines, even when conveying judicial standards, were simply a reference tool, and that their decisions were a product of individual judgement based on the evidence and could not be fettered by blind adherence to guidelines. A lawyer involved in the case later mentioned, as an aside, that in her experience, the independence of decision-makers typically is raised at the moment the accountability of decision-makers is at issue.[57]

The impact of judicial review on bureaucratic discretion in the 'humanitarian and compassionate' setting as a result of *Baker* has been, at first glance, dramatic. Procedurally, applicants are now routinely entitled to written reasons for decisions (although, importantly, only if written reasons are formally requested). Substantively, many applicants with children have had more favourable 'humanitarian and compassionate' determinations as a result of the Court's direction. However, it is more difficult to discern whether the values displayed in the officer's reasons at issue in *Baker* have been affected by the Court's intervention.

One of the central difficulties in coming to terms with the impact of *Baker* on front-line decision-making is that the Court left many of the key questions for decision-makers inadequately resolved—a fact not remedied by the operational memorandum which adopted much of the Court's language. After canvassing conflicting jurisprudence on the precise standards the Court imposed on decision-makers through *Baker*, Nadon J noted in *Legault v Canada (Minister of Citizenship and Immigration)*,[58]

> One of the difficulties arising from L'Heureux-Dubé J's decision is what does proper consideration of the children's interests mean. What does it mean, in fact, to be alert, alive and sensitive to the children's interests? Because there is no easy answer to these questions, either on a factual basis or on a principled basis, immigration officers and judges of this Court have struggled whenever confronted with these questions...
>
> In my respectful view, the difficulty which immigration officers are now confronted with stems in part from the Supreme Court's failure—by reason of its conclusions that there was a reasonable apprehension of bias and that the officer had not considered the children's best interests—to address the real issue in *Baker*, supra. That issue was whether the fact that Ms Baker would be a burden on taxpayers was a consideration which could outweigh the children's best interests. Could the officer in *Baker*, supra, give importance to, inter alia, the

---

[57] Interview with lawyer involved in *Baker*, 9 July 2002.
[58] [2001] 3 FC 277.

fact that Ms Baker had remained illegally in this country for over ten years? [footnotes omitted]⁵⁹

On appeal, the Federal Court of Appeal upheld Nadon J's ruling,[60] which was to dismiss an application for judicial review of a denial under section 114(2) of the *Act*, where Canadian born children were affected. The Federal Court of Appeal affirmed that 'public policy' grounds could outweigh the best interests of the children, without offending the standard established in *Baker*.[61] Thus, we are left to question what really will change when the 'best interests of the children' migrate from the policy guideline to the statutory grant of discretion itself.

While it is in the nature of significant judgments such as *Baker* to gloss over the minutiae of implementation, the lack of precision with respect to the Court's standards for the discretionary authority in *Baker* complicates the question of the impact of the Court's decision. For example, as lower courts whittle away at the scope of *Baker* and, significantly, as the Supreme Court itself comes to read *Baker* in narrower terms,[62] should this interpretive evolution be reflected by modifying policy guidelines dealing with this discretion? To the extent that concerns arise as to whether policy-makers and front line decision-makers are complying sufficiently or genuinely with the standards in *Baker*, these concerns must be contingent on the extent to which there is any consensus on precisely what standards the Court in *Baker* actually conveyed. Or, as Trevor Allan has characterised it, the continuing judicial refinement of standards defines the 'discretionary area of judgment' within which decision-makers may manoeuvre.[63]

At a minimum, however, by choosing to engage with the *Baker* case directly in the operational memorandum, and through subsequent training workshops, both policy-makers and decision-makers have been able to participate in a meaningful dialogue with each other (and with the courts as revised guidelines and novel decisions are judicially reviewed) regarding the scope and content of their discretionary authority. This, in my view, is

---

[59] *Ibid*, at paras 58, 62.
[60] 2002 FCA 125.
[61] As to the nature of these 'public policy' grounds, the Federal Court of Appeal looked, once again, to the policy guidelines. However, while devoting a substantial portion of the judgment to a consideration of the guidelines, Decary JA observes that the guidelines cannot fetter ministry decision-makers. *Baker* was relied upon solely for the proposition that the guidelines are 'of great assistance'. See *ibid*, para 20.
[62] The Supreme Court took the opportunity in *Suresh*, above n 20, of clarifying that *Baker* was an exceptional case of judicial intervention (in part, because of the issue of the departure from the ministry guidelines) and that normally, a higher degree of deference should be shown discretionary decision-making. See especially para 36. This narrowing of Baker's scope is discussed in David Mullan's contribution to this volume, 'Deference from *Baker* to *Suresh*—Interpreting the Conflicting Signals'.
[63] Allan, above n 22, at p 2.

a significant and necessary first step towards constructive judicial impact in settings of discretionary decision-making.

THE IMPACT OF JUDICIAL REVIEW AND THE RULE OF POLICY

Socio-legal approaches both to judicial review and bureaucratic decision-making begin from the premise that neither judicial nor bureaucratic statements should be taken as self-evident or straightforward. The exercise of administrative discretion constitutes both a complex social process,[64] and a 'collective enterprise',[65] which neither a particular judicial decision or policy guideline can control. However, both judicial review and administrative policy provide a valuable measure of accountability for discretionary decision-making—in some cases, the only such measure—and for this reason merit deeper scrutiny. Judicial review presents an opportunity not only to prevent abuse but also to shed light on the proper scope and purpose of discretionary authority.[66] As *Baker* illustrates, soft law serves as a site of interpretation and contestation over the meaning of discretionary authority, and by extension, as a forum for administrative bodies both to inform courts and respond to them regarding the proper criteria for decision-making.

Prevailing wisdom holds that judicial review is not an effective means of changing bureaucratic action, and that its utility, if any, lies in focusing public attention on particularly oppressive or discriminatory decision-making settings.[67] However, it is worth observing that the reverse may sometimes be true as well—in certain discretionary settings, judicial review is welcomed as an easy crutch to avoid the difficult and sometimes unpopular work of policy-making. For example, the determination of eligibility for charitable status in Canada under the *Income Tax Act* is a highly discretionary process which invites policy-makers and decision-makers to craft a

---

[64] For a discussion of discretion as a dialogic relationship, see J Handler, 'Dependent People, the State and the Modern/Postmodern Search for the Dialogic Community' (1988) 35 *UCLA Law Review* 999. See also L Sossin, 'Law and Intimacy in the Bureaucrat-Citizen Relationship' in N des Rosiers (ed), *No Person is an Island: Personal Relationships of Dependence and Independence* (Vancouver, University of British Columbia Press, 2002) 120–54.

[65] This characterisation of administrative discretion is borrowed from Hawkins, above n 29, at p 27.

[66] For a broader discussion of the relationship between law and discretion in the Canadian context, see N des Rosier and B Feldthusen, 'Discretion in Social Assistance Legislation' (1992) *Journal of Law and Social Policy* 204; L Sossin, 'The Politics of Discretion: Toward a Critical Theory of Public Administration' (1992) 36 *Canadian Public Administration* 364; and L Sossin, 'Redistributing Democracy: Authority, Discretion and the Possibility of Engagement in the Welfare State' (1994) 26 *Ottawa Law Review* 1.

[67] See P Robson, 'Judicial Review and Social Security' in T Buck (ed), *Judicial Review and Social Welfare* (London, Pinter, 1998), 105; also see generally, L Bridges, G Meszaros and M Sunkin, *Judicial Review in Perspective* (London, Cavendish, 1995).

principled approach to defining the scope of what constitutes a 'charity'.[68] Rather than take up this challenge, officials have simply deferred to the Courts, and in so doing, transformed judicially developed principles intended to guide administrative decision-making into rigid, legal requirements.[69] Neither indifference nor blind obedience to courts is likely to improve the quality and coherence of discretionary decision-making.

Not only is it difficult to agree on what we mean by the 'impact' of judicial review on bureaucratic decision-making, and more difficult still to assess it, but, even if we assume that we can overcome these conceptual challenges, a further hurdle is encountered in ascertaining whether greater or lesser impact is desirable. Notwithstanding chronic problems of delay, cost and access associated with litigation, judicial review continues to hold promise as a means of constructive influence on bureaucratic decision-making. By clarifying criteria for the reasonable exercise of discretion judicial review may serve as a catalyst, as in *Baker*, for reflection by policy-makers and decision-makers about the principles which ought to underlie the exercise of discretion.

While a detailed discussion of the proper conceptual framework to guide an understanding of the impact of judicial review is beyond the scope of this chapter, it would seem valuable as a preliminary step to such a framework to distinguish between different types of judicial influence, different methods of judicial influence and finally, different degrees of judicial influence.

Judicial review appears to influence bureaucratic decision-making in at least three discrete ways. First, judicial review may serve an individual dispute resolution role—a judicial order may uphold, modify or quash a particular administrative decision, and may apply directly to others in the same position. For example, it is certainly a relevant impact that Mavis Baker herself was granted permanent residency status once her application was reheard in light of the Court's decision. In this way, judicial review maps the boundaries of administrative discretion in individual cases or classes of cases. Second, judicial reasons may offer a new, changed or definitive interpretation of a legal standard which has broader implications for bureaucratic decision-making. Here, the reach of the judicial decision may extend far beyond the particular dispute. *Baker*'s reach extended beyond the case of Mavis Baker in a number of ways. Procedurally, it altered the standard of issuing written reasons in decision-making throughout immigration and

---

[68] For an analysis of administrative decision-making in this area, see L Sossin, 'Regulating Virtue: A Purposive Approach to the Administration of Charities in Canada', in J Phillips, *et al* (eds), *Charities: Between State and Market* (Kingston, McGill-Queen's Press, 2001), pp 373–406.
[69] Those standards are conveyed to decision-makers using yet another form of 'soft law'—a set of guidelines contained as part of an 'Employees Handbook', which summarise the judicial case law in the field of charitable eligibility, discussed in *ibid*.

refugee settings and beyond. Substantively, it altered the weight given to certain factors such as the best interests of the child in immigration and refugee decision-making (both within and outside the H&C setting), while clarifying that other factors would be irrelevant to these determinations. In this fashion, judicial review influences the direction of administrative policy. Finally, judicial review may also influence bureaucratic practices. Bureaucrats may attempt to avoid judicial review in the future by complying with established judicial standards, whether this compliance is cosmetic (for example, issuing reasons calculated to comply with the *Baker* standard rather than the candid disclosure of motivations and values which characterised the reasons actually at issue in *Baker*) or reflects a genuine change of heart, respect for the authority of the courts, or some combination of the above.

Classifying various kinds of influence, however, does not shed light on the method of the influence. Developing a framework for understanding *how* judicial review influence bureaucratic decision-making requires an examination of at least three sequential aspects of the administrative process.[70] First, a policy decision is made as to whether any soft law instruments require revision in light of a particular case, and if so, what the content and degree of the revision should be. While judicial review may be pursued with adversarial zeal by government lawyers, those same lawyers generally work to ensure bureaucratic compliance with judicial decisions.[71] Secondly, a further policy decision is made as to the form of the revision. Based on my interviews, this determination appears to be made most often on institutional and situational grounds—the consensus is that, due to bureaucratic inertia, revisions to guidelines tend to follow the same form as predecessors. In other words, policy-makers do not tend to consider afresh the question of whether to present a judicial standard in the form of a checklist, a set of principles or a detailed commentary but rather follow their own precedent as to how like standards were conveyed in the past. Finally, the third aspect of the administrative process which must be considered is the reception of policy change by front-line decision-makers. The frequency of post-*Baker* judicial reviews of negative H&C applications where applicants argued that the best interests of children were disregarded by immigration officers,[72] may attest to bureaucratic resistance to the *Baker* standards, or may simply attest to *Baker* providing a credible basis

---

[70] This sequential—or serial—view of discretion builds on the approach to discretion which views each exercise of discretionary authority as part of a sequence of decisions occurring in a network of legal relationships. For discussion of this 'holistic' view, see Hawkins, above n 29, at 28–32.
[71] See Hammond, 'Judicial Review: the continuing interplay between law and policy', [1998] *Public Law* 34 at 40–41.
[72] A search through Quicklaw yielded 20 such challenges which reached the Federal Court between January 2001 and November of 2002.

to challenge almost any negative determination of an H&C application where children are involved.

Alternatively, one could look at different methods of judicial influence from the standpoint of the judicial rather than the administrative process. In sketching what such a framework might include, Maurice Sunkin has distinguished between the impact of the process of judicial review litigation (this would include the discovery process, the publicity and public validation of claims against bureaucratic decision-making, the cost to government to defend against litigation), the impact of judgments in particular cases (this would include differentiating between the impact of successful challenges and the impact of unsuccessful ones) and the impact of the principles or values enshrined in judicial review.[73]

The third consideration is one of degree. While it is difficult to reach any conclusion regarding the extent of judicial impact,[74] which may turn on the perspectives of individual decision-makers across diverse settings, the aftermath of *Baker* suggests that front-line discretion was influenced by the Court's judgment, but as in many other cases, this has not occurred as quickly, comprehensively or coherently as the litigants (especially the interveners with broader policy interests) and the Court might have wished.

A conceptual framework of the impact of judicial review on bureaucratic discretion must also address the question: judicial impact on what? Bureaucracy is not a monolith and discretionary decision-making must never be seen as static. Judicial influence may also be classified according to different types of discretion. Bouchard and Carroll, for example, distinguish between procedural discretion, discretion as to criteria for substantive determinations and discretion as to outcome, and argue that different considerations may pertain to each.[75] *Baker* arguably had significant but different consequences for all three kinds of discretion. Alternatively, one could look at judicial impact from the broader standpoint of discretion over institutional design and structures. Again, in the context of *Baker*, this focus might lead to an analysis of the new procedures and resources required in order to comply with the expanded requirement of written reasons.

As Halliday has cautioned, one cannot approach the judicial-executive relationship as a linear cause-and-effect interaction. Rather, this relationship

---

[73] Maurice Sunkin, 'Methodological and Conceptual Issues in Researching the Impact of Judicial Review on Government Bureaucracies'. Paper presented to Tilburg Workshop on Judicial Review and Bureaucratic Impact, 7 November 2002.

[74] Bradley Canon suggests four degrees of response: (1) defiant non compliance, (2) evasion or avoidance, (3) cosmetic acceptance and (4) full compliance. See B Canon, 'Studying Bureaucratic Implementation of Judicial Policies: Conceptual Approaches'. Paper presented to Tilburg Workshop on *Judicial Review and Bureaucratic Impact*, 7 November 2002.

[75] Above n 34, at 248–253. Intriguingly, Bouchard and Carroll also attempt to distinguish between 'professional' and 'personal' discretion based on whether discretionary judgments are guided by institutional values or ones held by individuals.

should be conceived as fluid, organic and unstable. Baldwin and Hawkins saw it as 'a subtle and shifting affair which is a matter of seemingly endless human interpretive work'.[76] As government lawyers devise particular litigation strategies, or decide which cases to appeal or settle, as policy-makers interpret judgments through various instruments of soft law, and as decision-makers reinterpret those standards through their own social and personal rubric of values, the impact of judicial review mutates.[77] Moreover, as decisions are challenged, and courts defer to administrative expertise in discretionary settings, the relationship doubles back, with policy choices and bureaucratic practices influencing the nature and scope of judicial intervention.

As a result of the fluid and mutually reinforcing nature of the judicial-executive relationship, a framework for understanding judicial impact on bureaucratic discretion cannot be blind to political and bureaucratic contexts. Such a framework must take into consideration short and long term consequences as well as grapple with the fact that it may not be possible to know in advance whether a particular change, which is welcomed at the time, will be experienced as desirable in the long run or vice versa.[78]

Notwithstanding the complexity and uncertainty of judicial impact on bureaucratic discretion, there is good cause to advocate greater transparency and justification on the part of both administrative and judicial actors in relation to discretionary authority. Courts should provide clear and specific standards when responding to judicial challenges involving discretionary authority. Policy-makers should ensure that guidelines or other soft law instruments engage with judicial reasons as well as simply conveying the ruling. Where policy-makers interpret those standards, the rationale for their interpretation should be clear. Finally, decision-makers should specify when and why they have decided to depart from standards set out in guidelines. On this measure, *Baker* reflects some of the promise of soft law but also some of its dangers. If, as I have argued, soft law reflects a delicate and shifting balance between rules and discretion, law and policy, and offers a window into the dynamic relationship between front-line decision-makers, policy-makers and courts, then the ambiguity regarding the legal status of soft law reflected in *Baker*, and the absence of

---

[76] Baldwin and Hawkins, 'Discretionary Justice: David Reconsidered' [1984] *Public Law* 581.
[77] S Halliday, 'Researching the Impact of Judicial Review on Routine Administrative Decision-Making' in D Cowan (ed), *Housing, Participation, Exclusion* (1998), p 196.
[78] To take but one example, the attempt to reign in discretionary authority in the context of social welfare in the 1960s (in order to counter the arbitrary and discriminatory standards used to determine eligibility), brought about in large measure as a response to vigorous 'welfare rights' litigation and new judicially crafted procedural standards, contributed to a 'clericalization' of the welfare bureaucracy and a sharp increase in complexity and delay in processing applications. On this phenomenon, see W Simon, 'Legality, Bureaucracy and Class in the Welfare System' (1983) 92 *Yale Law Journal* 1198.

any accountability over its development, modification and application, is particularly troubling.

It is apparent that the binding/non-binding framework is too one-dimensional to account for the complex and symbiotic relationship between soft law and discretion. Soft law must be taken seriously as an integral aspect of the exercise of public authority, a domain in which judicial standards and executive preferences commingle, interact and inform one another. Soft law should be approached by courts from a contextual and realistic vantage, balancing the need for flexibility and judgment with the imperatives of accountability, transparency and justification. The sharp distinction drawn by Binnie J in *Little Sisters* between the 'legality of decisions' and the 'quality of the guidebook' cannot be sustained in discretionary settings where law and policy are inextricably intertwined. *Baker* stands for the enduring proposition that judicial review over administrative discretion provides a crucial check against arbitrary, discriminatory and unfair state action; however, until courts are prepared to engage in a coherent and sustained way with the rules of policy in discretionary settings, this check may prove illusory and the rule of law will remain an elusive ideal.

5

'Alert, alive and sensitive': Baker, *the Duty to Give Reasons, and the Ethos of Justification in Canadian Public Law*

MARY LISTON*

> It follows that I disagree with the Federal Court of Appeal's holding ... that a section 114(2) decision is 'wholly a matter of judgment and discretion' ... The wording of section 114(2) and of the Regulations shows that the discretion granted is confined within certain boundaries. ... While deference should be given to immigration officers on section 114(2) judicial review applications, decisions cannot stand when the manner in which the decision was made and the approach taken are in conflict with humanitarian and compassionate values. The Minister's guidelines themselves reflect this approach. ... The principles discussed above indicate that, for the exercise of the discretion to fall within the standard of reasonableness, the decision-maker should consider the children's best interests as an important factor, give them substantial weight, and be *alert, alive and sensitive* to them (emphasis added).[1]

INTRODUCTION

AN ADMINISTRATIVE DECISION was made in a manner that was not 'alert, alive and sensitive'[2] to the interests of Mavis Baker's Canadian-born children. L'Heureux-Dubé J's remarkable phrase,

---

* I would like to thank Jennifer Nedelsky, Lorne Sossin and James Tully for their extremely helpful comments. Special thanks go to David Dyzenhaus for his encouragement and assistance—and for not 'pulling any punches' when reviewing an earlier draft. Finally, I wish to acknowledge the unstinting support given to me by my partner, David Duff.
[1] L'Heureux-Dubé J writing for the Canadian Supreme Court in *Baker v Canada (Minister of Citizenship and Immigration)* [1999] 2 SCR 817 at paras 74–75 (citations omitted) [hereinafter *Baker*]. Mavis Baker was an immigrant who overstayed her visa and became subject to a deportation order after 11 years of illegal residence as a live-in domestic worker in Canada. During this time, she had four Canadian children and at the later part of her residency suffered post-partum psychosis, went on welfare, and had her children removed from her care. She

I will argue, comports with an emergent understanding of Canadian public law as an 'ethos of justification'[3] where citizens and residents are democratically and often constitutionally entitled to participate in decisions which affect their rights, interests and privileges as well as to have access to and understand the reasons for these decisions. Indeed, *Baker* has affirmed that any administrative decision which affects the rights, privileges or interests of an individual will trigger the application of a duty of fairness whose content may include the duty to give reasons.[4] Within this ethos of justification, the legal relationship between the individual and the state rests on fundamental normative considerations of dignity, rationality and respect.

Throughout this chapter, I will use the weighty phrase 'alert, alive and sensitive' as a shorthand to describe the ethos of justification. I will consider both the characteristics of and values suggested by this ethos and discuss the methodology that has emerged to complement this mode of analysis and judgement. I will then explore its connection with the duty to give reasons. I want to suggest that this ethos can be used to inform decision-making contexts other than the judicial and that it will therefore have relevance to related domains of administrative decision-making and even community decision-making as an ethical framework for evaluating and arriving at good judgements about good administration.

The chapter will first present and analyse the *Baker* methodology and what such a standard entails for decision-making. Then I will briefly describe how this ethical standard has appeared in pre-*Baker* caselaw before turning to examine several key post-*Baker* cases in section three. Section four conducts an assessment of the *Baker* landscape and discusses possible trends for Canadian administrative law. I will conclude by suggesting how the *Baker* ethos and its unified methodology complement and conform to a larger democratic, justificatory culture. The key claim that I make here is that this ethical standard functions to govern power relationships throughout the

---

submitted a humanitarian and compassionate grounds application to remain in Canada which was denied without reasons until, at counsel's request, she was provided with notes relevant to the decision which revealed inflammatory and impolitic language on the part of the investigating officer. S 114(2) was the relevant provision in the *Immigration Act*, RSC 1985, c I–2 (repealed, now article 25(1) of the *Immigration and Refugee Protection Act*, RSC 2001, c 27).

[2] See also *Baker* at para 73 which rephrases the introductory quote: 'I conclude that because the reasons for this decision do not indicate that it was made in a manner which was *alive, attentive, or sensitive* to the interests of Ms Baker's children, and did not consider them as an important factor in making the decision, it was an unreasonable exercise of the power conferred by the legislation, and must, therefore, be overturned' (emphasis added).

[3] I have borrowed this phrase from Supreme Court Chief Justice Beverley McLachlin in her article 'The Role of Administrative Tribunals and Courts in Maintaining the Rule of Law' (1999) 12 *Canadian Journal of Administrative Law and Practice* 171–89 at 174. I owe a much larger debt to the work of David Dyzenhaus as found in 'The Politics of Deference: Judicial Review and Democracy' in M Taggart (ed), *The Province of Administrative Law* (Oxford, Hart Publishing, 1997) at 278–307 and 'Law as Justification: Etienne Mureinik's Conception of Legal Culture' (1998) 14 *South African Journal of Human Rights* 11.

[4] *Baker*, n 1 at para 20.

Canadian polity, a polity which has embraced constitutional democracy and the rule of law as permanent tenets of this ethos.

EMBODYING *BAKER*: THE ETHOS OF ALIVE, ALERT AND SENSITIVE

The essence of the *Baker* decision, I claim, is the entrenchment of a unified methodological approach to the judicial review of discretionary decisions compatible with a notion of participatory democracy. In this section, I will explore two aspects of this methodological approach. First, I will describe the methods used in *Baker* for the review of discretionary decision-making and for the detection and protection of fundamental interests. Second, I will discuss the aims and concepts, the principles of reasoning, and the institutional relationships implicated in the *Baker* ethos.

1. The Methods Behind the Methodology, or, the Skeleton

From one perspective, it would seem that the Supreme Court in *Baker* used three different, distinct and unrelated methods to determine different aspects of the duty of fairness within the context of the case. From another perspective, and one that I advance, each is a particular application of a unified approach to reviewing discretionary decision-making in administrative law—an approach usually labelled 'pragmatic and functional'.[5] This section will set out the three methods within the overall methodology: determining the context of the procedural duty of fairness in an administrative context; selecting and applying a standard of review in an administrative context; and, discerning the presence of bias in an administrative decision.

(a) The Content of the Duty of Fairness

To understand the content of the procedural duty of fairness in *Baker*, the Supreme Court used the 'pragmatic and functional analysis' to outline five factors which assist in determining fairness in context:[6] 1) comparing how institutionally analogous the administrative process is to the judicial in order to determine how close the procedural protections are to those found in the trial model; 2) examining the statutory scheme to review potential violations of justice in administrative processes which have either no internal appeal procedures or where the decision is determinative; 3) ensuring that the procedural protections afforded conform to the importance of the

---
[5] *Ibid* at paras 51–56.
[6] *Ibid* at paras 21–27.

decision to the person(s) affected and, where the impact is greater, more stringent procedural protections will be required; 4) attending to the legitimate expectations of the person challenging the decision and according substantive procedural protection where the claimant had a legitimate expectation that a certain result might have been reached when, for example, representations regarding procedures, regular practices, or substantive promises have been contravened without significant or sufficient procedural protections;[7] and, 5) acknowledging and respecting the procedures deemed appropriate by the administrative agency where the agency has the ability and the expertise to choose its own procedures.

These factors are not exhaustive and others may apply in contexts where the duty of fairness is not related to participatory rights. Of these factors at play in *Baker*, factor four, the doctrine of legitimate expectations, was rejected outright in the decision and therefore did not affect the content of the duty of fairness.[8]

(b) The Standard of Review

A comparable set of methodological guides governs the selection and application of the three standards of review for errors of law in discretionary administrative decisions. Here the pragmatic and functional approach requires the reviewer to consider: 1) the absence or presence of a privative clause; 2) the expertise of the decision-maker; 3) the purpose of the provision and the Act in which it is found and a) whether open-textured legal principles are at play as well as b) whether the interest involved is individual or polycentric; and, 4) whether the decision is highly discretionary and fact-based.[9]

Greater deference is shown in the choice of the standard of patently unreasonable while greater intervention is signalled in the choice of correctness review. Reasonableness, the intermediate standard, was used in *Baker* because of the nature of decision-making in the immigration context.

(c) The Test for the Reasonable Apprehension of Bias

Lastly, the Supreme Court employed a reasonable person standard in *Baker* to access the values underlying the duty of fairness in the context of a potentially biased discretionary decision putatively made on humanitarian grounds. Importantly, the standard itself was part of the set of guidelines issued by Citizenship and Immigration Canada for immigration officers.[10]

---

[7] But, as L'Heureux- Dubé J hastened to affirm, legitimate expectations in Canadian jurisprudence 'cannot lead to substantive rights outside the procedural domain'. *Ibid* at para 26.
[8] *Ibid* at para 29.
[9] *Ibid* at paras 57–62.
[10] *Ibid* at para 16.

As with the other two tests, the test for apprehension of bias will vary according to context and the type of function performed by the administrative decision-maker involved.[11]

Employing this standard, the court examined whether or not the immigration officer's notes were biased and therefore disclosed an impartial or arbitrary decision. Looking to the form and content of the officer's notes, L'Heureux- Dubé J stated that his 'notes, and the manner in which they are written, do not disclose the existence of an open mind or a weighing of the particular circumstances of the case free from stereotypes'.[12] As a result, 'the well-informed member of the community would perceive bias when reading Officer Lorenz's comments'.[13] The contextual nature of the methodology is important here for *Baker* not only subjects specific behaviour of the officials involved but the entire chain of reasoning to scrutiny.[14]

(d) The Unifying Proposition within these Three Methods

Each one of these tests aims to conform to an ideal of what the Supreme Court calls 'deference as respect',[15] meaning that courts will respect administrative autonomy where decisions affecting important interests are reasonable. If an agency exhibits competency and good reasoning concerning a procedural or substantive issue, the complementary institutional response from the judiciary is to respect that institutional capability. Several underlying methodological aims and principles need to be unpacked from the conception of deference as respect.

2. Methodological Aims, or the Vitals

The three tests discussed in subsection one above allude to substantive underlying values in the duty of procedural fairness in which the democratic right to participate in decisions and laws affecting one's rights and interests is paramount. On this point, L'Heureux-Dubé J writes:

> I emphasize that underlying all these factors is the notion that the purpose of participatory rights contained within the duty of procedural fairness is to

---

[11] *Ibid* at para 47. However, this test is a bit 'looser', more discretionary, that the two approaches discussed above since it is not directed by an explicit set of considerations but, rather, imaginatively guided by the abstract personification of the 'reasonable Canadian'.
[12] *Ibid* at para 48.
[13] *Ibid*.
[14] Indeed, on a more formalistic approach, these two developments—concluding that the notes counted as reasons and subjecting the chain of reasoning to scrutiny—might well have been obstructed.
[15] *Baker* at para 65 quoting David Dyzenhaus's notion of deference as respect: deference 'requires not submission but a respectful attention to the reasons offered or which could be offered in support of a decision'. Quote taken from D Dyzenhaus, 'The Politics of Deference', n 3 at 286.

ensure that administrative decisions are made using a fair and open procedure, appropriate to the decision being made and its statutory, institutional, and social context, with an opportunity for those affected by the decision to put forward their views and evidence fully and have them considered by the decision-maker.[16]

Given this language, there is an obvious and tight connection between the values contained in the duty of fairness, the duty to give reasons, and the idea of the rule of law. The nexus of values hinges on the insight that no one is infallible and that no power is or ought be unbounded; humans exist in a world of limitation, much of it self-created and self-imposed.[17] 'Second-guessers'[18] are therefore necessary to scrutinise the content of and procedures used in discretionary decision in order to recognise and affirm whether or not fairness and reasonableness are sufficiently present.[19]

The kind of decision involved in *Baker* was one that required an 'open mind'[20] due to its individualised nature, the humanitarian and compassionate requirements as stipulated in the department's own guidelines, and its evocation of a disposition characterised by 'special sensitivity' and understanding which would recognise and attend to the importance of ethnocultural diversity—a diversity that is inseparable from the character of the Canadian political community. Finding bias in the notes meant that such a flaw or error tainted the entire process through which the final discretionary decision was made, ultimately by a superior in the department. The initial attitude, not corrected through the internal process, indicated that the approach taken was unreasonable as it was 'completely dismissive' of the children's interests and failed to give these interests 'serious weight'.[21] Notwithstanding the deference generally shown to discretionary decisions of this kind, these reasons were held to be inconsistent with the values underlying the grant of discretion—Canadian values which include respect

---

[16] *Ibid* at para 22. See also para 28.
[17] As Rand J wrote in *Roncarelli*, in public administration there can be 'no such thing as absolute and untrammelled "discretion", that is that action can be taken on any ground or for any reasons that can be suggested to the mind of the administrator'. Furthermore, no legislative Act can 'without express language, be taken to contemplate an unlimited arbitrary power exercised for any purpose, however capricious or irrelevant, regardless of the nature and the purpose of the statute' or the rule of law. *Roncarelli v Duplessis* [1959] SCR 121 at para 19.
[18] I borrow this term from Charles Taylor's essay 'What's wrong with negative liberty'. In *Philosophy and the Human Sciences: Philosophical Papers 2* (Cambridge, Cambridge University Press, 1985) 211–229 at 228. The Canadian landscape has a co-ordinate system of second-guessing at the constitutional level since Courts and Parliaments are allowed to trump each other respectively through constitutional remedies and a constitutionally-guaranteed legislative override of judicial decisions (s 33 of the *Canadian Charter of Rights and Freedoms*).
[19] Second-guessing in the administrative context can happen internally within agencies or externally through judicial review.
[20] *Baker*, n 1 at para 48. This requirement links up with an earlier judgment, *RDS,* discussed in notes 37–39 below in subsection 1 of s III.
[21] *Ibid* at para 65.

for diversity, family and children's rights and interests—and therefore did not meet the threshold of reasonableness which could command 'respect' from judicial review.[22]

L'Heureux-Dubé J's judgment canvassed several interpretive aids such as the purposes of the *Immigration Act*, international law,[23] and the Minister's own guidelines. However, consideration of the ministerial guidelines provides the ethical moment and it is at this point in the judgment that the introductory quote can be located.[24] The ministerial guidelines affirm the kind of treatment persons affected by the immigration regime can legitimately expect from officers in the department—they represent, in a very loose sense, a code of conduct. The guidelines also embody one aspect of the character of the Canadian political community which is manifested through political commitments to diversity, fairness and good administration. The 'manner' in which the decision was made contradicted all of these commitments, summed up as 'humanitarian and compassionate values', and therefore the decision stepped outside the boundaries of reasonableness.[25] In the *Baker* context, unreasonableness and dismissiveness in manner were originally signalled by the lack of reasons given to Baker and her counsel, a defect and a disrespect that the court's imposition of the duty to give reasons intended to remedy.

From *Baker*, it seems clear that reason-giving is valuable since such a practice may assist in determining when reviewable error exists. However reasons not only facilitate 'second-guessing' but also actualise several tenets of the rule of law in context.[26] Reason-giving may assist in ensuring fair and transparent decision-making as well as contribute to the guarantee of accuracy and accountability of decisions.[27] Reasons can satisfy the maxim

---

[22] *Ibid* quoting Dyzenhaus's notion of deference as respect. On Canadian values, see para 67.

[23] It is this aspect of the judgment where the *Convention on the Rights of the Child* and the *Universal Declaration of Human Rights* were used that animated the dissent. Iacobucci and Cory JJ dissented on the use of the executively-ratified but domestically unincorporated international documents which they held to be merely of interpretive guidance in an administrative law decision. They stated that they felt the majority had violated the separation of powers doctrine through 'backdoor' incorporation via statutory interpretation. Without incorporation, and outside of the *Charter* which invites consideration of international law as influential authority since its bears such kinship with these kind of international documents, the *Convention* was rendered 'irrelevant' (at para 81) by the dissent for administrative law even in these circumstances. *Ibid* at paras 78–81.

[24] For an important discussion of the usefulness of such 'soft law' in the process of justification, see Lorne Sossin in this volume as well as L Sossin and CW Smith, 'Hard Choices and Soft Law: Ethical Codes, Policy Guidelines and the Role of the Courts in Regulating Government' (2002) 40(4) *Alberta Law Review* 1–25.

[25] *Baker*, n 1 at para 74.

[26] I say the rule of law in context for, eg, transparency and consistency alone have no certain connection with either democratic legitimacy or a culture of justification since a totalitarian or authoritarian state can make 'mad' transparent rules consistently.

[27] *Baker*, n 1 at paras 35–39. On the importance of reasons, see generally: PP Craig, 'The Common Law, Reasons and Administrative Justice' (1994) 53 *Cambridge Law Journal*

that justice be done and must be seen to be done and contribute to overall legitimacy through recognition by the claimant that a negative result is nevertheless fair and reasonable. Finally, reasons attend to the dignity interests that are at the heart of post-World War II jurisprudence, as decisions which have profound importance compel a requirement of reasons: 'It would be unfair for a person subject to a decision such as this one which is so critical to their future not to be told why the result was reached'.[28] Within the framework I have proposed, then, reasons are essential for the realisation of the rule of law within a democracy and, furthermore, serve as a particular instantiation of the rule of law. The duty to give reasons, then, has both procedural and substantive value.

FROM SKELETAL TO FULL-BODIED: A LIVING, BREATHING *BAKER*?

In this section, I will examine a selection of pre- and post-*Baker* jurisprudence in order to illustrate this ethos in jurisprudential action. First, I will very briefly allude to earlier jurisprudential links to the *Baker* approach, a background I argue provides a bridge from *Baker* to important subsequent caselaw. Three trajectories will then be plotted: the elaboration of the common law duty to give reasons (*Sheppard*); consideration of the proper attitude intrinsic to judgement (*Legault*) as well as the resultant quality of the given reasons (*Hawthorne*); and, the nexus between reasons, standards of behaviour involving promises, and the remedies available for holding public actors to account (*Mount Sinai*).

1. Anticipating *Baker*: Embryonic Manifestations

Though each of the terms, 'alive', 'alert' and 'sensitive' have appeared individually in a multitude of judgments as predicates of a proper judicial mentality and indicators of good judgment, *Baker* is the case that brings them all together methodologically and metaphorically. What this earlier case-law discloses is a web of related concepts, including: vulnerability within rights to autonomy or self-determination, consent and trust, disclosure and context, deference and expertise, and equity and consistency. They suggest that the essence of judgement is to be alive, alert and sensitive and that deference, instead of acting as a cover for formalism or non-justiciability, at heart means respect for human dignity and respect for the rule of law.

282–302 at 283–84. For the Canadian context, see D Mullan, *Administrative Law* (Toronto, Irwin Law, 2001) at 306–18.

[28] *Ibid* at para 43.

Alertness in the administrative law context originates from Dickson J's (as he then was) notable dictum from *CUPE*, a case that, along with *Nicholson*,[29] changed the face of Canadian administrative law. In *CUPE*, after considering the historical and political relationship between the courts and labour tribunals in Canada, Dickson J concluded that:

> [t]he question of what is and is not jurisdictional is often very difficult to determine. The courts, in my view, should not be alert to brand as jurisdictional, and therefore subject to broader curial review, that which may be doubtfully so.[30]

Sensitivity to context was deemed paramount, meaning that the court would not upset the delicate political balance that had been achieved in Canadian labour relations—this disposition was captured in Dickson J's phrase that the labour board was 'entitled to "err"'[31] based on its comparative expertise and this created the foundation for the evolution of the pragmatic and functional approach in administrative law.[32]

CUPE discloses one aspect of the methodological approach which *Baker* unifies: institutionalised practices of deference as respect. Outside of administrative law, criminal law illustrates the necessity of being alive and attentive to complex issues in conflicted evidentiary contexts.[33] And, as we will see

---

[29] *Nicholson v Haldimand-Norfolk (Regional) Police Commissioners* [1979] 1 SCR 311. In addition to entrenching the duty to act fairly in Canadian administrative law, *Nicholson* dispensed with formalism in another guise as it found that 'at pleasure' dismissals were 'relics of Crown law' since there was more than one interest at play than the designated authority and such authority, despite its executive-like authority, needed to conform to procedural justice when dismissing an employee by providing a fair opportunity to be heard. *Nicholson* at para 15.

[30] *Canadian Union of Public Employees, Local 963 v New Brunswick Liquor Corp* [1979] 2 SCR 227 at para 10.

[31] *Ibid* at para 15. Though subsequent case law had to work through the legal tension between agency protection through statutory privative clauses, being entitled to err, and when intervention was necessary to correct error or to protect substantive interests that had been overridden.

[32] This form of analysis was introduced in *UES, Local 298 v Bibeault* [1988] 2 SCR 1048.

[33] See, eg: *R v Esau* [1997] 2 SCR 777 [hereinafter *Esau*]. The accused, a second-cousin of the complainant, had sexual intercourse with her after a party at her home. She was drunk and denied that she consented, saying that she had no memory of anything from the time she went to her bedroom until the next morning. She testified that she would never have had sex with a relative. The legal focus was on whether the trial judge erred in not putting the defence of mistaken belief about the complainant's consent to the jury because he held that there was no evidentiary basis for this defence. The appeal court found that the trial judge was correctly 'alive' to the issues raised by evidence. The Supreme Court divided along gender lines with the five male justices finding sufficient evidence to justify the defence while the two female justices dissented on the ground that there did not exist an 'air of reality' to the defence. McLachlin and L'Heureux-Dubé JJ's dissent demanded clear communication and explicit, not implied, consent and shifted the focus to the mens rea of the accused on whom the evidentiary burden rested. Increasingly, the accused must provide a good reason for his mistaken belief and show that he has taken reasonable steps to request and obtain actual consent from the complainant. The dissent's approach has since emerged as the standard. As an analogue for old-style

below in the discussion of *Sheppard*, institutional parallels exist between deference as respect in administrative law between reviewers and decision-makers and in criminal law where deference as respect requires the reviewing court to defer to the competence of trial court judges' findings of fact in complex criminal cases. Being attentive to the autonomy and vulnerability of parties in power-dependent relations constitutes a third aspect of the *Baker* approach and the ethos here can be summarised as being alert, alive and sensitive to abuses of power.[34] As an analogue to administrative law, for example, the citizen's position in the citizen-state relationship[35] can mirror that of the vulnerable party in tort law cases involving fiduciary relations.[36] Finally, cases concerning the importance of justificatory practices or reason-giving and impartial judging in the judicial context can inform what it means to have an 'open mind' and, conversely bias in

administrative law, the mistaken belief defence can sanction the discretionary judgement of the accused, shifts the burden of proof onto the injured party, conceives of consent thinly and formally instead of as an on-going relational matter which can be revoked at any time, and may allow the accused to circumvent the provision of a good reason for his mistaken belief. As such, this defence should be as rare as untrammelled executive discretion in the new-style administrative law context.

[34] See, eg: *Norberg v Wynrib* [1992] 2 SCR 226 at 228. This case hinged on consent and sexual conduct but this time within the context of a doctor-patient relationship. Here a doctor provided drugs to a drug-dependent woman in exchange for sex and, like *Esau*, the case revolved around whether the patient had consented to this arrangement and in what manner the doctor may have violated his duties by initiating and continuing to conduct this relationship. Grounds for liability included the tort of battery, breach of contract and breach of a fiduciary duty. As with sexual assault cases in the criminal context, a pragmatic and functional methodology is used to recognise individual autonomy and free will within the analysis of contexts involving 'power dependency' relationships where the distribution of power is unequal and one of the parties, as a result, is placed in a vulnerable position. The majority decided on the grounds of battery and used an equitably-derived community standards approach to find the doctor's conduct exploitative. Sopinka J located the liability in contract but, despite his finding of consent, concluded that the doctor's conduct was a contractual breach. L'Heureux-Dubé and McLachlin JJ's concurring judgment rested on breach of fiduciary duty. On their analysis, the foundation of the fiduciary obligation in the doctor-patient relationship is based on trust and this shifts the focus to the risks involved in the unequal distribution of power (notably power over another that is not inherently wrong), the rights and duties involved, and when an abuse of power has taken place.

[35] For recent work on the concept of public authority as a form of public political trust, see L Sossin, 'Public Fiduciary Obligations, Political Trusts and the Evolving Duty of Reasonableness in Administrative Law' (2003) 66 *Saskatchewan Law Review* 101–55. My own take, which accords with the equitable and justificatory approach taken by Sossin, is that in contrast to the unilateral nature of the fiduciary relationship, I would instead construct an analogous relationship which de-emphasises vulnerability and re-emphasises a code of behaviour whose authoritative source lies in the extra-legal power vested in judging citizens.

[36] Similar problems regarding autonomy, trust and consent carry over into public law where the courts have been loath to characterise the citizen-state relationship as fiduciary in nature. Canadian jurisprudence, with the notable exception of the fiduciary duty the Crown holds towards Aboriginal peoples, does not characterise the relationship between the state and its citizens in terms of trust and consent per se though an analogous framework, I claim, necessarily underpins any substantive conception of the basis of the political relationship between the state and the citizen and the circumscribed nature of political power in a liberal democracy.

decision-making contexts.³⁷ As discussed above, Officer Lorenz in *Baker* failed to appreciate Mavis Baker's circumstances by exhibiting a great degree of callousness in his notes. Moreover, he had inappropriately 'crossed the line' and made inappropriate use of the context to reach his conclusion; he had therefore unduly restricted his discretionary ambit. His judgment therefore manifested neither a 'conscious, contextual inquiry'³⁸ nor an open mind.³⁹

2. Reason-giving, or 'Sharing-the-World-with-Others'⁴⁰

The pre-*Baker* caselaw discloses several bases of the methodological approach which *Baker* unified including: contextualised and impartial judging, institutionalised practices of deference as respect, attention to the autonomy and vulnerability of parties in power-dependent relations, and

---

³⁷ See, eg: *R v RDS* [1997] 23 SCR 484 [hereinafter *RDS*]. In this case, a white police officer arrested RDS, an African-Canadian 15-year-old who had allegedly interfered with the arrest of another youth. The police officer and RDS were the only witnesses and their accounts of the events greatly differed from the other's. The Youth Court Judge, while delivering her oral reasons, responded to a rhetorical question put to her by the Crown—specifically, that there was no reason to question the credibility of the officer—by saying that police officers in Halifax had been known to mislead the court in the past and that they had been known to overreact particularly toward non-white groups. The trial judge therefore concluded that she was more likely to find the youth's version credible. All of the Supreme Court justices in *RDS* agreed that judges can at times make reference to prevailing social realities—such as the existence of racism in a particular community—as any reasonable person would. Judges, therefore, are not 'neutral ciphers'. Not only can judges not discount their life experiences, they ought not to according to the Supreme Court so long as these conclusions have been tested in the reasoning process. *Ibid* at para 38. Using the test for apprehension of bias discussed above in subsection 1c of s II, the majority concluded that judges should avoid making untested generalisations and here the judge's comments were 'close to the line' but acceptable. The dissent (Lamer CJ, Sopinka and Major JJ), however, found that the judge's comments were stereotypical concerning police officers and constituted an irreparable defect.
³⁸ *Ibid* at para 42. But, in contrast to *RDS* where much effort was devoted to inquiring into and evaluating the social context of Sparks J's judgment, the *Baker* court did not spend much time at all considering the social context of Officer Lorenz's notes. This would seem an important omission when determining reasonable apprehension of bias in context.
³⁹ McLachlin and L'Heureux-Dubé JJ (La Forest and Gonthier JJ concurring) approached the reasonable apprehension of bias test differently than the majority did and found that the judge's remarks were an 'entirely appropriate recognition of the facts ... and of the context'. The two justices provided a different characterisation of impartial judgment, suggesting that having an 'open mind' or the capacity for an 'enlargement of mind' is the essential precondition since it functions as a species of representative thinking which considers a multiplicity of standpoints about a certain issue. *Ibid* at paras 42–44 quoting J Nedelsky, 'Embodied Diversity and the Challenges to Law' (1997) 42 *McGill Law Journal* 91. Consequently, the judge's personal understanding of the factual and social context indicated that she was alive and alert to the context. *Ibid* at paras 57–59.
⁴⁰ This phrase originates with Hannah Arendt and her thoughts on the Kantian activity of judging in her essay 'The Crisis in Culture' in *Between Past and Future* (New York, Penguin, 1977) 173–226 at 221. See also 'Truth and Politics' 227–64. Arendt's work indirectly constituted a crucial source for the conception of impartial judgement in *RDS* as it was significantly relied on by Nedelsky in the article cited by the court in n 39.

the importance of justificatory practices or reason-giving. The addition of the duty to give reasons to the content of the duty to act fairly, however, constitutes the crucial advance in Canadian administrative law brought about by *Baker*. Though the duty to give reasons is not yet a general duty imposed on all statutory and prerogative authorities in Canada, I will argue that reading *Baker* in conjunction with the explication of a duty to give reasons in the criminal case *Sheppard*,[41] provides fruitful elaboration on the duty to give reasons in the administrative law context. Most importantly, *Sheppard* concerns a case where the reasons given by a trial judge failed to meet the obligation.[42] Using the *Baker* ethos of alert, alive and sensitive, I will show how the *Sheppard* decision gives greater specificity to the content of the duty to give reasons.

(a) The Bare Bones of Sheppard

The facts behind *Sheppard* involve an accused, Colin Sheppard, whose at times violent ex-girlfriend, Sandra Noseworthy, vowed to 'get him' after the break-up of their tempestuous relationship. She informed the police that he had confessed to her that he had stolen two windows for his home renovation, windows which were later discovered to have disappeared from a supplier's stock. No other evidence, verbal or physical, linked the accused to these missing windows; he had no prior criminal record or charges. Barnable J, the trial court judge, found the accused guilty based on the evidence and on the testimony of credible witnesses, including the ex-girlfriend as chief informant. His judgment, in its entirety, read:

> Having considered all the testimony in this case, and reminding myself of the burden on the Crown and the credibility of witnesses, and how this is to be assessed, I find the defendant guilty as charged.[43]

According to the Court of Appeal of Newfoundland, Barnable J's failure to provide reasons compelled intervention because he did not indicate that he was 'alive' to the issues and to let the judgment stand would 'encourage trial judges to deliberately structure judgments to frustrate appellate review or to mask a lazy or inadequate analysis'.[44] The Supreme Court agreed with the Court of Appeal and provided a detailed framework outlining the requirement of reasons, the propositions of which will be outlined below.

---

[41] *R v Sheppard* [2002] SCJ No 30, 2002 SCC 26 [hereinafter *Sheppard*]. Note that this judgment did not include Madame Justice L'Heureux-Dubé.
[42] For a significant early article concerning civil, not criminal, cases, see M Taggart, 'Should Canadian Judges be Legally Required to Give Reasoned Decisions in Civil Cases?' (1983) 33 *University of Toronto Law Journal* 1.
[43] *Sheppard*, n 41 at para 10.
[44] *Ibid* at paras 11–12.

(b) Was the Reason-giver Alert and Attentive?

Binnie J for the court in *Sheppard* considered that attentiveness to the context and the interests ensures some direction for the judicial mind about how the duty to give reasons ought to be fulfilled. Where it is plain why an accused has been acquitted or accused on the evidence, and where inadequate or absent reasons will not hinder the exercise of the right of appeal, the Supreme Court suggested that intervention with respect to reasons will not be required. However, where reasoning is murky or confused, where evidence is conflicting, where a variety of interpretations about the judge's reasons can be drawn, and where difficult areas of law were 'circumnavigated without explanation' [45] by the trial court judge, some or all of which might hinder appellate review, then deficiencies in reasons may be held an error of law.

Binnie J offered a ten-point framework outlining the duty of a trial judge to give reasons in the context of appellate intervention in a criminal case.[46] Briefly, he found that reasons satisfy demands for accountability, certainty and due process and that a decision which meets these demands provides assurance about the integrity of the appellate process. Reasons serve the purpose for the imposed duty within the particular context so that not every deficiency will provide a ground of appeal.[47] Reasons will also not be held to an abstract standard of perfection. However, judges are not infallible and especially in instances of unsettled law or evidentiary uncertainty, the presumption of competence is limited and justifies the role of appellate courts to 'cure' unintelligibility through substitution.

Significantly, Binnie J rejected 'floodgates' or efficiency-based arguments which suggest the duty to provide reasons significantly slows down the criminal justice system and imposes an onerous task on already overworked lower court judges. The response to this point was that if judges were alert during the trial process, then constructing reasons would not be so heavy a burden and therefore the arguments for reasons outweigh efficiency concerns:

> While, as suggested above, the act of formulating reasons may further focus and concentrate the judge's mind, and demands an additional effort of

---

[45] *Ibid* at para 46.
[46] *Ibid* at para 55.
[47] On this point, see *R v Zinck* [2003] SCJ No 5, 2003 SCC 6. The Supreme Court reviewed a trial judge's decisions to delay parole eligibility—a decision characterised as 'out of the ordinary' (at para 29)—and found that they did not breach the *Sheppard* standard despite being somewhat imprecise and curtailed. In contrast to *Baker*, though delayed parole is an extraordinary measure, the context did not require additional procedures apart from the sentencing decision and therefore the accused did not need any written notice that delayed parole would be applied for by the Crown. The offender, however, must be allowed to make submissions and introduce additional evidence in response, and is entitled to reasons (at paras 36–37). The court held that though a more detailed analysis 'should have been attempted', the reasons read in context with the evidence and submissions made at the hearing, permitted an appellate court to understand and review the decision (at para 39).

self-expression, the requirement of reasons as such is directed only to having the trial judge articulate the thinking process that presumed has already occurred in a fashion sufficient to satisfy the demand of appellate review.[48]

The Supreme Court concluded that where deficient reasons implicate fundamental principles which protect the interests, rights and privileges of a citizen, and which prevent the appellate court from being satisfied that fundamental principles have been properly applied, then deficiency of reasons may be converted into an error of law in the criminal context[49]—a proposition which I argue ought to extend to the administrative context. There exists, then, a 'necessary connection' between the failure to provide proper reasons and the frustration of rights of appeal in the appellate context rather than a more general duty to give reasons with a free-standing right of appeal.[50] Rights, however, must not be rendered 'illusory' or unexercisable which would make a sham of the system of justice within courts and, as I argue, within internal agency review.[51]

(c) Was the Reason-giver Alive to the Issues?

Barnable J in *Sheppard* erred in law by not providing sufficiently intelligible or adequate reasons in circumstances which 'cried out for some explanatory analysis' thereby substantially impeding appellate review.[52] Though the Supreme Court stated that no general duty to give reasons rests on the trial judge 'in the abstract and divorced from the circumstances of the particular case', nevertheless at the 'broadest level of accountability, the giving of reasoned judgments is central to the legitimacy of judicial institutions in the eyes of the public'.[53] Accordingly, reasons facilitate public scrutiny of the evolving law in order to arrive at agreement or criticism about the rules of conduct applicable to their activities. Furthermore, if no reasons are given in the judicial context, judges are prevented from judging the judges—a violation of a 'broad principle of governance' which translates into a specific rule concerning appellate review.[54] The trial judge's one-sentence 'skeletal' judgment, however, provided no toehold for review and was therefore unreasonable—to draw out the metaphor, both the legal body and mind were 'dead' and all that remained as evidence of a live process were reasons as vital as a pile of bones.

---

[48] *Sheppard*, n 41 at para 51.
[49] *Ibid* at para 43.
[50] *Ibid* at para 53.
[51] *Ibid* at para 66.
[52] *Ibid* at para 1.
[53] *Ibid* at paras 4–5.
[54] *Ibid* at para 5.

The starting point for the Supreme Court's analysis was the proposition that reasons are essential for judicial accountability because they are evidence that justice has been done and has been seen to be done.[55] For this proposition, the Supreme Court cited *Baker*, though hedged that the form and nature of the duty to give reasons conforms to each adjudicative setting and therefore must be understood as a spectrum of possibilities rather than one template.[56] Reasons are evidence the judicial mind has 'concentrated' on the problems in the case and show the path that explains and justifies the result.[57] Thus, the test is contextual, functional and pragmatic and the question to be asked becomes: does this particular decision provide sufficient reasoning or a rational basis to enable appellate review of the correctness of the decision? Any subsequent intervention is not based on the aesthetics of poor articulation per se.

In contrast, the companion case to *Sheppard*, *Braich*,[58] also involved contradictory evidence and the credibility of witnesses. Here, however, the trial judge was 'alive' to one complexity—the possibility of collusion between key witnesses—but after due and articulated consideration, rejected this finding.[59] The trial judge's reasons were sufficient to meet the functional test of allowing the appeal court to review the correctness of the trial decision[60] and the Court chastised the appellate judge for holding the trial judge to 'an unjustifiably high standard of perfection'.[61]

The appellate court was not permitted to substitute its views for that of the trial judge who provided an 'intelligible pathway through his reasons'.[62] In other words, the appellate court was not allowed to characterise the trial court judge's reasons as 'inadequate' in order to 'mask' what was, in effect, a disagreement about the result.[63] The institutional allocation of a decision

---

[55] *Ibid* at para 15.
[56] They cite the following passage: 'it is now appropriate to recognize that, in certain circumstances, the duty of procedural fairness will require the provision of a written explanation for a decision. The strong arguments demonstrating the advantages of written reasons suggest that, in cases such as this where the decision has important significance for the individual, when there is a statutory right of appeal, or in other circumstances, some form of reasons should be required'. See *Baker*, n 1 at para 43.
[57] *Sheppard*, n 41 at paras 23–24.
[58] *R v Braich* [2002] SCJ No 29, 2002 SCC 27.
[59] *Ibid* at para 26.
[60] In an interesting aside, Binnie J writing for the Court observed that the appellate judge, McEachern CJ who found the trial judge's reasons deficient, himself engaged in skimpy reasoning when McEachern CJ thought certain applicable law was so well-known and superfluous that he did not propose to discuss it. Binnie J commented: 'As the Court of Appeal thought it superfluous to discuss the applicable law, it was prepared to extend the same dispensation to the trial judge'. *Ibid* at para 33.
[61] *Ibid* at para 37.
[62] *Ibid* at para 42.
[63] *Ibid* at para 39. Binnie J suggests that the appellate court was driven by the peculiarities of the facts rather than the deficiency of the reasons: 'The majority judgment simply took the view that if the trial judge had thought harder about the problems and written a more extensive analysis, he might have reached a different conclusion'. *Ibid* at para 41.

about credibility that rests on findings of fact belongs to the trial court judge. As an analogue to administrative law, then, agencies and tribunals which exhibit competence in analysis and come to reasonable conclusions based on their understanding of the facts and context should be accorded the same measure of respect as a trial court judge is by a reviewing court. A similar scope of deference is accorded to a decision-maker's judgement of what the policy context requires in a particular matter.

(d) Was the Reason-giver Sensitive to the Context?

Barnable J's 'generic' reasons could 'apply with equal facility to almost any criminal case', a result which not only indicates a lack of reasoning but a lack of respect for the particularity of the case before him and therefore he showed disrespect to the particular accused who appeared before him.[64] His reasons were so '"generic" as to be no reasons at all' and provided no 'comfort' to the losing party concerning the fairness of the process.[65] However, brevity and efficiency in reason-giving were not held to be synonymous with bad reasons and the onus still remained on the appellant to show that a prejudicial deficiency in reasons impeded access to appellate review in the criminal context. While absent or inadequate reasons might support a conclusion of unreasonableness, that alone will not constitute a reviewable ground. Where law is unsettled, however, it would be 'wise'—albeit not obligatory—for a trial judge to provide reasons setting out the legal principles;[66] silence on settled points is acceptable but the absence of reasons in general was not 'blessed'.[67]

Looking at Barnable J's decision, the Supreme Court admonished him for solipsistically 'reminding himself' of his reasoning without articulating the 'pathway' he had taken.[68] He failed to appreciate, perhaps even completely disregarded, the public nature of his obligation to three audiences: the accused, the appellate court and the general public. He also failed to provide 'clarity, transparency and accessibility' to intelligible reasoning and in so doing frustrated the contextualisation of the rule of law.[69]

---

[64] *Sheppard*, n 41 at para 32.
[65] On this point, Binnie J quoted Green JA from the appellate level *Sheppard* decision: 'Particularly in a difficult case where hard choices have to be made, [reasons] may provide a modicum of comfort, especially to the losing party, that the process operated fairly ... It is cold comfort ... to an accused seeking an explanation for being convicted in a case where there was realistic chance of success, to be told he is not entitled to an explanation because judges are "too busy"'. *Ibid* at para 60.
[66] *Ibid* at para 40.
[67] *Ibid* at para 37.
[68] *Ibid* at paras 59, 61.
[69] *Ibid* at para 63.

3. Sensitivity, or Reminding the Head about the Heart

After the *Baker* decision was handed down, a backlash from the bench occurred based on the belief that this judgment warranted too much judicial intervention into discretionary decision-making and therefore disturbed the Canadian version of the separation of powers.[70] A Federal Court of Appeal case of just such a backlash, *Legault*, focused on how decision-making ought to consider the children's best interests and whether these interests 'trumped' or took precedence over all other considerations in humanitarian and compassionate grounds applications.[71] Décary JA found the trial court judge's reading of *Baker* 'excessive'.[72]

Looking to *Suresh*[73] and *Chieu*,[74] both of which 'clarified' *Baker* in light of this ambiguity, the appellate court affirmed that the weighing of relevant factors is the responsibility of the Minister or the Minister's delegate, not the court's responsibility. Procedural fairness in these circumstances does not dictate a particular outcome but includes the right to make written submissions to the immigration officer who actually makes the decision, a right to an unbiased decision-maker and a right to receive brief reasons for the decision. However, the officer must still illustrate that she is 'alert, alive and sensitive' to the various factors including the children's interests, but once she has identified and considered the facts, it is her judgement which then determines the weight accorded to each factor;[75] importantly, 'mere mention' of the children is not sufficient evidence of considered examination and weighing.[76] Here the immigration officer was found to have 'examined the interests of the children with a great deal of attention' and these were weighed against

---

[70] See n 23 and accompanying text.
[71] *Legault v Canada (Minister of Citizenship and Immigration)* [2002] 4 FC 358, FCJ No 457, FCA 125 (CA) [hereinafter *Legault*]. The individual was an American citizen and had been living in Canada for 20 years. He had two families in Canada—7 children by 2 ex-wives—and was the sole supporter of these families. He was indicted on a number of fraud-related offences and, after negative results to applications to stay based on permanent residence and refugee status, filed a humanitarian and compassionate grounds application which was also denied.
[72] Nadon J in the trial decision wrote: 'In conclusion, it is my view that the Supreme Court's decision in Baker ... calls for a certain result, and that result is that, save in exceptional cases, the children's best interests must prevail. ... As I have made it clear, I do not share the view expressed by the Supreme Court' *Legault v Canada (Minister of Citizenship and Immigration)* [2001] FCJ No 568, 2001 FCT 315 (FCTD) at paras 67–68.
[73] *Suresh v Canada (Minister of Citizenship and Immigration)* [2002] SCJ No 3, 2002 SCC 1 at paras 35–38: 'If the Minister has considered the appropriate factors in conformity with these constraints, the court must uphold her decision. It cannot set it aside even if it would have weighted the factors differently and arrived at a different conclusion'(at para 38).
[74] *Chieu v Canada (Minister of Citizenship and Immigration)* [2002] SCJ No 1, 2002 SCC 3 at para 70 where the Supreme Court declared that *Baker* stands as 'an example of an instance where the Minister's decision was procedurally deficient' rather than entailing any substantive considerations.
[75] *Legault*, n 71 at para 12.
[76] *Ibid* at para 13.

other factors in a reasonable decision. The Supreme Court denied leave to appeal.[77]

In *Hawthorne*,[78] the 'best interests of the child' factor received greater articulation than the discussion in *Legault*. The baseline that the Federal Court of Appeal found was 'absent exceptional circumstances ... the "child's best interests" factor will play in favour of the non-removal of the parent'.[79] In the majority and concurring judgements, the court held that the immigration officer was not 'alert, alive and sensitive' to the child's interests—a child who had permanent resident status—because the officer subsumed these particular interests under the separate category of inquiry around the hardship of removal of the parent on the child.[80] Moreover, the officer, in the written reasons to Ms Hawthorne outlining why her application was denied, clearly appeared quite heartless about the child's concerns which were provided to the officer by Suzette in a formal statement.

The concurring decision by Evans JA elucidated the broader and explicitly normative perspective and provided guidance on how to interpret the degree of harm in this particular context.[81] He too found that the officer provided insufficient treatment of the child's interests, writing: 'The summary, or less than responsive, treatment of the principal submissions made to the officer is indicative or a dismissive attitude towards her best interests'.[82] And, importantly, although he noted that properly formulated reasons which 'clearly demonstrate that the best interests of an affected child have received careful attention' no doubt impose an administrative burden,

---

[77] *Legault v Canada (Minister of Citizenship and Immigration)* [2002] SCCA No 220—no reasons given.

[78] *Hawthorne v Canada (Minister of Citizenship and Immigration)* [2002] FCJ No 1687, 2002 FCA 475 (CA). Daphney Hawthorne left Jamaica to live with the father of her daughter Suzette in 1992. Ms Hawthorne and the father of Suzette had separated in 1994 after he abused her; he subsequently married another woman and had children. Suzette, the daughter, remained in Jamaica with her grandmothers until her father sponsored her in 1999; her mother sent her financial assistance throughout this period. After coming to Canada, Suzette lived with and was supported by her mother. Ms Hawthorne had no legal status in Canada and in the midst of a humanitarian and compassionate grounds application to regularise her immigration status, was ordered deported in 2000. At this time, Suzette was in her early teens, did not want to live with her father as he was suspected of abusing one of his children, had no other relatives in Canada, and was not old enough to live on her own.

[79] *Ibid* at para 5 in the majority judgment by Décary and Rothstein JJA.

[80] *Ibid* at para 10.

[81] For example, Evans JA took seriously the Immigration Manual guidelines, calling them the 'normative framework' within which humanitarian and compassionate grounds decisions are made. *Ibid* at para 30. Evans JA's position on such 'soft law' accords with and supports that taken by Sossin and Smith: 'As cases such as *Baker* ... illustrate, although courts have often been unwilling to treat guidelines and codes as law, soft law has significant potential to serve as a conduit for a judicial-executive dialogue concerning the nature and scope of bureaucratic decision-making'. See Sossin and Smith, n 24 at 24.

[82] *Ibid* at para 50. Evans JA stated that the immigration officer had failed to treat Suzette's interests properly because an incorrect comparison was made. The relevant comparison ought to have been Suzette's present life in Canada and the choice of either losing her mother or her residency, not what her life would be like in Jamaica if she 'opted' to leave with her mother.

this is as it should be. Rigorous process requirements are fully justified for the determination of subsection 114(2) applications that may adversely affect the welfare of children with the right to reside in Canada: vital interests of the vulnerable are at stake and opportunities for substantive review are limited.[83]

Left for another day was the question of whether post-*Baker* cases like *Suresh* in fact preclude inquiry into the substantive unreasonableness[84] of the exercise of discretion when important individual interests are unreasonably or capriciously harmed—that is, interests that are either non-*Charter* or outside of traditional ultra vires categories.

4. Promises, or Footing the Remedy

The Mount Sinai hospital case provides a fascinating example of the murky line between the scope of discretion and the finality of a decision.[85] At play in this decision were a wide variety of unusual factors including the inconsistent behaviour of a government official, an overt promise, judicial reconstruction of the public interest and a contextualised approach to the determination of an ongoing web of relationships—the combination of which led to a rare instance of *mandamus* as a remedy to compel issuance of an operating permit from the Crown.

Of the two judgments, judgments which agree regarding the result but not in the method, the minority judgment written by Binnie J with the concurrence of McLachlin CJ evokes the language of *Baker*.[86] This judgment

---

[83] *Ibid* at para 52.
[84] Evans JA suggested that '[d]iscretion is exercised unreasonably or capriciously when the damage to important individual interests is disproportionate to the benefit produced by the decision'. *Ibid* at para 35.
[85] *Mount Sinai Hospital Center v Quebec (Minister of Health and Social Services)* [2001] SCJ No 43, 2001 SCC 41 [hereinafter *Mount Sinai*]. Since the 1950s, Mount Sinai hospital had possessed an operating permit which did not reflect its mix of long-term and short-term facilities, a situation known to the provincial government all along. In the 1980s, Mount Sinai and the government began negotiations to move the Center to Montreal and the Minister promised the Center that it would alter the permit to reflect reality upon the move, a promise which was reaffirmed on many occasions. In 1991, the Center moved and applied to have its permit regularised but, without giving the Center an opportunity to respond, the Minister retracted the promise and said the Center would have to operate under the terms of the old permit.
[86] In contrast, the majority judgment written by Bastarache J found a particular 'moment' where the Minister had exercised his discretion—the 1991 move. This meant that the Minster's discretion was not under review, as in *Baker* and in Binnie J's judgment, because it was 'spent' in January 1991. In October the Center received a letter revoking the promise and reversing the discretion and the question became whether this decision constituted a valid reversal. In light of the Minister's subsequent inconsistent behaviour with this supposed reversal, Bastarache J found that a later letter was an invalid exercise of discretion: 'The Minister cannot promise the Center to issue the modified permit when the move to Montreal is made, refuse to issue that permit, and then continue to treat the Center as if the permit had in fact been issued'. *Ibid* at para 114.

also illustrates an interesting nexus between public and private law in understanding a 'web of understandings and incremental agreements' on which the Center relied and which, over time, came to embody a specific public interest.[87] Binnie J reviewed the various grounds of appeal (eg, an acquired right, failure to observe procedural fairness, legitimate expectations, public promissory estoppel, and abuse of discretion) and considered failure to observe procedural fairness and abuse of discretion (citing *Baker*) as the appropriate grounds to find the Minister's decision patently unreasonable.[88] On this standard, the Minister showed a 'total lack of regard for the implications for the respondents of the Minister's broken promises' and the court was unable to mitigate this finding since the Minister offered no 'serious policy reason' for a redefinition of the public interest.[89] Indeed, the court suggested that it would have been 'sensitive' to any serious policy reason the Minister might have put forward.[90] As a result, 10 years after the broken promise and without any supporting reasons, the Minister was not allowed to advance a new vision of the public interest and the only option left open to him was to issue the modified permit.[91]

What is particularly novel and encouraging about the *Mount Sinai* decision is that the court undertook a probing review of an executive decision under the rubric of abuse of discretion *and* concluded that such an abuse demands a very intrusive remedy. But, as with *Baker*, the evidentiary requirements—the reasons—possess an air of contingency about them which makes assertion of an ethos a tenuous and variable claim for, as Binnie J states:

> The communications from the Minister are not simply evidence of the state of the Minister's mind, but are the source of the respondents' entitlement. In other words, if the successive Ministers had gone through the same cogitations and deliberations as they did between 1984 and 1991, *but kept their thoughts to themselves*, I think it unlikely that the respondents would succeed in obtaining the order they seek (emphasis added).[92]

In other words, if public officials keep their cogitations private and do not provide any evidence of reasoning, then the duty to give reasons can be no more than a sham.

---

[87] *Ibid* at para 8. Binnie J writes: 'If this were a private law situation there would likely be a breach of contract. This is not, of course, a private law situation'.

[88] Unfortunately, this decision has set back the development of both legitimate expectations and public law estoppel for some time in Canada.

[89] *Ibid* at paras 64–65. Bastarache J also held that the 'Minister cannot now invoke a vague and ungrounded funding concern as a reason for reversing a prior exercise of discretion in these circumstances'. *Ibid* at para 109.

[90] *Ibid* at para 65.

[91] *Ibid* at para 67.

[92] *Ibid* at para 4.

SEVERAL IMPLICATIONS OF THE *BAKER* ETHOS FOR CANADIAN ADMINISTRATIVE LAW

Binnie J's statement directly above regarding the contingent evidentiary foundation in the *Mount Sinai* case sounds a necessary cautionary note about the potential sanguinity of my approach to *Baker*. In this section, I hope to flesh out the argument against the possibility that *Baker* can provide no purchase regarding the quality of the reason-giving exercise and therefore may further a substandard relationship between the administrative decision-maker and the affected individuals or citizens, particularly vulnerable persons.[93]

1. Fleshing Out the Reasons Requirement

Critics of the duty to provide reasons usually warn that reasons may do very little to facilitate the free and fair exchange of information in the administrative setting. They may also do very little to produce accountability, transparency, or legitimacy in either the administrative or judicial spheres. Indeed, Lorne Sossin goes so far as to suggest that *Baker* may act as a disincentive as decision-makers may perversely use reasons to circumvent judicial review of the decision.[94] Cursory, formulaic, vague, unclear, uninformative, inauthentic—'boilerplate' or bureaucratic—reasons could emerge as a standard and, in some administrative contexts, be held acceptable by a reviewer based on functional grounds alone—that is to say, that a lack of reasons would not frustrate review of the decision. Lastly, the absence of reasons and the inadequacy of reasons are also not free-standing grounds of appeal—in this respect both *Baker* and *Sheppard* represent the failings of law for some.

Nevertheless, review for the reasonableness of decisions has expanded and I suggest that the absence or inadequacy of reasons may no longer be acceptable.[95] Fairness considerations could and should be used to challenge this outcome and I argue that where reasons are deficient and

---

[93] See, eg: L Sossin, 'An Intimate Approach to Fairness, Impartiality and Reasonableness in Administrative Law' (2002) 27 *Queen's Law Journal* 809–858. In his article, Sossin suggests replacing the current fairness model with a proposed 'framework of intimacy' which conceives of the exchange of knowledge as the basis for justifying decisions to the affected parties and the public, not as the means to legitimating adverse decisions. *Ibid* at 826–27. Such a framework would include a standard on which to assess and evaluate reasons in order to spur the production of 'fuller, clearer, more comprehensive, genuine reasons'. Sossin, however, does not disclose what this standard of meaningfulness looks like or how it will operate. *Ibid* at 837–38.
[94] As Sossin notes, fairness depends on the disclosure of knowledge by both parties where the decision-maker is obliged to provide some information to the individual and the affected party has the right to have certain information considered by the decision-maker. *Ibid* at 824 and 836.
[95] On the desirability of a general duty of to give reasons at common law, see Craig, n 27 at 301–02.

reveal an inattentive or arbitrary disposition, or where insupportable and unsupported conclusions are drawn, such deficiencies will provide a justification for greater scrutiny and a demand for reasons.

(a) Absent Reasons

Reading *Baker* through *Sheppard* tells us that not every administrative law decision will attract the duty to give reasons nor in the same way. However, where significant interests and rights are at play, it would be prudent public policy for the decision-maker to provide an intelligible rationale in order to satisfy the individual, the reviewer (either agency or judicial), and the general public. Determining evidence and weighing relevant factors will, in general, be the domain of the decision-maker who has first-hand knowledge of the context.

The absence of reasons could evoke a continuum of responses on the pragmatic and functional approach ranging from undeferential suspicion, to a probing examination, to soliciting respectful attention from the reviewer, and all the way to—though I would argue almost never—endorsement and full deference. *Mount Sinai*, for example, provided an example where the Supreme Court engaged in a respectful examination of the policy context while *Sheppard* stood somewhere between undeferential suspicion and a probing examination.

Outside of the criminal law context, the Montfort Hospital decision, *Lalonde*,[96] illustrates greater scrutiny of a discretionary decision. The Ontario Court of Appeal in *Lalonde* reviewed a discretionary decision to close the sole francophone hospital in Ontario, a decision purporting to be made in the public interest. Looking to the context and approaching language rights purposively in the pragmatic and functional approach,[97] the Ontario court identified several underlying constitutional principles and used these principles to interpret the statutory boundaries within which the Ontario government could act. Here the court used *Baker* for the proposition that the 'the review of discretionary decisions on the basis of fundamental Canadian constitutional and societal values' is possible and, despite being accorded deference, are not immune.[98] The statute required that a

---

[96] *Lalonde v Ontario (Commission de restructuration des services de santé)* [2001] OJ No 4767, 56 OR (3d) 505 (OCA) [hereinafter *Lalonde*]. The Ontario Court of Appeal found that a fundamental unwritten principle of the constitutional order, protection of minorities, served to protect Ontario's sole francophone hospital from both closure and substantial reduction in services. The Minister's directions were quashed because they failed to take into account the importance of francophone institutions and the preservation of the Franco-Ontarian culture.
[97] Weiler and Sharpe JJA approvingly cite Supreme Court jurisprudence which states that language rights 'must be given a purposive interpretation, taking into account the historical and social context, past injustices, and the importance of rights and institutions to the minority language community affected'. *Ibid* at para 138.
[98] *Ibid* at para 177.

right to receive French language services existed and could only be limited if all reasonable and necessary measures to comply with the statute had been exhausted. Montfort was explicitly designated as a francophone hospital for the Ottawa-Carleton community and the decision to restructure was a shift in policy for which no explanation was given. Given this absence, the court was compelled to scrutinise the gap:

> Although it is impossible to specify precisely what is encompassed by the words 'reasonable and necessary' and 'all reasonable measures', at a minimum they require some justification or explanation for the directions limiting the rights of francophones to benefit from Montfort as a community hospital.[99]

While the Minister could exercise discretion to change and even limit the provision of these services, 'it cannot simply invoke administrative convenience and vague funding concerns as the reasons for doing so ... '.[100] The Health Services Commission forfeited its entitlement to deference by providing no justificatory policy for impinging on fundamental constitutional values and its decision would have been found, on *any* standard of review, incorrect or unreasonable.[101]

(b) Inadequate Reasons

The adequacy of reasons is an area demanding greater jurisprudential elaboration as well. In the criminal case *Braich* discussed in subsection 2c of part III, what remained unresolved was the on-going puzzle of when a lack of genuine 'hard thought' on the part of the original decision-maker will constitute an improper or unreasonable step in the margin of discretionary manoeuvrability so that a reviewer can say with legitimacy and certainty that a different conclusion ought to have been reached in the context of a particular case. Whether such occurrences remain the exception remains to be charted.

Gray v Ontario[102] is a case that grapples with the fairness dimension of reasons in an examination of the 'quality' of reasons in the statutory context.

---

[99] *Ibid* at para 166.
[100] *Ibid* at 168. This language concerning the nature of the governmental justification strongly echoes that found in the *Mount Sinai* case above. See n 89 above and text therein.
[101] *Ibid* at 186.
[102] *Gray v Ontario (Disability Support Program, Director)* [2002] OJ No 1531 (CA) [hereinafter *Gray*]. The appellant claimed disability benefits on the basis that migraines and other ailments precluded her from holding down any form of employment. The Social Benefits Tribunal found that, although the appellant was credible in her testimony about her condition, she could cope on a day-to-day basis, was not substantially impaired, and therefore was not a person with a disability. It was unclear on what evidence the Tribunal relied in reaching this conclusion.

McMurtry CJO affirmed an earlier dictum that the duty to give reasons is 'only fulfilled if the reasons provided are adequate...[and] serve the functions for which the duty to provide them was imposed'.[103] The Ontario Court of Appeal unanimously held that a decision-maker must set out findings of fact as well as the principal evidence upon which the findings are based—particularly when the statutory regime implicates vulnerable persons such as people with disabilities. Not only did the tribunal provide 'little or no explanation of the reasoning process',[104] the tribunal asked itself the wrong question.[105] Mirroring *Sheppard*, *Gray* stands for the proposition in the administrative context that when a tribunal 'asks itself the wrong question' and fails to give reasons that are statutorily required, both of these flaws will be considered a reviewable error of law—errors which do not entitle a tribunal to deference.[106]

2. Conclusions and Further Problems

Post-*Baker* caselaw suggests that the absence or inadequacy of reasons will not serve as complete bars to a demand for justification. They point to a baseline that where an important interest has been negatively affected by a discretionary decision, justification is required.[107] Indeed, caselaw suggests that absence or inadequacy of reasons can inform grounds for review under the duty of fairness and its contents. Finally, *Baker* and its progeny tell us that a variety of authorities can be used to call the decision-maker to account including international law, fundamental norms both written and unwritten, and policy guidelines. Several problems, however, remain unresolved and I will mention a few here.

First, given the balance of power between the discretionary decision-maker and the affected individual(s), and as Binnie J alluded to in *Mount Sinai*, the element of contingency will almost certainly remain an evidentiary challenge for administrative law cases. Secondly, save legislative amendment or further judicial extension, these cases do not address the concern left open by *Baker* that reasons need not be contemporaneous with the decision

---

[103] *Ibid* at para 22 quoting *VIA Rail Canada Inc v Canada (National Transportation Agency)* [2001] 2 FC 25 (FCA).
[104] *Ibid* at para 24.
[105] The Court of Appeal stated that the question was not whether the appellant could cope on a day-to-day basis but whether or not she could function in the workplace and the community or attend to her personal care. *Ibid* at para 25.
[106] *Ibid* at paras 25–26. This would suggest that the appropriate standard of review on these issues, depending on the context, is correctness or reasonableness.
[107] See R Macdonald and D Lametti, 'Reasons for Decisions in Administrative Law' (1990) 3 *Canadian Journal of Law and Administrative Practice* 123 at 151–58 and MH Morris, 'Administrative Decision-makers and the Duty to Give Reasons: An Emerging Debate' (1998) 11 *Canadian Journal of Law and Administrative Practice* 155 at 177–78.

but may be obtained after the fact and upon request.[108] Thirdly, despite the guidance provided by the pragmatic and functional approach, these cases do not yet adequately address the problem of the appropriate standard of review of substantively unreasonable discretionary decisions that different decision-makers might reach.[109] And fourthly, the case-law has not yet resolved the underlying problem of when the courts will intervene in substantively unreasonable discretionary decisions and how they might remedy such decisions. For different reasons, both *Braich* and *Suresh* suggest that reweighing and resort to substantive remedies will occur infrequently.

Nevertheless, *Baker*, *Sheppard*, *Mount Sinai*, *Lalonde*, *Hawthorne* and *Gray* together suggest that deference will not be granted to a public body if it appears that not all the evidence was considered, if the court cannot determine how or if fair decision-making was engaged, or if reasons are sparse, incoherent and otherwise indefensible.[110] And, it is clear that a variety of remedies exist including *mandamus*, which can be used to order the issuance of reasons, and *certiorari* to quash a decision which failed to meet the common law requirement to give reasons and remit it for reconsideration.[111] For now, *Mount Sinai* stands as a rare example of a more substantive remedy—the direct grant of the benefit sought.[112]

---

[108] Thanks to Lorne Sossin for alerting me to this point—as he suggests, the line between justification as transparency and justification as immunity from accountability is a thin one.
[109] On this last point, see David Mullan's chapter in this volume. He argues that the courts, using *Baker*, have confirmed and increased deference to discretionary and executive decision-making, particularly with respect to the national security concerns including access to sensitive information. In administrative law in general and national security contexts in particular, Mullan argues that what has not yet resulted is optimal coherence within administrative law jurisprudence around standards of review. The courts have not calibrated deference so that it is most intense where it is most needed and there remains a persistent tendency to revert to categorical labelling as a solution when confronted by difficult conflicts of fact and law.
[110] See *Canada (Director of Investigation & Research) v Southam Inc* [1997] 1 SCR 748 on expertise at para 62: 'Expertise loses a right to deference when it is not defensible'. Iacobucci J for the court suggested that expertise is demonstrated in an administrative decision through well-informed, rational, cogent, and coherent conclusions.
[111] See JLH Sprague, 'Remedies for the Failure to Provide Reasons' (2000) 13 *Canadian Journal of Administrative Law and Practice* 209–23. Sprague argues that the proper remedy for a failure to give reasons should be *mandamus* whereas *certiorari* should be reserved for the rare case when it is impossible to provide reasons and 'even then only when such action is justified by the role played by the reasons in the particular scheme'. On Sprague's account, reasons do not go to the correctness/validity of the decision or its fairness. *Ibid* at 222–23. In contrast, David Mullan suggests that no hard and fast rule regarding the appropriate remedy exists. However, quashing and remission may be the most appropriate response to the failure to provide reasons while ordering the provision of reasons may satisfy the functional concern regarding effective review or appeal. He recommends that the substantive approach—the grant or a direction to grant the benefit the applicant is seeking—'remain a reserve possibility'. Mullan, *Administrative Law*, n 27 at 317–18.
[112] Both decisions employed *mandamus* to compel the issuance of the permit, albeit for different reasons. The remedy is all the more extraordinary since it was used against the Crown and the court specifically rejected the argument put forward that the Crown should retain immunity from this writ (*Mount Sinai*, n 85 at para 117).

THE *BAKER* ETHOS: THE AORTA OF CANADIAN PUBLIC LAW?

Many commentators would concur in the assessment that *Baker* is one of the 'most significant administrative law judgements ever delivered by the Supreme Court of Canada'.[113] *Baker* confirms the existence of a unified methodology: a pragmatic and contextual application of three standards of review revealing an overall 'deference as respect' approach to the administrative state, combined with a framework deeply evocative of a substantive conception of the rule of law. The 'bottom line' significance is that discretionary decisions must be exercised in accordance with the 'boundaries imposed in the statute, the principles of the rule of law, the principles of administrative law, the fundamental values of Canadian society, and the principles of the *Charter*';[114] otherwise, they will not be respected by either the courts or the general public.

In this concluding section, however, I will assert that *Baker* is more important than even initially thought for three reasons. First, the duty to give reasons stands as a substantive instantiation of the rule of law.[115] Therefore, what many judges labelled a 'substantive' as opposed to a purely procedural approach was the correct characterisation of the *Baker* ethos.[116] However, I do not agree that such an approach always intrudes on the merits of the initial decision or that it always guarantees the result that the claimant would like. As I have argued, a competent and fair decision-making process combined with a decision that recognises individual rights and interests and provides adequate reasons should usually command respect from a reviewer.

Secondly, *Baker*'s unified approach may inform the legal order as a whole. Looking at the pre-and post-*Baker* landscape illustrates that this methodology is not only confined to *Baker* and administrative law, but is pertinent for all public law[117] and perhaps beyond to specific

---

[113] D Mullan, '*Baker v Canada (Minister of Citizenship and Immigration)*—A Defining Moment in Canadian Administrative Law' (1999) 7 *Reid's Administrative Law* 145 at 146. See also L Sossin, 'Developments in Administrative Law: The 1998–99 Term' (2000) 11 *Supreme Court Law Review* (2d) 37 at 99.

[114] *Baker* n 1 at para 56.

[115] David Dyzenhaus and Evan Fox-Decent suggest that *Baker* exemplifies the principle of legality. See 'Rethinking the Process/Substance Distinction' (2001) 51 *University of Toronto Law Journal* 193–242 at 238–42.

[116] Here I disagree with Binnie J in *Mount Sinai* in his discussion about why the doctrine of legitimate expectations is limited to procedural rather than substantive relief. He uses this discussion to affirm the distinction between the procedural and the substantive though he acknowledges that 'in some cases it is difficult to distinguish the procedural from the substantive' (n 85 at para 35). At least with respect to reasons and reasonableness, I concur with Dyzenhaus and Fox-Decent that *Baker* fuses them. See above n 115.

[117] Analogous approaches can be found in *Charter* cases both in approaches to analysing rights in context and in relation to the specific provisions in the *Charter*, in s 1, and in the standard technique of statutory interpretation. See also D Mullan in *Administrative Law*, n 27 at 108, characterising *Baker*'s extension of the pragmatic and functional approach to abuse of discretion

instances of private law.[118] Indeed, equitable concerns about standards and proper behaviour inform both private and public law.[119] Such an approach avoids formalism and positivism in order to ground a decision in the substantive context and enables the judicial decision-maker to call into play many kinds of authority.[120] One interesting nexus concerning fairness between the private and the public has occurred in cases involving mistreatment of individuals within certain corporate communal organisations such as religious colonies.[121] It would seem that a modified version of the body of public law regarding procedural justice I have outlined here could apply to decisions made that impinge on individual rights and interests within such communities. In contrast to private law, however, the standard used to judge behaviour in administration and governance is constitutive of the character of the polity—in Canada, then, a liberal and constitutional democracy combined with a rule-of-law state.

Finally, the *Baker* ethos provides the strongest jurisprudential link between the rule of law and democracy. The idea of the justificatory democratic state may be best exemplified in the finding of the duty to give reasons in public law and coheres with the substantive understanding of the rule of law the Supreme Court has recently articulated in

as the provision of 'an overarching or unifying theory for review of the substantive decision of all manner of statutory and prerogative decision makers'.

[118] For a decision that applies *Sheppard* to the family law context, see *CAS v Alberta (Director of Child Welfare)* [2002] AJ No 895, 2002 ABQB 631.

[119] Equity has often supervised economic relations to impose standards of behaviour. See Sossin for an argument why the duty to give reasons in administrative law is equitable and that equitable principles inform public law duties based on a reconception of the fiduciary model in public law relationships and of authority as political trust. See 'Public Fiduciary Obligations', n 35.

[120] According to Jeffery Berryman, the methodology employed in courts of equity did not distinguish between fact and law resulting in an approach characterised as 'pragmatic, robust, and highly contextualized'. J Berryman, *The Law of Equitable Remedies* (Toronto, Irwin Law, 2000) at 2.

[121] See most recently *Waldner v Ponderosa Hutterian Brethren* [2003] AJ No 7, 2003 ABQB 6 which is a subsidiary case to a larger claim about procedural impropriety. This case concerns whether several members were improperly expelled from a Hutterian religious community because they were not afforded proper notice of the proposed expulsion nor were they given explicit reasons for such expulsion; significant property interests were at play as property is held in common in these communities and members are cared for until death. In an interesting link to *Baker*, the member who brought forward the suit was expelled but his wife was allowed to remain in the community. As with *Mount Sinai*, this case provides an example of overlapping public and private law doctrines as expulsion here could be thought analogous to wrongful dismissal. The Alberta court declared that the expulsion was invalid and granted an interim injunction to require reinstatement to his status before expulsion pending completion of the action regarding the evidence about procedural merits of the expulsion. The court would not interfere with what sanctions the community imposed prior to the wrongful expulsion and cautioned that the final determination of appropriate discipline rested in the decision-making body of the community. Other cases of this type include *Hofer v Wollman*, [1992] 3 SCR 165 and several early cases concerning memberships in associations.

the *Secession Reference*.[122] In this new understanding, administrative tribunals remain the 'front-line embodiments of the Rule of Law'[123] while the courts' participation in democratic governance actualises the rule of law norms of accountability and transparency. The view that I advance complements the picture of the rule of law outlined by Chief Justice Beverley McLachlin:

> Where a society is marked by a culture of justification, an exercise of public power is only appropriate where it can be justified to citizens in terms of *rationality and fairness*. Arbitrary decision and rules are seen as illegitimate ... most importantly, the ability to call for such a justification as a precondition to the legitimate exercise of public power is regarded by citizens as their *right*, a right which only illegitimate institutions and laws venture to infringe. The prevalence of such a cultural expectation is, in my view, the definitive marker of a mature Rule of Law.[124]

Rather than a standard account of the court's role which might focus, for example, on the counter-majoritarian principle, the *Baker* ethos presents a different and deeper explanation and justification, tapping into an ethical framework where the courts evaluate and legitimate a democratically originating, rule-governed way of life. The exercise of public power that affects individual rights must be justified to citizens on the bases of fairness, rationality, and reasonableness. Skeletal, generic, boilerplate, formulaic reasons cannot serve the function of reminding the political, social and legal order of the rules of conduct we believe are necessary to regulate our activities.

The rule of law therefore necessitates the multiple supervision of the exercise of public power between the executive, the legislative, the administrative state, the judiciary and the citizenry.[125] Determining the scope of duties owed by government officials in a decision-making context is a joint task shared between the legislatures which elaborate public purposes, the executive which animates these purposes and the courts which ensure reasonableness of government action.[126] But rather than a contest with only one winner, the object of the game of public law is for the players to better understand the rules of the game through their mutual participation

---

[122] In the *Secession Reference*, the Supreme Court suggested that: 'A political system must also possess legitimacy, and in our political culture, that requires an interaction between the rule of law and the democratic principle'. *Reference re Secession of Quebec* [1998] 2 SCR 217 at para 67.
[123] McLachlin, n 3 at 189.
[124] *Ibid* at 174.
[125] D Dyzenhaus, 'Constituting the Rule of Law: Fundamental Values in Administrative Law', (2002) 27 *Queen's Law Journal* 445–509 at 501–02. See also K Roach, *The Supreme Court on Trial: Judicial Activism or Democratic Dialogue* (Toronto, Irwin Law, 2001).
[126] *Ibid* at 175.

in the process of challenging, explaining, and applying these rules in concrete situations.[127] Courts and tribunals should be co-operative players in the game of administrative justice. Deference as respect ought then to facilitate power-sharing and aim to foster institutional respect for other bodies' competencies—this is the type of co-ordination intended by *Baker*.[128]

It is, of course, the affected individual or individuals, citizen or non-citizen, who provide the participatory stamp because they themselves have engaged the process. The procedural protection afforded by the duty to give reasons accords with a view of democracy that is participatory and therefore respects individual agency by facilitating the exercise of moral responsibility and by providing fair procedures that treat the individual as a whole person thereby respecting human dignity.[129] The *Baker* ethos manifests a sophisticated conception of participation in legal processes which complements democratic participation in political processes. I have argued that the *Baker* ethos embeds this conception in the duty to give reasons.

---

[127] For a brief analysis of this 'activity-oriented' view of democracy and constitutionalism, see J Tully, 'The Unattained Yet Attainable Democracy: Canada and Quebec Face the New Century' (Montréal, Programme d'études sur le Québec de l'Université McGill, 2000). In this essay, he writes: that '[c]onstitutional democracy must thus be seen as an activity, a system of discursive practices of rule following and rule modifying in which diversity is reconciled with unity through the continuous exchange of public reasons'. *Ibid* at 17.

[128] Geneviève Cartier calls this the '*Baker* effect', a term that she unpacks in her paper in this volume.

[129] See DJ Galligan, *Due Process and Fair Procedures A Study of Administrative Procedures* (Oxford, Clarendon Press, 1996), TRS Allan's review of this book, 'Procedural Fairness and the Duty of Respect' (1998) 18 *Oxford Journal of Legal Studies* 497–515, and P Craig, 'Public Law, Political Theory and Legal Theory' (2000) *Public Law* 211–39.

6

The Internal Morality of Administration: The Form and Structure of Reasonableness[1]

EVAN FOX-DECENT

One of the difficulties arising from L'Heureux-Dubé J's decision in *Baker*[2] is what does proper consideration of the children's interests mean. What does it mean, in fact, to be alert, alive and sensitive to the children's interests? Because there is no easy answer to these questions, either on a factual basis or on a principled basis, immigration officers and judges of this Court have struggled whenever confronted with these questions…

In my respectful view, the difficulty which immigration officers are now confronted with stems in part from the Supreme Court's failure—by reason of its conclusions that there was a reasonable apprehension of bias and that the officer had not considered the children's best interests—to address the real issue in *Baker*. That issue was whether the fact that Ms Baker would be a burden on taxpayers was a consideration which could outweigh the children's best interests. Could the officer in *Baker* give importance to, inter alia, the fact that Ms Baker had remained illegally in this country for over ten years.[3]

INTRODUCTION

THE MAIN ISSUE in *Baker* was the legality of a discretionary decision made by an immigration officer charged with determining whether there were humanitarian and compassionate grounds to

---

[1] I would like to thank the Social Science and Humanities Research Council for its generous support of the research that made this paper possible. The ideas presented here owe a debt to the papers and oral interventions at the conference 'The Authority of Reasons?' held at the University of Toronto in January, 2003, and especially to the papers by Geneviève Cartier, David Mullan and Lorne Sossin that are reproduced in this collection. I am also grateful to those authors and David Dyzenhaus for insightful comments on an earlier draft.
[2] *Baker v Canada (Minister of Citizenship and Immigration)* [1999] 2 SCR 817 [hereinafter *Baker*].
[3] Excerpted from the judgment of Nadon J (as he then was) in *Legault v Canada (Minister of Citizenship and Immigration)* [2001] FCJ No 568, 2001 FCT 315 (FCTD) [hereinafter *Legault*] at paras 58, 62.

grant Mavis Baker relief from a deportation order.⁴ A Jamaican, Ms Baker overstayed on a visitor's visa and spent 11 years in Canada working for the most part as a domestic employee. During that time she had four children. The Supreme Court held that a fundamental value of Canadian society is a concern for children's best interests, and that the decision-maker had to do more than simply indicate that he had taken those interests into account as one of many relevant factors. Writing for the Court,⁵ L'Heureux-Dubé J said that an exercise of discretion in these circumstances must give the children's best interests 'serious weight and consideration',⁶ 'close attention',⁷ and a kind of consideration she characterised as 'alive, attentive, or sensitive'.⁸ In summary, 'the decision-maker should consider children's best interests as an important factor, give them substantial weight, and be alert, alive and sensitive to them'.⁹ Because the officer failed in this regard (among others),¹⁰ she ruled that his exercise of discretionary authority was unreasonable and therefore illegal.

Baker is perhaps the most important case in Canadian administrative law because, more than any other, it specifies the democratic, substantive and equitable requirements of the legal duty of reasonableness. As we shall see, the demands of reasonable decision-making are democratic in that they take the form of an overarching duty to give reasons, the rationale for which is to justify and thereby make accountable the exercise of public power. The requirements of reasonableness are substantive in the sense that they explicitly require decision-makers to be 'alert, alive and sensitive' to fundamental and substantive values such as children's best interests. Fundamental values such as these need not have a basis in either the Canadian *Charter* or past common law, and do not depend on express statutory words for their authority. Lastly, the requirements of reasonableness are equitable in that they reflect the sense in which arbitrariness is anathema to public authority while fairness is constitutive of it, and so decision-makers must take seriously the critical interests and views of those

---

⁴ Subsection 114 (2) of the *Immigration Act*, RSC 1985, c I–2 (repealed, now Art 25(1) of the *Immigration and Refugee Protection Act*, RSC 2001, c 27) [hereinafter *Immigration Act*] gives the Minister authority to exempt an individual from the usual requirements and regulations concerning immigration if the Minister is satisfied 'that the person's admission should be facilitated owing to the existence of compassionate or humanitarian considerations'.

⁵ Iacobucci and Cory JJ dissented in part, but not on this point.
⁶ *Baker*, n 2 at para 65.
⁷ *Ibid*, at para 67.
⁸ *Ibid*, at para 73.
⁹ *Ibid*, at para 75.
¹⁰ The failure was quite spectacular, and captured graphically in the notes of the front line officer. The notes are so riddled with prejudice and stereotype that the Court held that they gave rise to a reasonable apprehension of bias. The notes are reproduced in full in L Sossin's, 'The Rule of Policy: *Baker* and the Impact of Judicial Review on Administrative Discretion', ch 4 of this volume.

persons immediately affected by their decisions.[11] In short, *Baker* holds out the promise of a conception of the rule of law that is at once democratic, substantive and equitable. Underlying and uniting these three elements is a profound commitment to respect the human dignity of each person subject to legal authority, and to do so in a manner that is sensitive to the vulnerability of the individual affected by an exercise of public power.

My hope in this chapter is to elaborate a rights-oriented framework to address the 'real issue' and the questions to which Nadon J in the epigraph above says 'there is no easy answer'. The framework involves a particular approach to administrative decision-making and judicial review, one that seeks to do justice to *Baker's* democratic, substantive and equitable rule of law message while maintaining the distinction between review of legality and review on the merits. Although the legality/merits distinction necessarily becomes complicated in light of *Baker*, I argue that a version of it may be sustained which permits us to hold on to a robust sense of curial deference. In keeping with the title of this volume, I defend a conception of public law that draws support and a sense of unity from Canadian constitutional jurisprudence as well as from the European doctrine of proportionality. First, however, it is important to see why Nadon J supposes there is no easy answer to what it means to be alert, alive, and sensitive to fundamental values, and why he thinks that in any event the courts are not the institution to provide the answer.

RELEVANCE AND WEIGHT, LEGALITY AND MERITS

The legal context in *Legault* was similar to *Baker* in that an individual with Canadian-born children and subject to deportation sought to remain in Canada on the basis of humanitarian and compassionate considerations. Like Baker, Legault had spent many years in Canada illegally. In addition, Legault had been indicted in the United States on fraud-related charges. The issue for Nadon J was whether the immigration officer had given sufficient importance to the children's best interests when she weighed those

---

[11] For extended treatment of the idea that the duty of reasonableness in *Baker* is a public equitable obligation, see L Sossin, 'Public Fiduciary Obligations, Political Trusts and the Evolving Duty of Reasonableness in Administrative Law' (2003) 66 *Saskatchewan Law Review* (forthcoming). For discussion of the idea that the relationship between state and subject is fiduciary (and therefore equitable) in nature, see P Finn, 'The Forgotten "Trust": The People and the State' in M Cope (ed), *Equity Issues and Trends, 1995* (The Foundation Press, 1995). For the argument that the state-subject fiduciary relationship arises from the conditions inherent to sovereignty (ie, entrusted authority, power and discretion on the one side; reposed trust and vulnerability on the other), and that this relationship justifies free-standing public duties of fairness and reasonableness, see E Fox-Decent, 'Sovereignty's Promise: The State as Fiduciary', (PhD thesis, University of Toronto, Department of Philosophy, 2003).

interests against other factors, factors which he thought should include Legault's prior illegal residence in Canada[12] and the allegations of fraud.

After reviewing the relevant cases that had come before the Federal Court since *Baker*, the judge discerned two 'contradictory approaches' to review of reasonableness, a 'process' approach and a 'substantive' approach.[13] As we will see, his characterisation of each—as well as their alleged mutual exclusivity—is instructive:

> Under the process approach, the Court will examine whether the immigration officer has taken into consideration the effects which the parents' departure from Canada might have upon the children. If the immigration officer has taken into consideration these effects, the Court will not intervene, even though the decision made is not a favourable one to the applicant. On the other hand, under the substantive approach, the Court will not only verify whether the officer has considered the effects of a refusal of the parents' application under subsection 114(2), but will go further and assess whether the ultimate decision is the correct one.[14]

Nadon J left no doubt that he preferred the 'process' approach, saying that '[i]n my view, the best interests of children, whether they be Canadian or foreign born, is only one of the considerations which an immigration officer should take into account', and that '[t]o direct the Minister to give more weight to one factor, namely, the children's best interests, is, in my respectful view, tantamount to fettering the Minister's discretion'.[15] None the less, he understood L'Heureux-Dubé J's judgment to endorse the 'substantive' approach, and so, despite his disagreement with it, he held that *Baker* 'calls for a certain result, and that result is that, save in exceptional circumstances, the children's best interests must prevail'.[16] Nadon J found that:

> there will be few cases where the immigration officer will be able to conclude that the children's best interests do not require that their parents' application for an exemption be granted.[17]

In the result, he allowed Legault's application, reversing the front-line officer.

Nadon J's characterisation of process and substance is instructive because it reveals the sense in which he and many judges take process and substance to track two further distinctions familiar to public lawyers: the

---

[12] Nadon J lamented that '[t]he fact that Ms Baker remained illegally in this country for over 10 years does not appear to have been a relevant consideration in so far as the Supreme Court was concerned. Nowhere in the decision can one find any condemnation or reproach concerning Ms Baker's conduct in disregarding the law'. *Legault*, n 4 at para 64.
[13] *Legault*, n 4 at para 55.
[14] *Ibid*.
[15] *Ibid*, at paras 63, 66.
[16] *Ibid*, at para 67.
[17] *Ibid*.

distinction between relevance and weight, on the one hand, and review of legality and review of the merits, on the other. The distinction between the relevance of a factor and the weight accorded it is all important to these judges, since the relevance/weight distinction underpins the hallowed distinction between review of legality and review on the merits. Thus, Nadon J took *Holder*[18] to be a 'clear example of the substantive approach' because in that case Tremblay-Lamer J closely reviewed the evidence of humanitarian considerations warranting an exemption, and so according to Nadon J, 'the learned Judge was "intruding" into the merits of the matter'.[19]

Nadon J's characterisation of process and substance is also instructive in that it suggests that review of the substance or reasons for a decision is invariably tantamount to review of the merits on a standard of correctness. A reviewing court that adopts the substantive approach must 'assess whether the ultimate decision is the correct one'.[20] The trial judge leaves little room for review on a standard of reasonableness because the officer's decision must align with the court's view of the correct outcome regardless of the strength of the reasons the decision-maker provides. And with respect to the 'process' approach, he adopts a restrictive view here as well, since in principle review under this approach need not involve anything more than simply noting that the decision-maker has in some manner or other taken the relevant considerations into account.

The Federal Court of Appeal reversed Nadon J, saying that his reading of *Baker* was 'excessive' because L'Heureux-Dubé J's judgment does not state that outcome of the decision must be dictated by the children's best interests.[21] Décary JA cited the Supreme Court's finding in *Suresh*[22] that:

> *Baker* does not authorise courts reviewing decisions on the discretionary end of the spectrum to engage in a new weighing process, but draws on an

---

[18] *Holder v Canada (Minister of Citizenship and Immigration)* [2001] FCJ No 267, 2001 FCT 119 (FCTD).
[19] *Legault*, n 4 at para 56.
[20] *Ibid*, above n 14.
[21] *Legault v Canada (Minister of Citizenship and Immigration) (CA)* [2002] FCA 125 at para 7 [hereinafter *Legault (FCA)*]. The reasons were delivered for a unanimous court by Décary JA. Décary JA had penned *Langner v Canada (Minister of Employment and Immigration)* [1995] FCJ No 469 (FCA) [hereinafter *Langner*], the case on which his brother Strayer JA relied most heavily when Décary JA joined him in the judgment L'Heureux-Dubé J would subsequently overturn in *Baker*. In *Langner*, Décary JA had said at para 6 that '[t]he appellant parents' decision to take their children to Poland with them or to leave them with family members living in Canada is a decision which is their own to make and which, to all appearances, they will make in the best interests of the children. The Canadian Government has nothing to do with this decision, which is of a strictly private interest'. Décary JA had also signed onto the reversed decision of Robertson JA in *Suresh v Canada (Minister of Citizenship and Immigration)* (2000), 183 DLR (4th) 629 (FCA). Lastly, to bring the point full circle, Décary JA in *Legault (FCA)* at para 12 cites his decision in *Langner* for the proposition that 'Parliament has not decided, as of yet, that the presence of children in Canada constitutes in itself an impediment to any "refoulement" of a parent illegally residing in Canada'.
[22] *Suresh v Canada (Minister of Citizenship and Immigration)* [2002] SCJ No 3, 2002 SCC 1 [hereinafter *Suresh*] at para 37.

established line of cases concerning the failure of ministerial delegates to consider and weigh implied limitations and/or patently relevant factors. (Citations omitted.)[23]

Décary JA concluded that:

> [i]t is up to the immigration officer to determine the appropriate weight to be accorded to this factor [the children's interests] in the circumstances of the case. It is not the role of the courts to re-examine the weight given to the different factors by the officers.[24]

In other words, the officer's task is to engage in a balancing exercise in which they 'examine and weigh' the children's interests against other factors.[25] So long as the decision-maker has:

> well identified and defined this factor [the interests of the children], it is up to her to determine what weight, in her view, it must be given in the circumstances.[26]

The Supreme Court denied leave to appeal.[27]

Reliance on a 'process' approach that draws a bright line between relevance and weight to insulate review of legality from review of the merits, however, offers little guidance to the primary decision-maker with respect to the important substantive issue of just how much weight in the circumstances the decision-maker ought to give to the children's best interests. This is not surprising, since the argument that underlies mapping relevance and weight onto legality and merits is a formal argument concerning the separation of powers, and hence not an argument concerned with the actual values at play at the level of decision-making.[28]

---

[23] *Legault (FCA)*, n 21 at para 9.
[24] *Ibid*, at para 11. To similar effect, Décary JA cites *Chieu v Canada (Minister of Citizenship and Immigration)* [2002] SCJ No 1, 2002 SCC 3 at para 70 for Iacobucci J's dictum that *Baker* is an 'example of an instance where the Minister's decision was procedurally deficient'.
[25] *Legault (FCA)*, n 21 at para 13. And here Décary JA suggests reading down 'children's best interests' to 'the interests of the children', since the former may lead the decision-maker to believe that this factor is 'before all others, more important'.
[26] *Ibid*, at para 12.
[27] *Legault v Canada (Minister of Citizenship and Immigration)* [2002] SCCA No 220—no reasons given.
[28] *Suresh*, n 22, at para 38, cited by Décary JA in *Legault (FCA)*, provides one of the more positivist illustrations of this argument in recent jurisprudence: 'This [deferential] standard appropriately reflects the different obligations of Parliament, the Minister, and the reviewing court. Parliament's task is to establish the criteria and procedures governing deportation, within the limits of the Constitution. The Minister's task is to make a decision that conforms to Parliament's criteria and procedures as well as the Constitution. The court's task, if called upon to review the Minister's decision, is to determine whether the Minister has exercised her decision-making power within the constraints imposed by Parliament's legislation and the Constitution. If the Minister has considered the appropriate factors in conformity with these constraints, the court must uphold her decision. It cannot set it aside even if it would have weighed the factors differently and arrived at a different conclusion'.

It follows that even if the 'process' approach to fundamental values adopted in *Legault (FCA)* and *Suresh* is a faithful reading of *Baker*,[29] primary decision-makers are still left with Nadon J's 'real issue'; ie, the problem of figuring out just how much importance fundamental values are to receive when weighed against other considerations. And, even if this issue is settled in principle, there still remains the question of the extent to which courts may review the legality of decisions involving fundamental values without becoming involved in straightforward merits review. Whether judges engage in a wholesale reweighing of the factors or not, any review of whether a decision-maker has been 'alert, alive, and sensitive' to fundamental values implies a review of substance that pre-*Baker* would usually have been left to the discretion of the legislature's delegates, with curial admonitions about the danger of the courts substituting their view of the merits for the view of the primary decision-maker. This engagement with substance necessarily strains the legality/merits distinction, and so just below the surface and closely related to the challenge of rearticulating deference is a need to rearticulate the content of legality itself.

THE INTERNAL MORALITY

General Features

In what follows I suggest that a certain structure of justification lends itself well to the principle of legality with which *Baker* constrains and justifies administrative decision-making. The overall framework may be thought of as an internal morality of administration, for it is a compendium of principles which set out the formal requirements and structure of the justification we should expect from public authorities when critical interests are at stake.[30] As such, at its weakest, the internal morality does not determine the relative weights to be accorded the various considerations that may be in play. The task of weighing, as a rule, falls to the primary decision-maker.[31]

---

[29] Below I argue that Evans JA's concurring judgment in *Hawthorne v Canada (Minister of Citizenship and Immigration)*, 2002 FCA 475 (28 November 2002) [hereinafter *Hawthorne*] better captures *Baker*'s spirit than *Legault (FCA)* and *Suresh*.
[30] The term and the idea is taken from Lon L Fuller's 'internal morality of law', a set of formal constraints on legislation and administration (eg, publicity, generality, nonretroactivity, clarity, etc) that Fuller took to comprise part of the concept of law. While these constraints have substantive implications in that they exclude certain exercises of power from counting as law properly understood as such, they do not reflect the law's substantive policy goals, and so in this sense Fuller considered them to be formal rather than substantive in nature. I make a similar claim with respect to the internal morality of administration, and pin the legality/merits distinction on it. See Lon L Fuller, *The Morality of Law*, rev edn (New Haven, Yale University Press, 1969). See especially: ch 2.
[31] However, I claim below that if fundamental values or explicit constitutional rights are in play (such as those based in the *Canadian Charter of Rights and Freedoms*, Part I of the *Constitution Act, 1982*, being Schedule B to the *Canada Act 1982* (UK), 1982, c 11

But what the internal morality does do is make abundantly clear the basis for the decision, for the very duty to give reasons which themselves respect the contours of the internal morality requires just that.

As we shall see, the internal morality requires the decision-maker to engage in a number of comparative and inferential justificatory practices. These practices do not themselves entail particular outcomes. Nor do they guarantee favourable results for the individual. But they do have substantive implications in the sense that they limit the range of outcomes and results to those which are capable of being justified. Moreover, the comparative and inferential practices of the internal morality reveal the policies and values underlying a particular decision, not just the factors or considerations that may be in play. As a consequence, the internal morality brings to the surface the relative priority the decision-maker gives to policies and values that infringe on fundamental values and critical interests.

The internal morality is internal to administration and to law in the following related ways. First, it is internal in Fuller's sense that it does not prejudge nor predetermine the success or failure of the legitimate policy goals the law hopes to achieve.[32] Rather, the internal morality facilitates and enables the law to realise its ambitions in a manner that is democratic and equitable, and does so by giving a particular form and structure to legal duties of fairness and reasonableness. Secondly, the internal morality is internal in the sense that it reflects the commitment of the administration and the courts to exercise public power in a manner that is democratic and equitable, a commitment that is embodied in legal duties of fairness and reasonableness, but one which rests on the trust and authority these institutions enjoy for the purpose of securing legal order and governing through law.[33] Thirdly, the internal morality is peculiarly internal to law in that it establishes an overarching structure of justification which is based on legal ideals of fairness and reasonableness, and those ideals themselves are ultimately grounded in human dignity, the legal ideal that underlies respect for all human rights.

The argument for the internal morality of administration follows up on Geneviève Cartier's suggestion that there is no reason to suppose that a bright line distinguishes the methodology appropriate to administrative law from the approach used in cases that deal explicitly with

---

[hereinafter the *Charter*]), then the courts are justified in reviewing the weight given the factors which are alleged to warrant their infringement. I agree with Mullan on this, and later adopt the argument he advances to show that deference can survive a judicial willingness to consider the weight given to considerations on which the protection of fundamental values depends. See D Mullan, 'Deference from *Baker* to *Suresh* and Beyond—Interpreting the Conflicting Signals', ch 2 of this volume.

[32] I leave to one side the thorny problem of overtly wicked laws, and what the internal morality would have to say about them.

[33] Here too I borrow from Fuller, in this case from his idea that the relationship between law-giver and legal subject is best characterised as one of reciprocity rather than a 'one way projection of authority'. See Fuller, n 30 at 204–10.

Charter rights.³⁴ To that end, the internal morality's justificatory structure adopts criteria familiar to constitutional tests such as the ones found in *Oakes*³⁵ and the European principle of proportionality.³⁶ What is common to the structures of justification found in these tests is that they provide a framework that a decision-maker may use to assign particular weights to particular considerations and thereby attempt to justify a decision that is adverse to the individual or group immediately affected by the decision. However, while the tests limit the range of lawful outcomes to those capable of justification, they themselves do not assign weight to the factors that ultimately determine the result. As a consequence, courts may properly be said to review legality independently of the merits whenever they simply inquire into whether the decision-maker in fact uses the legal framework of the internal morality to justify her decision. We might expect the default standard of the review regarding the decision-maker's good faith use of the internal morality to be reasonableness, for determining whether the decision-maker has in fact engaged the internal morality will require a 'somewhat probing examination' of the reasons she gives.³⁷

As we shall see, subscribing to the internal morality in merely this procedural sense gets us pretty far down the road toward a satisfying conception of legality. But the legality/merits line becomes less clear for judges who

---

³⁴ See G Cartier, 'The *Baker* Effect: A New Interface between the *Canadian Charter of Rights and Freedoms* and Administrative Law—The Case of Discretion', in this volume. Administrative law's greatest challenge, Cartier argues, is the development of a structured analysis within which to integrate and apply the values articulated by the various participants in legal order: the legislature, the judiciary, the executive and the individuals. The internal morality of administration is one reply to that challenge, an effort to flesh out the implications of an insightful comment by JM Evans: 'The *Charter* has undermined the artificial barriers that have for too long separated administrative and constitutional law, and revealed the concerns and methodology that they share as components of our public law'. JM Evans 'The Principles of Fundamental Justice: The Constitution and the Common Law', (1991) 29 *Osgoode Hall Law Journal* 51 at 92.
³⁵ *R v Oakes* [1986] 1 SCR 103 [hereinafter *Oakes*].
³⁶ Cartier argues that *Baker* is to administrative law what *Oakes* is to constitutional doctrine in the sense that both cases force public authority to justify its intended exercise of power in terms of a concern for the values that ultimately justify the authority's power. See G Cartier, 'Administrative Law Twenty Years After the *Charter*', (2003) *Revue du Barreau du Québec*, *Numéro spécial* 197 (forthcoming). I agree. Drawing a similar parallel, during the conference Paul Craig suggested that *Baker* would have been settled in the UK with a fairly unconventional application of proportionality doctrine. (Art 8 of the European Convention on Human Rights asserts family life as a right, and the UK Human Rights Act (1998) incorporates this and other provisions of the ECHR, as well as proportionality, into UK municipal law.) For Craig's argument that proportionality has been a quiet but steady part of UK law independently of the Human Rights Act (1998), and that this is a good thing which does not threaten a collapse of legality/merits, see his 'Unreasonableness and Proportionality in UK Law' in Evelyn Ellis (ed), *The Principle of Proportionality in the Laws of Europe* (Oxford, Hart Publishing, 1999). So, my argument here follows a course that Craig too has already charted.
³⁷ The 'somewhat probing examination' test for reasonableness is from *Canada (Director of Investigation and Research) v Southam* [1997] 1 SCR 748 [hereinafter *Southam*] at para 56, reaffirmed in *Baker*, n 2 at para 63, discussed below at n 45.

follow L'Heureux-Dubé J's lead in *Baker* and review the weight attributed to fundamental values. And so a principle is needed to justify and explain this kind of review of substance.

The principle, I suggest, is simply judicial responsibility for the rule of law, with the important qualifier that discharging this responsibility presupposes a conception of the rule of law that includes review of weight if (and only if) there is reason to think that, within the relevant legal context, taking account of a particular consideration in fact implies giving it a certain weight.[38] Evidence to support giving more than minimal weight to a certain factor may come from a variety of sources, including of course relevant domestic legislation and the common law, but also international human rights instruments and 'soft law' (ministerial guidelines, policy memoranda, accepted patterns of decision-making, and so on). In *Baker*, L'Heureux-Dubé J evoked both the *Convention on the Rights of the Child* and ministerial guidelines to suggest that children's best interests are not simply one factor among many, but a consideration that must be given special notice.[39]

In this regard, soft law and international instruments form part of the legal context that determines the legality of the weight accorded to factors such as fundamental values and critical interests, and the idea that weight has a legal component implies that weight is to some extent reviewable. Further, soft law and international law may play an indispensable role, as they did in *Baker*, in identifying just what those rights-bearing fundamental values and critical interests are.

The last general feature of the internal morality worth flagging is its rights-oriented nature. While the discussion thus far has turned on the distinction between relevance and weight, the rights-oriented approach inherent to the internal morality takes as its starting point a careful characterisation of the right or interest that is vulnerable to the decision-maker's discretion. The nature of the right or interest is to be inferred from the full legal context, including international law and soft law, and only then does inquiry proceed to consider whether infringement of the interest is justifiable, taking into account all relevant considerations and their appropriate weight. As we shall see, this is essentially the approach adopted by Evans JA in *Hawthorne*, and differs considerably from the balancing exercise engaged in by Décary JA in *Legault (FCA)*, one which stops to characterise the vulnerable interest as an afterthought, once the issue has been decided, and then only to water down 'the children's best interests' to simply 'the children's interests'.[40] The methodological differences between the

---

[38] The idea that weight can be subsumed within a sufficiently broad notion of taking a factor into account is the point Mullan makes, noted in n 31 above.
[39] *Baker*, n 2 at paras 69–72.
[40] See n 25 above.

rights-based and the balancing approach are revealed in the structure of the principles of the internal morality discussed below in the section 'A Public Structure of Justification'.

Baker's Starting Points

Before moving on to the principles of the internal morality, it is important to have before us two of L'Heureux-Dubé J's starting points for review in *Baker*. One is the 'pragmatic and functional' test,[41] the other is David Dyzenhaus' idea of deference as respect.[42] As we will see, each starting point adds a critical dimension to her framework for review, and each lays the groundwork that makes the internal morality possible. But neither (either separately or jointly) make explicit the resources necessary to answer Nadon J's worry concerning the relative importance of fundamental values.

Until *Baker*, the pragmatic and functional test had been applied exclusively to determine the standard of review appropriate for a court reviewing a tribunal's interpretation of its constitutive or enabling statute. The test posits standards of review that range in intensity from correctness to reasonableness to patent unreasonableness, with the appropriate standard being determined by evaluating the presence and weight of a series of contextual factors. Judges are instructed to consider factors such as the importance of the interest at stake, whether the decision is final or one from which there is a statutory right of appeal, whether there is a privative clause, the relative expertise of the tribunal, whether the decision involves primarily a determination of fact or law or a mixture of both, whether the decision-making context is one that pits the state against the individual, and whether the decision is of a policy or legislative rather than quasi-judicial nature.[43]

---

[41] See *Pushpanathan v Canada (Minister of Citizenship and Immigration)* [1998] 1 SCR 982 at paras 27–38 [hereinafter *Pushpanathan*]; *Baker*, n 2 at paras 55, 56.

[42] David Dyzenhaus, 'The Politics of Deference: Judicial Review and Democracy' in M Taggart (ed), *The Province of Administrative Law* (Oxford, Hart Publishing, 1997) cited in *Baker*, n 2 at para 65.

[43] See *Pushpanathan*, n 41 above; *Baker*, n 2 at paras 58–62. Murray Hunt adopts similar criteria in his articulation of an issue-focused 'due deference' approach: M Hunt, 'Sovereignty's Blight: Why Contemporary Public Law Needs the Concept of "Due Deference"' in N Bamforth and P Leyland, (eds), *Public Law in a Multi-Layered Constitution* (Oxford, Hart Publishing, forthcoming). But Hunt adds an important principle of democratic accountability to the mix, one that is at best merely implicit in the Canadian pragmatic and functional test. He suggests that an important contextual factor to bear in mind when determining the intensity of review is the degree of democratic accountability of the primary decision-maker. In practice, this principle may usefully distinguish the deference due a labour board with representation from both affected parties (labour and management), on the one hand, and the deference to be accorded an anonymous immigration official deciding the fate of a non-citizen, on the other.

Determining the appropriate standard of review, however, only takes one so far. Once a court determines, for example, that the standard is reasonableness, it must still say what reasonableness is, or at least what it is not.[44] In *Southam*, cited in *Baker*, the Supreme Court said that:

> [a]n unreasonable decision is one that, in the main, is not supported by any reasons that can stand up to a somewhat probing examination. Accordingly, a court reviewing a conclusion on the reasonableness standard must look to see whether any reasons support it. The defect, if there is one, could presumably be in the evidentiary foundation itself or in the logical process by which conclusions are sought to be drawn from it.[45]

So, a reasonable decision is one that must be supported by some reasons which can stand up to a 'somewhat probing examination'. This sounds nice, but does not get us much closer to an idea of the form or content we might expect those reasons to possess, nor does it tell us how we are to assign weight to considerations that pull in different directions.

Generally, determining the standard of review suggests something about the degree of intensity with which review may occur, but does not, without more, inform us of the principles appropriate to carrying out such review. *Baker* gives us a detailed articulation of what those principles may be, with fundamental values figuring prominently in the catalogue.[46] But the

---

[44] Courts may often be able to sidestep the necessarily difficult task of giving a complete account of reasonableness by limiting their observations to a negative claim about what reasonableness cannot be in a given set of circumstances. L'Heureux-Dubé J followed this approach in *Baker*. Working from a negative account of reasonableness is less problematic than attempting a thorough-going positive characterisation, since the latter but not the former carries with it a presumption that what is put forward is in some sense a full and complete account of the concept. An analogy to justice is apt. There is general agreement on a wide range of things which are unjust (eg, arbitrariness, corruption, fraud, etc.), but less agreement on exactly what the best account of justice is. The same is true of reasonableness. Courts reviewing on a standard of reasonableness only need to be able to say if a particular exercise of power is unreasonable. If it is not unreasonable so far as its legality is concerned, then it passes muster regardless of whether it is reasonable or not on the merits, all things considered.

[45] *Southam*, n 37 at para 56; *Baker*, n 2 at para 63.

[46] L'Heureux-Dubé J held at para 56 that 'discretion must be exercised in accordance with the boundaries imposed in the statute, the principles of the rule of law, the principles of administrative law, the fundamental values of Canadian society, and the principles of the *Charter*'. One might be tempted to think that, fundamental values aside, this catalogue just states what we already knew. But given the international law aspect of *Baker*, the catalogue has a significant implication, for the majority in *Baker* affirmed that ratified but unincorporated human rights treaties form part of the relevant legal context within which domestic legislation is enacted and discretionary decisions are made, and therefore international instruments may inform critical, rights-determining interpretations of domestic legislation on which discretionary decisions rely. The significant implication is found in L'Heureux-Dubé J's explicit reference in her catalogue to the rule of law, for only the idea of the rule of law is of sufficient generality and plasticity to let consideration of human rights instruments into its fold. It follows that international human rights law is now an integral part of Canada's conception of the rule of law.

difficulty again resurfaces for the primary decision-maker and judge alike who find themselves confronted with the task of having to determine the role of fundamental values such that consideration of them in relation to other factors conforms to the requirements of legality. Nadon J's 'real issue' is still left lurking.

Complementing the pragmatic and functional approach, L'Heureux-Dubé J cited with approval Dyzenhaus' idea that deference is best thought of as deference as respect, where the object of respect is the reasons given, or which could be given, for a decision. If the reasons offered (or which could be offered) justify the decision, then deference is due regardless of whether the court would have come to a different conclusion had it considered the matter afresh. Deference as respect is most at home with a reasonableness standard of review, since reasonableness invites a 'somewhat probing examination' of the reasons said to justify the decision. Moreover, deference as respect is fully consistent with the possibility that there may be more than one justifiable outcome or more than one reasonable interpretation of a statute.[47] Reason is not necessarily univocal in its prescriptions, and so judges may recognise in appropriate circumstances that a decision is justifiable, and therefore reasonable and legal, notwithstanding that they may have reached a different conclusion on the merits.

As Hunt points out, deference as respect provides a healthy antidote to the conventional view of deference, a view that relies on spatial metaphors involving 'spheres' or 'areas' in which judges would interfere on only narrow grounds.[48] Spheres or areas which courts have generally deemed immune from review include immigration, social and economic policy, matters related to national security, and decisions based upon a statutory grant of wide discretionary authority. In the result, determinations made in these areas have often been thought to take place in a legal void, free from judicial review of the reasons that may support them (and usually free from even a duty to give reasons).[49]

---

[47] See, for example, *Canadian Union of Public Employees, Local 963 v New Brunswick Liquor Corporation* [1979] 2 SCR 227, where Dickson J recognised that one could quite reasonably give a meaning to the ambiguous but critical term 'employee' that favoured either side. The case turned on this interpretation.

[48] Hunt, n 43 above. These grounds arise from *Associated Provincial Picture Houses Ltd v Wednesbury Corporation* [1948] 1 KB 223, and are usually put in terms of not taking into account irrelevant considerations, taking account of all relevant considerations, not deciding on the basis of improper purposes, exercising discretion in good faith and so on. The Canadian analogue is *Roncarelli v Duplessis* [1959] SCR 121 [hereinafter *Roncarelli*]. In the Canadian case, Rand J held that Roncarelli, a restaurant owner, was entitled to compensation from the former Premier of Quebec, Maurice Duplessis, because Duplessis had abused his office to compel revocation of Roncarelli's liquor license, effectively putting Roncarelli out of business. Duplessis had ordered the arrest of Jehovah's Witnesses in an attempt to impede their efforts to proselytise their creed. Roncarelli supplied bail guarantees for the arrested Witnesses, a move which infuriated Duplessis and led him to order the cancellation of Roncarelli's license.

[49] For an excellent recent example of the legal void position, see the judgment of Strayer JA that *Baker* reversed. The clearest statement of the legal void thesis is Masten JA's dictum in

Like any theory of respect,[50] however, the hard work lies in specifying the details, which in the case of deference means specifying the sense in which judges may evaluate and respect the reasons given for a decision without converting review of legality into review of the merits. Suppose the test for reasonableness or legality is put in terms of whether the decision is justifiable in the sense of whether it is defensible, taking all the important considerations into account.[51] The key issue with respect to deference, again, is determining just what it means for a reviewing judge to take all the important considerations into account without collapsing the legality/merits distinction. The central issue with respect to legality is establishing a general framework of justification which compels recognition of all the important considerations and provides some guidance as to the relative weight legality demands of them. Deference as respect invites engagement with these issues; the internal morality of administration fleshes out the implications of that engagement.

A Public Structure of Justification

I have argued that saying that reasonable decisions must conform to indicia such as the principles of the rule of law and fundamental values indicates the starting point rather than the conclusion of the administrator's analytical journey toward a reasonable decision. As a starting point, these indicia give the decision-maker a sense of bearing, but without more they do not indicate which fundamental values or rule of law principles are to apply in any given case, nor the weight to be accorded them.

Of course, it would be foolhardy to expect *a priori* guidelines of uniform application which are capable of neatly determining the relevance and weight of such considerations in every context. Nor is such precision desirable. The broad range and peculiarities of public law regimes suggest that administration is not so much a science as a moral art.[52] Like any art, administration

---

re *Ashby et al* [1934] OR 421 (quoted enthusiastically by Cartwright J, as he then was, at 167–68 for the minority in *Roncarelli*, n 48), where he said at 428 that an administrative tribunal, within its province, is a 'law unto itself'.

[50] Two such theories come quickly to mind. One is Kant's view that persons must be treated with respect in that they must never be treated as mere means to another's ends. The other is Dworkin's theory of equality, a theory that prefers equality of respect to equality of outcome.
[51] This is the formulation Dyzenhaus uses to distinguish review of legality from review of correctness. Correctness review concerns itself with merely the coincidence of outcome between the primary decision-maker and the court, whereas review of legality concerns itself with the relationship between the reasons and the outcome of the decision. See D Dyzenhaus, 'Law as Justification: Etienne Mureinik's Conception of Legal Culture' (1998) 14 SAJHR 11 at 27–28.
[52] Fuller characterises administration as an enterprise, but his intent was to convey the sense in which the achievement of legal order is secured through the conscientious and purpose-driven efforts of public authorities. See eg: Fuller, n 30 at 91. I prefer 'art' because the term connotes

has normative features which present the artist with a value-laden framework within which to ply her craft and expertise. Hence, the major practices of administration—interpretation of constitutive or enabling statutes and discretionary decision-making—may be seen as the practices of a moral art oriented toward the fulfillment of purposive obligations.

When these practices manifest themselves in a transparent structure of justification, they let the affected individual know that public authority is not indifferent to her, and that such authority will be used to her detriment only if there are compelling reasons to justify it. In this way, giving reasons demonstrates respect for the autonomy and dignity of the individual, and to that extent exercises of public power live up to the democratic and equitable aspirations of legality.

Here I briefly introduce nine principles that are at least implicit in *Baker*, and which together comprise a rough guide to the internal morality of administration. There are surely more.[53] And conversely, in many cases the facts will be such that some of these principles do not apply. So, strictly speaking, the foregoing principles are not necessary conditions of an overarching principle of legality. Nor is any particular collection of them sufficient to guarantee that the demands of legality will be met in every case. Nevertheless, while the principles are not necessary and sufficient conditions of legality, they do represent a structure of justification that aspires to say to each person that he or she will be counted, and that it is in the equal dignity of each that the authorisation and trust enjoyed by public authority ultimately lies.

Evans JA's reasons in *Hawthorne* supply a good illustration of the first principle, a careful analysis and characterisation of the right or interest at stake. As in *Baker*, *Hawthorne* is a case of an individual who applies for relief against a deportation order based on humanitarian and compassionate considerations pursuant to subsection 114(2) of the *Immigration Act*. At the time of her application, Ms Hawthorne was a single mother whose 15-year-old daughter, Suzette (a permanent resident), lived with her and attended high school in Toronto. Because Suzette had come to Canada in 1999, after living in Jamaica and separated from her mother since 1992,

---

an activity with qualitative normative standards that guide the artist, but which leave ample room for interpretive judgment that is itself valuable, whereas 'enterprise' in this context is (needlessly) less committal.

[53] Issues of fraud, bias and legitimate expectations, for example, may arise independently. But the assumption here is that we have an administrator who seeks to make a fair and reasonable decision in good faith, and so the internal morality of administration is directed toward the benchmarks against which she can test the reasons of her good faith decision for fairness and reasonableness. Because legitimate expectation in Canada has been eclipsed by procedural fairness as a common law duty, I do not discuss it here. One place it could play a fruitful role, however, is in the determination of the weight to be given to fundamental values, discussed below.

the officer concluded that 'one cannot consider it a major hardship if she were to be separated from her again'.[54] Evans JA held that the officer mistook the relevant interest as an interest based on the harm Suzette would suffer considering her life circumstances prior to becoming a permanent resident in Canada, whereas the appropriate starting point was the best interests of Suzette (interests which included residence in Canada with her mother) at the time of the decision.[55] In virtue of the officer's mischaracterisation of the nature and importance of the interest at stake, Evans JA found that the decision-maker had failed to be alert, alive and sensitive to Suzette's best interests. He dismissed the appeal in Ms Hawthorne's favour, noting that because:

> the error identified in the officer's decision occurred before she weighed the H & C factors against law enforcement considerations, the statement in *Suresh* that *Baker* does not permit the Court to weigh the various factors is not germane to the disposition of this appeal.[56]

From Evans JA's reasons we may infer that the decision-maker must begin with a careful analysis and characterisation of the interest or right that is vulnerable to her exercise of discretion. As indicated above, relevant to the analysis and characterisation of the interest is the full legal context in which the decision is made, a context which includes international human rights instruments and soft law. And, as in *Baker*, we might expect some indication of the legal significance of the right or interest to flow from this analysis. For example, a decision-maker would contribute to the transparency of her deliberations if she indicates whether or not she thinks the interest embodies a fundamental value of Canadian society. This articulation of the vulnerable interest is a necessary starting point because, as we shall see, the remaining principles are triggered in virtue of that interest, as legality's response to the threat discretionary power poses to it. Without a fairly clear idea of the nature and importance of the interest at stake, it is difficult to say which factors and considerations may or may not justify its infringement. The subsequent principles, then, spell out the kinds of justificatory burdens a decision-maker must satisfy to infringe on critical interests and fundamental values.

The second principle is that any administrative decision which adversely affects interests critical to a person's future must be shown to be based on a policy which is compelling and substantial in light of the legislative purpose

---

[54] *Hawthorne*, n 29 at para 26.
[55] *Ibid* at paras 41–45. At para 44 Evans JA follows L'Heureux-Dubé J's example in a further respect, citing the *Convention on the Rights of the Child* for 'indirect guidance on the range of considerations that constitute the best interests of the child in the context of H & C [humanitarian and compassionate] applications'.
[56] *Ibid* at para 51.

it is intended to satisfy. At a minimum, we would expect there to be a rational connection between the administrative policy and the purpose of the legislation. This idea essentially captures the rule of law principle that public power may not be used for improper purposes or on the basis of irrelevant considerations.[57] For instance, in the context of immigration cases determined on the basis of humanitarian and compassionate considerations, a policy of sensitivity to the best interests of children has a clear and rational connection to the stated legislative objective of facilitating 'the reunion in Canada of Canadian citizens and permanent residents with their close relatives from abroad'.[58]

Thirdly, the policy on which the decision is based must satisfy a narrow proportionality requirement which ensures that the cure is not worse than the disease the policy is intended to remedy. As the pithy phrase goes, one should not use a steam hammer to crack a nut. For example, one disproportionate mismatch of means and ends would be a policy that sought to restrict immigration through a roundup and deportation of all visitors. A less extreme case would be a policy that urged rejection of subsection 114(2) applications if the individual were found to have depended on social assistance.[59]

Fourthly, there must be an effective consultation with the potentially affected individual or group. Consultation here is simply the right from procedural fairness to know the case one faces and to have an opportunity to respond. The opportunity may take the form of an oral hearing, but written submissions may also be sufficient, depending on the circumstances. In *Baker* L'Heureux-Dubé J made a point of this, upholding the administration's choice of procedure, and reiterating her dictum in *Knight*[60] that 'the concept of procedural fairness is eminently variable'.[61] Hence, Ms Baker could provide written submissions, but was not given an oral hearing.[62]

Fifthly, *Baker* also suggests that the decision-maker must consider seriously the views and arguments of the affected individual.[63] An adverse decision must indicate why the arguments presented were irrelevant or of

---

[57] See eg, *Roncarelli*, n 48 at 142.
[58] *Immigration Act*, s 3(c), cited by L'Heureux-Dubé J to make a similar point in *Baker*, n 2 at para 68.
[59] In *Baker*, n 2 at para 48, L'Heureux-Dubé J questions this sort of policy in her discussion of bias. Speaking to the content of the officer's notes, she finds that '[m]ost unfortunate is the fact that they seem to make a link between Ms Baker's mental illness, her training as a domestic worker, the fact that she has several children, and the conclusion that she would therefore be a strain on our social welfare system for the rest of her life'.
[60] *Knight v Indian Head School Division No 19* [1990] 1 SCR 653 [hereinafter *Knight*].
[61] *Ibid* at 682, cited in *Baker*, n 2 at para 21.
[62] *Baker*, n 2 at paras 30–34.
[63] See eg, *Ibid* at para 32, where L'Heureux-Dubé J says that part of procedural fairness involves giving the individual and others whose important interests are affected a 'meaningful opportunity to present the various types of evidence relevant to their case and have it fully and fairly considered'.

insufficient weight given countervailing considerations. It may be that the decision is unrelated to the person's competency or conduct, and based entirely on a broad policy (eg, reducing the size of the police force, cutting medical services, etc), but then the policy must be clearly stated. As well, there should be some explanation of why the decision is necessary for the policy to succeed.[64] Further, if there is some doubt as to the credibility of the individual's submissions, the decision-maker may owe the applicant a duty to investigate. Evans JA criticised the immigration officer in *Hawthorne* for not taking seriously Suzette's concern over the prospect of living with her estranged father, whom she believed had been charged with sexual abuse of his step-daughter. Evans JA found that 'given the relatively high procedural content of the duty of fairness owed by officers deciding H & C applications, the officer ought not to have rejected the submission without further inquiries'.[65]

Sixthly, a reasonable decision should minimally impair the important interest of the individual subject to it. The minimal impairment condition says that if two equally convenient means to the same end present themselves and one does less harm than the other, there can be no justification for the more injurious means. The administrator is presumed to exercise her powers for the public good, and so can have no reason to cause more harm than is necessary if doing so yields no further benefit to the public. The difficult cases, of course, are those where the public could conceivably derive some benefit from a means to an end that does more harm to the affected individual than an alternative. In those cases, the justification must explain why the benefit to the public at large outweighs the injury to those immediately affected. So, for example, if Canada wished to deport a person but the individual faced a serious risk of torture if deported to his place of origin (as would have been the facts in *Suresh* but for the Supreme Court reversing the decision of the Federal Court of Appeal), Canada would have an obligation to attempt to deport the individual to a third-party state where he would not face torture.

Seventhly, *Baker* tells us that the decision-maker must show an alert and attentive regard for fundamental values that inform the legal context in which the decision is made. As in *Baker*, evidence for these values and their relative importance to Canadian society may be inferred from a wide variety of sources, such as the object of the legislation, ministerial guidelines, and international law. But it is not the source *per se* that makes the fundamental value legally significant. Rather, it is the fact that the value embodies some important aspect of the public good that has achieved—or should achieve—recognition as a legal principle in the case at hand.

---

[64] As we shall see below, this is one of the three elements of the European test for proportionality.
[65] *Hawthorne*, n 29 at para 47.

In most cases where fundamental values are alleged to be at stake, the challenge will not be to cut an entirely new path of principle, but rather to determine and to characterise a recognised fundamental value in a manner that gives it the scope and weight appropriate to a particular decision-making context. Here, more than anywhere, the decision-maker must engage the issue as a moral artist sensitive to the dignity of those whose interests depend most on the characterisation and importance of the alleged fundamental value. The practical consequences of this endeavour are evident from the distinct approaches utilised, and outcomes reached, by Décary JA in *Legault (FCA)*, on the one hand, and Evans JA in *Hawthorne*, on the other.

Sensitivity to the human dignity to which fundamental values respond implies that if a decision infringes on a fundamental value, the decision-maker must clearly identify the public good to be secured at the expense of the value. Having made that initial identification, some argument must be given to show why the competing good takes priority over the infringed fundamental value.

It follows that fundamental values are always at least mandatory relevant considerations in the sense that decision-makers must always, in some fashion, take them into account.[66] If this is all they were, then in theory the decision-maker could satisfy the requirement to take them into account through a token mention of them or a box-ticking exercise. However, the justificatory burden outlined above suggests that they are primary considerations in the sense that they place a heavy onus on the decision-maker who seeks to infringe them. An official cannot simply engage in a box-ticking exercise and say that he has noted the affected party's interests and concerns, and here is his adverse decision. Within the reasons for the decision must be an argument—or at least an indication of an argument[67]—that can

---

[66] If fundamental values were merely relevant considerations, then the decision-maker would not be required to take them into account, since by definition they would not be 'mandatory'.

[67] Naturally, it is implausible to think that administrators must always produce reasons as nicely packaged as I suggest. This is why the full structure of justification is triggered only if important interests are at stake, interests critical to the lives of those affected. And even then, the test is not simply what reasons are in fact produced, but what reasons could be produced in defence of the decision. The internal morality of administration, then, applies as much to a reviewing court as it does to the administration. Thus, when lesser interests are at stake, the decision must still be justifiable, but the primary decision-maker's duty to articulate its justification may be less onerous. This may also be the case when the standard of review is patent unreasonableness rather than reasonableness. While I have expressly limited application of the internal morality to contexts where the standard of review is the reasonableness standard articulated in *Baker* and other cases, the generality of the arguments in favour of the internal morality may seem to suggest that it applies to discretionary decision-making contexts across the board, including where the standard of review is determined to be patent unreasonableness. If this is so, then it may be the case that the pragmatic and functional test for determining the standard of review will require rethinking, for review of patent unreasonableness would seem to collapse into review of reasonableness. And even if the collapse is resisted by assuming that the difference between review of reasonableness and patent unreasonableness respectively is a difference in *intensity* and *degree* of scrutiny rather than a difference in the *kind* of review

stand up to a 'somewhat probing examination' on the issue of whether the decision discloses a satisfactory justification for infringing a fundamental value.[68]

Eighth, as we have seen in *Baker* and *Hawthorne*, the decision-maker must take account of the norms and provisions contained in any relevant international human rights instruments. This inquiry may be subsumed within the broader inquiry into fundamental values, but is valuable in its own right for the purposes of both interpreting domestic legislation and making discretionary decisions whenever critical interests are engaged. Ratification and incorporation are significant, but only in the sense that they increase the justificatory burden the administration must discharge to infringe on values contained within the instrument.

Ratification increases the burden because it is unconscionable to imagine that an administration entrusted to act solely for the public good may announce its commitment to human rights through ratification and then, without more, betray that commitment in its decision-making practices.[69]

Incorporation of an international instrument into domestic legislation raises the bar further, since Parliament has in effect declared its intention to enact laws consistent with the instrument. Thus, only a very substantial justification will suffice, since the instrument assumes an explicit constitutional character.[70]

---

that is undertaken (ie the justificatory structure within which review occurs is largely the same in both contexts), supposing that the kind of review sanctioned in *Baker* may be extended to review of patent unreasonability is a significant extension of *Baker*. Arguably, this extension stands in some tension with the current understanding of the pragmatic and functional test. I do not pursue this further here.

[68] The standard of a 'somewhat probing examination' was reaffirmed by Evans JA in *Hawthorne*, n 29 at para 34, as the intensity of review to be applied to determine the reasonableness of an immigration officer's consideration of the best interests of the child. The non-box-ticking approach to reasons has found additional support in *Via Rail Canada Inc v National Transportation Agency* [2001] 2 FC 25 (FCA) where Sexton JA said at 36 that '[t]he obligation to provide adequate reasons is not satisfied by merely reciting the submissions and evidence of the parties and stating a conclusion. Rather, the decision maker must set out its findings of fact and the principal evidence upon which those findings were based. The reasons must address the major points in issue. The reasoning process followed by the decision maker must be set out and must reflect consideration of the main relevant factors'. See also *Gray v Director of the Ontario Disability Support Program* [2002] OJ No 1531 (CA), where the Ontario Court of Appeal reversed a tribunal for failing to explain the reasoning process that had led the tribunal to reject Ms Gray's application for disability benefits. McMurtry CJO at para 23 found the tribunal's reasons to be lacking because it was 'simply unclear what relevant evidence the Tribunal accepted and what it rejected'.

[69] On this point, see M Moran, 'Authority, Influence and Persuasion: *Baker*, *Charter* Values and the Puzzle of Method', ch 15 of this volume.

[70] In Canada, the instrument would have authority comparable to the pre-*Charter Bill of Rights*, and we might expect the debate over Parliamentary sovereignty to resurface with regard to whether Parliament through ordinary legislation can bind itself and future Parliaments.

Note, however, that because international human rights instruments articulate norms that seek to crystallise respect for human dignity, a decision-maker ought to give some account of any measure that would infringe them, regardless of whether or not ratification or incorporation has taken place.[71] In principle, the justification may be put in terms of an explicit denial that a particular provision of an instrument reflects an underlying legal value or an aspect of the public good. But one kind of justification that is not open to the administration is the retort that the instrument is irrelevant because neither ratification nor incorporation have occurred. This retort presupposes that the appropriate attitude of public authority to human rights is indifference unless there is a positive statutory indication to the contrary, and so to that extent it betrays the trust and authority the administration enjoys to exercise its powers in a manner sensitive to human dignity.

Lastly, as L'Heureux-Dubé J points out in *Baker*, while soft law is not in a strict sense binding on decision-makers, it is 'of great assistance' in determining what will count as a reasonable exercise of discretion.[72] So one would expect the decision-maker to take account of relevant policy guidelines, directives and practices, and to justify divergences from them. Soft law translates judicial standards of necessarily general application into context-sensitive instructions of greater specificity for front-line decision-makers. As Sossin observes, soft law is especially important where broad discretionary authority is concerned, and doubly so where the decision-maker is instructed to consider whether in the circumstances a value as amorphous as compassion provides a sufficient reason to exempt an applicant from deportation.[73] Where the rule of law becomes, in effect, the rule of policy, decision-makers must explain departures from it.

If the reasons for the decision satisfy (or could satisfy) this requirement and the others that together constitute the internal morality of administration, then we have the basis for a strong presumption that the decision-maker has acted with a due regard for the impartiality, fairness and reasonableness one ought to expect of a public body entrusted to act exclusively for the public good.

This initial presumption suggests that a measure of deference is due. And while the presumption is rebuttable, its basis implies that a reviewing court will have to discharge a significant burden to overcome it. A court that set aside a decision without discharging its burden would put as great a strain on legality as a primary decision-maker who breached her duty to give reasons by simply failing to do so.

---

[71] In this regard, it is worth noting that in the wake of *Baker* even judges who ultimately deny the domestic effect or relevance of international law nevertheless take pains to show that their reasons conform to it. See, for example, the judgment of Robertson JA for the Federal Court of Appeal in *Suresh*.
[72] *Baker*, n 2 at para 72.
[73] See Sossin, n 10.

ANALAGOUS STRUCTURES OF JUSTIFICATION

The internal morality of administration is not especially novel. Similar structures of justification may be found in the European doctrine of proportionality, as well as in Canadian constitutional law. I briefly discuss proportionality and *Oakes* to underscore the similarity of the structural features they share with the internal morality. My hope in this regard is to suggest that the internal morality just applies a familiar justificatory framework to a new range of cases, those involving critical interests and fundamental values in which the individual may have no statutory or pre-existent rights.

The structure of justification most familiar to Canadian lawyers is the analytical framework based on the test laid out in *Oakes* to determine whether a piece of infringing legislation can be saved by section one of the *Charter*.[74] In *Oakes*, the Supreme Court established a two stage test for determining whether impugned legislation could be saved by section one.[75]

First, the Crown must establish that the objective of the legislation is 'pressing and substantial', or 'of sufficient importance' to be capable of justifying an infringement of a constitutional right.

Secondly, the Crown must satisfy a three part proportionality requirement with respect to the intended means to achieve the objective. There must be a rational connection between the means and the objective in the sense that the means must not be arbitrary. In addition, the limiting measure must impair the right as little as possible (the minimal impairment condition). And lastly, there must be a sense of proportionality between the limiting measure and the objective it is intended to secure (proportionality in the narrow sense). In *Oakes*, then, we find an analytical framework that has much in common with the internal morality.

The European proportionality principle has its origins in German administrative law, and has three parts, as summarised by Jurgen Schwarze:[76]

(1) the measure must be appropriate for attaining the objective;
(2) it must be necessary, in the sense that no other measure is available which is less restrictive of freedom;
(3) the measure must not be disproportionate to its aim (proportionality in the narrower sense).

---

[74] Section one of the *Charter* stipulates the following: 'The *Canadian Charter of Rights and Freedoms* guarantees the rights and freedoms set out in it subject only to such reasonable limits prescribed by law as can be demonstrably justified in a free and democratic society'.
[75] *Oakes*, n 35 at 138–42.
[76] Jurgen Schwarze, *European Administrative Law* (London, Sweet & Maxwell, 1992) at p 687, cited in Francis G Jacobs, 'Recent Developments in the Principle of Proportionality in European Community Law', in Ellis (ed), n 36 at 1.

As stated above, the principle concerns itself strictly with the means adopted to achieve a legislative end or objective. There is nothing here that licenses a court to review the objective. But in Britain, proportionality seems to have assumed a wider compass.

Paul Craig characterises the third part of the test as an inquiry into simply whether the measure imposes 'excessive burdens on the individual, (the proportionality inquiry in the narrow sense)'.[77] Craig insists that:

> [t]here will be instances where, even though a measure is suited and necessary to attain the end in view, it is felt none the less that the burden on those affected is simply too great.[78]

The difference between Craig's formulation and Schwarze's is subtle but important. The Craig formula but not Schwarze's says that political ends cannot be pursued if doing so would impose excessive burdens on the individual. Whereas Schwarze's conception limits proportionality inquiry to a formal consideration of the relationship between means and ends, Craig's view imposes a substantive limit on the kinds of ends public authority may adopt. The rationale for the substantive limit is that human dignity precludes unilaterally imposing extreme hardship on individuals for the sake of a policy goal.

The internal morality favours Craig's approach, for it is animated by the idea that public bodies are entrusted and authorised to exercise their powers strictly for the public good, consistent with respect for dignity, and so there are some ends to which their powers cannot be put. Moreover, within the ambit of permissible ends, those ends themselves must be shown to be compelling if pursuing them necessarily entails prejudice to a critical interest or a fundamental value. So in this sense too the internal morality looks beyond the means, and to the policy's objective, in order to demand justification of any objective that entails an excessive burden.

I turn now to two objections to the internal morality and the kind of approach it presupposes.

WHAT IS REASONABLE? VS WHO DECIDES?

As we have seen in *Suresh* and *Legault*, a familiar complaint against any proposal that appears to expand the grounds of judicial review is that it threatens to let judges substitute their view of the merits for the view of the primary decision-maker. The fundamental issue, it is alleged, is not a determination

---

[77] Craig, n 36 at 99–100.
[78] *Ibid*, at 101.

of what is reasonable, but rather one of who decides, the courts or the legislature's delegates. As Lord Hoffmann puts it:

> No minister, accused of an irrational exercise of power, responds by denying that he is obliged to act rationally.... The minister's answer is that in his opinion his action has been rational and proportional. The application of the principle [of proportionality] is common to both sides: the true issue is whether the court should accept the minister's judgment that his action complies with the principle or impose its own view of the matter. This is the heart of any problem of judicial review.[79]

However, there are several things that may be said to allay the worry that review based on either proportionality or the internal morality implies an illegitimate review of the merits.

First, one of the virtues of the internal morality is that it requires decision-makers to express very clearly the reasons for their determinations, including the reasons taken to justify the weight and importance they have attributed to policy objectives. This exercise in reason-giving contributes to the transparency of the decision-making process, and with transparency comes a decreased likelihood that decisions will contain reviewable errors of fact and of law.[80]

Secondly, when primary decision-makers justify their decisions along the lines suggested by the internal morality, they make it more rather than less difficult for a court to set them aside, for the decision-maker creates a presumption that the reviewing court must overcome to show that the reasons offered fail to justify the decision. Put slightly differently, reasons embody in an objective and public form the substantive rationale for deference, since they permit the decision-maker to showcase the expertise and institutional competence that make her fit to reconcile the requirements of the rule of law with the relevant policy goals. Making essentially the same point in *Southam*, Iacobucci J quotes approvingly RP Kerans' view of the connection between expertise and reasons:

> Experts, in our society, are called that precisely because they can arrive at well-informed and rational conclusions. If that is so, they should be able to

---

[79] The Rt Hon Lord Hoffmann, 'The Influence of the European Principle of Proportionality upon UK Law' in Ellis (ed), n 36 at p 109.
[80] In *Baker*, n 2 at para 39, L'Heureux-Dubé J endorses the idea that reasons 'foster better decision making by ensuring that issues and reasoning are well articulated and, therefore, more carefully thought out. The process of writing reasons for a decision by itself may be a guarantee of a better decision'. Speaking to the transparency reasons afford, at para 38 she cites Estey J's dictum on the desirability of reasons from *Northwestern Utilities Ltd v City of Edmonton* [1979] 1 SCR 684 at 706: 'It reduces to a considerable degree the chances of arbitrary or capricious decisions, reinforces public confidence in the judgment and fairness of administrative tribunals, and affords parties to administrative proceedings an opportunity to assess the question of appeal...'.

explain, to a fair-minded but less well-informed observer, the reasons for their conclusions. If they cannot, they are not very expert. If something is worth knowing and relying upon, it is worth telling. Expertise commands deference only when the expert is coherent. Expertise loses a right to deference when it is not defensible. That said, it seems obvious that [appellate courts] manifestly *must give great weight* to cogent views thus articulated. (Emphasis added by Iacobucci J in *Southam*.)[81]

Thirdly, to characterise the 'heart of any problem of judicial review' as simply an issue of who decides is to oversimplify drastically the problem of articulating an adequate conception of judicial review. Telling judges that the central issue they need to resolve is whether or not they have review authority tells them nothing about how that authority ought to be exercised. In other words, determining who decides tells us nothing about what counts as a reasonable decision.

Fourthly, and related, to frame the issue as one of who decides is to assert the nihilist or legal void thesis that administration, within its province, is a law unto itself. Just under the surface of 'who decides' is Dicey's scepticism of the legitimacy of the administrative state, ie, scepticism that within administration legal standards operate at all. But the nihilist view is at deep odds with *Baker*, even on the 'process' interpretation.

Fifthly, if the legislature wishes to infringe on fundamental and common law values the courts have protected, generally it can do so through legislation that uses clear and express language. Parliament is sovereign in this respect, but it must be clear that it intends to trump entitlements that have found recognition in the courts.

Finally, the methodology that animates the 'pragmatic and functional' approach to determining the standard of review, a methodology driven by sensitivity to legal context, may be used by judges to determine more than simply whether they should review on a standard of correctness, reasonableness or patent unreasonableness. Sensitivity to the full legal context within which a decision is made may also let judges determine the intensity and nature of review *within* reasonableness itself. I explain and defend this claim immediately below, within a broader discussion regarding the legality/merits distinction.

WHAT IS LEFT OF LEGALITY/MERITS?

A separate objection from the one concerning the threat of judicial activism takes us back to where we started, with the problem of understanding *Baker* in a way that still leaves room for the distinction between review of

---

[81] RP Kerans, *Standards of Review Employed by Appellate Courts* (Edmonton, Juriliber, 1994) at 17, cited in *Southam*, n 37 at para 62.

legality and review of the merits. One might think that the intensity of review mandated by the internal morality is so severe that the distinction between legality and merits cannot survive.

All that cannot survive, however, is a rigid mapping of relevance and weight onto legality and merits. As noted above, one important and legally relevant factor within a decision-making context may be the weight that a particular consideration deserves. Now, as a rule, primary responsibility for assigning weight lies with the primary decision-maker. But there may be circumstances, such as those in *Baker*, where the evidence from the full legal context suggests that the decision-maker must give substantial weight to factors such as fundamental values and critical interests.

Part of the difficulty in articulating a conception of judicial review that can include review of weight in appropriate circumstances, however, lies in the dominant approach to decision-making in public law. The dominant approach conceives of the decision-maker as engaged chiefly in the balancing of competing social interests. Call this the balancing paradigm. The issue of weight becomes problematic because weighing factors against one another is inherent to the idea of balancing, and as we saw in *Suresh* and *Legault*, the view of many judges is that they should resist getting caught up in the messy contingencies of determining weight. Issues of weight admit of few bright lines because weight is something that applies as a matter of degree. Relevance, it seems, is much sharper, for one can say flat out whether or not a factor is a relevant consideration.

Be that as it may, there is no reason to think that legality is incompatible with messy concepts that lack bright lines. Laskin CJ's rejection of the quasi-judicial/administrative distinction, a distinction that had been used to determine whether the rules of natural justice run, was premised on the idea that:

> the classification of statutory functions as judicial, quasi-judicial or administrative is often very difficult, to say the least; and to endow some with procedural protection while denying others any at all would work injustice when the results of the statutory decisions raise the same serious consequences for those adversely affected.[82]

So, the reach of the duty of fairness was extended, in part, just because bright lines are hard to come by in public law.[83]

Furthermore, there is reason to think that the considerations that suggest deference to the primary decision-maker's determinations of weight may

---

[82] *Nicholson v Haldimand-Norfolk Regional Board of Commissioners of Police* [1979] 1 SCR 62 at 137.
[83] Another case that involves balancing and few bright lines is the 'pragmatic and functional' test for the standard of review, where judges must consider and weigh contextual factors against one another.

also apply to her determinations of what is to count as a relevant factor. L'Heureux-Dubé J makes this point in *Baker*: 'deferential standards of review may give substantial leeway to the discretionary decision-maker in determining the "proper purposes" or "relevant considerations" involved in making a given determination'.[84] So even within the balancing paradigm, so long as it takes deference seriously, there is reason to think that review of weight in certain circumstances is not as problematic as it is sometimes taken to be.

The starting point for the balancing paradigm is the view that all relevant factors can (and should) be weighed against one another. No factor in and of itself is necessarily more important than any other, and this explains why Décary JA in *Legault (FCA)* thought it wise to eject the 'best' from 'children's best interests'. It is not the individual's right to a reasonable decision that occupies centre stage, but rather an inquiry into whether the decision itself is reasonable, with the individual's interest figuring as just one of the relevant considerations.

The rights-oriented approach taken by the internal morality, on the other hand, does start from the perspective of the individual's right to a reasonable decision. This starting point has the salutary effect of inherently extending and limiting review to those factors which must be taken into account to determine the precise nature and content of the right to reasonableness in the circumstances. The internal morality is well-suited to this kind of rights-based inquiry, since the justificatory burden it imposes is one that must be satisfied relative to the protected interest the administration would infringe with an adverse decision. By sharpening inquiry to focus on the case-specific nature and content of a right to reasonableness, we engage directly the legal dimension of the individual's threatened interest.

Within the rights model, the right to reasonableness is there from the outset as a matter of principle, a function of the trust and authority enjoyed by public authority to exercise power exclusively for the public good. The specific content of the duty of reasonableness may vary considerably from case to case, depending on the interest and the underlying values at stake, as well as contextual considerations. But the nature of the inquiry into the content of the duty is quite different than one concerned primarily with making a tally of all the relevant factors, assigning them each a certain weight, and then balancing one off against the other. In a rights-based analysis, the starting point is an assumption that reasonableness is due as a matter of right, and that part of what reasonableness means is that any impairment of a critical interest or infringement of a fundamental value must be accompanied by a substantive justification that makes explicit (among other things) both the reason for the infringement and the efforts made to minimise it.

---

[84] *Baker*, n 2 at 56.

Now, within the rights paradigm judges will sometimes have to engage in some form of balancing as they strive to determine the appropriate content of the individual's right to reasonableness, since the content of the right is simply the justificatory burden that must be overcome to infringe on the protected interest. So the difference between the rights model and the balancing paradigm is one of starting points, and of emphasis and degree. But it is also one of overall approach, since the rights model alone looks to the relevant factors at play for the sole purpose of characterising the nature and content of the individual's lawful entitlement to reasonableness.

The singularness of this purpose underwrites the distinction between review of legality and review on the merits. Thus, for example, on the merits a decision may be questionable because of its impact on the environment, or perhaps because it may adversely affect third-parties unrepresented at trial and with no connection to the complainant. However, these are considerations beyond the scope of a court reviewing the reasonableness of a decision with respect to a particular individual because these considerations, while related to the merits all things considered, are irrelevant to an inquiry into the specific content of this particular individual's right to reasonableness.

Within the range of factors that are relevant to the content of the individual's right to reasonableness are those which inform the full legal context within which the decision is made, since the context supplies indications of what counts as a reasonable decision. In this regard, considerations of soft law and international human rights are relevant to the weight of the justificatory burden that an official must discharge, and thus they inform the content of the individual's actual right to reasonableness in the circumstances. So long as a court connects its evaluation of the weight the primary decision-maker gives to a particular factor with an articulation of the individual's right to reasonableness in the circumstances—ie, the individual's right to receive reasons that satisfy a certain justificatory threshold—there is reason to suppose that the court conducts its review within the confines of legality. And conversely, so long as the decision-maker's justification engages the full legal context such that it can stand up to a 'somewhat probing examination', the decision conforms with the rule of law regardless of whether a reviewing court would have reached a different outcome all things considered.

CONCLUSION

I have argued that administrative law does not need to reinvent public law to live up to the democratic, substantive and equitable aspirations that *Baker* sets for it. We can look to other instances where public law imposes structures of justification to reconcile the demands of human dignity with the need for governance. These include the European test for proportionality and the *Oakes* test. The internal morality of administration borrows from these in an effort to ensure that the reasons for the exercise of public power are justified and made known to those most vulnerable to it.

In a sense, Nadon J is correct in saying that there is no easy answer to the question of what it means to be alert, alive and sensitive to fundamental values. None the less, what the internal morality and the rights approach attempt to do is establish a framework within which decision-makers and courts alike may justify their decisions in a manner that pays close attention to the demands of legality, while leaving responsibility for the merits with the officials entrusted to consider them.

7

The State of Law's Borders and the Law of States' Borders

AUDREY MACKLIN

INTRODUCTION

A CASUAL SURVEY of Canadian jurisprudence about the application of international human rights norms in domestic law will quickly reveal two tendencies. First, most case law emerges from the administrative realm and secondly, most of those administrative cases concern some aspect of immigration or refugee law. *Baker v Canada (Minister of Citizenship and Immigration)*[1] is no longer even the most recent example of this trend.[2] This trend is true not only of Canada but also of New Zealand, Australia and even England. Significantly, the first three jurisdictions understand themselves to be 'countries of immigration', and all partake broadly in the British common law tradition in respect of judicial review of government action and the domestic incorporation of international law.[3] Canada is unique among the three in possessing an entrenched *Charter of Rights of Freedoms*,[4] which provides a third metric of human rights norms against which courts evaluate state conduct.[5]

---

[1] [1999] 2 SCR 817 [hereafter *Baker*].
[2] See *Suresh v Canada (Minister of Citizenship and Immigration)* [2002] 1 SCR 3, and *Ahani v Canada (Attorney General)* (2002) 58 OR (3d) 107, discussed below.
[3] The United States' approach to both spheres of law is distinct: Though a land of immigration, its 'plenary powers' doctrine has a peculiarly insulating effect on judicial scrutiny of immigration law. The constitutional structure of government in the US also differentiates that country's doctrine regarding domestic application of international law. For its part, the UK conceives of itself less as a country of immigration, which perhaps account for the relative under-representation of immigration cases in its jurisprudence.
[4] Part I of the *Constitution Act 1982*, being Schedule B of the *Canada Act*, 1982 (UK) 1982, c 11 [hereafter *Charter*].
[5] The UK Human Rights Act 1998 obliges British courts to respect the European Convention on Human Rights. S 3 requires courts to 'interpret legislation so as to uphold [European Convention on Human Rights] unless the legislation itself is so clearly incompatible with the Convention that it is impossible to do so'. S 4 authorises courts to make a declaration of incompatibility where no compatible interpretation is possible, but such declaration neither invalidates the legislation nor binds the parties.

Why do so many of the cases raising international human rights law before the courts emerge from the field of immigration and refugee law? One reason is that immigration and refugee lawyers are more likely than other lawyers to raise the arguments. This point is not entirely banal: the very subject of immigration and refugee law enlarges one's horizons beyond national borders to the global realm. Over the years, a small but intrepid coterie of immigration and refugee lawyers have educated themselves about Canada's international human rights undertakings. Where Canadian courts have rendered adverse decisions, these lawyers have not hesitated to approach the United Nations Human Rights Committee, or the Organization of American States' Inter-American Commission on Human Rights in order to lodge complaints against Canada. Some of these lawyers have also established links with advocates in other jurisdictions, and can access jurisprudence from other supra-national jurisdictions, such as the European Court of Human Rights.

In addition to taking Canada to court in the international arena, these same lawyers have brought international law to Canadian courts. Despite right-wing rhetoric proclaiming that the *Charter* pries open Canadian borders to all comers, the *Charter* remains a national constitutional document, rooted in a historic liberal tradition where membership in the nation-state (as evinced in the juridical status of citizenship) is the pre-requisite to the enjoyment of rights and liberties. Of course, the *Charter* is also the product of post-World War II human rights consciousness, where entitlement to fundamental rights is predicated on the moral equality and dignity of all human beings. The erratic pattern traced by *Charter* cases involving non-citizens manifests the tension between these two visions. Sometimes, the Supreme Court of Canada seems downright solicitous of the interests of non-citizens, particularly those with professional qualifications and, most recently, persons facing torture or the death penalty.[6] At other moments, the Court seems almost disdainful of non-citizens' attempts to assert their entitlement to rights.[7]

The social and legal status of non-citizens has certainly not benefited from the events of 11 September 2001. Nine months after the attack on the World Trade Center, the Supreme Court of Canada heard the appeals of two refugees ordered deported from Canada, one on grounds that he fundraised for a terrorist organisation, the other because he directly engaged in terrorism. The judgments in *Suresh v Canada (Minister of Citizenship and Immigration)*[8] and *Ahani v Canada (Minister of Citizenship and Immigration)*[9] attempt to

---

[6] See, eg, *Singh v Canada (Minister of Employment and Immigration)*, [1985] 1 SCR 177; *Andrews v Law Society of British Columbia*, [1989] 1 SCR 143, *United States v Burns*, [2001] 1 SCR 283.
[7] See, eg, *Canada (Minister of Employment and Immigration) v Chiarelli*, [1992] 1 SCR 711; *Dehghani v Canada (Minister of Employment and Immigration)*, [1993] 1 SCR 1053; *Lavoie v Canada*, [2002] 1 SCR 769.
[8] See above n 2.
[9] [2002] 1 SCR 72.

balance the prohibition on returning a person to face torture against putative threats to national security. The decision in *Suresh* reads as a victory for human rights to the extent that the Supreme Court of Canada rules that a person should virtually never be deported to another country to face a substantial risk of torture. The companion case of *Ahani*, however, tells a different story, by assuring the executive that the courts will be very deferential in reviewing the Minister's determination of whether the person concerned actually faces a substantial risk of torture: the *Charter* giveth, administrative law taketh away.

The point is that non-citizens remain foreigners to national rights protection in important ways, whether by explicit exclusion from the ambit of protection or by eviscerating the right of any meaningful content, or by circumscribing access to judicial review of rights-limiting state action. Conversely, every individual is a full 'citizen' of the human community defined under international human rights law simply by virtue of being human, and is therefore entitled to the equal protection of those norms. When immigration lawyers invoke international law in aid of a *Charter* challenge, they call upon on the cosmopolitan antecedents of the *Charter*. When they invoke international law directly in aid of statutory interpretation, they encourage the internalisation of universal normative commitments within the national legal frame.

Prior to the *Charter*, the relationship between domestic law and international law was intelligible, if not ideal. The advent of the *Charter* has ruptured this dyad, however, and supplanted it with three relationships where once there was one. Instead of international law/domestic law, we must now contend with administrative law/international law, *Charter*/administrative law, and *Charter*/international law. Each of these dyads submits to its own internal logic, and the rules of mobility between regimes. Yet the three dyads do not triangulate. For example, the rules governing the relationship between administrative law and international law disrupt the coherence of the rules governing the relationship between the *Charter* and administrative law, and so on. The result is a legal ordering of administrative law, the *Charter*, and international law that is at best, disjointed, and at worst, irreconcilable. Like the migrants whose lives become the site for this discursive wrangling, we find that boundaries are at once porous, arbitrary and highly contested.

THREE RELATIONSHIPS THAT (SORT OF) WORK

Administrative Law and International Law

Statutory interpretation is formally constrained by the doctrine of parliamentary supremacy, as expressed by the premise that giving effect to the intention of the legislature drives the process of interpretation. Where the language of the statute expressly or by implication conflicts with a rule of common law, the former prevails. In construing a statutory provision (or, more commonly, in construing statutory silence), judges may resort to Canada's international legal obligations to fill the gap. Where an international treaty has been incorporated into Canadian law, the implementing statute must be interpreted in a manner consistent with the international obligation. Even where an international norm has not been implemented, it should inform the task of statutory interpretation. In *Baker*, L'Heureux-Dubé J cites with approval the following maxim:

> [T]he legislature is presumed to respect the values and principles enshrined in international law, both customary and conventional. These constitute a part of the legal context in which legislation is enacted and read. *In so far as possible, therefore, interpretations that reflect these values and principles are preferred.* [Emphasis in judgment.][10]

The question as to whether a given statute incorporates an international norm arises at various points in Canadian immigration legislation. Section 97 of the *Immigration and Refugee Protection Act*[11] (IRPA) incorporates by reference the definition of torture as contained in the *Convention Against Torture*. Section 96 reproduces almost verbatim the *UN Convention Relating to the Status of Refugees* (the *Refugee Convention*) definition of a refugee, while section 98 replicates the provisions excluding an applicant from the scope of that definition. These should provide uncontroversial illustrations of incorporation. However, the IRPA provisions governing *refoulement* (removal of a refugee to the country of his/her nationality) do not replicate the language of Article 33 of the *Refugee Convention*,[12] and it seems clear that the IRPA erects fewer impediments to *refoulement* than does the *Refugee Convention*.

Section 3(3)(h) of IRPA is both the most general and the most expansive of the provisions addressing international law. It provides that the IRPA shall be 'construed and applied in a manner that ... complies with international

---

[10] See Baker, above n 1, at para 70, quoting Ruth Sullivan, *Driedger on the Construction of Statutes* 3rd edn, (Butterworths, Markham, 1994), at 330.
[11] SCC 2001, c 27.
[12] 1. No Contracting State shall expel or return ('refouler') a refugee in any manner whatsoever to the frontiers of territories where his life or freedom would be threatened on account of his race, religion, nationality, membership or a particular social group or opinion.
  2. The benefit of the present provision may not, however, be claimed by a refugee whom there are reasonable grounds for regarding as a danger to the security of the country in which he is, or who, having been convicted by a final judgment of a particularly serious crime, constitutes a danger to the community of that country.

human rights instruments to which Canada is signatory'. This guide to statutory construction requires judges to interpret the IRPA consistent with Canada's international legal obligations, whether or not they have been formally incorporated into domestic law. Apart from the *Refugee Convention*, the *Convention Against Torture*[13] (CAT), the *Convention on the Rights of the Child*,[14] the *International Covenant on Civil and Political Rights*[15] (ICCPR) and the *Optional Protocol*[16] are the most significant international instruments binding on Canada that purport to constrain the power to remove a non-citizen.

Some contributors in this volume disagree about the weight Mme Justice L'Heureux-Dubé attaches to international law in *Baker* as a tool for interpreting the *Immigration Act*, the predecessor to the IRPA. The stronger version, as articulated by Moran, views Canada's unincorporated international obligations as influential legal authority. On this reading, the values expressed by an international instrument demand attention and assert justificatory force, even if the precise articulation of the value does not bind. Thus, in *Baker*, the 'best interests of the child' standard expressed in the *Convention on the Rights of the Child* constitutes a norm that demands attention and justifies an exercise of humanitarian and compassionate discretion consistent with that value. However, since the *Convention on the Rights of the Child* is not incorporated into Canadian law, the requirement under Article 3(1) that the best interests of the child be 'a primary consideration' in decisions affecting children does not bind Canadian decision-makers. This means that the Court can take the international *Convention on the Rights of the Child* into account by chastising the decision maker for failing to attend to 'the best interests of the child', while declining to endorse the rule that the best interests be 'a primary consideration'.

The weaker version, as endorsed by Brunnée and Toope, sees *Baker* as deploying Canada's international obligations under the *Convention on the Rights of the Child* as one (but only one) source of guidance in interpreting the statutory grant of humanitarian and compassionate discretion. On this reading, the Court adopted the 'best interests of the child' standard but veered away from the specific requirement that it be a 'primary consideration' simply because it was persuaded by the former, but not by the latter. Moran, on the other hand suggests that the general norm asserts greater force than its precise formulation under Article 3(1) because of its quality as a fundamental value.

---

[13] Convention against Torture and Other Cruel, Inhuman or Degrading Treatment or Punishment, G.A. res. 39/46, 39 U.N. GAOR Supp. (No 51) at 197, U.N. Doc. A/39/51 (1984).
[14] Can. T.S. 1992 No 3.
[15] 999 UNTS 171.
[16] 999 UNTS 302, entered into force 23 March 1976.

I confess to greater sympathy for Brunnée and Toope's analysis of Justice L'Heureux-Dubé's judgment.[17] Before turning to international law, L'Heureux-Dube J declares that '[c]hildren's rights, and attention to their interests, are central humanitarian and compassionate values in Canadian society',[18] thus signalling that international law was not the only, or even the most compelling, source of the norm. The distinctive contribution that the *Convention on the Rights of the Child* could make to the analysis is the elevation of that interest to 'a primary consideration' in all actions concerning children. The deliberate and conspicuous choice not to endorse this aspect of the *Convention on the Rights of the Child* reveals, in my view, less respect for the influential role of international law than Moran would claim, and rather more of the instrumentalist approach described by Brunnée and Toope.

Significantly, the *Immigration Act* (the predecessor to the IRPA) was silent about the role of international law as an interpretive aid. However, the IRPA arguably imposes a stricter duty on decision-makers. As noted earlier, section 3(3) of the IRPA instructs decision-makers to interpret and apply the legislation such that it 'complies with international human rights instruments to which Canada is a signatory'. Section 3(3) contains five other principles of statutory interpretation, but none are phrased in the mandatory language of compliance.[19] Except in situations where the legislative provision simply does not admit of ambiguity, it would seem that Canada's obligations at international law—be they general or specific, incorporated or not—will henceforth bind judges in their interpretive function under the IRPA. To make the point concrete, I would argue that nothing in the language of the statutory grant of humanitarian and compassionate discretion, and no other principle guiding the interpretation of the IRPA, prevents or precludes interpreting humanitarian and compassionate discretion

---

[17] On the one hand, L'Heureux-Dubé J supports using the Convention on the Rights of the Child to set the parameters on the scope of discretion. On the other hand, she conspicuously refrains from adopting the specific language of Art 3 of the *Convention on the Rights of the Child*, which states that 'the best interests of the child shall be a primary consideration'. I infer from this a reluctance to give international law the appearance of carrying decisive weight.
[18] See above n 1, para 67.
[19] In addition to the reference to international law, sub-section 3(3) of IRPA directs decision-makers to interpret the statute in a manner that:

(a) furthers the domestic and international interests of Canada
(b) promotes accountability and transparency by enhancing public awareness of immigration and refugee programs;
(c) facilitates cooperation between the Government of Canada, provincial governments, foreign states, international organizations and non-governmental organizations;
(d) ensures that decisions taken under this Act are consistent with the *Canadian Charter of Rights and Freedoms*, including its principles of equality and freedom from discrimination and of the equality of English and French as the official languages of Canada;
(e) supports the commitment of the Government of Canada to enhance the vitality of the English and French linguistic minority communities in Canada; ...

to comply with the duty in the Convention on the Rights of the Child to make the best interests of the child 'a primary consideration'. If I am correct on this point, Canada's obligation to abide by its international obligations has been considerably strengthened by the particularly statutory language of the IRPA, which neither incorporates the *Convention on the Rights of the Child*, nor ignores it.

The *Charter* and International Law

Since the entrenchment of the *Charter* in 1982, claims by non-citizens have gradually been telescoped into the equality provision under section 15 and section 7,[20] subject of course to the limiting provision under section 1. For present purposes, section 7 and section 1 are most pertinent:

> 7. Everyone has the right to life, liberty and security of the person, and the right not to be deprived thereof except in accordance with the principles of fundamental justice.
>
> ...
>
> 1. The Canadian *Charter* of Rights and Freedoms guarantees the rights and freedoms set out in it subject only to such reasonable limits prescribed by law as can be demonstrably justified in a free and democratic society.

In the course of giving meaning to these rights and limitations, Canadian courts have opted to enfold international human rights norms into the domestic constitutional sphere on a tentative, selective basis. The effect is to preserve enough judicial space to invoke international law when it is instrumentally useful, while leaving enough 'wiggle room' to avoid being bound by it when it is not. This is particularly true in relation to *Charter* interpretation, as typified by the remarks of the late Chief Justice Dickson:

> [T]hough I do not believe the judiciary is bound by the norms of international law in interpreting the *Charter*, these norms provide a relevant and persuasive source for interpretation of the provisions of the *Charter*, especially when they arise out of Canada's international obligations under human rights conventions.[21]

In virtually the same breath, Dickson CJ expresses the view that 'the *Charter* should generally be presumed to provide protection at least as great

---

[20] 15. (1) Every individual is equal before and under the law and has the right to the equal protection and equal benefit of the law without discrimination and, in particular, without discrimination based on race, national or ethnic origin, colour, religion, sex, age or mental or physical disability.

[21] *In the Matter of a Reference re Public Service Employee Relations Act (Alta)*, [1987] 1 SCR 313, 349–50.

as that afforded by similar provisions in international human rights documents which Canada has ratified'.[22]

I suggest that the subtext of this presumption is that the *Charter* was partly inspired by, and drafted in the shadow of, Canada's extant human rights obligations. Perhaps more contentiously, I also suspect that Dickson CJ's presumption reflects a certain confidence that Canada's status as a Western democratic state puts it at the vanguard of human rights protection, such that it has nothing to fear—and perhaps little to gain—from the application of less rigorous international standards. In other words, the distinction between binding and non-binding international law, which is so important to international lawyers, matters less to judges who take it for granted that the benchmark set by international norms will not exceed whatever the *Charter* mandates.

The highly general expression of norms contained in international human rights instruments provides relatively little guidance to their application in specific cases. Unfortunately, Canadian courts rarely refer to the growing body of jurisprudence emanating from treaty bodies such as the Human Rights Committee, which hears communications regarding violations of the *Optional Protocol* to the ICCPR. By confining attention solely to the general norm contained in an international instrument—as opposed to its interpretation and application by international bodies—domestic judges can usually avoid the awkwardness of contradicting the conclusion reached by another judicial or quasi-judicial body authorised to interpret international law.

Evasion is not always possible, however. In *Suresh*, the Supreme Court of Canada held, as a matter of principle, that the *Charter* did not place an absolute prohibition on returning an individual to a country where he or she faces a substantial risk of torture. The *Convention Against Torture* does impose an absolute prohibition and most international jurists agree that the prohibition on torture is *jus cogens*—a peremptory norm of international law that is universally binding and non-derogable. Despite this discernible trend in international law, the Court ultimately declined to acknowledge the prohibition on torture as *jus cogens* and, contrary to what Moran's theory might suggest, the Court did not feel compelled to justify its rejection of international legal authority. I believe the Court's hesitation signified a discomfort with effectively allowing an external norm to dictate the meaning of a constitutional provision.

Yet in *Suresh* itself, the Court found that returning Suresh to Sri Lanka would violate section 7, so any actual conflict with the putative international norm was avoided. In *Ahani*, the Court adopted the Minister's finding that

---

[22] *Ibid*. See also *Slaight Communications Inc v Davidson*, [1989] 1 SCR 38. While Dickson CJ was writing in dissent in *PSERA*, his dicta regarding international law were incorporated into the majority judgment in *Slaight*.

Ahani did not face a substantial risk of torture in Iran, thereby circumventing the problem altogether.

But not quite. Under the terms of the *Optional Protocol*, The United Nations Human Rights Committee has jurisdiction to hear complaints from individuals alleging violations of the ICCPR by a State Party. After the Supreme Court of Canada issued its ruling in *Ahani*, his counsel filed a communication with the Human Rights Committee for relief under the International Protocol. Ahani's petition alleged that *refoulement* to Iran would put Canada in breach of various obligations owed to Ahani under the ICCPR, including Ahani's right to life and his right not to be subjected to cruel and inhuman treatment. The Human Rights Committee requested, and Canada refused, to delay Ahani's *refoulement* to Iran until the Committee considered Ahani's communication. The *Optional Protocol* sets out the procedure by which the Human Rights Committee receives communications and may request interim measures (including a stay) from the affected State Party, but does not explicitly require the State Party to actually grant the request for interim measures, or to implement any remedy proposed by the Human Rights Committee. Moreover, neither the ICCPR nor the *Optional Protocol* have been expressly incorporated into Canadian law.

The case reached the Ontario Court of Appeal, which ruled that Canada had not breached the *Charter* or Ahani's legitimate expectations by refusing a stay of removal pending the Human Rights Committee's determination.[23] Writing for the majority, Laskin JA characterises Ahani's *Charter* section 7 argument as the contention that 'the principles of fundamental justice include the right to remain in Canada until his international law remedies have been exhausted'.[24] Laskin JA's short answer to this proposition is that since Canada has incorporated neither the ICCPR nor the *Optional Protocol*, neither can have legal effect within Canada. Furthermore, the very terms of the *Optional Protocol* do not require Canada to respect the Committee's process (by awaiting a determination before removing Ahani) or the Committee's ultimate determination on the merits (by refraining from action that would violate Canada's international obligations under the ICCPR).

Although Laskin JA acknowledges that 'Canada's international human rights commitments may still inform the content of the principles of fundamental justice under section 7 of the *Charter*', he views Ahani's tactic as deploying section 7 to 'enforce Canada's international commitments in a domestic court. This he cannot do'.

I will return to this judgment later, but for present purposes, suffice to say that the majority judgment revives the stark distinction between incorporated and unincorporated international norms by deeming the latter irrelevant to

---

[23] See above n 2.
[24] *Ibid*, para 28.

interpreting the scope of 'fundamental justice' under section 7. Brunnée and Toope query the prior assertion that the ICCPR and Protocol have not been incorporated into Canadian law, and rely on implicit implementation through the *Charter*, as well as Canada's own declarations of conformity with the ICCPR in reports to various United Nations bodies. However, Brunnée and Toope readily concede that the majority decision is 'undoubtedly correct' in relation to the non-compulsory aspect of Committee process and outcome.

Administrative Law and the *Charter*

Twenty years after the entrenchment of the *Charter*, basic features of the relationship between administrative law and the *Charter* remain ambiguous. It seems reasonably certain that the *Charter* section 7 rights to life, liberty and security of the person cast a narrower compass than the range of interests that will trigger a duty of procedural fairness under administrative law. The obverse proposition is that in circumstances where life, liberty or security of the person gives rise to the entitlement to fundamental justice, chances are high that a duty of fairness under the common law will also obtain. Resort to section 7 of the *Charter* becomes necessary where the statutory provision in question resists an interpretation consistent with the duty of fairness.

For instance, in *Singh v Canada (Minister of Employment and Immigration)*,[25] the Supreme Court of Canada found that the detailed roadmap of the refugee determination process contained in the *Immigration Act (circa 1985)* precluded reading in a requirement of a hearing before the actual decision-maker. A hearing could only be imposed by striking down the legislative scheme as a violation of section 7 of the *Charter*, which the Court then proceeded to do.

Seven years later, in *Chiarelli v Canada (Minister of Employment and Immigration)*,[26] resort to the *Charter* was again necessary to challenge the *Immigration Act*'s regime of secret hearings, non-disclosure and revocation of certain appeal rights, in relation to permanent residents alleged to be engaged in terrorism, subversion or organised crime. In *Chiarelli*, the statutory scheme withstood the section 7 challenge on all fronts, and the process leading to deportation emerged unscathed. Indeed, it provided a model for Canada's post 9/11 anti-terrorism legislation. The *Criminal Code* now sanctions a process of non-disclosure of evidence and exclusion of an accused from segments of his or her own trial for terrorism-related offences.[27]

---

[25] See above n 6.
[26] See above n 7.
[27] *Criminal Code*, RSC 1985, c C–46, as am., ss 83.01–83.33, ss 183–96.

In *Baker*, it appeared that the Supreme Court of Canada might revisit the relationship between administrative law and the *Charter* in the context of expulsion of non-citizens. Ms Baker was a non-status migrant seeking exemption from the rule that non-citizens shall not be admitted or permitted to remain in Canada without legal authorisation. A general 'humanitarian and compassionate discretion' existed in immigration legislation that enabled the Minister to grant her permanent resident status. Section 114(2) of the *Immigration Act*[28] authorised the Governor-in-Council to enact a humanitarian and compassionate exemption; section 2.1 of the *Immigration Regulations*[29] was that exemption:

> The Minister is hereby authorised to exempt any person from any regulation made under section 114(1) of the Act or otherwise facilitate the admission to Canada of any person where the Minister is satisfied that the person's admission should be facilitated owing to the existence of compassionate or humanitarian considerations.

One strategy pursued by Ms Baker and various intervenors was to challenge the constitutionality of the grant of humanitarian and compassionate discretion to the extent that it permitted deportation of a parent without attention to the best interests of children in Canada. As it happened, the administrative law issues raised in the case extended beyond the review of discretion, and included procedural fairness (oral hearing, duty to give reasons) and reasonable apprehension of bias. L'Heureux-Dubé J embarked on her reasons by announcing that:

> [B]ecause, in my view, the issues raised can be resolved under the principles of administrative law and statutory interpretation, I find it unnecessary to consider the various *Charter* issues raised by the appellant and the interveners who supported her position.[30]

L'Heureux-Dubé J's approach seems sensible and uncontroversial; if one can set aside a decision as a breach of procedural fairness or because of a reasonable apprehension of bias, why go further and venture into the *Charter*?

But she does go further, mainly because the question explicitly posed to the Court on appeal concerned the exercise of discretion. The Supreme Court of Canada had occasion to address the relationship between the *Charter* and administrative review of discretion in two earlier judgments. The first case was *Slaight Communications Inc v Davidson*,[31] analysed in detail by Cartier. In the subsequent case of *Ross v New Brunswick School*

---

[28] Now s 25 of IRPA.
[29] SOR/78–172.
[30] See above n 1, para 11.
[31] [1989] 1 SCR 1038.

District No 15,[32] LaForest J attempted to clarify and synthesise the rather opaque dicta of both Lamer J and Dickson CJ in *Slaight Communications*.

Malcolm Ross was a public school teacher and also a notorious Holocaust-denier in his spare time. The school board that employed him was alleged to have engaged in discriminatory behaviour, contrary to the *New Brunswick Human Rights Act*, by failing to discipline him appropriately for his extra-curricular activities. One issue in *Ross* concerned a remedial order issued by the New Brunswick human rights board of inquiry that mandated Ross' dismissal from the school board if he wrote, published or sold anti-Semitic materials. Ross challenged the order both as an unlawful exercise of the remedial discretion granted the board of inquiry under the NB Human Rights Act, and also as a violation of his freedom of expression under section 2(b) of the *Charter*.

The initial task of the Court was to decide whether to review the legality of the order under the principles of administrative law, the *Charter*, or both. LaForest J's unanimous judgment describes *Charter* review as inherently more exacting than administrative review, such that a provision that is 'demonstrably justified in a free and democratic society' under section 1 of the *Charter* will, by definition, not be a 'patently unreasonable' exercise of discretion. Where a given challenge could be framed either as a *Charter* violation or as *ultra vires*, LaForest J offers the following test:

> When the issues involved are untouched by the *Charter*, the appropriate administrative law standard is properly applied as a standard of review. ... As Dickson CJ noted, the more sophisticated and structured analysis of section 1 is the proper framework within which to review *Charter* values.[33]

As Geneviève Cartier observes, the operative—and problematic—assumption in Justice LaForest's synthesis is that administrative review and *Charter* review are commensurate in object, structure and method. Designating 'basic values' as a matter for *Charter* analysis proceeds from this presupposition and simply cabins off a certain range of topics and allocates them exclusively to *Charter* review. In the result, the Court in *Ross* did not ask whether the infringement on expression effected by the remedial order rendered the exercise of discretion patently unreasonable. Instead, the Court confronted the remedy directly as a potential *Charter* violation and considered any justifications under section 1.

The final aspect of the relationship between administrative and constitutional review warranting attention is the question of whether decision-makers who are not judges possess authority to consider and rule upon constitutional

---

[32] [1996] 1 SCR 825. Geneviève Cartier convincingly argues that Justice LaForest's apparent reconciliation elides the discrepancies between the two judges' reasoning.
[33] *Ibid*, para 32.

challenges to legsislation. In the United States, for example, administrative decision-makers do not have jurisdiction to consider and apply the US Bill of Rights to their constitutive legislation. In Canada, Lamer CJ (as he then was), delivered a forceful dissent in *Cooper v Canada (Canadian Human Rights Commission)*,[34] in which he exhorted his fellow judges to retreat from the path they had embarked upon in earlier cases and to follow in the footsteps of their US cohorts. His rationale rests on the separation of powers between Parliament, the judiciary, and the executive:

> The constitutional status of the judiciary, flowing as it does from the separation of powers, requires that certain functions be exclusively exercised by judicial bodies. Although the judiciary certainly does not have an interpretive monopoly over questions of law, in my opinion, it must have exclusive jurisdiction over challenges to the validity of legislation under the Constitution of Canada, and particularly the *Charter*. The reason is that only courts have the requisite *independence* to be entrusted with the constitutional scrutiny of legislation when that scrutiny leads a court to declare invalid an enactment of the legislature. Mere creatures of the legislature, whose very existence can be terminated at the stroke of a legislative pen, whose members, while the tribunal is in existence, usually serve at the pleasure of the government of the day, and whose decisions in some circumstances are properly governed by guidelines established by the executive branch of government, are not suited to this task.[35]

The majority of the Supreme Court of Canada rejected Lamer CJ's categorical approach, and instead attempted to devise an approach that would assess the individual administrative body's capacity to undertake a *Charter* analysis. The Supreme Court of Canada initially set out its test in three cases known collectively as the *Cuddy Chicks* trilogy: *Cuddy Chicks Ltd v Ontario (Labour Relations Board)*;[36] *Tétreault-Gadoury v Canada (Employment and Immigration Commission)*;[37] *Douglas/Kwantlen Faculty Assn v Douglas College*.[38] It later revisited the issue in *Cooper v Canada (Human Rights Commission)*, wherein Lamer CJ (who had not participated in the *Cuddy Chicks* trilogy) launched his rear-guard action.

These cases are not without ambiguity, but one rule that appears reasonably clear is that a necessary pre-requisite for a tribunal to consider a *Charter* challenge to its own legislation is express or implied power to consider questions of law.[39] The Court has not hesitated to find that authority

---

[34] [1996] 3 SCR 854.
[35] *Ibid*, para 13.
[36] [1991] 2 SCR 5.
[37] [1991] 2 SCR 22.
[38] [1990] 3 SCR 570.
[39] Expertise, expedience, evidentiary and efficiency concerns may also influence the court's assessment of whether the legislature notionally considered the particular administrative actor competent to consider the *Charter*.

lacking in certain cases.⁴⁰ Having said that, explicit or implicit authority to determine questions of law seems a tenuous hook upon which to hang *Charter* jurisdiction. At some point it becomes difficult to defend the distinction between a power to determine questions of law that can be derived from statutory language and putative legislative intention, versus the inevitable necessity of interpreting law as an incident of implementing virtually any legislative scheme.

Another principle that emerges from the jurisprudence is that *Charter* rulings by administrative decision-makers can lead no further than a refusal in the particular case to apply a statutory provision that appears to violate the *Charter*. The determination attracts no judicial deference, and courts will readily set it aside if they deem it incorrect.

ONE MESSY MÉNAGE À TROIS

To a greater or lesser extent, each of the foregoing dyads—administrative law/international law, *Charter*/international law, administrative law/*Charter*—make sense on their own terms. That is not to deny the existence of internal tensions: one notable example is the resistance of the courts to recognising an international norm, such as the prohibition on torture, as *jus cogens*. Such recognition would effectively determine the scope of the corresponding *Charter* right to be free from cruel and unusual treatment or punishment, and would also determine whether deporting a person to face torture violated section 7.

Nevertheless, I suggest that only when one attempts to triangulate the three dyads into one coherent legal order do the fissures rise to the surface. And nowhere do the cracks appear more dramatically than in cases involving non-citizens.

Consider first the relationship between administrative law and the *Charter*. In stating that the *Charter* is the supreme law, we have an intuition not only that it 'trumps' conflicting statutory and common law, but also that it must provide at least as much protection as a non-constitutional source of rights, at least where both legal regimes potentially operate. Where life, liberty and security of the person are affected, we expect that fundamental justice will guarantee the same or greater procedural entitlements as would the common law doctrine of procedural fairness. Thus, in *Ross*, LaForest J could simply assert that it was 'obvious that a review of values on an administrative law standard should not impose a more onerous standard upon government than under the *Charter* review'.⁴¹

---

⁴⁰ See, eg, *Tetreault-Gadoury*, above n 37 and *Cooper*, above n 34.
⁴¹ See above n 32, at para 32. It is true that the principles of procedural fairness extend to deprivation of property, whereas s 7 almost certainly does not. In *Blencoe v British Columbia*

While this dictum was uttered in the context of a review of discretion, I suspect the same attitude would prevail in the context of procedure.

I concede that I have not subjected this assumption to rigorous empirical testing. Perhaps section 7 is not *necessarily* more generous than the common law. However, one of the resources that supplies content to 'fundamental justice' is the common law standard of procedural fairness. The only way the content of fundamental justice could guarantee less than procedural fairness is if a countervailing legal principle 'cancelled out' or otherwise diminished the contribution of procedural fairness to the content of fundamental justice. In other words, if fundamental justice encompasses procedural fairness, fundamental justice cannot furnish less protection than procedural fairness unless it simultaneously draws inspiration from other norms that would detract from, or outweigh, the principles of procedural fairness. In sum, it would be odd if the principles of administrative law provided greater protection than the *Charter* in circumstances where the interests at stake would trigger a duty of fairness or fundamental justice.[42]

In *Chiarelli*, the Supreme Court of Canada had little difficulty upholding the constitutionality of deporting permanent residents deemed to be involved in organised crime or to activities threatening to national security.[43] The process employed to arrive at a determination regarding involvement in organised crime or national security was characterised by secret hearings, non-disclosure of evidence to the subject of the process, and disqualification from a statutory appeal on humanitarian and compassionate grounds.

Speaking for the Court, Justice Sopinka declared at the outset that it was unnecessary to determine whether life, liberty or security of the person interest was infringed by deportation, because the procedural scheme violated no principle of fundamental justice in any event. He did remark, however, that:

> The most fundamental principle of immigration law is that non-citizens do not have an unqualified right to enter or remain in the country. At common law an alien has no right to enter or remain in the country.
>
> ...

(Human Rights Commission), [2000] 2 SCR 307, the appellant complained of an unreasonable delay in adjudicating a sexual harassment complaint made against him under the British Columbia Human Rights Act. Blencoe alleged that the delay constituted both a violation of the administrative duty of procedural fairness, and a violation of s 7 of the Charter. The majority of the Supreme Court of Canada first determined that no life, liberty or security of the person interest was engaged by the delay in adjudicating a human rights complaint against the appellant. Ultimately, the validity of the delay was measured against common law principles of abuse of process.

[42] One could argue that judges engaging in constitutional adjudication ought to incorporate a greater sense of deference to the legislature in their analysis than they employ in statutory interpretation. After all, the *Charter* enables them to defeat the will of an elected Parliament by striking down legislation, whereas statutory interpretation is predicated on the fiction of implementing the intention of the legislature. Even if this is correct, however, one would expect the deference to appear at the stage of a s 1 analysis, not in the determination of fundamental justice.
[43] Permanent residents are legal immigrants who have not (yet) acquired citizenship. One is eligible to apply for citizenship after three years of permanent residence, but for various reasons, eligible people may reside in Canada indefinitely without applying for citizenship.

> [T]here is one element common to all persons who fall within the class of permanent residents [convicted of a serious crime]. They have all deliberately violated an essential condition under which they were permitted to remain in Canada. In such a situation, there is no breach of fundamental justice in giving practical effect to the termination of their right to remain in Canada.... It is not necessary, in order to comply with fundamental justice, to look beyond this fact to other aggravating or mitigating circumstances.[43a]

Put bluntly, deporting a non-citizen does not in and of itself breach principles of fundamental justice, no matter how long the person has lived in Canada, what she would leave behind if deported, and what awaits her (short of persecution as interpreted within the refugee definition) upon arrival in the country of nationality. By refusing to determine whether deportation violates a right to life, liberty and security of the person before ruling on the requirements of fundamental justice, Sopinka J adopts a de-contextualised methodology that purports to calculate what fundamental justice requires without any inquiry into the stakes for an individual facing deportation. By ignoring the human impact of deportation, the Court tacitly finds that any infringement of security of the person is legally inconsequential because of the contingent legal entitlement of permanent residents to remain in Canada.

If the section 7 rights of a permanent resident are so flimsy, how would a non-status (so-called 'illegal') migrant fare under the *Charter*—someone like, for example, Mrs Baker? One might expect that she would be in an even more vulnerable position vis-à-vis section 7 than Mr Chiarelli, who at least had the legal status of permanent resident in Canada. If fundamental justice requires so little in circumstances where an individual is a permanent resident, one cannot but suspect that it requires virtually nothing where the person has no legal entitlement to be in Canada in the first place.

Yet in *Baker*, the Supreme Court avoided confronting and reconsidering the sterile and restrictive approach it took in *Chiarelli* by pursuing an administrative law analysis instead. I do not suggest that the Court was wrong to do so with respect to the doctrines of procedural fairness or reasonable apprehension of bias, though I believe it to be problematic with respect to discretion.

In assessing the content of the common law duty of fairness, the Court noted that one of the factors is 'the importance of the decision to the individual or individuals affected'.[44] Later, L'Heureux-Dubé J finds that:

> this is a decision that in practice has exceptional importance to the lives of those with an interest in its result—the claimant and his or her close family

---

[43a] See above n 1, 714–15.
[44] See above n 1, para 25.

members—and this leads to the content of the duty of fairness being more extensive.⁴⁵

In other words, deportation profoundly affects important interests, and therefore a duty of fairness is owed. Compare this to *Chiarelli*:

> The fact of a deliberate violation of the condition [that one not be convicted of a serious criminal offence] is sufficient to justify a deportation order. It is not necessary, in order to comply with fundamental justice, to look beyond this fact to other aggravating or mitigating circumstances.⁴⁶

The contrast between the situated subject of administrative law and the deracinated constitutional subject could not be more stark.

Placing *Chiarelli* side by side with *Baker* exposes the anomaly that common law principles of administrative law currently accord greater concern and respect to non-citizens facing expulsion than does section 7 of the *Charter*. Ironically, one can trace *Chiarelli*'s peremptory disregard of non-citizens' interests to the old common law insistence that immigration was a privilege and not a right, and thus lacked the normative heft to support a claim to natural justice. This view was renounced for *Charter* purposes in *Singh*, then reinscribed in *Chiarelli*; *Baker*, in turn, ignores *Chiarelli*, and upgrades the status of the non-citizen at common law.

Another site of friction between administrative law and the *Charter* clash are the dicta in *Slaight Communication* and *Ross*. As stated earlier, the rule appears to be that if the exercise of discretion engages fundamental *Charter* values, then the *Charter* is the appropriate normative framework for review. Both *Slaight Communication* and *Ross* concerned remedial orders limiting the individual actor's freedom of expression. While *Slaight* is notoriously opaque in its reasoning, *Ross* quite clearly proceeds from the position that the human rights tribunal's discretionary order should be subject to a *Charter* analysis, rather than an administrative law analysis.

In *Baker*, the Court was concerned with the impact of a discretionary decision to exempt Mrs Baker from deportation. Based on *Singh*, it seems easy to cast the issues at stake in a deportation decision ('best interests of children', impact of deportation on individual etc) as *Charter* values. Put another way, if the best interests of the child is an international human rights norm, surely it is a likely candidate for a *Charter* value. That being the case, *Slaight* and *Ross* would appear to militate in favour of assessing the exercise of humanitarian and compassionate discretion against section 7 of the *Charter*, and not according to common law principles of discretion.

Of course, the reasoning that leads to this conclusion presents at least two related problems: First, the implicit separation of *Charter* values and

---

⁴⁵ See above n 1, para 31.
⁴⁶ See *Chiarelli*, above n 7, at p 715.

administrative law values stunts the natural evolution of the common law and, by implication, the refinement of a democratic conception of the rule of law. As Justice Lebel complained in *Blencoe*,

> Assuming that the *Charter* must solve every legal problem would be a recipe for freezing and sterilising the natural and necessary evolution of the common law and the civil law of this country.[47]

Second, the insistence on a clear bifurcation between common law and *Charter* norms overlooks the fact that the content of fundamental justice has been and will continue to be shaped by common law antecedents. The inevitable reciprocity of this encounter is expressly endorsed by L'Heureux-Dubé J's instruction in *Baker* that the *Charter* should function as an internal constraint informing the exercise of discretion. But if discretion must be exercised in accordance with 'the principles of the *Charter*',[48] the neat line that *Slaight* and *Ross* attempt to draw between *Charter* values and administrative law values as applied to discretion blurs as the two legal regimes bleed into one another. How can one distinguish between '*Charter* values' and 'non-*Charter* values' if each informs the other?

Despite—or because of—its virtues in extending the analytical approach to legal error to review of discretion, *Baker* has also confounded prior jurisprudence relating to the expertise of administrative decision-makers in the realm of the *Charter*. On the one hand, *Baker* instructs decision-makers that '*Charter* values' may circumscribe the permissible exercise of discretion. On the other hand, the *Cuddy Chicks* trilogy, and the subsequent case of *Cooper v Canada (Human Rights Commission)* purport to set up a gatekeeping test to limit which administrative decision-makers can consider *Charter* questions. Only administrative actors with the power to determine questions of law will gain admission to the *Charter* citadel.

It seems reasonable to anticipate that not every repository of statutory discretion will also (or necessarily) have express power to interpret questions of law, and therefore possess jurisdiction to consider *Charter* issues. It is also conceivable that some decision-makers will find themselves exercising discretion in circumstances that warrant attention to *Charter* values in the terms used by L'Heureux-Dubé J in *Baker*. It is not clear how these administrative actors can both honour the spirit of *Baker* (which requires adherence to *Charter* values where germane) and obey the letter of the *Cuddy Chicks* trilogy and *Cooper* (which will deny them jurisdiction to do so).

One might attempt to differentiate between subjecting a legal rule to *Charter* scrutiny and taking *Charter* values into account in the exercise of

---

[47] See above n 41, at para 189.
[48] See above n 1, para 56.

discretion in order to justify jurisdiction in the latter but not the former case. Yet L'Heureux-Dubé J herself undermines any attempt to draw a clear conceptual boundary between the interpreting law and exercising discretion. As she states in *Baker*:

> It is, however, inaccurate to speak of a rigid dichotomy of 'discretionary' or 'non-discretionary' decisions. Most administrative decisions involve the exercise of implicit discretion in relation to many aspects of decision-making. To give just one example, decision-makers may have considerable discretion as to the remedies they order. In addition, there is no easy distinction to be made between interpretation and the exercise of discretion; interpreting legal rules involves considerable discretion to clarify, fill in legislative gaps, and make choices among various options.[49]

Given L'Heureux-Dubé J's cogent argument about why the distinction between law and discretion is overstated, it seems awkward to rely on that same distinction for purposes of affording *Charter* jurisdiction to administrative decision-makers when exercising discretion, but not when dealing with a direct challenge to the constitutionality of a legal rule. Suggesting that decision-makers exercise discretion 'in accordance with ... the principles of the *Charter*' only obscures the problem by implying that this activity represents a qualitatively different exercise than actually subjecting discretion to systematic *Charter* scrutiny.

I am persuaded by L'Heureux-Dubé J's claim that legal interpretation and exercise of discretion share many of the same features; I also take the view that a methodological distinction between conducting a *Charter* analysis and taking '*Charter* values' into account cannot be sustained upon close scrutiny. The result is that one cannot simultaneously abide by *Baker*'s instruction to exercise discretion in accordance with the *Charter*, *Ross*' assumption that administrative review for abuse of discretion (unlike *Charter* review) does not engage fundamental values,[50] and the strict limits imposed by the *Cuddy Chicks* trilogy and *Cooper* on the jurisdiction of administrative decision-makers to consider the *Charter*.

Even assuming one could clear these jurisdictional hurdles, further confusion awaits at the deference checkpoint. Over the last 20 years, Canadian administrative law has elaborated a complex set of standards of judicial review by which a court will subject administrative decisions to scrutiny of varying intensity. The greater the expertise of the decision-maker, the more deference owed it by the judiciary, and the less exacting the standard of review. Thus, decision-makers worthy of the most deference in reference to a given determination will be set aside only if the decision is 'patently unreasonable'. Decision-makers in the middle range only have to meet a standard

---

[49] See above n 1, para 54.
[50] Geneviève Cartier provides a very cogent elaboration of this point.

of 'reasonableness *simpliciter*', while decision-makers entitled to the least deference will be reviewed on a standard of 'correctness'.

The standard of review may vary according to the subject matter as well as the identity of the decision-maker. For example, *Charter* analyses will always be assessed on a standard of correctness, since all administrative actors are deemed relatively inexpert in matters constitutional in comparison to the judiciary.

While the sliding scale of deference was initially reserved for legal interpretation, *Baker* heralded the extension of this approach to the realm of discretion. This raised the problem of whether discretion could be subjected to different levels of scrutiny. On the one hand, it seems to defy the very nature of discretion to subject it to a correctness standard of review. After all, the exercise of discretion is predicated on the absence of a single correct answer. One might expect that the standard of review for statutory grants of discretion to always be either reasonableness *simpliciter* (as it was in *Baker*) or patent unreasonableness. On the other hand, it is equally clear that administrative decision-makers who possess jurisdiction to consider *Charter* issues enjoy no deference whatsoever in respect of their determination, and will be judged against a correctness standard. The unresolved question then is whether discretion *per se* is subject to a single standard of review (as *Baker* suggests), or whether the various components that comprise its exercise (facts, *Charter*, other legal sources, non-legal factors) may be subject to different levels of deference in accordance with the expertise of the decision-maker in relation to that element.

The Supreme Court of Canada's decisions in *Suresh* and *Ahani* pursue the latter approach while purporting to follow *Baker*: in evaluating the exercise of ministerial discretion to deport a person deemed to be a security risk, the question of whether deportation to face torture would violate section 7 of the *Charter* is hived off—and tacitly reviewed on a correctness standard—from the determination of whether the individual faces a substantial risk of torture if deported, a factual finding to which the Court readily defers.

At present, all one can surmise with confidence is that *Baker* is on a collision course with key dicta in the Supreme Court of Canada's judgments in *Chiarelli, Slaight Communications, Ross, Cuddy Chicks, Cooper* and *Ahani*. I predict that the vehicle most likely to instigate this multi-case pile-up will be an immigration case involving a long-term permanent resident who faces automatic deportation under the new *Immigration and Refugee Protection Act*. The statute provides for automatic deportation of permanent residents with no right of appeal if they are convicted of a crime and sentenced to more than two years imprisonment.[51] The IRPA is silent on any mitigating circumstances, and provides no formal process by which a

---

[51] IRPA, ss 36, 64(2).

permanent resident can contest deportation for serious criminality. Even if one could argue that the legislative gap regarding process could be filled with common law presumptions, it seems unlikely that the failure to articulate even a single principle of mitigation could also be resolved through generating discretion where none appears in the legislation. If I am incorrect on this latter point, the Court will still have to choose between the *Charter* and administrative law in evaluating any particular deportation decision. Eventually, I expect that a reviewing court will have to contend with the post-*Baker* viability of *Chiarelli*'s narrow section 7 analysis, *Slaight Communication*'s rationale and methodology for choosing between the *Charter* and administrative law frameworks, and *Cuddy Chicks'* and *Cooper's* restrictive approach to *Charter* jurisdiction of administrative decision-makers.

The Ontario Court of Appeal decision in *Ahani (Ahani (OCA))* exposes the latest crack in the façade of one harmonious legal order containing administrative, international and constitutional law. The case arose after the Supreme Court rendered judgment, and represented an eleventh-hour attempt to prevent Mr Ahani's deportation by appealing to the international forum. Mr Ahani submitted a communication to the Human Rights Committee alleging that deporting Mr Ahani to Iran would violate Canada's obligations under the ICCPR. The Human Rights Committee issued a request to the government of Canada for interim measures to prevent Mr Ahani's deportation before the Committee had an opportunity to consider the communication. The government refused. The argument before the Ontario Court of Appeal was that deporting Mr Ahani to Iran without awaiting the UN Human Rights Committee's final Views on the merits of his Communication would violate Ahani's section 7 *Charter* rights.

Brunnée and Toope have provided a careful and thoughtful analysis of the majority and dissenting opinions on the question of the application of non-binding, non-mandatory international norms to *Charter* adjudication.[52] I will not comment on the impact of *Ahani (OCA)* on the internal nature of the *Charter*/international law relationship, except to note the position taken by Martin Scheinin, an international law scholar and member of the ICCPR Human Rights Committee. Scheinin argues forcefully that contrary to the assumption that a request for interim measures imposes no duty on a State Party, a State Party commits a 'grave breach' of its obligations under the Protocol by refusing to accede to a request. Based on recent jurisprudence from the Human Rights Committee, Scheinin concludes that:

[w]hen the obligation to afford interim protection in order to avoid irreparable damage is derived directly from the ratification of the Optional Protocol,

---

[52] By non-binding I mean that neither the ICCPR nor the Optional Protocol were formally incorporated into Canadian law by implementing legislation. By non-mandatory, I mean that

it is fully justified to state that such an obligation has a *stronger* legally binding force than the Committee's final Views or its specific pronouncements on the right to an effective remedy.[53]

In other words, Scheinin insists that accession to the interim requests by the State Party is *not* optional under international law where denying the request would irrevocably negate the petitioner's rights. Of course, this does not resolve the question of the status of the interim request process under Canadian law.

Writing for the majority of the Ontario Court of Appeal, Laskin JA does not refer to any jurisprudence from the Human Rights Committee regarding the status of interim requests under international law. Instead, he presses hard on the claim that the Protocol is unimplemented in Canada and therefore legally impotent. This perfunctory dismissal of ratified but unincorporated norms seems incongruous with the spirit of *Baker*, which demonstrated a willingness to grant non-binding norms at least persuasive value. Moreover, it also seems inconsistent with Dickson CJ's view that international human rights are generally apposite to *Charter* interpretation.

Laskin JA insists that giving effect to Ahani's argument that section 7 required granting a stay pending the outcome of the international process:

> would convert a non-binding request, in a Protocol which has never been part of Canadian law, into a binding obligation enforceable in Canada by a Canadian court, and more, into a constitutional principle of fundamental justice.[54]

In effect, Laskin JA believes that *Baker* endorsed the use of a non-binding, substantive international norm only as a source of guidance, whereas Ahani was attempting to assert a putatively optional, non-binding procedural norm as determinative.

Yet the majority arguably misrepresents the source of the compulsion. Even if one rejects Scheinin's claim that the interim request is binding upon States Party as a matter of international law, it is not international law but rather a constitutional entitlement to fundamental justice under section 7 that drives the argument. The claim is that section 7 entitles Ahani to fundamental justice, and fundamental justice requires that the Human Rights

---

the *Optional Protocol* did not mandate that Canada respect the Committee's views, or even delay action until the Committee expressed its views.

[53] M Scheinin, 'The Human Rights Committee's Pronouncements on the Right to an Effective Remedy—an Illustration of the Legal Nature of the Committee's Work under the Optional Protocol', unpublished 2002. Scheinin supports his argument by citing the Human Rights Committee case of *Piandiong et al v The Philippines*, Communication No 869/1999, where the Philippines executed several individuals who had submitted communications to the Committee, contrary to the request for interim measures made by the Committee.

[54] See above n 2, at para 31.

Committee have an opportunity to consider his communication before irrevocable action is taken.

I suspect that what really causes Laskin JA to insist on the legal irrelevance of the Protocol is the apparent absence of any other legal source that speaks to the question of whether fundamental justice requires allowing the international process to run its course. That an international norm is neither mandatory in its terms nor binding as a matter of domestic law does not mean that it lacks persuasive force. The fact is that Laskin JA could locate no principled reason *not* to be persuaded to honour an international process that Canada had ratified, and to stay Ahani's deportation until the Human Rights Committee ruled on his Communication. There was no evidence that national security would be put at risk, or that time was of the essence. After all, Mr Ahani had already spent seven years in detention. Laskin JA insists that 'Ahani is not merely asking this court to interpret section 7 in a way that is consistent with international human rights norms', but instead is trying to 'use section 7 to enforce Canada's international commitments in a domestic court'.[55] Laskin JA's implicit juxtaposition of the two legal strategies implies that they are mutually exclusive. In fact, interpreting section 7 consistent with international human rights norms *will* have the effect of enforcing Canada's international commitments domestically, but so what? It is section 7 doing the work, not the ICCPR or Optional Protocol themselves.[56]

Of course, the practical difference between a legal norm that is persuasive and one that is binding becomes attenuated if there is only one legal norm in play. The Ontario Court of Appeal could invoke no norm to justify the refusal to accede to the Human Rights Committee's request for a stay. That being the case, it becomes difficult to distinguish between persuasion and compulsion. Better to avoid the appearance of being compelled to act by an external norm by simply saying that the legal norm is disqualified from the game.

I wonder if the temptation to discount the norm in *Ahani (OCA)* was compounded by the fact that it would require giving space to a foreign voice in a matter that is viewed as quintessentially domestic, namely, who shall be expelled from the country. The UN Human Rights Committee actually has the mandate, the expertise, and the ability to adjudicate an alleged violation of the ICCPR by the Canadian government. However, in the usual

---

[55] See above n 2, para 31.
[56] The Supreme Court of Canada's judgment in *United States v Burns and Rafay*, [2001] 1 SCR 283 offers a useful precedent. Art 6 of the Extradition Treaty between Canada and the United States of America, Can TS 1976 No 3. grants the Minister of Justice discretion to refuse to extradite a fugitive unless the United States provides assurances that the death penalty will neither be sought nor imposed. In *Burns and Rafay*, the Supreme Court of Canada ruled that s 7 fundamental justice required the Minister of Justice to seek assurances in virtually all cases. While the language of the Treaty was optional, s 7 of the *Charter* effectively rendered in mandatory.

case where international law enters the domestic sphere, it is through the medium of national judges who interpret them.

In *Ahani (OCA),* the Ontario Court of Appeal was faced with the prospect of an international body (the Human Rights Committee) speaking directly to the interpretation and application of an international norm in the case before the court. That is to say, giving effect to Ahani's position would acknowledge the competence of another norm-generating body outside the domestic legal order capable of speaking to the validity of a state's decision to expel a non-citizen to face possible torture.

David Dyzenhaus recently referred to an attitude he labels 'judicial supremacism—the idea that judges are at the apex of legal order as sole guardians of its fundamental values'.[57] Most international human rights norms are articulated at a level of generality that enables national courts to interpret them in a manner that comports with the domestic legal order. If an international body is authorised to interpret the norm outside that order, and that interpretation can subsequently be imported into a *Charter* analysis, judicial supremacy is diminished. In a sense, disqualifying the Human Rights Committee's interim request mechanism from *Charter* consideration because the Protocol is unincorporated is the functional equivalent to disqualifying domestic administrative bodies from considering the *Charter* because they lack express power to interpret law: both moves preserve judicial supremacy.

As a final illustration of the leakiness of borders between legal regimes, let me suggest a way in which Ahani might have located support in common law doctrine for his argument that fundamental justice required permitting the international legal process to run its course. In *Knight v Indian Head School District No 19*,[58] L'Heureux-Dubé J took on the challenge of justifying why a duty of fairness was owed to a person who was appointed 'at pleasure' to his position, and was subsequently not renewed. The significance of characterising the appointment as 'at pleasure' is that the appointee can be fired for any reason, or no reason at all. This makes it rather difficult to argue that the individual is entitled to notice of the reasons for termination and an opportunity to respond—after all, what's the point? Writing for the majority, L'Heureux-Dubé J provides the following justification:

> The argument to the effect that, since the employer can dismiss his employee for unreasonable or capricious reasons, the giving of an opportunity to participate in the decision-making would be meaningless, is unconvincing. In both the situation of an office held at pleasure and an office from which one can be dismissed only for cause, one of the purposes of the imposition on the

[57] David Dyzenhaus, 'Constituting the Rule of Law: Fundamental Values in Administrative Law' (2002) *Queen's LJ* 445 at 488.
[58] [1990] 1 SCR 653.

administrative body of a duty to act fairly is the same, ie, enabling the employee to try to change the employer's mind about the dismissal. The value of such an opportunity should not be dependent on the grounds triggering the dismissal.

...

There is also a wider public policy argument militating in favour of the imposition of a duty to Act fairly on administrative bodies making decisions similar to the one impugned in the case at bar. The powers exercised by the appellant Board are delegated statutory powers which, as much as the statutory powers exercised directly by the government, should be put only to legitimate use.[59]

The key principle is that even where an employer genuinely has virtually untrammelled discretion to dismiss, fairness requires that the decision-maker maintains the opportunity to receive all the relevant information prior to rendering a final decision. In the typical employment context, that information would be provided by the employee, and thus notice and an opportunity to respond are the appropriate mechanisms for bringing the information to the attention of the decision-maker.

In Mr Ahani's situation, the Minister certainly possesses authority to determine the likely consequences to Mr Ahani if deported to Iran. The Minister arguably has no obligation under international or domestic law to accept contrary views from Ahani or from the UN Human Rights Committee.[60] Indeed, *Suresh* even reserves to the Minister residual power to deport someone to face torture in some undefined circumstance. Nevertheless, following *Knight*, fairness may well require that the Minister receive the expression of the Human Rights Committee's view on whether deportation violates Canada's international obligations before rendering a final decision. The purpose would be for the Minister to assure himself, Ahani, and the public, that the power to deport is being exercised legitimately and appropriately. The final link in this chain of reasoning is the assertion that if the principles of procedural fairness require awaiting the views of the UN Human Rights Committee, so too the principles of fundamental justice.

CONCLUSION

Migration law asks three questions: Who gets in? On what terms? Who decides who gets in? For at least the last 100 years, the typical answer has

---

[59] *Ibid*, at 675.
[60] Once again, Scheinin disagrees. While the Views of the Committee regarding a remedy are not binding on the State Party, once a violation has been found, a State Party is obliged under Art 3(a) of the ICCPR to 'ensure that any person whose rights or freedoms as herein recognized are violated shall have an effective remedy'. See above n 20.

been that nation-states will decide who gets in on whatever terms the state decrees to be in accordance with its self-interest.

The actual ability of states to control admittance is compromised by many factors, but two of the main limiting conditions are the irremediable porosity of borders, and the adoption of the *UN Refugee Convention*. The former is a practical obstacle while the latter is a legal constraint. Of course, states expend considerable effort attempting to deter and deflect those who might arrive at its borders seeking entry as refugees or as migrants.

Judicial management of boundary crossings between legal regimes also asks three questions: What gets in? On what terms? Who decides? The characterisation of international law as implemented or not, binding versus persuasive, mandatory versus optional, are all mechanisms for deciding which norms may enter the domestic legal order, and the terms upon which those norms will operate. Simultaneously, but elsewhere along the border, other rules set out the legal norms (international human rights, *Charter* values, common law principles) that must be admitted and allowed to play inside the arena of discretionary power. Administrative standards of review, from patently unreasonable, to reasonableness *simpliciter*, to correctness, dictate who—as between the judiciary and the government—has the 'last word' on deciding the meaning of law.

One of the lessons from the evolving jurisprudence is that the boundaries between domains of law is no longer reducible *ex ante* to formal categories and rules. Nor can the confusion be resolved by supplementing existing categories with new formal categories. Rather, the rules of admission are fluid, and vary in accordance with the character of the entity seeking admission as well as the relationship between the parties on both sides of the border.

Let me illustrate with two examples from the preceding text. Under the *Immigration Act*, the rules of admission for international law into the statute were governed by rules of interpretation and the incorporated/unincorporated status of the international instrument. Section 3(3) of the new *Immigration and Refugee Protection Act* arguably imposes a duty to interpret the legislation in compliance with international law that differs by degree from the common law presumption of conformity, exceeds Moran's conception of influential authority, yet falls short of actual incorporation. In *Ahani (OCA)*, the Court was confronted with an array of sources and degrees of compulsion within the *Optional Protocol*, between the *Optional Protocol* and Canada as State Party, and finally between the ICCPR, the *Optional Protocol* and the Canadian *Charter*. The utter complexity of these relationships, both alone and in combination, confound any attempt to pluck a ready-made rule of admission off the shelf and apply it in a satisfactory way.

Borders between legal orders, just like borders between states, rarely work the way we imagine, and we are constantly adapting and applying new rules for new prospective entrants and new situations. Seldom are we able to fully anticipate the consequences of these attempts to police entry and conditions of residence. Border crossings produce rich new possibilities, hybridities and permutations unforeseen, as well as confusion and disorientation. In law as in life, we are still learning to live with the results. More than any other legal subject, the foreigner perches precariously on these borders, seeking entry *qua* human being into the normative terrain of human rights discourse, yet too often denied shelter under the rights of citizenship precisely because she is not a citizen. Sometimes lucky, sometimes not. If there is a deeper, more coherent normative logic buttressing these borders and their operation, it eludes this author as much as it does most migrants.

8

Refugees, Asylum Seekers, the Rule of Law and Human Rights

COLIN HARVEY*

INTRODUCTION

FORCED DISPLACEMENT HAS played a prominent part in human history. The aim of the forcibly displaced is usually to seek the conditions which might make a fully human life possible. The reasons for flight are often varied and can be political, social or economic. The number of displaced persons continues to be significant,[1] and forced migration is accorded a central place in political discussions at all levels. In law distinctions are made between refugees, asylum seekers and other migrants. A range of legal standards exists at the international, regional and national levels.

The focus of this chapter is on refugees and asylum seekers. There are broader debates about the interaction between legal regulation and migration. I do not address these matters here. The specific intention is to explore the implications of the rule of law for refugees and asylum seekers, with reference to a debate that has emerged in the United Kingdom (UK) on the role of the courts in asylum cases. My concern is primarily with how the senior judiciary addresses arguments over the meaning of asylum law and policy. Are there, for example, any patterns in the approach adopted thus far? Politicians in the UK have suggested that the courts are interfering excessively in government asylum policy and on occasions have undermined the will of Parliament. In contrast, commentators and human rights advocates argue that deference to executive decision-making is the major problem. From this perspective judges have not gone far enough in defence of the rights of asylum seekers. The arguments are familiar ones and reflect long-established

---

* I am grateful to David Dyzenhaus for his comments on an earlier version of this paper.
[1] UNHCR, *Statistical Yearbook 2001: Refugees, Asylum-seekers and Other Persons of Concern-Trends in Displacement, Protection and Solutions* (UNHCR, October 2002).

debates within constitutional democracies. These arguments, which continue in asylum law, are therefore not unique.

In this chapter I suggest that the senior judiciary is not engaged in an attempt to undermine government asylum policy in the UK. The evidence does not exist to support this conclusion. The senior judiciary is aware of its institutional and constitutional roles, but is prepared to advance incrementally the interpretation of refugee law and on occasions question executive and administrative decision-making. The debate has become polarised between those who are sceptical of the judicial role and those who believe the judges do not go far enough in defence of the rights of asylum seekers. In my view, this suggests the need for an approach which recognises both the importance of parliamentary democracy (properly understood) and the robust judicial protection of the rights of vulnerable groups (through the common law and statute law). I believe this will not be found in excessive deference to the wishes of the executive in the area of asylum law. It will also not be discovered in attempts to place too much strain on the judicial role. Reconciling these approaches is not straightforward, but a start might be made by switching the attention to legal argumentation and to those arguments which deserve recognition within a constitutional democracy which is committed to the rule of law. This approach places considerable emphasis on the values which underpin legal order and the arguments which best serve those values.[2]

THE RULE OF LAW, REFUGEES AND ASYLUM SEEKERS

Reference is often made to the importance of the rule of law to the citizen. But what about the 'person'? Does the rule of law, as a political ideal, depend upon national status, or is physical presence within the state sufficient? How can law be legitimate for asylum seekers? The straightforward answer is that in law the asylum seeker is protected. Both common law and statute law recognise the asylum seeker. But in general discussions the link is still made between citizenship and legality.

There is no universal agreement on the meaning of the rule of law or the values which attach to it. Disagreement exists over what it means to govern within a legal order. Does it, for example, mean that judges should defer consistently to the express wishes of the democratic branch of government? Are there values which stand above ordinary law? If not, are there values which inhere in the process of interpretation and application of the law?

---

[2] D Dyzenhaus 'Reuniting the Brain: The Democratic Basis of Judicial Review' (1998) 9 *Public Law Review* 98.

Debates on the meaning of the rule of law continue. To the human rights lawyer or activist some of these discussions will appear unnecessarily abstract. However, in my view, the outcome of debates on the politics of law matters in the practical interpretation and application of substantive areas of legal regulation. But what views are expressed about the meaning of the rule of law?

First, there is what may be termed the 'formal tradition'. Writing from within this tradition Joseph Raz notes that legal rules must be general, prospective, open, clear and stable.[3] There is little in the description that one would wish to disagree with. In legal theory, the ongoing debate is on whether legal order is devoid of substantive moral or political content. The label 'formal tradition' is a simplification of the issues, but it captures a shared belief in the importance of separating legal validity from moral or political views.

Secondly, there are 'value-based' schools of thought on the rule of law. Albert Venn Dicey famously linked the concept to the supremacy of regular law as opposed to arbitrary power.[4] The basic idea is that extensive discretion is incompatible with the rule of law. This distrust of discretionary power is reflected in a number of accounts of the concept. It is one that has particular relevance in the asylum context. A significant concern in asylum law is the discretion which the legal framework affords. Dicey's approach, often now described as constitutional law orthodoxy, remains important. This is the case, as asylum law demonstrates, even when it is accepted that discretion can be exercised in a number of ways. As I suggest below, arbitrary power in the asylum context has raised questions about the basic fairness of procedures.

For Dicey, no one could be punished except by law, everyone must be equal before the law (in the sense that all classes of persons are subject to it) and it must be administered by the ordinary courts.[5] His key ideas are the applicability of the law to officials and citizens alike and a preference for specific protections rather than grand declarations of rights. The key themes identified by Dicey are evident in other conceptions of the rule of law which reflect a distrust of arbitrary power and a commitment to equality before the law. These core values underpin modern understandings of the rule of law, even if one accepts that law is, by nature, arguable. In my view, they are values which have particular significance for marginalised groups. One fear of extensive discretionary power, for example, is precisely that vulnerable individuals and groups will suffer as a result. How this approach is classified in legal theory is, in my view, of less interest than the values which it reflects and seeks to promote.

---

[3] J Raz 'The Rule of Law and its Virtues' (1977) 93 *Law Quarterly Review* 195.
[4] AV Dicey, *Introduction to the Study of the Law of the Constitution* 10th edn, (London, Macmillan, 1959).
[5] *Ibid.*

And finally, some prefer to view the rule of law as political rhetoric and as, potentially, an obstacle to the achievement of social change. For this group, legal order is inherently political in an indeterminate sense. In other words, law simply reflects power relations within wider society and should be approached from a strategic and instrumental perspective. The commitment to legal order thus becomes a tactical one and law is used as a tool, in appropriate circumstances, to advance wider political struggles. This strategic attitude towards the rule of law is often discussed in the human rights context.

The disagreement over the meaning of the rule of law reflects basic disputes in law and politics. My own view is that modern approaches which aim to hold onto a substantive understanding of the rule of law remain the more convincing. The traditional categories in legal theory are not always helpful in this respect. I believe the aim should be to highlight the arguable and dynamic nature of law and its basis in distinct values.[6] The focus should be on the substance of legal argumentation, as opposed to the sometimes oppressive institutional focus of the debate in the UK. Many of the values are reflected in the traditional approach of Dicey and others. The idea of equality before the law and the distrust of arbitrary power are part of this. The attention thus shifts to the contribution the rule of law makes to the promotion of a general political culture of rational justification and the values which underpin it. The argument is that it means something, in substantive political terms, to be committed to legal order as opposed to discretionary power administered on a case-by-case basis. The rule of law, in this understanding, is essential to the construction of a democratic culture in which people are treated equally, but the debate shifts towards legal reasoning as opposed to a rigid focus on the decision-maker.

But how is this relevant to the debate on refugees and asylum seekers? Surely this simply brings instability and uncertainty with it? These are genuine concerns and many democracies do not have a proud record on protecting the rights of asylum seekers. However, legal orders generate mechanisms to resolve disagreement on the basis of enacted norms and, often, foundational constitutional norms and values. Law is arguable, but it is not indeterminate. The turn to rational argumentation is convincing as a way to move the debate beyond the current preoccupation with 'who decides'. The obsession with the decision-maker eventually weakens the protection of vulnerable groups in constitutional democracies and in some cases simply exacerbates the problem of Westminster executive dominance in the UK's democratic order. This is therefore not just a debate in legal theory. It has practical implications in this area of law. The emphasis should be

---

[6] D Dyzenhaus 'Recrafting the Rule of Law' in David Dyzenhaus (ed), *Recrafting the Rule of Law* (Oxford, Hart Publishing, 1999), 1–12; N MacCormick 'Rhetoric and the Rule of Law' in Dyzenhaus (ed) *ibid* 163–77.

on continuing conversation over the terms of asylum policy but within the constraints of legal order. These are constraints which protect vulnerable individuals and groups. The political ideal of the rule of law is important not simply for citizens within the state, but for all persons who are subject to the jurisdiction of the state. In particular, this is because the rule of law promotes a democratic culture of equal concern and respect. And in the asylum context this becomes significant as it assists in the task of promoting a reasoned approach to this highly contested area of public policy. The justification of policy within law must *deserve* recognition within the terms of legal argumentation, and not solely on the basis of its pedigree. In the asylum context, it is not enough for judges to defer to executive decisions on the basis that Ministers are best placed to make them. In my view, the judges are obliged to address the substance of the legal arguments even in cases where immigration, asylum and national security collide. In this respect, Dicey's emphasis on the ordinary courts and concerns about discretionary power retain their significance in asylum law and policy. The strength of the approach rests, in my view, on respect for the individual and the basic principles of fairness which this implies. In asylum law, where there are often extensive pressures placed on government and public administration to deliver quick results, the insistence on the importance of each individual is of particular significance. A commitment to legalism thus has an ethical dimension.

JUDGING ASYLUM

The Legal Framework

Asylum law in the UK has developed in the last decade as a specific area of public law.[7] There is now an extensive statutory framework and a substantial body of case-law.[8] In addition, the Human Rights Act 1998 changes the human rights context and the full impact of the Act requires careful assessment over time.[9] My aim in this section is to focus on the role of the judges in the context of the English asylum process.

The rule of law has implications for all the institutions of government, including the executive. The Westminster Parliament has debated asylum

---

[7] See generally: C Harvey, *Seeking Asylum in the UK: Problems and Prospects* (London, Butterworths, 2000).
[8] Nationality, Immigration and Asylum Act 2002, Immigration and Asylum Act 1999, Asylum and Immigration Act 1996, Asylum and Immigration Appeals Act 1993.
[9] There is an extensive literature on the Human Rights Act 1998. See generally: C Gearty 'Reconciling Parliamentary Democracy and Human Rights' (2002) 118 *LQR* 248; J Wadham 'The Human Rights Act: One Year On' [2001] *EHRLR* 620; K Ewing 'The Human Rights Act and Parliamentary Democracy' (1999) 62 *MLR* 79; K Ewing and C Gearty 'Rocky Foundations for Labour's New Rights' [1997] *EHRLR* 146.

on numerous occasions and in the last decade several legislative initiatives have been undertaken. Government policy is regularly examined in the courts and this judicial assessment of policy provides a useful case study for the purpose of this chapter. What emerges is a dynamic relationship between government, administrators, adjudicators and the courts. The evidence does not suggest a senior judiciary intent on undermining asylum policy. There are cases where judges have taken a firm stand on the progressive development of asylum law. However, the senior judiciary, in particular, continues to display an acute awareness of executive policy preferences. The resulting danger is that excessive deference is accorded to the decision-maker rather than the substance of the legal argument. The results are troubling for those concerned with the effective legal protection of human rights in the UK.

Human Rights and the Management of the Asylum Process

In order to advance the argument I will highlight three themes in asylum law: the contested meaning of refugee status; the treatment of asylum seekers awaiting a determination of their claim; and national security. A pattern emerges in the case-law and it is one which does not support the argument that the judges are undermining asylum policy in the UK. What it does suggest is a senior judiciary intent on bringing clarity to the meaning of refugee law and mindful of its institutional role. This does not mean that agreement with executive decision-making is always the result, but it does demonstrate a willingness to try to combine fairness to the individual with effective management of the asylum process. This tension, evident throughout public law, becomes particularly problematic in this area. The problem is that in this area the management of the process and the concerns of the executive are accorded excessive weight. The danger at present is that the substantive legal arguments can lose out to managerial imperatives in the asylum process.

Refugee status determination is at the core of the asylum process. Who is a refugee in law? The definition is contained in the 1951 Convention relating to the Status of Refugees.[10] An individual is a refugee if he or she has a well-founded fear of persecution for a 'Convention reason' and is unwilling or unable to seek the protection of his or her state of origin.[11] This is the definition which is applied in domestic law in the UK. The House of Lords has attempted to establish a clear approach which will facilitate asylum decision-making. It has also, on some occasions, been prepared to advance the interpretation of the definition to reflect the purpose of the law and modern legal developments in the protection of human rights.

[10] 189 UNTS 154, entry into force: 22 April 1954.
[11] Art 1A(2).

In *R v Secretary of State for the Home Department, ex parte Sivakumaran*, for example, the issue was whether six Tamil asylum seekers were entitled to refugee status.[12] Their applications for asylum were refused by the Home Secretary. At first instance their applications for judicial review were rejected. However, on appeal to the Court of Appeal they were successful and the Home Secretary appealed. The Court of Appeal concluded that, from the perspective of someone of reasonable courage, the 'fear' (in 'well-founded fear') could be shown to be misconceived, but this fact alone did not necessarily transform its subjective nature. While the court accepted that fears which were simply paranoid could be discounted, those which were fully justified on the face of the situation could not be ignored, even if they were subsequently shown, by objective evidence, to have been misconceived. This approach was challenged in the House of Lords (the Court of Appeal did not find that the appellants were entitled to refugee status, this was a matter for the Home Secretary in the light of the new test). Lord Keith was critical of the reasoning. He shifted the attention back to the 'well-founded' nature of the fear. In other words, he stressed that the fear had to be objectively shown to be justified and not merely subjectively felt by the individual. Lord Keith stated:

> In my opinion the requirement that the applicant's fear of persecution should be well-founded means that there has to be demonstrated a reasonable degree of likelihood that he will be persecuted for a Convention reason if returned to his own country.[13]

Lord Templeman followed the same approach:

> My Lords, in order for a 'fear' of 'persecution' to be 'well-founded' there must exist a danger that if the claimant for refugee status is returned to his country of origin he will meet with persecution. The Convention does not enable the claimant to decide whether the danger of persecution exists.[14]

The approach of the Court of Appeal was rejected and the House of Lords opted for an interpretation which, in its view, would assist the process of asylum adjudication. By placing the emphasis on the 'well-founded' nature of the 'fear' the ruling guaranteed that, in practice, the objective element in the test would trump any subjective considerations. The focus thus shifted decisively to the assessment of the conditions in the state of origin as the principal matter in the assessment of asylum claims. In the first important disagreement over the meaning of refugee law to reach the House of Lords,

---

[12] [1988] 1 AC 958 (HL).
[13] *Ibid*, 994.
[14] *Ibid*, 996.

the Law Lords opted for an interpretation which reflected the government's preferred view of the refugee definition.

Disagreements are evident within states on the meaning of refugee law. These are resolved by domestic courts and tribunals. However, in the context of European integration, difficulties have arisen over divergent interpretations between member states of the European Union (EU). What happens when states disagree over the meaning of refugee law when a system is in place to transfer responsibility for the substantive assessment of claims? This question arises from the ongoing attempts to promote a common approach to asylum in the EU. The issues were addressed in *R v Secretary of State for the Home Department, ex parte Adan*.[15] The case involved two appeals before the House of Lords from decisions in the Court of Appeal on applications for judicial review. Adan, a citizen of Somalia, had unsuccessfully sought asylum in Germany. After the refusal of her claim she travelled to the UK and claimed asylum. The Home Secretary determined, however, that the Dublin Convention 1990 (a treaty designed to facilitate the transfer of responsibility for asylum claims) was applicable and that Germany should take responsibility for Adan. The German authorities accepted responsibility and her claim for asylum in the UK was refused without consideration of the merits. Adan sought leave to move for judicial review of the certification of her case. The Divisional Court dismissed the application but the Court of Appeal allowed Adan's appeal.

Aitseguer, a citizen of Algeria, had travelled through France on his way to the UK. He claimed to be at risk from an armed group in Algeria and that the government was unable to protect him. The Home Secretary determined that Aitseguer should be returned to France in line with the Dublin Convention 1990. The French authorities agreed to take him back and his case was certified. Aitseguer successfully challenged the decision in judicial review proceedings on the basis that the Home Secretary had not taken the French position fully into account. This decision was subsequently upheld by the Court of Appeal.

In both cases the approach of the courts had serious implications for government policy and for hundreds of other similar cases. The problem involved the contested meaning of the refugee definition in different states and the impact this had on the operation of the Dublin Convention 1990. As Lord Steyn noted, a minority of states confined protection to those who could link persecution to the state. France and Germany followed this approach. The UK did not take this view. The subsequent problems, of conflicting interpretations of refugee law within the EU, were well illustrated in both these cases. Adan feared persecution in Somalia as a result of being a member of a persecuted minority clan, while Aitseguer claimed to be the target of the Groupe Islamique Armé in Algeria. The feared persecution

---

[15] [2001] 2 AC 477 (HL).

could not be attributed directly to the state. The Home Secretary accepted the argument that if returned both might be sent to their states of origin, due to the interpretation of the Convention applied in Germany and France. The Home Secretary did, however, suggest that there were alternative forms of protection in both states which might offer protection to Adan and Aitseguer. An important question emerged in this case. Is there a true and 'international meaning' of the 1951 Convention, or do a range of possible interpretations exist, some of which the Home Secretary is entitled to regard as legitimate? Lord Steyn stated that the Refugee Convention did have a relevant autonomous and 'international meaning' and that this included persecution which emanated from non-state agents. Lord Slynn stated:

> The question is not whether the Secretary of State thinks that the alternative view is reasonable or permissible or legitimate or arguable but whether the Secretary of State is satisfied that the application of the other state's interpretation of the Convention would mean that the individual will still not be sent back otherwise than in accordance with the Convention. The Secretary of State must form his view as to what the Convention requires.... His is the relevant view and the relevant obligation is that of the United Kingdom.[16]

He rejected the argument that the Home Secretary could simply adopt a list of permissible interpretations of the Convention. The appeals by the Home Secretary were therefore dismissed. What the case demonstrated was a judicial insistence that the UK fulfil its obligations in refugee law by forming a view of the correct interpretation of the law. The question for the Home Secretary was not whether some other form of protection might be available in France or Germany, but what the 1951 Convention required. Would the individual in fact be sent back to his or her state of origin? In my view, by directing the Home Secretary to the correct interpretation of refugee law, the House of Lords effectively defended the notion that refugee law has a determinate content even in the face of disagreement in the EU. In particular, the Home Secretary was not permitted to evade responsibility by insisting that a range of reasonable interpretations existed outside of the UK. This case reflects a judicial insistence on the importance of according a determinate content to legal norms and the judges laid down important guidance on the approach that should be taken in the UK to refugee status in the context of European integration. The case is a useful example of how the law, through the process of adjudication, places a value on coherence and determinate outcomes in the context of ongoing disagreement.

It is difficult to view this as a case of the court stepping beyond the law to interfere with public administration. Even though the judgment had an impact on the application of the safe third country rule in other cases, the Law Lords were not prepared to defer to the argument of the

---

[16] *Ibid*, 509.

Home Secretary. Their approach was based on the fundamental value of respect for the individual and the protection of the person in the determination of asylum cases. In my view, this judgment suggests where the limits to disagreement rest within refugee law and why those limits should exist. The Law Lords, in this case, accepted that disagreement over the meaning of refugee law existed, but then advanced an approach which openly acknowledged the potential unfairness and risk to the individual. If the Home Secretary was allowed simply to rely on reasonable disagreement within Europe in this context then risks would follow for the individual asylum seeker. The Home Secretary was thus obliged in law to reach a definite view of the true meaning of the refugee definition. The case highlights neatly an instance of how the legal system finds a determinate way out of disagreement, and in this case, in a way which reflects a concern for the rights of the individual. Values thus enter the process of legal interpretation and co-exist with the need for determinate outcomes in individual cases. In my view, what underpins this is respect for the value of individual human dignity and a concern with the fairness of procedures.

Two further cases reveal the tensions in the contests over the meaning of refugee law. In the first case, *Horvath v Secretary of State for the Home Department*,[17] the appellant was a member of the Roma community and a citizen of the Republic of Slovakia. He left Slovakia and came to the UK with his family to claim asylum. He argued that he feared persecution from skinhead groups which targeted Roma and that the Slovak police had failed to provide adequate protection. His application was refused and a special adjudicator dismissed his appeal on the basis that he was not a credible witness. The Immigration Appeal Tribunal (IAT), however, did find his evidence to be consistent and reviewed the finding on credibility. The IAT accepted that he had a well-founded fear of violence by skinheads, but that this was not persecution because he had not demonstrated that he was unable or unwilling to seek the protection of the state. The Court of Appeal dismissed his appeal.

The issue for the House of Lords was the failure of the state to provide protection. What was the link to the persecution feared? Lord Hope noted that the purpose of the 1951 Convention was to offer surrogate protection when an individual no longer enjoyed the protection of his state of origin. He further stated that this purpose had implications for the interpretation of the word 'persecution'. Lord Hope suggested that the failure of state protection was central to the entire system of refugee law. He concluded that the word 'persecution':

> implies a failure by the state to make protection available against the ill-treatment or violence which the person suffers at the hands of his persecutors.[18]

[17] [2000] 1 AC 489 (HL).
[18] *Ibid*, 497.

The House of Lords dismissed the appeal. The case is a useful example of the government's concerns about asylum policy entering fully into the assessment of the interpretation of refugee status. Rather than decide on the meaning of 'persecution', as a distinct concept, the Law Lords were more focused on the availability of protection in the state of origin. The case also reveals an unwillingness to accept that treatment in other European states might generate a valid refugee claim. In particular, the House of Lords relied heavily on an argument about the surrogate nature of refugee protection in its assessment of the meaning of the term 'persecution'. The assumption in this case, and one that is evident in other cases, is that sufficient protection is available in other European states.

The case can be contrasted with *R v Immigration Appeal Tribunal, ex parte Shah; Islam and others v Secretary of State for the Home Department*.[19] The appellants were two Pakistani women who had been forced from their home by their husbands and risked being falsely accused of adultery. They argued that they would be unprotected by the state if sent back and that they ran the risk of criminal proceedings for sexual immorality. They sought asylum in the UK on the basis that they had a well-founded fear of persecution as a result of membership in a particular social group within the meaning of the 1951 Convention. The issue before the House of Lords was the precise meaning to be given to 'membership in a particular social group'. A majority of the House of Lords concluded (Lord Millett dissenting) that the phrase could be applied to groups which might be regarded as coming within the Convention's anti-discriminatory objectives. This meant it applied to those groups which shared a common immutable characteristic and were discriminated against in matters of fundamental human rights. In certain circumstances women could constitute such a group if they lived in societies like Pakistan. Unlike in *Horvath,* the majority in the House of Lords was here prepared to be generous in the interpretation of refugee law and in its assessment of the conditions in Pakistan. This can be contrasted with the views expressed in the 'European' context of *Horvath*.

Although *Shah/Islam* might appear to extend the applicability of refugee law widely, the Law Lords were careful to stress the particular circumstances of the cases. The exercise of a more purposive interpretation within refugee law thus promotes at best incremental advances. The case highlights, in my view, the fact that the law is not static and is subject to development on the basis of the values which refugee law protects. The Law Lords were influenced by arguments about what a modern interpretation of refugee status should be in the light of ongoing developments in human rights law. This conclusion was reached on the basis of the values which refugee law serves.

---

[19] [1999] 2 All ER 545 (HL).

The second main area of dispute in asylum policy is the treatment of asylum seekers while awaiting a decision and the decision-making process itself. Disagreement between some members of the judiciary and the executive is evident from the case-law.[20] The tensions were demonstrated in *R v Secretary of State for the Home Department, ex parte Saadi*.[21] Saadi was one of four asylum seekers who appealed against the decision of the Court of Appeal that his detention at Oakington detention centre was lawful. At first instance it was held to be unlawful with reference to Article 5 of the European Convention on Human Rights.[22]

A fast-track procedure was introduced at the centre in 2000 whereby asylum seekers could be detained for seven days if it was felt that their claims could be determined quickly. Saadi and others challenged their detention. The first instance decision in their favour was subsequently reversed by the Court of Appeal. Their appeal to the House of Lords was also dismissed. The House of Lords concluded that their compulsory detention could not be said to have been arbitrary or disproportionate. In fact, the court argued, the process was highly structured and tightly managed. The Law Lords concluded that this structure would be disrupted if asylum seekers were able to live wherever they wished. The Law Lords stated that a balance had to be struck between the deprivation of liberty and the need for speedy decisions in order to prevent long delays. The House of Lords argued that conditions at Oakington were reasonable and that the periods of detention were not excessive. As a result, the balance was in favour of recognising that detention at Oakington was reasonable and proportionate. The judgment demonstrated a willingness to defer to the overall objectives of asylum policy and judicial 'understanding' of the concerns of public administration. The government's argument that detention was required in order to facilitate the speedy processing of selected asylum claims was found to be persuasive. In reaching this conclusion the Law Lords were evidently influenced by concerns about the overall management of the asylum process. The first instance judgment had, in particular, triggered an angry reaction from the Home Secretary. The result was, however, based on an interpretation of the meaning of the limitations to Article 5 which suggested that the deprivation of liberty could be justified in this context.

The Home Secretary was also not impressed with the first instance decision of Justice Collins in *R (Q and others) v Secretary of State for the Home Department*.[23] The applicants here challenged the lawfulness of a

---

[20] See *R v Secretary of State for the Home Department, ex parte Joint Council for the Welfare of Immigrants* [1997] 1 WLR 275 (CA).
[21] [2002] UKHL 41.
[22] Art 5 guarantees the right to liberty and the security of the person. It is not an absolute right and there are listed limitations.
[23] [2003] EWHC 195 (Admin).

policy adopted under section 55 of the Nationality, Immigration and Asylum Act 2002. In order to meet government targets on the reduction of the number of asylum claims, the Home Secretary embarked on a policy of refusing welfare support to asylum seekers who did not make a claim 'as soon as reasonably practicable' upon entering the UK. The 2002 Act prohibits the provision of support to the destitute,[24] but allows the Home Secretary to offer support if it is necessary in order to prevent a breach of Convention rights. The precise meaning of section 55 was unclear, but more significantly the Act and its practical implementation were having a negative impact on groups of asylum seekers in various parts of Britain.

All the applicants were asylum seekers who were refused support because they had not made their claims as soon as reasonably practicable upon entering the UK. The applicants challenged the lawfulness of the decision and argued that their human rights were violated because the refusal to offer support meant they had no way of gaining access to food and shelter. Justice Collins held that the policy was unlawful. He found flaws in the decision-making process relating to a general failure to consider each case on its merits. He concluded that there was a real risk of a violation of Article 3 (prohibition on torture or inhuman or degrading treatment or punishment) and Article 8(1) (the right to privacy) of the European Convention on the basis that a person would be left destitute once benefits were refused. He also held that there had been a violation of Article 6 (right to a fair trial) with respect to the flawed procedures for challenging the initial refusal of support. In his judgment, Justice Collins referred to the fact that the Joint Committee on Human Rights at Westminster had noted possible problems under Article 3 and Article 8. The Home Secretary therefore had access to information suggesting problems during the legislative stage.

The Home Secretary appealed. The Court of Appeal, in rejecting the appeal, clarified the meaning of the relevant provision of the 2002 Act with reference, in particular, to Article 3 of the ECHR. But the more significant aspect of the judgment related to the assessment of the overall fairness of the procedures. The court held that the process was unfair for a range of reasons including: the flaws in the interview process; the fact that the purpose of the interview was not fully explained; that the Home Secretary had not taken into account the state of mind of the individuals involved; and the use of standard form questionnaires. The Home Secretary opted not to appeal and reforms to the asylum process were promised.

The importance of this case rests in the strict scrutiny of the procedures applied and the emphasis, at first instance and in the Court of Appeal, on the importance of a proper assessment of each individual case. This aspect of the application of the rule of law is sometimes neglected, but in a climate

---

[24] S 55(1).

of hostility towards asylum seekers, the stress on the fairness of procedures, and the precise factors which need to be incorporated, is valuable. Here the judges fulfil an important role in ensuring that equality before the law has meaning in practice for each individual. The stress on fairness is essential in the face of an asylum process which is under severe pressure from the executive to deliver quick results.

This rigorous assessment of asylum procedures has a history. An early example of concern about aspects of the asylum process is *Bugdaycay v Secretary of State for the Home Department*.[25] The appellants in this case were granted temporary leave to stay in the UK and had remained beyond their designated leave. They were arrested and admitted that they had lied about their reasons for coming to the UK. They stated that they did not wish to return as they feared that they would be arrested for their political activities. Their applications for asylum were refused. As Lord Bridge acknowledged, this was the first time the House of Lords had to consider the 1951 Convention.[26] In rejecting the argument of the appellants (that the immigration rules prohibited their removal), Lord Bridge noted that the matter was essentially a question of fact to be determined by an immigration officer or the Secretary of State and thus only open to challenge in the courts (at that time) on *Wednesbury* principles.[27] He stated:

> There is no ground for treating the question raised by a claim to refugee status as an exception to this rule.[28]

The first three appellants also sought to argue that the UK would be acting against recommendations advanced by the Executive Committee of the United Nations High Commissioner for Refugees (UNHCR) and that this was contrary to the obligation contained in Article 35 of the 1951 Convention.[29] Article 35 contains an undertaking by state parties to co-operate with UNHCR in the exercise of its functions. On this Lord Bridge stated:

> I express no opinion on that question, since it is as it seems to me, neither necessary nor desirable that this House should attempt to interpret an instrument of this character which is of no binding force either in municipal or international law.[30]

Lord Bridge rejected their argument. The case of the other appellant (Musisi) raised a distinct issue. He was a Ugandan national, and in this instance the Secretary of State argued that even if he was a refugee, there

[25] [1987] AC 514 (HL).
[26] *Ibid*, 521.
[27] *Ibid*, 523.
[28] *Ibid*.
[29] Art 35 deals with the obligation on states to co-operate with UNHCR.
[30] Above n 25, at 524.

was no obstacle to him being returned to Kenya. The issue to be addressed was whether there was any available ground by which the discretionary decision to remove Musisi to Kenya could be challenged in judicial review. On this Lord Bridge noted:

> a detailed examination of the way in which the application made by the appellant for asylum was dealt with by the immigration authorities gives cause for grave concern.[31]

Lord Bridge was critical of the original asylum interview conducted by the immigration officer.[32] In particular, he was surprised to see such an important interview being undertaken by an immigration official with no knowledge of the country of origin.[33] The immigration officer effectively rejected the appellant's arguments, but this view was not the one eventually relied on by the Home Office. The Home Office preferred to leave the question of refugee status 'open' in this case. The thrust of the argument was that a safe country (Kenya) existed to which he could be returned. After stating the limitations on the role of the court in judicial review proceedings Lord Bridge noted:

> Within those limitations the court must, I think, be entitled to subject an administrative decision to the more rigorous examination, to ensure that it is in no way flawed, according to the gravity of the issue which the decision determines. The most fundamental of all human rights is the individual's right to life and when an administrative decision under challenge is said to be one which may put the applicant's life at risk, the basis of the decision must surely call for the most anxious scrutiny.[34]

Applying this test to the case of Musisi, Lord Bridge concluded in the appellant's favour. The Secretary of State's decision to place faith in the Kenyan authorities was, according to Lord Bridge, misplaced.[35] Following a similar approach Lord Templeman stated:

> In my opinion where the result of a flawed decision may imperil life or liberty a special responsibility lies on the court in the examination of the decision-making process.[36]

The case is an example of the judicial use of rights discourse in administrative law long before the Human Rights Act 1998. It revealed a concern with the

---

[31] *Ibid*, 526–27.
[32] *Ibid*, 528.
[33] *Ibid*.
[34] *Ibid*, 531.
[35] *Ibid*, 533.
[36] *Ibid*, 537.

treatment of the individual in the asylum context and an acknowledgement of the serious human rights implications. As Nicholas Blake notes, the introduction of the 'anxious scrutiny' test in this case resulted in a sharp rise in judicial review applications and effectively assisted in the eventual creation of a comprehensive appeals system.[37] The judgment recognised that where fundamental rights are at risk (in this instance the right to life), the courts, in judicial review proceedings, should examine the decision-making process very closely to ensure that there is no unfairness to the individual. The House of Lords in this case therefore introduced a more rigorous assessment of the asylum decision-making process which had a practical impact on government policy.

The third area of relevance to this chapter is national security and the immigration and asylum process. Here a willingness to defer to executive decision-making is particularly marked. This is a trend which is not confined to immigration and asylum law. The first case of interest concerned the exclusion clauses in refugee law. In *T v Home Secretary*[38] the appellant was an Algerian citizen who claimed asylum in the UK. His claim was rejected by the Home Secretary and his appeal to a special adjudicator was unsuccessful. The appellant had been involved in a bomb attack on Algiers airport in which ten people were killed and then on a raid on an army barracks in which one person was killed. The special adjudicator concluded that this brought him within the exclusion clause in Article 1F(b)[39] because, as provided in that provision, 'there were serious reasons for considering' that he had committed serious non-political crimes. His appeals to the IAT and the Court of Appeal failed. The House of Lords also dismissed his appeal. However, the ruling contains extensive consideration of the meaning of 'serious non-political crime' within the context of refugee law. It demonstrated again the role of the House of Lords in resolving a disagreement over the meaning of refugee law with extensive reference to the values the law was intended to promote. The House of Lords concluded that there were serious reasons for considering that he had committed a serious non-political crime. The result was that the appellant could be legitimately excluded from refugee status. The debate in this case primarily involved the precision of the exclusion clauses rather than whether or not he should have been excluded. The Law Lords displayed a desire to advance a clear definition which could be straightforwardly applied in the process of decision-making and adjudication. Underpinning this, however, was a view of the purpose of refugee law and the values it is intended to uphold. In

---

[37] In this collection at ch 9.
[38] [1996] AC 742 (HL).
[39] A1F(b) provides: 'The provisions of this Convention shall not apply to a person with respect to whom there are serious reasons for considering that: ... (b) he has committed a serious non-political crime outside the country of refuge prior to his admission to that country as a refugee'.

particular, in this case, that some individuals should be excluded from refugee status because of their criminal activity.

As in other states, anxiety about terrorism has dominated political discussion in the UK since 11 September 2001. Many of the concerns raised have already been addressed in past cases in asylum and immigration law. What the past cases reveal is that when national security, immigration and asylum collide then the judges are likely to defer extensively to the views of the executive. This trend, remains the dominant one. This was confirmed in *Secretary of State for the Home Department v Rehman*.[40] The appellant, a Pakistani national, arrived in the UK in February 1993 after being given entry clearance to work as a minister of religion in Oldham. Both his parents were British citizens. His application for indefinite leave to remain was refused. The Home Secretary cited information which linked the appellant to an Islamic terrorist organisation and argued that his deportation from the UK would be conducive to the public good in the interests of national security. Rehman appealed to the Special Immigration Appeals Commission (SIAC). SIAC was established under the Special Immigration Appeals Commission Act 1997. It was created in response to the judgment of the European Court of Human Rights in *Chahal v UK* and the concerns raised in that case about the procedures for challenging deportation in the national security context.[41]

In his open statement to the Commission, the Home Secretary stated that the appellant had directly supported terrorism in the Indian subcontinent and as a result he was a threat to national security. The Commission held, contrary to the argument of the Home Secretary, that the term 'national security' should be narrowly defined. The Commission stated:

> we adopt the position that a person may be said to offend against national security if he engages in, promotes, or encourages violent activity which is targeted at the United Kingdom, its system of government or its people. This includes activities directed against the overthrow or destabilisation of a foreign government if that foreign government is likely to take reprisals against the United Kingdom which affect the security of the United Kingdom or of its nationals. National security extends also to situations where United Kingdom citizens are targeted, wherever they may be.[42]

The Commission concluded that it had not been established in fact that the appellant was likely to be a threat to national security. The test adopted was that of a high civil balance of probabilities. The Home Secretary appealed successfully to the Court of Appeal.[43] The Court of Appeal considered that too narrow a view of national security had been adopted by

[40] [2001] UKHL 47.
[41] (1996) 23 EHRR 413.
[42] Above n 40, at para 2.
[43] [2000] 3 WLR 1240 (CA).

the Commission. On appeal to the House of Lords, Lord Slynn acknowledged that the term 'in the interests of national security' could not be used to justify any reason the Home Secretary had for seeking the deportation of an individual.[44] However, he did not accept the narrow interpretation suggested by the appellant.

> I accept that there must be a real possibility of an adverse affect on the United Kingdom for what is done by the individual under inquiry but I do not accept that it has to be direct or immediate. Whether there is a real possibility is a matter which has to be weighed up by the Secretary of State and balanced against the possible injustice to that individual if a deportation order is made.[45]

Lord Slynn stressed the need for the Commission to give due weight to the assessment and conclusions of the Home Secretary in the light of his responsibilities.[46] Lord Steyn agreed with the reasoning of Lord Slynn and added that 'even democracies are entitled to protect themselves, *and* the executive is the best judge of the need for international co-operation to combat terrorism and counter-terrorist strategies'.[47] In rejecting the Commission's reliance on the civil standard of proof, Lord Steyn made reference to the events of 11 September 2001.[48] He concluded by acknowledging the well-established position that issues of national security do not fall beyond the competence of the courts, however, he stated that it was, 'self-evidently right that national courts must give great weight to the views of the executive on matters of national security'.[49] Lord Hoffmann continued this theme stating that the Commission had failed to acknowledge the inherent limitations of the judicial function which flowed from the doctrine of the separation of powers.[50] This brought with it the need 'in matters of judgment and evaluation of evidence, to show proper deference to the primary decision-maker'.[51] This restraint did not limit the appellate jurisdiction of the Commission and the need for it 'flows from a common-sense recognition of the nature of the issue and the differences in the decision-making

---

[44] Above n 40, at para 15.
[45] *Ibid*, para 16.
[46] *Ibid*, para 26.
[47] *Ibid*, para 28.
[48] 'While I came to this conclusion by the end of the hearing of the appeal, the tragic events of 11 September 2001 in New York reinforce compellingly that no other approach is possible'. *Ibid*, para 29. For developments in Canada see *Suresh v Canada (Minister of Citizenship and Immigration)* [2002] SCC 1; RJ Daniels, P Macklem and K Roach (eds), *The Security of Freedom: Essays on Canada's Anti-Terrorism Bill* (Toronto, University of Toronto Press, 2001).
[49] Above n 40, at para 31.
[50] *Ibid*, para 49.
[51] *Ibid*.

processes and responsibilities of the Home Secretary and the Commission'.[52] In a postscript Lord Hoffmann stated:

> I wrote this speech some three months before the recent events in New York and Washington. They are a reminder that in matters of national security, the cost of failure can be high. This seems to me to underline the need for the judicial arm of government to respect the decisions of ministers of the Crown on the question of whether support for terrorist activities in a foreign country constitutes a threat to national security ... If the people are to accept the consequences of such decisions, they must be made by persons whom the people have elected and whom they can remove.[53]

The ruling endorsed a very broad interpretation of 'national security'. The notion that the executive must be deferred to because of its democratic legitimacy, particularly in times of crisis, raises several problems. Lord Hoffmann's comments suggest that the executive can step outside the normal application of the rule of law in times of public emergency by making its own decision about what the law is. In my view, the doctrine of the rule of law does not permit this abdication of judicial responsibility. The risk in this approach is basic unfairness to the individual.

As Trevor Allan suggests, surely the focus should be on the quality of the reasons advanced.[54] The main question should be whether the legal reasoning is worthy of support or not in the individual case. It is problematic for judges to defer mainly because the executive has made a decision based on rather sweeping assessments of the national security threat. This view is reinforced if one considers that in the national security context there is a heightened risk to the human rights and civil liberties of the individual. It is on these occasions that the rule of law is tested. By according conclusive weight to the views of the executive, the judges are not discharging their responsibilities. It is for the judges to take a view on the meaning of law, and not to defer to the meaning preferred by the executive. If the courts do not do this they risk abandoning one of the values of the rule of law: the defence of the person against arbitrary power. Why the House of Lords was prepared to insist on its approach in *Shah/Islam* and *ex parte Adan* and not in *Rehman* remains unclear in my view.

Although dealing with a different issue, similar trends are evident in *A and others v Secretary of State for the Home Department*.[55] The case concerned a challenge by a number of individuals detained under the provisions of the Anti-terrorism, Crime and Security Act 2001. The Act, and the Human Rights Act 1998 (Designated Derogation) Order 2001,

---

[52] *Ibid*, para 58.
[53] *Ibid*, para 62.
[54] In this collection ch 11.
[55] [2002] EWCA Civ 1502.

were introduced after the terrorist attacks of 11 September 2001. A challenge was brought against the provisions of the 2001 Act which allow the Home Secretary to detain indefinitely foreign nationals who are suspected of links with terrorist activity or organisations but who cannot be deported, extradited or removed from the UK. The government derogated from Article 5 of the Convention for the specific purpose of these provisions in order to allow the detention of selected individuals indefinitely (and subject to prescribed safeguards). SIAC held that the measures were discriminatory in effect, and were contrary to Articles 5 and 14 of the European Convention, as they did not apply equally to British nationals.

On appeal against the SIAC decision the Court of Appeal reached a different conclusion. Following a similar approach to that expressed in *Rehman* Lord Woolf stated:

> Decisions as to what is required in the interest of national security are self-evidently within the category of decisions in relation to which the court is required to show considerable deference to the Secretary of State because he is better qualified to make an assessment as to what action is called for.[56]

Lord Justice Brooke adopted a similar line of reasoning.[57]

The Court of Appeal held that British nationals were not in the same position as foreign nationals in this context. Lord Woolf noted that the non-nationals involved in this case no longer had a right to remain, only a right not to be removed.[58] This distinguished their plight from that of nationals. He also stressed that international law recognised the distinction between the treatment of nationals and non-nationals. The court accepted that Parliament was entitled to limit the measures to foreign nationals on the basis that Article 15 of the European Convention permitted measures that derogate only 'to the extent strictly required by the exigencies of the situation'. The tension between Article 14 and Article 15 had, Lord Woolf argued, an important impact. The Secretary of State was obliged to derogate only to the extent necessary and widening the powers of indefinite detention would, Lord Woolf stated, conflict with this objective.

While acknowledging the importance of human rights protection, the Court of Appeal also accepted that it had to accord a degree of deference to the views of the executive in this area. Lord Woolf stated:

> The unfortunate fact is that the emergency which the government believes to exist justifies the taking of action which would not otherwise be acceptable.

---

[56] *Ibid*, para 39.
[57] *Ibid*, para 81(6): 'The events of 11th September are a reminder that in matters of national security the cost of failure can be high. Decisions by ministers on such questions, with serious potential rights for the community ... require a legitimacy which can be conferred only by entrusting them to persons responsible to the community through the democratic process'.
[58] *Ibid*, para 47.

The ECHR recognises that there can be circumstances where action of this sort is fully justified. It is my conclusion here, as a matter of law, and that is what we are concerned with, that action is justified. The important point is that the courts are able to protect the rule of law.[59]

The case reveals again the measure of deference accorded to the executive when national security is raised. Lord Woolf's reference to the rule of law rests uneasily with other aspects of the case. What the statement reveals is, in this case, a concern to check that the government's policy could be justified with reference to established legal norms. But there was not the sort of rigorous assessment which has emerged in other immigration and asylum cases. It is also evident from the SIAC ruling that scope for disagreement on the content of the law existed in this case.

The weight given to the views of the executive (by both SIAC and the Court of Appeal) on what was necessary in this context, and whether there was in fact an emergency which threatened the life of the nation, is revealing. Again, there is evidence that the views of the Home Secretary are being accorded excessive weight. This is an area where 'anxious scrutiny' of the reasons provided is most needed. In my view, this is not happening when national security is raised. As noted in the cases above, beyond the national security context the views of the Home Secretary, and the administrative perspective, are accorded significant weight, but they are not generally regarded as a decisive argument. While one can understand a certain judicial unease in addressing national security matters, excessive deference to the views of the executive is inappropriate if there is a principled commitment to the rule of law. Evidence suggests that this is precisely the time when the values which underpin the rule of law need to be upheld. While the Home Secretary will have access to more detailed factual information and is an elected politician, I am still not persuaded of the view that the courts should therefore automatically defer to his or her understanding of the substantive content of the law. This view is reinforced when one considers that human rights are now a secure part of domestic law in the UK in the form of the Human Rights Act 1998. The judges have a responsibility to ensure that the law, properly understood, is applied to all on an equal basis.

Disagreement and the Meaning of Asylum Law

The cases examined address some key areas of disagreement over the meaning of asylum law. Questions were raised over the definition of 'refugee', the management of the asylum process, the effective implementation of international agreements, as well as the matter of national security. The House of Lords has now clarified central elements of the refugee

---

[59] *Ibid*, para 64.

definition in an attempt to resolve disputes within the process of adjudication. The Law Lords, in my view, have not adopted an approach which can be easily reduced to a single or unified theme. However, it is inaccurate to describe the approach as a concerted attempt to undermine government asylum policy. While there have been incremental advances in doctrinal development, and in ensuring procedures are applied fairly to each individual, the senior judiciary consistently displays a measure of deference toward the executive and, in my view, a rather generous understanding of the problems faced by successive governments. The risk in this approach is that the value which the rule of law attaches to the protection of the individual is steadily eroded.

On national security, decisions reveal an established trend of excessive deference toward the government's view. This is evident in *A and others* and *Rehman*.[60] In these cases, the judges selected an approach designed to facilitate government policy and which relied on deferring to the executive on the basis of its democratic mandate. The reference made to the rule of law in *A and others* by Lord Woolf reflects a rather 'thin' version of the concept. This general 'facilitative approach' goes beyond national security and is evident in the other cases examined above.

The cases reveal a senior judiciary which places considerable weight on the overall management implications of judicial decision-making and which is inclined to defer excessively to the executive, particularly if national security is raised. From the analysis of these cases (most decided before the Human Rights Act 1998), concern expressed by politicians about judicial activism appears to have little validity. In my view, this is a cause for concern. Even in areas where a clash with the government is likely, the judges should insist on following the legal argument which is the most persuasive in the context of the asylum case before it. Fairness to the individual and equality before the law (both inherent in a proper understanding of what it means to function within a legal order) should not be abandoned when judges are faced with difficult choices. These values are more (not less) important when national security concerns are raised or when a marginalised group is at risk. In this context, each individual (whatever the collective ambitions of government policy) relies on a robust judiciary which is willing to remain consistently focused on the rule of law and the values which underpin it.

CONCLUSION

My suggestion in this chapter is that the traditional values associated with the rule of law are of particular significance for refugees and asylum seekers.

---

[60] This trend was also evident in *R (Farrakhan) v Secretary of State for the Home Department* [2002] 3 WLR 481 (CA).

The protection against arbitrary power and the basic principles of fairness, which are built into legal order, are important for marginalised groups in society. The judges have a duty to uphold the rule of law even when they risk serious public criticism. The protection from arbitrary power that the concept should bring is undermined if judges refuse to engage with contested areas of public policy. In my view, there are two problems which have as a result arisen in asylum law.

First, the judges are too often influenced by the broader policy debates on asylum and the problems which the government has experienced in trying to manage the process in an efficient and effective way. These factors should not be discounted, but if they become the dominant concern, there is an increased risk of unfairness in individual cases.

Secondly, there is evidence of a willingness to defer to the views of the executive at times when rigorous scrutiny of the merits of legal arguments is required. The obvious example is in the national security, immigration and asylum context. I am not persuaded that reference to national security should be enough to deter the judges from a close assessment of the law and its proper application.

Adherence to the rule of law brings with it a commitment to respect for the dignity of the individual. In my view, the judges have on occasions demonstrated an understanding of this fact in asylum law. However, when national security is raised, there is a danger of excessive deference undermining a thorough examination of the substantive legal issues. Asylum seekers, in particular, depend on judges and decision-makers who are prepared to uphold the values which underpin legal order.

9

Judicial Review of Expulsion Decisions: Reflections on the UK Experience

NICHOLAS BLAKE QC

OUTLINE

IN THIS CHAPTER I review the role of human rights and other international legal obligations of the state in opening up a bastion of the prerogative power to judicial scrutiny, namely the admission and expulsion of foreigners. I attempt to describe the development of British law from common law concepts of the exercise of prerogative powers with respect to aliens through to a legal regime giving domestic effect to both the European Convention on Human Rights (hereafter ECHR) and the obligations with respect to aliens under European Community law (hereafter EC law). I suggest that the latter may have had particular importance in persuading judges that aliens have rights that require enforcement against the executive or cogent justification for necessary restrictions. This perhaps is one reason why international obligation seems to have played a somewhat more significant role in the case-law of the United Kingdom than in some jurisdictions in North America. In the second section I review the sequence of national security cases leading to the decision of the European Court of Human Rights in the case of *Chahal v United Kingdom* and the legislative and judicial responses to it in the UK. This includes the new statutory regimes in both the Special Immigration Appeals Commission Act 1997 and the Anti-Terrorism Crime and Security Act 2001. However, the content of these fragile rights and the extent to which the judiciary enforce them against the executive, turns on the critical question of judicial deference to the discretionary area of judgement afforded to the executive. Here judicial opinions and the resulting case-law are divided. The events of 9/11 have resulted in much of the constitutional space being yielded to the executive, who promptly derogated from the right to freedom from arbitrary detention in the case of suspected international terrorists who cannot be removed because of the risk of torture. The judicial scrutiny of these detentions is now a matter of acute controversy. In the concluding remarks, I attempt to make the case for the virtues of intensive judicial scrutiny of justification for interference with human rights under the common law or whatever legislative instrument has been enacted within the particular jurisdiction to give effect to these rights.

INTRODUCTION

The UK celebrated the first anniversary of the coming into force of its Human Rights Act 1998 (HRA) by derogating[1] from the protection against arbitrary detention afforded by Article 5 of the ECHR.[2] This is, at first blush, an unfortunate foundation for the suggestion that international human rights law has made a significant contribution to the judicial protection of aliens in the UK. It may be, however, that the derogation was perceived by the executive to be necessary in a human rights culture where prolonged detention, of asylum seekers would be seen as an affront to normal standards of justice precisely because human rights had made a difference. The derogation, itself subject to strict scrutiny in both the national and the international courts, could thus be seen as a reflection of how far judicial supervision of executive actions had established itself as a constitutional principle within the discourse of public law in the UK.

It would no doubt have astonished the British delegation who participated in the drafting and adoption of the European Convention in the1950s that the modest instrument they had designed to promote the virtues of a liberal democracy against the excesses of fascist and communist terror could have resulted in such a course of events.[3] Aliens were given no rights under the Convention itself. Indeed aliens are mentioned twice in the first 17 substantive Articles of the Convention. In Article 5(1)(f) their detention with a view to extradition or deportation is acknowledged to be a legitimate justification of interference with the right to liberty.[4] In Article 16,

---

[1] Anti Terrorism Crime and Security Act 2001 ss 21 to 23; Derogation Order effective from 13 November 2001.
[2] Art 5(1) provides:

> Everyone has the right to liberty and security of person. No one shall be deprived of his liberty save in the following cases and in accordance with a procedure prescribed by law: ... f) the lawful arrest or detention of a person to prevent his unauthorised entry into a country or of a person against whom action is being taken with a view to deportation or extradition.

[3] See AWB Simpson, *Human Rights and the End of Empire: Britain and the Genesis of the European Convention* (Oxford, Oxford University Press, 2001).
[4] The meaning of Art 5(1)(f) has recently been considered by the *R (Saadi) v Secretary of State for the Home Department* [2002] UKHL 41; [2002] INLR 523 where their Lordships concluded that detention to prevent unauthorised entry included the power to detain an asylum seeker to examine whether he or she had a lawful claim to enter. They rejected the proposition that the power was limited to detaining those who might otherwise abscond.

it is provided that nothing in the Convention is designed to preclude restrictions on the right of freedom of expression in respect of aliens.[5]

As a text therefore the ECHR appeared to be a distinctively uninviting instrument on which to found submissions on judicial control of immigration policy. The Fourth Protocol to the Convention[6] made express reference to immigration rights: the right of own nationals to enter their own country; freedom from collective expulsions; and a right to a hearing before a lawfully resident alien was deported from the jurisdiction. However, the UK, for reasons bound up with its peculiar problems in defining who its nationals were, never ratified the Fourth Protocol. An examination of the precise meaning of British subject, British national and British citizen for the purpose of national and international law is irrelevant to the present theme,[7] for the purpose of the law, the critical distinction was between aliens, who were subject to the prerogative, and British subjects, who were not. Until 1983, a British subject was the same as a Commonwealth citizen.[8] Until 1962,[9] such a person could enter and remain in the United Kingdom wherever he or she was born and of whatever colour, race, religion or gender. From 1973,[10] 'non-patrial British subjects'[11] required the same leave to enter as other foreigners, but the memory of the era when a nationality status gave rise to a right of entry shaped one form of judicial response to executive acts of immigration control. Whether a person was a British subject was a matter of precedent fact to be determined by the

---

[5] This obscure provision of the ECHR was not repeated in the subsequent ICCPR but was enacted into the HRA 1998. It was considered by the Court of Appeal in the case of *R (Farrakhan) v Secretary of State for the Home Department* [2002] 3 WLR 481, where it was considered to be largely obsolete.

[6] Opened for signature in 1963. For a recent application of the prohibition against mass expulsions see *Conka v Belgium* 05/02/2002; App No 0051564/99.

[7] From 1962 immigration restrictions were placed on certain classes of citizens of the [UK] and Colonies. The intensification of these restrictions in 1968 led to an early decision of the European Commission of Human Rights that this was degrading treatment directed against British nationals of Asian origin: the *East African Asian* case 3 EHRR 76. With the end of British sovereignty in Hong Kong, the favourable treatment given to British nationals from the Falkland Islands, and the continuing disgrace of the British overseas citizens coming to adverse international attention, measures were recently adopted to enable all British nationals to acquire the single privileged status of British citizen.

[8] On this date the British Nationality Act 1981 came into force.

[9] The Commonwealth Immigrants Act 1962 was the first set of laws requiring Commonwealth citizens to submit to examination on arrival. A more draconian regime was rushed through in 1968 in response to the expulsion of UK citizens from East Africa. The humiliating treatment meted out to these UK citizens without the right of abode, gave rise to the conclusion of the European Commission of Human Rights in the case of *East African Asians v UK* 3 EHRR 76 that the UK was guilty of degrading treatment contrary to Art 3 ECHR.

[10] The year when the regime of control established by the Immigration Act 1971 came into force.

[11] The term 'partial' was introduced by the Immigration Act 1971 until it was replaced by a statutory definition of citizen for immigration purposes by the British Nationality Act 1981. It referred to a citizen of the United Kingdom and Colonies and certain other British subjects who had a connection with the United Kingdom itself by reason of ancestry, residence, consular registration or marriage.

judiciary and not a matter of rational exercise of discretion for the assessment of the executive.[12] In the seminal case of *Khawaja*,[13] the House of Lords decided that a similar test was to be applied in examining executive claims that a non-citizen had entered the United Kingdom by deception. It was insufficient that the executive honestly and reasonably thought that such people were illegal entrants, the question was whether they were. Ultimately the journey described in this chapter is a narrative of the selection and use of different judicial techniques of review, whether so intensive as to amount to examination of jurisdictional facts (the correctness standard), a review of executive decisions concerning human rights with 'anxious scrutiny', or a review of discretion so deferential that it amounts to effective abstention (the so called super *Wednesbury* approach[14]).

JURISDICTION AND DISCRETION

The independent assertion of primary judicial power in the common law is most associated with the venerated writ of *habeas corpus*, by which the judges call for the executive to justify interference with the liberty of the subject, and the review is of the correctness of the executive assertion of authority to detain as a matter of fact or law.[15] The use of the term subject is not intended to amount to a special rule for citizens but rather those who are subject to the authority or jurisdiction of the Crown acting in right of the government of the UK.[16]

By contrast with the writ of *habeas* there are the former prerogative writs, now gathered together in the modern procedure for judicial review

---

[12] *R v Governor of Brixton Prison ex parte Guerin*, (1907) 51 Solicitors Journal 571 for the jurisdictional fact approach to questions of nationality. See *DPP v Bhagwan* [1972] AC 60 for a discussion of the former common law right of entry of Commonwealth citizens.

[13] *R v Secretary of State for the Home Department ex parte Khawaja* [1984] AC 74; [1983] 2 WLR 321.

[14] In fact there was always one test that applied a different level of scrutiny according to the subject matter. For the rejection of a super *Wednesbury* approach in the field of immigration and where subordinate legislation was quashed as irrational see *R v Secretary of State for the Home Department ex parte Javed and Ahmed* [2001] 3 WLR 323; [2002] QB 129.

[15] For the classic account of the scope of the writ in the Commonwealth see RJ Sharpe, *The Law of Habeas Corpus*, 2nd edn, (Oxford, Clarendon Press, 1995). Justice Sharpe of the Ontario Court of Appeal kindly brought to my attention his recent review of another proposal to subordinate the writ to the judicial review procedure. See Sharpe's review of D Clark and G McCoy's 'The Most Fundamental Legal Right: Habeas Corpus and the Commonwealth', 1 *Oxford Journal of Commonwealth Law* 287.

[16] This was made plain by Lord Scarman in *Khawaja* [1984], above n 13. The contrast with the position under the US Constitution was one reason for the Courts concerns in the case of *Abbasi* (see below n 21). Habeas is thus a means of reviewing the legitimacy of detention with a view to expulsion of any non-citizen: see *Tan Te Lam v Superintendent of Tai Chau Detention Centre* [1997] AC 97.

in the UK[17] that have developed as the primary procedure for public law challenges. A once-obscure decision as to the nature of the court's function when reviewing a decision of a local authority licensing committee, has for long given rise to the so-called *Wednesbury* principles for judicial review.[18] This case has been important in creating a proper constitutional space for democratically accountable policy-making and in permitting the exercise of truly discretionary powers granted to local authorities and other decision-makers.[19] This is properly the field of judicial deference and constitutional restraint. In both the UK and Canada, over-enthusiastic judicial meddling in labour relations cases, has prompted legislative intervention and judicial self-denial. It is not, however, a helpful or even a coherent test when dealing with human rights decisions, evaluation of risks of persecution or justification of immigration decisions interfering with human rights. Where the statutory regime is itself silent as to the relevant criteria what is then a relevant circumstance to be taken into account, and what is an irrelevant consideration to be disregarded? What above all is the meaning of the resonant tautology of a decision so unreasonable that no reasonable decision maker could have arrived at it? Surely a mature democracy and an evolving common law constitution requires something a little more grown-up than this?

The prestige of the writ of *habeas* and its celebrated role in the constitutional struggles of the seventeenth and eighteenth century reflect the constitutional principle of the separation of powers, judicial independence and the subordination of the executive to the rule of law. The vitality of this tradition ensures that it emerges from time to time in unexpected ways in the modern era: from Lord Atkin's famous dissent in *Liversidge v Anderson*[20] to the UK Court of Appeal's concerns in the case of *Abassi*[21] at the absence of any court in the USA able to review the legality of the detention of aliens held as 'unlawful combatants' in Guantanamo Bay, a state of affairs it described as 'a legal black hole'. At a time when it was widely believed that there was no power in judicial review to obtain an interim injunction against the Crown to stay implementation of an expulsion decision, *habeas*

---

[17] For the classic account of judicial review, see De Smith, 4th edn, *Judicial Review of Administrative Action* (London, Sweet & Maxwell, 1995) and Supplement (1998).
[18] *Associated Provincial Picture Houses v Wednesbury Corporation* [1948] 1 KB 223.
[19] See JAG Griffith, *The Politics of the Judiciary* (London, Penguin Books, 1977) and Trevor Allen's chapter in this volume 'Common law reasons and the limits of judicial deference'. Judges have frequently looked foolish and damaged respect for the rule of law when they sought to impose their values on local democracy: see *Roberts v Hopwood* [1925] AC 578.
[20] [1942] AC 206. He rejected the proposition that the executive were to be the sole judge of whether there were reasonable grounds to detain in war time with the celebrated citation of Lewis Carroll and the Humpty Dumpty principle of statutory construction. See also B Simpson *In the Highest Degree Odious: Detention Without Trial in Wartime Britain* (Oxford, Clarendon Press, 1992) for a critical review of the conflict between judiciary and executive on the question of preventive detention during World War II.
[21] *R (Abassi) v Secretary of State for Foreign and Commonwealth Affairs* [2002] EWCA Civ 1598; Times LR 8.11.2002, where Lord Atkin was cited.

corpus could fill the procedural hiatus by requiring the detainee to be brought before the court[22] before the expulsion decision was implemented. The House of Lords declined to apply the *habeas* jurisdictional fact text to whether someone was a refugee within the meaning of the UN Refugee Convention 1951[23] but opted instead for a review of anxious scrutiny of the executive decision where life and liberty was engaged. This gave rise to so many judicial reviews of the procedural propriety of executive decisions rejecting asylum claims, that a comprehensive system of in-country appeals in all refugee cases was implemented in 1993, and has remained with numerous statutory adjustments, ever since.

ALIENS AND THE COMMON LAW

Before the modern era of uniform immigration control emerged in the UK with the Immigration Act 1971, immigration control depended on status as a British subject or an alien. The former could come and go as they pleased if they could establish who they were by any appropriate evidence. The latter had always been subject to control by the royal prerogative subject to occasional intrusions of legislative power. By the early twentieth century, friendly aliens were generally welcomed if they were self-sufficient, but anarchists, socialists and the poor Jews associated with the pogroms in Russia in the East were not. They were subject to the first Aliens Act in 1905 that was replaced by a second on the outbreak of the First World War in the Aliens Restriction Act 1914. Aliens were thus associated with German spies, Bolshevik revolutionaries and other threats to the stability and security of the realm. Control of aliens was part of the prerogative power to preserve national security, by control of the borders, registration with the police and the maintenance of surveillance and intelligence gathering. Until 1971, control of the entry and residence of foreigners was still regulated in the UK by Aliens Orders made under the 1914 statute.

Once a person was identified as an alien, there were no rights of entry, merely a right to seek permission to enter. Judicial review of the refusal of such permission was rare to the point of non-existence. Lord Justice Widgery summarised the position in 1969 thus:

> when an alien approaching this country is refused leave to land, he has no right capable of being infringed ... [I]n such a situation the alien's desire to

[22] *R v Secretary of State for the Home Department ex parte Muboyayi* [1992] QB 244. See also *M v Home Office* [1994] 1 AC 377 when the executive appealed a finding of contempt of court for its failure to reverse a decision to expel a failed asylum seeker to Nigeria despite a court order to the contrary. The House of Lords dismissed as absurd the executive's contention that its past obedience to the writ of *habeas corpus* had been a voluntary cooperation with an essentially advisory judgment of the courts.
[23] *R v Secretary of State ex parte Bugdacay and Musisi* [1987] AC 514.

land can be rejected for good reason or bad, for sensible reason or fanciful reason or for no reason at all.[24]

Even where immigration expulsion operated as a disguised form of extradition, the courts were unwilling to impose duties on the executive that interfered with the exercise of prerogative discretion.[25] There were no immigration appeals.[26] There was no judicial review of the merits of decisions on entry—whether the subject matter was admission as a refugee, or deportation after years of residence. Manifestly, such decisions would be considered non-justiciable if the executive asserted that they raised questions of national security and public policy. It did not occur to anybody that international law had anything much to say as to the propriety of this state of affairs. Three overlapping sources of international law have radically altered the position in the UK: European Community (EC) law, refugee law and the developing principles of the ECHR.

First and foremost in terms of hard-edged international rules taking precedence over other national laws is EC law. In 1973, with the coming into force of the Immigration Act 1971, Commonwealth nationals (although still British subjects with the right to vote, serve in the armed forces and on juries) finally lost the last remnants of their privileged immigration status. All persons who did not have the right of abode required permission to enter or remain under the immigration rules.[27] At the same time, the UK entered the European Economic Community, as it was then called (now the EC, part of the EU). A treaty right to enter and remain for economic purposes was afforded to a privileged category of alien. This treaty right, directly enforceable in domestic law, superimposed a new regime of rights for immigrants over the discretionary and permissive regime of immigration control.[28] There were now new issues of jurisdictional fact for judicial examination: was a claimant a worker or a family member of a worker and thus entitled to remain without more, subject to the requirements of public policy?[29] Further, and of direct relevance to the present account, executive discretion to expel those whose presence was considered to be undesirable was now circumscribed by EC rules requiring

---

[24] *Schmidt v Secretary of State* [1969] 2 Ch 149. There was no citation or consideration of international law principles in this decision.
[25] *R v Governor of Brixton prison ex parte Soblen* [1963] 2 QB 243.
[26] In this respect the Immigration Act 1971 granting a system of immigration appeals to aliens and Commonwealth citizens alike, was a substantial improvement in the procedural rights of the former class.
[27] Immigration Act 1971 s 1.
[28] See *Van Duyn* [1974] ECR 1337; [1975] 3 All ER 190, and *R v Pieck* [1981] QB 571, where it was held that the granting of a permission to enter the territory was unlawful and inconsistent with the direct right of entry granted under what was then Art 48 of the EC Treaty.
[29] It was unlawful to grant a EC worker a limited leave to enter the United Kingdom, or prosecute them for breach of conditions because there was a right to enter and remain directly applicable from the EC Treaty and not dependent on state permission: see *R v Pieck*, above n 28.

an independent assessment as to whether someone was a threat to public policy.[30] It was not a sufficient foundation for an expulsion decision that someone had criminal convictions, they also had to be a present threat to public policy, and in most cases this required proof by the executive of a propensity to re-offend.[31] The use of deportation as part of a policy to deter anti-social behaviour by migrants was not consistent with EC rules.[32] The resulting case-law presents a remarkable contrast with US rules of mandatory deportation for aliens who commit offences. Serious offenders who no longer represent a threat to society on their release from prison are unlikely to face deportation if they come within EU rules. Where there was a balance of competing interests, the approach was not the deferential one of whether a reasonable Home Secretary could conclude that the public interest justified the expulsion, a more intensive and intrusive principle of judicially supervised proportionality was called for. In exercising the judgment as to the proper balance, regard was to be had to the ECHR as part of the constitutional foundation of the EU.[33] Where EC rights of residence were allied with rights to enjoy family life that would be disrupted if a family member were removed, it was for the executive to justify the interference as necessary in a democratic society.[34]

The contrast with Commonwealth citizens and the unprivileged class of aliens became very marked and has continued to broaden to this day. Those outside the charmed circle of EC law were subject to immigration rules that became progressively stricter and more complex in their requirements. The terms of the immigration rules or any policies designed to supplement the exercise of discretion were for the executive who had responsibility for immigration policy. True these policies were designed to reflect international obligations under the ECHR, but the executive, not the judges decided what those obligations required in immigration law. Application of the rules and policies might be ensured by appeals and judicial review. On its particular facts, the decision of the Supreme Court in *Baker v Canada (Minister of Citizenship and Immigration)*[35] looks like a decision that the individual officer departed from departmental policy without just cause

---

[30] EC Directive 64/221 of 1964 as interpreted in the cases of *R v Bouchereau* [1978] QB 732; *Bonsignore (Angelo), Cologne v Oberstadtdirektor of the City of Cologne* [1975] ECR 297.
[31] See the decision of the Court of Appeal in *B v Secretary of State for the Home Department* [2000] Imm AR 478.
[32] See *Bonsignore*, above n 30. This test then applied when EC principles were extended to workers admitted under Association Agreements. Thus in *Nazli v Stadt* [2000] 1–ECR p 957, where a Turkish worker who benefited from the public policy provisions of the Turkish Association Agreement with the EU could not be expelled despite having committed an offence of trafficking 1.5 kilos of heroin. For the contrasting position for aliens generally see *R (Samaroo) v Secretary of State for the Home Department* [2001] INLR 55.
[33] *Nold* [1974] ECR 491; ECJ see also *Carpenter* below n 34.
[34] *Carpenter v Secretary of State* [2003] 2 WLR 267; see also the discussion in *B v Secretary of State for the Home Department* see above n 31.
[35] [1999] 2 SCR 817.

or sufficient enquiry. This would not have been considered a remarkable decision in the UK. Policies are matters that the executive cannot ignore without good reason, and the doctrine of either the principle of legitimate expectation or good administration in the equal treatment of claimants rendered failures to apply and adhere to the terms of a policy subject to judicial review on the grounds of procedural impropriety.[36] But rules and policies can be changed from time to time, and are an insubstantial basis for the foundation of the assertion of the rights of the alien against a host state, particularly where countervailing considerations like national security come into play. A similar experience results from using legitimate expectation as a basis for requiring the state to act compatibly with international law rights that are not binding in domestic law.[37]

The second international obligation that restrained the freedom of manoeuvre of the executive in its dealings with aliens is the UN Refugee Convention of 1951. We have noted that the Refugee Convention appeared to provide a basis for entry to the territory to those who could not comply with the immigration rules. Immigration applications and challenges became focused on asylum claims under the UN Refugee Convention, where there were a set of criteria not dependent solely on executive policy and therefore revocable at will. The test for a well-founded fear of persecution has always been a high one, and even where there was a well-founded fear of significant harm, refugee claims might fail on the basis that there was no Convention reason for the feared persecution.[38] As is well-known, the 1951 Refugee Convention does not impose absolute standards in its core provisions. The right of 'non-refoulement' did not extend to cases where the claimant had been convicted, since arrival, of a particular serious offence or was regarded as a danger to national security.[39] Further, refugee status could be excluded by reference to conduct that was a serious non-political offence, a war crime or acts contrary to the principles of the United Nations.[40]

---

[36] See *Asif Khan v IAT* [1985] 1 All ER 40; [1984] 1 WLR 1337; for a failure to comply with a policy designed to implement human rights decisions see *R v Secretary of State for the Home Department ex parte Amankwah* [1994] Imm AR 240.

[37] *Ahmed and Patel v Secretary of State for the Home Department* [1998] INLR 570 where the Court of Appeal indicated that it would have endorsed the Teoh approach of the Australian High Court (*Minister for Immigration and Ethnic Affairs v Teoh* (1995) 183 CLR 273 (HCA)) but for the fact that the UK maintained an immigration reservation to the UN Convention on the Rights of the Child.

[38] See *R v Secretary of State for the Home Department ex parte Ravichandran* [1996] Imm AR 418 where detention of young Tamils was held not to be persecution: see also the case of *Horvath v Secretary of State for the Home Department* [2001] 1 AC 489 where it was held that a Czech Roma had a sufficiency of protection against racist assault notwithstanding a well-founded fear.

[39] See Art 33(2) of the UN Convention on the Status of Refugees 1951. See *Chahal v Secretary of State for the Home Department* [1995] 1 WLR 526 for the Court of Appeal decision in the UK.

[40] See *T v Secretary of State for the Home Department* [1996] AC 742 where Commonwealth authorities on the exclusion clauses are examined. I have brought this review up to date in an article to be published in the *European Journal of Migration and Law* [2003] 4, 425.

Thirdly, there has been, in the background of UK law and practice, the influence of the European Convention on Human Rights. The immigration rules and the executive policies relating to children and family ties were inspired by the principles of respect for family life recognised in Article 8 of the ECHR, although the stringent family reunion directives of EC law did not apply to spouses of British citizens who had not exercised EC rights of free movement.[41] The contrast between the application of the ECHR as an aspect of EU law and its background status before the Human Rights Act came into force as a mere international obligation of the UK is striking.[42]

Article 8 of the ECHR had been recognised to have application to immigration decisions and the requirement to maintain non-discriminatory immigration rules in the case of *Abdulaziz*[43] and others. In this case women who were not British citizens were lawfully resident in the United Kingdom. They sought to sponsor their husbands who resided abroad. The men did not qualify for admission as husbands under the immigration rules that were more generous to men settled in the UK bringing in their wives. The women complained that they had been the subject of sexual and racial discrimination in the formulation of immigration policy. The UK Government's first argument was that the ECHR could not apply at all, as the province of immigration was confined to the Fourth Protocol to the Convention to which the UK was not a party. Where a supplementary instrument is adopted later to extend the scope of the Convention and spells out in detail rights relating to immigration, the original articles of the Convention cannot be said to have been intended to restrain the state's powers in a field where international law recognised it had the right to control its frontiers and determine its asylum policy.[44] In *Abdulaziz*, however, the Court ruled that immigration decisions could affect the substantive enjoyment of other rights, even though there was no right to enter or remain in the territory of

---

[41] *R v Immigration Appeal Tribunal ex parte Secretary of State and Surinder Singh*; ECJ Case C 370/90 [1992] Imm AR 565 established that EC law did apply where the UK national has worked elsewhere in the EC and then re-entered the UK. A UK national could accordingly rely on the more favourable migration rules for spouses of EC workers, rather than be governed solely by national law. The *Carpenter* case (see above n 34) extends this principle to UK nationals resident in the UK who provide commercial services in the EC.

[42] Compare the results in *R v Secretary of State ex parte Phull* [1996] Imm AR 72, where a non-national spouse of a British citizen who had not exercised treaty rights could be removed for overstaying leave to remain with *Carpenter v Secretary of State for the Home Department* Case C–60/00 [2003] 2 WLR 267 where the removal of an alien wife of a British citizen was held to be an interference with the husband's community law rights to provide services because it was a disproportionate interference with family life.

[43] (1985) 7 EHRR 471.

[44] This was an argument that the French Government were to replicate with greater success in the case of *Maouia v France* 05/10/2000 App No 00039652/98, where the European Court held that the fair trial rights of Art 6 rights did not apply to immigration expulsions as the procedures in such cases were regulated by Protocol 4.

a foreign state. Immigration powers had to be exercised subject to and consistent with international obligations under human rights treaties.

Although Strasbourg case law on the duty to admit family members has been sparse and inconsistent, it does provide a minimum standard to which the UK must adhere in its immigration policies.[45] The answer will usually lie in the rules and policies adopted to give effect to international obligations rather than a free-standing appeal to respect for human rights itself. Executive discretion to waive provisions of the rules was soon reduced to a series of stringent policies, of which the executive was the sole judge. Attempts to challenge the terms of these policies or their application have usually foundered on the basis that the executive has a wide margin of discretion when formulating policies about the admission of migrants to and removal from the UK.[46] The Strasbourg case-law restraining deportation that interferes with family life has been more pro-active.[47] It is now recognised that a decision to expel on the basis of criminal offending must be a proportionate response to family or private life established in the UK, and must be a fair balance between the public and private interests that fall to be taken into consideration.

EXPULSIONS FOR REASONS OF NATIONAL SECURITY

The Immigration Act 1971 introduced a general scheme of immigration appeals to cover most cases of expulsion of someone who had been lawfully permitted to enter the UK. There was always the exceptional case, however, of decisions that were taken personally by the Secretary of State 'as being in the interests of national security, or of the relations between the UK and any other country or other reasons of a political nature'.[48] In this class of case the prerogative powers of the Crown with respect to aliens were preserved free from appellate scrutiny and the risk that an independent person might decide that the discretion should have been exercised differently. The only remedy in respect of such decisions was judicial review, but judicial review was inherently inappropriate to review the factual foundation of the decision, particularly where the executive declined to reveal the source of the information or indeed specific details of the allegation on the ground that to do so might jeopardise the security services' methods of investigation.

---

[45] *Sen v Netherlands* [2003] 36 EHRR 7.
[46] See *Ahmad and Patel v Secretary of State for the Home Department* [1998] Imm AR 22 CA where the expectation that the UK would act compatibly with the Convention on the rights of the child was held to be defeated by the terms of a reservation to that Treaty not applying it to immigration control decisions.
[47] See two key decisions determining that expulsion based on criminal conduct was disproportionate: *Boultif v Switzerland* [2001] EHRR 50; *Amrollahi v Denmark* 11/07/2002 App No 00056811/00.
[48] See s 15(3) Immigration Act.

One such decision concerned the deportation of the American journalists Mark Hosenball and Philip Agee. The expulsion of the former, who had a British spouse and no apparent connections with espionage, seemed particularly harsh. Nevertheless the Court of Appeal concluded that the assertion of the interests of national security by the executive precluded judicial scrutiny of the evidence relied on in justifying the decision.[49] There was therefore no deportation appeal to an adjudicator, and no effective remedy by way of judicial review of the decision. National security was a sufficient basis to justify expulsion and interference with residence rights and family life, and the Court concluded that there was no alternative but for the immigrant to trust the decision of the executive in such matters. The only procedure offered in such cases was a personal interview with a board of advisers who were not permitted to disclose the evidence to the immigrant, conduct an appeal with legal representation or give a reasoned decision binding on the executive.[50] The procedure was based on security vetting in the civil service.

It was in these circumstances that Agee prayed in aid international human rights obligations to provide some basis of challenge to the decision. This was an unpromising case to establish a human rights challenge. He had no persecution or ill-treatment fears back in the United States of America and no family life established in the UK. The case law of the Commission recently approved by the Strasbourg Court was to the effect that immigration decisions did not involve the determination of civil rights. There was no right not to be expelled and therefore the fair trial criteria of Article 6 of the ECHR did not apply. Neither Agee nor Hosenball was detained and so no procedural rights of access to an independent court for the review of detention arose under Article 5. Agee attempted to argue that his deportation contravened his right to freedom of expression under Article 10, but the claim was declared inadmissible as there was no basis for a belief that the expulsion had been ordered because of his views or their expression.[51]

The UK courts were equally unwilling or unable to assist in the case of a Palestinian asylum seeker with family connections in the UK who was excluded on security grounds, even though the Court found that he had a well-founded fear of persecution.[52] It concluded that the Secretary of State was entitled to be satisfied that the Article 33(2) exception to the principle of *non-refoulement* provided for in the Refugee Convention applied. If the exception applied, the Court of Appeal concluded that there was no

---

[49] *R v Secretary of State for the Home Department ex parte Hosenball* [1977] 1 WLR 766.
[50] See also *R. v Secretary of State for the Home Department ex parte Cheblak* [1991] 2 All ER 319. For a further description of the due process deficit of such an arrangement see the ECtHr decision in *Chahal v UK* [1996] 23 EHRR.
[51] *Agee v UK Commission* (1976) 7 D & R 164.
[52] *NSH v SSHD* [1988] Imm AR 389.

balancing factor as between the seriousness of the threat to national security on the one hand and the threat to the individual on the other. The prerogative of expulsion and exclusion on national security grounds had survived undamaged a second direct attempt to subjugate it to principles of international legality.

CHAHAL

This was the case-law background to the *Chahal* case that was decided in the Strasbourg court in November 1996, but started its long procession through the domestic legal process with Chahal's detention some six years earlier in 1990. After an earlier quashing of a rejection of Chahal's asylum appeal, the case proceeded to the Court of Appeal on asylum and human rights grounds.[53] This was a case of national security deportation of a long-resident Indian national with substantial family connections to the UK. The Secretary of State alleged that he was a prominent organiser of Sikh terrorist extremism in the UK and thus a candidate for deportation. He was offered the same internal scrutiny procedure as adopted in the *Hosenball* case with predictably negative results. His asylum claim continued to be rejected on the merits despite cogent concerns of the treatment of suspected Sikh militants by the Indian security forces. The Home Secretary indicated, however, that even if Chahal's fear of persecution was well-founded he would apply the Article 33(2) exclusion clause to deny him the protection of the principle of *non refoulement*. In addition, Chahal raised Article 3 of the ECHR as a reason to preclude deportation, irrespective of the Refugee Convention. In response the Home Secretary submitted that return to India was permissible because he had carefully considered the human rights claim, but nevertheless concluded that deportation was required in the public interest. The risks of ill-treatment were said to be remote, particularly after the UK's concerns had been drawn to the attention of the Indian authorities. Further the risks were not the result of state policy but of the conduct of aberrant police officers not condoned by the state. It was suggested that Chahal could relocate elsewhere in India outside the Punjab. In any event, the risk of torture or inhuman or degrading treatment did not preclude the exercise of the prerogative powers to expel a person vulnerable to the power in the interests of national security. In the Home Secretary's view, this human rights obligation was a factor the executive had to take into account, but was not an absolute obstacle to removal.

We have already noted the *Abdulaziz* decision whereby the Strasbourg court was able to read into the concept of respect for family life protected by Article 8 of the ECHR, an obligation in certain circumstances to use

[53] *Chahal v SSHD* [1995] 1 WLR 526.

immigration powers proportionately so as not to divide families that could not be reasonably expected to live together in another country. A second key decision to apply the ECHR to a case of immigration expulsion where the Convention itself was silent about such matters was the case of *Soering*.[54] In this case a German national faced extradition from the UK to the state of Virginia where he faced the death penalty for a double murder. As in the *Abdulaziz* case the UK Government disputed the application of the Convention to immigration decisions. It argued that the prohibition on torture, inhuman or degrading treatment was not intended to apply to acts committed outside the territorial jurisdiction of Contracting States. The USA was not a party to the European Convention. The UK government was not responsible for the Acts of the USA. Article 3 could never have been intended by the drafters to apply to immigration cases, particularly as the international community had adopted the Refugee Convention at about the same time as the European Convention where the balanced rights of protection were recognised. The Court was not persuaded by all this, and in a judgment whose implications are still being considered daily in the UK's immigration courts and tribunals, explained that the UK's international obligations are engaged where it treats someone who is subject to its jurisdiction in a way that causes them to be exposed to ill-treatment (torture, inhuman or degrading treatment) that is contrary to the standards of Article 3, in whatever state the foreseeable consequences occur.

The judgment in *Soering* was given on the day that argument in *Chahal* was heard before the European Commission. The UK government maintained its *a priori* objection to the supposedly 'extra territorial' application of the ECHR. It also developed a subsidiary argument as to the scope of Article 3 or the application of the *Soering* principle in expulsion cases where national security was engaged as a reason for the deportation. Reliance was placed on the exceptions and exclusions from the Refugee Convention as indicating that the drafters could not have intended to create an absolute obligation against expulsion by implication where a limited obligation was undertaken in the appropriate instrument devoted to the topic. In any event, in *Soering* the Court itself had pointed out that inherent in the whole of the Convention is a balance between the interests of the community and the interests of the individual. The claimant responded to this argument by demonstrating that although there was a need for a balance of all the relevant circumstances to determine whether treatment was inhuman or degrading (particularly in a case where the Convention had not abolished the death penalty itself) once the treatment reached the minimum level of severity there was no room for a further balance to justify such treatment. As to the supposed original meaning, the Government failed to appreciate that the Convention was to be construed as a living instrument adapting to

[54] (1989) 11 EHRR 439.

changed circumstances and developing in the light of international norms in a manner designed to ensure that its provisions were practical and effective in respect for human rights. Further, by this stage the international community had adopted Article 3 of the UN Convention Against Torture 1984 that expressly prohibited, without exception, returns or removals to countries where torture might be practised.[55]

In its judgment in *Chahal*, the European Court of Human Rights made two significant inroads into the prerogative powers of the state to expel aliens where it considered such a course conducive to the interests of national security. First, and most significantly, it was held that an expulsion was precluded where there were substantial grounds to fear that the individual faced a real risk of torture or inhuman treatment on his deportation and removal. The Court expressly acknowledged that it was giving a wider meaning to the protection against *non-refoulement* contained in the Refugee Convention, but concluded it was appropriate to do so given the absolute and non-derogable standard contained in Article 3 that prevented governments exposing individuals to torture by any means whatsoever. This applied even if the national authority concluded that the individual was a threat to national security. If exposure was not permitted in times of national emergency, it could not be justified by the broad exigencies on which states rely in defence of their national interests in expelling aliens.

Secondly, it introduced an element of due process into the determination whether the individual was indeed a threat to national security. It did so by focusing on the prolonged detention, and Chahal's inability to get bail because of government reliance on the interest of national security that precluded judges from examining the evidence and deciding the matter for themselves. The advisory procedure was held to violate Article 5(4) of the ECHR that required a right of a person detained for immigration purposes to appear before a court to challenge the legality of his detention. In order to review whether detention was lawful under the extended definition of that term given in Convention jurisprudence, the reviewing Court must be able to assess the material that is relied on by the state to justify the detention: here the self same national security data relied on to justify the expulsion. If the High Court on *habeas corpus* or judicial review could not examine this material for itself under the long-standing self-denying ordinance applied in such cases, it could not review all the questions necessary to determine whether the detention was proportionate and in accordance with the law. The internal advisers procedure might have had access to the material,

---

[55] The nature of this obligation has been considered recently in Canada by the Supreme Court in *Suresh v Canada (Minister of Citizenship and Immigration)* 2002 SCC 1. The eccentric approach to construction of this Treaty by the Federal Court of Appeal whereby Art 16 of UNCAT was read as permitting Art 3 to be subject to any lesser protection in other human rights treaties cases, was rejected, although an approach that gives Art 3 unrestricted dominance over interests of national security was also not accepted.

but despite the distinguished character of its chair, a serving Law Lord and Security Commissioner, its procedures prevented it from being considered to be an independent court within the meaning of Article 5(4). An advisory body appointed by the executive *pro tem*, whose conclusions were both secret and non-binding, could hardly have that status. A new way of proceeding in such cases was thus needed.

Henceforth, if the Government were going to seek to remove anybody on national security grounds, it was going to need a procedure that at least enabled any interim detention to be carefully reviewed. This was the genesis of the Special Immigration Appeal Commission that would determine all asylum, human rights and detention questions in future national security expulsions or exclusions. An equal incentive to fundamental procedural review was required as a result of a Community law case concerning the procedural rights of EU nationals being removed on national security grounds. The joined cases of *Radiom and Shingara*[56] were pending before the European Court of Justice at the time of the *Chahal* judgment. Here a French Sikh and an Irish Iranian complained that they had not had the right of appeal or judicial scrutiny required by EC law of decisions to exclude them on national security grounds. Although the eventual decision of the Court did not engage with the question, the Advocate General concluded that judicial review was not an adequate mechanism for the purpose of this task, because the Court only reviewed the opinion of the executive with a view to procedural or legal error, and could not review the factual conclusions on which the case was based. The procedure did not marry up to an effective judicial remedy required wherever there was to be any interference with Community law rights of entry and residence.

The establishment of a Special Immigration Appeals Commission (SIAC) was intended to resolve the dichotomy between a fair hearing for the suspect and the preservation of secrecy for informer material and other intelligence data that could not be disclosed to suspects without compromising future operations. The scheme was based on remarks in the *Chahal* judgment (itself based on the submissions of the intervener, Liberty) that Canada had been able to achieve a fairer procedure in certain of its immigration decision-making by such a scheme. In the UK version, a special advocate is appointed where the Home Secretary intends to rely on sensitive material. The special advocate represents the interests of, but not the proposed deportee (the appellant) directly, who has his own legal team. The special advocate can meet and converse with, and obtain information from the appellant, until service of the sensitive or closed material that is not served on the appellant or his legal team. Thereafter the special advocate cannot communicate with the appellant or his lawyers about the case,

---

[56] [1997] 3 CMLR 703. See also the subsequent Court of Appeal decision about the exclusion of a Dutch national suspected of migrant trafficking *Yiadom v SSHD* [1998] EWCA Civ 660.

for fear that questions may inadvertently disclose the nature of the closed material. Submissions are then made that some closed material should be disclosed in whole or in gist to achieve as fair a hearing as possible and commensurate with the public interest. The substantive appeal then proceeds to an open and closed part with the state's case for exclusion tested by the special advocate in the absence of the appellant.

A third element of the *Chahal* decision was its finding that the UK had violated the applicant's rights under Article 13 of the ECHR: the right to an effective remedy whenever an arguable breach of the subject's Convention rights was engaged on the evidence. The Court of Appeal had asked the traditional judicial review question 'could a reasonable Secretary of State have concluded that there was no real risk of torture'. It then suggested that as long as he had conscientiously examined the materials, the Court would be unable to intervene with the decision unless it reached the conclusion that the decision was irrational or perverse, applying a high degree of deference to the conclusions of the decision-maker, informed by a variety of material that is not usually placed before the domestic court. For the Strasbourg Court this would not do. It stressed in its judgment that because of the absolute nature of the obligations involved, the judicial body had to carefully examine all the evidence to determine whether there were substantial grounds for fearing a real risk of harm. The domestic court had not done so because all it required was that the executive had examined the evidence of the risk, and, because of the national security implications, the court of review had gone no further.

This part of the judgment has general significance for the development of judicial review as an instrument of scrutiny of executive decisions where human rights are concerned. It undoubtedly added to the clamour for the introduction of the Human Rights Act whereby the domestic court could perform the functions presently reserved for the international tribunal. The Strasbourg Court was prepared to believe that the common law could develop a 'correctness' standard where risk of inhuman or degrading treatment was concerned as long as national security or other irrelevant considerations did not obscure the stark nature of the duty.

In the case of *D v UK*,[57] the Strasbourg Court found Article 3 was violated by the proposed removal of a convicted drug smuggler dying of AIDS to an island where he would receive inadequate medical treatment. Despite this notable conclusion extending the scope of Article 3 to inhuman and degrading treatment that was not deliberate infliction of harm, no violation of Article 13 was found. Judicial review was seen in principle as being a sufficient method of enforcing Convention rights even before the

---

[57] (1997) 24 EHRR 423. A similar conclusion was reached in the case of *Hilal v UK* (2001) 33 EHRR 2. By contrast see the case of *Smith and Brady v UK* (2000) 29 EHRR 493 where there was a violation of Art 13 because the Court of Appeal was unable to examine the proportionality of the justification for excluding homosexuals from the armed services.

HRA came into force. A remedy is an effective remedy if it is capable, in principle, of delivering the result that the Convention requires, and not whether it in fact did so in the particular case. In the international understanding of common law principles, judicial review had at least the capacity to give effect to international human rights as part of the common law, even if it failed to arrive at decisions that protected the right in question.

The common law response to the specific challenges faced by international human rights developments was the 'anxious scrutiny' review of executive decisions that touched on human rights. The phrase was used in a House of Lords case where the jurisdictional fact approach to the determination of whether an asylum seeker was a refugee was rejected.[58] Anxious scrutiny is not therefore a full 'correctness' standard as a matter of primary judicial fact finding, but an intense scrutiny of relevant executive decisions to see that they are in no way flawed in their procedure, or their reasoning process. A test case for a post-*Chahal* intensity of review was *Turgut*,[59] decided after the enactment of the HRA but before it came into force. Here the Court of Appeal concluded that it could receive original material as evidence of risk that the appellant faced in Turkey, and evaluate it for itself, as it was as well placed as the Secretary of State to make the evaluation. It stressed it was still performing a review of whether a reasonable Secretary of State could reach the decision he had, rather than substituting itself as part of the primary decision-making process. The old excuse for deference in such an area that the Secretary of State had access to better sources of information than the court would not do. If he had relevant data he was duty bound to place it before the Court. If the data objectively reviewed pointed to the existence of a risk, then a reasonable Secretary of State could not lawfully arrive at a rational conclusion that there was no risk. Where the data was uncertain and required evaluation some deference would be afforded to the evaluative judgment of the executive within proper limits. Anxious scrutiny thus enabled a hard-edged test to be applied to certain questions, almost but not quite as intense as jurisdictional fact.

Where anxious scrutiny was applied to an executive decision affecting human rights that involved the exercise of judgment or discretion, different considerations were factored in. A constitutional deference re-emerged as a basis for relaxing the intensity of the review. In *Smith v Minister of Defence*,[60] the case concerned with the legitimacy of the Ministry's policy of dismissing homosexual servicemen from the armed forces, the Court of Appeal recognised the severely intrusive interference with the human right to respect for private life, but indicated that it was not in a position to make a judgement on the justification for the interference as proportionate and necessary for some legitimate interest of security. The Strasbourg Court had

---

[58] *R v Secretary of State ex parte Bugdacay* [1987] AC 514.
[59] *R v Secretary of State for the Home Department ex parte Turgut* [2001] 1 All ER 719.
[60] [1996] 2 WLR 305.

no such qualms and found a violation of both Article 8 (the right to respect for private life) and Article 13 (the right to an effective remedy). It concluded that the failure to adjudicate on proportionality deprived the claimants of an effective remedy to vindicate their Convention rights. Once again the case for the HRA was restored, domestic judges had to do more by way of judicial review if they were to secure respect for human rights in domestic law.

SPECIAL IMMIGRATION ACT COMMISSION

We have already noted the next phase of the legislative developments in response to *Chahal*. If national security were to be relied on as the basis for the exclusion of foreigners in the future, there would have to be a fundamentally new procedure, to ensure a fair hearing or as fair a hearing as possible. The Special Immigration Appeal Commission Act 1997 was intended to have precisely this effect. Three substantive decisions have emerged from that body since the legislation came into force in 1999. To some extent the Commission has vindicated its ability to take an independent line, by finding in part for the detainees in all three cases. In 1999, in the case of *Rehman*, it concluded that it should decide for itself what meaning was to be given to the term 'national security' in deportation cases, and review as primary fact finder whether the Secretary of State had proved his case. In the second case the Commission was satisfied that the appellants were indeed a threat to national security but could not be returned to India for the same reasons as in the *Chahal* case, the continued risk of torture. The appellants were accordingly released from custody. The third decision was in *A and others* where it had to consider whether there was a sufficient emergency to justify derogation. In a bold decision on the meaning of discrimination in the field of detention SIAC concluded that the UK's derogation from Article 5 of the ECHR was unlawful when set against the non-discrimination principles proclaimed in Article 14 of the ECHR. The threat to national security came from both British citizens and foreigners who could not be deported by reason of the risk of torture. However, only the foreigners were to be detained without trial. Unfortunately, the first and the third decision have been reversed by the higher courts and the second has been severely limited by statute and the derogation from Article 5.[60a]

REHMAN

The decision in *Rehman*[61] proceeded to the House of Lords where judgment was given in October 2001 and has now led the way for a new mood

---

[60a] See *Rehman* n 61 below, *A v Secretary of State* [2003] 2 WLR 564.
[61] [2001] UKHL 47; [2001] 3 WLR 877.

of international judicial restraint in reviewing the security decisions of the executive, a mood reflected in Canada by the decision of the Supreme Court in *Suresh*.[62] There was no question of persecution or Article 3 harm in this case. The issue was whether SIAC should have been satisfied that deportation was appropriate for reasons of national security namely the international fight against terrorism. Here SIAC accepted submissions that the Secretary of State had to prove behaviour that resulted in the appellant being a danger to the host community in which he resided. National security was equated with the defence of the realm rather than the protection of friendly relations with other states whose nationals had been the subject of violent attacks by others. SIAC was not satisfied that Rehman was a risk applying this definition and allowed the appeal. The Secretary of State's appeal to the Court of Appeal was allowed and upheld in the subsequent decision of the House of Lords. The decision is notable for Lord Hoffmann's forceful assertion that SIAC was obliged to defer to the Secretary of State's assessment as to what the interests of national security required, even though it had a statutory power to determine that the discretion should have been exercised differently. This deference was owed not merely because the subject matter was national security where the executive with its expert advisers was better placed and equipped to make the necessary judgment, but also because there was a constitutional duty of deference owed by courts to the executive on questions where Parliament could and should hold the Secretary of State to account.[63] Lord Hoffmann stressed that the judgment was written before the 9/11 attacks, but those events were:

> a reminder that in matters of national security, the costs of failure can be high. This seems to me to underline the need for the judicial arm of government to respect the decisions of ministers of the Crown on the question of whether support for terrorist activities in a foreign country constitutes a threat to national security. It is not only that the executive has access to special information and expertise in these matters. It is also that such decisions with serious potential results for the community acquire a legitimacy which can be acquired only by entrusting them to persons responsible to the community through the democratic process. If the people are to accept the consequences of such decisions they must be made by persons whom the people have elected and whom they can remove.[64]

As other chapters in this book have noted, this set the stage for a retreat from judicial firmness against the encroachment of the executive. Subsequently the English Court of Appeal overturned the first instance

---
[62] See above n 55.
[63] See above n 21, at paras 57–8.
[64] At para 62.

decision quashing the ban on entry in the *Farrakhan* case,⁶⁵ despite paucity of both evidence and reasoning process in support of the interference with free speech with express reference to Lord Hoffmann's conception of deference and judicial restraint. Lord Hoffmann did recognise that the Article 3 function of the courts was not a matter of deference and the risk of torture would have to be anxiously examined. It is somewhat surprising that this part of the reasoning did not seem to attract the support of the Supreme Court in *Suresh*.

The events of 9/11 give a kind of validity to the approach of placing responsibility for leaving the requirements of national security firmly with the executive, but there must be limits to the process if the rule of law is to survive as a constitutional bulwark in troubled times. In his address to the judges at the European Court of Human Rights on the opening of the judicial year at Strasbourg in January 2003, Lord Woolf CJ noted Lord Hoffmann's above quoted remarks and added:

> The good sense and force of the comments of Lord Hoffmann cannot be denied but this does not mean that the courts, while bearing those remarks in mind, do not have to scrutinise carefully the action which the executive and the legislature has taken, to see whether those actions accord with the fundamental rights of the individual under the European Convention.⁶⁶

There is at the end, a clash of philosophical and constitutional viewpoints on a question of such magnitude as to the limits of the judicial function in defending human rights at a time of crisis. It should not be imagined that all Lord Hoffmann's conclusions on institutional (as opposed to functional or subject matter) deference represent judicial consensus on this topic.⁶⁷ Functional deference to an assessment of what the requirements of national security are in any given situation seems understandable; courts would be reluctant to gain-say the executive in terms of predicting from where serious threats to the whole community might emerge and who might support them. Equally, it is probably inappropriate in a global community to restrict the interests of national security to a narrow sovereign review of the defence requirements of the realm against foreign invasion or specific

---

⁶⁵ See above n 5.
⁶⁶ For the full speech see Strasbourg web site www.echr.coe.int (last visited 17th February 2003).
⁶⁷ The debate is reflected in a series of very marked divisions of opinion in the Judicial Committee of the Privy Council sitting on appeal from the courts of the Caribbean in death penalty cases. The contentious issue as to the relevance of permitting the condemned man access to the regional human rights body, has been marked by the distinctive but fatal jurisprudence in a number of cases culminating in Lord Hoffmann's virulent dissent in *Lewis v Attorney General of Jamaica* [2001] 2 AC 50. More recently, their Lordships split 3–2 on the question of whether the Constitution of the Bahamas permitted the reintroduction of flogging previously recognised to be a barbarous form of torture: *Pinder v Attorney General Bahamas* [2002] 3 WLR 1443. Lord Hoffmann and the majority were of the opinion that the will of Parliament must prevail in reintroducing punishment considered to be torture.

terrorist attack. In a world where criminal acts against civilians are the subject of international co-ordination respecting no borders, states are entitled to make an international response.

It is the assertion that the judges must defer to the executive irrespective of the particular subject-matter, because they are unelected judges and not democratically accountable decision-makers that risks running against the grain of an emergence of constitutional principles from the human rights developments hitherto discussed. At a certain point in the spectrum of intervention, deference can amount to abstention from the performance of judicial duty. In the UK, the executive enjoys unparalleled powers to create policy, promote the legislative powers that it needs, and push them through a largely servile House of Commons where it enjoys a massive majority. Laws are passed and promoted with a minimum of informed scrutiny in the lower house. Victorian theories of parliamentary sovereignty predate the decline of the independent MP and the rise of party patronage, the corrosive influence of the mass media and the diversity of interests in a society that cannot be reflected in a modest share of the votes polled in a progressively declining turnout with no constitutional institution able to control the executive in its frenzy of law-making.

Legislative scrutiny by the more independent House of Lords is kept in check by the convention that the un-elected House should not flout the will of the people as reflected by the make-up of the Commons. It is ironic that the government's programme of constitutional reforms has baulked at the idea of turning the House of Lords into an electorally accountable Senate.

Lord Hoffmann has added to his speech in *Rehman* in an extra-judicial lecture where he makes the point that the rule of law is not the same as the rule of lawyers.[68] But the notion that the so called High Court of Parliament is a safe or sufficient repository for the protection of these values is an eccentric one in an era where the UK seems set to re-write the norms of criminal due process, remove the safeguards in the law of extradition, take preventive civil powers of detention of the mentally ill and the threatening foreigner, and intrude into privacy and property rights in support of the greater good. Unless judges critically define the scope of these powers, and articulate values that protect the vulnerable individual from the over-mighty state, then the rule of law is in danger of becoming an empty vacuity, long in rhetoric, short on substance. It can be argued that the rule of law is not the same thing as the rules of the politicians. Law is a set of rules based on values and not just from the means by which it is promoted. It also matters what the law says and how far it is consistent with the human rights order recognised in charters, conventions and declarations. In this sense democracy = electoral accountability plus due process, implying that due process has an ethical and not merely a procedural content. If the separation of powers is to mean

[68] COMBAR lecture reproduced in Judicial Review [2002] Vol 7 (3), para 14.

anything at times of high crisis, it is a separation that cannot always be lubricated by deference to executive and legislative acts that disproportionately intrude into fundamental norms of fairness, certainty and the burden of proof.

The *Rehman* case is unlikely to be the last word on judicial scrutiny of the grounds for the decision to expel in national security cases. If the cases of executive internment of suspected terrorists now proceeding through the SIAC system do not provide a suitable opportunity for revisiting the limits of deference, then it is likely that the EU law may at some stage set limits of its own. Unlike the domestic application of human rights, with its generous margins of discretionary areas of judgments, the ECJ does look like a constitutional court, sitting over both the judicial and legislative organs of Member States, and setting aside legislation that infringes Treaty rights of free movement and free trade. Lord Hoffmann's deferential approach does not appear to match up to EC concepts of proportionality in justification of interference with fundamental rights even where suspected terrorists are concerned.[69] Community law and its more intrusive application of ECHR norms may yet come back to restrict the executive's freedom of manoeuvre in its wide ranging measures against those supporting political organisations engaged in violent struggle in their own countries.[70] Indeed I would suggest that the binding nature of the UK's obligations under Community law are part of the reason why the Strasbourg jurisprudence is now regarded as a solemn international obligation and not merely the opinions of some ill-advised bunch of misguided bleeding hearts. These are not merely theoretical obligations: they are practical and effective ones, reflecting shared values of a civilised society, refining, improving, updating and developing principles that form the central foundation to the legitimacy of state power in the twenty-first century.

It is surely not too metaphysical or autocratic to argue now that even fairly elected governments have no authority to deprive citizens or minorities within society of their human rights. The content of these rights, civil and political, social and economic, must grow according to universal and international values about the environment, free movement, social diversity and the like. The repository for the impartial protection of these values in a society that distributes the exercise of public power between institutions must be the independent judiciary. True, the judges cannot be social tyrants imposing outdated personal values on a powerless nation. Judges are not a substitute for popularly elected governments fulfilling a social agenda as to

---

[69] See *Gough v Chief Constable of Derbyshire* [2002] EWCA Civ 351 (20th March 2002), a case concerning justification of restriction of free movement of football hooligans, or *Roth International v Secretary of State* [2002] EWCA Civ 158 (22 February 2002).
[70] The EU is considering adopting a legally binding Charter of Human Rights.

the raising and distribution of revenue, and the promotion of economic and social justice. Judicial independence consists of integrity of intellectual reasoning and adherence to the values of the rule of law, whatever the exigencies of the executive or the baying chorus of mass-circulation newspapers. The internment and expulsion of foreigners suspected of threatening national security is a great challenge for this judicial function. Here at the heart of the prerogative powers of the state, lie the unpopular, the marginalised, the strange, the deviant and the foreign. Anxious scrutiny rather than institutional deference is precisely what is called for to discharge this challenge. There is some comfort in the *Rehman* saga—a few months ago the executive reviewed its original decision and decided that he was no longer such a threat, and has now been allowed to remain with his family. Perhaps the original judgment of SIAC had a continuing resonance after all. As for the future legitimacy of the UK's derogation from Article 5, this is a question that will have to be reviewed by the House of Lords in the derogation case of *S v SSHD*[71] and thereafter in Strasbourg itself.

The security crisis generated by 9/11 enabled the executive to promote the anti-terrorist legislation to circumvent the impact of the *Chahal* decision with respect to detention pending deportation of suspected international terrorists. A number of suspects are currently held in indefinite detention. SIAC concluded that there was an emergency threatening the life of the nation but the power to detain had been exercised in a discriminatory fashion. The Court of Appeal disagreed with SIAC and concluded that the international right to expel aliens and protect the borders of the state was a sufficient distinction between the detained group and the comparator class of British citizens. The Court of Appeal rejected SIAC's argument that to impose an overall scheme of internment on suspected terrorists that could not be prosecuted was excessive and disproportionate.

CONCLUSION

It is a paradox that the logic of the discrimination argument was that human rights groups should have been calling for the government to either abandon or introduce a more generalised system of internment to combat the terrorist threat rather than selective internment of immigration detainees. It could be said that this takes discrimination to an excessive degree of punctiliousness. Nevertheless it is unfortunate that more attention was not paid to the contribution of EU law to the question. The principle of non-discrimination between own nationals and aliens with Treaty rights of free movement has given rise to a precise set of standards, rather than a general deference to the executive. In the rulings given on the public

[71] See above n 60a.

policy exception to free movement rights, the ECJ has stated that expulsion is not permitted where it is in respect of conduct that is not the subject of genuine measures of repression if performed by own nationals. Thus in one recent case Polish prostitutes[72] could not be expelled from the Netherlands for plying an immoral trade, if repressive measures were not taken against Dutch nationals for plying the same trade. Once the identical conduct is the subject of repressive measures against both groups, it does not matter that the form of the repression taken against foreigners includes action that could not be taken against own nationals for well-established reasons of international law. It would then have been necessary for the security services to show what repressive measures they were taking against British adherents to Al Quaida and its activities.

This seems to be a solution consistent with common sense and principle. A state would rightly be criticised for doing nothing with respect to serious suspected terrorists in its midst. The primary response should be in the field of criminal law, and it remains a peculiarity why the UK's laws of criminal evidence do not permit the admission of intercept material, that may be probative of guilt of terrorist planning when forensic use of such evidence seems common-place in other jurisdictions. Where the state cannot institute criminal proceedings with a reasonable prospect of success consistent with its fair trial obligations, other forms of repression whether by way of surveillance, civil confiscation of assets, restrictions on travel for the duration of the emergency, or whatever, may then be adopted against alien and citizen alike. In the extreme class of case where the alien represents such a significant and urgent threat to the public interest, then detention for a finite and proportionate period may be considered necessary, provided that a strict SIAC review of the cogency of the data relied on for the internment decision is conducted and a judgment reached.

On this issue at least, principle suggests that the *Rehman* scrutiny test will surely have to be revisited, and Lord Woolf's observations as to the limits of the approach addressed. It may be one thing to require a judicial body to ask whether the Secretary of State's assessment that deportation promotes his policy on national security is rational where there is no threat to the life, liberty or bodily integrity of the individual. It is another to adopt such a loose and deferential review where indefinite internment in lieu of torture abroad is relied on. An intrusive scrutiny doing the best that fairness can provide in difficult and sensitive circumstances can thus make an informed and responsible contribution to both the safety of the public and the interests of the community in having an independent judiciary.

The working title for the seminar that inspired this chapter was the 'Authority of Reasons'. David Dyzenhaus has explained in the introduction

---

[72] *Jany v Staatssecretaris van Justitie* 20/11/2001 [2001] ECR I–8615; [2003] All ER (EC) 193; Case No 268/99.

to this volume how debate shifted from the duty to give reasons to the divergence of principles in Canadian and English law on review of administrative decisions, respect for refugees and foreigners and different approaches in the field of human rights. As this paper has been revised for publication I wonder whether 'The Authority of Reason' is a different title that would reflect many of my concerns. It is not a case of a court merely explaining its decision to the parties and the interested bystander, but of allocating the legal and ethical values underlying its approach to its proper place in the task in hand. The judicial task can range from the correctness review where life, liberty and security are concerned to the extreme self-denial in cases of Parliamentary decisions relating to fiscal activity. The substance of these values, I have suggested can be found or at least supported by the body of international norms reflected in the international bill of rights and regional emanations of the UN Declaration of 1948. When fused with common law principles this amounts to a rich corpus of constitutional restraint that governments must respect in their treatment of aliens.

Ten years ago, Commonwealth judges who drew support for their conclusions on contested questions of public law from international standards might be seen to be brave or eccentric or both, particularly in the field of immigration control. The notorious dualism of the common law as applied in the UK tended to regard treaties unincorporated into domestic law with suspicion or indifference. Treaties were the field of foreign affairs and the prerogatives of the Crown. Perhaps there is a continuity of distaste extending back to the extravagant luxuries of the Stuart Court in seventeenth-century Protestant Britain, when treaties like foreign marriages were seen as royalist devices to undermine the rights of the free-born Englishman. Now it is the executive who denies the forensic relevance of its adherence to international resolutions and Conventions. Whilst treaties unincorporated into domestic law cannot normally be the foundation of enforceable private law rights between individuals, there can be no coherent objection that a Treaty signed and ratified by a state in order to provide additional protection for the human rights of those subject to its jurisdiction is not a proper consideration for the judiciary in making public law determinations as to the legality of acts of the executive of the ratifying state.

Incorporation of a Charter of Rights in Canada or the HRA in the UK marks a qualitative shift in this process of engagement, but as Lord Cooke has pertinently pointed out in his concurring comments in the case of *Daly*,[73] conventions and other international instruments often merely declare what the law already is rather than create new sources of obligations and rights.[74] The European case law and the UK experience may

---

[73] *R (Daly) v Secretary of State for the Home Department* [2001] UKHL 26; [2001] 2 AC 532.
[74] See also Lord Bingham's recent comments in Saunders and others [2002] UKHL and Murray Hunt, *Using Human Rights Law in English Courts* (Oxford, Hart Publishing, 1997).

thus be relevant to inform other jurisdictions where similar human rights obligations are known, notwithstanding the reluctance of the Canadian Supreme Court to apply the *Chahal* principle in *Suresh*.

In one field of law, British judges have completed a quiet revolution, drawing inspiration from the Canadian Charter of Rights and Freedoms and the consistent jurisprudence of Madam Justice Claire L'Heureux-Dubé on the question of sexual preference orientation in the field of social welfare legislation. The Strasbourg case-law had shown little indication that same sex partners should be treated as family members for the purpose of tenancy protection and welfare and pension payments. The UK Parliament had been unwilling to grasp the nettle, indeed its last effort had been the embarrassing proscription of local authorities from teaching that same sex relationships should be equated to family life under clause 28 of the Local Government Act. Nevertheless when the House of Lords had to consider the question of whether a same sex partner could come within the phrase 'member of the family' of the deceased tenant in *Fitzpatrick v Sterling Housing*[75] a majority of the Lords decided that he could. The principles of statutory interpretation relied on was the 'always speaking' approach enabling a word to develop a broader meaning than from the date of enactment. This is a domestic equivalent of the living instrument approach applied by human rights bodies. The decision was greeted with relief and gratitude by Parliament and other courts, and shortly afterwards unmarried same sex partners were provided for in the immigration rules. Recently in the case of *Mendoza*,[76] the Court of Appeal went further and now applying the non-discrimination principle of the HRA has concluded that same-sex partners are to be treated not merely as family members but the same as common law spouses, giving greater security of tenure. Similarly in the case of *Bellinger*,[77] the Court of Appeal invited Strasbourg to reconsider its case-law with respect to transsexuals, where Parliament had failed to address the problems of gender diaspora after 16 years of human rights litigation. Strasbourg promptly responded and in the case of *Goodwin*,[78] reversed its previous decision and concluded that transsexuals should have the right to marry in their new identity.

Judicial decision-making is thus about setting standards, reflecting such norms as the right to dignity and keeping up to date with modern societal developments. It is not all about deference and waiting for the legislature to remedy problems and get it right. It is about setting standards of decency as the boundaries for executive action, particularly where the objects of this action are an unpopular and marginalised group in society. In these cases justice was done despite the reluctance of the executive or the legislative to

---

[75] [1999] 3 WLR 1113.
[76] *Mendoza v Ghaidam* [2002] EWCA Civ 1533 2002) 4 All ER 1162.
[77] *Bellinger v Bellinger* [2001] EWCA Civ 1140 (2002) 1 All ER 311: (2002) 2 WLR 411.
[78] *Goodwin v United Kingdom* (2002) 35 EHRR 447.

address problems that would give little electoral advantage. In no field of law is this function more critically in need than in immigration and asylum questions. Within that field nowhere is there a greater need for judicial supervision than in the field of national security as applied to vulnerable individuals. The derogation from Article 5 pays a backhanded compliment to the importance of human rights values. It certainly keeps the issue politically sensitive and high-profile. Ultimately the justification for the UK's decision will have to be examined by a court of largely foreign judges, concerned to ensure that stringent standards are set for a continent determined to march forward to higher standards of decency for citizen and foreigner alike. International human rights obligations outside the province of domestic dilution and compromise, are thus a source of reason amidst the rancour of political controversy and provide the values and the intellectual tools for domestic judges to explain how and why they act. Whilst civilised states permit these values to nourish their laws and policies and judges continue to fearlessly ask the right questions, then it can truly be said that the laws are not silent in times of war.

10

Rights in the Balance: Non-Citizens and State Sovereignty Under the Charter

NINETTE KELLEY*

INTRODUCTION

One of the rights possessed by the supreme power in every State is the right to refuse to permit an alien to enter that State, to annex what conditions it pleases to the permission to enter it, and to expel or deport from the State, at pleasure, even a friendly alien, especially if it considers his presence in the State opposed to its peace, order and good government, or to its social or material interests.
Attorney General of Canada v Cain [1906] AC 542, 546.

FEW COUNTRIES IN the world can claim to have been shaped more profoundly in as short a time by immigrant hands than Canada. Yet the frequently acknowledged debt to immigrants in building the nation has not diminished the constant, century-old concerns regarding who should be allowed entry, in what numbers, and on what conditions they should be permitted to remain. Throughout Canada's 150 years of being an immigrant receiving nation, these fundamental and often emotive questions at the heart of immigration policy, have frequently been central to national policy debates. In fact, in any period in the country's history one can find that immigration policy was seen to be, and continues to be seen as 'in crisis', both by advocates of more immigration and proponents of less.

At the core of these controversies are two conflicting interests: the sovereign right of the state to control admission and membership in the community, and the right of the individual (citizen and non-citizen alike) to respect and protection of his or her fundamental human rights. For most of

---

* With thanks to Reva Devins and David Dyzenhaus for helpful comments on an earlier draft.

our history, whenever the state's right and the right(s) of the non-citizen collided, the state's interest dominated, at times at great human cost to those who were excluded or removed on racial and political grounds.[1] In this chapter I look at what impact, if any, the entrenchment of the *Canadian Charter of Rights and Freedoms* (the '*Charter*'), has had in the balancing of the state's interest in controlling community membership against the rights of non-citizens in Canada. I begin by providing a historical perspective to modern rights adjudication in immigration matters showing how, until the late 1960s, the executive branch of government was accorded relatively unfettered discretion in matters of immigrant admission and deportation decisions. I then examine a number of post-*Charter* constitutional challenges to these decisions, observing that the *Charter* has had little impact on protecting the rights of non-citizens, largely because of the deference the Supreme Court of Canada (the 'Court') has shown to the executive, particularly where matters of criminality or state security are concerned. Finally, I review a number of major changes introduced in 2002, in the new *Immigration and Refugee Protection Act* (IRPA), which draw directly from the Court's jurisprudence. As a result of these changes, non-citizens today have fewer rights than they did before the *Charter* was entrenched and I conclude that given the pattern of judicial reasoning, challenges to the new legislation are unlikely to succeed.

HISTORICAL CONTEXT

For over 75 years following Confederation, immigration acts were characterised by broad statutory classifications of admissible and inadmissible immigrants. The executive was given enormous discretion to determine, through regulation and cabinet directives, those who would be permitted entry and those who could be excluded or expelled.[2] It was a system that provided maximum flexibility, enabling the Cabinet to alter admissibility and removal policies quickly, unencumbered by judicial or parliamentary scrutiny. At the turn of the century, when immigrants were needed to settle the West, provide a consumer base to support the economy and to supply needed labour to expanding industries, admission criteria were relatively few. Hundreds of thousands of immigrants each year took advantage of this

---

[1] See discussion and accompanying notes regarding the exclusion of Asians, African Americans, Chinese, Japanese and Jewish immigrants during the first half of this century and the removal of those who became sick, destitute, or who advocated political or labour reform, at pp 255–7.

[2] A thorough summary of the history of Canadian immigration policy is beyond the scope of this paper. For a more detailed analysis see N Kelley and M Trebilcock, *The Making of the Mosaic: A History of Canadian Immigration Policy*, (Toronto, University of Toronto Press, 1998).

relatively open-door policy.³ During the 1930s, when a depressed economy and surging welfare roles made immigrant arrivals less desirable, the doors were effectively shut simply by executive decision.⁴ Not only was the system easily adjusted to control the number of immigrants, but also their racial composition.⁵ It was through regulations and Cabinet directives that Asian, African-American, Jewish and Armenian immigrants were excluded.⁶ Similarly, immigrants who were found unsuitable after admission, because of poverty, criminality or political activism, were shown the door, all on the assumption that it was the state's sovereign right to control membership in the community.⁷ Throughout this exclusionary period in Canadian history the courts were largely silent. This was due in part to the privative clauses reproduced in successive immigration acts,⁸ and in part because the judiciary shared the same values that informed the immigration policy of the day.⁹

---

[3] Between 1896 and 1914 over 3 million people immigrated to Canada, transforming not just the social landscape but the economic one as well. *Ibid*, ch 4.

[4] *Ibid*, ch 6.

[5] These powers were made explicit in successive immigration Acts from 1867–1952. For example, amendments to the Immigration Act in 1919 gave the Cabinet power to prohibit any race, nationality, or class of immigrant by reason of 'economic, industrial, or other condition temporarily existing in Canada'; or because such immigrants were unsuitable given the social, economic and labour requirements of the country; or simply because of their 'peculiar habits, modes of life and methods of holding property' and their 'probable inability to become readily assimilated or assume the responsibilities and duties of Canadian citizenship within a reasonable period of time'. *An Act to Amend the Immigration Act* SC 1919, ch 25, s 3. In the 1952 Act only certain classes of immigrants were admissible, and the power to exclude found in earlier Acts was conferred on senior immigration officers. Immigration Act SC 1952, s 20 (1).

[6] For a discussion of the various orders-in-council and immigration department directives that were used to limit specific classes of immigrants see Kelley and Trebilcock above n 2, pp 146–49, 199, 328–29 (re Asian immigrants); 151–56 (re African American immigrants); 201 (re Armenian); 200, 260, 268–71 (re Jewish Immigrants). Chinese immigration was restricted by the terms of the Chinese Immigration Act, the amendments in 1923 effectively ending immigration from China for over 20 years, pp 97, 109–10, 152–53, 203–04, 22–23, 314.

[7] Early immigration Acts contained provisions for removing those who were found to be medically inadmissible after arrival or who had relied on public relief ('public charge') and for reasons of criminality. Initially an immigrant could only be removed within one year of arrival, by 1910 this probationary period had been expanded to three years after which time the person gained 'domicile'. Medical grounds made up the bulk of early removals. *Ibid*, pp 156–58, 206–09. Those removed for becoming a public charge tended to make up a significantly high proportion of annual removals during depressed economic times. Pp 229–34. Deportation was also used to remove from Canada suspected communists and labour activists especially evident during the depression years as part of the government's 'war on communism'. Pp 234–47. In the second half of the century removal for public charge reasons fell and other reasons such as entering by stealth or misrepresentation and removal for security or criminal grounds correspondingly rose. Pp 367–71, 430–35.

[8] S 23 of the Immigration Act 1910 is a typical example: 'No court, and no judge or officer thereof, shall have jurisdiction to review, quash, reverse, restrain or otherwise interfere with any proceeding, decision, or order of the Minister or of any Board of Inquiry, or officer in charge ... relating to the detention, deportation of any rejected immigrant ... upon any ground whatsoever'.

[9] The comments of Justice McPhillips in the case of *Re Munshi Singh* (1914) 20 BCR 243 (CA) are representative. In upholding the deportation of Singh under a regulation designed to

Restrictive and racist admission policies and judicial restraint reached their height during World War II with the exclusion of Jewish refugees, the incarceration of hundreds of 'enemy aliens', suspected fascists and communists and the forced internment of nearly the entire Canadian population of Japanese descent.[10] While there was a growing recognition that Canadian treatment of immigrants was inconsistent with the ideals and values Canada had fought for during the war, change was slow. It was not until 1962 that explicit racially discriminatory admission provisions were eliminated and replaced by criteria for independent immigrants that emphasised skills, education and training.[11] This was a watershed in Canadian immigration policy history. It marked the beginning of a new modern policy characterised by increased public contribution to immigration policy formation,[12] more transparent admissions criteria, due process protections for non-citizens refused entry or subject to removal and a greater willingness on the part of the judiciary to review immigration admissibility and deportation decisions.[13] The most significant development in the latter regard was the creation of the Immigration Appeal Board (IAB) in 1967, a quasi-judicial body, independent of the Immigration department. The IAB heard appeals from deportation orders and refusals to approve family sponsorship applications on the basis of fact, law and on humanitarian and compassionate grounds. Its decisions were final, subject only to appeal on

---

prohibit East Indian arrivals, McPhillips stated: 'Better that the people's of non-assimilative—and by nature properly non-assimilative—races should not come to Canada, but rather that they should remain of residence in their country of origin and there do their share, as they have in the past, in the preservation and development of the Empire'. The notion that certain races were inferior and non-assimilative also informed judicial decisions upholding racially discriminatory provincial legislation that disenfranchised certain races and imposed restrictions on employment, property and residence rights on the basis of race. See Kelley and Trebilcock, above n 2, 98, 141, 205, 209 and 228. See also N Blake's chapter 'National Security and Judicial Review of Immigration Control: Reflections on the United Kingdom Experience' regarding the unwillingness of British courts to interfere with the exercise of executive discretion.

[10] *Ibid*, ch 7.
[11] PC 1962–86 (18 January 1962).
[12] Initially this was by representations to the Senate Standing Committee on Immigration and Labour, established in 1946 to consider immigration policy options. Over the years, representations were regularly made to both the House and the Senate Standing committees. The 1976 Immigration Act introduced the requirement that the Minister consult with the provinces as well as with other individuals and institutions regarding future levels of immigration. In 1993 the legislation was amended to require the Minister submit an annual immigration plan to Parliament.
[13] See for example *Podlaszecka v MMI* (1972) 23 DLR 3d 331 (SCC) (deportation cannot be on the basis of technical non compliance alone); *Leiba v MMI* (1972) 23 DLR (3d) 476 (SCC) (immigration officers had to follow the procedures set out in the Immigration Act); *Gana v MMI* [1970] SCR 699 (points assessment can be varied by the IAB); *Re Gooliah and Minister of Citizenship and Immigration* 91967), 63 DLR (2d) 224 (Man CA) (deportation quashed because immigration officer biased).

Non-Citizens and State Sovereignty Under the Charter 257

questions of law to the Federal Court of Appeal.[14] These changes were consolidated and expanded with the Immigration Act (the 'Act') of 1976, which preserved transparent admissibility criteria and due process protections for those refused admission or ordered removed. It also contained a formal recognition of Canada's international obligations with respect to refugees. In some areas ministerial discretion was maintained, including the power to issue a Minister's permit to allow entry of those who did not satisfy admission criteria. The Minister also retained the authority to issue certificates against those considered to be security risks, which, as a consequence, limited their right to appeal deportation orders made against them.[15]

THE SUPREME COURT WEIGHS IN

Refugee Status Determination: *Singh*[16]

The next major development in modern immigration policy was the repatriation of the constitution and adoption of the *Charter*. The impact of the *Charter* on the rights of non-citizens was tested in 1985 with the Supreme Court of Canada decision in *Singh*. *Singh* involved a challenge to the refugee determination procedures under the 1976 Act. The Act had adopted the definition of a refugee found in the international *Convention relating to the Status of Refugees*: a person with a well founded fear of persecution in his or her country of origin for reasons of race, religion, nationality, membership in a particular social group or political opinion.[17] Under the Act, refugees were accorded certain rights including the right not to be removed to a country where their life or freedom would be threatened. Individuals claiming refugee status were first interviewed by an immigration officer concerning the basis of their refugee claim. The decision to grant refugee status rested with the Minister's delegate, and was made after having considered the transcript of the interview along with other relevant information, which was not disclosed to the claimant.[18] A negative decision from the Minister could be appealed to the IAB and an oral hearing on the merits accorded, however, only if the claimant first satisfied the IAB that there

---

[14] Following the establishment of the Federal Court (Trial Division) in 1971, IAB decisions were subject to judicial review by the Federal Court with leave. Federal Court Act RSC 1985, F-7.
[15] The operation of security certificates is canvassed below at p 265.
[16] *Singh v Canada (Minister of Employment and Immigration)* [1985] 1 SCR 177.
[17] CSR51, Art 1A(2) and *Protocol relating to The Status of Refugees*, 31 January 1967 (CSRP67); Immigration Act, 1976–77 (Can) c 52, s 2(1).
[18] Under the Act, the Minister could delegate this authority to the registrar of the Refugee Status Advisory Committee. Immigration Act, above n 17, s 45.

were 'reasonable grounds to believe that a claim could, upon the hearing of the application, be established'. The refugee claimants in *Singh* all had their claims rejected by the Minister and had been denied a hearing by the IAB. They argued that the refugee determination procedure was unconstitutional. Specifically, they claimed that it violated their rights under section 7 of the *Charter*, 'to life, liberty and security of the person and the right not to be deprived thereof except in accordance with the principles of fundamental justice', because the procedure did not provide them a meaningful opportunity to present their claims or to know the case they had to meet.

The Court issued two concurring judgments. Justice Wilson (Dickson CJ and Lamer J concurring) held that the procedures violated section 7 entitlements under the *Charter*, and Justice Beetz, (Estey and McIntyre JJ concurring) found that the procedures were in conflict with section 2 (e) of the *Canadian Bill of Rights*. For our purposes the former is of most interest, both in its reasoning and the result. Justice Wilson's analysis starts with the observation that the rights in section 7 extend to 'everyone' which she held included 'every human being who is physically present in Canada and by virtue of such presence amenable to Canadian law', and therefore included refugee claimants. The right to security of the person was engaged in the refugee determination process, she reasoned, because security of the person encompassed freedom from the threat of physical punishment or suffering as well as such punishment itself.[19]

> Given the potential consequences for the appellants of a denial of the status if they are in fact persons with a 'well-founded fear of persecution', it seems to me unthinkable that the *Charter* would not apply to entitle them to fundamental justice in the adjudication of their status.[20]

In considering the content of fundamental justice, Wilson J held that at a minimum this includes the notion of procedural fairness: a person has to have an opportunity to state his or her case and to know the case he or she has to meet. She acknowledged that procedural fairness may demand different things in different contexts and that an oral hearing may therefore not be necessary in every case where section 7 is engaged. However, where a serious issue of credibility is involved 'fundamental justice requires that credibility be determined on the basis of an oral hearing'.[21] In *Singh*, the claimants' right to fundamental justice had been breached because an oral hearing was predicated on their showing that the Minister's decision was wrong, a decision based in part on information and policies that they could not access and therefore could not know. Wilson J concluded further

---

[19] *Singh* above n 16 para 47.
[20] *Ibid*, para 52.
[21] *Ibid*, para 58.

that the procedures were not saved under section 1. In her opinion, the 'unreasonable burden' on the Board's resources that the government argued would be caused by providing an oral hearing to every refugee claimant, had not been substantiated with evidence. More importantly she doubted that this type of utilitarian analysis could justify a limitation of *Charter* rights. The guarantees of the *Charter* would be 'illusory' she wrote 'if they could be ignored because it was administratively convenient to do so'.[22]

The Court's decision in *Singh* set in motion a number of very significant changes to the procedure for determining refugee status that significantly enhanced due process protections accorded to refugee claimants. Although the fairness of the refugee determination procedure had been debated long before the decision in *Singh,* the latter provoked further review and public comment that led to a radical institutional restructuring of immigration decision-making.[23] In 1989 the Immigration and Refugee Board (IRB) was created. This was an independent quasi-judicial tribunal consisting of the Immigration Appeal Division (IAD) and the Convention Refugee Determination Division (CRDD). The former was responsible for hearing appeals of deportation decision and refusals of family sponsorship applications while the latter was responsible for determining refugee status determination. Both divisions conducted oral hearings in which the appellant and/or claimant had full disclosure of evidence to be considered, a right to submit documentation of their own, a right to be heard orally and the right to written decisions.[24]

Extradition: *Kindler*[25]

In 1991, the Court considered the case of Kindler, an American fugitive who had been ordered extradited to the United States where he faced the death penalty. *Kindler* brought into sharp relief the conflict between the state's interest in preserving its right to determine the terms and conditions upon which non-citizens could remain in Canada and the interest of the non-citizen in not being expelled. The Court's analysis of the constitutional issues in *Kindler* was substantially different from its approach six years

---

[22] *Ibid*, para 70.
[23] In the interim the government passed Bill C–55, which provided for an oral hearing on appeals before the IAB. This attempt to provide oral hearings for refugee claimants within the existing framework eventually resulted in a large backlog of cases which was relieved by the application of a partial amnesty to those claimants who could show that they were likely to establish in Canada.
[24] In 1993 the Immigration Adjudication Division was added to the IRB, which was responsible for conducting immigration admissibility hearings for certain categories of people believed to be inadmissible to, or removable from, Canada and conducting detention reviews for those detained under the Act. Adjudicators are appointed under the Public Service Employment Act.
[25] *Kindler v Canada (Minister of Justice)* [1991] 2 SCR 779.

earlier in *Singh*. In the intervening years the political and legal landscape had changed in important respects. First the annual number of refugee claimants had soared from approximately 5,000 in 1984 to nearly 37,000 in 1991. The growing number of annual arrivals provoked increasing concern about the ability of the country to maintain control over its borders. The sensitivity surrounding the issue was dramatically illustrated in August 1987 with the arrival of 174 Sikh refugee claimants off the east coast. Their entry sparked a national outcry sufficiently strong to support the government's call for an emergency session of Parliament for what was sensationally characterised as a matter of 'grave national importance'.[26] The result of the emergency session was the introduction of Bill C-84 which broadened the powers of immigration officers to order the detention of those who arrived at the border without proper documentation and which further expanded the power of the Minister of Immigration together with the Solicitor General to deport those they certified were a threat to security. Notwithstanding some vocal opposition expressed both in the House and by various legal and immigration interest groups, the Bill was passed with what seemed widespread public approval.

The years between *Singh* and *Kindler* had also seen significant shifts in the composition of the Court and the legal analysis it used in *Charter* adjudication. Of the six judges who had participated in the *Singh* decision, only Justice Lamer remained in 1991 when *Kindler* was decided. A detailed analysis of how the composition of the Court affected the pattern of *Charter* reasoning is beyond the scope of this chapter. However, two observations are worthy of mention. The first concerns the Court's application of section 1. In 1986, the year following its decision in *Singh*, the Court handed down its landmark ruling in *Oakes* which pulled together the various tests it had developed for determining whether measures that infringed a *Charter* right were demonstrably justified in a free and democratic society. In *Oakes* the Court said the objective to be served by the measures had to be sufficiently important to warrant overriding a constitutionally protected right or freedom. Secondly, the party invoking section 1 had to show the means were proportional: fair, rationally connected to the objective, and impaired the right in question as little as possible.[27] In subsequent cases, however, the Court emphasised that the *Oakes* test should not be applied in too rigid a fashion and that the nature of the proportionality test would vary according to the circumstances. It necessitated a weighing

---

[26] Although arrivals at sea have consistently constituted a very small fraction of total refugee claimants, they tend to illicit disproportionately strong responses. For a more recent example recall the hostile reaction to the arrival of Chinese migrants in boats off the coast of British Columbia in the summer of 1999. Nearly all of the approximately 600 who arrived claimed refugee status—representing less than 3% of the total number of refugee claimant's that year.
[27] *R v Oakes* [1986] 1 SCR 103.

of values and often a balancing of competing interests.[28] Where the objective of the challenged law or practice was pressing and substantial, in the Court's view the legislature had to be given reasonable room to achieve that objective.[29] Moreover, in areas involving complex consideration of interests, where the executive/legislature is better informed than the courts, the Court held that it should proceed cautiously, conferring discretion on the executive/legislature.[30]

Another significant development in *Charter* jurisprudence between the Court's decisions in *Singh* and *Kindler* was the Court's limitation of its power to review laws or actions under the *Charter* to those that were directly connected to legislative or executive action. In a range of cases it had found the *Charter* was not applicable where the rights infringement could not be directly attributed to the government.[31] For example, in a series of extradition cases, the Court concluded that generally *Charter* protections did not apply if the infringement of the right was due to the actions of a foreign government.[32] Only in exceptional situations, where the manner in which the foreign state would treat the fugitive on surrender 'sufficiently shocks the conscience', such as torturing the person, would the surrender breach the principles of fundamental justice enshrined in section 7.[33] Kindler argued that the circumstances of his case fell within this exception.

In *Kindler*, the Court was asked to decide whether the Minister's decision to extradite Kindler to the United States, without obtaining an assurance that the death penalty would not be carried out, infringed his *Charter* rights. Kindler argued that his section 12 right (not to be subjected to cruel and unusual punishment or treatment) and his section 7 rights had been violated by the Minister's decision, and that the infringements were not justified under section 1. The Court split, four to three, in favour of upholding the constitutionality of the legislative provisions which gave the Minister the discretion whether or not to seek assurances. Justices McLachlin and LaForest wrote separate reasons, both of which were signed

---

[28] *R v Edwards Books* [1986] 2 SCR 713.
[29] *United States of America v Cotroni* [1989] 1 SCR 1469; *R v Schwartz* [1988] 2 SCR 443.
[30] *Cotroni ibid*; *Irwin Toy v AG Quebec* [1989] 1 SCR 927.
[31] So, for example, the *Charter* was found not to be applicable in the following: *Retail, Wholesale and Department Store Union, Local 580 v Dolphin Delivery Ltd* [1986] 2 SCR 573 (private litigation/picketing); *McKinney v University of Guelph* [1990] 3 SCR 229 (university mandatory retirement policies); *Stoffman v Vancouver General Hospital* [1990] 3 SCR 483 (non renewal of admitting licence to physicians over age 64); *Tremblay v Daigle* [1989] 2 SCR 530 (civil action/injunction preventing a woman from having an abortion). See also extradition cases n 32.
[32] *Canada v Schmidt* [1987] 1 SCR 500 (double jeopardy and application of s 7); *Argentina v Mellino* [1987] 1 SCR 536 (delay in prosecution and ss 7 and 11(b)); *United States v Allard*, [1987] 1 SCR 564 (delay in prosecution and s 7).
[33] *Schmidt ibid*.

by Gonthier and L'Heureux-Dubé JJ.[34] Two dissenting judgments, (both of which were concurred in by Lamer CJ), were delivered by Sopinka J, who held that the extradition provision was an unjustified infringement of section 7, and Cory J who found that it unjustifiably infringed section 12.

The reasoning of the dissenting judges was similar to the reasoning of the Court in *Singh*. Sopinka J held that extradition violated Kindler's section 7 rights because it exposed him to the threat of the death penalty. On a similar basis, Cory J held that Kindler's section 12 rights were also engaged because its prohibition against cruel or unusual treatment or punishment included protection from the 'threat' of such action. For Cory J there was no doubt that the death penalty was a form of cruel and unusual treatment.[35] All three dissenting judges agreed that the violation of Kindler's *Charter* rights were not demonstrably justified under section 1. They found that the government had not provided any evidentiary foundation for its claim that the purposes of extradition policy (ie international comity, preventing criminals from escaping justice) would be undermined by requiring assurances in death penalty cases.[36] They concluded that by seeking assurances in death penalty cases it was possible to achieve the goals of extradition policy in a manner that did not deprive the fugitive of the protection of the *Charter*.

The analytical approach adopted by the judges upholding the Minister's decision was different in emphasis from the reasons of the minority and reflected a sharp departure away from the approach Wilson J had set in *Singh*. Although both McLachlin and LaForest JJ acknowledged that Kindler's section 7 rights were engaged in the extradition decision, they rejected his claim that his section 12 rights were involved. Neither thought that his extradition could be characterised as 'punishment'. Moreover, they held that the Minister's decision did not subject Kindler to cruel and unusual 'treatment', since the death penalty would be imposed by the United States and not the Government of Canada. Neither McLachlin nor LaForest JJ explained why the rights infringement under section 12 had to be directly imposed by the Canadian government yet indirect action by the government was sufficient to engage section 7.

McLachlin and LaForest JJ's approach to the requirements of fundamental justice also differed significantly from the approach in *Singh*. In *Singh*, the Court addressed this question from the perspective of procedural fairness: did the process give the person an opportunity to state his or her

[34] LaForest J stated that he was in substantial agreement with McLachlin J's reasons and his reasons do not depart from hers in material respects.
[35] He noted the evidence of the excruciating pain and suffering attendant on death by execution and/or lethal gas and the Court's previous jurisprudence finding non-fatal forms of treatment (corporal punishment, lobotomies, castration) to be cruel and unusual punishment within the meaning of s 12. Above n 25 para 81–88.
[36] They pointed to the fact that there was nothing in past experience to support such a finding nor was it supported by the experience of European states that routinely requested assurances in death penalty extradition cases. *Ibid* paras 111–13.

Non-Citizens and State Sovereignty Under the Charter 263

case and know the case he or she has to meet? If not, then the Court had to consider whether the limitation was reasonable and demonstrably justified in a free and democratic society within the meaning of section 1. In *Kindler,* many of the considerations relevant to the section 1 analysis were incorporated into the assessment of what fundamental justice required in that case. Whether fundamental justice prohibited extradition without assurances was held to depend on a variety of factors including: the nature of the offence; the justice system in the requesting state; the consequences of requesting assurances in death penalty cases; and whether the practice under review was consistent with fundamental conceptions of what is fair and right in Canadian society. They said that the question to be asked was, considering these factors, is extradition to face the death penalty 'simply unacceptable' such that it 'sufficiently shocks' the Canadian conscience, offending the Canadian sense of what is fair, right and just.

In starting from the premise that the requirements of fundamental justice were to be determined by consideration of a complex set of factors, the Court endorsed a very open-ended framework of analysis that was unlikely to yield consistent results since it allowed each judge to approach and weigh the factors differently. A comparison of the majority and minority opinions is illustrative. For example, unlike the dissenting judges, those in the majority were prepared to accept the government's assertion that seeking assurances would frustrate the legitimate purposes of extradition policy, without requiring evidence to support the argument. Similarly, while those in the minority held that the parliamentary rejection of the death penalty reflected the Canadian view that the death penalty was inconsistent with human dignity, the majority dismissed this view on the basis that the votes were too close to make such an assertion. The two sides also drew different conclusions from the practice of other states. Cory J highlighted the international instruments that favoured the abolition of the death penalty, and the European Court of Human Rights decision in *Soering,* that held that extradition to face the death penalty constituted cruel and unusual punishment under the European Convention.[37] LaForest J, by contrast, argued that all but one of these international instruments fell short of abolishing the death penalty and McLachlin J cited a European Commission for Human Rights decision in *Kirkwood,*[38] to support her view that the court should not lightly interfere in extradition decisions.[39]

---

[37] *Soering case,* judgment of 7 July 1989, Series A No 161. Art 3 of the *European Convention for the Protection of Human Rights and Fundamental Freedoms* provides that no one shall be subjected to torture or inhuman or degrading treatment or punishment. Cory J also noted decisions of the European Commission of Human Rights that held that the extradition to a place where the person could be tortured was a violation of Art 3, above n 25 para 101–07.
[38] *Kirkwood v United Kingdom,* 12 March 1984, DR 37, p 158; Eur Court.
[39] Ten years later in *States v Burns* [2001] 1 SCR 283, a case involving extradition to the United States of two Canadians citizens to stand trial for murder, the Court came to the opposite conclusion from the one it had reached in *Kindler*. It relied on essentially the same factors

Overall the majority judgment in *Kindler* illustrated a clear move away from *Singh*. First, like pre-Charter court decisions, *Kindler* took a deferential approach towards the state's exercise of control over the conditions on which non-citizens could remain in Canada. Its ruling that many factors had to be considered in determining whether the principles of fundamental justice were breached allowed the majority to be very deferential to the Minister's decision to extradite without assurances. A second change in the Court's approach, was its limitation of section 12, finding it inapplicable because the government of Canada was not directly responsible for the imposition of the death penalty without addressing why section 12 should be read more restrictively than section 7 which encompassed direct and indirect rights infringements. Thirdly, in bringing many of the factors associated with the section 1 analysis (international comity, apprehension of criminals), the Court added to the appellant's burden of establishing a section 7 violation. Had the Court required evidence in support of the government's arguments that extradition with assurances would permit criminals to go free and render Canada a safe haven for fugitives, the burden of proof would have been borne by the government. Finally, in reasoning that Parliament's defeat of a motion to reinstate the death penalty was by too narrow a margin to establish Canadian values on the issue, the Court further raised the appellant's burden by inferring that only broad consensus of opinion is indicative of what Canadians feel is fair and just, thereby further insulating executive decisions from judicial scrutiny unless sufficient public opposition to them encourages judicial intervention.[40]

With its decision in *Kindler,* the Court had marked two very different lines of analysis. In its subsequent decisions regarding the constitutionality of the government's removal powers and procedures under the Immigration Act, the analytical methods used in *Kindler* proved to be decisive. This was clearly evident in the decision it rendered in *Chiarelli* the following year, concerning the constitutionality of the deportation provisions of the Act.

Deportation: *Chiarelli*[41]

In *Chiarelli* the Court was faced with another contest between the right of the state to control the terms of entry and residence and the interests of a

---

to determine the requirements of fundamental justice, but with different emphasis. Although the Court suggested that some of those factors had gained more importance in the intervening decade, such as concern over wrongful convictions, most of the evidence it relied upon in *Burns* was substantially similar to that used by the dissenting judges in *Kindler*. The fact that the Court could come to opposite results on similar evidence without saying it was reversing itself, illustrates the open-ended nature of the Court's balancing method.

[40] Although LaForest J said that courts should not use statistical measurements exclusively, he did indicate that they provided insight into the public values of the community. *Kindler*, above n 25, para 129.
[41] *Canada (Minister of Employment and Immigration) v Chiarelli* [1992] 1 SCR 711.

non-citizen in not being removed. This time the conflict was between a permanent resident, Chiarelli who had resided in Canada for ten years since the age of 15. Chiarelli had been ordered deported because of two criminal convictions.[42] The Minister had also issued a security certificate against Chiarelli on the basis that there were reasonable grounds to believe he would engage in organised crime. The effect of the security certificate was that it limited Chiarelli's grounds to appeal the deportation order to errors of fact and/or law, revoking his right to have the order reviewed on the basis of 'all the circumstances of the case' (compassionate considerations). In cases of this kind, an appeal for compassionate consideration was the most common ground of appeal. It permitted considerations of factors such as: the seriousness of the offence, the chance of rehabilitation, the length or residence, family ties and establishment in Canada. Chiarelli argued that the deportation provisions of the Act, and the procedures under which the security certificate were issued, were unconstitutional. In a unanimous judgment, delivered by Sopinka J, the Court upheld the constitutionality of the challenged provisions.

With respect to the deportation provisions, Chiarelli claimed that the mandatory issuing of a deportation order without regard to the circumstances of the offence or the offender was a violation of section 7. And he argued that the removal of the right to appeal his deportation on compassionate grounds once a security certificate had been issued also violated his section 7 rights. At the heart of both arguments was his contention that deportation was a deprivation of liberty and security of the person and therefore had to be in accordance with fundamental justice. This, he claimed, required consideration of all the circumstances of his case. Given the wide range of offences, including less serious ones, that could trigger a deportation order, and the different personal circumstances of the offender, deportation without consideration of those circumstances offended the values of fairness and proportionality underlying the *Charter* protection.

Sopinka J held that it was unnecessary for him to determine whether deportation involved a deprivation of liberty because in his view there was no breach of fundamental justice. The starting point for determining the content of fundamental justice, he reasoned, was the principles and policies underlying the Immigration Act, the most fundamental one being the common law principle that 'non citizens do not have an unqualified right to enter or remain in the country'. From this principle it followed that Parliament had a right to set conditions under which non-citizens were permitted to enter and remain in Canada. The condition that a person not be convicted of a crime was a legitimate one. Sopinka J characterised those

---

[42] These were for unlawfully uttering threats to cause injury and possession of a narcotic for the purposes of trafficking. Although Chiarelli received a suspended sentence for the first conviction and six months imprisonment for the second, he was ordered deported because the offences carried a possible sentence of five years or more.

who had breached that condition as having 'deliberately violated an essential condition under which they were permitted to remain in Canada' and as such there was 'no breach of fundamental justice in giving practical effect to the termination of their right to remain in Canada'.[43] He continued by reasoning that, to the extent that fundamental justice required an appeal of a deportation order, an appeal on fact and law was sufficient. He drew support for this from historical practice, noting that a right of an appeal on compassionate grounds was only introduced in 1967 and that since then the Minister had retained the power to exclude that ground of appeal in cases involving security interests.

Just as the Court's analysis in *Kindler* had favoured the Minister's position, so too did the Court's analysis of the deportation provisions in *Chiarelli*. The Court's willingness to consider the content of fundamental justice without considering whether and to what extent Chiarelli's right to liberty was at stake (ie the impact of deportation on his life) rendered it easier for the Court to find that his deportation without a review of all the circumstances of the case was not a disproportionate response. Moreover, the Court's reference to the underlying common law principles of the Immigration Act to determine the content of a *Charter* right, rather than using the values underlying the *Charter* to determine the constitutionality of the provisions of the Act, effectively denied the supremacy of the *Charter*. It accorded almost complete deference to the legislature. As the legislative provisions were consistent with the statute's general rationale, they were immune from scrutiny.

Additionally, the Court's characterisation of the underlying principle of the Immigration Act, and of the historical record, was very selective and supportive of the Minister's position. In much the same manner as the Privy Council in 1906, the Court in *Chiarelli* stated that the most fundamental principle in immigration law was that non-citizens do not have an unqualified right to enter or remain in the country. The Court did not acknowledge the much wider range of purposes enumerated in the Immigration Act, including demographic, social, cultural, humanitarian and health and security objectives.[44] Similarly, the Court's characterisation of the historical record was incomplete. It is true that relief from a deportation decision on compassionate grounds prior to 1967 was purely at the discretion of the executive. However, it was precisely the unfettered and arbitrary use of this discretion that prompted the legislative changes in 1967, enabling a person to appeal a deportation order to an independent tribunal on the basis of fact, law and compassionate grounds, although excluding the latter ground from those considered a security risk. Moreover, until 1976, most grounds for deportation only applied to those without domicile (less than five years residence).

---

[43] *Chiarelli* above n 41, para 27.
[44] Above n 17, s 3.

With the 1976 Immigration Act this concept was removed, permitting the deportation of long-term residents, but providing a right to appeal their deportation on compassionate grounds except when a security certificate had been issued against them. Viewed in this light, the historical record could be seen as reinforcing the notion that a right of review on compassionate grounds, subject to limited exceptions, was a value recognised for over 25 years and in keeping with the values underlying the requirement of fundamental justice enshrined in section 7 of the *Charter*.

The Court's characterisation of those who breached the conditions of their residence, as having done so 'deliberately' and therefore there was nothing inherently unjust about deporting them, was also much too broad. Although the Court's emphasis on the 'deliberate' nature of the breach fit the facts of *Chiarelli*, it does not accord with the circumstances of many others who are subject to deportation for breaches of conditions that are not intentional including those who incur criminal convictions when suffering from mental illness, drug or alcohol addiction and those who are deported for non-criminal breaches of their conditions of residence over which they have no control.[45]

The Court's reasoning in support of the constitutionality of the security certificate procedures was also weighted in favour of the government. Under the legislation, Chiarelli was only entitled to a summary of the Minister's case against him. Although he was allowed to submit evidence and make oral arguments before the reviewing tribunal,[46] he was not entitled to be present during, or to have access to, the representations made by the Minister. The government claimed that these limitations were necessary to protect the investigatory techniques of the police. Chiarelli argued that they were too broad, because he was excluded from hearing any of the Minister's case, and not simply those aspects of it that were necessary to safeguard protected information. As such he claimed that they violated the principles of fundamental justice.

The analysis the Court relied on in rejecting Chiarelli's argument was similar to its analysis of the deportation provisions in so far as it concluded that the procedures accorded with the principles of fundamental justice without deciding whether Chiarelli's rights to liberty or security of the person were engaged. Although the Court acknowledged that the content of fundamental justice would vary with the context and interests at stake, it narrowly described Chiarelli's interest as being in a fair procedure, which

---

[45] Eg fiancés whose sponsors refuse to marry them after arrival or entrepreneurs who face unexpected and insurmountable economic barriers during the time they are required to establish an enterprise.

[46] Security certificates were reviewed by the Security Intelligence Review Committee, which was required to conduct an investigation and then make a report to Cabinet with a conclusion of whether or not the certificate should be issued. *Security Intelligence Review Committee Act*, SC 1984 c 21, ss 43, 44, 48–52.

had to be balanced against the interest of the state in effectively conducting national security and criminal intelligence investigations and protecting police sources. Narrowly defining Chiarelli's interest in this way affected its overall weight. Moreover, as in *Kindler,* the balancing of Chiarelli's interest against the interests of the state in section 7, rather than in section 1, further limited the breadth of the *Charter* protection since the weight of Chiarelli's interest was counterbalanced by that of the state. And again it relieved the government of having to justify why giving the reviewing tribunal complete discretion with respect to how much of the government's case it should reveal to Chiarelli, rather than limiting non-disclosure to only evidence that was required to protect police sources, was reasonably justified under section 1.

The significance of the Court's decision in *Chiarelli* transcended the facts of that case. In limiting the reach of the *Charter* in the way it did, the Court endorsed the right of the state to impose conditions on residence in a relatively unfettered manner and reinforced the lack of any corresponding right on the part of the non-citizen to challenge the exercise of state sovereignty except on the narrowest of grounds. What a non-citizen now could expect from the *Charter* was actually less than what had been provided by immigration legislation before the entrenchment of the *Charter*.

Right to Counsel: *Dehghani*[47]

One year after its decision in *Chiarelli*, the Court was asked to rule on the constitutionality of provisions of the Immigration Act governing the questioning of non-citizens entering Canada. Dehghani, a citizen of Iran, arrived in Canada without travel or identity documents and claimed refugee status before the immigration officer who first examined him. He was then referred to a secondary examination in a different part of the airport where, after a four-hour wait, another immigration officer interviewed him. This examination lasted two hours and consisted of questions relating to his admissibility and concerning his reasons for making a refugee claim. In the course of this interview, Dehghani omitted important factual details regarding his refugee claim. Following the interview, he was scheduled to appear at an inquiry to determine whether there was a credible basis to his refugee claim and, if so, to refer him to the IRB for an oral hearing on the merits of the claim.[48] At the inquiry he was represented by counsel. He was found not to be credible, largely because of his failure to state fully the reasons for

---

[47] *Dehghani v Canada (Minister of Employment and Immigration)* [1993] 1 SCR 1053.
[48] A hearing before an immigration adjudicator of the Adjudication Division of the IRB. Credible basis inquiries were discontinued in 1993 because of the unnecessary delay and expense they added to the refugee determination process.

his refugee claim at the secondary examination: the expectation being that a person with a genuine fear of persecution would be forthright when first questioned about the reasons for that fear. Dehghani was therefore denied an opportunity to have his claim determined by the IRB and was ordered removed from Canada.

Dehghani argued that his *Charter* rights had been violated at the airport because he was not given the opportunity to retain and instruct counsel prior to being interviewed at the secondary examination. Specifically, he claimed that he was detained and therefore had a right under section 10, upon arrest or detention to retain and instruct counsel without delay and be informed of that right. He also claimed that the denial of the right to counsel infringed his section 7 right not to be deprived of life, liberty and the security of the person unless in accordance with fundamental justice. In another unanimous judgment, this time written by Justice Iacobucci, the Court again upheld the constitutionality of the statutory procedures.

Iacobucci J reasoned that the claimant was not detained within the meaning of section 10. Referring to the Court's previous section 10 jurisprudence, he noted that detention was held to be a restraint of liberty by a state agent, which may have significant legal consequences, and in which a person may reasonably require the assistance of counsel. It involves a degree of coercion or compulsion, and can include psychological compulsion where the person reasonably believes that he or she has no choice but to submit to the restraint of his or her liberty. He further noted that the Court had previously held that routine questioning at the border which every traveller undergoes, accompanied at times by a search of luggage or a frisk, is not a detention within the meaning of section 10 but that border strip searches did fall within its provisions.[49] According to Iacobucci J, the claimant's secondary examination was more like the former than the latter.

In reaching this conclusion Iacobucci J, like Sopinka J in *Chiarelli*, started from the premise that 'there is no right of a non-citizen to enter or remain in Canada'.[50] He then highlighted three characteristics of the second examination, which he reasoned supported his conclusion that it was not a detention in the constitutional sense. First, the examination was conducted for a proper purpose, which he said was to determine the appropriate procedures to be invoked to deal with Dehghani's refugee claim. Secondly, it was not an abnormal procedure since both citizens and non-citizens alike could be sent to a secondary examination. Thirdly, he held that the secondary examination was simply a continuation of the first, a reasonable way to conduct a port of entry examination of those who require more time without holding up the primary examination line. Although he acknowledged that Dehghani was required to answer the questions asked,

---

[49] Above n 47 paras 21–32.
[50] *Ibid*, para 33.

and could be criminally prosecuted for failing to do so, in Iacobucci J's view this did not lead to the conclusion that Dehghani was detained since these 'provisions are both logically and rationally connected to the role of immigration officials in examining those persons seeking to enter the country'.[51]

Here again, as it had in *Chiarelli*, the Court used the purpose of the legislative provision to determine the content of a *Charter* right, in effect placing the *Charter* in a subordinate position to the legislation. In addition, the Court did not address the other indicia that Dehghani was detained within the meaning of section 10 including: immigration authorities had assumed control over the movement of Dehghani; he assumed that he had no choice but to proceed to the secondary examination; and there were very significant legal consequences to the answers he provided at that examination since they could lead to a rejection of his refugee claim and his return to the country where he claimed to fear persecution. Its reasoning in this regard underscored what was evident in *Kindler*, that even where the Court lists a set of factors to guide its interpretation of the law, it does not always rigorously apply them to the facts of the case.

With respect to whether Dehghani's section 7 rights had been violated at the secondary interview, the Court's reasoning paralleled its analysis in *Chiarelli*. Iacobucci J held that he did not need to consider whether the procedures engaged section 7 rights because the principles of fundamental justice had been observed. With respect to the content of fundamental justice, it depended on context. Factual situations, which are closer or analogous to criminal proceedings, he reasoned, required greater vigilance by the courts. While a right to counsel may be required at hearings, including refugee status hearings as per *Singh*, this right, he said, did not extend to the pre-inquiry or pre-hearing stage. A secondary examination was not a hearing nor analogous to a criminal proceeding, rather it was a routine information-gathering exercise.

In declining to address whether a section 7 liberty interest was engaged, as in *Chiarelli*, the scale automatically tipped in favour of finding the requirements of fundamental justice had been met. Also like *Chiarelli*, the Court ascribed a relatively narrow purpose to the process in question: for routine information gathering.[52] Yet according to the Act, the purpose of the examination was to determine whether the person should be allowed to come into Canada.[53] Dehghani's interview was two hours in length, involving detailed questions regarding how he arrived in Canada, whether he had past criminal convictions and the factual basis of his refugee claim. The information gathered was not just to determine the appropriate procedures to be invoked to deal with his application for refugee status, but also for

---

[51] *Ibid*, para 41.
[52] *Ibid*, para 37.
[53] Above n 17 s 12 (1).

the purpose of testing his credibility at the subsequent 'credible basis' inquiry. In those respects, it was not similar to the routine procedure that most citizen and visitors expect to endure when they arrive at the border. By not considering the consequences to Dehghani arising from the responses he provided at the secondary interview, the Court made it easier to reach the conclusion that the process accorded with the principles of fundamental justice.[54]

It is clear that the Court was very concerned with the implications of providing a right to counsel at every secondary examination, especially in light of the fact that Dehghani did have a right to counsel at his credible basis inquiry, which he exercised. To recognise a right to counsel at the secondary interview, Iacobucci J reasoned, would be equivalent to adding another inquiry to the process, possibly just as complex and prolonged as already provided and would 'constitute unnecessary duplication'.[55] This evidence could have supported a finding that although Dehghani's constitutional rights were infringed, the infringements were reasonably and demonstrably justified. However, the Court chose not to engage in a section 1 analysis. Rather, it shrunk the scope of the *Charter* protections, and gave the government wider leeway in not having to justify its position.

Ministerial Discretion: *Baker*[56]

In 1999, six years after its decision in *Dehghani*, the Court was asked to review the Minister's refusal to approve an application for permanent residence status made by Mavis Baker. Baker was a citizen of Jamaica who came to Canada on a visitor's visa in 1981. She overstayed her visa, and continued to live and work illegally in Canada for 11 years. In 1992 she

---

[54] Lower courts have adopted the analytical approach used by the Court in *Chiarelli* and in *Dehghani*. The case of *Ahani v Canada* [1995] 3 FC 669 (TD) aff [1996] FCJ No 937 (CA) is one prominent example. Ahani was a Convention refugee who was detained after a certificate was issued against him on the basis he was inadmissible on terrorism grounds. Ahani challenged the constitutionality of the provisions, including the absence of a right for him to apply for release from detention. By the time the Trial Division considered his challenge, he had been detained for 2 years, and it was a further 4 years before the Federal Court of Appeal upheld the Trial Division's decision that the provisions were constitutional. Ahani argued that the Federal Court review of the reasonableness of the certificate engaged his liberty and security rights including the loss of liberty from detention and the threat to his life if the certificate were upheld and he were repatriated to his country. The Court held that it was unnecessary to determine the issue because in its view the procedures conformed with the principles of fundamental justice, the content of which was determined according to the underlying principles and policies of the immigration act (and not criminal law standards) and in regard to the competing interests of the state and the person in question. Ahani's interest was narrowly characterised as pre-detention release that had to be balanced against the state's interest in combating terrorism. Leave to appeal to the Supreme Court was denied, 3 July 1997.
[55] Above n 47, paras 49–50.
[56] *Baker v Minister (Citizenship and Immigration)* [1999] 2 SCR 817.

was ordered deported. She then applied to the Minister to permit her to remain in Canada and allow her application for permanent residence status on compassionate and humanitarian grounds.[57] An immigration officer considered Baker's application and supporting documentation. His notes, which formed the basis for the rejection of her application, alluded to the harmful effect her removal would have on her and her children, but concluded that her situation was an indictment of the Canadian system given her illegal residence, mental illness, lack of qualifications, eight children and that fact that, in his opinion, she would be a strain on the Canadian social system for the rest of her life. Baker was not provided with reasons for the negative decision. Upon request of her counsel, she was given a copy of the immigration officer's notes. Baker argued that she was not accorded procedural fairness in the making of the Minister's decision and that the decision was unreasonable. In a unanimous decision of the Court, delivered by L'Heureux-Dubé J, the Court agreed.[58] The Minister's decision was quashed and sent back for redetermination.

No constitutional questioned was raised in *Baker*. Baker did argue, however, that the principles of procedural fairness in administrative proceedings were informed by *Charter* values. The Court held that it was unnecessary to consider the *Charter* issues because the case could be resolved under the principles of administrative law and statutory interpretation. Although it is not a *Charter* case, *Baker* is relevant to our inquiry because it involved a non-citizen who, as in the other cases we have covered, challenged the fairness of the procedures and the substance of a Ministerial decision having to do with her removal from Canada. The Court's use of administrative law, which is subject to the *Charter*, to determine the scope of protection to which Baker was entitled, provides an interesting comparison to the Court's reasoning in cases where the *Charter* is engaged.

Baker argued that the procedure by which her application was reviewed was unfair because it failed to provide her and her children with an oral interview before the immigration officer, did not supply her with written reasons for decision and was tainted with bias. In addressing this issue, L'Heureux-Dubé J began by noting that underlying the duty of procedural fairness was the principle that those affected by a decision should have an opportunity to present their case and have it fully and fairly considered by the decision-maker. Whether more or less extensive procedural rights were required, depended on the specific context of each case. Factors that minimised the procedural rights to which Baker was entitled included: the

---

[57] Had Baker been assessed according to regular immigration criteria, she would not have met the admissibility requirements of the Regulations.
[58] Justices Cory and Iacobucci dissented only in regard to the effect on the exercise of ministerial discretion of an international convention not yet incorporated into domestic legislation. Unlike their colleagues, they held that it had no effect for the reasons delivered by Iacobucci J.

discretionary, non-judicial nature of the Minister's decision; the lack of a legitimate expectation that another procedure would be followed[59] and the statute's conferral on the Minister of considerable flexibility in the choice of procedure. Factors that militated in favour of more stringent protections were the absence of an appeal procedure and 'the exceptional importance to the lives of those with an interest in the result'.[60] Balancing these factors, she concluded that the duty of fairness required that those affected by such an important decision have a meaningful opportunity to present the various types of evidence relevant to their case, have it fully and fairly considered and be provided with a written explanation for the decision.

L'Heureux–Dubé J was clear that an oral hearing was not essential in humanitarian and compassionate decisions and that an opportunity to put forward, in written form, argument and evidence in support of the application satisfied the participatory rights required by a duty of fairness in this context. Baker had been given this opportunity and so her participatory rights had not been infringed. Nor did the failure to issue her formal reasons infringe her rights. L'Heureux-Dubé J anticipated that various types of written explanations could be sufficient to meet the 'reasons for decision' requirement and that in Baker's case, the immigration officer's notes, which Baker had received and upon which the refusal of her application was based, were satisfactory. The duty of fairness had been breached, however, because the immigration officer's notes gave the impression that he did not approach the decision with an open mind but was influenced by stereotypes relating to Baker's mental illness, her status as a domestic worker and the number of children she had.

Its conclusion that the Minister's decision was not free from a reasonable apprehension of bias was sufficient to dispose of the appeal. However, the Court went on to consider whether the decision was also unreasonable for failing to consider the best interests of Baker's children. L'Heureux-Dubé J began by acknowledging that traditionally courts have only reviewed such discretionary decisions on limited grounds to ensure that they had not been made in bad faith, for an improper purpose, or on the basis of irrelevant considerations. These restricted grounds of review were premised on the idea that the statutory grant of discretion reflected the legislative intention to confer broad choices on the decision-maker, which should not be lightly interfered with by a court. L'Heureux-Dubé reasoned, however, that as a practical matter the degree of discretion in a grant of power varied and

---

[59] The Court rejected Baker's argument that she had a 'legitimate expectation' that certain procedures would be followed as a result of Canada's ratification of the *Convention on the Rights of the Child*. The Court held that this was not equivalent to a government representation about how humanitarian and compassionate applications would be handled. For more on this, and the implications of the decision on children's rights more generally see S Aiken and S Scott, 'Baker v Canada (Minister of Citizenship and Immigration) and the Rights of Children' *Journal of Law and Social Policy* Volume 14, 2002, 211.
[60] Above n 56, para 31.

therefore a 'pragmatic and functional' analysis was required to determine which of three standards of review applied: correctness, reasonableness or patent unreasonableness.[61] Using the pragmatic and functional analysis, she reviewed the factors the Court had previously identified as being relevant. Again she saw factors going in different directions in Baker's case. Factors that militated in favour of a deferential standard were the statute's conferral of broad discretion on the Minister, with limited rights of review,[62] and the fact-based nature of the decision in an area where the Minister and his or her delegates have considerable expertise. Factors pointing to a stricter standard of review, were the absence of a privative clause, and the individual nature of the decision, as opposed to one calling for the management or balancing of competing rights of different groups. Considered together, she concluded that the appropriate standard of review was the intermediate one of reasonableness.

Early in her analysis, L'Heureux-Dubé J emphasised that all discretion must be exercised 'in accordance with the boundaries imposed in the statute, the principles of the rule of law, principles of the administrative law, the fundamental values of Canadian society, and the principles of the Charter'.[63] As it had in *Kindler*, the Court relied specifically on what it understood Canadian values to stand for in its review of the Minister's decision. Specifically, in *Baker* the Court held that children's rights and attention to their interests are central compassionate and humanitarian values in Canadian society, reflected in the purposes of the statute, international instruments and the Minister's guidelines. Therefore they must be considered in discretionary decisions on humanitarian and compassionate grounds. In a marked contrast from *Chiarelli* and *Dehghani*, where the Court had isolated as the most fundamental principle underlying the Immigration Act, the absence of a right of non-citizens to remain in Canada, in *Baker* the Court pointed to the explicit purposes of the Act 'to facilitate the reunion of Canadians or Canadian citizens with their close relatives from abroad', to show that Parliament placed a high value on keeping together citizens and permanent residents with their close relatives in Canada. Moreover, whereas in *Kindler* the Court had not found international instruments persuasive, in *Baker* the Court held that the importance of children's rights and attention to their interests are central to the *Convention on the Rights of the Child*, (which had been ratified but not implemented by Parliament), and were values that should be reflected in the exercise of discretion. In addition, the guidelines issued by the Minister also recognised the need to be attentive to children's interests for they

---

[61] *Ibid* para 65.
[62] Only with leave to the Federal Court Trial Division, and upon certification of a serious question to the Federal Court of Appeal.
[63] Above n 56, para 56.

instructed immigration officers to be alert to the consequences a negative decision would impose on the applicant and family members. The Court concluded that the Minister's decision to reject Baker's application was unreasonable because the decision did not appear to have been made in a manner which was 'alive, attentive or sensitive' to the interests of her children.[64]

The decision in *Baker* provoked considerable scholarly comment and speculation regarding its impact on administrative law.[65] The decision was also significant from an immigration law perspective. Baker was a non-citizen, with no right to be in Canada, who successfully challenged the Minister's refusal to exercise discretion and allow her to remain. Why did the Court, relying on administrative law principles, not show the same degree of deference to the government as it had in previous immigration cases when applying the *Charter*? For some, the decision in *Baker* suggested that perhaps the Court was moving into a new phase, one where non-citizen rights would be more rigorously examined. The Court's imposition of a reasons requirement for humanitarian and compassionate decisions, its review of the Minister's decision according to a fairly probing standard of review, and its conclusion that the Minister had to be attentive to the interest's of Baker's children, suggested that the Court was perhaps becoming more attentive to the interests of non-citizens in decisions fundamentally affecting their lives. If administrative law principles provided enhanced protection to non-citizens, surely *Charter* protections would also be expanded.

Others however, viewed the decision more cautiously. While the Court acknowledged the exceptional importance of the Minister's decision on Baker and her children, it did not extend participatory rights beyond the provision of written argument and evidence, and did not specifically consider whether giving this opportunity to Baker was sufficient to ensure that her children were given notice and an opportunity for meaningful participation as well.[66] Additionally, while the Court held that the appropriate standard of review for the decision in that case was one of reasonableness, this did not necessarily suggest that a similar standard would be applied to other areas of discretionary decision-making. As David Mullan points out in his chapter, 'Deference from *Baker* to *Suresh* and Beyond—Interpreting the Conflicting Signals', L'Heureux-Dubé J specifically indicates in her

---

[64] *Ibid* para 73.
[65] D Mullan 'Baker v Canada (Minister of Citizenship and Immigration)—A Defining Moment in Canadian Immigration Law' (1999) 7 *Reid's Administrative Law* 145; L Sossin, 'Developments in Administrative Law: The 1997–98 and 1998–99 Terms' (2000) 11 *Supreme Court LR* (2d) 37; D Dyzenhaus and E Fox-Decent, 'Rethinking the Process/Substance Distinction: Baker v Canada' (2001) 51 *University of Toronto Law Journal* 193, D Dyzenhaus, 'Constituting the Rule of Law: Fundamental Values in Administrative Law' (2002), 27 *Queen's Law Journal* 445; D Brown and J Evans 'Discretionary Justice: Reasons and Reasonableness: Case Comment on Baker' www. brownandevans.com/case.
[66] See eg Aiken and Scott, above n 59, pp 232–33.

reasoning that the pragmatic and functional analysis can take account of the fact that the more discretion that is given to the decision-maker, the more reluctant the courts should be to interfere.[67] Finally, the Court's reliance on the 'fundamental values of Canadian society' in its review of the reasonableness of the Minister's decision, left the test itself highly indeterminate, giving the courts considerable leeway to determine what those values reflected in any given case and therefore whether judicial intervention was warranted.

Deportation to Torture: *Suresh*[68]

Ambiguity on which way the Court was moving after *Baker* was soon resolved in *Suresh*, a case that was argued before but not decided until after the 11 September terrorist attack on the World Trade Centre.[69] Manickavasagam Suresh was a Convention refugee who was ordered deported to Sri Lanka, where he faced torture, because the Minister had decided that Suresh was a member of a terrorist organisation (the 'LTTE')[70] and a threat to the security of Canada. The case raised a number of important issues, including whether deportation to torture was permitted by the Constitution, whether the procedures under which Suresh was found to be a security risk were fair, and what standard of review the Court should use in reviewing the Minister's decision to deport Suresh. In a per curiam judgment, the Court allowed the appeal because it found that Suresh, who had made a prima facie case that he faced a substantial risk of torture if expelled to Sri Lanka, was entitled to certain procedural protections in the determination of whether he constituted a danger to the security of Canada. Having decided the case on procedural grounds, it was unnecessary for the Court to review the Minister's decision that Suresh constituted such a risk. Nevertheless, for the purposes of assisting courts in future ministerial review, the Court commented that a deferential approach was required for these types of decisions and that the Court would only set aside the Minister's discretionary decision if it was patently unreasonable.

The Court accepted Suresh's argument that deportation to face torture may deprive a refugee of section 7 rights to liberty, security and perhaps even life. The question therefore was whether the deprivation was in accordance with fundamental justice. Drawing on its previous decisions in *Kindler* and in *Burns*,[71] the Court reiterated that the relevant principles of

[67] Above n 56, para 56.
[68] *Suresh v Canada (Minister of Citizenship and Immigration)* 2002 SCC 1.
[69] The Court refused the government's request, made after the attack, to reconvene to hear additional arguments, however, it is clear that the event had an impact on its reasons for decision.
[70] Liberation Tigers of Tamil Eelam.
[71] Regarding *Burns* see above n 39.

fundamental justice must be determined by a contextual approach, one that requires the Court to balance a variety of factors. In Suresh's case the Court had to consider Canada's interest in combating terrorism and the refugee's interest in not being deported to torture. The essential issue was whether the government's proposed response was reasonable (ie proportionate) in relation to the threat. The Court reasoned that Canadian law and international law were relevant in making this determination. The rejection of all forms of state sanctioned torture in Canada, the *Charter's* proscription of cruel and unusual punishment or treatment in section 12, and the Court's previous pronouncements that extraditing a person to face torture would be inconsistent with fundamental justice, showed that Canadians do not accept torture as fair or compatible with justice. Moreover, the Court held that international declarations, covenants and judicial decisions all suggested that the prohibition of torture is an emerging if not established peremptory norm. Although there was evidence before the Court that freedom from torture was a non-derogable right, not sanctioned even where national security is at stake, the Court held that it was a right 'not easily derogated from'. It therefore concluded that domestic and international jurisprudence suggested that torture almost always would be disproportionate to the interests of the state, but left open the possibility that in exceptional circumstances it might be justified either as a consequence of the balancing process in section 7 or under section 1 in cases arising out of exceptional conditions, such as 'natural disasters, the outbreak of war, epidemics and the like'.[72] Since deportation to torture may pass the test of fundamental justice in exceptional cases, the statutory provision permitting such removal was constitutional.

The Minister's position was that Suresh's removal was an exceptional case because there were reasonable grounds to believe he was a member of an organisation that engaged in 'terrorism' and because he was a 'danger to the security of Canada'. Neither statutory term was defined in the Act, and Suresh argued that both terms were unconstitutionally vague. Noting that a law could be unconstitutionally vague either because it fails to give those that fall within its ambit fair notice of the consequences of their actions or because it fails to adequately limit the law's enforcement, the Court held that none of the language could be characterised as such, notwithstanding the fact that the Court itself pointed to no authoritative definition for either. In regard to 'terrorism' the Court observed that 'one searches in vain for an authoritative definition'[73], one not provided in the Act nor accepted internationally. Rather than sending it back to the legislature to define, however, the Court concluded that the definition in the *International*

---

[72] Above n 68, para 78 quoting from its earlier s 7 jurisprudence.
[73] *Ibid* para 94.

Convention for the Suppression of the Financing of Terrorism[74] catches in essence what the world understands by the term. 'Danger to the security of Canada' was even less open to an exact meaning, but the Court concluded that a flexible approach was required, recognising that the term was fact-based and political. While historically there may have been validity in insisting that the term require proof of a direct danger to Canada, the Court said that in a post-September 11 world, this was to set the bar too high.[75] While there must be a real and serious possibility of an adverse effect on Canada, it need not be direct and could be grounded in distant events that could indirectly harm Canada. The Court provided no guidance as to what kinds of threats may be included, nor any other limiting considerations such as the requirement that there be a real connection between the refugee and prospective risk and that the removal of the refugee would significantly reduce that risk.

Having concluded that it was not contrary to the Constitution to deport a refugee to torture in exceptional cases where the refugee constitutes a danger to the security of Canada, the Court went on to consider whether the procedures used by the Minister to do so were constitutional. Under those procedures, Suresh had been notified that the Minister was considering issuing an opinion declaring him to be a danger to the security of Canada, an opinion that would therefore permit him to be removed to Sri Lanka. Suresh submitted written arguments and documentation concerning his activities in Canada and his risk of torture in Sri Lanka. These were then considered by an immigration officer who subsequently recommended to the Minister that despite the non-violent nature of Suresh's work for LTTE, and the risks he faced upon return to Sri Lanka, he nevertheless constituted a danger to the security of Canada. Moreover, in the officer's view there were insufficient humanitarian and compassionate considerations to warrant special consideration. Accordingly, the Minister issued an opinion that Suresh constituted a danger to the security of Canada and should be deported. Suresh was not provided with a copy of the immigration officer's memorandum, nor was he given an opportunity to respond to it, and he was not provided with reasons for the Minister's opinion.

Quoting from *Singh*, the Court noted that the 'the principles of fundamental justice demand, at a minimum, compliance with the common law requirements'. Although the reference to *Singh* suggested that fundamental justice requirements under section 7 may demand more than what would

---

[74] *Ibid* para 96. Art 2(a), defining 'terrorism' as '[a]n Act which constitutes an offence within the scope of and as defined in one of the treaties listed in the annex' and Art 2(1)(b) 'Any ... Act intended to cause death or serious bodily injury to a civilian, or to any other person not taking an active part in the hostilities in a situation of armed conflict, when the purpose of such Act, by its nature or context, is to intimidate a population, or to compel a government or an international organization to do or to abstain from doing any Act'.
[75] *Ibid*, para 88.

be provided at common law, this was mentioned but not pursued in the case of Suresh. Instead the Court used the common law factors elaborated in *Baker* to determine whether the procedures provided to Suresh 'satisfy the demands of section 7'. In *Baker* the Court held that the discretionary nature of the decision, and the absence of legitimate expectation that more procedural safeguards would be provided, had to be balanced against those factors that militated in favour of more procedural safeguards namely, the potential consequences of the decision and the limited right of appeal. Applying the same approach in *Suresh*, the Court concluded that the procedural protections required by section 7 in Suresh's case required more than what he had received.

The procedural protections, the Court concluded, that must be accorded to a person facing deportation to torture for reasons of national security were limited and only came into play once the person had established a prima facie case that there is a substantial risk of torture. A full judicial process was not necessary nor was the Minister required to conduct an oral hearing. Once a prima facie case had been established, all the person was entitled to was the material upon which the Minister's decision was based (subject to privilege or other valid reason for reduced disclosure in the interests of security), an opportunity to respond by presenting evidence and legal argument, and written reasons for the decision emanating from the Minister. The failure to provide these basic procedural protections to Suresh could not be justified by section 1. In the Court's opinion, the fact the government had a valid purpose for removing a refugee to a place of risk did not justify the failure of the Minister to provide fair procedures where the danger to the refugee was torture.[76]

Although Suresh prevailed in his personal fight to remain in Canada, the Court's analysis of the procedural protections required by fundamental justice does not bode well for future refugees facing removal. It effectively diluted the Court's earlier position in *Singh*, and did not meet the expectations it had raised after *Baker*. In *Singh* the Court had concluded that fundamental justice required an oral hearing for the determination of refugee status given that serious issues of credibility were involved and the potential consequences of a denial of refugee status: the return to a country where the person's life or freedom was threatened. This level of protection was necessary even though a refugee claimant has not established a prima facie case of risk. In *Suresh*, however, where the prima facie case of a substantial risk of torture was established, and credibility was at issue, no oral hearing was mandated and no explanation provided for the apparent abandonment of the principles in *Singh*. Even more limiting was the Court's emphasis that the level of procedural safeguards required for those that

---

[76] *Ibid*, para 128.

faced deportation to torture 'need not be invoked in every case' where a Convention refugee was being removed from Canada on security grounds to a place where his or her life or freedom would be threatened. The Court reasoned that this was because not all refugees whose life or freedom would be threatened by removal will be at risk of torture or similar abuses.[77] This raises the question of what types of threats to life or security would fall short of torture and not warrant the limited procedural guarantees afforded to Suresh. For example, would the risk of generalised violence, famine, long-term indefinite detention and other forms of persecution recognised by the Convention be insufficiently severe to warrant the procedural protections required in Suresh's case?

It is worth noting in this regard that the protections that the Court said should have been extended to Suresh were not that different from those it concluded had to be provided to Baker. In fact the main distinction is that in *Suresh* the Court held that he was entitled to reasons for the decisions emanating from the Minister and not from the Minister's delegate, which was permitted in *Baker*. Aside from that requirement, the level of procedural protections mandated by the Court for admissibility decisions where there was no risk to life or freedom and where there was no protected *Charter* interest, was the same as provided to those facing removal to a place where there was a substantial risk of torture and whose *Charter* interests were engaged. Moreover, those who faced other risks to life or freedom, short of torture and similar abuses, were not entitled to the same level of protections afforded to Baker even thought they may face more egregious forms of harm from an unfavourable decision. *Suresh* suggests that in matters involving national security, the requirements of fundamental justice will be relaxed in all but the exceptional case. This seems inconsistent with the spirit of *Baker* that the procedural protections required depend not just on the nature of the decision but on the interests and personal circumstances involved. It is, however, consistent with *Chiarelli* where the Court also accorded considerable deference to the procedural choices of the Minister in removing non-citizens for reasons of national security.[78]

The Court's reasoning with respect to the appropriate standard of review of the Minister's decision signalled that its decision in *Baker* did not represent a shift from the more deferential approach it had taken in *Chiarelli*.

---

[77] *Ibid* paras 128–29.
[78] *Suresh* was applied in *Ahani v Canada (Minister of Citizenship and Immigration)*, 2002 SCC 2 which also involved the removal of a Convention refugee under s 53(1)(b). The Court held that Ahani had not cleared the evidentiary threshold required to access the protection guaranteed by s 7 because he had not made out a prima facie case that there was a substantial risk of torture upon deportation. In this case, unlike *Suresh*, the Court held that the Minister had provided adequate procedural protections. Although the procedures may not have precisely complied with those suggested in *Suresh*, the Court held that Ahani had not been prejudiced because he was fully informed of the Minister's case against him and given a full opportunity to respond.

In Suresh's case, two decisions were required of the Minister. These were whether Suresh constituted a danger to the security of Canada and whether he faced a substantial risk of torture should he be removed to Sri Lanka. The Court characterised the latter decision as being factual and not constitutional. It required consideration of the human rights record in the destination country, the personal risk faced by the claimant there, and may involve a consideration of whether a third country is willing to accept the refugee.[79] The Court stated that these were matters largely outside the expertise of the reviewing court, and 'possess a negligible legal dimension'. The Minister's decision regarding whether a person faces a substantial risk of torture therefore warranted a lot of deference.[80] A court should only intervene if the decision was not supported by the evidence or failed to consider appropriate factors.[81] It was once a prima facie risk of torture was established, according to the Court, that the claimant's section 7 interests were engaged and the constitutional test was whether it would shock the Canadian conscience to deport the person on the grounds of national security. The Court concluded that this decision also merited much deference. In supporting this conclusion, the Court listed the same set of recognised criteria that it had used in *Baker* to determine the appropriate standard of review, but in Suresh's case it focused almost exclusively on those that argued for it to be deferential. The limited right of review, the fact-based nature of the inquiry in an area where the Minister had expertise, and the need to balance the interests of Suresh against the security interests of Canadian society, the Court said, pointed to deference. It is clear from its reasons that the Court's greatest concern was that the Minister's decision touched matters of national security. It quoted with approval the statements of Lord Hoffmann in the House of Lords case of *Rehman*, stressing the need for the judiciary to respect executive decisions regarding national security, on the basis that not only did the executive have access to special information and expertise in such matters, but also, only the elected branch of government had the legitimacy to make decisions of such serious consequences to the community.[82] *Rehman* and *Suresh* suggest that in a post-11 September world, national security is an issue that judges are not willing to touch.

With respect to the standard of review, the Court reaffirmed that the traditional restricted grounds for review were appropriate for decisions based

---

[79] For a criticism of the Court's fact/law distinction, and its inconsistency in this area see D Mullan's 'Baker and Deference—Interpreting the Conflicting Signals', ch 2 of this volume.
[80] The Court suggested that when evaluating assurances by a foreign government, 'the Minister *may* also wish to take into account the human rights record' of that government and its ability to 'fulfill the assurances'. [emphasis added] *Suresh* above n 68 para 125.
[81] *Ibid*, para 39.
[82] *Secretary of State for the Home Department v Rehman*, [2001] 3 WLR 877 at para 62.

on broad discretion and characterised its acknowledgement in *Baker* of a range of standards as simply a recognition that in 'special situations' traditionally discretionary decisions will be best reviewed according to a less deferential standard.[83] There is no reference to the overarching principle stressed in *Baker* that even though discretionary decisions will generally be given considerable respect:

> discretion must be exercised in accordance with the boundaries imposed in the statute, the principles of the rule of law, the principles of administrative law, the fundamental values of Canadian society, and the principles of the *Charter*.[84]

In *Baker*, the Court held that the Minister's delegate had not been attentive enough to the interests of Baker's children and had failed to give 'sufficient weight' to the hardship that a return to Jamaica would cause her. In *Suresh*, however, the Court held that the weight to be given the factors relevant to the exercise of discretion was entirely the Minister's task. It distinguished its reasoning in *Baker* by suggesting that to the extent the Court reviewed the Minister's discretion in that case, its decision was based on the failure of the Minister's delegate to comply with self-imposed guidelines. Yet this is not supported by the reasons for the decision in that case, in which L'Heureux-Dubé J spent considerable time illustrating how the interests of children were an important value in international law, as well as Canadian immigration law and that the exercise of discretion had to reflect those values, which the decision in question had not.

Although the Court's decision in *Suresh* did extend *Charter* protections to those facing extreme harm of torture or similar abuses upon removal, the victory was a narrow one because it simultaneously gave the Minister considerable leeway to determine when such protections apply. So, although the *Charter* prohibits deportation to torture in all but exceptional circumstances, the Minister's decision regarding whether those circumstances are present in any given case will attract deference from a reviewing court. The terrorism ground for removal has now been defined and therefore more precise than before yet whether someone is a 'danger to the security of Canada' has been left relatively open-ended to enable the Minister to flexibly respond to threats as she or he sees fit. If in doing so, the response is to remove a refugee to a place where his or her life or freedom is at risk, the Minister has to accord basic procedural protections to the refugee, but only if the refugee establishes a prima facie case of a substantial risk of torture or equivalent harm.

---

[83] Above n 68, para 35.
[84] *Baker* above n 56 para 56.

THE IMMIGRATION AND REFUGEE PROTECTION ACT

In June 2002 a new immigration Act was passed, the Immigration and Refugee Protection Act (IRPA), which bears the mark of the Court's jurisprudence. There are some aspects of the legislation that draw directly from the jurisprudence and work to the benefit of non-citizens and many others that do not. On the benefit side of the balance is the requirement, set out in the objectives of the Act and in keeping with the Court's analysis in *Baker* and *Suresh*, that the Act be construed and applied 'in a manner that complies with international human rights instruments to which Canada is a signatory'.[85] In addition, the Act provides for an oral hearing for those who are found eligible to make a refugee claim, as required by *Singh*. Moreover, the Act affords protection from torture, as per *Suresh*, as well as from risks to life, cruel and unusual treatment or punishment[86] and from persecution for Convention refugee grounds. In addition, discretionary decisions made on the basis of humanitarian and compassionate grounds, must include consideration of the best interests of the child, again reflecting the Court's analysis in *Baker*.

On the deficit side of the balance, from the perspective of the non-citizen, are the broad degree of discretion conferred on the executive in setting admission and removal policy, the restrictions on access to the refugee protection determination procedure, the expanded grounds for deportation, and the narrowing of the grounds to appeal various removal orders. These changes can also find support in the Court's recent jurisprudence. For example, unlike the 1976 Act, the IRPA is skeletal legislation, most of the details left to regulations, and of those, only a relatively few are required to be put before Parliament for review. In this respect, the IRPA is similar to the pre-1976 immigration Acts, which provided the basic framework of immigration policy while conferring wide discretion on the Cabinet, the responsible Minister and his or her delegates to formulate and administer immigration policy free from parliamentary oversight. In immigration cases, the Court has often emphasised the right of the legislature to confer discretionary powers on the Minister, and for the Court to accord deference to those decisions in areas where the Minister has comparative expertise such as the criteria for admission and removal of non-citizens and the assessment of risks to national security or threats to life upon removal.

The Act also expands the grounds for refusing to allow a refugee claimant access to the refugee determination process of the IRB, and does so in a manner that the Court's jurisprudence suggests will be immune from

---

[85] SC 2001, ch 27, assented to 1 November 2001, s 3.
[86] Provided such risks are not faced by the general population, are not incidental to lawful sanctions and are not caused by the inability of the country to provide adequate health care. *Ibid*, s 97.

Charter challenges. Those who are not entitled to have their claims heard by the IRB include: those who have made a prior claim to refugee protection; persons who could have claimed protection in a country prescribed by the regulations as 'safe' before arriving in Canada; and those who are inadmissible on grounds of security, violating human rights, or serious criminality.[87] These persons are only entitled to request relief from removal from the Minister through a pre-removal risk assessment process, which is by way of written application: an oral interview is provided only if the Minister, on the basis of prescribed factors, is of the opinion that one is necessary.[88]

One can foresee various *Charter* arguments being raised concerning both the substantive and procedural aspects of these ineligibility provisions of the Act and Regulations, although given the Court's jurisprudence such challenges are unlikely to succeed. Each of the grounds of ineligibility can be seen as serving a legitimate public policy objective: preventing abuse of the system (by excluding repeat claims, claims of persons already found to be Convention refugees, and those who could have claimed elsewhere); not extending protection to the undeserving (war criminals and those guilty of crimes against humanity); not providing sanctuary to fugitives from justice; and protecting the security of Canada by excluding those who pose a threat (terrorists, serious criminals.) On the basis of the Court's balancing approach, the public interest behind such restrictions would weigh in favour of upholding them, particularly since the Act provides for an administrative consideration of risk prior to removal. With respect to that risk assessment procedure, the Court's analysis in *Chiarelli* and *Suresh* suggest that it would likely find that the requirements of procedural fairness do not mandate an oral interview in all cases, and that the discretion to provide one is properly left to the Minister guided by the criteria set out in the Regulations.

The third significant change in the new Act, which cuts back significantly on the rights non-citizens had under the previous legislation, is in the deportation provisions. Under the old Act all permanent residents, except those found to be security risks, had a right to appeal a deportation order to the IAD on compassionate grounds. The new Act removes the right to appeal to the IAD from permanent residents who have been sentenced to two or more years of imprisonment, or have been found to be inadmissible on grounds of security, violating human or international rights, or organised

---

[87] *Ibid*, s 101. It also includes those the Minister considers a danger to the public in Canada and who have who have been convicted outside Canada of an offence that, if committed here, is punishable by a maximum penalty of at least 10 years.

[88] *Ibid*, ss 112 and 113(b). Those found to be ineligible for reasons of security and criminality can only apply for a stay of the removal order while others can apply for protected refugee status.

criminality.[89] They retain a right to appeal for leave to appeal to the Federal Court on the limited grounds of fact or law. However, they cannot have their appeal considered on the basis of all the circumstances of the case to determine whether removal is a proportionate response and justified in the public interest. In this respect, the provisions of the new Act are more restrictive than any other post 1967 immigration legislation.

Again these new provisions find support in the Court's jurisprudence. In *Chiarelli* the Court said that if fundamental justice required a right to appeal a deportation order, an appeal on fact or law would be sufficient to meet that requirement. While it could be argued that the leave requirement of the Federal Court does not provide the deportee with sufficient protection, the Court's clear statements in *Chiarelli*, upholding the constitutionality of a mandatory deportation order, suggest that this argument would also not succeed. It is the loss of the right of appeal on all the circumstances of the case that is most significant, given that this has been the ground of appeal most relied upon in the past. In *Chiarelli*, without considering whether a liberty interest was at stake, the Court concluded that this ground of appeal was not a constitutionally protected right. It partly justified its conclusion because of the 'deliberate' nature of the breach. If confronted with a case where the liberty interest is clearly at issue (eg risk of serious harm), would the Court find that mandatory removal without an independent review on all the circumstances of the case unconstitutional? Probably not, because a person who faces a risk of torture, a risk to life or a risk of cruel or unusual treatment, retains the right to apply for an administrative pre-removal risk assessment. It is unlikely the Court would find that anything more was constitutionally required.

What about a case where, unlike in *Chiarelli*, the breach of the condition prompting the deportation order and excluding an appeal on compassionate considerations was not deliberate (eg because of mental incompetence), or where the consequences of removal are severe but not of a life threatening magnitude required of the pre-removal risk assessment process? In these cases there is no avenue to challenge the removal on the grounds that the consequences of removal are disproportionate to the objectives of the Act. To challenge successfully the constitutionality of the process, the person would have to satisfy the Court that his or her section 7 liberty interests were engaged and that fundamental justice demanded a review of all the circumstances. This has already been argued in the case of a severely mentally disabled man who had lived in Canada since he was an infant and was ordered deported under the provisions of the old Act for criminality. The Court refused to hear his appeal from the decision of the lower court,

---

[89] *Ibid*, s 64. See also Nicholas Blake's description of recent British restrictions on the right of review of deportation orders, above n 9.

which, applying *Chiarelli*, concluded that fundamental justice did not require a consideration of all the circumstances of the case.[90]

CONCLUSION

In 1906 the Privy Council affirmed that the state has an unfettered right to determine who can enter the country and the corresponding right to expel or deport at pleasure those whose presence do not serve the interests of the state. For most of our history this power has been conferred through legislation to the Minister and his or her delegates. For many years non-citizens were regarded as having no right to demand fairness or humanitarian consideration in their requests for admission to Canada or in decisions deporting them. It was only in the 1960s that Immigration Acts began to define more clearly the limits of executive discretion, by setting out more precise, transparent and non-racial admission criteria and by providing appeal rights to those ordered deported. However, there remained broad areas of Ministerial discretion, which were all but immune to legal challenge. The entrenchment of a bill of rights raised the expectation that the interests of the non-citizen in matters fundamentally affecting their lives would gain constitutional recognition. After 20 years of *Charter* litigation, however, very little has changed.

Substantively the *Charter* has been held by the Court to prohibit the state from removing a non-citizen to death or torture unless exceptional circumstances prevail. In other situations, however, the state remains relatively free to determine the substantive grounds and the procedures under which non-citizens can be removed. As the Court made clear in *Chiarelli*, the *Charter* does not mandate a consideration of mitigating circumstances (ie whether removal is a proportionate response) before a person can be deported. At a procedural level, the *Charter* requires an oral hearing in refugee status determinations as held in *Singh*, but an oral hearing is not necessarily required for those who face removal to a place were their life or freedom may be at risk, as the Court made clear in *Suresh*.

The analytical approach the Court has used in these cases, which has limited the *Charter's* reach in all but a narrow range of circumstances, is consistent with, and seems motivated by the same view of state sovereignty set out by the Privy Council in 1906 and reiterated by the Court in both *Chiarelli* and *Dehghani*: 'non-citizens do not have an unqualified right to enter or remain in the country'. In using the balancing approach to determine the requirements of fundamental justice, generally the state's interests have been seen to carry extra weight. When the Court has not considered

---

[90] *Romans v Canada (Minister of Citizenship and Immigration)*; [2001] FCJ No 740 (FCTD); upheld 2001 FCA 27 Decision on the application for leave to appeal, Gonthier, Major and Binnie JJ dismissed, with costs 06 December 2001. Docket 28806.

the non-citizen's interest, or defined it narrowly, the balance has automatically tipped in the government's favour. Its characterisation of certain decisions as primarily 'factual' rather than 'legal', even when a *Charter* right is at stake, has further distanced executive decisions from judicial scrutiny. Moreover, and perhaps most significantly, the incorporation of section 1 factors in the fundamental justice analysis in section 7 has favoured the government by relieving it from having to justify a *Charter* infringement according to principles of proportionality.

Although the Court has been reluctant to extend *Charter* protections to non-citizens in admission and removal proceedings, this does not mean that non-citizens have never received favourable results from the Court. They have, but with the exception of *Singh* and *Suresh* concerning procedural fairness, not on *Charter* grounds. On the basis of statutory interpretation and the application of administrative law principles, refugee claimants and permanent residents have successfully argued that the statutory provisions concerning their status applications were interpreted incorrectly.[91] As one of these cases, *Baker* particularly stands out because of the Court's willingness to depart from its customary deference to the exercise of Ministerial discretion, finding that both in process and in substance the decision was reviewable. Does this suggest that non-citizens can expect more protection under administrative law than under the constitution?[92] To reach this conclusion one would have to read more into *Baker* than the reasons or the Court's subsequent decision in *Suresh* can support. It must be kept in mind that factually Baker presented a compelling case. Although illegally in Canada, she was a hardworking woman whose continuous work history was interrupted by the onset of psychological problems, over which she had no control. She had four Canadian children who depended on her for support and she was making progress in overcoming her difficulties. Her removal would be harmful to both her and her children. The Court was able to give her relief without widening the constitutional protections that it had so narrowly limited with respect to non-citizens in *Chiarelli* and *Dehghani*. Significantly, it also explicitly left open the possibility that courts

---

[91] *Canada (Attorney General) v Ward*, [1993] 2 SCR 689 (re convention refugee definition, meaning to be ascribed to the 'persecution' of a particular social group and political opinion); *Pushpanathan v Canada (Minister of Citizenship and Immigration)*, [1998] 1 SCR 1222 (re conspiring to traffic in a narcotic is not included in the grounds for excluding a person from Convention refugee status) *Chieu v Canada (Minister of Citizenship and Immigration)*, 2002 SCC 3 and *Al Sagban v Canada (Minister of Citizenship and Immigration)* 2002 SCC 4 (re IAD is entitled to consider potential foreign hardship as part of all the circumstances of the case, when deciding to quash or stay a removal order made against a permanent resident, provided that a likely country of removal has been established); *Chen v Canada (Minister of Employment and Immigration)* [1995] 1 SCR (re the scope of the discretionary power given to a visa officer).

[92] Which would follow if Audrey Macklin is correct in saying that currently common law principles under administrative law accord greater concern and respect to non-citizens than does s 7. See 'The State of Law's Borders and the Law of State Borders', ch 7 of this volume.

could continue to accord deference to highly discretionary ministerial decisions.

When *Baker* is viewed in this light, and within the historical context of judicial review of admission and removal decisions, *Suresh* comes as no surprise. *Suresh* is consistent with the traditional deference courts have shown executive removal decisions: a deference that historically led to excesses, which the immigration legislation of the 1960s and 1970s attempted to address. The protections introduced in the legislation of that latter period, however, have now been significantly clawed back under the new Act by limiting access to protection, expanding the grounds for deportation and restricting the right to appeal removal orders. These changes have been implemented in a manner that draws directly from the Court's *Charter* jurisprudence. Paradoxically, and contrary to initial expectations, the way the Court has interpreted the *Charter* has supported fewer protections being accorded to non-citizens in immigration decisions which profoundly affect their lives.

11

Common Law Reason and the Limits of Judicial Deference

TRS ALLAN*

INTRODUCTION

ADVERSARIAL ADJUDICATION, IN the common law tradition, expresses fundamental moral and constitutional values. The power of the litigants to fashion their dispute in their own way and the judge's duty to determine the issues arising, on the basis of the submissions presented, reflect the special character of the adversarial trial. The purpose is not merely to resolve the dispute but to *justify* the resolution to the parties. Where the litigant's claim is brought against the state, the judge is an independent arbitrator between the governors and the governed; and where he rejects an allegation of injustice or impropriety, he seeks not merely to offer reasons for his decision but reasons for the disappointed claimant to *accept* it as a just outcome. The constitutional role of adjudication is informed by the ideal of consent implicit in the rule of law. The law makes a moral claim to the citizen's obedience, asserting its compliance with standards of justice that she should accept; and the judge must address her complaint that, for the reasons she offers, these standards have been violated by public officials.[1]

It follows that the judge's reasons are as important as those of the minister or public authority; for whereas the authority must attempt to defend its actions when these impinge on the complainant's rights or interests, the judge must seek to justify his decision that that defence succeeds or fails. If it succeeds, he must demonstrate the flaws in the complainant's case, providing reasons for his own acceptance of the arguments made on behalf of the public authority. He cannot merely endorse the authority's response

---

* The helpful comments of David Dyzenhaus, Gerald Heckman and other conference participants are gratefully acknowledged.
[1] See TRS Allan, *Constitutional Justice: A Liberal Theory of the Rule of Law* (Oxford, Oxford University Press, 2001), ch 3.

on the grounds of its superior access to information or expertise; for such a stance would undermine the substance of judicial independence, revealing the citizen's rights as little more than aspirations, without genuine legal support. In everyday decision-making, we defer constantly to the opinions of those we perceive to possess knowledge and expertise that we lack ourselves; but we are not then making and announcing judgments of legal or constitutional right. A judge who defers to official claims to superior wisdom forfeits his neutrality: he allows his own assessment of the merits of the claim to be displaced by the views of the public officials whose decision he is supposed to be reviewing.

It is none the less generally thought that some element of judicial deference is entailed by the doctrine of separation of powers. There are reasons of fairness for allowing democratically accountable legislators to determine what, in the relevant context, constitutional rights require—or what limits are necessary—at least within certain boundaries of good faith and reasonableness. Similar considerations may apply to executive agencies when power is delegated to them for particular purposes; and such agencies may develop a specialist expertise that courts would be incompetent to usurp even if they could do so with constitutional propriety. In the United Kingdom, it is now widely accepted that, in construing and applying the European Convention rights given domestic legal status by the Human Rights Act 1998, the courts should defer, in some degree, to the wisdom of the other branches of government.[2] It has been observed that while:

> a national court does not accord the margin of appreciation recognised by the European Court as a supra-national court, it will give weight to the decisions of a representative legislature and a democratic government within the discretionary area of judgment accorded to those bodies.[3]

The important questions here, however, are what 'giving weight' to such decisions actually means and whether the 'discretionary area of judgment' is something distinct from the scope of discretion, if any, conferred by the relevant constitutional right on its correct interpretation. Few rights are absolute and even those that, in principle, allow no qualifications, such as an immunity from torture or inhuman treatment, must be capable of definition: whether or not specific conduct violates a person's rights may depend on whether it truly amounts to torture or inhuman treatment. When such questions are disputed, the courts must decide whether there is any infringement of the relevant right, on its correct interpretation, and if such

---

[2] See P Craig, 'The Courts, the Human Rights Act and Judicial Review' (2001) 117 *Law Quarterly Review* 589. For a more skeptical view, see I Leigh, 'Taking Rights Proportionately: Judicial Review, the Human Rights Act and Strasbourg' [2002] *Public Law* 265.
[3] *Brown v Stott (Procurator Fiscal, Dunfermline)* [2001] 2 WLR 817, at p 835.

infringements may under certain conditions be excused, whether those conditions obtain in the particular case. Since there may be various means whereby government may pursue its legitimate ends without improperly infringing rights, constitutional adjudication does not entail the elimination of administrative discretion. Legal principles limit executive freedom but do not simply substitute judicial direction for ministerial decision.

There is symmetry between the enforcement of specific constitutional rights and the preservation of administrative legality more generally: each is a requirement of equality, or equal citizenship, which may fairly claim to ground the unity of public law. Judicial deference, properly understood, is merely a function of the generality of legal standards that equality entails. The reasons in favour of an administrative decision include its conformity to whatever general considerations of policy are compatible with relevant legislation, provided that those criteria are fairly and consistently applied in other comparable cases. The separation of powers between courts and the executive is secured by judges' acceptance of the proper sphere of administrative discretion, defined by the relevant statutory conditions and purposes, interpreted in accordance with constitutional principle. It is those statutory conditions and purposes, correctly ascertained, that will determine the administrator's scope to balance public and private interests afresh, according to the demands of the particular case; and the larger that scope, the more urgent the need for judicial scrutiny to maintain the value of legal rights. Conversely, the greater the administrator's reliance on general policy judgements or established guidelines, where that is legitimate, the smaller the scope for judicial intervention to disturb a conclusion reached in good faith.

Correctly understood, therefore, the 'discretionary area of judgement' is determined by the proper scope and meaning of the legal right in question. Its extent will reflect the balance of public and private interests, attuned to the facts of the particular case; and the court will respect a legitimate governmental purpose in judging the extent to which the individual must endure its adverse consequences for his own position. The court will also respect a governmental assessment of the merits of the particular case, in the sense that it will examine the arguments presented in the government's favour. But there is no apparent need for any further element of judicial reticence. If talk of 'deference' and 'margins of discretion' is merely a confusing reference to the idea that the executive and judicial functions are distinct and independent, it may serve only to obscure and weaken our grasp of constitutional theory. What is crucial, at any rate, is to observe and maintain the distinction between deference as 'respect', on the one hand, and deference as 'submission', on the other.[4] Deference is not due to an administrative decision merely on the ground of its source or 'pedigree', but

---

[4] Cf D Dyzenhaus, 'The Politics of Deference: Judicial Review and Democracy' in M Taggart (ed), *The Province of Administrative Law* (Oxford, Hart Publishing, 1997), p 286.

only in the sense (and to the extent) that it is supported by reasons that can withstand proper scrutiny.

The court cannot abdicate its own responsibility for legal judgment. It cannot therefore acknowledge the legality of a decision that, on the balance of reasons, appears to be an unjustified infringement of a complainant's legitimate interests or constitutional rights. A proper deference is established by the reasons that exist *in the particular case* for affirming the validity of an impugned decision: such deference must yield to contrary reasons for denying such validity when in the court's view the latter are stronger. There is no 'discretionary area of judgement', or 'margin of manoeuvre', beyond the strict constraints of reason, as they apply in all the circumstances; there is no yardstick by which the proper scope or degree of any further judicial deference could be quantified or measured. We should therefore be skeptical of *doctrines* of judicial deference, for such doctrines may invoke general categories or standard criteria as a substitute for judgement more closely attuned to the facts of the particular case. In the context of perceived threats to national security, in particular, legal and constitutional rights are likely under such conditions to prove illusory.

THE SEPARATION OF POWERS AND THE RULE OF LAW

Administrative discretion is consistent with the ideal of the rule of law when its exercise satisfies the basic principles of due process and equality. Due process or procedural fairness is intended to ensure not only that particular cases are decided on the basis of the relevant facts and circumstances, correctly ascertained, but that the individuals affected can participate in the deliberations of the public authority. In the absence of any dialogue with such an authority, there is little reason to accept its conclusions as truly meeting the genuine needs of the common good, acknowledging that certain rights or interests must be overridden. Ideally, the dialogue extends to the proper interpretation of the legal standards by which the requirements of the common good are authoritatively determined.

The legitimacy of the relevant legal standards depends on their meeting the requirements of constitutional equality, which ensure that everyone is treated with the respect that his dignity as an equal citizen demands. Equality requires governmental acts and decisions to be capable of justification on the basis of a plausible conception of the common good—a conception that specifies criteria which are consistently applied and open to uninhibited public debate and moral criticism. It explains the virtue of generality as a characteristic of legislation, properly so called, and enables administrative discretion to meet the demands of the rule of law by excluding arbitrary discrimination between persons. There must be a reasonable balance between public and private interests: the individual right or interest must not be unfairly sacrificed for the general good; and judgements of fairness will reflect the nature and degree of the burdens borne by other persons in comparable situations, according to the urgency of the public need.[5]

The nature and degree of judicial deference should reflect these general principles of the rule of law, making the separation of powers subservient to our most fundamental constitutional values. Democratic constitutionalism entails judicial deference to general rules and policies, whether enacted by the legislature or adopted by the executive, in so far as such rules and policies do not discriminate unfairly between persons or groups. The specific content of, and limits to, legal and constitutional rights are properly matters for legislative and democratic determination; it is only where exceptions or qualifications systematically disfavour certain categories of person in ways that undermine their equal status that judicial deference is inappropriate. Conversely, however, the more a person's treatment is a matter of administrative discretion, where general rules or policies surrender to *ad hoc* judgements of the public interest, case by case, the stronger the judicial scrutiny normally required. In these circumstances, constitutional equality is most readily undermined, and objections to judicial interference on grounds of democratic legitimacy are also very much weaker.

It follows that Iacobucci J's suggestion, in *Southam*, that very general and abstract conclusions of law merit less judicial deference than their more specific legal consequences, should be confined to its immediate context.[6] When a tribunal is empowered to determine questions concerning commercial competition, it may be appropriate for courts to accept that mixed questions of law and fact are usually matters of judgement for the tribunal. The weight appropriately attached to each of the relevant factors may vary from case to case, according to the tribunal's specialist expertise. The reasonableness standard of review makes proper allowance for the differences of functions and expertise between court and agency:

> Where the purposes of the statute and of the decision-maker are conceived not primarily in terms of establishing rights as between parties ... but rather as a delicate balancing between different constituencies, then the appropriateness of court supervision diminishes.[7]

In many contexts, however, an agency's specific conclusions, dependent on particular judgements of relevance and weight, should provoke a closer scrutiny than the abstract principles or general policies from which they proceed. The distinction between law and fact is not determinative: the 'creation

---

[5] See generally Allan, *Constitutional Justice*, n 1 above, esp ch 5.
[6] *Canada (Director of Investigation and Research) v Southam Inc.* [1997] 1 SCR 748, at pp 776–71.
[7] *Pushpanathan v Canada (Minister of Citizenship and Immigration)* [1998] 1 SCR 982, p 1008.

of a legislative "scheme" combined with the creation of a highly specialised administrative decision-maker' may entail 'an expansive deference even over extremely general questions of law'.[8] More specific questions of justice, where law and fact will inevitably be harder to disentangle, may by contrast demand more rigorous attention. The court's chief concern in preserving the rule of law must be that generally accepted standards, whatever their intrinsic merits, should be fairly applied to the particular case; and where the proper treatment of individuals is the primary focus of an administrative decision, there will be much less scope for permissible error than in the determination of what may be highly contestable (and hence less 'justiciable') matters of public interest, broadly conceived.

The more abstract the relevant legal standards, within statutory and constitutional—'jurisdictional'—limits, the greater the elements of value judgement and expertise that normally command judicial deference on constitutional grounds. It is a well-established principle, reflecting requirements of the separation of powers, that the courts should not usurp policy-making functions conferred on the executive. Provided that the relevant policy is itself a lawful and legitimate means of structuring an agency's discretion, the court must acknowledge its authority in the particular case unless there are special reasons for treating that case as exceptional. Moreover, the legality of the relevant policy cannot be dependent on the court's own determination of the public interest: the court must respect the public agency's right to act on its own judgements of the public good, within whatever boundaries the law provides. Equally fundamental, however, is the agency's duty to apply its standards consistently, without arbitrary qualifications or exceptions.

Like legal rules, policies vary in their generality. The more concrete the policy, in the sense that it entails conclusions about the appropriate treatment of particular persons, the smaller the scope for deference. And the more serious the consequences for individuals adversely affected, moreover, the greater the importance that the general policy should give way to more precise judgements based on the properly substantiated facts of the particular case. A general policy, however reasonable in the abstract, must be finely tuned in its application to those whose rights or important interests are most at risk. At the concrete level, questions of fact (whether as regards past events or the probability of future ones) are likely to dominate the agency's assessment; and such matters will inevitably turn on evidence and specific experience, susceptible of close analysis and reasoned explanation. The court can properly demand to be convinced: it need not defer to an expertise that claims a technical authority beyond judicial competence.

---

[8] *Ibid*, p 1011.

Interpreted as an elastic principle, sensitive to the particularity of the state's intrusion into personal freedom, the separation of powers needs no further and independent doctrine of judicial deference. It is likely that any such doctrine would prove to be arbitrary in practical application, distinguishing between claims of legal or constitutional right on grounds that fail to reflect their intrinsic and individual merits. The assumption, for example, that the courts will be readier to intervene in the sphere of criminal justice than in that of economic or social policy may well be defensible as a descriptive generalisation; but judicial remedies can only be fairly granted or denied on the basis of specific complaints in regard to concrete events. Free-standing principles of judicial deference—detached from analysis of specific legal duties and constitutional rights—reproduce the dubious distinctions characteristic of general doctrines of justiciability. In so far as they enable courts to dispense with detailed scrutiny of claims, on the ground that they relate to administrative functions or powers inherently resistant to judicial review, such doctrines threaten the integrity of the rule of law.[9]

If, in constitutional cases, judicial review is more 'intensive', it is because a judge who is committed to the defence of fundamental rights will be harder to convince that encroachments on such rights are justified. His skepticism about the strength of the reasons offered for such encroachments will match the citizen's sense of injury—a perception of unfair or unequal treatment that only cogent reasons of public interest can assuage. The judge, like the individual affected, may readily accept the general grounds for restricting a right, abstractly stated; but he will be far more guarded when assessing the specific consequences, or alleged consequences, as they apply to the facts of the particular case. At this concrete level, the principles of due process and equality will be most fully and powerfully engaged.

EQUALITY AND RATIONALITY

The decision of the Supreme Court of Canada in *Baker* shows that the validity of a discretionary administrative decision depends on a judicial assessment that is appropriately sensitive to context.[10] A general standard of reasonableness enabled the court to do justice within the constraints of the separation of powers. Applying a 'pragmatic and functional approach', it was held that the standard of review should reflect the nature of the minister's decision, which permitted him a 'considerable choice' in deciding when humanitarian and compassionate considerations warranted an exemption from the general requirements of the Immigration Act. The minister's expertise in immigration matters also pointed towards a greater,

---
[9] Allan, *Constitutional Justice*, ch 6.
[10] *Baker v Canada (Minister of Citizenship and Immigration)* (1999) 174 DLR (4th) 193.

rather than smaller, judicial deference; yet the nature of the decision, as one directly affecting 'the rights and interests of an individual in relation to government', closely dependent on assessment of the facts of the particular case, argued in favour of a stricter scrutiny.

The court's concern with the scope of the minister's discretion, however, was in danger of obscuring the critical issue, which was whether or not the rejection of Baker's plea for favourable treatment could be reconciled with whatever standards or policies the minister had adopted or authorised. It does not follow from the fact that the statute grants a broad discretion to the minister, as a matter of general policy, that a similar freedom of choice should be permitted to his officials in specific instances. It understated the importance of the ministerial guidelines to say merely that they were a 'useful indicator of what constitutes a reasonable interpretation of the power conferred':[11] they were clearly the principal means for transforming an otherwise arbitrary power into a properly regulated discretion, capable of equitable application between different claimants. The fact that the immigration officer's decision contravened the tenor of the guidelines was surely conclusive of its irrationality, in the absence of special circumstances that might warrant such a contravention.

The tri-partite scale of review endorsed by the Supreme Court may impose an unfortunate rigidity, deflecting our attention from matters of substance toward rather arbitrary questions of categorisation. In view of the central focus of the power on considerations of humanity and compassion, as they apply in the circumstances of particular cases, it must be doubted whether the court was right to conclude that 'considerable deference should be accorded' to immigration officers' decisions.[12] At the level of specific decisions, the opposite conclusion is more compelling. If, for example, the interests of the applicant's children were truly entitled to 'serious weight and consideration', there would need to be cogent reasons, clearly articulated, for overriding such interests in any particular instance. The only 'reasonable' decision will often be the one that is 'correct'. An officer who is 'alert, alive and sensitive' to the children's interests could not decide to override them without persuasive grounds.[13]

The critical question in *Baker*, as regards the scope of review, was not, then, whether a standard of reasonableness ought to be applied, but rather how searching and skeptical the court's examination of the decision should properly be within the constraints of that highly flexible standard.[14] In regard to *that* question, the various factors regarded as pointing in the

---

[11] *Ibid*, p 232.
[12] *Ibid*, p 228.
[13] *Ibid*, p 233.
[14] Cf D Dyzenhaus, 'Constituting the Rule of Law: Fundamental Values in Administrative Law' (2002) 27 *Queen's Law Journal* 445, at pp 493–95.

direction of judicial deference may be viewed in a different light. The width of the discretion conferred on the minister is, in context, a reason for closer scrutiny: in the absence of generally applicable norms, limiting the opportunity for arbitrary choices, the individual is highly vulnerable to unfair treatment. Nor does her request for exemption from the general statutory requirements impose a necessary duty of judicial restraint; for the appellant was entitled to consideration on the same terms as other persons in a similar position, without unjustified discrimination. Nor is the minister's expertise a ground for such restraint in the absence of compelling reasons for the decision: a general expertise is no guarantee against unfairness in the particular case.

The proper standard of deference is therefore a function of the appellant's right to equality: the more dependent the decision on the specific facts of her case, and the smaller its impact on the national welfare or the public good, the weaker the objection to the court's intervention as an infringement of the separation of powers. We should not accept the suggestion, offered in support of the 'pragmatic and functional approach', that the greater the discretion conferred by the statute, 'the more reluctant courts should be to interfere with the manner in which decision-makers have made choices among various options'.[15] That is so only where the various options represent competing assessments of the general public interest, as opposed to determinations of the rights or interests or needs of specific individuals. L'Heureux-Dubé J's suggestion is effectively cancelled in the latter case by the qualification that administrative discretion must be exercised, not only within its statutory boundaries, but in accordance with 'the principles of the rule of law, the principles of administrative law, the fundamental values of Canadian society, and the principles of the *Charter*'.

Interpreted appropriately, the traditional *Wednesbury* principle of English administrative law also contains all appropriate requirements of constitutional deference within it.[16] A finding of 'unreasonableness' expresses the conclusion that a decision lies beyond the legitimate boundaries of administrative discretion, lacking any defensible legal basis. Its chief virtue as a principle of legality is its intrinsic adaptability to context: its meaning is precisely a function of the rational power of a complaint of injustice in all the circumstances. Although it has generated specious sub-divisions—super-*Wednesbury* and sub-*Wednesbury*, as they are sometimes called—the varying degrees of judicial oversight are only the natural consequence of applying an abstract principle to an infinite range of circumstances.[17] A requirement, for example, that decisions relating to economic policy must exhibit

---

[15] *Baker v Canada* 174 DLR (4th) 193, at p 226 (L'Heureux-Dube J).
[16] *Associated Provincial Picture Houses Ltd v Wednesbury Corporation* [1948] 1 KB 223.
[17] Cf Sir John Laws, 'Wednesbury', in C Forsyth and I Hare, *The Golden Metwand and the Crooked Cord: Essays on Public Law in Honour of Sir William Wade* (Oxford, Clarendon Press, 1998).

evidence of improper motive or 'manifest absurdity', before falling foul of the rationality standard, asserts a generalisation about the scope or strength of any relevant legal or constitutional rights.[18] 'Absurdity' has no more concrete content, divorced from an argument about legal or factual error, than irrationality or unreasonableness.

It is now accepted in English law that administrative acts may give rise to substantive legitimate expectations, not merely expectations regarding procedure, and that such an expectation can be extinguished by an overriding public interest only when such a balance of interests meets acceptable standards of fairness. The courts' proper insistence that the decision to override a legitimate expectation must be reasonable, or not wholly unreasonable, has given way, inevitably, to the further recognition that the court must itself undertake some weighing of interests: a reasonable decision is one that treats the citizen fairly in all the circumstances. In the result, a capacious judicial discretion must be applied with great sensitivity to the administrative context: 'The more the decision challenged lies in what may ... be called the macro-political field, the less intrusive will be the court's supervision'.[19]

Laws LJ's appeal to a scale of 'intrusiveness' is only metaphor, however, for the consequences of a genuine balancing of interests: it does not, on the most persuasive understanding, import an independent doctrine of judicial deference. The more wide-ranging the issues of general policy and the larger the number of persons whose reasonable expectations may have to be dashed for the wider public good, the stronger will be the defence that no impermissible infringements of equality are entailed. The principle of equality itself reflects the tension between law and politics, acknowledging that one gradually merges with the other. As the judge himself accepts, in the macro-political field:

> true abuse of power is less likely to be found, since within it changes of policy, fuelled by broad conceptions of the public interest, may more readily be accepted as taking precedence over the interests of groups which enjoyed expectations generated by an earlier policy.[20]

Abuse of power is less likely to be found because the relevant distinctions between persons, as regards their treatment by the state, can be more easily justified as consistent with constitutional equality.[21]

---

[18] See *R v Secretary of State for the Environment ex parte Hammersmith & Fulham LBC* [1991] 1 AC 521, at pp 594–97.
[19] *R v Secretary of State for Education and Employment ex parte Begbie* [2000] 1 WLR 1115, at p 1131 (Laws LJ).
[20] *Ibid.*
[21] For an analogous approach to polycentric questions, involving numerous interests and interrelated issues, see *Pushpanathan*, above at p 1009.

If, then, the court is 'entitled to subject an administrative decision to the more rigorous examination, to ensure that it is in no way flawed, according to the gravity of the issue' being decided,[22] that is because relatively more serious encroachments on an individual's rights or interests need relatively more demanding justification. Rationality is a function of constitutional equality: the pursuit of public ends, however admirable, should not entail unfair or disproportionately deleterious consequences for particular persons. The appropriate degree of deference to executive discretion is determined by the court's assessment of the balance of public and private interests in the light of the reasons presented to it, informed by the evidence adduced in their support. It represents in a sense the *outcome*, rather than the guiding principle, of the court's decision. There is no additional requirement of judicial restraint on constitutional grounds: placing further weight on the public side of the scales denies the countervailing private right its due.

The failure of the English courts to protect the applicants' rights of privacy and personhood, in *ex parte Smith*, provides an apt illustration.[23] The applicants had been compulsorily discharged from the British armed forces on the sole ground of their homosexual orientation. The courts' conclusion that their treatment was not irrational flew in the teeth of their own assessment of the merits of the complaint. Government fears of damage to morale, if homosexual men and women were allowed to serve, were apparently based on little more than a perception of general prejudice. In the absence of evidence of specific past experience that might have supported such fears, Simon Brown LJ (in the Divisional Court) held that the 'balance of argument' lay clearly in favour of the applicants; and Sir Thomas Bingham MR (in the Court of Appeal) acknowledged the 'very considerable cogency' of the arguments made on their behalf.[24] The orthodox wisdom, that the rationality test had proved incapable of protecting constitutional rights, is not persuasive: it overlooks both the elastic or open-ended nature of the test and the importance of judicial skepticism in the face of executive claims to superior wisdom.

According to Sir Thomas Bingham, a government policy that had been endorsed by a select committee of the House of Commons, whose report 'reflected the overwhelming consensus of service and official opinion', could not be condemned as irrational. Relaxation of the former ban on homosexuals in the armed forces of Canada, Australia and New Zealand was too recent to yield useful experience. But such deference to official opinion contravened the rationality requirements properly applicable. The importance of the human rights context was expressly acknowledged; it would colour

---

[22] *R v Secretary of State for the Home Department ex parte Brind* [1987] AC 514, at p 531.
[23] *R v Ministry of Defence ex parte Smith* [1995] 4 All ER 427 and [1996] 1 All ER 257.
[24] Cf Thorpe LJ at [1996] 1 All ER 257, pp 273–74.

the court's assessment of whether the decision was unreasonable in the sense that it lay 'beyond the range of responses open to a reasonable decision-maker': the 'more substantial the interference with human rights, the more the court will require by way of justification before it is satisfied that the decision is reasonable' in the sense specified. On that approach, however, the court could not properly be satisfied on the basis of official opinion that did not rest on truly persuasive grounds.

The difference between the judgments of the English courts and that of the European Court of Human Rights is that, whereas the former submitted, without conviction, to the supposedly superior wisdom of the executive, the latter asserted its own intellectual autonomy.[25] The Strasbourg court declined to accept the findings of the Homosexuality Policy Assessment Team, established by the Ministry of Defence: the report's independence was open to question, and in so far as it was representative of opinion throughout the armed forces, which was doubtful, it reflected a general bias against, or hostility towards, a homosexual minority. There was no concrete evidence to substantiate the alleged damage to morale and fighting power that a change of policy would entail; a strict code of conduct, applicable to all service personnel, would serve to deal with any genuine disciplinary problems. Accordingly, the policy of excluding homosexuals had not been justified by 'convincing and weighty reasons'.

A legitimate constitutional deference is implicit in the court's recognition of the policy-making role of the executive; but the scope of that role must reflect the demands of constitutional equality. Executive freedom to fashion defence policy, and prohibit practices likely to undermine staff morale, is curtailed only by its duty to respect constitutional rights. The court may properly defer to governmental assessments of defence needs until the point is reached where such assessments, or the policies they inform, result in serious deprivations of liberty or security for particular persons, singled out for special treatment. The question is then whether, having regard to such plainly proper governmental aims as enhancing national defence or security, there is a 'pressing social need' for the imposition of the particular restrictions or deprivations on those affected.

If the infringement of a prima facie right must be justified in the sense of meeting a 'pressing social need', so that the individual interest is not unfairly sacrificed to the general good, the court must exercise its own judgement on the basis of the evidence adduced, as explained and tested by the respective parties. There is always the danger that the court's focus on the individual right will obscure less tangible consequences for the public interest, which may be hard to predict or formulate with desirable precision; but such dangers are simply inherent in the enforcement of constitutional rights. The executive is entitled to a fair hearing on the same terms as

---

[25] See *Smith and Grady v United Kingdom* (2000) 29 EHRR 493.

the victim of the action impugned; but it has no right that its case should be favourably received merely on the ground of its governmental status, charged with pursuit of the public good.

The English courts in *Smith* confused the legitimate species of deference, inherent in acknowledging the responsibility of the executive for defence and security, with an unjustified acceptance of decisions that were poorly grounded in reason. These courts submitted to the executive decision as such, rather than acknowledging the force of any reasons actually offered in its defence. Since there was no guarantee that those who shared the official and military consensus had given serious attention to the human rights dimension of the issue—let alone that they had accorded it sufficient weight—the court's deference to such opinion was illegitimate. The presumptive expertise of the executive was improperly substituted for the court's judgement of the legal merits, at the level where a general policy affected the rights of specific individuals; the applicants' constitutional rights were accordingly denied.

NATIONAL SECURITY AND PUBLIC ORDER

In *Rehman*, the courts acknowledged the widest amplitude of power to deport someone on grounds of national security: in view of the need for international co-operation against terrorism, it was not necessary that the perceived threat must be aimed specifically at the United Kingdom.[26] Lord Hoffmann explained that whether or not something was 'in the interests' of national security was a 'matter of judgment and policy' rather than law; and the Special Immigration Appeals Commission was:

> not entitled to differ from the opinion of the Secretary of State on the question of whether, for example, the promotion of terrorism in a foreign country by a United Kingdom resident would be contrary to the interests of national security.[27]

Notwithstanding the wide jurisdiction of the Commission to examine the minister's exercise of discretion, as well as deciding questions of law and fact, its powers of intervention were constrained by its judicial status, conferred as a means of ensuring compliance with Article 6 of the European Convention on Human Rights. As 'a member of the judicial branch of government', the Commission must not usurp the legitimate sphere of the executive.

There is an obvious danger here that the constraints of the separation of powers, articulated through the medium of 'policy', will undermine the

---

[26] *Secretary of State for the Home Department v Rehman* [2001] 3 WLR 877.
[27] *Ibid*, p 894.

protection for the suspect's rights that the creation of the Commission was intended to secure. It is true that the suspect's specific acts must be proved by evidence, where these are relied on to illustrate the perceived danger; but, though important, this requirement confers only limited protection because the minister is entitled to act on the basis of his suspicion that future activities may prove harmful to national security. If, then, the Commission is to serve its intended purpose it must be free to reassess the minister's estimation of the risk of such future harmful activities, as well as the degree to which such activities would actually present a danger to the United Kingdom. Questions of policy are largely displaced, at this level, by judgements of fact and assessment of evidence. Yet the House of Lords was unwilling to concede even this responsibility to the Commission, substituting a more limited review function for a truly appellate one. Lord Hoffmann considered that in evaluating risks an appellate body should allow a 'considerable margin to the primary decision-maker'. The Home Secretary had 'the advantage of a wide range of advice from people with day-to-day involvement in security matters which the Commission, despite its specialist membership, cannot match'.[28]

Hoffmann's invocation of the separation of powers is too blunt, making insufficient allowance for the peculiar dependence of the decision on the specific facts of the particular case. The scope of the minister's discretion demanded a more rigorous, rather than more deferential, scrutiny. There was no genuine question here of public policy being even-handedly applied: instead, a somewhat indeterminate public purpose was pleaded to justify the most stringent measures against an allegedly dangerous individual. In these circumstances, constitutional propriety requires the highest standards of due process: the individual is otherwise at the mercy of an essentially arbitrary discretion. Our understanding of the separation of powers must, then, be attuned to the nature of the threat to the fundamental values of equality and due process. The weaker the legal constraints on the scope of the minister's discretion—the more closely it resembles an unfettered discretion to act in pursuit of his own conception of the public good—the greater the need for *quasi-judicial* safeguards. The downgrading of the Commission's role in *Rehman* jeopardises those safeguards in defiance of a proper understanding of the rule of law.

The dual constraints on the Commission, reflecting both the separation of powers and the limitations of the appellate process, as Hoffmann construes them, threaten to eliminate any genuine protection for the suspect's rights in a context where they are especially vulnerable. Together they deprive the tribunal of the true independence from the executive that the judicial protection of constitutional rights demands. The requirement for the Commission to defer to the minister's superior knowledge is also

---

[28] *Ibid*, p 896.

unnecessary because its procedures have been specially adapted to allow sensitive information to be received in the absence of the suspect. Following the Canadian model, commended by the European Court in *Chahal*,[29] the rules allow the proceedings to be conducted partly in private, the appellant being represented by a special advocate appointed by the Attorney-General. In these circumstances, it should be perfectly possible for the executive to place all relevant facts and opinions before the Commission, allowing it to form an independent judgement on their cogency.

When a court is deprived of relevant information on national security grounds, procedural fairness is radically undermined; and in consequence the court's recognition of rights against the executive is largely empty, incapable of generating legal protection against arbitrary treatment.[30] In such circumstances, it is only the existence of adequate safeguards *outside* the ordinary courts that can give such rights any genuine content. Viewed as a *quasi-judicial* body, the Special Immigration Appeals Commission can provide the intensive scrutiny for which the courts, with their standard public procedures, may be thought unsuitable. If, however, the tribunal is itself denied the full jurisdiction that its appellate function implies, the gravest incursions into ordinary principles of natural justice must be accepted without any compensating rigour in the quality of the substantive protection. The indignities inflicted at a procedural level are compounded by a lack of appropriately independent scrutiny of executive claims and judgements.

A dramatic illustration of the deleterious consequences of *Rehman* for the judicial protection of rights, even where national security was not strictly engaged, is provided by the outcome of a recent challenge to the Home Secretary's exclusion of Louis Farrakhan, the American leader of the 'Nation of Islam'.[31] The exclusion order was based on the minister's fear that Farrakhan's proposed visit to the United Kingdom would damage relations between the Muslim and Jewish communities and thereby pose a threat to public order. The judge at first instance quashed the decision on the basis that the Secretary of State had failed to demonstrate objective justification for the interference with freedom of speech under Article 10 of the European Convention: a purely 'nominal risk' of harm to community relations would not suffice.

Reversing the judge's decision, however, the Court of Appeal held it 'appropriate to accord a particularly wide margin of discretion' to the Home Secretary, citing *Rehman* in support of its approach. A number of matters were alleged to affect the proper standard of review. The case concerned an immigration decision and under international law a state is

---

[29] *Chahal v United Kingdom* (1996) 23 EHRR 413.
[30] See, eg, *R v Secretary of State for the Home Department ex parte McQuillan* [1995] 4 All ER 400.
[31] *R (Farrakhan) v Secretary of State for the Home Department* [2002] 3 WLR 481.

entitled to control immigration into its territory; it involved a personal decision of the Home Secretary, who had consulted widely; the minister was democratically accountable for his decision; and he was 'far better placed to reach an informed decision as to the likely consequences' of admitting the applicant than was the court. The minister had sources of information available to him, the nature and purport of which he had 'not chosen to describe'. Even more remarkably, the court rejected a submission that the absence of any right of appeal strengthened the need for a 'particularly rigorous scrutiny' by way of judicial review: that submission, it was held, contradicted the statutory scheme.[32]

Even if these various factors confirmed the case for according the minister's reasons proper respect, in so far as he had articulated the grounds on which his judgement was based, none justified submission to an outcome that could not be defended by evidence and argument that the court itself found persuasive. The court's conclusion, that the minister had 'provided sufficient explanation' to show that his decision did not involve a disproportionate interference with freedom of expression, is hard to square—in a case where the merits were conceded to be 'finely balanced'—with the judges' regret that he had been so 'diffident about explaining the nature of the information and advice that he had received'.[33] By invoking general grounds for judicial deference, detached from its judgement of the merits of the particular claim, the court effectively eliminated the rights it had earlier purported to affirm.

The considerations that recommended deference, in the court's opinion, bear a striking resemblance to those emphasised by the Canadian Supreme Court when adopting a similar stance in relation to deportation decisions, taken on grounds of national security.[34] The Immigration Act permits the deportation of a refugee, otherwise entitled to asylum, where the minister considers him a danger to Canada's security, even if he faces a substantial risk of torture at the hands of the authorities in his country of origin. The court has held in *Suresh* that the minister's decision that a refugee's presence endangers national security should be quashed only if 'it is patently unreasonable in the sense that it was made arbitrarily or in bad faith, it cannot be supported on the evidence, or the minister failed to consider the appropriate factors'.[35] The court could not interfere on the basis that the relevant factors had been erroneously weighed.

Parliament had apparently intended only a limited right of appeal, requiring leave of the Federal Court—Trial Division. The minister enjoyed a special expertise, and he was better able to balance the respective public

---

[32] *Ibid*, pp 502–504.
[33] *Ibid*, p 504.
[34] *Suresh v Canada (Minister of Citizenship and Immigration)* 2002 SCC 1.
[35] *Ibid*, para 29.

and private interests than the court. *Rehman* was cited in support. Even on the question of whether the refugee faced a substantial risk of torture, a large measure of deference was required: the relevant factual issues were 'largely outside the realm of expertise of reviewing courts' and possessed 'a negligible legal dimension'.[36]

Although the 'principles of fundamental justice', entrenched by section 7 of the *Charter*, imposed basic requirements of procedural fairness—the right to make written submissions in the light of the advice on which the minister proposed to act—the refugee's security enjoys little protection in substance. The highly discretionary nature of the minister's decision, whereby a person's most basic interests are vulnerable to assessments not guided by the 'application or interpretation of definitive legal rules',[37] demands a stricter rather than a looser judicial oversight. Nor is there any legitimate basis for the court's distinction between review of matters relevant to a decision, on the one hand, and judgements of weight, on the other. Attachments of weight are fully as susceptible to error and arbitrariness—of varying degrees—as a minister's identification of material considerations. Where the values of the rule of law are most urgently at stake, such narrow distinctions between formal categories of error are of doubtful assistance.

Admittedly, the court held that the minister should normally decline to deport a refugee who does face a substantial risk of torture: the balance of interests must conform to the principles of fundamental justice. Presumably, therefore, there is greater scope for judicial scrutiny at this point: the minister cannot be the sole judge of her own compliance with section 7 of the *Charter*. If, however, there is no serious appraisal of the minister's conclusions as regards either national security or the risk of torture, any review of the balance of interests is bound to be extremely superficial, wholly dependent on the minister's own construction of the dilemma to be resolved. The court's dubious reliance on formal distinctions, as regards the scope of legitimate review, goes hand in hand with its proclamation of the merits of deference. It is an approach that insulates the exercise of a dangerous discretion against the intrusion of rule of law constraints that, in this context, the court appears unwilling to defend.

CONCLUSION

I have argued that judicial deference to the executive should reflect the balance of reason in particular cases, rather than constituting an automatic and overriding reason for judicial restraint in sensitive areas, such as those relating to national security. A general principle or independent doctrine of

[36] *Ibid*, para 39.
[37] *Ibid*, para 31.

judicial deference is capable of undermining the protection of legal and constitutional rights, and when such a doctrine is invoked in the context of national defence or security such rights are likely to be eliminated. Since respect for the expertise and policy-making functions of the executive is an integral feature of judicial review—a practical and constitutional requirement already reflected in ordinary doctrinal analysis—there is no case for a further, free-standing doctrine of deference. Such a doctrine serves only to frustrate the critical assessment of particular administrative decisions by erecting false barriers to judicial review. It rests on crude distinctions between the spheres of court and agency, insufficiently attuned to the circumstances of the particular case. It reflects a formalist conception of the separation of powers.

The formalist conception marks the division between court and agency according to the scope of the discretionary powers conferred on the latter. An open-ended power attracts only minimal judicial scrutiny, allowing maximum freedom to the executive to implement its policies as it sees fit. When we grasp the true meaning of the fundamental precepts of equality and due process, however, we can see why the formalist conception is unacceptable. The separation of judicial power is intended to secure an intellectual autonomy, which is compromised by a deference to the other branches of government beyond that recommended by reason—a common law reason, sensitive to all relevant circumstances, where the demands of the rule of law provide the chief determinants of relevance.

A broadly framed discretion poses a graver challenge to the rule of law than a relatively more specific power, inviting a greater danger of unfairness or arbitrariness, even when its exercise is properly directed towards the public good. The danger can be averted only by close attention to the consequences of such an exercise of power in particular cases; and at the level of the particular, as opposed to the general, the gulf between judicial and administrative expertise, or between law and policy, is sharply diminished. In the context of evidence and argument directed to the circumstances of the particular case, reason can come to grips with policy and principle. The ideal of equality can be given more concrete content, forcing the executive to justify the exceptional treatment of individuals. The common law can oversee the conflict between the authorised defenders of the public interest and those whom they allege to be its enemies.

12

Of Cocoons and Small 'c' Constitutionalism: The Principle of Legality and an Australian Perspective on Baker

MARGARET ALLARS

INTRODUCTION

THE ASSERTION THAT the rule of law is a vital component of the Australian legal system surfaces in judicial pronouncements and is purveyed in political debate in Australia. However invocation of the idea is occasional and confused. If only we knew what the rule of law was, or is. Tense may be important, since a concept employed to do the work of radically opposed juristic or political forces, without the compensating benefit of illuminating the issues at stake, may be justifiably jettisoned. In a legal system marked by the absence of a bill of rights, parliamentary sovereignty may say all there is to say about the rule of law. The 'rule of parliament' may more truly describe the lie of the legal landscape in Australia.

Whether this paints a bleak picture depends on what the rule of law might offer. According to the most minimalist account, the rule of law means a principle of legality. Legal rules with a core meaning are to be applied and bind judges, administrators and citizens. At the opposite end of the spectrum, the rule of law embodies a substantive theory of democratic justice which supplements the principle of legality, sanctioning departure from a legal rule which the judge determines to be invalid on account of its evil content.

In the territory between these extremes of the principle of legality and theories of justice, the rule of law lurks as a standard which may be capable of providing a deep 'constitutional' justification for the resolution of tensions between fundamental values of the common law and the operation of parliamentary sovereignty. I defer for the moment dealing with the objection which would be raised at this point by writers such as Paul Craig who would say that some standards which claim to be versions of the rule of law are not properly so described because they are truly theories of justice. This chapter explores that territory by examining the decision of the Supreme Court of Canada in *Baker v Minister for Immigration*[1] from an Australian perspective, with regard to the issues of reasoned decision-making, privative clauses and the content of a fair hearing.

The warning should be given that 'constitutionalism' in this essay does not denote respect for the Commonwealth Constitution, which provides scant protection of the liberty of the individual. Rather, 'constitutionalism' connotes the small 'c' constitutionalism of the values protected by the common law. This encompasses the fundamental rights traditionally recognised by the common law, including the right to a fair trial, to liberty, to the privilege against self-incrimination and legal professional privilege. Constitutionalism extends to broader conceptions of the proper function of courts within the doctrines of separation of powers, representative democracy and responsible government and accountability of the executive branch to the courts by reference to values of openness, rationality and fairness.

In the context of the exercise of discretion by the executive branch, and its judicial scrutiny, a contest has emerged in Australia as to whether the principle of legality delivers neat answers, or whether there is scope for the operation of these common law rights, doctrines and values.

If the first view is correct, the principle of legality operates in a cocoon, unsullied by the messy common law world of constitutionalism. Parliament speaks and the courts obey. The work of judges is easy. They apply the rules. They dutifully tend to keeping tidy the internal recesses of the cocoon.

If the second view prevails, constitutionalism infuses the principle of legality and judges have no choice but to negotiate the contested territory where competing conceptions of the rule of law point to different answers to issues of interpretation of statutes and common law.

RULE OF LAW AS A CONTESTED STANDARD

Clustered at legalism's end of the spectrum are the positivists, while the anti-positivists camp at various places ranging across the opposite end of the spectrum.[2] Those who eschew the furthest extreme of the spectrum, occupied by the natural law theorists, populate the less comfortable territory in between, straining under the burden of giving some meaning to the rule of law without working unacceptable damage to the fabric of rules, both statutory and common law.

[1] [1999] 2 SCR 817.
[2] D Dyzenhaus, 'The Politics of Deference—Judicial Review and Democracy' in M Taggart (ed), *The Province of Administrative Law* (Oxford, Hart Publishing, 1997) 279, 280–81.

However there is common ground between the positivists and the anti-positivists.[3] While Joseph Raz tends to be ranked amongst the positivists at legality's end of the spectrum, the eight principles comprising the rule of law, identified in his earlier account, are identical with those espoused by leading natural law theorists as part of the minimum content of a legal system.[4] The principles provide a useful means for exploring the interface between legality and constitutionalism in the contested territory.[5]

Considered in isolation from the other principles, Raz's first three principles reflect a position most closely aligned to legality. The principles require that all laws should be prospective, open and clear; that laws should be relatively stable; and that the making of particular legal orders should be guided by open, stable, clear and general rules. The degree to which a legal system departs from these principles, and thereby undermines the values associated with the rule of law, depends upon judgments of degree. For example, retrospectively operating laws are valid, and involve a degree of derogation from the rule of law. Whether retrospectively operating criminal laws are acceptable is a large question, even for those who regard the rule of law as confined to the principle of legality.[6]

A second threat to a rigid legality is posed by the third principle. In what sense are particular legal orders, understood to be adjudicative decisions made by the executive branch, to be guided by legal rules which are open, prospective and clear? Welcome to the ultra vires doctrine and the rich jurisprudence of the common law which it encompasses.

Further, if Raz's reference to particular legal orders is understood as a reference to adjudicative decisions made by judges, how much of judicial adjudication is indeed guided by legal rules? To accept that legal rules run out and that judicial discretion may be exercised is to abandon reliance upon a principle of legality as a complete account of the basis for decision. Considering all of the offerings in the feast of theoretical analyses of judicial adjudication, whether conceding resort in hard cases to moral and political norms, or drawing upon the application of competing legal principles, or professing adherence to a structured and deep political justification for judicial decisions as advocated by Dworkin, a shared feature is the abandonment of reliance upon a narrow principle of legality as a simple solution to the problem of judicial discretion. In any event Raz only asked, after all, that particular legal orders be 'guided' by more general legal rules. Understood as limited in this way, his third principle of the rule of law tells

---

[3] Ibid.
[4] L Fuller, *The Morality of Law*, rev'd edn, (New Haven, Yale University Press, 1969); J Finnis, *Natural Law and Natural Rights* (Oxford, Clarendon Press, 1980).
[5] J Raz, *The Authority of Law: Essays on Law and Morality* (Oxford, Clarendon Press, 1979) p 214. For Raz's later account modifying his position to take account of cultural differences between legal systems, see J Raz, 'The Politics of the Rule of Law' (1990) 3 *Ratio Juris* 331.
[6] *Polyukovich v Commonwealth* (1991) 172 CLR 501.

the executive and judicial branches of government nothing about how those general legal rules are properly to be interpreted to enable particular legal rules to be made in accordance with the law.

Focusing upon judicial review of executive action, the meaning of the rule of law presents itself at two levels. What are the boundaries of executive power and how are those boundaries to be determined by a judge?

The contribution of common law constitutionalism to an understanding of the boundaries of executive power is most powerfully evident in the principles of abuse of power, including duties of administrative decision-makers to take into account relevant considerations, act for proper purposes, reasonably and on the basis of probative evidence. These are principles developed at common law, extending the reach the ultra vires doctrine in a way which could never be gleaned by reading the statute. However, these principles have been argued to reflect the will of the legislature that the ultra vires doctrine should operate in this extended way.[7] To allow the ultra vires doctrine to account for all judicial review by reference to legislative will, procedural fairness is characterised as no more than an implied condition of the exercise of statutory power. The courts exceed their proper function if they review a decision otherwise than for its conformity to a statute. This special legislative lens upon the ultra vires doctrine provides a positivist approach to the theory of judicial adjudication, incorporating a version of the rule of law which is synonymous with the principle of legality. This is a version of the rule of law which means much the same as the rule of parliament.

However, as TRS Allan argues, this is an entirely fictional account of legislative will.[8] Moreover it does violence to the principle of legality. Statutes which import a hidden baggage of abuse of power principles, staggering in its size and complexity, are hardly open, prospective and clear, within Raz's first principle of the rule of law. And all that is claimed to supply the adhesive between this baggage and the statutory provisions is the silence of the legislature. Again that is hardly a legal rule which is open, prospective and clear. It is a common law principle of interpretation. Struggle as one might, obedience to legislative will cannot, on its own, account for the way in which laws constraining the executive branch are understood and applied by the courts. There is inevitably a common law constitutional dimension to the operation of statutory rules governing the

---

[7] See, eg: D Oliver, 'Is the Ultra Vires Rule the Basis of Judicial Review?' [1987] 543; C Forsyth, 'Of Fig Leaves and Fairy Tales: The Ultra Vires Doctrine, The Sovereignty of Parliament and Judicial Review' (1996) 55 *Cambridge Law Journal* 122; P Craig, 'Competing Models of Judicial Review' [1999] *Public Law* 428; J Jowell, 'Of Vires and Vacuums: The Constitutional Context of Judicial Review' [1999] *Public Law* 448; M Elliott, *The Constitutional Foundations of Judicial Review* (Oxford, Hart Publishing, 2001) pp 109–110.
[8] TRS Allan, 'Fairness, Equality, Rationality: Constitutional Theory and Judicial Review' in C Forsyth and I Hare (eds), *The Golden Metwand and the Crooked Cord* (Oxford, Clarendon Press, 1998) 15, 20.

executive branch and that dimension is critical to ensuring compliance with the rule of law.

When judges impose the narrowest requirement of the ultra vires doctrine, that administrators act within the boundaries of statutory power, difficult issues of interpretation are frequently raised. Even if the ultra vires doctrine, and conformity to legislative will were accepted to be the basis for judicial review, the principle of legality can be shown to have failed to give a complete and final account of the boundaries of executive power. This failure is neatly illustrated by the duties which interpretation statutes now place upon judges to consider extraneous material such as explanatory memoranda, second reading speeches and law reform reports.[9] It is legislative will that the judge look beyond the text of the statute, but the legislature itself neither creates nor controls the content of these non-legislative materials to which it directs the interpretive enterprise.

There is another more telling way in which narrow ultra vires requires the judge to resort to small 'c' constitutionalism. In cases of ambiguity or uncertainty in statutory provisions, common law principles require a judge to turn to fundamental common law rights and international law, which includes international human rights jurisprudence.[10] Moreover since Australia's accession in 1991 to the First Optional Protocol to the International Covenant on Civil and Political Rights ('ICCPR'), a new common law principle has emerged of treating the ICCPR as a 'legitimate influence' on the development of the common law.[11] In the absence of unswerving denial of ambiguity or uncertainty in the law, an administrator or judge concerned to make a decision in accordance with the rules expressed by parliament is directed to international human rights which, while having some counterparts in fundamental common law rights, are not part of Australian domestic law. The cocoon of legality is breached.

The difference between the positivists and the anti-positivists is not simply a matter of uninvited excursions beyond legality. The difference often lies in the degree of preparedness to find a chink in the wall of a statute, in the form of an uncertainty or ambiguity. Does the statute speak clearly, overriding fundamental common law rights? Or does a chink exist, inviting the anti-positivist to claim a common law duty, imposed by principles of statutory interpretation, to read down the statute so that fundamental rights are not violated?

The remaining five principles of the rule of law identified by Raz are even more readily seen to introduce standards which go beyond the

---

[9] Acts Interpretation Act 1901 (Cth) s 15AB.
[10] *Coco v R* (1994) 179 CLR 427, 437; *Re Bolton Ex parte Beane* (1987) 162 CLR 514; *Balog v Independent Commission Against Corruption* (1990) 169 CLR 625; *Minister for Immigration and Ethnic Affairs v Teoh* (1995) 183 CLR 273, 287.
[11] *Mabo v Queensland (No 2)* (1992) 175 CLR 1, 42 per Brennan J; *Dietrich v R* (1992) 177 CLR 292, 391.

principle of legality. These are that the independence of the judiciary must be guaranteed; the principles of natural justice must be observed; the courts should have review powers over the implementation of the other principles; the courts should be easily accessible; and the discretion of the crime-preventing agencies should not be allowed to pervert the law.[12]

Two of these principles are highlighted now, for it will be necessary to return to them in the analysis of *Baker*. The principles of natural justice, or procedural fairness, embody a rich jurisprudence which has evolved by elaboration of the common law. The content of the principles differs from one common law country to another, and can be highly controversial, as demonstrated by *Minister for Immigration and Ethnic Affairs v Teoh*,[13] a High Court decision exploring the interface between administrative law and international human rights. As the Australian counterpart to *Baker*, *Teoh* is considered later. It is one of the cases that indicate that procedural fairness owes its development to the common law, rather than to a narrow ultra vires doctrine whose rationale barely extends beyond the doctrine of parliamentary sovereignty.

The second principle which is readily seen to incorporate a substantive theory of justice is the requirement that the courts have a role in reviewing the implementation of the other principles. Whittling away the availability of judicial review of administrative action effectively undermines the other principles of the rule of law. Yet the scope of a reviewing court's jurisdiction and the enactment of privative clauses lie within the province of parliament. How courts should respond to legal rules which dilute the operation of the principle of legality is considered further below in connection with a privative clause purporting to oust judicial review of migration decisions.

Paul Craig has argued that even within a positivist theory of the rule of law a distinction must be made between a formal conception of the rule of law, say incorporating Raz's first three principles, and a substantive conception of the rule of law, incorporating the balance of Raz's principles.[14] However the substantive conception of the rule of law becomes synonymous with the theory of justice one espouses. There is then no occasion for utilising a conception of the 'rule of law'. Theorists who use the expression do so inappropriately because they are describing a rights based theory of law and adjudication.

The principle of legality is the formal conception of the rule of law to which Craig refers. It is argued in this chapter that even a formal and procedural conception of the rule of law involves a substantive commitment to rights and values found in the common law. The dissolution of the distinction

---

[12] J Raz, *The Authority of Law: Essays on Law and Morality* (Oxford, Clarendon Press, 1979), p 215.
[13] (1995) 183 CLR 273.
[14] P Craig, 'Formal and Substantive Conceptions of the Rule of Law: An Analytical Framework' [1997] *Public Law* 467.

between formal and substantive conceptions of the rule of law does not, however, indicate that it is time to cease use of the expression the 'rule of law'. A conception of the rule of law potentially provides a basis for identifying common ground between different theories of justice and adjudication, a minimum set of rules understood within a particular legal tradition, as Raz envisaged. It is on that basis that its analysis remains a valuable enterprise.

JUDICIAL PERCEPTIONS OF THE RULE OF LAW

Only a small band of Australian appellate judges have articulated their conceptions of the rule of law.[15] This is fortunate, for such pronouncements generally leave in their wake a miscellany of confusion as to any settled or enduring concept, combined with pessimism as to what contribution any conception might make to Australian jurisprudence.

The views which have been expressed are divergent. The dominating view is a traditionalist version of the principle of legality, often sliding into strict legalism, and asserting that there are clear lines between the valid application of legal rules and political contest about the substance of the rules. Writing extra-judicially the Chief Justice of Australia has equated the rule of law with the principle of legality:

> The rule of law is meant to be a safeguard, not a menace. It operates in many aspects of our lives. Our system of government is infused by the principle of legality. ... the civil law is working at its best when people do not need to go to court to make claims or enforce rights, because legal obligations are known, and accepted.[16]

Underlying this approach is the view that the application of the law always admits of one correct answer, a view more clearly evident in the conception

---

[15] K Mason QC, 'The Rule of Law' in P Finn (ed), *Essays on Law and Government Vol 1 Principles and Values* (Sydney, Law Book Co, 1995) p 114; Justice Toohey, 'A Government of Laws, Not Men?' (1993) 4 *Public Law Review* 159; The Hon J Doyle, 'Accountability: Parliament, the Executive and the Judiciary' in S Kneebone (ed), *Administrative Law and the Rule of Law: Still Part of the Same Package?* 1998 Administrative Law Forum (Canberra, AIAL, 1999) p 18; The Hon Murray Gleeson, *The Rule of Law and the Constitution* Boyer Lectures 2000 (Sydney, ABC Books, 2000); The Hon Justice Dyson Heydon, 'Judicial Activism and the Death of the Rule of Law' (2003) 47 *Quadrant* 9.

[16] The Hon Murray Gleeson, *The Rule of Law and the Constitution* Boyer Lectures 2000 (Sydney, ABC Books, 2000) p 2 [footnote omitted]. In *Minister for Immigration and Multicultural Affairs v Jia* (2001) 178 CLR 42 at para 61 Gleeson CJ in a joint judgment with Gummow J said that the Minister for Immigration, being a member of parliament with political accountability to the electorate, and a member of the executive government with responsibility to parliament, functions 'in the arena of public debate, political controversy, and democratic accountability'. The rule of law is seen to operate as a brake on this: 'At the same time, the minister's exercise of statutory powers is subject to the rule of law, and the form of accountability which that entails': *ibid*. Here the rule of law is invoked in order to emphasise its separateness from the sphere of morals and politics.

of the rule of law espoused by the justice most recently appointed to the High Court:

> The duty of a judge is to decide the case. It entails a duty to say what is necessary to explain why it was decided as it was, and a duty to say no more than what is necessary. To breach the latter duty is a form of activism capable of causing insidious harm to the rule of law.[17]

By contrast, Gaudron J has expressed a view which takes her into the contested territory of small 'c' constitutionalism. In a case where the High Court reinvigorated the jurisdictional fact doctrine, *Corporation of the City of Enfield v Development Assessment Commission*,[18] Gaudron J anchored her separate judgment to the third and sixth principles of the rule of law:

> Once it is appreciated that it is the rule of law that requires the courts to grant whatever remedies are available and appropriate to ensure that those possessed of executive and administrative powers exercise them only in accordance with the laws which govern their exercise, it follows that there is very limited scope for the notion of 'judicial deference' with respect to findings by an administrative body of jurisdictional facts.[19]

These Australian approaches may be compared with *Baker v Minister for Immigration*,[20] where L'Heureux-Dubé J invoked the 'rule of law' at the outset of her discussion of deference and the pragmatic and functional approach to judicial review:

> However, discretion must still be exercised in a manner that is within a reasonable interpretation of the margin of manouevre contemplated by the legislature, in accordance with the principles of the rule of law (*Roncarelli v Duplessis* [1959] SCR 121, in line with general principles of administrative law governing the exercise of discretion, and consistent with the [Charter] ... [21]

The rule of law thus appears to be a fundamental constitutional doctrine which underlies administrative law and is consistent with the Charter. A further reference in *Baker* suggests the rule of law is fundamental but is ranked alongside the relevant statute, the Charter and the fundamental values of Canadian society:

> though discretionary decisions will generally be given considerable respect, that discretion must be exercised in accordance with the boundaries imposed

---

[17] The Hon Justice Dyson Heydon, 'Judicial Activism and the Death of the Rule of Law' (2003) 47 *Quadrant* 9, 16.
[18] (2000) 199 CLR 135.
[19] *Ibid*, 158 at para 59.
[20] See above n 1.
[21] See above n 1, at para 53.

in the statute, the principles of the rule of law, the principles of administrative law, the fundamental values of Canadian society and the principles of the Charter.[22]

REASONS FOR DECISIONS

Baker and *Osmond*

A duty to give reasons does not feature in Raz's categorisation of principles of the rule of law. Yet *Baker* is generally regarded as having revolutionised the common law in Canada by introducing a duty of administrators at common law to give reasons for their decisions.

In *Baker* L'Heureux-Dubé J considered the leading Australian authority, *Public Service Board of New South Wales v Osmond*,[23] a decision which reflects the common law principle that administrators have no duty to give reasons for their decisions. In *Osmond* the High Court firmly rejected the course taken in *Baker*, giving as its own reasons, inter alia, the policy concerns that introduction of such a duty at common law could impose a burden on the executive branch, and a lack of candour in decision-making. However, L'Heureux-Dubé J found that there were countervailing arguments supporting the introduction of such a duty:

> Reasons, it has been argued, foster better decision-making by ensuring that issues and reasoning are well articulated and, therefore, more carefully thought out. The process of writing reasons for decision by itself may be a guarantee of a better decision. Reasons also allow parties to see that the applicable issues have been carefully considered, and are invaluable if a decision is to be appealed, questioned, or considered on judicial review. ... Those affected may be more likely to feel they were treated fairly and appropriately if reasons are given ... .[24]

L'Heureux-Dubé J swept away the policy concerns identified in *Osmond*, apparently by characterising the duty as one which depends upon the circumstances of the particular case.[25] That approach is consistent with the way in which a common law duty to give reasons was introduced in the United Kingdom from the early 1990s.[26]

L'Heureux-Dubé J provided minimal guidance as to the kind of circumstances which would warrant the giving of reasons, save that the decision

---

[22] See above n 1, at para 56.
[23] (1986) 159 CLR 656.
[24] See above n 1, at para 39.
[25] See above n 1, at para 40.
[26] *R v Civil Service Appeal Board; Ex parte Cunningham* [1991] 4 All ER 310; *R v Secretary of State for the Home Department; Ex parte Doody* [1994] 1 AC 531.

must have 'important significance for the individual', as in the determination of migration status, when 'there is no statutory right of appeal' or 'in other circumstances'.[27]

The central plank in the reasoning of the High Court in *Osmond*, which L'Heureux-Dubé J did not mention, was the view that it was not the proper function of the court to introduce such a duty, this being a matter of general law reform to be undertaken by the legislature. True it is that *Baker* was decided in a context of developing authority in Canadian appellate courts that a common law duty arises in particular decision-making contexts, such as decisions of parole boards and decisions subject to statutory appeal. *Osmond* was not decided in such a context but rather as a response by the High Court to a New South Wales Court of Appeal decision which sought to introduce a broadly-framed general duty from which exceptions would need to be carved in subsequent cases. The circumstances provided a poor test case, concerning a disappointed applicant for a promotion in the public service. *Baker* provided a much more compelling context of immigration status, threatened deportation of the mother of children who were Canadian citizens raised in Canada, and a departmental report containing florid and prejudicial language.

Shifts in Australia

Miniscule shifts have occurred in Australia since *Osmond*. This has been due more to enduring dissatisfaction in some quarters with *Osmond* than because the way was shown by *Baker* or by *R v Secretary of State for the Home Department; Ex parte Doody*,[28] a United Kingdom decision expanding the scope for finding a duty to give reasons is part of the content of a fair hearing.

One shift is found in a handful of cases, chiefly decided in state Supreme Courts, where reasons have been held to be a component of the content of a fair hearing.[29] Those decisions have sought support in the judgment of

---

[27] See above n 1, at para 43.
[28] See *Doody*, above n 26.
[29] *Coope v Iuliano* (1996) 65 SASR 405 raised the question of the duty of a Promotion Appeal Board to give reasons for its dismissal of a police officer's promotion appeal. While *Osmond* applied, the Supreme Court of South Australia held that in the current climate of judicial opinion, as a matter of statutory interpretation, courts are alert to the possibility of finding a legislative intention that reasons be supplied to a person whose property or legitimate expectations may be in jeopardy by reason of the decision. However, no implication should be made in the circumstances of the present case. The Court made it clear that had this been a case concerning disciplinary provisions the result would have been different. The Court relied upon Deane J in *Osmond* and made no reference to *Doody*. In *Yung v Adams* (1997) 150 ALR 436, 463 Davies J held, referring to *Doody*, that a Professional Services Review Tribunal had an implied duty to give reasons for its conclusion that the medical practitioner had engaged in excessive servicing. The empowering statute did not impose an express duty to give reasons but, as noted by Davies J, the Tribunal was chaired by a judicial officer, and an appeal lay to the Federal Court. On appeal the Full Federal Court upheld the conclusion of Davies J that the Tribunal's determination gave inadequate reasons, without elaboration or reference to *Doody*:

Deane J in *Osmond*. While agreeing with Gibbs CJ that there was no common law duty to give reasons, Deane J held that the common law principles of procedural justice are:

> neither standardized nor immutable. The procedural consequences of their application depend upon the particular statutory framework within which they apply and upon the exigencies of the particular case. Their content may vary with changes in contemporary practice and standards.[30]

With dramatic flair reminiscent of the Court of Appeal's decision in *Osmond*, the new Chief Justice of New South Wales instigated another shift, by issuing a practice note with respect to proceedings brought in the Administrative Law List of the Supreme Court of New South Wales. The practice note requires respondent administrative agencies to file in the court their reasons for decision if they have not already been provided.[31] Whether a duty to give reasons in respect of a decision which is the subject of a judicial review challenge can be introduced by this technique is a novel question, given the absence of any express statutory power to issue a practice note on this subject. No respondent has yet challenged it.

Statutory Duties

The debate about a common law duty to give reasons has in any event become something of a side show to the main action in Australia because of the extensive statutory duties to give reasons. These apply to most federal tribunals and primary decision-makers in high volume areas of decision-making, including migration, social security, taxation, veterans' affairs and freedom of information. Where the empowering statute does not impose a duty to give reasons automatically, then provided the decision is justiciable in the Federal Court under the Administrative Decisions (Judicial Review) Act 1977 (Cth) ('ADJR Act') a person with standing to seek review is entitled to request a statement of reasons for the decision.[32]

The statutory duties are far reaching, requiring decision-makers to set out their findings on material questions of fact, referring to the evidence or other material on which those findings were based, and giving the reasons for the decision.[33] Section 13 was included in the ADJR Act in order to overcome the deficiencies of the common law and enable applicants to

---

Adams v Yung (1998) 83 FCR 248. See also *Croatia Sydney Soccer Football Club v Soccer Australia Ltd* (unreported) Supreme Court of NSW, Einstein J, 23 September 1997, p 61; *McIlraith v Institute of Chartered Accountants* [2003] NSWSC 208 at [38]–[41].

[30] See above n 23, 676.
[31] Supreme Court of New South Wales Practice Note No 119.
[32] Administrative Decisions (Judicial Review) Act 1977 (Cth) ('ADJR Act') s 13. Certain classes of decision are excepted from this duty by the ADJR Act s 13(11), Sch 2.
[33] ADJR Act s 13(1). As to recommendations for the further refinement of the principles governing statements under s 13, see Administrative Review Council, *Review of the*

ascertain from the statement whether the decision-maker has made an error of law.[34] The statement is intended to overcome the real sense of grievance people experience when not told why something affecting them has been done.[35] A further policy of the legislative scheme to which section 13 belongs was to improve decision-making by imposing on administrators the intellectual discipline of identifying for themselves the reasons for their decisions.[36]

Common Law Interpretation of Statutory Duties

Two strands of common law have developed in connection with statutory duties to give statements of reasons. The first is that the decision-maker must include in the statement the true reasons for the decision, rather than censor the statement, removing findings or reasons which in the light of a pending review application appear to reflect an error.[37] The statement should not be an ex post facto justification of the decision so as to allow the statement to stand up in court.[38]

Second, in scrutinising a statement of reasons for legal error the court is to bear in mind that it is not a document necessarily prepared by a lawyer and should not subject it to microscopic study for some error of law. In *Minister for Immigration and Ethnic Affairs v Wu Shan Liang* [39] the High Court held that:

> the reasons of an administrative decision-maker are meant to inform and not to be scrutinised upon over-zealous judicial review by seeking to discern whether some inadequacy may be gleaned from the way in which the reasons are expressed ... any court reviewing a decision upon refugee status must beware of turning a review of the reasons of the decision-maker upon proper principles into a reconsideration of the merits of the decision.[40]

While some commentators believed *Wu Shan Liang* heralded a new era of deference towards administrative decisions, it truly did no more than affirm a line of authority in the Federal Court that scrutiny of statements of reasons

---

Administrative Decisions (Judicial Review) Act: Statements of Reasons for Decisions Report No 33 (1991).

[34] See Commonwealth Administrative Review Committee, *Report*, PP No 144 of 1977 ('Kerr Committee Report').
[35] *Burns v Australian National University* (1982) 40 ALR 707, 715 per Ellicott J; reversed on another point in *Australian National University v Burns* (1982) 43 ALR 25; *Minister for Immigration Local Government and Ethnic Affairs v Taveli* (1990) 23 FCR 162; *Powell v Evreniades* (1989) 21 FCR 252.
[36] See *Taveli ibid*, per French J.
[37] See *ibid*, 179 per French J.
[38] See *ibid*.
[39] (1996) 185 CLR 259.
[40] *Ibid*, 491.

should not be overzealous. The Federal Court decision which the High Court reversed in *Wu Shan Liang* was indeed overzealous review, discerning legal error in unhappy phraseology of the tribunal's description of the standard of proof required of an applicant for refugee status.

An exercise of parliamentary sovereignty secured a duty of the executive branch at the federal level to provide reasoned decision-making. However, even those statutory duties defy mechanistic application. Beyond the cocoon of legality, courts are called upon to balance the value of openness in administrative decision-making with the legality/merits distinction, which is but one aspect of the separation of powers. To reach a proper interpretation of the duty to give reasons requires a resolution of the tension between these components of constitutionalism.

With regard to reasoned decision-making, generally in Australia small 'c' constitutionalism failed the anti-positivists. In *Osmond* the common law declined to match the federal statutory duties. Yet there are good common law constitutional arguments for adding reason-giving by the executive branch to Raz's list of principles of the rule of law. Such an additional principle would be consistent with the general rationale of the rule of law: that the law should be capable of guiding individuals. It is not enough for administrative decisions to be reasoned. That reasoning must be disclosed to the person who seeks to be guided by it. In the course of giving guidance, the reasoning is exposed to critical scrutiny. This buttresses other principles of the rule of law, such as the third principle. It facilitates assessment of whether the administrative decision was indeed guided by general rules which are open, prospective and clear.

Revision of the decision in *Osmond* has appeared desirable, but not urgent. The more pressing issue which has confronted Australian courts in the last two years, in particular the Federal Court in its migration jurisdiction, is not the standard of reason-giving, but whether the decision is amenable to judicial review. Even if the court has jurisdiction and identifies a legal error in the statement of reasons, it may be precluded from applying traditional grounds of review. These are questions which turn on the effectiveness of privative clauses.

PRIVATIVE CLAUSES

According to traditional principles of administrative law, a comprehensive privative clause is ineffective to oust judicial review for jurisdictional error but is effective to oust review for non-jurisdictional error of law on the face of the record.[41] Where an agency acts in excess of jurisdiction it has not

---

[41] *Hockey v Yelland* (1984) 157 CLR 124; *Houssein v Under Secretary Department of Industrial Relations and Technology* (1982) 148 CLR 88.

made a 'decision', as contemplated by the statute, therefore there is nothing for the privative clause to protect. It is wholly ineffective. As Street CJ said in *Ex parte Wurth; Re Tully*:[42]

> it would be an extraordinary interpretation to put upon the [privative clause] that the [Crown Employees Appeal Board] was to have unfettered and unchallengeable power to define the extent of its own jurisdiction, and to give any decision or embark upon any proceeding without any liability to correction.[43]

The approach of the House of Lords in *Anisminic Ltd v Foreign Compensation Commission*[44] was the same. The privative clause could not protect a purported decision which was a nullity by reason of the agency's jurisdictional error.

The implications of this traditional judicial disdain for privative clauses depend upon whether a distinction is maintained between jurisdictional and non-jurisdictional errors of law. The High Court maintained the distinction for inferior courts whilst indicating in *Craig v South Australia*[45] that in many circumstances a tribunal's errors go to jurisdiction. Although the position has been left in a rather uncertain state, it appears that more prominent tribunals comprised of judicial officers and with a clear role in determining legal issues enjoy the protection of a distinction between jurisdictional and non-jurisdictional errors.

Maintenance of a distinction between jurisdictional and non-jurisdictional errors of law is consistent with the positivist approach. The inconsistency between the legislative restriction of the ambit of the agency's power and the legislative prohibition upon the court's jurisdiction to enforce that restriction, is reconciled by allowing jurisdictional scrutiny of only the outer boundaries of the agency's power. For positivists the rule of law requires no more.

In this kind of context, the interpretation of the privative clause is not so radical. A supervisory court will be free to review the decisions of most tribunals for virtually the full range of errors but will defer to inferior courts and tribunals comprised of judicial officers in the case of non-jurisdictional errors, unless they appear on the face of the record. The principle of legality is applied to ensure that the agency has jurisdiction. Beyond that, the agency is free to make errors of the abuse of power variety. Common law constitutionalism is kept at bay. None the less there remains scope for the principles of interpretation, which respect fundamental common law rights and international human rights jurisprudence, to operate in the interpretation of the statutory description of the agency's powers.

---

[42] (1954) 55 SR (NSW) 47.
[43] *Ibid*, 53.
[44] [1969] 2 AC 147.
[45] (1995) 184 CLR 163, 179.

The Principle of Legality and an Australian Perspective on Baker 321

Restriction of Jurisdiction of Courts

From 1989 migration law and policy in Australia was thrust into a new era of complex and constantly changing statutory regulation, leaving behind as historical relics notions of compassion and humanitarianism such as those considered in *Baker*.[46] This was underlined by the removal of 'strong compassionate or humanitarian grounds' as a basis for obtaining permanent resident status.[47]

From 1994 a new Part 8 was inserted into the Migration Act, removing from the Federal Court its jurisdiction to review primary migration decisions. The intention was that applicants for visas should utilise review by the Migration Review Tribunal or the Refugee Review Tribunal, before seeking judicial review. Where judicial review was sought of decision made by these tribunals, strict time limits applied to lodgment of applications and the grounds of review were limited. In particular the new Part 8 excluded review on the grounds of *Wednesbury* unreasonableness and certain other types of abuse of power, together with denial of procedural fairness, although actual bias was retained as an available ground.[48]

The governmental objective was to remove the facility for review on those grounds which had delivered most success to immigrant applicants in Federal Court decisions perceived to involve judicial activism. Still available were actual bias, narrow jurisdictional error, and one or two types of abuse of power which presumably were regarded as less troublesome to the executive branch. The amended Act was designed to eliminate or radically restrict the scope for judicial importation of common law conceptions of procedural fairness and abuse of power, let alone constitutional values of the humanitarian or compassionate variety.

This statutory exclusion of grounds of review was fatally undermined when in *Minister for Immigration and Multicultural Affairs v Yusuf*[49] the High Court said what had been clear from *Craig*. Jurisdictional error embraces a number of different kinds of legal error, including identifying a wrong issue, asking a wrong question and ignoring relevant material, such that the decision is vitiated. The attempt to limit judicial review to a

---

[46] See generally: M Allars, 'One Small Step for Legal Doctrine, One Giant Leap Towards Integrity in Government: *Teoh's case* and the Internationalisation of Administrative Law' (1995) 17 *Sydney Law Review* 204, 210–216, setting out the demise of cases like *Fuduche v Minister for Immigration, Local Government and Ethnic Affairs* (1993) 117 ALR 418 and *Chaudhary v Minister for Immigration and Ethnic Affairs* (1994) 121 ALR 315 where the Federal Court had adopted a 'broad and generous' interpretive approach in favour of immigrants.
[47] Repeal of s 6A(1)(c) of the Migration Act 1958 (Cth).
[48] Migration Act 1958 (Cth) s 476.
[49] (2001) 180 ALR 1 at par 82 per McHugh, Gummow and Hayne JJ.

narrow jurisdictional ground was shattered. Jurisdictional error, to the surprise of the executive branch and its handmaiden the parliament, covered most types of abuse of power. The legislative response was swift. It was a privative clause.

Hickman Revival

From the 1990s a test for determining the effectiveness of privative clauses, set out by Dixon J in *R v Hickman; Ex parte Fox and Clinton*[50] (the *Hickman* principle), enjoyed a revival in Australia. There is an apparent inconsistency between a statutory provision which seems to limit the jurisdiction of the tribunal and the privative clause, which seems to contemplate that the tribunal's decisions operate free from any restriction. The *Hickman* principle is a rule of construction which requires that the provisions be read together and effect given to each.[51] The apparent inconsistency is resolved so that a comprehensive privative clause protects a decision from judicial review if three factors are satisfied. The decision must be a bona fide attempt to exercise the power given; it must relate to the subject matter of the legislation; and it must be reasonably capable of reference to the power given to the tribunal.[52] A privative clause therefore protects against errors by altering the substantive law (the statutory provision describing the jurisdiction of the tribunal) to expand the jurisdiction of the tribunal, ensuring that the impugned decision is valid.

The *Hickman* principle is no more than a common law principle of statutory interpretation.[53] However, it operates to invert the traditional principle that a privative clause does not protect against jurisdictional error. It does so in an attempt to give some effect to the privative clause, and hence to legislative will. It offers a *via media* between ignoring the privative clause as having no effect, and giving the clause effect according to its terms with the result that it shuts out judicial review.

Parliament set out to ensure that the Federal Court understood its intention, by expressly invoking the *Hickman* principle in the explanatory memorandum to the Bill which introduced it. The explanatory memorandum recited the government's reliance upon the dictum of Dixon J in *Hickman*. What moved the legislative draftsperson to locate the proper interpretation in the explanatory memorandum in preference to setting out the three *Hickman* provisos in the Act is unknown. The irony of the entire endeavour

---

[50] (1945) 70 CLR 598, 615.
[51] *O'Toole v Charles David Pty Ltd* (1990) 171 CLR 232, 248–49 per Mason CJ, 275 per Brennan J, 287 per Deane, Gaudron and McHugh JJ; *Darling Casino Ltd v New South Wales Casino Control Authority* (1997) 191 CLR 602, 631 per Gaudron and Gummow JJ.
[52] See above n 50, 616–17.
[53] *Ibid* at 195 per Brennan J; see also *Darling Casino* at n 51, 631 per Gaudron and Gummow JJ.

is that the parliament sought to exclude constitutionalism but did so by depending upon statutory rules of interpretation which directed attention to an explanatory memorandum, which in turn directed attention to an arguably neglected common law solution to the problem of statutory interpretation posed by a privative clause.

Dixon J espoused a positivism which may not have extended beyond the principle of legality. What his dictum so readily shut out was Australian administrative law as it stood in the mid 1940s. The welfare state had not developed. *Ridge v Baldwin*[54] had not been decided. The Australian landmark case *Kioa v West*,[55] which developed a general and liberal test for implication of procedural fairness would not be decided for another 40 years. Lord Greene MR had yet to set out the *Wednesbury* principles which were also applied in Australia. These later developments in administrative law in Australia are not inconsistent with positivism, but are likely to be inconsistent with the brand of positivism which Dixon J avowed. Yet perhaps even Dixon J would have blanched at the prospective exclusionary effect of his simple test, innocently proposed at a time when administrative law truly did not exist in Australia.

Another complication neglected by the draftsperson was that a judicial dictum is likely to generate some incremental case-law. In the decades following *Hickman* the High Court held, mainly in cases involving complex issues of industrial law, that the *Hickman* principle does not protect a decision made in breach of an 'inviolable limitation' upon the tribunal's jurisdiction.[56] These inviolable limitations certainly include statutory preconditions to the exercise of jurisdiction. The contentious question is whether they extend to common law restrictions upon the exercise of jurisdiction, including abuse of power principles and procedural fairness. Acceptance of the latter view of course would result in the matter coming full circle again as it did in *Yusuf*.[57] All errors are exposed to review. Constitutionalism is restored.

As the first cases were decided, conflicting interpretations of the new privative clause were delivered by positivist and anti-positivist Federal Court judges. A specially convened Full Federal Court comprised of five justices heard together five appeals invoking interpretation of the privative clause. All the justices in *NAAV v Minister for Immigration and Multicultural Affairs*[58] agreed that the effect of a privative clause is a question of statutory construction.[59] Beaumont and von Doussa JJ held that in each of the five appeals no breach of the *Hickman* provisos or of any inviolable statutory

---

[54] [1964] AC 40.
[55] (1985) 159 CLR 550.
[56] *R v Murray; Ex parte Proctor* (1949) 77 CLR 387.
[57] See above n 49.
[58] [2002] FCAFC 228.
[59] *Ibid*, at para 500 per French J.

condition had been established. Black CJ joined these justices in three of the appeals but in two others held that statutory conditions precedent had been violated and the privative clause did not protect the decision from review.

Wilcox and French JJ dissented, holding that in those cases where the tribunal had made an error of law, the privative clause did not protect it from review. French J alone invoked the rule of law. In his view it did not matter whether the ultra vires theory, discussed in section 1 above, best describes the proper basis for judicial review in Australia because the question of the effectiveness of a privative clause would be determined by the doctrine of parliamentary sovereignty.[60] The *Hickman* test should not be elevated into a rigid rule of construction so that the three *Hickman* criteria are sufficient for validity.

French J regarded fraud, bad faith and actual bias as bases for establishing that a decision was not made bona fides for the purposes of the first *Hickman* proviso. Inviolable conditions included excess of jurisdiction, including for lack of a jurisdictional fact, improper purpose and denial of procedural fairness. The common law assumes that it is the legislature's intention that the rules of procedural fairness be implied because the legislature has the power to displace the rules by using clear words. This is such a well known common law rule that it is a legitimate way of determining legislative intention.[61] It followed that common law procedural fairness on its own could constitute an inviolable limitation upon statutory power whose breach was not protected by the privative clause:

> In some cases the power to be exercised by an official decision-maker may be so dramatic in its effect on the life or liberty of an individual that, absent explicit exclusion, attribution of an implied legislative intent to exclude procedural fairness would offend common concepts of justice.[62]

On the basis of the authority of the majority decision of the Full Federal Court in *NAAV*, a privative clause appeared to protect the executive branch from the scrutiny of the courts in a way which was not previously possible.[63] Blatant error could be apparent in the reasons of the Refugee Review Tribunal, indicating a failure to take into account a relevant consideration, the receipt of some adverse allegation from another source which was not disclosed to the applicant, or a closed mind indicating an appearance of bias, possibly actual bias. The Court on review would often identify the error, but then pronounce itself bound not to interfere on account of the privative clause.

Were the circumstances of *Baker* to be replicated in Australia, with the florid and prejudicial terms of the immigration officer's recommendation

[60] *Ibid*, at para 480 (subject to any limits on statutory interference with the High Court's original jurisdiction under s 75(v) of the Commonwealth Constitution).
[61] *Ibid*, at para 484.
[62] *Ibid*, at para 536.
[63] See *Darling Casino* above n 51 per Gaudron and Gummow JJ.

being reproduced in a decision of the Migration Review Tribunal, on the basis of *NAAV* it was likely that no relief would be available. In such a case clearly the second and third *Hickman* conditions would have been satisfied for the Tribunal's decision relates to the grant of a visa under the Act and is reasonably capable of reference to the power given to the tribunal. Of the *Hickman* provisos only the first, lack of bona fides, would have appeared to offer scope for argument. But that test has tended to be interpreted as requiring something more than actual bias. To meet that test Ms Baker would need to show that the tribunal's decision was infected by bad faith in the sense of 'a lack of an honest or genuine attempt to undertake the task in a way meriting personal criticism of the Tribunal or officer in question'.[64] Clearly such a test would have been met only in extraordinary circumstances.

Six months after the decision in *NAAV*, the High Court delivered judgment in *Plaintiff S157/2002 v Commonwealth of Australia* ('*Plaintiff S157/2002*'),[65] a test case on the privative clause, brought directly in its original jurisdiction. The High Court held unanimously that the privative clause did not, properly interpreted, purport to deprive the High Court of jurisdiction, and so did not violate the Commonwealth Constitution.[66]

As for its general interpretation, the Court held that there is 'no general rule as to the meaning or effect of privative clauses'.[67] However, reaching a result directly opposed to that of the majority in *NAAV*, the unanimous High Court held that a 'decision...made under this Act', which the privative clause purported to protect from review, was to be interpreted as a decision which involves neither a failure to exercise jurisdiction nor an excess of jurisdiction;[68] In *Plaintiff S157/2002* the ground of review argued was denial of procedural fairness. The decision, which was flawed for reasons of a failure to comply with the principles of procedural fairness, was not protected by the privative clause and was amenable to the issue of the prerogative remedies.[69]

Consistently with *Plaintiff S157/2002*, there are some errors of law which do not amount to jurisdictional errors so as to escape the operation of the privative clause.[70] The question whether the Tribunal has committed a jurisdictional error requires the Court to examine the statutory limitations

---

[64] See *NAAV* above n 58, at paras 107–108. That test was not met in the case of *NAAV* itself.
[65] [2003] 195 ALR 24 (High Court, Gleeson CJ, Gaudron, McHugh, Gummow, Kirby, Hayne and Callinan JJ, 4 February 2003).
[66] *Ibid*, at paras 3–22 per Gleeson CJ, at paras 71, 79–83 per Gaudron, McHugh, Gummow, Kirby, Hayne JJ, at para 163 per Callinan J.
[67] *Ibid*, at para 60 per Gaudron, McHugh, Gummow, Kirby, Hayne JJ.
[68] *Ibid*, at para 19 per Gleeson CJ, at para 76 per Gaudron, McHugh, Gummow, Kirby, Hayne JJ, at para 162 per Callinan J.
[69] *Ibid*, at paras 36–38 per Gleeson CJ, at para 83 per Gaudron, McHugh, Gummow, Kirby, Hayne JJ, at para 159 per Callinan J, suggesting that a grave or serious breach is required.
[70] *Lobo v Minister for Immigration and Multicultural and Indigenous Affairs* [2003] FCA 144 (unreported, Federal Court, Gyles J, 6 March 2003).

or requirements placed on the decision-maker in order to ascertain whether the Tribunal has failed to observe them in a way which results in jurisdictional error.[71] The privative clause does prevent the issue of certiorari in a case of non-jurisdictional error of law on the face of the record.[72]

The decision in *Plaintiff S157/2002* reinstates Raz's sixth principle, that the courts should have review powers over the implementation of the other principles of the rule of law. Gleeson CJ sought support in the rule of law. He held that that the original jurisdiction of the High Court to issue prerogative remedies, in the case of the High Court called the constitutional writs, was a 'basic element of the rule of law'.[73] That invocation of the rule of law is not surprising. It is capital 'C' constitutionalism, concerned with the proper interpretation of section 75(v) of the Commonwealth Constitution, which vests this original jurisdiction in the High Court.

However, Gleeson CJ offered some more broadly-based incantations of the rule of law. He quoted from Denning LJ:

> If tribunals were to be at liberty to exceed their jurisdiction without any check by the courts the rule of law would be at an end.[74]

Gleeson CJ then sought to summarise the principles of interpretation which might assist in reconciling the privative clause with the provisions describing the statutory boundaries of the jurisdiction of the Refugee Review Tribunal. Amongst the five principles identified was this:

> Thirdly, the Australian Constitution is framed upon the assumption of the rule of law (*Australian Communist Party v The Commonwealth* (1951) 83 CLR 1 at 193 per Dixon J). Brennan J said (*Church of Scientology v Woodward* (1982) 154 CLR 25 at 70):
> > 'Judicial review is neither more nor less than the enforcement of the rule of law. over executive action; it is the means by which executive action is prevented from exceeding the powers and functions assigned to the executive by law and the interests of the individual are protected accordingly'.[77]

The other justices eschewed the language of the rule of law.

Another principle adopted by Gleeson CJ, and in the joint judgment of Gaudron, McHugh, Gummow, Kirby and Hayne JJ, was the presumption

---

[71] See above n 65, at paras 20–21, 33–6 per Gleeson CJ, at para 76 per Gaudron, McHugh, Gummow, Kirby, Hayne JJ, at para 162 per Callinan J; *Re Minister for Immigration and Multicultural and Indigenous Affairs; Ex parte Applicants S134/2002 Prosecutors* [2003] HCA 1 at para 72 per Gaudron and Kirby JJ.
[72] See above n 65, at para 81 per Gaudron, McHugh, Gummow, Kirby, Hayne JJ.
[73] See above n 65, at para 5.
[74] See above n 65, at para 8, quoting Denning LJ in *R v Medical Appeal Tribunal; Ex parte Gilmore* [1957] 1 QB 574, 586.
[77] See above n 65, at para 31.

that the legislature does not intend to deprive the citizen of the fundamental right of access to the courts unless by express language or necessary implication.[78]

While Gleeson CJ, writing extra-judicially in 2000, equated the rule of law with the principle of legality,[79] in *Plaintiff S157/2002* he ventures into territory which recognises the role of small 'c' constitutionalism in the interpretation of statutes. That step, no doubt intended not to take him beyond the positivist terrain, occurred in a context which went to the very core of the accountability of the executive branch to the judicial branch. Raz's fifth principle (requiring that natural justice be observed), sixth principle (the courts should have review powers over implementation of other principles), and seventh principle (accessibility of the courts) were at stake. The concept of the rule of law appears to be invoked only in relation to the sixth principle. However there is much to support the conclusion that this is a judgment which relies heavily on small 'c' constitutionalism, unlike that of the joint judgment which is timid in its invocation of general principles and doctrine.

A FAIR HEARING

The general approach to the implication of procedural fairness reflected in *Baker*, namely that it is implied when an administrative decision affects the rights, privileges or interests of an individual,[80] is consistent with the approach taken in Australia. The High Court has held that it is now settled that when a statute confers power upon a public official to destroy, defeat or prejudice a person's rights, interests or legitimate expectations, the principles of procedural fairness regulate the exercise of that power unless they are excluded by plain words of necessary intendment.[81] An intention of parliament to exclude procedural fairness cannot be assumed, nor spelled out from indirect references, uncertain inferences or equivocal considerations.[82]

Immigrants seeking a visa apply in writing, and undergo an interview. If the application is refused, they are entitled to an oral hearing in the course of a merits review by either the Migration Review Tribunal or the Refugee Review Tribunal, unless the decision is made on the papers because it is substantially in favour of the immigrant. With one exception, these statutory provisions for a hearing do not exclude procedural fairness,

---

[78] See above n 65, at paras 32, 72.
[79] See text accompanying above n 11.
[80] *Baker v Minister of Citizenship and Immigration* [1999] 2 SCR 817 at para 20.
[81] *Annetts v McCann* (1990) 170 CLR 596 at 598–99; *Ainsworth v Criminal Justice Commission* (1992) 175 CLR 564.
[82] *Commissioner of Police v Tanos* (1958) 98 CLR 383, 396.

which is implied.[83] However, as explained above, absent the decision in *Plaintiff 5157/2002*, the privative clause in the Act apparently ousts judicial review on the ground of procedural fairness.

Baker, in a relaxed way, accepts that the existence of a legitimate expectation affects the content of the duty to give a hearing. In Australia the legitimate expectation developed as a vehicle for expanding the test for implication of procedural fairness. As explained in *Baker,* its practical significance now lies in the kind of hearing which it requires the decision-maker to give, although Australian courts have yet to acknowledge this explicitly. The statement in *Baker* of how legitimate expectations only provide a procedural protection rather than substantive rights,[84] is consistent with the position in Australia. Australian courts have emphasised that a legitimate expectation cannot prevent a decision-maker from changing policy or compel a particular decision in a person's favour.[85]

While promises, regular practices and representations as to procedure generate legitimate expectations, L'Heureux-Dubé J held, delivering the judgment of the court in *Baker*, that in the circumstances of this case ratification of an international convention did not.[86] The Convention on the Rights of the Child did not give rise to a legitimate expectation that Ms Baker would be accorded 'specific procedural rights' beyond the normal rights of procedural fairness, or that a 'positive finding would be made, or particular criteria would be complied with'.[87] Ratification of a convention did not, in this case, amount to a governmental representation about how humanitarian and compassionate applications would be decided. In observing that it was unnecessary to decide whether an international instrument ratified by Canada could, in other circumstances, give rise to a legitimate expectation, L'Heureux–Dubé J left the door open for a case where, unlike *Baker*, a legitimate expectation is generated.

L'Heureux–Dubé J did not refer to *Teoh*, the 1995 decision of the High Court of Australia accepting the very argument which she now rejected. In *Teoh* a majority of the High Court held that Australia's ratification of Article 3.1 of the Convention generated a legitimate expectation on the part of children of a deportee, that the decision-maker would not depart from Article 3.1 without first giving them a hearing. The Court was able to reach that conclusion because it accepted that the entitlement to a hearing on this issue does not afford a substantive protection, and that ratification of a convention does amount to a representation by government as to how it will make administrative decisions. L'Heureux-Dubé J appeared to regard

---

[83] Pursuant to the Migration Act 1958 (Cth) s 501(5) where the Minister cancels a visa on character grounds, procedural fairness is expressly excluded.
[84] See above n 1, at para 26.
[85] *Attorney-General (NSW) v Quin* (1990) 170 CLR 1.
[86] See above n 1, at para 29.
[87] *Ibid*, at para 29.

this kind of approach as one which would afford a substantive protection. This is apparent in a later passage where she summarised her findings as inter alia, that 'the doctrine of legitimate expectations does not mandate a result consistent with the wording of any international instruments'.[88]

Reasonableness Review

None the less L'Heureux-Dubé J reached the same destination as did the High Court in *Teoh*, by a different route, within the framework of the pragmatic and functional approach to judicial review. That approach incorporates consideration of the presence of a privative clause, the expertise of the decision-maker, the purpose of the particular provision and object of the statute as a whole, and the nature of the question. This is a more holistic approach than that in Australia, where review may founder at the outset on a privative clause, and is not subject to any highly developed doctrine of deference.

L'Heureux-Dubé J concluded that given the absence of a privative clause together with other factors, the standard applicable to the particular type of migration decision determining whether the case was an exceptional one for humanitarian and compassionate reasons, was that of reasonableness *simpliciter* rather than patent unreasonableness. Applying that test in the circumstances of the case, the case officer's failure to give serious weight and consideration to the interests of the children constituted an unreasonable exercise of the discretion, notwithstanding the operation of a requirement of deference.[89]

The upshot of the application of reasonableness *simpliciter* was:

> While deference should be given ... the decision cannot stand when the manner in which the decision was made and the approach taken are in conflict with humanitarian and compassionate values.[90]

Instead of answering the certified question in terms of the Convention generating a legitimate expectation that the interests of the children must be a primary consideration when assessing an immigrant's status under the relevant provisions, the question is answered in terms of the children's best interests being considered as important facts and given substantial weight. The net result is a more powerful basis for review than affording protection through the legitimate expectation doctrine. The officer must be 'alert alive and sensitive'[91] to the interests of the children or else the decision fails the

[88] *Ibid*, at para 74.
[89] *Ibid*, at para 65.
[90] *Ibid*, at para 74.
[91] *Ibid*, at para 75.

standard of reasonableness. This resembles a principle of abuse of power in Australia which requires a decision-maker not to apply policy inflexibly but to consider the merits of the case by always being willing to listen to something new.

Focusing however on comparison of *Baker* and *Teoh*, the approach taken by L'Heureux-Dubé J is similar to the view taken by Gaudron J in *Teoh*. While the other justices in the majority held that the decision-maker had a duty to give Teoh a hearing on the issue of departure from the Convention, Gaudron J did not base her decision on the Convention's having generated a legitimate expectation. Without reference to the rule of law, Gaudron J based her conclusion on a broad common law notion of human rights of children as citizens:

> The significance of the Convention, in my view, is that it gives expression to a fundamental human right which is taken for granted by Australian society, in the sense that it is valued and respected here as in other civilised countries. And if there were any doubt whether that were so, ratification would tend to confirm the significance of the right within our society. Given that the Convention gives expression to an important right valued by the Australian community, it is reasonable to speak of an expectation that the Convention would be given effect. However that may not be so in the case of a treaty or convention that is not in harmony with community values and expectations ....[92]

Clearly the positions of Gaudron J and L'Heureux-Dubé J are similar if not identical. L'Heureux-Dubé J held that the case officer's failure to accord proper weight or consideration to the interests of the children is assessed by reference to 'the values underlying the grant of discretion',[93] which were described as follows:

> a reasonable exercise of the power conferred by the section requires close attention to the interests and needs of children. Children's rights, and attention to their interests are central humanitarian and compassionate values in Canadian society. Indications of children's interests as important considerations governing the manner in which H & C powers should be exercised may be found, for example in the purpose of the Act, in international instruments, and in the guidelines for making H & C decisions published by the Minister herself.[94]

Both judges are anti-positivist and allow small 'c' constitutionalism to guide the development of the common law as a brake upon parliamentary sovereignty. Gaudron J finds fundamental common law rights in Australian society, and hence presumably in the common law. So does

---

[92] See *Teoh* above n 10, 304–05.
[93] See above n 1, at para 65.
[94] *Ibid*, at para 67.

L'Heureux-Dubé J, Gaudron J tempers that by saying that ratification of a treaty which gives expression to a fundamental human right which is taken for granted in Australian society confirms the significance of the right, perhaps giving it more force. So does L'Heureux-Dubé J, although she also relies upon the purpose of the statute and relevant policy to support her conclusion that children's rights are central humanitarian and compassionate values in Canadian society.[95] Gaudron J, on the other hand, qualified the relevance of a ratified treaty by discounting the importance of one which is not in harmony with community values and expectations. The noticeable distinguishing factor between the two approaches is that on this occasion Gaudron J does not invoke the rule of law.

None the less, L'Heureux-Dubé J's exposition of each of the three indicators of the importance of children's interests under the Act would not be accepted in Australian administrative law. Even in *Teoh*, Gaudron J was alone in her approach. L'Heureux-Dubé's first indicator is a common law approach to interpretation of the Act by reference to 'a large and liberal interpretation of the values underlying this legislation'.[96] In days long past in Australia this approach might have been called the 'compassionate and humanitarian' approach to the interpretation of migration legislation. It is a feature of what came to be seen as judicial activism of the 1980s. Such an approach is now incompatible with migration legislation whose objects clearly are elimination of ministerial discretion which might be exercised on compassionate or humanitarian grounds, minute control of excessively technical categories and requirements for the grant of visas, procedural complexity in decision-making, and more recently the policy of 'border control'.

In expounding the content of the second indicator, international law, L'Heureux-Dubé J reverted to elevating the importance of international conventions in statutory interpretation, effectively in the same way that *Teoh* does. She relied, inter alia, upon the New Zealand case of *Tavita v Minister of Immigration*[97] for a limited principle of interpretation, namely that human rights play a part in the interpretation for domestic law. Yet, as we have seen, curiously L'Heureux-Dubé J appeared deliberately to avoid citing *Teoh*, where the same principles were summarised.

Iacobucci and Cory JJ dissented in *Baker* with respect to that part of the judgment dealing with the effect of international law on the exercise of ministerial discretion. An international instrument which has not been incorporated into domestic law does not have the role in statutory interpretation which L'Heureux-Dubé J sought to give it. Iacobucci J held that the 'underlying values' of an international convention which has not been incorporated do not have an effect as a principle of statutory interpretation.[98]

---

[95] *Ibid*, at para 67.
[96] *Ibid*, at para 68.
[97] (1994) 2 NZLR 257.
[98] See above n 1, at 79.

Their rejection of 'incorporation by the back door',[99] is similar to that of McHugh J in *Teoh*, although McHugh J dissented in much stronger terms.

L'Heureux-Dubé's third indicator, ministerial guidelines which emphasise humanitarian factors, is one which reflects a very different ministerial policy in each country. Since the 1980s Australian ministerial policies in the migration area have placed more weight on the national interest, say in removing drug offenders from Australia, and satisfaction of technical requirements, than humanitarian or compassionate factors. Indeed the anti-*Teoh* policies issued after *Teoh* provide a very different indicator from that which L'Heureux-Dubé J considered in *Baker*.[100]

L'Heureux-Dubé J's threefold test as to whether the decision-maker gave adequate weight or 'close attention' to various considerations will gain little support in Australian courts. First, the prohibition upon courts trespassing upon the merits operates as a powerful constraint upon judicial review, effectively a traditional common law form of deference. Secondly the test of reasonableness *simpliciter* appears to be equivalent in Australian terms to accepting that international instruments are mandatory relevant considerations which a decision-maker is bound to take into account. That view has been rejected in Australia.[101] International instruments which have not been incorporated into domestic law are not irrelevant considerations which the decision-maker is bound not to take into account. They are not mandatory relevant considerations which the decision-maker is bound to take into account. Whether they are taken into account truly lies within the discretion of the decision-maker. While *Teoh* comes close to saying that international instruments are mandatory relevant considerations, it does not go quite so far. It preserves a distinction between a procedural protection and a substantive protection, the former being achieved by procedural fairness. The latter is achievable by the mandatory relevant considerations requirement in the abuse of power doctrine, but this has not been introduced in relation to international instruments. It is true, however, that in the practical realm of decision-making the distinction is likely to make little difference.

Baker will not influence Australian decisions in relation to legitimate expectations, save that the short rejection by Iacobucci and Cory JJ of legitimate expectations generated by ratification of international instruments will provide further support for those who argue that *Teoh* reflects back-door incorporation. Despite the similarities in the conclusions reached by Gaudron J in *Teoh* and L'Heureux-Dubé J in *Baker*, the judgment of L'Heureux-Dubé J provides no support for *Teoh*. Her embrace of underlying values and the rule of law in the context of migration review can give no

---

[99] *Ibid*, at 80.
[100] M Allars, 'Human Rights, Ukases and Merits Review Tribunals: The Impact of *Teoh's case* on the Administrative Appeals Tribunal in Australia' in M Harris and M Partington (eds), *Administrative Justice in the Twenty First Century* (Oxford, Hart Publishing, 1999) p 337.
[101] See *Kioa* above n 55, 571, 604, 630.

succour to those jurists in Australia who endorse such an approach. The Australian Act and parliamentary sovereignty makes such an approach impossible. Even a differently constituted High Court is unlikely to travel so far into the territory of anti-positivism. The invocation of the rule of law by Gleeson CJ in *Plaintiff S157/2002* occurred in a very different context. The interpretation of the privative clause in that case did not raise questions of trespassing into the merits of the decision under review.

The influence of *Baker* in Australia will be confined to the question whether an appearance of bias on the part of an adviser or other decision-maker in a process can be visited upon the actual decision-maker so as to vitiate the decision. This has not been a prominent issue, but arose for decision by the High Court in *Hot Holdings Pty Ltd v Creasy*.[102] The approach taken in *Baker* to this issue was approved, although it will be relevant to ask whether the officer affected by bias participated in a significant manner in the process.

CONCLUSIONS

So long as the principles applied in judicial review are sourced in common law they are likely to develop in a manner sympathetic to the anti-positivists, allowing more scope for judicial activism. Supplementing the bare boundaries of the empowering statute, the common law mediates to set proper limits upon executive discretion. It does not follow that parliamentary sovereignty is flouted. The common law fills in the gaps left by uncertainty or ambiguity in the expression of legislative will in the statute. The common law may also supply presumptions, for example, that very plain and unambiguous statutory language must be employed in order to displace fundamental common law rights of access to the courts or procedural fairness. To go further and say that the common law may override the statute is to adopt an extreme version of anti-positivism, at the natural law end of the spectrum.

Does the idea of the rule of law contribute to this debate? Raz's first three principles of the rule of law, focusing upon requiring open, prospective and clear legal rules, cannot stand alone, free from substantive commitments. Attempts to identify the meaning of the rule of law demonstrate that the principle of legality cannot operate except with the support of some elements of small 'c' constitutionalism. There is no cocoon of legal rules within which judges may shelter, sustained by nothing more than parliamentary sovereignty. Whether the issue be reasons for decisions, privative clauses or the content of a fair hearing, the extent and manner in which constitutionalism

---

[102] [2002] 193 ALR 90.

may sustain and enrich the principle of legality will remain contested. *Baker* and *Teoh* illustrate the very different routes taken by appellate courts in Canada and Australia to reach similar conclusions, with *Teoh* placing greater emphasis upon the principle of legality.

Substantive rules, drawn from small 'c' constitutionalism, inevitably intrude upon formal and procedural conceptions of the rule of law. It does not follow that conceptions of the rule of law should be abandoned. Analysis of the constitutional role of the common law in relation to all the principles identified by Raz provides a valuable basis for development of the proper approach of courts to review of the executive branch within a particular legal tradition.

The High Court's decision in *Plaintiff S157/2002* disposed of an approach to interpretation of a privative clause, adopted in *NAAV*, which had severely truncated the scope of judicial review of migration decisions in Australia, allowing parliamentary sovereignty to operate virtually untrammelled by constitutionalism. That was a new development, making Australian administrative law unrecognisable to jurists in other common law countries. However neither the result in *Plaintiff S157/2002*, nor the Chief Justice's references to the rule of law in that case, can be taken to indicate that small 'c' constitutionalism is commencing a new ascendancy. The constitutional contribution of the common law to the principles of the rule of law remains vulnerable.

13

Judicial Review, Intensity and Deference in EU Law

PAUL CRAIG

THERE IS A very considerable volume of EU case law dealing with review of both Community and Member State action. It is therefore not surprising that this jurisprudence raises many of the issues concerning the relationship between courts, legislature and executive that have been explored in the other chapters of this book. The present discussion will pick up some of these central themes and consider how they have been dealt with by the Community courts. Particular attention will be given to the way in which the Community courts vary the intensity of review within different contexts, and the way in which this casts light on the degree of deference/respect that courts ought to afford to other branches of government when reviewing their action.

THE STRUCTURE OF EU JUDICIAL REVIEW

Applicants can seek judicial review of Community action either directly or indirectly. These will be considered in turn.

The direct action for judicial review is based on Article 230 EC (ex Article 173). This provides the substantive criteria for review and also delineates the rules of standing that apply in the context of direct actions:

> The Court of Justice shall review the legality of Acts adopted jointly by the European Parliament and the Council, of Acts of the Council, of the Commission, and of the ECB other than recommendations and opinions, and Acts of the European Parliament intended to produce legal effects *vis-à-vis* third parties.
>
> It shall for this purpose have jurisdiction in actions brought by a Member State, the European Parliament, the Council or the Commission on the grounds of lack of competence, infringement of an essential procedural requirement, infringement of this Treaty or of any rule of law relating to its application, or misuse of powers.

> The Court shall have jurisdiction under the same conditions in actions brought by the Court of Auditors and by the ECB for the purpose of protecting their prerogatives.
>
> Any natural or legal person may, under the same conditions, institute proceedings against a decision addressed to that person or against a decision which, although in the form of a regulation or decision addressed to another person, is of direct and individual concern to the former.
>
> The proceedings provided for in this Article shall be instituted within two months of the publication of the measure, or of its notification to the plaintiff, or, in the absence thereof, of the day on which it came to the knowledge of the latter, as the case may be.

Indirect challenge to the legality of Community action is through Article 234 EC (ex Article 177). This Article establishes a mechanism whereby a national court can seek a preliminary ruling on a point of Community law where that is necessary for the resolution of the case. Article 234 reads as follows:

> The Court of Justice shall have jurisdiction to give preliminary rulings concerning:
>
> (a) the interpretation of the Treaty;
> (b) the validity and interpretation of Acts of the institutions of the Community and of the ECB;
> (c) the interpretation of the statutes of bodies established by an Act of the Council, where those statutes so provide.
>
> Where such a question is raised before any court or tribunal of a Member State, that court or tribunal may, if it considers that a decision on the question is necessary to enable it to give judgment, request the Court of Justice to give a ruling thereon.
>
> Where any such question is raised in a case pending before a court or tribunal of a Member State, against whose decision there is no judicial remedy under national law, that court or tribunal shall bring the matter before the Court of Justice.

It is for the national court to decide whether to seek a preliminary ruling, and in that sense, Article 234 creates a reference system, not an appellate one. The individual has no right to take the case to the ECJ from the national court, should the latter refuse to make a reference. Preliminary rulings are important as a method of indirect challenge to the legality of Community action. Article 234(1)(b) allows national courts to refer to the ECJ questions concerning the 'validity and interpretation of Acts of the institutions of the Community'. This provision has assumed an increased importance for private applicants because of the Court's narrow construction of the standing criteria under Article 230.[1] This has meant that a reference

---

[1] P Craig and G de Búrca *EU Law, Text, Cases and Materials* 3rd edn (Oxford, Oxford University Press, 2002) ch 12.

under Article 234 is often the only mechanism whereby such parties may contest the legality of Community norms. It may be helpful to set out a paradigm case in order to understand how Article 234 is used in this context. A common situation is of a Common Agricultural Policy (CAP) regulation, which cannot be contested under Article 230, either because the applicant lacks standing, or because of the time limit. The regulations will normally be applied at national level by a national intervention agency. A regulation may, for example, require in certain circumstances the forfeiture of a deposit that has been given by a trader. The trader believes that this forfeiture and the regulation are contrary to Community law, because it is disproportionate, or discriminatory. If the security is forfeited the trader may then institute judicial review proceedings in the national court, claiming that the regulation is invalid.[2] It will be for the national court to decide whether to refer the matter to the ECJ under Article 234(1)(b). An alternative way in which the action can arise is where there is a regulation, under which a trader is liable to pay a levy, which it believes to be in breach of EU law. The trader might decide to resist payment, be sued by the national agency, and then raise the alleged invalidity of the regulation on which the demand is based by way of defence. It would then be for the national court to decide whether to refer the matter to the ECJ.

THE SOURCES OF EU ADMINISTRATIVE LAW

The sources of the principles of judicial review applied by the ECJ and the CFI are eclectic. They are derived from the Treaty, Community legislation, the jurisprudence of the Community courts and soft law. These will be considered in turn.

The *EC Treaty* contains certain Articles that deal with principles, both procedural and substantive, that are directly relevant for judicial review. Thus, for example, Article 253 EC (ex Article 190) establishes a duty to give reasons that applies to regulations, decisions, and directives adopted either by the Council, Commission, and Parliament, or by the Council and Commission alone. It is noteworthy that Article 253 imposes a duty to give reasons not only for administrative decisions, but also for legislative norms, such as regulations or directives. Article 255 EC deals with access to information. It provides that any citizen of the Union, and any natural or legal person residing or having their registered office in a Member State, shall have a right of access to European Parliament, Council and Commission documents, subject to certain principles and conditions. Non-discrimination provides an example of a substantive principle within the Treaty that is of direct relevance for judicial review. Thus Article 12 (ex Article 6) contains a

---

[2] See, eg, Case 181/84 *R v Intervention Board for Agricultural Produce, ex parte E D & F Man (Sugar) Ltd* [1985] ECR 2889.

general proscription of discrimination on the grounds of nationality, and this same proscription is to be found in the specific Treaty articles dealing with free movement of workers, freedom of establishment and the provision of services. Non-discrimination on the grounds of gender is dealt with by Articles 137 and 141 EC (ex Articles 118 and 119). There are also provisions dealing with non-discrimination as between producers or consumers in the field of agriculture, Article 34(2) (ex Article 40(3), and specific provisions such as Article 90 (ex Article 95), prohibiting discriminatory taxation.

Community legislation made pursuant to the Treaty may also deal with the principles of judicial review. This legislation may flesh out a principle contained in a Treaty article. This was the case in relation to the legislation adopted pursuant to Article 255 EC, dealing with access to information.[3] Community legislation may also establish what is in effect a code of administrative procedure that is to apply in a particular area, as exemplified in the context of EC competition policy.

It has, however, been the *Community courts* that have made the major contribution to the development of a set of administrative law principles that are to govern the legality of Community decision-making. The ECJ and the CFI have read principles such as proportionality, fundamental rights, legal certainty, legitimate expectations, equality and procedural justice into the Treaty, and used them as the foundation for judicial review, under Articles 230 or 234. It is important at this juncture to understand in juridical terms how these principles were read into the Treaty. The ECJ used the 'window' of Article 230(2). This sets out, in general terms, the grounds of judicial review. The administrative law principles adumbrated above were read into the Treaty more specifically through the provision in Article 230(2) that allows for review on the ground of infringement of any rule of law relating to the application of the Treaty. This open textured provision allowed the Community courts to fashion a detailed administrative law jurisprudence that it had lacked hitherto. In developing these principles the Community courts drew upon administrative law doctrine from the Member States. The ECJ and CFI did not systematically trawl through the legal systems of each of the Member States in order to find principles that they had in common, which could then be transferred to the Community context. Their approach was, rather, to consider principles found in the major legal systems of the Member States, to use those that were felt to be best developed and to fashion them to suit the Community's own needs. German law was perhaps the most influential in this regard. It was German jurisprudence on, for example, proportionality and legitimate expectations that was of principal significance for the development of Community law in these areas.

---

[3] S Peers 'The New Regulation on Access to Documents: A Critical Analysis' (2002) 21 *Yearbook of European Law*.

Judicial Review, Intensity and Deference in EU Law

It should also be recognised that *soft law* has played a role in the evolution of the principles of Community administrative law. This is exemplified by Inter-Institutional Agreements, which are agreements between the Council, Commission and the Parliament. Such agreements have been made on topics of constitutional significance such as subsidiarity, transparency and participation rights.

JUDICIAL REVIEW, INTENSITY AND DEFERENCE

There is considerable evidence of the ECJ and the CFI applying the principles of judicial review with varying degrees of intensity, and according varying degrees of deference to the initial decision-maker. The discussion within this section will focus on this in relation to a number of areas.

1. Intensity of Review and Jurisdictional Conditions

A reader will look in vain for any 'heading' in a book on EU law dealing with the administrative law category commonly known as jurisdictional error. The reality is that the substantive issue underlying this 'heading' gives rise to disputes in EU law, in much the same way that it does in domestic law. The initial decision-maker, which will normally be the Commission, will be accorded power to do certain things on certain conditions. The conditional grant of power may be contained in a Treaty article, or in Community legislation, but this makes no difference for the point at issue. A claimant will contend that the Commission has committed an error in the interpretation of the conditions that establish its jurisdiction over the relevant topic. It will then be for the Community courts to decide on the existence of this error, and it will be for the Community courts to decide on the appropriate test for review to be employed in such circumstances. There is, as is well known, a range of possibilities concerning the test for review. Courts may apply a correctness test, whereby they substitute judgment on the meaning of the contested term. They can alternatively apply a less intrusive test, framed in terms of rationality, and only overturn the contested decision if it fails to meet this criterion. There is, in EU law, no case equivalent to *Chevron*[4] in the USA, in which the ECJ has articulated a general approach to problems of this kind. A reading of the case law makes it clear none the less that the ECJ has in fact adopted a variable test for review when dealing with cases of this kind.

---

[4] *Chevron USA Inc v NRDC* 467 US 837 (1984).

In some situations it will simply substitute judgment on the matter at hand, specifying the interpretation that the contested words must have, and striking down the measure if it fails to accord with that interpretation.

In other situations the ECJ has, however, adopted a test for review that is in substantive terms equivalent to rationality scrutiny. It has moreover done so for the same type of reasons that have influenced national courts in this respect. The nature of the subject matter, the relative expertise of the initial decision-maker and the specificity of the jurisdictional condition have been of particular importance in this respect. This can be exemplified by the case-law on state aids, and the Common Agricultural Policy (CAP).

The basic principle is that *state aid* is contrary to EU law, since it distorts the ideal of a level playing field between competitors in different Member States. The Commission is, however, afforded power to authorise state aid in certain circumstances laid down in the Treaty. Thus Article 87(3)(a) (ex 92(3)(a)) provides that 'aid to promote the economic development of areas where the standard of living is abnormally low or where there is serious under-employment' may be considered to be compatible with the common market. The meaning of this provision came before the ECJ in the *Philip Morris Holland* case.[5] The Dutch Government gave aid to a tobacco manufacturer. The Commission found that the aid did not come within Article 87(3)(a), and this was challenged by the applicant. It argued, inter alia, that the Commission was wrong to hold that the standard of living in the relevant area was not 'abnormally low', and was wrong to conclude that the area did not suffer serious 'under employment' within the meaning of Article 87(3)(a). The ECJ rejected the argument. It held that in the assessment of what was a jurisdictional condition the Commission had a discretion, the exercise of which involved economic and social assessments that had to be made in a Community context.[6] The Commission had advanced good reasons for assessing the standard of living and serious under-employment in the relevant area, not with reference to the national average in the Netherlands but in relation to the Community level.

The same judicial approach is evident in other decisions concerning state aids, made pursuant to Article 87(3)(c). This provides that 'aid to facilitate the development of certain economic activities or of certain economic areas, where such aid does not adversely affect trading conditions to an extent contrary to the common interest' may be compatible with the common market. This Article is the provision through which a State can seek to justify aid to a particular depressed region as judged by national criteria. This nationally based criterion is not, however, unqualified. It is still necessary to consider the impact of the aid on inter-Community trade, and its sectoral repercussions at Community level. The meaning of this Article is considered

---

[5] Case 730/79 *Philip Morris Holland BV v Commission* [1980] ECR 2671.
[6] *Ibid*, para 24.

in the *Glaverbel* case.⁷ The Belgian Government gave aid to certain glass producers. The Commission found that the aid did not come within Article 87(3). This was because the aid, which was for periodic plant renovation, did not satisfy the requirement that there must be economic development of the relevant sector, without this adversely affecting trading conditions to an extent contrary to the common interest. The applicant argued that the Commission had misinterpreted the Treaty Article. The ECJ rejected the claim. It held that the Commission's reasoning was comprehensible, and that the Commission should be accorded a power of appraisal when applying the criteria in Article 87(3)(c). The applicant had not shown that the Commission had misused its powers or committed a manifest error, and hence the claim was dismissed.

The ECJ has also undertaken less intensive review of jurisdictional conditions in other areas, such as the *Common Agricultural Policy (CAP)*. The Community regulations or decisions often contain terms that premise Community action on the existence of 'serious disturbances' on the relevant market, or where 'economic difficulties' might be caused by a change in prices or currency values. The Court could undertake an extensive re-evaluation of the factual and legal issues, in order to determine whether such circumstances existed. This would, however, be time-consuming. It would encourage applicants to ask the Court to second-guess evaluations made by the Community institutions. It would moreover involve intensive review of measures that are often adopted under severe time constraints, or in situations where there is an urgent need for measures to combat a temporary problem in the market.⁸ The ECJ's predominant approach has, therefore, not been one of complete substitution of judgment, or of a complete rehearing of issues of fact or mixed fact and law. This is exemplified by *CNTA*.⁹ The applicant complained of the withdrawal of monetary compensatory amounts (MCAS). These could be given to compensate for exchange-rate movements, in circumstances where those movements might otherwise disturb trade in agricultural products. The Court held that the Commission possessed a large degree of discretion in determining whether alterations in monetary values as a result of exchange-rate movements might lead to such disturbances in trade and, therefore, whether MCAS were warranted. The Court also held that the Commission could properly take account of broader economic factors, and was not confined to considering only monetary values. The same approach is apparent in the *Deuka* case.¹⁰ The applicant

---

⁷ Cases 62 and 72/87 *Executif Régional Wallon and Glaverbel SA v Commission* [1988] ECR 1573.
⁸ Lord Mackenzie Stuart *The European Communities and the Rule of Law* (1977) pp 91, 96.
⁹ Case 74/74, *CNTA SA v Commission* [1975] ECR 533.
¹⁰ Case 78/74 *Deuka, Deutsche Kraftfutter GmbH, BJ Stolp v Einfuhr-und Vorratsstelle für Getreide und Futtermittel* [1975] ECR 421, 432. See also Case 57/72 *Westzucker GmbH v Einfuhr-und Vorratsstelle für Zucker* [1973] ECR 321; Case 98/78 *Firma A Racke v Hauptzollamt Mainz* [1979] ECR 69.

sought to test the legality of a particular regulation under which premiums payable on wheat were modified. It was argued that this was illegal, on the ground that the basic regulation on these matters only permitted adjustments 'where the balance of the market in cereals is likely to be disturbed'. The Court rejected the claim. It stated that the Commission had a 'significant freedom of evaluation' in deciding on both the existence of a disturbance, and the method of dealing with it. The ECJ would only intervene if there were a patent error or a misuse of power.[11]

2. Intensity of Review and Proportionality

The relative intensity of judicial review is also apparent in the jurisprudence on proportionality. It is a general principle of Community law, which has been brought into the Community legal order in the manner explicated above. The principle is also enshrined in Article 5 EC, which provides that action by the Community shall not go beyond what is necessary to achieve the objectives of the Treaty, and its requirements are further fleshed out in a protocol to the Treaty. Proportionality can be used to challenge Community action, and the legality of state action that falls within the sphere of application of Community law. The proportionality inquiry will normally require the court to decide whether the measure was suitable to achieve the desired end; whether it was necessary to achieve the desired end; and whether the measure imposed a burden on the individual that was excessive in relation to the objective sought to be achieved, (proportionality *stricto sensu*). The ECJ may articulate and apply all three steps of the inquiry. It will not do so where the case can be resolved at one of the earlier stages. Moreover, in some cases the ECJ may distinguish stages two and three of the inquiry, in others it may in effect 'fold' stage three of the inquiry back into stage two.

The ECJ will decide how intensively to apply the proportionality test. As de Búrca states,

> the way the proportionality principle is applied by the Court of Justice covers a spectrum ranging from a very deferential approach, to quite a rigorous and searching examination of the justification for a measure which has been challenged.[12]

The courts express this deference through a number of juridical devices.[13]

> The ways in which a court may defer in such circumstances range from deeming the measure to be non-justiciable, to refusing to look closely at the

---

[11] *Ibid*, 432.
[12] See G de Búrca 'The Principle of Proportionality and its Application in EC Law' (1993) 13 *Yearbook of European Law* 105, 111.
[13] *Ibid*, p 112.

justification for the restrictive effects of the measure, to placing the onus of proof on the challenger who is claiming that the measure is disproportionate. Courts tend to be deferential in their review in cases which highlight the non-representative nature of the judiciary, the limited evidentiary and procedural processes of adjudication, and the difficulty of providing a defined individual remedy in contexts which involve complex political and economic policies.

Three broad types of case can be distinguished, and the intensity of proportionality review differs in these types of case.

There are cases concerning rights, which prompt the most intensive scrutiny. In *Hauer*[14] the applicant challenged a Community regulation that placed limitations on the planting of new vines. The Court found that this did not, in itself, constitute an invalid restriction on property rights. It then considered whether the planting restrictions were disproportionate, 'impinging upon the very substance of the right to property'.[15] The Court found that they were not, but it did carefully examine the purpose of the general scheme within which the contested regulation fell. The objects of this scheme were to attain a balanced wine market, with fair prices for consumers and a fair return for producers; the eradication of surpluses; and an improvement in the quality of wine. The disputed regulation, which prohibited new plantings, was part of this overall plan. It was not disproportionate in the light of the legitimate, general Community policy for this area. This policy was designed to deal with an immediate problem of surpluses, while at the same time laying the foundation for more permanent measures to facilitate a balanced wine market. In *Hautala*[16] an MEP sought access to a Council document concerning arms exports. The Council refused to grant access, on the ground that this could be harmful to the EU's relations with third countries, and sought to justify this under Article 4(1) of Decision 93/731,[17] governing access to Council documentation. The ECJ held that the right of access to documents was to be broadly construed so as to include access to information contained in the document, not just the document itself. The principle of proportionality required the Council to consider partial access to a document that contained information the disclosure of which could endanger one of the interests protected by Article 4(1). Proportionality also required that derogation from the right of access be limited to what was appropriate and necessary for achieving the aim in view.

There are cases where the attack is on the penalty imposed—the claim being that it is excessive. The Community courts are reasonably searching

---

[14] Case 44/79 *Hauer v Land Rheinland-Pfalz* [1979] ECR 3727.
[15] *Ibid*, para 23.
[16] Case C-353/99P *Council v Hautala*, 6 December 2001.
[17] [1993] OJ L340/43.

in this type of case too, since they can normally strike down a particular penalty without thereby undermining the entirety of the administrative policy with which it is connected. In *Man (Sugar)*[18] the applicant was required to give a security deposit to the Board when seeking a licence to export sugar outside the Community. The applicant was then late, but only by four hours, in completing the relevant paperwork. The Board, acting pursuant to a Community regulation, declared the entire deposit of £1,670,370 to be forfeit. The Court held that the automatic forfeiture of the entire deposit in the event of any failure to fulfil the time requirement was too drastic, given the function performed by the system of export licences. In addition to cases dealing with penalties *stricto sensu* the Court has applied proportionality in the field of economic regulation, scrutinising the level of charges imposed by the Community institutions.[19] Complaints about the burden imposed by a Community norm have given rise to many cases. Thus in *Portugal v Commission*,[20] Portugal argued that an export ban on meat products, imposed in response to mad cow disease, was disproportionate. This was because Portugal was not a significant meat exporter, and it was therefore easier to regulate low-volume exports as compared to the large volume exports from the UK. The ECJ rejected the argument. Beef exports from the UK had not been allowed until the UK had put in place export arrangements of a kind advocated by a certain health code. This had not been done at the time when the ban was imposed on Portugal.

The third type of case is where the individual argues that the policy choice made by the administration is disproportionate, because, for example, the costs are excessive in relation to the benefits, or because the measure is not suitable or necessary to achieve the end in view. The Community courts will often be more circumspect in this type of case, especially where the contested measure relates to social and economic regulatory policy.[21] Proportionality still applies in such instances, but the judicial tendency is only to overturn the policy choice if it is clearly or manifestly disproportionate. This is exemplified by the *Fedesa* case.[22] The applicants were manufacturers and distributors of veterinary medicine who challenged the validity of a national legislative measure implementing a Directive that prohibited the use in livestock farming of certain hormonal substances. They argued that the Directive infringed, inter alia, the principle of proportionality.

---

[18] Case 181/84 *R v Intervention Board, ex parte E D & F Man (Sugar) Ltd* [1985] ECR 2889.
[19] Case 114/76 *Bela-Mühle Josef Bergman KG v Grows-Farm GmbH & Co KG* [1977] ECR 1211.
[20] Case C-365/99, [2001] ECR I-5645.
[21] C Vajda 'Some Aspects of Judicial Review within the Common Agricultural Policy—Part II' (1979) 4 *ELRev* 341, 347–48; T Tridimas *The General Principles of EC Law* (Oxford, Oxford University Press, 1999), ch 3.
[22] Case C-331/88 *R v Minister for Agriculture, Fisheries and Food, ex parte Fedesa* [1990] ECR 4023.

The applicants contended, more specifically, that the prohibition on the hormones was inappropriate to attain the declared objectives, since it would be impossible to apply in practice and would lead to the creation of a dangerous black market. They argued further that the prohibition was not necessary, because consumer anxieties could be allayed by the dissemination of information and advice. In relation to the third part of the proportionality inquiry, the applicants contended that the prohibition entailed excessive disadvantages to the concerned traders, who would suffer considerable financial loss, and that this outweighed the alleged benefits to the general interest.

The Court acknowledged that proportionality was one of the general principles of Community law. The lawfulness of the prohibition of an economic activity was therefore subject to the condition that the prohibitory measures were appropriate and necessary in order to achieve the objectives legitimately pursued by the legislation. When there was a choice between several appropriate measures recourse must be had to the least onerous, and the disadvantages caused must not be disproportionate to the aims pursued. The ECJ then continued in the following vein:[23]

> However, with regard to judicial review of compliance with those conditions it must be stated that in matters concerning the common agricultural policy the Community legislature has a discretionary power which corresponds to the political responsibilities given to it by the Treaty. Consequently, the legality of a measure adopted in that sphere can be affected only if the measure is manifestly inappropriate having regard to the objective which the competent institution is seeking to pursue.

The applicants had therefore to show that the measure was manifestly inappropriate and the Court concluded that they had not discharged this burden.[24] The prohibition, even though it might have caused financial loss to some traders, could not be regarded as manifestly inappropriate.

A similar judicial reluctance to engage in intensive review is also apparent in other areas in which the Commission is possessed of discretionary power requiring it to make complex evaluative choices, as in the case of state aids,[25] dumping[26] and safeguard measures.[27]

---

[23] *Ibid*, para 14.
[24] See also Case C–8/89 *Vincenzo Zardi v Consorzio Agrario Provinciale di Ferrara* [1990] ECR I–2515, 2532–33; Case T–30/99 *Bocchi Food Trade International GmbH v Commission* [2001] ECR II–943, para 92.
[25] Case T–380/94 *AIUFFASS v Commission* [1996] ECR II–2169; Case T–358/94 *Compagnie Nationale Air France v Commission* [1996] ECR II–2109.
[26] Case T–118/96 *Thai Bicycle Industry Co Ltd v Council* [1998] ECR II–2991.
[27] Case C–390/95P *Antillean Rice Mills NV v Commission* [1999] ECR I–769, para 48.

3. Intensity of Review of Member State Action

The discussion thus far has been concerned with the intensity of review of Community action. The ECJ can also review the legality of Member State action in areas covered by Community law. The normal way this arises is as follows. The Community has competence in many areas. The four freedoms are, however, central to the Community ideal of creating a single market. These are free movement of goods, workers, capital and freedom of establishment and the provision of services. The structure of the relevant Treaty provisions in these areas is largely the same. There will be a proscription of discrimination on the grounds of nationality, a power to make more detailed norms where necessary and a provision enabling the Member State to exclude goods, workers etc on grounds such as public policy, public health and the like. The paradigm case that comes before the ECJ is one in which the Member State has acted in violation of the provisions on free movement and then seeks to justify its action, by arguing that it was necessary on grounds of public health, safety etc. These cases come to the ECJ from the national courts via Article 234. It will be for the ECJ to decide whether the Member State's action comes within one of the allowable exceptions, and whether it was proportionate. In these cases the Court tends to engage in fairly intensive review, in order to determine whether the restriction which the Member State has imposed on an important right granted by the Treaties really is necessary or warranted.

Thus the ECJ has insisted that derogation from the principle of free movement of workers can only be sanctioned in cases which pose a genuine and serious threat to public policy, and even then the measure must be the least restrictive possible in the circumstances.[28] The same principle is evident in cases on freedom to provide services. In *Van Binsbergen*[29] the Court held that residence requirements limiting this freedom might be justified, but only where they were strictly necessary to prevent the evasion, by those outside the territory, of professional rules applicable to the activity in question. In *Canal*[30] the ECJ considered the legality of national legislation requiring operators of certain television services to register details of their equipment in a national register. It held that such a measure could not satisfy the necessity requirement of the proportionality test if the registration requirement duplicated controls that had already been carried out, either in the same state or in another Member State. The same approach is applied to cases

---

[28] Case 36/75 *Rutili v Ministre de l'Intérieur* [1975] ECR 1219; Case 30/77 *R v Bouchereau* [1977] ECR 1999.
[29] Case 33/74 *Van Binsbergen v Bestuur van de Bedrijfsvereniging Metaalnijverheid* [1974] ECR 1299; Case 39/75 *Coenen v Social Economische Raad* [1975] ECR 1547.
[30] Case C-390/99 *Canal Satelite Digital SL v Aministacion General del Estado and Distribuidora de Television Gigital SA (DTS)*, 22 January 2002.

concerned with the free movement of goods. Thus in *Cassis de Dijon*[31] the Court decided that a German rule which prescribed the minimum alcohol content for a certain alcoholic beverage could constitute an impediment to the free movement of goods. The Court then considered whether the rule was necessary in order to protect consumers from being misled. It rejected the defence, because the interests of consumers could be safeguarded in other, less restrictive ways, by displaying the alcohol content on the packaging of the drinks.

4. Intensity of Review and Rights

The significance of rights for judicial review has been touched on in the previous discussion concerning proportionality. Many of the contributions to this volume have addressed in detail the relationship between rights, deference and judicial review within national legal systems, especially Canada and the UK. It is therefore appropriate to consider this issue in more detail in the context of the EU.

(a) The Development of Fundamental Rights in the EU: The Judicial Contribution

It is important to begin by making clear the origins of fundamental rights in the EU.[32] This story is well-known and therefore only the bare outlines will be related here.[33]

---

[31] Case 120/78 *Rewe Zentrale v Bundesmonopolverwaltung für Branntwein* [1979] ECR 649.
[32] A Cassese, A Clapham and J Weiler (eds), *Human Rights and the European Community* (Baden-Baden, Nomos, 1991); N Neuwahl and R Rosas (eds) *The European Union and Human Rights* (The Hague, Martinus Nijhoff Publishers, 1995); P Alston (ed), *The EU and Human Rights* (New York, Oxford University Press, 1999); M Dauses 'The Protection of Fundamental Rights in the Community Legal Order' (1985) 10 *European Law Review* 398; A Clapham 'A Human Rights Policy for the European Community' (1990) 10 *Yearbook of European Law* 309; K Lenaerts 'Fundamental Rights to be Included in a Community Catalogue' (1991) 16 *European Law Review* 367; J Weiler 'Thou Shalt not Oppress a Stranger: On the Judicial Protection of the Human Rights of Non-Community Nationals—a Critique' (1992) *European Journal of International Law* 65; J Coppel and A O'Neill 'The European Court of Justice: Taking Rights Seriously?' (1992) 12 *Legal Studies: The Journal of the Society of Public Teachers of Law* 227; D Phelan 'Right to Life of the Unborn v Promotion of Trade in Services: The European Court of Justice and the Normative Shaping of the European Union' (1992) 55 *Modern Law Review* 670; G de Búrca 'Fundamental Human Rights and the Reach of EC law' (1993) 13 *Oxford Journal of Legal Studies* 283; P Twomey 'The European Union: Three Pillars without a Human Rights Foundation' in D O'Keeffe and P Twomey (eds), *Legal Issues of the Maastricht Treaty* (London, Chancery Law, 1994) p 121; J Weiler and N Lockhart '"Taking Rights Seriously" Seriously: The European Court and its Fundamental Rights Jurisprudence' (1995) 32 *Common Market Law Review* 51, 579; S O'Leary 'The Relationship between Community Citizenship and the Protection of Fundamental Rights in Community Law' (1995) 32 *Common Market Law Review* 519.
[33] See B de Witte 'The Past and Future Role of the European Court of Justice in the Protection of Human Rights', in P Alston (ed), *The EU and Human Rights*, above n 32, ch 27.

The original Treaties contained no express provisions for the protection of human rights. This may have been a reaction to the failure of the ambitious attempts to found a European Political Community (EPC) in the mid-1950s. The protection of human rights was integral to the EPC. The failure of the EPC convinced advocates of closer integration to scale down their plans. The 1957 EEC Treaty focused on economic integration and contained no mention of human rights. The absence of human rights may also have been because the framers did not realise that the EEC Treaty, with its economic focus, could encroach on traditionally protected fundamental human rights. This was belied by subsequent events. It quickly became apparent that Community action could affect social and political, as well as economic, issues. The expansion of Community competences attendant upon successive Treaty amendments reinforced this.

It was the ECJ that developed what amounts to an unwritten *charter* of rights. The ECJ's early approach was unreceptive to rights-based claims.[34] In *Stauder* there were none the less indications that fundamental rights would be protected in the Community order by the ECJ.[35] It was however *Internationale Handelsgesselschaft* which secured fundamental rights within the Community legal order.[36] The applicant, a German import–export company, argued that a Community regulation, which required forfeiture of a deposit if goods were not exported within a specified time, was contrary to principles of German constitutional law. The ECJ's response was a mixture of stick and carrot. It forcefully denied that the validity of a Community measure could be judged against principles of national constitutional law. It then held that respect for fundamental rights formed an integral part of the general principles of Community law protected by the ECJ. The ECJ would therefore decide whether the deposit system infringed these fundamental rights. In subsequent case law the ECJ emphasised that it would draw inspiration from the constitutional traditions of the Member States, from international human rights Treaties,[37] and especially from the European Convention on Human Rights (ECHR).[38]

The early case-law was concerned with the compatibility of Community norms with fundamental rights. The ECJ later confirmed that these rights

---

[34] Case 1/58 *Stork v High Authority* [1959] ECR 17; Cases 36, 37, 38 and 40/59, *Geitling v High Authority* [1960] ECR 423; Case 40/64, *Sgarlata and others v Commission* [1965] ECR 215.
[35] Case 29/69 *Stauder v City of Ulm* [1969] ECR 419, para 7.
[36] Case 11/70 *Internationale Handelsgesellschaft v Einfuhr- und Vorratstelle für Getreide und Futtermittel* [1970] ECR 1125.
[37] Case 149/77 *Defrenne v Sabena* [1978] ECR 1365.
[38] Case 4/73 *Nold v Commission* [1974] ECR 491; Case 44/79 *Hauer v Land Rheinland-Pfalz* [1979] ECR 3727.

could be binding on the Member States when they acted within the sphere of Community law. This covered situations where Member States were applying provisions of Community Law which were themselves based on protection for human rights.³⁹ It applied to the many important areas where a Member State acted as agent for the Community in the application of EC law within its own country, *Wachauf*.⁴⁰ The ECJ held further in *ERT* that Member States which sought to derogate from EC law on free movement, by relying on public policy, public health and the like, would be subject to the requirements of fundamental rights when deciding whether the derogation was lawful.⁴¹ The ECJ will not, however, allow fundamental rights to be pleaded against a Member State where there is no real connection with EC law.⁴²

While the ECJ stated repeatedly that it gave particular attention to the ECHR, it held in *Opinion 2/94* that the Community lacked competence under the EC Treaty to accede to the ECHR.⁴³ The ECJ acknowledged that the Community might have an implied as well as an express international Treaty-making competence: an express internal power could generate an implied external power. However there was, said the ECJ, no such express internal power in the field of human rights. Nor could Article 235 (now 308) be used to fill the gap. That Article could not widen the scope of Community powers beyond the general framework created by the provisions of the Treaty as a whole. It could not be used as a basis for the 'adoption of provisions whose effect would, in substance, be to amend the Treaty without following the procedure which it provides for that purpose'.⁴⁴ The ECJ accepted that respect for human rights was a condition for the lawfulness of Community Acts. The Court held, however, that accession to the Convention would entail a substantial change in the existing Community system. The Community would thereby be entering a distinct international institutional system, the provisions of which would have to be integrated into the Community legal order. This could not be done through Article 235, but only through a Treaty amendment.

---

³⁹ Case 222/84 *Johnston v Chief Constable of the Royal Ulster Constabulary* [1986] ECR 1651.
⁴⁰ Case 5/88 *Wachauf v Germany* [1989] ECR 2609; Cases C–74/95 and 129/95 *Criminal Proceedings against X* [1996] ECR I–6609.
⁴¹ Case C–260/89 *Elliniki Radiophonia Tileorassi AE v Dimotiki Etairia Pliroforissis and Sotirios Kouvelas* [1991] ECR I–2925; Case C–368/95 *Vereinigte Familiapress Zeitungsverlags- und vertriebs GmbH v Heinrich Bauer Verlag* [1997] ECR I–3689.
⁴² Case C–144/95 *Maurin* [1996] ECR I–2909; Case C–299/95 *Kremzow v Austria* [1997] ECR I–2629; Case C–309/96 *Annibaldi v Sindaco del Commune di Guidonia and Presidente Regione Lazio* [1997] ECR I–7493.
⁴³ *Opinion 2/94 on Accession by the Community to the ECHR* [1996] ECR I–1759.
⁴⁴ *Ibid*, para 30. Cf *Brunner v European Union Treaty* [1994] 1 CMLR 57, para 99.

(b) The Development of Fundamental Rights in the EU: The Political and Legislative Contribution

It would be mistaken to think that the ECJ made the sole contribution to the evolution of human rights within the Community. The Treaty itself contained certain provisions that would find a place in any modern Bill of Rights. Non-discrimination on the grounds of nationality was secured by Article 12, and also more specifically in the Treaty provisions on free movement. Gender equality was protected by Article 141 and the legislation made thereunder.[45]

The ECJ's approach to fundamental rights was cloaked with legitimacy in a declaration of the three major Community institutions on 5 April 1977.[46] They emphasised the prime importance of fundamental rights, as derived in particular from the constitutions of the Member States and the ECHR, and stated that they would respect them in the exercise of their powers. This was followed by several other non-binding political initiatives. These included a Joint Declaration of the three institutions in 1986; various declarations and resolutions on racism and xenophobia by the European Council;[47] a Declaration of Fundamental Rights and Freedoms by the European Parliament in 1989;[48] a Community Charter of Fundamental Social Rights, signed by 11 of the then 12 Member States in 1989;[49] as well as lofty references in the preamble to the SEA to the ECHR, the European Social Charter and to 'equality and social justice'.

The 'soft law' approach manifested in the preceding declarations was given added 'hard law' force by the TEU. Article 177 EC (ex Article 130u) provided that Community policy in relation to development cooperation 'shall contribute to the general objective of developing and consolidating democracy and the rule of law, and to that of respecting human rights and fundamental freedoms'. Article F(2) of the TEU, which was not at that stage justiciable, provided that the Union would respect the fundamental rights guaranteed by the ECHR and by national constitutional traditions. Respect for human rights and fundamental freedoms was also mentioned in the two other 'pillars' of the TEU.

The Amsterdam Treaty (ToA) made further changes. Article 6 (old Article F) of the TEU was strengthened. It had previously stated that the Union would respect fundamental rights etc. The amended provision

---

[45] C Barnard 'Gender Equality in the EU: A Balance Sheet', in P Alston (ed), *The EU and Human Rights*, above n 32, ch 8.
[46] [1977] OJ C103/1. See generally: K St C Bradley, 'Reflections on the Human Rights Role of the European Parliament, in P Alston (ed) *The EU and Human Rights*, above n 32, ch 26.
[47] See, eg, [1986] OJ C158/1, Bull EC 5–1990, 1.2.247., Bull EC 6–1991, I.45, and Bull EC 12–1991, I.19.
[48] [1989] OJ C120/51.
[49] COM(89)471 Final See Bull EC 12–1989, 2.1.104.

declared that the Union 'is founded on' the principles of liberty, democracy and respect for human rights and fundamental freedoms. This provision was made justiciable. The ECJ has jurisdiction not only under the EC Treaty, but under any provision of the other two pillars over which it has been given jurisdiction (which is primarily pillar three), to review the conduct of the European institutions for compliance with these principles. The new Article 7 enables the Council to suspend certain Member State rights under the TEU, where it has committed serious and persistent breach of the fundamental principles on which the Union is founded. The state's voting rights under the EC Treaty, and other rights may also be suspended by the Council. Following the Treaty of Amsterdam (ToA), respect for these fundamental principles has also been made a condition of application for membership of the European Union. The ToA also added an important new head of legislative competence. Article 13 EC provides that the Community legislature may, within the limits of the Community's powers, take 'appropriate action to combat discrimination based on sex, racial or ethnic origin, religion or belief, disability, age or sexual orientation'.[50] This is not in itself a prohibition on discrimination on grounds of race, disability, sexual orientation etc, but instead enables the Community to adopt measures to combat such discrimination within the scope of the policies and powers otherwise granted in the Treaty.[51]

(c) Rights and Review in the Community Order Prior to the Community Charter of Fundamental Rights

There were a number of concerns about the place of rights in the Community order and the role of the Community courts prior to the adoption of the Community Charter of Rights. The discussion within this section will focus on those concerns that are relevant to the relationship between rights and judicial review.

In structural terms, the relationship between the EC and the ECHR in the sphere of human rights has given rise to much comment. A number of different, albeit connected points, have been made about this relationship. There is concern about the possibility of overlap and potential conflict between the pronouncements of the two courts. This has happened on occasion,[52] although commentators differ as to how seriously they

---

[50] L Flynn 'The Implications of Article 13—After Amsterdam Will Some Forms of Discrimination be More Equal than Others?' (1999) 36 *Common Market Law Review* 1127.
[51] See especially: G de Búrca 'The Role of Equality in European Community Law' in S O'Leary and A Dashwood (eds), *The Principle of Equal Treatment in EC Law* (London, Sweet & Maxwell, 1997).
[52] Above n 1, ch 8; D Spielmann, 'Human Rights Case Law in the Strasbourg and Luxembourg Courts: Conflicts, Inconsistencies and Complementarities', in P Alston (ed) *The EU and Human Rights*, above n 32, ch 23.

regard this problem.⁵³ There is the oft-voiced critique that the Community should be subject to the ECHR system. The ECJ's decision denying that the EC had competence to accede without a Treaty amendment has been subject to critical scrutiny. What appeared to place accession to the ECHR beyond the scope of Community competence, in the ECJ's view, was not the fact that it would entail concluding an agreement for the protection of fundamental rights. It was rather that the agreement would bring fundamental institutional and constitutional changes, which would require a Treaty amendment, rather than merely Community legislation under Articles 308. Analogous arguments did not, however, serve to prevent the ECJ holding that the EC could sign up to the WTO.⁵⁴ For many, the real nub of the issue in relation to the ECHR was that the ECJ did not wish to be subject to a superior court in the form of the European Court of Human Rights.

It has been argued that the ECJ conceives of fundamental rights in terms of general principles, and that it thereby accords them less force than if they had been conceptualised specifically as rights, as they are within Member States.⁵⁵ This critique is misconceived. It elides and confuses the conceptual basis through which the ECJ has read fundamental rights into the Community legal order, with the interpretation of those rights within that order. The window through which fundamental rights were brought into EC law was as general principles of law. This was in accord with Article 230, which lays down the grounds for judicial review, and includes breach of the Treaty or any rule of law relating to its application. Fundamental rights were regarded as one such rule of law, as were principles such as proportionality, legitimate expectations and the like. However, once they were read into the Treaty, the fundamental rights were interpreted in the same general manner as they are in domestic legal orders. The claim that there is some major difference between a 'specific requirements approach', and 'a general formula' is equally suspect. Under the former approach, each provision protecting a particular right will lay down specific requirements in order for the infringement of the right to be legal. Under the latter approach, a court will determine in general terms the weight to be given to the right in the light of other competing principles and in accord with proportionality. It has been shown that the specific requirement approach has proven to be impracticable within some national legal orders, and that in

---

⁵³ F Jacobs and R White *The European Convention on Human Rights* 2nd edn, (Oxford, Oxford University Press, 1996), pp 410–14; P Van Dijk and G Van Hoof *Theory and Practice of the European Convention on Human Rights* 3rd edn, (Netherlands, Kluwer, 1998), pp 18–21, 117.
⁵⁴ J Weiler and S Fries 'A Human Rights Policy for the European Community and Union: The Question of Competences', in P Alston (ed) *The EU and Human Rights*, above n 32, ch 5.
⁵⁵ L Besselink 'Entrapped by the Maximum Standard: On Fundamental Rights, Pluralism and Subsidiarity in the European Union' (1998) 35 *Common Market Law Review* 629, 633–38.

reality the courts adopt a general formula.[56] There is, moreover, scant evidence that the ECJ has ignored the type of specific limitations that attach to rights in regimes such as the ECHR.

A further concern that has been voiced is that the ECJ has not 'taken rights seriously'. It has been argued that the Court has manipulated the language of rights while in reality advancing the commercial goals of EC, that it is biased towards 'market rights' instead of protecting values that are genuinely fundamental to the human condition.[57] This view has been vigorously contested.[58] It is important to distinguish in this respect between challenges to Community action and challenges to Member State action.

It is true that claimants have found it difficult to succeed when challenging the legality of Community norms for violation of fundamental rights. Many such claims were, however, factually weak, and it is doubtful whether they would have been any more successful if brought before a national court. It should also be remembered that a number of such cases concerned the allegation that a property right had been infringed. It is generally accepted that such rights are not absolute and must be subject to qualification in order to enable other regulatory goals to be attained. These other goals will normally have the imprimatur of the Treaty itself, or legislation made pursuant thereto.

It is challenges to Member State action that have provoked the most ire from those critical of the ECJ. The argument that the Court has favoured market rights over more traditional human values requires more careful analysis than that accorded by the critics. The fact that the ECJ might place in the balance some species of market right with a more traditional human value does not mean that the former will outweigh the latter. It is, moreover, mistaken to think of Treaty rights concerning free movement and the like attaching to individuals simply as factors of production. Community aims and freedoms derived initially from a Treaty primarily concerned with economic integration may also have moral and social importance beyond their economic significance.[59]

It should most importantly not be forgotten how cases concerned with Member State action and fundamental rights arise. The paradigm case is that a Member State has been found to be in breach of one of the four freedoms discussed above. The Member State seeks to justify this restriction on grounds of public policy, health, etc. This may then raise issues concerning the compatibility of this defence with a fundamental right such as free speech.

---

[56] See A von Bogdany 'The European Union as a Human Rights Organization? Human Rights and the Core of the European Union' (2000) 37 *Common Market Law Review* 1307, 1330–32.
[57] Coppel and O'Neill, above n 32; Phelan, n 32.
[58] Weiler and Lockhart, above n 32.
[59] G de Búrca, above n 32.

This can be exemplified by the *ERT* case.⁶⁰ ERT was a Greek radio and television company to which the Greek State had granted exclusive rights under statute. ERT sought an injunction from a domestic court against the two respondents, who had set up a television station and had begun to broadcast programmes in defiance of the applicants' exclusive statutory rights. The defence relied mainly on the provisions of Community law relating to the free movement of goods and to the rules on competition and monopolies, as well as on the provisions of the ECHR concerning freedom of expression. The ECJ held that where a Member State relied on defences to justify rules that obstructed the freedom to provide services, such justification had to be interpreted in the light, inter alia, of fundamental rights. This included freedom of expression, as embodied in Article 10 of the ECHR. The same pattern emerged in *Familiapress*.⁶¹ In that case the Member State sought to defend a national rule that impeded the free movement of goods by prohibiting the sale of magazines with competitions for prizes, on the ground that it promoted press diversity. The ECJ held that this justification had to be interpreted in the light of general principles of Community law and fundamental rights, including the freedom of expression of the publisher under Article 10 ECHR.

(d) Rights and Review in the Community Order under the Community Charter of Fundamental Rights

The catalyst for the Charter of Fundamental Rights came from the European Council. In June 1999 the Cologne European Council⁶² decided that there should be a European Union Charter of Fundamental Rights to consolidate the fundamental rights applicable at Union Level and to make their overriding importance and relevance more visible to the citizens of the Union. The Charter was to contain fundamental rights and freedoms, as well as the basic procedural rights guaranteed by the ECHR. It was to embrace the rights derived from the constitutional traditions common to the Member States that had been recognised as general principles of Community law. It was also made clear at the inception that the document should include economic and social rights, as contained in the European Social Charter and the Community Charter of Social Rights of Workers. The institutional structure for the discussions about the Charter was laid down in the Tampere European Council in October 1999.⁶³ It was decided

---

⁶⁰ Case C-260/89 *Elliniki Radiophonia Tileorassi AE v Dimotiki Etairia Pliroforissis and Sotirios Kouvelas* [1991] ECR I-2925.
⁶¹ Case C-368/95 *Vereinigte Familiapress Zeitungsverlags-und Vertriebs-GmbH v Heinrich Bauer Verlag* [1997] ECR I-3689.
⁶² 3–4 June 1999.
⁶³ 15–16 October 1999.

to establish a body called the Convention. It consisted of representatives of the Member States, a member of the Commission, members of the EP, and representatives from national Parliaments. The first meeting took place in December 1999. The Convention was instructed to conclude its work in time for the Nice European Council in December 2000. The discussion in the Convention was therefore conducted in parallel with the Intergovernmental Conference concerning the institutional consequences of enlargement that led to the Nice Treaty. The Charter was approved by the European Council. It was drafted so as to be capable of being legally binding. The precise legal status of the Charter was left undecided in Nice, but it now seems, in the light of the discussion at the Convention on the Future of Europe, that it will be binding as part of a new Constitutional Treaty for the EU.

There is little doubt that the Charter, given legal force within a Constitutional Treaty, will have a profound effect on judicial review within the EU. Many claims will be presented in rights-based terms, in the same manner as occurred in the UK, as a result of the Human Rights Act 1998. This is more especially so, given that the Charter embraces a very broad range of rights, civil, political, social and economic.[64] These rights are defined in differing degrees of detail.

The Community courts will perforce have to decide which rights are enforceable directly. The issue was addressed by Commissioner Vitorino, the Commission representative to the Convention.[65] He distinguished between rights enforceable in the courts and principles that could be relied on against official authorities. The Commissioner argued that rights could be pleaded directly in the courts. Principles, by way of contrast, were mandatory in relation to the authorities that had to comply with them when exercising their powers, and could be used as a basis for censuring their Acts. Private individuals would not, however, be able to bring a legal action to enforce them. This same issue was addressed, albeit indirectly, by the Convention in two explanatory memorandums.[66] Thus health care and access to services of general economic interest were, for example, said to be principles and not rights. This issue was addressed yet again in Working Group II of the Laeken Convention, which considered the issue of rights. It recommended a modification to the Charter, by the inclusion of what would be Article 52(5). This would provide that the provisions of the Charter that contain principles may be implemented by legislative and executive Acts taken by the EU institutions, and by Acts of the Member States when implementing EU law. They are, however, to be judicially cognisable only in

---

[64] *Charter of Fundamental Rights of the European Union* [2000] OJ C364/1.
[65] A Vitorino, *The Charter of Fundamental Rights as a Foundation for the Area of Freedom, Justice and Security* (Centre for European Legal Studies, Exeter Paper in European Law, No 4, 2001), p 25–6.
[66] Charte 4423/00, Convent 46, 31 July 2000, p 24; Charte 4473/00, Convent 49, 11 October 2000, pp 31–2.

the interpretation of such Acts when ruling on their legality.[67] It would be for the ECJ to decide as to which articles fell into the categories of rights and principles. The final version of the draft EU Constitution has modified the original version of the Charter and has embodied the distinction between rights and principles.

The Community courts will also face an increasing number of cases that raise the issue of the appropriate level of deference or respect to accord to the Community legislature, where the legislation is contested for compliance with Charter rights. The EU will not escape the tensions that have been apparent within national legal orders. The way in which those tensions 'play out', and the way in which they are resolved, will however be shaped by the nature of the Community order itself. It should be remembered in this respect that while the list of Charter rights is broad, the areas in which the Community has competence is also very broad. The Treaty contains moreover considerable detail as to how the Community's objectives are to be attained. These features will be bound to have an impact on clashes between Community rights embodied in the Charter and Community legislation made to effectuate detailed Treaty objectives.

---

[67] CONV 354/02, *Final Report of Working Group II*, 22 October 2002, p 8.

14

A Hesitant Embrace: Baker *and the Application of International Law by Canadian Courts*

JUTTA BRUNNÉE & STEPHEN J TOOPE*

INTRODUCTION

TODAY, COURTS APPEAR to recognise the relevance of international norms whether or not they have been implemented through Canadian legislation, and whether or not they are binding on Canada. In *Baker*, the majority of the Supreme Court held that 'the values reflected in international human rights law may help inform the contextual approach to statutory interpretation and judicial review'.[1] Canadian courts, then, are grappling more and more with the 'practical application' of international law. However, for all their declared openness to international law, they are not yet meeting all the challenges that its domestic application poses. We venture to say that our courts are still inclined to avoid deciding cases on the basis of international law. This does not mean that international law is given no effect, or that its broad relevance is denied. The avoidance strategy is more subtle: even when they invoke or refer to international law, Canadian courts generally do not give international norms concrete legal effect in individual cases. Especially following the Supreme

---

* This chapter is a shortened and modified version of 'A Hesitant Embrace: The Application of International Law by Canadian Courts' (2002) 40 *Canadian Yearbook of International Law* 3. The idea for the original paper arose from the participation of Toope in the 2001 conference of the International Association of Women Judges, and of Brunnée and Toope in annual education seminars of the Ontario Court of Appeal, the BC courts and the Federal Court of Canada. We thank the many judges whose probing questions have helped us to clarify our analysis. We also benefited from lively discussions with David Dyzenhaus, Karen Knop and Irit Weiser about various themes explored in this paper. We thank them for their perceptive comments on earlier drafts. We are indebted to Sean Rehaag and Ranjan Agarwal for their excellent research assistance.
[1] *Baker v Canada (Minister of Citizenship and Immigration)* [1999] 2 SCR 817 at para 70 [hereinafter *Baker*].

Court's decision in *Baker*, there appears to be a trend towards treating all of international law, whether custom or treaty, binding on Canada or not, implemented or unimplemented, in the same manner—as relevant and perhaps persuasive, but not as determinative, dare we say obligatory.

Some commentators have read *Baker* as signalling a positive paradigm shift, with the Supreme Court embracing a more nuanced search for persuasive norms, rather than focusing on binary distinctions between binding and non-binding norms.[2] We agree that subtlety is required in the evaluation of sources of legal influence; it would be misleading to see the distinction between binding and non-binding norms as a simple on-off switch. However, we caution against throwing out the entire distinction when discussing the interplay between international and domestic law.

As we will illustrate, within the Canadian legal order the question of the 'bindingness' of international law is closely intertwined with the manner in which it comes to influence the interpretation of domestic law. We will show that, in the case of norms that are binding on Canada under international law, Canadian courts have an obligation to interpret domestic law in conformity with the relevant international norms, as far as this is possible. For domestic administrative lawyers, a more accessible terminology may be that a binding international norm is a 'mandatory relevant factor' in judicial decision making and in the exercise of administrative discretion. By contrast, norms that do not bind Canada internationally (eg soft law, or provisions of treaties not ratified by Canada) can help inform the interpretation of domestic law and, depending on the norm in question and the case at issue, may even be persuasive. Courts may, and in some cases should, draw upon such norms for interpretative purposes, but they are not strictly speaking required to do so. In short, in the domestic application of international law, the distinction between norms that bind Canada under international law and those that do not actually matters because of its implications for the manner in which courts should approach their interpretative tasks.

At least some of the factors that underpin the seemingly new approach of Canadian courts to international law are far more mundane than shifting paradigms, and one should be careful not to read too much into the recent cases. In part, these factors relate to the delicate balancing tasks that courts face in the application of international law.[3] Courts must balance Canada's international commitments, made by the federal government, and

---

[2] K Knop, 'Here and There: International Law in Domestic Courts' (2000) 32 *New York University Journal of International Law and Politics* 501. Knop's argument concerning the importance of persuasive authority builds on the work of HP Glenn, 'Persuasive Authority' (1987) 32 *McGill Law Journal* 261.

[3] See generally: G van Ert, 'Using Treaties in Canadian Courts' (2000) 38 *Canadian Yearbook of International Law* 3 at 4–9.

legislative supremacy over the laws that apply in Canada.[4] Similarly, courts must balance the federal government's authority to bind Canada internationally and provincial legislative jurisdiction. Finally, and not least, courts must carefully delineate their own role in giving domestic effect to international law. Treating international law as persuasive but not mandatory may be one way to manage these multiple balancing acts. International law is brought to bear on a growing range of questions, yet its potential impact is tempered—and we fear largely eviscerated—because it is merely one factor in the application and interpretation of domestic law.[5]

The inclination to temper the effect of international law may also be fed by the unease that many judges continue to feel in identifying applicable international law, particularly customary law, and determining its precise legal effect in Canada. Noting the increased use by counsel of international law in cases before the Supreme Court, Justice LeBel observed:

> Arguments are advanced before us on the basis of a bewildering number of sources, international instruments, declarations, decisions of other tribunals, and too often there is little attempt at defining the kind of law we are dealing with, or, if we are discussing international norms, customs or practice, of actually trying to establish that there is really such a practice.[6]

By treating all international norms, of whatever status and purported effect, as potentially relevant and persuasive, courts avoid the thorny details of the application of international law.

To be sure, the Supreme Court has not explicitly decided that all international law should be given persuasive rather than mandatory effect. Nor, we assume, did it intend for others to pull its decisions in this direction. Yet, the ambiguities in *Baker* and several other of the Supreme Court's recent decisions do provide considerable room for other courts to apply international law in ways that might end up reducing rather than increasing,

---

[4] See, eg, dissent of Justices Iacobucci and Cory in *Baker*, above n 1 at para 80 (noting that the effect of the majority's approach was 'to give force and effect within the domestic legal system to international obligations undertaken by the executive alone that have yet to be subject to the democratic will of Parliament').
[5] See, eg, *Suresh v Canada (Minister of Citizenship and Immigration)* (2002) 208 DLR (4th) 1 at para 46 [hereinafter *Suresh*]. The Supreme Court implies that 'soft' law, unimplemented treaties, custom and even *jus cogens* all simply help 'inform' the interpretation of the *Charter*. For a detailed discussion of this aspect of the Court's decision in *Suresh*, see below nn 101–109 and accompanying text.
[6] Quoted in L Chwialkowska, 'Global law emerging, judge tells conference—Canada struggling to accommodate international treaties and tribunals' *The National Post* (13 April 2002) A6. For a full version of Justice LeBel's comments, see Justice L LeBel and G Chao, 'The Rise of International Law in Canadian Constitutional Litigation: Fugue or Fusion? Recent Developments and Challenges in Internalising International Law' (Fifth Annual Analysis of the Constitutional Decisions of the Supreme Court of Canada, *Osgoode Hall Law School*, 12 April 2002) at 6 [unpublished, on file with authors].

and confusing rather than clarifying, its domestic impact. We are pleased, therefore, that Justice LeBel also stressed the need for more rigour 'in the definition and identification of international rules and the process of internalization'.[7] Indeed, he called upon lawyers and scholars to increase their efforts in this regard.

In this article we take up the challenge. We wholeheartedly agree with Justice LeBel that what is needed most in the growing domestic engagement with international law is greater analytical rigour. However, the challenge is not just one for lawyers and scholars. Courts too must approach international law in a principled and coherent manner, providing clarity as to precisely what effect is accorded to international law in a given case, and why. Indeed, the judicial role is of particular importance because domestic courts influence the development not only of domestic law but of international law as well.[8] Especially in the context of customary international law, domestic courts participate in the continuous weaving of the fabric of international law. It is particularly important that Canadian courts carefully distinguish between the different threads that together make up a strong and resilient cloth. As we will argue, it is not enough to treat *all* normative threads as potentially persuasive but not mandatory—over time this approach risks weakening the fabric of the law. Our concern is that if international law is merely persuasive, it becomes purely optional, and can be ignored at the discretion of the judge.

To establish the context in which the *Baker* case can best be understood, we review the principles that govern the internalisation of international law and the approaches that Canadian courts have taken in this context. Much has been written on these topics over the last five years.[9] Our purpose is not to retrace this literature, but to use it to spotlight the ambiguities and potential contradictions in the judicial treatment of international law to which we have alluded. We will focus on several interrelated questions and distinctions that, we believe, are crucial to the development of a consistent approach to the application of international law in Canada: When is international law directly applicable in Canada? To what extent are the legal

---

[7] *Ibid.*
[8] According to Art 38(1)(d) of the *Statute of the International Court of Justice*, 26 June 1945, Can TS 1945 No 7 (entered into force 24 October 1945) [hereinafter ICJ *Statute*], the decisions of domestic courts are a subsidiary means for the determination of international law.
[9] See van Ert, above n 3. And see E Brandon, 'Does international law mean anything in Canadian Courts?' (2002) 11 *Journal of Environmental Law and Practice* 397; J Brunnée, 'A Long and Winding Road: Bringing International Environmental Law into Canadian Courts' in M Anderson and P Galizzi (eds), *International Environmental Law in National Courts* (London, British Institute of International and Comparative Law, 2002) 45; HM Kindred, 'The Use of Unimplemented Treaties in Canada: Practice and Prospects in the Supreme Court' in C Carmody *et al* (eds), *Trilateral Perspectives on International Legal Issues: Conflict and Coherence* (Washington DC, American Society of International Law, 2003) 3; Knop, above n 2; WA Schabas, 'Twenty-five Years of Public International Law at the Supreme Court of Canada' (2000) 79 *Canadian Bar Review* 174; SJ Toope, 'The Uses of Metaphor: International Law and

effects of international law in Canada dependent upon its domestic implementation? What constitutes implementation? Under what circumstances can international law that is binding *on* Canada have legal effects *in* Canada? Under what circumstances, if any, can international norms that are not binding on Canada, or not legally binding at all, have legal effects in Canada?

THE INTERPLAY OF INTERNATIONAL LAW AND DOMESTIC LAW

International treaties are not directly applicable in Canada but require transformation.[10] Beneath the surface of this straightforward proposition, however, lie an array of twists and turns that make the domestic application of treaties complex territory to navigate. Yet, if the law concerning the interplay of treaties and Canadian domestic law is complex, the law governing the domestic application of international customary law is at best ambiguous. Whereas, in the context of treaty law, it is clear at least that the basic outlook of the Canadian constitutional framework is dualist, our senior courts have never clarified whether customary law is directly applicable in Canada, as most commentators assume,[11] or not.

1. The Application of International Treaties

Canadian courts struggle not only to determine when international norms require implementation through legislation but also to determine whether such implementation has actually occurred.[12] They wrestle as well with the

---

the Supreme Court of Canada' (2001) 80 *Canadian Bar Review* 534; SJ Toope, 'Inside and Out: The Stories of International Law and Domestic Law' (2001) 50 *Universiy of New Brunswick Law Journal* 11[hereinafter 'Inside & Out']; SJ Toope, 'Canada and International Law' (1998) 27 *Canadian Council of International Law Proceedings* 33; G van Ert, *Using International Law in Canadian Courts* (New York, Kluwer Law International, 2002); I Weiser, 'Effect in Domestic Law of International Human Rights Treaties Ratified Without Implementing Legislation' (1998) 27 *Canadian Council of International Law Proceedings* 132; I Weiser, 'Undressing the Window: A Proposal for Making International Human Rights Law Meaningful in the Canadian Commonwealth System' (September 2002; on file with authors) [hereinafter 'Undressing the Window'].

[10] See generally: R St J Macdonald, 'The Relationship between International Law and Domestic Law in Canada' in R St J Macdonald, G Morris and DM Johnston (eds), *Canadian Perspectives on International Law and Organization* (Toronto, University of Toronto Press, 1974) 88.

[11] See, eg: Kindred, above n 9 at 5; Macdonald, *ibid* at 109; Schabas, above n 9 at 182; van Ert, above n 3 at 4. Note that a recent decision of the Superior Court of Ontario states directly that customary international law forms part of the law of Canada. See *Bouzari v Iran* (1 May 2002), Toronto 00–CV–201372 (Ont Sup Ct) at para 39 [hereinafter *Bouzari*].

[12] As we have argued elsewhere, there are many forms of incorporation. See the detailed discussion in J Brunnée and SJ Toope, *A Hesitant Embrace: The Application of International Law by Canadian Courts* (2002) 40 *Canadian Yearbook of International Law* 3.

implications of the common law principle that 'Parliament is not presumed to legislate in breach of a treaty or in a manner inconsistent with the comity of nations and the established rules of international law'.[13] In the case law, it remains unclear when this principle comes into play, and how it relates to the implementation requirement. There is concern that too wide an application of the presumption would undermine the requirement that international treaties must be transformed to apply in Canada.[14] We argue that it is also unclear exactly what effect the presumption accords to international law in Canada's domestic legal system. Is it merely to 'help inform' a contextual approach to statutory interpretation and judicial review,[15] or must courts, to the extent possible, interpret domestic statutes consistently with international law?[16] In this context, does it matter whether the international norm in question is legally binding on Canada or not? Further, does the application of the presumption depend upon whether international law is used to interpret the *Canadian Charter of Rights and Freedoms*[17] or ordinary statute law?

Implemented Treaties

When a treaty has been explicitly transformed into Canadian law, its provisions should be determinative in the interpretation of domestic legislation. As Justice Bastarache observed in *Pushpanathan*, when the purpose of a statute is to implement an international treaty, 'the Court must adopt an interpretation consistent with Canada's obligations under the [treaty]'.[18] More specifically, a court must rely on the treaty to interpret the statute, and on the international rules of treaty interpretation to interpret the treaty and resolve any textual ambiguities.[19] Of course, reliance on the treaty underlying an implementing statute is subject to the prerogative of

---

[13] *Daniels v R*, [1968] SCR 517 at 541. For a recent restatement of the vitality of this doctrine, see *Schreiber v Canada (Attorney General)*, 2002 SCC 62, para 50 [hereinafter *Schreiber*]. See also R Sullivan, *Driedger on the Construction of Statutes*, 3 edn (Markham, Ont, Butterworths, 1994) at 330.

[14] See *Baker*, above n 1 at para 80 (per Iacobucci and Cory JJ). But see D Dyzenhaus, M Hunt and M Taggart, 'The Principle of Legality in Administrative Law: Internationalisation as Constitutionalisation' (2001) 1 *Oxford University Commonwealth Law Journal* 5 (challenging the validity of concerns over the legitimacy of reference to international norms in the judicial review of the exercise of executive authority).

[15] *Baker, ibid.* at para 70.

[16] See eg *National Corn Growers Association v Canada (Import Tribunal)* [1992] 2 SCR 1324 at 1369 [hereinafter *National Corn Growers*]. Note that *National Corn Growers* was concerned with the interpretation of a statute designed to implement an international treaty. However, a similar approach should apply to all statutes, whether implementing legislation or not. See below n 52 and accompanying text.

[17] *Canadian Charter of Rights and Freedoms*, Part I of the *Constitution Act, 1982*, being Sch B to the *Canada Act 1982* (UK), 1982, c 11.

[18] *Pushpanathan v Canada (Minister of Citizenship and Immigration)* [1998] 1 SCR 982 at para 51 [hereinafter *Pushpanathan*].

[19] *Ibid.* For a detailed discussion of the Court's interpretative approach in *Pushpanathan*, see Schabas, above n 9 at 180.

Parliament and provincial legislatures to enact legislation that deviates from Canada's treaty commitments.[20]

In cases where it is uncertain whether, or to what extent, a statute is implementing a treaty, courts can resort to various interpretative presumptions. Notably, since the Supreme Court's decision in *National Corn Growers Association v Canada*,[21] it has become well-established that the treaty text may be relied upon not merely to resolve a patent ambiguity in the domestic legislation. Courts may also draw upon the treaty at the very beginning of their analysis to determine whether the domestic legislation is ambiguous.[22] The focus on ambiguity links this approach back to the above-mentioned presumption of legislative intent to act consistently with Canada's international obligations.[23] Thus, unless the legislators' intent to deviate from international treaty obligations is evident, courts should not only resort to the relevant treaty to identify ambiguities, but must strive to resolve them through an interpretation of the statute that is consistent with international law.[24] The latter presumption has been most widely invoked in *Charter* cases.

In cases where there was no specific legislative transformation but Canadian law is in conformity with a treaty due to prior statutory, common law, or even administrative policy, we suggest that the treaty is also implemented for the purposes of domestic law.[25] We are mindful that courts and academic commentators frequently note that '[i]nternational treaties and conventions are not part of Canadian law unless they have been implemented by statute', as did the majority of the Supreme Court in *Baker*.[26] However, in the foundational *Labour Conventions* case, Lord Atkin observed:

---

[20] See, eg: *Reference re Powers of Ottawa (City) & Rockcliffe Park (Village) to Levy Rates on Foreign Legations and High Commissioners Residences* [1943] SCR 208 at 231 [hereinafter *Re Foreign Legations*]; *Capital Cities Inc v Canada (CRTC)* [1978] SCR 141 at 173 [hereinafter *Capital Cities*].
[21] *National Corn Growers*, above n 16.
[22] The restrictive approach of *Schavernoch v Canada (Foreign Claims Commission)* [1982] 1 SCR 1092 at 1098 (per Estey J); and *Capital Cities*, ibid at 173 (per Laskin CJ) (where only manifest statutory 'ambiguity' would allow reference to an underlying treaty obligation for purposes of interpretation), has not recently been followed, with the Supreme Court moving to the position established in 1984 by the Ontario Court of Appeal. See *R. v Palacios*, (1984) 45 OR (2d) 269 (CA); *National Corn Growers*, above n 16; *Canada (AG) v Ward*, [1993] 2 SCR 689; and *Pushpanathan*, above n 18.
[23] See above n 13.
[24] *Re Arrow River & Tributaries Slide & Boom Co*, [1931] 2 DLR 216 at 217 (Ont SC (App Div)) [hereinafter *Re Arrow River*]. See also M Hunt, *Using Human Rights Law in English Courts* (Oxford, Hart Publishing, 1997) at 40 ('So instead of asking if there is ambiguity which can be resolved with the "assistance" of international law, on this approach the court should ask, having automatically considered the international law alongside the national law, whether the domestic law is unambiguously (in the sense of irreconcilably) in conflict with the international norm'.).
[25] See also Brandon, above n 9 at 401–407.
[26] See eg *Baker*, above n 1 at para 70. And see the majority decision of the Ontario Court of Appeal in *Ahani v Canada (AG)* (2002), 58 OR (3d) 107 at para 31 (CA) [hereinafter *Ahani*] ('Absent implementing legislation, neither [the *ICCPR* nor its *First Optional Protocol*] has any legal effect in Canada'.)

> Within the British Empire there is a well-established rule that the making of a treaty is an executive Act, while the performance of its obligations, *if they entail alteration of the existing domestic law*, requires legislative action .... If the national executive, the government of the day, decide to incur the obligations of a treaty *which involve alteration of law* they have to run the risk of obtaining the assent of Parliament to the necessary statute or statutes.[27]

This latter passage indicates that, traditionally, Canadian law did not categorically require statutory implementation and that the flat assertion that treaties are not part of Canadian law unless they have been implemented *by statute*, is overly restrictive.[28]

Canadian courts have none the less tended towards a much narrower construction of the implementation requirement, effectively equating implementation with statutory implementaion. The recent decision of the Ontario Court of Appeal in *Ahani v Canada (AG)* is an illuminating case in point.[29] *Ahani* was the companion case to *Suresh v Canada*, both decided by the Supreme Court in January 2002.[30] Before the Supreme Court, the central issue in both cases was whether or not Canada was prevented from deporting a person accused of links to terrorist activity if that person was likely to be subject to torture in the receiving state. The Court decided unanimously that deportation to torture remains possible under section 53(1)(b) of the *Immigration Act*, which permits the Minister to deport a refugee deemed a danger to Canadian security.[31] However, the principles of fundamental justice under section 7 of the *Charter* will generally militate against deportation where there is evidence of a substantial risk of torture.[32] In *Suresh*, the Supreme Court found that the appellant was entitled to a new deportation hearing.[33] By contrast, in *Ahani* it held that the facts did not warrant interference with the Government's determination that Ahani faced only a minimal risk of torture if returned to his native Iran.[34] Having exhausted all Canadian remedies and facing deportation, Ahani petitioned the UN Human Rights Committee under the *Optional Protocol* to the *ICCPR*.[35] The Committee requested that Canada stay the deportation order

---

[27] *Canada (AG) v Ontario (AG)*, [1937] AC 326 (PC) at 347 (per Lord Atkin) [hereinafter *Labour Conventions Case*] (emphasis added). See also *Francis v R*, [1956] SCR 618 at 626 [hereinafter *Francis*].
[28] See also JH Currie, *Public International Law* (Toronto, Irwin Law, 2001) at 209, n 33; Kindred, above n 9 at 7, 9; van Ert, above n 3 at 16.
[29] *Ahani*, above n 26 and accompanying text.
[30] *Suresh*, above n 5; *Ahani v Canada (Minister of Citizenship and Immigration)* (2002), 208 DLR (4th) 57 (SCC) [hereinafter *Ahani, SCC*].
[31] *Suresh, ibid* at para 79.
[32] *Ibid* at para 129.
[33] *Ibid* at para 130.
[34] *Ahani, SCC*, above n 30 at para 25–26.
[35] *Optional Protocol to the International Covenant on Civil and Political Rights*, 16 December 1966, Can. TS 1976 No 47 (entered into force 23 March 23 1976) [hereinafter *Optional Protocol*].

until it had considered Ahani's petition. Taking the view that the Committee's interim measures request was non-binding, Canada refused the request.[36] Ahani then applied to the Ontario Superior Court for an injunction restraining his deportation pending the Committee's consideration of his petition. The trial judge denied the stay;[37] the majority of the Court of Appeal declined to overturn that decision.[38]

The majority concluded that, as a matter of treaty law, the access accorded to individuals to the Human Rights Committee by Canada's ratification of the Option Protocol is conditioned by two key points. First, on the terms of the *Optional Protocol*, the Human Rights Committee has no power to bind Canada—even its final determination is merely recommendatory.[39] Secondly, in ratifying the *Optional Protocol*, Canada did not consent to stay domestic proceedings.[40] Thus, the appellant could not be allowed to 'convert a non-binding request in a Protocol, which has never been part of Canadian law, into a binding obligation enforceable in Canada by a Canadian court'.[41] The majority decision is arguably correct in so far as it is based on the non-binding nature of the Committee process. However, to the extent that the decision treats the *ICCPR* and the *Optional Protocol* as unimplemented,[42] on the principles that we outlined above, it is questionable whether the majority was correct. The majority did not consider whether the two treaties might have been implicitly implemented through the *Charter*. Instead, it expounded the narrow view that 'Canada has never incorporated either the Covenant or the Protocol into Canadian law *by implementing legislation*. Absent *implementing legislation*, neither has any legal effect in Canada'.[43]

---

[36] As it has done in previous instances of such requests. See Schabas, above n 9 at 194.
[37] *Ahani v Canada (Minister of Citizenship and Immigration)* (2002), 18 Imm LR (3d) 193 (Ont SCJ).
[38] *Ahani*, above n 26.
[39] *Ibid* at para 31.
[40] *Ibid* at para 32.
[41] *Ibid* at para 33.
[42] Note that, given the focus on the non-binding nature of the *Optional Protocol*'s committee process, it should not have mattered, from a strictly legal standpoint, whether or not the relevant provisions were implemented in Canadian law (unless, of course, Canadian law had provided a right to have deportation orders stayed pending the outcome of the Committee process).
[43] *Ahani*, above n 26 at para 31 (emphasis added). The majority went on to say that a court may none the less rely upon international human rights commitments to interpret s 7 of the *Charter* in way that is consistent with them. See also D Dyzenhaus and E Fox-Decent, 'Rethinking the process/substance distinction: *Baker v Canada*' (2001) 51 *University of Toronto Law Journal* 193 at 232–236. Dyzenhaus and Fox-Decent argue that the insistence on statutory transformation of international obligations would logically have to be matched by an insistence that common rules can only bind if they are transformed into statute law. The justification for the requirement of statutory implementation is typically rooted in supposed considerations of democratic legitimacy, that is in the requirement of majoritarian legislative action. Pointing to this logical connection reveals a fundamental flaw in the 'transformation' requirement.

The dissent by Justice Rosenberg epitomises the lingering dissatisfaction with this conclusion and, perhaps more importantly, with some of the arguments that the Canadian government presented in this case. As we suggested earlier, in international forums Canada routinely argues that it is in compliance with the *ICCPR* because of the *Charter*.[44] Thus, while there was no express incorporation of the treaty, we would argue that it has been implicitly incorporated into Canadian law. The same argument can be made concerning the purely procedural obligations voluntarily accepted by Canada under the *Optional Protocol*. As Justice Rosenberg makes clear, the mere fact that Ahani could ask the Human Rights Committee to review his situation in the light of Canada's obligations under the *ICCPR* does not mean that a substantive remedy would have been available. However, it seems odd for Canada to agree to the procedural right to petition the Committee and then, by declining the Committee's request for a stay of deportation proceedings, effectively to deny it randomly in concrete cases. Has not the procedural right been incorporated into Canadian law by virtue of the Government's regular engagement with the Committee, both in specific cases and in fulfilling reporting obligations? Or is the solemn commitment of the Government nothing more than a discretion unshaped by any legal duties? When, before the Ontario Court of Appeal, the Canadian Government then argued that international conventions are not binding in Canada unless specifically incorporated,[45] one cannot but question the good faith of its position.[46] Indeed, one may also share Justice Rosenberg's frustration with the Government's reliance on the non-binding nature of the Committee process 'to shield the executive from the consequences of its voluntary decision to enter into and therefore be bound by the Covenant and the Protocol'.[47] Thus, although we reiterate that the majority decision on this particular point was correct

---

[44] Human Rights Committee, *Consideration of reports submitted by states under Art 40 of the Covenant: Fourth periodic report of States parties due in 1995: Canada*, UN CCPROR, 1995, UN Doc CCPR/C/103/Add.5, online: Office of the United Nations High Commissioner for Human Rights <http://www.unhchr.ch/tbs/doc.nsf/(Symbol)/ CCPR.C.135.En? Opendocument> (date accessed: 4 July 2002).

[45] See *Ahani*, above n 26 at para 91 (Rosenberg dissent).

[46] See also J Harrington, 'The Year in Review: Developments in International Law and Its Application in Canada' (Presentation to the Canadian Bar Association Conference on Directions in International Law and Practice, Ottawa, 30 March 2002) at 8 [unpublished, on file with authors].

[47] *Ahani*, above n 26 at para 92. Justice Rosenberg specifically noted his dissatisfaction with the government's insistence on the non-binding nature of the Committee process when, on a government website, it asserts that: '[i]t accepts the authority of the UN Human Rights Committee to hear complaints from Canadian citizens under the *Optional Protocol to the International Covenant on Civil and Political Rights*. These undertakings strengthen Canada's reputation as a guarantor of its citizen's rights and enhance our credentials to urge other governments to respect international standards'.

Ibid at para 103, citing Canada, Department of Foreign Affairs and International Trade, 'Human Rights in Canadian Foreign Policy', online: Department of Foreign Affairs and International Trade <http://www.dfait-maeci.gc.ca/foreign_policy/human-rights/forpol-en.asp> (last modified: September 1998). For a similar view, see Harrington, *ibid* at 8–9.

as a matter of law, we have considerable sympathy for Justice Rosenberg's decision to accord to the appellant a procedural right to have a court determine whether 'the balance of convenience favours his remaining in Canada'.[48]

Unimplemented Treaties

There are, of course, cases where treaties that are in force for Canada remain genuinely unimplemented in domestic law. For example, it is conceivable that, due to complex stakeholder debates or federal-provincial disagreements, transformation of a treaty lags behind Canada's international obligations. One can easily imagine this scenario unfolding in the case of the Kyoto Protocol, assuming the protocol enters into force. What is the legal effect of a genuinely unimplemented treaty in Canada?[49]

We submit that a treaty that is binding *on* Canada, while not directly applicable *in* Canada, is none the less subject to the presumption of legislative intent to Act consistently with Canada's international obligations. As we understand this presumption, it applies to all of Canada's international obligations, be they treaty-based or rooted in customary international law.[50] This understanding leads to the inference that courts should make every effort to interpret Canadian law (legislation or the common law) so as to conform to Canada's international obligations.[51] Furthermore, the principle that domestic law should, if possible, be interpreted consistently with Canada's treaty obligations, applies not merely to implementing legislation but to all its domestic law.[52]

Unfortunately, Canadian case law has not taken a consistent approach to the presumption of conformity with international law. First, there is uncertainty regarding the effect that the presumption produces in the

---

[48] Justice Rosenberg would have remitted the case to the Superior Court for determination of whether the applicant would suffer irreparable harm if returned to Iran, and which of the parties would suffer greater harm from the granting of refusal of the remedy pending the outcome of the Committee process. *Ibid* at paras 107–111.

[49] We use the phrase 'genuinely unimplemented treaty' to distinguish this category from the spectrum of situations in which, as we have argued, treaties are implemented, albeit not necessarily through specific statutory transformation.

[50] See above nn 13–17 and 25–28 and accompanying text. As we will suggest below, a different approach should apply to international legal norms that do not bind Canada or to international soft law. See below nn 113–114 and accompanying text. For a detailed discussion of the presumption in the context of the use of human rights law by English courts, see M Hunt, above n 24 at 13–25, 297–324.

[51] For a detailed discussion of why the presumption should be equally applicable to legislation enacted prior to a given international commitment, see van Ert, above n 3 at 38–46.

[52] See van Ert, above n 3 at 35–38. Kindred, above n 9 at 12; Schabas, above n 9 at 183; Weiser, 'Effect in Domestic Law', above n 9 at 138, argue that the presumption of conformity should apply to all statutes. However, in 'Undressing the Window', above n 9, at n. 116, Weiser concludes that, since the Supreme Court does not mention the presumption in the bulk of its decisions involving international law, the presumption does not currently exist with respect to statutes other than implementing legislation.

context of *Charter* interpretation. Secondly, the case-law, notably since *Baker*, is unclear on whether the presumption applies equally to Canada's international obligations and non-binding international norms.

As far as the *Charter* is concerned, Supreme Court decisions appear to invoke the presumption of conformity to interpret the *Charter* in the light of international human rights law, but then to eviscerate the presumption in practice.[53] At the end of the day, international (human rights) law is treated as highly 'relevant and persuasive', coming close to but stopping short of the ordinary presumption of conformity. This approach is reflected in Chief Justice Dickson's dissenting judgment in *Reference re Public Service Employee Relations Act*:

> I believe the *Charter* should generally be presumed to provide protection at least as great as that afforded by similar provisions in international human rights documents which Canada has ratified.
>
> In short, though I do not believe the judiciary is bound by the norms of international law in interpreting the *Charter*, these norms provide a relevant and persuasive source for interpretation of the provisions of the *Charter*, especially when they arise out of Canada's international obligations under human rights conventions.[54]

Building on the idea that international law is 'relevant and persuasive', the Supreme Court has tended to draw upon international norms merely to 'inform' its interpretation of the *Charter*, without, however, seeing itself as required to strive for an interpretation that is consistent with international norms.[55] The cumulative effect is that international law is not treated as a base-line measure, as suggested by Chief Justice Dickson, but simply as an instructive aid. Thus, in the *Charter* context, a weaker version of the presumption of conformity appears to have emerged. Irit Weiser argues that this approach is the appropriate way for courts to deal with unimplemented treaties in *Charter* interpretation. Weiser's concern is that the ordinary presumption of conformity would effectively eliminate domestic democratic controls over the legal system and entrench the relevant international obligation.

---

[53] In *R v Keegstra*, [1990] 3 SCR 697 at 837–38 [hereinafter *Keegstra*] (per McLachlin J), even the dissenters held that s 2 (b) of the *Charter* should be interpreted 'as a matter of construction' in a manner consistent with international approaches. But their concern was not to allow international law to restrict the full scope of *Charter* rights. On the latter point, see also *R v Cook*, [1998] 2 SCR 597 at para 148 (per Bastarache J).

[54] *Reference re Public Service Employee Relations Act (Alberta)*, [1987] 1 SCR 313 at 349 [hereinafter *Reference re Public Service Employee Relations Act*] (per Dickson CJC in dissent, though not on this point). See also the discussion in GV La Forest, 'The Use of International and Foreign Materials in the Supreme Court of Canada' (1988) 17 *Canadian Council of International Lawyers Proceedings* 230 at 232–33.

[55] See eg *Slaight Communications Inc v Davidson*, [1989] 1 SCR 1038 at 1056–057 [hereinafter *Slaight Communications*]; *R v Keegstra*, above n 53 at 837; *United States v Burns*, [2001] 1 SCR 283 at paras 79–81; *Baker*, above n 1 at para 70; *Suresh*, above n 5 at para 60.

Unlike in the case of ordinary statutes, since the treaty provision would be incorporated into *Charter* interpretation, Parliament could not legislate in deviation from international law, except on the basis of section 33.[56] One might be sympathetic to this concern, notably with regard to treaty obligations that would restrict the scope of *Charter* rights. Yet, Dyzenhaus argues convincingly that 'democratic deficit' arguments are often rooted in impoverished conceptions of democratic governance. They typically equate democracy with majoritarian legislative action. Dyzenhaus suggests that a rich view of democratic legitimacy can account for public engagement with international and common law norms outside the framework of statutory intervention.[57] In any event, the problem pointed to by Weiser would arise only in a relatively small number of cases. Many human rights treaties are in fact implemented implicitly, including through the *Charter* itself, or due to prior conformity of Canadian law. Thus, courts have considerable scope for resorting to the presumption of conformity. In cases of genuinely unimplemented treaties, the primary concern should be that international human rights law serve as 'floor' rather than 'ceiling' for the rights enshrined in the *Charter*. In fact, this concern, nicely encapsulated in the above quotation from Chief Justice Dickson's judgment in 1987 *Reference re Public Service Employee Relations Act*, has already shaped the approach of the Canadian judiciary. Canadian courts have been intent not to allow international law to restrict the scope of *Charter* rights.[58]

While the Supreme Court has thus built on Chief Justice Dickson's approach to international law as potentially relevant and persuasive—rather than obligatory—sources for *Charter* interpretation, it has not pursued his attempt to distinguish between international norms that are binding on Canada and other international norms.[59] The Court frequently cites a mixture of binding and non-binding sources, apparently according

---

[56] Weiser, 'Effect in Domestic Law', above n 9 at 138–39. In our view, requiring the invocation of s 33 of the *Charter* might well be appropriate where Parliament wishes to assert an interpretation of the *Charter* that restricts human rights provided by an international treaty to which Canada is a party.

[57] D Dyzenhaus, 'Constituting the Rule of Law: Fundamental Values in Administrative Law' (2002) 27 *Queen's Law Journal* 445 at 501–02. See also Dyzenhaus & Fox-Decent, above n 43.

[58] See eg *Slaight Communications Inc*, above n 55 at 1056; *R v Cook*, above n 53 at para 148 (per Bastarache J) (emphasising that 'the presumption of statutory interpretation that Parliament intended to legislate in conformity with international law must be applied with great care in the *Charter* context. The *Charter* is the fundamental expression of the minimum obligations owed to individuals in our society; I would not be inclined to accept that Canada's international law obligations could truncate rights defined by the *Charter*').

[59] While Dickson did not consider international law to bind courts in *Charter* interpretation, he did consider it relevant to the Court's interpretative task that, by ratifying a treaty, Canada 'oblige[s] itself internationally to ensure within its borders the protection of certain fundamental rights and freedoms'. *Reference re Public Service Employee Relations Act*, above n 54 at 349. Note that Justice Bastarache, in a recent paper, endorsed Dickson's approach. He suggested that '[t]he Supreme Court will consider inherently non-binding instruments..., as well as instruments to which Canada is a party... The first group, like international case law, are a guide to interpretation, while the second are a "relevant and persuasive" factor in

them the same interpretative weight. For example, in *Suresh*, the Supreme Court suggests that 'soft' law, unimplemented treaties, custom and even *jus cogens* all simply help 'inform' the interpretation of the *Charter*.[60] The lack of clarity on this issue has been compounded by the fact that the Supreme Court's treatment of international law as relevant and persuasive in the interpretation of the *Charter* seems to have carried over to the interpretation of ordinary statutes. In other words, there are some indications that this approach is implanting itself in the very context in which the presumption of conformity originated, and where it should have full application: the interpretation of domestic legislation in light of Canada's international obligations.

The ambiguous state of the case-law in this regard is reflected in the Supreme Court's decision in *Baker*, and is carried further in subsequent decisions of the Supreme Court and other Canadian courts. One of the principal casualties of this lack of clarity is customary international law. We turn first to a more detailed discussion of the Supreme Court's decision in *Baker* on the effect of unimplemented international treaties. In our subsequent discussion of customary law, we will then examine how later decisions have applied the ruling in *Baker* and what the potential implications of these decisions are for the status of international custom in Canadian law.

Baker involved both the statutory basis for, and the proper scope of, Ministerial discretion concerning a deportation order.[61] To prevent her deportation, and the consequent separation from her Canadian children, for two of whom she was sole caregiver, Ms Baker requested an exemption from the rule that one must apply for permanent residency from outside Canada; under the *Immigration Act*[62] and Regulations,[63] an exception that was available on humanitarian or compassionate grounds. Her application was denied, a decision subjected to judicial review. The Supreme Court's decision, per Justice L'Heureux-Dubé, was complex and wide-ranging, necessarily focusing upon process standards in administrative law, and upon substantive standards for judicial review. For our purposes, the central ruling was that even though Canada had never explicitly transformed its obligations under the *Convention on the Rights of the Child*[64] into domestic law, the

---

Charter interpretation'. Justice M Bastarache, 'The Honourable GV La Forest's Use of Foreign Materials in the Supreme Court of Canada and His Influence on Foreign Courts' in R Johnson et al (eds) *Gérard V La Forest at the Supreme Court of Canada 1985–1997* (Winnipeg, Canadian Legal History Project, 2000) 433 at 434.

[60] *Suresh*, above n 5 at para 46. See also below nn 101–109 and accompanying text.
[61] For the summary of the *Baker case*, we rely on Toope, 'Inside & Out', above n 9 at 19–21.
[62] RSC 1985, c I–2, s 114(2), as rep by *An Act respecting immigration to Canada and the granting of refugee protection to persons who are displaced, persecuted or in danger*, SC 2001, c 27, s 274(a).
[63] SOR/78–172, s 2.1.
[64] *Convention on the Rights of the Child*, 20 November 1989, Can TS 1992 No 3 (entered into force 2 September 1990).

immigration official was bound to consider the 'values' expressed in that *Convention* when exercising discretion. Therefore, the *Convention's* emphasis upon 'the best interests of the child' should have weighed heavily in considering Ms Baker's application.

Of greatest interest for our discussion is how the majority arrived at the conclusion that 'the values reflected in international human rights law may help inform the contextual approach to statutory interpretation and judicial review'.[65] More specifically, the central question is how the majority conceived of this principle in relation to the traditional presumption of statutory conformity with international obligations. Justice L'Heureux-Dubé supported the passage quoted above through the following statement, quoted from *Driedger on the Construction of Statutes*:

> [T]he legislature is presumed to respect the values and principles contained in international law, both customary and conventional. These constitute a part of the legal context in which legislation is enacted and read. *In so far as possible, therefore, interpretations that reflect these values and principles are preferred.*[66]

It would seem that the primary question for the majority with respect to the *Convention on the Rights of the Child* was how to give effect to the unimplemented treaty. As noted earlier, the majority took a narrow view on the question of implementation and observed that, absent implementation by Parliament, '[i]ts provisions...have no direct application in Canadian law'.[67] Yet, the 'values' reflected in the *Convention* could shape statutory interpretation. It is conceivable that, in distinguishing the *Convention's* provisions from its values, the majority was looking for a compromise formula that would make the consideration of unimplemented treaties more broadly acceptable.[68] However, in our view, the majority erred on the side of caution, for at least two reasons.

First, while the provisions of the *Convention* were not directly applicable *in* Canadian law, they were binding *on* Canada and, therefore, relevant to statutory interpretation through the presumption of conformity. From the standpoint of the presumption, the Court did not have to distinguish between provisions and values—it could have had recourse to both. By drawing the distinction, the majority implied that Canada's international obligations, as expressed in the provisions of the unimplemented *Convention*, are not covered by the presumption of statutory conformity. Curiously, it took this approach to the presumption notwithstanding the

---

[65] *Baker*, above n 1 at para 70.
[66] *Ibid* at para 69, quoting Sullivan, above n 13 at 330 (emphasis in Supreme Court decision).
[67] *Ibid* at para 69. See also above n 59 and accompanying text.
[68] None the less, Iacobucci and Cory JJ objected to the majority's approach to the convention. See below nn 78–81 and accompanying text.

very passage in *Driedger* that it quoted, in part, to support its reliance on the values expressed in the *Convention*. In full, the relevant passage describes the scope of the presumption of conformity as follows:

> there are two aspects to the presumption. First, the legislature is presumed to comply with the obligations owed by Canada as a signatory [*sic*] of international instruments and more generally as a member of the international community. In choosing among possible interpretations, therefore, the courts avoid interpretations that would put Canada in breach of any of its international obligations. Second, the legislature is presumed to respect the values and principles enshrined in international law, both customary and conventional. These constitute a part of the legal context in which legislation is enacted and read. In so far as possible, therefore, interpretations that reflect these values and principles are preferred.[69]

It was fully open to the majority to hold that Canada's immigration officers are bound to consider the best interests of the child within the framework of the *Immigration Act*,[70] so as to interpret it in conformity with international obligations binding on Canada.[71]

Our second concern relates to the effect of the presumption of conformity on the interpretative task of the Court. The *Convention on the Rights of the Child* should not merely have been at the Court's discretion to 'help inform' its interpretative effort—something less than what is required by the traditional presumption of conformity.[72] Instead, the Court was obliged to strive, to the extent possible, for an interpretation that is consistent with

---

[69] Sullivan, above n 13 at 330. There is some irony in the fact that the *Baker* decision, in quoting *Driedger*, deviates from the very approach that the passage suggests courts take to the presumption.
[70] Above n 62.
[71] One might object that the Court had to tread especially carefully since it was not merely interpreting a domestic statute in light of an unimplemented treaty but was also reviewing the exercise of administrative discretion granted by the statute. In other words, the Court had to avoid both trespassing upon parliamentary supremacy *and* unduly constraining discretionary power. While, as a general matter, both considerations deserve deference, we do not believe that the exercise of administrative discretion warrants different treatment in the context of the presumption of conformity. After all, if Parliament is presumed to intend conformity with Canada's international obligations, it makes little sense to assume that it granted administrative decision-makers discretion to ignore those obligations. Thus, in reviewing the exercise of discretion in the light of applicable international law, a court would not be constraining discretion let alone usurping the role of the decision-maker. It would merely identify the statutory bounds of the discretion. See also the detailed discussion of this issue in Dyzenhaus *et al*, above n 14 at 24–29. Dyzenhaus *et al*, at 27, point out that '[t]he fear of negating discretion assumes that the intention or the effect of applying the interpretative principle to discretionary power is to substitute the court's view of the merits for that of the primary decision-maker. There is no such intention, and it will not have that effect'.
[72] See also Currie, above n 28 at 225. But see Kindred, above n 9 at 23, who argues that the approach of the Supreme Court in *Baker* actually went beyond the principle that, to the extent possible, statutes should be interpreted in conformity with international law. According to Kindred, the judgment 'demands that courts make affirmative use of international law ... in the interpretation of domestic statutes'.

the legal commitments that Canada made by ratifying the *Convention*.[73] The difference between the provisions of the treaty and its spirit should have manifested itself in the relatively greater interpretative scope that open-textured concepts, such as 'values and principles', provide. The difference should not have affected the initial onus on the Court in approaching the relevant norms.

In our view, a lesser interpretative onus ('may help inform' rather than the onus to 'strive to interpret consistently') would have been warranted only if the majority had seen itself as working with non-binding international norms. In other words, had the Court looked to norms that were not binding on Canada, such as non-binding values and principles reflected in international treaties or other soft law, it would have quite correctly allowed statutory interpretation or judicial review to be 'informed' by them. The Court would then have gone beyond the traditional reach of the presumption of conformity and accepted that a broader range of international norms than Canada's international obligations are potentially relevant to the interpretation of statutes.[74] This subtle extension of international law's influence on the domestic sphere, we submit, would have been both desirable and appropriate. However, given the focus on the fact that the *Convention of the Rights of the Child* was an unimplemented treaty, it is not clear that the majority intended the articulation of a principle that non-binding international law can inform statutory interpretation and judicial review.[75]

From the standpoint of international law, then, the *Baker* decision puts into the spotlight two questions about the binding quality of international law. How should courts approach international treaty norms that are binding on Canada but, absent implementation, not directly applicable in Canada? How should they approach norms that do not bind Canada internationally but that none the less reflect important international values?

Karen Knop has suggested that international law may be best seen as 'foreign' law that needs to be translated into domestic systems such as Canada's, interpreted into local culture.[76] According to Knop, comparative law methodology, which seeks out persuasive authority, is better suited to the internalisation of international law than an application of international law that is dependent upon a rigid distinction between binding and non-binding norms. She argues that this distinction, if applied uncritically, risks

---

[73] For a compelling discussion of the judicial obligation to interpret domestic law consistently with international law, at least as concerns human rights law, see Hunt, above n 24 at 297–324.
[74] See Kindred, above n 9 at 23.
[75] But it is possible to read the Court's subsequent decision in *Spraytech* as drawing upon *Baker* to precisely this effect. We return to this issue in our discussion of customary law in the next section. See below nn 91–100 and accompanying text.
[76] Knop, above n 2 at 525.

caricaturing the influence of international law as an all or nothing proposition. On the one hand, some norms risk being ignored altogether, simply because they are not legally binding. On the other hand, legally binding norms produce a false sense of certainty when it is assumed that they require nothing other than 'mechanical' application by a judge. According to Knop, an approach focused on persuasiveness of norms can improve the domestic application of both types of norms. In the case of non-binding norms, a search for persuasiveness is *necessary* to justify reliance on individual norms. In the case of binding international law, it can assist the interpretative tasks inherent in applying international law. Knop interprets the majority decision in *Baker* as embracing just such a more flexible and more nuanced methodology and thus as signalling a significant and welcome shift in the approach of the Supreme Court to international law.[77]

While we agree with the argument that Knop advances regarding the pitfalls of a mechanical focus on the binding and non-binding distinction, it should be evident from the preceding discussion that we are less confident that *Baker* signals a positive shift. Our worry is that the majority decision places the Supreme Court on a path towards treating all international law as persuasive authority, which the Court *may* use to 'inform' its interpretation of domestic law. In other words, by treating both binding and non-binding international norms in this manner, courts move away from their duty to strive for an interpretation that is consistent with Canada's international obligations. Thus, as appealing as the comparative law metaphor may seem at first glance, it too bears risks.

We fear that the approach, if not carefully applied as a *supplementary* analytical tool, could easily lead to less rather than more nuance. The temptation may be great to treat all international law, whether binding on Canada or not, as 'optional information' and to disregard the particular interpretative onus that is placed upon courts by the presumption of conformity with Canada's international obligations. There is a significant difference between international law that is binding on Canada, and other international norms. The former is not only potentially persuasive, it is obligatory. This distinction matters—when we fail to uphold our obligations, we undermine respect for law internationally. The distinction also provides the rationale for the traditional common law presumption of conformity with Canada's international obligations, and for treating international norms that do not legally bind Canada differently. A more limited version of the presumption, treating international law as relevant and persuasive, appears to have evolved in the context of *Charter* interpretation. This approach may or may not be warranted in the unique circumstances of the *Charter*. But the ordinary presumption of conformity should have unfettered application in all other cases. Traditionally, that presumption did apply to the interpretation of

[77] *Ibid* at 535.

statutory and common law and there is no rationale for importing a different approach from case-law regarding *Charter* interpretation.

For all these reasons, we also believe that the dissent of Justices Iacobucci and Cory in *Baker* miscast the issues at hand. For the dissenters, the majority ruling was 'not in accordance with the Court's jurisprudence concerning the status of international law within the domestic legal system'.[78] However, the concern of the dissenters was not merely the idea that international 'values' should shape Canadian law. Rather, the real concern seems to have been that the majority transgressed the principle that an unimplemented treaty has no direct application in Canada. Thus, Iacobucci and Cory considered that the majority had effected the 'adoption of a principle of law which permits reference to an unincorporated convention during the process of statutory interpretation'.[79] One may or may not share the dissenters' concern that this type of principle ultimately 'give[s] force and effect within the domestic legal system to international obligations undertaken by the executive alone that have yet to be subject to the democratic will of Parliament'.[80] However, as far as the domestic effect of a binding but unimplemented treaty obligation is concerned, the principle in question was most certainly not 'adopted' by the majority in *Baker*. Indeed, it has long existed in the shape of the presumption of conformity with Canada's international obligations.[81]

2. The Application of Customary International Law

The proper application of customary international law in Canada emerged in a series of cases after *Baker* as a major question for the Supreme Court. To what extent can international customary law inform domestic legal processes?[82] The Court's treatment of this question leads to new concerns about the already troubled status of customary international law in Canada.

Given the primacy of the common law tradition in the public law of Canada, the best view appears to be that customary law can operate directly within the Canadian legal system.[83] Yet, this point needs to be

---

[78] *Baker*, above n 1 at para 79, per Iacobucci J (dissenting in part).
[79] *Ibid* at para 80.
[80] *Ibid*. Once again we see revealed a narrow and majoritarian conception of democratic governance. See above n 43. Also see above n 57 and accompanying text.
[81] Justices Iacobucci and Cory seemed to assume that this presumption applied only to the interpretation of the *Charter*. See *Baker, ibid* at para 81. We have already explained that we believe that this assumption is wrong. See also Dyzenhaus and Fox-Decent, above n 43 at 236.
[82] Indeed, it is worth noting that customary international law has seen something of a renaissance in Canadian courts. A search on legal databases by the authors in May 2002 revealed 67 cases in Canadian courts citing customary law; two-thirds of these were decided during the previous three years.
[83] A wonderfully clear example of such direct application of customary law is the recent decision of the Ontario Superior Court of Justice in *Bouzari*, above n 11 at para 39. At paras 57–73, Swinton J provides a nuanced discussion of the prohibition on torture as *jus cogens* and of its impact on the interpretation of Canada's *State Immunity Act*, RSC 1985, c S–18. See also the

clarified by senior Canadian courts.[84] Regrettably, the decisions of the Supreme Court over the last decade or so have further muddied the waters. Indeed, there have been indications that the Court was inching its way towards a dualist position vis-à-vis customary international law; the course may have been corrected in the recent *Schreiber* decision.[85]

In a number of important decisions, the Supreme Court did not take up the opportunity to focus its attention on customary international law. For example, in the *Quebec Secession Reference*, the amicus curiae had asserted that the Supreme Court would not have jurisdiction to apply 'pure international law'.[86] Without discussion, the Supreme Court implicitly adopted that view, leaving others to divine the implications for the status of international law. The implication could be simply that customary law becomes part of 'the laws of Canada' for the purposes of the Court's jurisdiction under section 3 of the *Supreme Court Act*.[87] However, the implication could also be that the Supreme Court cannot directly apply international customary law because it is *not* part of Canadian law. The fact that the Supreme Court's international law analysis in the *Secession Reference* failed completely to engage with the customary law on self-determination, suggests that a dualist position may implicitly have been adopted.[88]

Baker was another missed opportunity, where the Court might have helped to clarify the status of customary international law within Canadian law.[89] Rather than engage in the debate on the domestic effect of unimplemented treaties, it would have been open to the Supreme Court in *Baker* to conclude that the 'best interests of the child' test had solidified as a norm of

---

Ontario Court of Appeal in *Mack v Canada (AG)*, OJ No 3488, at para 32 (CA)(QL) [hereinafter *Mack*] (implying that customary law is directly applicable within the domestic legal system unless ousted by unambiguous legislation).

[84] In some decisions, customary law seemed to be treated as part of the law of Canada and thus as directly applicable. See *Saint John (City) v Fraser-Brace Overseas Corp*, [1958] SCR 263 (seeming to favour direct incorporation); *Schreiber*, above n 13, at paras 48 to 50 (suggesting that customary law is relevant to the interpretation of domestic law, and that *jus cogens* ousts ordinary customary norms and requires its direct application within domestic law); and *Mack*, above n 83, at paras 18 to 33 (treating customary law as directly applicable, unless ousted by contrary dometic legislation). Other decisions would appear to point in the opposite direction, or remain ambiguous. See *Congo v Venne*, [1971] SCR 997 (where changes to customary law did not operate automatically within Canadian law); *Reference Re Mining and Other Natural Resources of the Continental Shelf*, (1983) 41 Nfld & PEIR 271 (Nfld CA) (implicitly requiring transformation of customary law).

[85] *Schreiber*, above n 13, para 50 (hinting that customary law is directly applicable within the domestic legal system unless ousted by unambiguous legislation).

[86] *Reference re Secession of Quebec*, [1998] 2 SCR 217 [hereinafter *Quebec Secession Reference*]. See also SJ Toope, Case Comment on *Quebec Secession Reference* (1999) 93 *American Journal of International Law* 519 at 523.

[87] RSC 1985, c S–26, s 3. See also Currie, above n 28 at 204 (noting that the decision could be read 'as an endorsement of the direct legal effect or relevance of customary international law').

[88] See Toope, above n 86 at 523–525.

[89] See also Schabas, above n 9 at 182.

customary international law. Was the Court looking to avoid the complexities of determining whether a customary norm indeed existed; did it wish to avoid the question whether international customary law forms part of the law of Canada;[90] or did it simply miss the customary law angle altogether?

Far more troubling than the Supreme Court's failure to engage with customary law is the shadow that the majority's approach to international norms has since cast on the status of customary law in Canada. In a number of decisions since *Baker*, the Court has referred to the *Baker* approach to statutory interpretation in the context of questions that involved customary international law. What are the implications of linking the principle that international values and principles can help inform the interpretation of domestic law to the application of customary international law?

In *Spraytech*, the Supreme Court had to decide whether or not it was within the jurisdiction of a municipality to regulate the use of lawn chemicals. Although Justice L'Heureux-Dubé, writing for the majority, did not need to address this issue for the purposes of the decision, she chose to note that reading the relevant by-law as permitting the municipality to regulate pesticide use 'is consistent with principles of international law and policy'.[91] She went on to quote from her decision in *Baker* the passage that held that 'the values reflected in international human rights law may help inform the contextual approach to statutory interpretation and judicial review' and that quoted *Driedger*'s rendition of the presumption of conformity with international law.[92] L'Heureux-Dubé J concluded that the by-law respected international law's 'precautionary principle',[93] pursuant to which measures to address significant risks of environmental harm should not be postponed due to lack of full scientific certainty.[94] She then went on to observe:

> Scholars have documented the precautionary principle's inclusion "in virtually every recently adopted treaty and policy document related to the protection of the environment"... As a result, there may be "currently sufficient state practice to allow a good argument that the precautionary principle is a principle

---

[90] On this and the previous point, see LeBel and Chao, above n 6 at 11 (offering the following cryptic statement: 'unless the impugned custom is formally ratified and adopted into national legislation, it could be difficult to situate the custom in the domestic legal order'). At the risk of pedantry, it is important to emphasise that custom cannot ever be 'formally ratified' as it emerges from practice when read with the requisite *opinio juris*. And the common law tradition, in both the UK and the USA at least, is clear that no adoption into national legislation is necessary.
[91] See eg *114957 Canada Ltée (Spraytech, Société d'arrosage) v Hudson (Town)*, [2001] 2 SCR 241 at para 30 [hereinafter *Spraytech*].
[92] *Ibid*. For the text of the *Driedger* quote, see supra n 69 and accompanying text.
[93] *Ibid* at para 31.
[94] The most recent and most comprehensive analysis of the precautionary principle can be found in A Trouwborst, *Evolution and Status of the Precautionary Principle in International Law* (Boston, Kluwer Law International, 2002).

of customary international law"... The Supreme Court of India considers the precautionary principle to be "part of Customary International Law".[95]

In view of the fact that international environmental law has not played a significant role in Canadian courts,[96] the Supreme Court's references to the precautionary principle should be welcomed. For the purposes of our inquiry into the application of international law by Canadian courts, two aspects of the decision deserve closer attention.

First, although a good case can indeed be made that the precautionary principle is custom, the issue arguably remains unresolved. It is worth asking, therefore, what contribution the *Spraytech* decision might make to the further development of international law.[97] Although the Court ultimately leaves open the question whether the precautionary principle has acquired customary law status, its citation of strong evidence to that effect would tend to strengthen future customary law arguments. However, by quoting a definition of the precautionary principle that is not the most widely accepted one, the Court may also end up assisting those who insist that the precautionary principle is at best emerging international law. The Supreme Court's choice of definition may have been in part prompted by the fact that the Canadian government had actually advocated the inclusion of the precautionary principle in the *Bergen Ministerial Declaration on Sustainable Development*, the document cited by the Court.[98] None the less, the definitional issue is of some importance because the existence of multiple textual versions of the principle is the main basis for the assertion, including very recently by Canada, that no single version has crystallised into custom.[99]

The second and, for present purposes, most important question is what message *Spraytech* sends regarding the linkages between the *Baker* approach and the application of customary international law in Canada. The decision could be read as implying that a customary norm merely helps inform statutory interpretation. We assume that the Court did not intend any such implication, given that it did not actually decide the question of

---

[95] *Spraytech*, above n 91 at para 32 (sources omitted).
[96] See Brunnée, above n 9.
[97] See above n 8 and accompanying text on the role of national courts in the development of international law.
[98] See *Spraytech*, above n 91, at para 31. The Court quotes the definition of the precautionary principle in the *Bergen Ministerial Declaration on Sustainable Development in the ECE Region*, (1990) 1 *Yearbook of International Environmental Law* 429. The most widely cited definition is found in Principle 15 of the *Rio Declaration on Environment and Development*, (1992) 31 *International Legal Materials* 876.
[99] See Canada, *A Canadian Perspective on the Precautionary Approach/Principle—Proposed Guiding Principles* (September 2001) at 5, online: Department of Foreign Affairs and International Trade <http://www.dfait-maeci.gc.ca/tna-nac/prec-booklet-e.pdf> (last modified: September 2001).

the precautionary principle's customary law status, and given that the impact on the interplay between Canadian and international law would be enormous. Not only would the necessary implication be that customary law is not directly applicable in Canada; the result may also be that customary international law, which is binding on Canada, is treated as if it were soft law—as a potentially relevant and persuasive source for courts' interpretative tasks, but not as obligatory. We hope, therefore, that the Supreme Court intended to suggest instead that the precautionary principle can inform statutory interpretation even if it should not yet have become customary international law. If this reading is correct, the Court would have confirmed a principle that, in *Baker*, it at best alluded to: in appropriate cases, international norms that are not legally binding on Canada may inform statutory interpretation and judicial review.

In assessing the implications of the *Spraytech* decision, it is important to note that the precautionary principle, and the question of its legal status, were not argued by either of the principal parties to the case. Rather, the principle and its role in statutory interpretation were brought into play by some of the interveners.[100] In view of this fact, the Court was unlikely to go very far in its treatment of the relevant issues. Therefore, caution is warranted in drawing conclusions regarding the Court's stance on the domestic application of customary international law, and the role of the *Baker* approach. It is safe to say, however, that the *Spraytech* decision does not clarify the matter.

Another case in which the Supreme Court commented on customary law and cited its decision in *Baker* was *Suresh*.[101] Yet again we confront a case that should not be cast as the last word on the interplay of customary international law and Canadian law. Simply put, *Suresh* involved the interpretation of the Canadian *Charter*, and we have already argued that when the *Charter* is at play, the Court backs away from a clear presumption of conformity. In *Suresh*, the Court offered a nicely nuanced analysis of whether or not the prohibition of torture had become a norm of international *jus cogens*.[102] As the Court observes, a norm of *jus cogens* is 'a peremptory norm of customary international law' and emerges by general consensus of the international community.[103] Such norms prevail over other customary or treaty norms and can be modified only by a subsequent norm of the same character.[104] While the Supreme Court stops just short of concluding that

---

[100] See factum of the intervenors Federation of Canadian Municipalities, Nature-Action Québec Inc. and World Wildlife Fund Canada, paras 20–25 (on file with authors).
[101] *Suresh*, above n 5.
[102] *Ibid* at paras 61–5.
[103] *Ibid.* at para 61.
[104] *Vienna Convention on the Law of Treaties*, 23 May 1969, Can TS 1980 No 37 (entered into force 27 January 1980) Art 53 [hereinafter *Vienna Convention*].

the prohibition of torture is indeed *jus cogens*,[105] it does emphasise that there are 'compelling indicia' that this is the case.[106]

Notwithstanding strong statements about the complete illegality of torture, the Court then finds that a residual discretion exists in the Minister of Citizenship and Immigration to deport to feared torture, either as a result of the balancing process required by the principles of fundamental justice under section 7 or because the section 7 right of the claimant can be overridden under section 1 of the *Charter* on grounds of national security. However, in deference to the powerful anti-torture norm, the deportation to torture on these grounds would be permitted only in 'exceptional circumstances'.[107]

Although it may seem as if the Supreme Court did a masterful job in squaring the circle, it ultimately failed. The central problem with its analysis is that if the Court is right that the prohibition on torture is *jus cogens* (and deportation to torture would have to be an included prohibition), no 'balancing' would be appropriate. *Jus cogens* norms are a particularly compelling form of customary law, and should have been directly controlling within Canadian law to preclude deportation. Still, citing inter alia its decision in *Baker*, the Supreme Court opined that

> [t]he inquiry into the principles of fundamental justice is informed not only by Canadian experience and jurisprudence, but also by international law, including *jus cogens*.[108]

This formulation is consistent with the interpretative approach that the Court has developed in the *Charter* context. Yet, even if one accepts that approach in principle, we suggest that one should question its application to a norm of *jus cogens*.[109] In part, the Court's approach may be explained by its focus on international treaty norms, in particular those in the *ICCPR* and the *Convention against Torture and Other Cruel, Inhuman or Degrading Treatment or Punishment*.[110] Canada has ratified both treaties but has not explicitly implemented them by statute. Thus, the Supreme Court's attention may have been focused on what it deemed to be two

---

[105] *Suresh*, above n 5 at para 65.
[106] *Ibid.* at paras 62–64. It is worth noting that in *Bouzari*, above n 11 at para 61, Swinton J concluded without much ado that the prohibition on torture is *jus cogens*. While she noted that the Supreme Court, in *Suresh*, did not have to finally decide the issue, she felt that her conclusion was well supported by the sources set out in that decision.
[107] *Ibid* at paras 76–79.
[108] *Ibid* at para 46.
[109] We suggested in n 56 above that requiring resort to s 33 of the *Charter* may be appropriate where Parliament wishes to assert an interpretation of the *Charter* that restricts human rights provided by an international treaty to which Canada is a party. This argument applies with even greater force when norms of *jus cogens* are at issue.
[110] 10 December 1984, Can TS 1987 No 36 (entered into force 26 June 1987). The Court also relied upon the *Convention Relating to the Status of Refugees*, 28 July 1951, Can TS 1969 No 6 (entered into force 22 April 1954), which Canada has implemented by statute.

unimplemented treaties. None the less, even if the Court's approach was correct with respect to these treaties as such, it should have considered the direct application of the customary prohibition on torture.

3. Summary

We can now offer an outline of the principles that should govern the domestic application of international law in Canada, and a summary of the approaches that Canadian courts actually take.

Customary International Law

Customary international law should be directly applicable—it is part of Canadian law. This means that Canadian courts, to the extent possible, should strive to interpret both statutes and the common law to be consistent with Canada's obligations under customary law. However, the approach of senior Canadian courts to customary international law is utterly unclear. There is no unequivocal statement on whether custom is part of Canadian law or not. If anything, there are some indications that our courts may be retreating from custom. The Supreme Court's decisions in *Spraytech* and *Suresh* leave room to be interpreted as suggesting that customary law, including even *jus cogens*, is not directly binding in Canada.[111] The two decisions permit the inference that custom merely helps inform a contextual approach to statutory interpretation, furnishing a potentially relevant and persuasive source for this purpose, but nothing more. Indeed, in applying customary law in this fashion, Canadian courts would not even be treating it as binding *on* Canada. If it were so treated, custom should not merely 'help inform' statutory interpretation. It should give rise to the presumption of statutory conformity with Canada's international obligations. The recent *Schreiber* decision can be read as returning the Court to the possiblity of direct application of customary law within Canada, and to reliance on the traditional common law presumption of conformity. However, the discussion is not unambiguous, and the Court is careful to emphasise that the presumption will rarely be applied.[112]

International Treaty Law

A treaty that has been explicitly implemented by statute is part of our domestic law and should be determinative in the interpretation of Canadian

---

[111] But see *Bouzari*, above n 11 at para 60. Swinton J cites the Supreme Court's decision in *Suresh* in support of the proposition that customary law is directly incorporated into Canadian domestic law.
[112] *Schreiber*, above n 13, at para 50. See also *Mack*, above n 83, at para 32.

statutes. Courts must interpret implementing legislation in conformity with the underlying treaty. The interpretative effort must be focused on clarifying the meaning of the treaty, and must employ the rules of treaty interpretation set out in the *Vienna Convention*. These principles are in fact the only ones on which there is complete agreement in the context of the domestic application of international law in Canada. Canadian courts now consistently handle the application of transformed treaties in this fashion.

Treaties can also be transformed implicitly, or on account of prior conformity of Canadian law and policy with the treaty obligations (including the *Charter*). Such treaties should be subject to the same interpretative principles as other international obligations that are part of Canadian law. However, Canadian courts tend to rely on an unduly narrow conception of transformation, holding that treaties are not part of Canadian law unless they have been implemented by statute. As a result, they are treating this category of treaties as unimplemented.

Treaties that Canada has ratified but not implemented are not binding *in* Canada as part of domestic law. None the less, because such treaties are binding *on* Canada under international law, the presumption of conformity should apply. The onus is on Canadian courts, where possible, to interpret domestic law in a manner that comports with Canada's obligations under these treaties. By contrast, apparently drawing upon the Supreme Court's *Charter* jurisprudence, Canadian courts seem increasingly inclined to approach unimplemented treaties merely as relevant and persuasive sources that can help inform statutory interpretation. While this approach would be appropriate in the case of a treaty that Canada has not ratified, it fails to take due account of the fact that international legal obligations arise from all treaties that Canada ratifies. We argue that a principled approach to the domestic application of international treaties must reflect the legal difference between a treaty that produces obligations for Canada and one that does not.

To summarise, all forms of international law canvassed up to this point are binding *on* Canada. While only customary law and implemented treaties are binding *in* Canada and should be applied as part of Canadian law, all of Canada's international legal obligations give rise to the presumption of conformity. This does not mean that Canadian courts are reduced to applying binding international norms in mechanical fashion. Indeed, it is difficult to imagine any circumstances in which the judicial role would be exhausted by such an approach. Courts must search for interpretations of domestic law that are compatible with Canada's international obligations, but they are not deprived of the margins of appreciation inherent in all their interpretative tasks. Applying the presumption of conformity to all of Canada's international obligations also does not mean that the legislative authority of Parliament or the provincial legislatures would be undermined. As we have stressed at various points, with the possible exception of the

Charter, for which a different interpretative approach appears to have evolved in any event, Canadian legislatures retain control over domestic law. The presumption of conformity is to be applied only 'where possible' and, of course, it can be rebutted by an explicit legislative Act. If Canadian legislators choose to ignore Canada's international obligations, they can do so. However, Canada would then be in breach of its international obligations, and could suffer from the remedies accorded to other states under public international law.

International Law that is not Binding on Canada—International Soft Law

Finally, there is an array of international normative statements that may not legally bind Canada but that Canadian courts may none the less find relevant to the interpretation of a domestic statute. For example, Canadian courts might encounter: non-binding parts (such as preambular statements, or provisions phrased in non-obligatory terms) of a treaty that is otherwise binding; international treaties to which Canada is not a party; decisions of international tribunals; or a range of 'soft' international norms (such as declarations, codes of conduct, or principles that have not yet crystallised into custom). There is no reason why Canadian courts should not draw upon these types of norms, so long as they do so in a manner that recognises their non-binding legal quality.

We argue that these non-binding norms—and *only* these norms—should be treated as potentially relevant and persuasive sources for the interpretation of domestic law. Courts may, and in cases of particularly compelling norms *should*, draw upon such norms for interpretative purposes, but they are not strictly speaking required to do so.[113] This approach was first suggested for *Charter* interpretation by then Chief Justice Dickson in *Reference re Public Service Employee Relations Act*.[114] In *Baker*, the Supreme Court may have alluded to a similar approach to ordinary statutes and the exercise of discretion under statutes, although a number of factors militate against this interpretation of the decision. However, there is good reason to read the Court's decision in *Spraytech* as endorsing the principle that, in

---

[113] An example of a 'particularly compelling' non-binding norm might be one that is widely supported, or even close to crystallising into customary law. Of course, one might also argue that at least some non-binding norms should not be applied by courts at all. For example, where Canada has specifically chosen not to sign a treaty, it may be inappropriate for a Canadian court to rely upon it in the interpretation of domestic law. This consideration underscores the importance of careful evaluation of each norm, its international stature, and Canada's position. It is in this very context, that an analytical focus on why the norm is relevant and why it should be persuasive can be of assistance. We are grateful to Karen Knop for the observation, offered in comments on an earlier draft, that 'persuasion is not a synonym for non-binding [international law], only for the maximum status it can have [in domestic application]' (on file with authors).
[114] *Reference re Public Service Employee Relations Act*, above n 54.

appropriate cases, non-binding international law may inform statutory interpretation and judicial review. *Spraytech* also confirms that the approach is applicable to legislative action at all jurisdictional levels—federal, provincial and even municipal. We applaud these developments but emphasise once again that the *Baker* approach should be limited to non-binding international norms and should not be applied to Canada's customary or treaty obligations. There is no need for the *Baker* approach in the domestic application of Canada's international obligations. The ordinary presumption of conformity is available and would be the appropriate interpretative device for these cases.

CONCLUSION

We welcome the recent openness of Canadian courts, particularly the Supreme Court, to international influences. However, as Justice LeBel suggested, greater precision is required in distinguishing between mandatory and persuasive influences.[115] Our worry is that the inclination appears to be to treat all international law as inspirational but not obligatory. Indeed, the recent paper by Justice LeBel and Gloria Chao on the internalisation of international law in Canada betrays this very inclination. The following quotation reveals exactly the assumptions that have given rise to the confusion against which the judge warns: 'As international law is generally non-binding or without effective control mechanisms, it does not suffice to simply state that international law requires a certain outcome'.[116] We would highlight several concerns. First, international law *is* binding. This is a separate question from how it relates to a domestic legal system. Secondly, international law does possess so-called 'control mechanisms'. They simply do not look exactly the same as the mechanisms that exist in national legal systems. Moreover, the statement obscures the role that national courts play in the internalisation of international law.[117] Domestic courts are in many circumstances the very 'control mechanisms' that Justice LeBel suggests do not exist.[118]

Why does the distinction between binding and non-binding norms matter? Why not simplify the domestic application of international law by treating all international norms, whether binding on Canada or not, as potentially persuasive, and nothing more?

---

[115] See above n 6 and accompanying text.
[116] LeBel and Chao, above n 6 at 48.
[117] See HH Koh, 'Bringing International Law Home' (1998) 35 *Houston Law Review* 623.
[118] Koh argues that the internalisation of international law through domestic political and legal processes is an important avenue for implanting a genuine sense of obligation in a state, and for promoting its compliance with international law. See *ibid*; and see HH Koh, 'Why Do Nations Obey International Law?' (1997) 106 *Yale Law Journal* 2599. In Justice Lebel's own reasons in *Schreiber*, above n 13, at para 49, he stresses that customary law or *jus cogens* might 'allow domestic courts to entertain claims'.

First, we want to be clear that our conclusion that it matters in domestic litigation whether or not an international norm is binding upon Canada should not lead to the inference that we believe that international soft law is inherently less valuable than binding international law—on the contrary. The simple fact that a rule is enshrined in a treaty does not necessarily mean that it will be influential in international relations. Conversely, the fact that a rule is not binding as treaty or customary law does not necessarily mean that it cannot shape state conduct in international society.[119] In the international legal system, formal indicators alone do not account for a norm's power. Rather than operating through hierarchical processes of adjudication or enforcement, international law most commonly works horizontally, through processes such as normative discourse and negotiation among relevant actors. In these processes, a norm's legitimacy and attendant persuasiveness are likely more important to its influence than its formal pedigree.[120] Mark Walter's discussion in chapter 16, 'The Common Law Constitution and Legal Cosmopolitanism', underscores this point. 'Legal black holes' can increasingly be filled with values derived from transnational legal, especially judicial, discourse.

However, in domestic judicial processes the yardstick for legal influence is law that would at least colloquially be described as 'binding', even if in practice this means that it is a mandatory consideration.[121] While it is true that binding rules, be they rooted in statutes or the common law (or *droit commune*), are formally the basis of parties' arguments and courts' decisions, non-binding principles and values are in fact influential, especially in

---

[119] In the words of Professor Chinkin: 'While soft law may not be directly used to found a cause of action it has both a legitimising and a delegitimising direct effect: it is extremely difficult for a State that rejected some instrument of soft law to argue that behaviour in conformity with it by those who accepted it is illegitimate'.
C Chinkin, 'The Challenge of Soft-Law: Development and Change in International Law' (1989) 38 *International and Comparative Law Quarterly* 850, at 850–51. See also J Brunnée and SJ Toope, 'International Law and Constructivism: Elements of an Interactional Theory of International Law' (2000) 39 *Columbian Journal of Transnational Law* 19 [hereinafter 'Constructivism']; V Lowe, 'The Politics of Law-Making: Are the Method and Character of Norm Creation Changing?' in M Byers (ed) *The Role of Law in International Politics: Essays in International Relations and International Law* (New York, Oxford University Press, 2000), 207.
[120] See Brunnée and Toope, *ibid*; and J Brunnée and SJ Toope, 'The Changing Nile Basin Regime: Does Law Matter?' (2002) 43 *Harvard International Law Journal* 105.
[121] It is, of course, perfectly possible—even desirable—for domestic legal processes to evade or escape from the paradigm of formally binding law. The so-called legal pluralists have explored this issue in great detail. See eg B Santos, *Toward a New Common Sense: Law, Science and Politics in the Paradigmatic Transition* (London, Routledge, 1995); J Belley, 'Law as *terra incognita*: Constructing Legal Pluralism' (1997) 12(2) *Canadian Journal of Law and Society* 17; and RA Macdonald, 'Metaphors of Multiplicity: Civil Society, Regimes and Legal Pluralism' (1998) 15 *Arizona Journal of Comparative and International Law* 69. Lon Fuller argues that even judging, the seeming epitome of formal decision-making rooted in binding law, is actually a process of mutual deliberation in which the parties and the judge articulate shared purposes. See LL Fuller, 'Human Purpose and Natural Law' (1958) 3 *Naural Law Forum F* 68 at 73–74; Brunnée and Toope, 'Constructivism', above n 119 at 43–53.

constitutional adjudication, as the *Quebec Secession Reference*[122] makes clear. However, this influence is intentionally limited by assertions that the court is not 'bound' to invoke these principles and values. We worry that by treating all international norms merely as potentially persuasive—at the discretionary disposal of judges—courts view all international law as 'soft' law, if indeed it is seen as law at all. So while international law can, in this conception, play the same role as 'principles and values', it can never amount to an obligation that actually constrains the discretion of a judge. We may have here a perfectly vicious circle. Because of an inclination to cast international law as 'generally non-binding' and thus not as real law—viz the LeBel and Chao view—courts may lean towards the *Baker* approach. In turn, the more international norms are seen as merely helpful in informing statutory interpretation, the more the initial assumptions about the 'softness' of international law are reinforced.

We share Moran's preoccupation in chapter 15, 'Authority, Influence and Persuasion: *Baker, Charter* Values and the Puzzle of Method', with the need to find a category that fills the interpretative space between the extremes of purely optional considerations and rules that formally bind courts and other decision makers. We believe that our discussion of the presumption of conformity, leading to the mandatory consideration of binding international law, is very close to Moran's treatment of ratified but unimplemented treaties as 'influential authority'. The central difference between our approach and Moran's is methodological. Moran seeks to identify reasons for treating certain norms as influential. We suggest that the differences between international norms that bind Canada and those that do not are central to that very task.

This is why it is important to resist the idea that the application of international law is merely an exercise in comparative law, whereby 'foreign' legal norms are translated into domestic law, and may or may not be found to be persuasive. Comparative law may provide helpful supplementary methods, particularly in identifying the appropriate domestic influence of international norms that are not legally binding on Canada. But, as we have illustrated throughout this chapter, many international legal rules bind Canada; some are part of Canadian law. They should be treated accordingly.[123]

---

[122] Above n 86. See also *Reference Re Amendment of Constitution of Canada*, [1981] 1 SCR 753.
[123] In discussing binding international human rights norms, the Senate Standing Committee on Human Rights, made the following forceful observation: 'International human rights obligations are no less binding upon us than our domestic guarantees.... International human rights are not simply promises we make to other countries or to the international community as a whole. They are rights that all people have and that we have pledged to respect and implement in our country. Human rights belong to the people, not to the states who ratify the treaties. Part of the problem in Canada is that the domestic/international dichotomy that is so firmly embedded in our legal system pervades our thinking outside the courts as well'.
Canada, Senate Standing Committee on Human Rights, *Promises to Keep: Implementing Canada's Human Rights Obligations* (Ottawa, Standing Committee on Human Rights, 2001) (Chair: Andreychuk).

In applying international law, domestic courts are not merely engaged in the internalisation of international norms into the domestic legal system.[124] They are also involved in the continuous process of the development of international law, particularly customary law. For this reason too it is important that Canadian courts carefully distinguish between treaty, customary and non-binding norms. For example, when a Canadian court concludes that a given norm has become customary international law, it actually contributes to the process of establishing evidence for the status of the norm. This contribution may consist in the analysis conducted by the court and the evidence it assembled in the process. The court's decision itself may also constitute evidence of the state practice or *opinio juris* that help build custom. By the same token, if the court's analysis is not sufficiently careful, its decision may come to undermine the crystallisation of customary law,[125] or the development of its normative content.[126]

For all these reasons, we return again to Justice LeBel's plea for greater rigour 'in the definition and identification of international rules and the process of internalisation'. In this article, we have highlighted a number of areas of ambiguity that, we believe, negatively affect both the definition and identification of international rules, and their internalisation into Canadian law. In their joint paper, LeBel and Chao argue that:

> the reception of international law into the Canadian legal system must in itself form part of the argument advanced by counsel. In other words, if parties wish to rely on a certain principle of international law as binding obligation, they should endeavour to establish how that principle became binding and how it applies to their case.[127]

---

[124] The importance of domestic internalisation, in the context of international environmental law, was recently reaffirmed by leading judges from around the globe in the *Johannesburg Principles on the Role of Law and Sustainable Development*. United Nations Environment Programme, News Release 2002/58, 'Senior Judges Adopt Ground-breaking Action Plan To Strengthen World's Environment-related Laws' (27 August 2002), online: United Nations Environment Programme <http://www.unep.org/Documents/Default.asp?DocumentID=259&ArticleID=3115> (date accessed: 29 August 2002).

[125] See our earlier discussion of the Supreme Court's comments on the precautionary principle in *Spraytech*, above nn 91–100 and accompanying text.

[126] In the *Quebec Secession Reference*, above n 86, the Supreme Court's failure to engage with customary law and, notably, with the evolving state practice and *opinio juris* in Europe, caused it to neglect potential shifts in the right to self-determination beyond what the Court considered to be the content of that right. On this point see Schabas, above n 9 at 192–193; Toope, above n 86 at 524–25. The Court's opinion has since been widely referred to by other courts and academic writers from around the world. Thus, its partial analysis of the evolving right to self-determination may reinforce those voices that seek to limit the scope of the right. Our point here is not that the right should be narrowly or widely construed. It is simply to illustrate that the decisions of domestic courts can have a significant impact on the development of international law. See eg VP Nanda, 'Self-Determination and Secession under International Law', (2001) 29 *Denver Journal of International Law and Policy* 305 at 315–19 (discussing the *Quebec Secession Reference* in detail).

[127] LeBel and Chao, above n 6 at 20.

We fully agree that it is incumbent upon lawyers appearing before the courts to provide detailed and rigorous arguments regarding the international norms on which they rely. Indeed, when international law arguments are employed frivolously or without appropriate nuance, this may reinforce judicial attitudes treating international law as uncertain and irrelevant. However, Canadian courts for their part must provide clear signals as to what international law will matter (custom, treaty or soft law), when it will matter (the transformation issues), and how it will matter (the presumption issues).

Justice LaForest is right that Canadian courts are 'becoming international courts'.[128] This development is an under-appreciated aspect of the increasing global integration prompted by trade, by the evolution of international human rights, by attempts to address environmental degradation, and even by security concerns. But the current crop of judges finds itself in a strange new world, and understandably resists changes in the judicial role that are not well specified, and not well argued by counsel. If it is any consolation to our judges, the rise in importance of international law within Canadian courts echoes the changes in judicial role brought about by the promulgation of the *Canadian Charter of Rights and Freedoms*.[129] In our view, Canadian judges have proven themselves to be resilient and flexible in adapting to the new world of the *Charter*, and its effect upon domestic law. There is every reason to expect that they will be equally successful in negotiating their way through the new world of international law. So far, they have been unduly hesitant, but recent cases suggest the possibility of a warm embrace, one prompted by a recognition of the normative richness of international law and a desire to contribute to its flourishing.

---

[128] GV LaForest, 'The Expanding Role of the Supreme Court of Canada in International Law Issues' (1996) 34 *Canadian Yearbook of International Law* 89 at 100.
[129] Above n 17.

15

Authority, Influence and Persuasion: Baker, Charter Values and the Puzzle of Method

MAYO MORAN[1]

INTRODUCTION

THE CONTOURS OF legal judgment are in flux. Courts and commentators note the increasing use of comparative law and international materials in decision-making. And legal boundaries other than those between states are also coming under increasing scrutiny and strain. Thus we witness new attentiveness to the kinds of relationships that might exist between what have generally been considered the relatively discrete categories of private law. So too do we see a changing relationship between public law and private law. In the midst of this foment, the very theory of judgment has also begun to show signs of wear. And perhaps no aspect of the traditional model of judgment seems more under siege than its commitment to the exclusive salience of 'binding' sources or rules, a commitment most dramatically expressed in the dualist understanding of the relationship between the international and domestic spheres but also apparent in the other kinds of 'boundary' questions that courts increasingly face.

In an important article in 1987, Patrick Glenn outlined how the old concept of persuasive authority might hold out some hope as our faith in the nationalist ideals of binding law crumbles from without and from within.[2] And indeed, the idea of persuasive authority has been invoked both by decision-makers and by commentators as providing a more illuminating

---

[1] This article is part of a larger project with Karen Knop on the changing nature of legal judgment, sources of law and role of justification that attends the declining significance of the traditional 'binding law' model. The discussion herein has benefited in innumerable ways from her input. I am also grateful to the participants in the conference for their input and most especially to David Dyzenhaus whose comments led to many revisions to this paper.
[2] 'Persuasive Authority' (1987) 32 *McGill Law Journal* 262.

lens for viewing recent developments in the relationship between domestic and international law, including of course the important decision in *Baker v Canada*.[3] The fact that the majority in *Baker* did not invoke the traditional apparatus of binding authority can thus be seen as part of a larger shift away from the theory of judgment dominated by that understanding in favour of one that posits a deeper connection to the task of justification.[4] And using this insight as a point of departure, it is also possible to situate the methodology of *Baker* within a related, slightly larger framework. In a world dominated by the binding sources model, it was possible to term everything else 'persuasive'. In this sense, persuasive authority may look significantly indebted to the traditional model. Yet the increasing importance of persuasive authority is, in a sense, self-defeating. In the shifting world of legal judgement, it is gradually becoming clear that what we once termed 'persuasive authority' captures a whole range of norms that have complex relations to each other and to the relevant decision. Attention to this phenomenon thus provides the impetus to refine our vocabulary in order to capture the increasingly complex range of legal sources and their relation to judgment, inside the state and beyond. In this way, the development of a more fine-grained understanding of what we would formerly have called persuasive authority heralds both the triumph and the demise of that important idea.

In common with the jurisprudence that considers another 'boundary' problem—the relationship of the *Charter* to private law—cases like *Baker* alert us to how more general *values* as well as more specific claims of entitlement and obligation (rights) exert demands on legal judgment. This in turn suggests a potentially important refinement to the old idea of persuasive authority. Thus, within the rubric that the traditional picture would have termed persuasive sources, or have had difficulty classifying, it is possible to locate a category of what we might call 'influential authority' which is reducible neither to binding authority nor to what we might call the permissive extreme of persuasive authority.[5] Like what have traditionally been termed 'binding' sources, its demands are mandatory not permissive but its

---

[3] [1999] 2 SCR 817; Madam Justice L'Heureux-Dubé, 'From Many Different Stones: A House of Justice', Notes for an Address to the International Association of Women Judges, Montreal 10 November, 2001 (Manuscript on file with the author) at 13 ff discussing persuasive authority of international law. K Knop, 'Here and There: International Law in Domestic Courts' (2000) 32 *NYU Journal of International Law and Politics* 507 arguing that it may be more illuminating to view recourse to international law in cases like *Baker* through the lens of persuasive authority than through the traditional bindingness model.

[4] Knop, *ibid*; D Dyzenhaus, M Hunt and M Taggart, 'The Principle of Legality in Administrative Law: Internationalisation as Constitutionalisation' (2001) 1 *Oxford University Commonwealth Law Journal* 5.

[5] I term this far end of the spectrum 'pure persuasive authority' to highlight the fact that the traditional term persuasive authority encompasses everything from the truly permissive extreme of a source from another unrelated jurisdiction ('pure persuasive authority') to sources that seem to bear in a more 'demanding' way on the question at issue. Thus, what may seem a

demands tend to take shape at the level of *values*. And so like pure persuasive authority, it exerts its influence primarily at the level of justification. Its ultimate challenge however is systemic in nature.

Paying attention to the dynamics of influential authority seems to place increasing strain on the traditional theory of sources dominated by the ideal of binding law. For at least in cases like *Baker* and in those involving the *Charter*/common law relation, the problematic of influential authority is occupied with a fundamentally different conception of boundary. Boundary in the imagination of the binding law model is the border, with fixed and regulated points of entry. Pure persuasive authority, on this view, is the fluidity characterised by the absence of this kind of formal delineation. But cases like *Baker* and the *Charter*/common law cases direct our attention to the inadequacy of this understanding. Problems of influential authority are occupied with boundaries that deserve some kind of systematic attention and respect and yet are in fundamental ways inherently and necessarily permeable. So while the permeable nature of the boundary does not obliterate difference, it poses a challenge about how to construct and understand the nature both of that difference and what would constitute a proper relation across it, so to speak. If the binding law model notionally solved the legal question through unique invocation of the binding source, and pure persuasive authority freed the judge to examine a wide array of sources and to justify the best outcome, influential authority demands attentiveness to the very different salience and weight of a wide array of reasons and directs our efforts towards constructing the relation between them.

And so while it may well be possible to try to fit the nature of influential authority into the traditional model, this may not be the most illuminating response. For the problematic of influential authority turns on questions of relation, fusion and distillation of the implications of various sets of norms that might operate at different levels with different justifications and different weights. The model of judgment that attentiveness to influential authority thus implicates is inevitably directed to rather different issues than those that preoccupy the traditional model. By attending to the nature of those differences as we juxtapose two case studies of influential authority (*Baker* and related cases on the one hand, and the *Charter*/common law relation

---

comparative exercise may in fact have more pressing salience that distinguishes the source from the purely permissive source. So in the American tort of torture cases, the courts commonly describe international law as their binding source, only to invoke the domestic criminal and civil law of the jurisdiction where the acts occurred and are being litigated: M Moran, 'An Uncivil Action: The Tort of Torture and Cosmopolitan Private Law' in C Scott (ed) *Torture as Tort* (Oxford, Hart Publishing, 2001). As I note there, the claim to binding authority may belie the actual complexity of sources which are *essential* to the task of justification. As Karen Knop has pointed out to me, it is possible to understand the apparently 'comparative' exercise in extradition cases like *United States v Burns* [2001] 1 SCR 283 as involving a more demanding conception of sources than 'pure persuasive authority'. In this sense, what looks like purely permissive comparative law may actually be understood as influential authority, as discussed in the text.

cases on the other), we can begin to develop a sharper understanding of this alternative picture of legal judgement.

AUTHORITY AND INFLUENCE: SOME PRELIMINARY OBSERVATIONS

The decision of the Supreme Court of Canada in *Baker* has rightly been heralded as groundbreaking on a number of issues. In administrative law terms, *Baker* makes important contributions to our understanding of reasonableness, discretion and the duty to give reasons. In addition, *Baker* addresses difficult questions concerned with bias in administrative decision-making and holds important lessons for the immigration law context. Beyond this, commentators have also noted and debated its significance for the reception and effect of international law norms, particularly treaty-based norms, within the domestic legal system. On the question of the domestic effect of international law norms, the majority decision in *Baker* points to a more fluid, persuasive understanding of authority and a more complex array of relevant norms than that typically associated with the traditional binding/non-binding distinction. But it also seems profitable to position the approach of *Baker* and subsequent cases to ratified but unincorporated treaties in international law against another set of cases that involve a similar dynamic of judgment.

In this context, *Baker* may be seen as part of a shift towards an alternative conception of the relationship between decision-maker, types of reasons and authority. So the approach that we see at work in *Baker* is not confined to the difficult question of the domestic effect of international law, though that may serve as a particularly pointed illustration of it. In fact, reading *Baker* and related cases more closely suggests that the picture of judgment that it implicates is complex in part because it turns on weight and significance, in contrast with the relatively binary nature of bindingness. Thus in these cases, courts seek some terrain between the unpalatable extremes of the traditional model in an effort to capture what seems legally salient about ratified treaties without raising the 'backdoor incorporation' worry—the worry, that is, about circumventing the ordinary requirement of domestic incorporation. The understanding of legal norms the cases invoke suggests that such norms may have weight and effect that is not exhausted by the traditional assessment of their force. In this sense, then, the picture of judgment in these cases takes apart what has heretofore been the relatively automatic equation of force and effect. We may, of course, be tempted to dismiss what courts are doing here as simply error or confusion but we should not, I think, be too quick to do so.

One important reason not to be too dismissive of these impulses can be found in the fact that what the courts strain towards in cases like *Baker* is also evident elsewhere as our courts come up against other relatively new boundary problems. A particularly salient example can be found in the somewhat embryonic judicial efforts to think through the relation of constitutional norms to traditional private law and common law rights. Here too we see the inadequacy of the traditional model of binding/non-binding sources as courts attempt to capture what is, on the traditional model, a rather puzzling relation. In Canada, it is well settled that the *Charter* does not apply to private common law litigation. In this sense then, the *Charter* has no force or direct application. None the less, it is also a commonplace that the *Charter*, notwithstanding its lack of force [or direct application], demands attention in the development of private and other bodies of law to which it does not directly apply. So, it is also uncontroversial that the common law must be developed in accordance with the principles and fundamental values which underlie the *Charter*. But as courts attempt to think through what this entails in any discrete case, they too strain against the confines of the traditional model in ways reminiscent of *Baker* and related cases.

Thus, bringing together these two instances of what I shall term 'influential authority' may help to illuminate how courts respond to the increasingly complex challenges of judgement across boundaries of space and time. If the traditional picture had a relatively simple understanding of sources (either binding or not) and their effect (dispositive or irrelevant), the contours of this alternative are rather different. While some norms carry very significant weight as a matter of 'pedigree' (hence may be called 'binding'), the fact that the norm does not possess this kind of 'force' does not mean that it does not have 'effect'. But while force in the way that it is traditionally used tends to be binary in nature (has force/lacks force), the same cannot be said of effect. The majority decision in *Baker* and the other cases examined here all point to something not captured by either the idea of binding authority or by pure persuasive authority. Instead, the idea of influence, of effect, of what Dworkin in another context called 'gravitational force',[6] seems to point to some rather different set of possibilities regarding the significance of various kinds of norms that carry their own distinctive set of demands.

The methodological cue of cases like *Baker* and the *Charter*/common law cases thus may provide an impetus to develop a more refined understanding of the influence or effect of norms that the traditional model would term 'non-binding'. The argument elaborated here is that there are distinct requirements associated with authorities whose claims would not

---

[6] Interestingly, Guido Calabresi appropriated the term 'gravitational force' from Dworkin's article 'Hard Cases', R Dworkin, *Taking Rights Seriously* (Cambridge, Mass., Harvard University Press, 1978) 121–23, and used it to try to capture the influence of constitutional norms on private law: G Calabresi, *Ideals, Beliefs and Attitudes: Private Law Perspectives on a Public Law Problem* (Syracuse, Syracuse University Press, 1985).

normally be termed 'binding' but that are not best understood as purely persuasive either. Poised between the relatively insistent and content-neutral claims of pedigree that characterise 'binding' norms and the voluntarism of purely persuasive sources like those found in comparative law, influential authorities incorporate elements of both ends of the spectrum of authority, though they can be reduced to neither. Influential authority shares with binding sources the fact that its demand for attention is grounded in part on reasons that extend beyond the simple persuasiveness or appeal of its substantive values (though of course we hope that these qualities will co-exist). Unlike pure persuasive authority therefore, a judgment that fails to address or discuss an influential authority is open to a different ground of criticism.

However, the demands of influential authority also share an affinity with traditional 'persuasive' authorities in that they are felt primarily at the level of justification. The nature of an influential source is such that whenever it bears upon an issue, any decision that purports to resolve that issue must address the role of that authority in the justification of its resolution or on that ground be found legally wanting. But because influential norms operate at the level of values rather than discrete entitlements and obligations, their salience takes hold at a level that is not easily assimilated to 'binding' sources. Instead, influential norms engage the adequacy of justification, demanding that they be given appropriate weight in the articulation of discrete rights and obligations. In this respect too influential authority differs from 'pure' persuasive authority. Normally we cannot insist that purely persuasive norms be addressed in any act of judgment. An act of judgment can, of course, establish through its argument the persuasiveness of any particular authority. However, where the authority is also influential any judgment that fails to address it will fail to that degree as a justification.[7] It is thus this ability to insist that it be addressed and respected that helps to distinguish influential authority. With this in mind, let us begin our examination by looking at *Baker* and related cases.

BAKER AND THE IDEA OF INFLUENTIAL AUTHORITY

When the Supreme Court of Canada decision in *Baker v Canada* was released in 1999, there was considerable interest in the few short paragraphs of the majority decision that addressed the question of the relevance of international law.[8] Indeed, this issue forms the only point of disagreement

---

[7] This suggests that Glenn may have somewhat overstated the relation between the common law method and persuasive authority for presumably some common law sources are actually influential in the sense that they demand justification. This should remind us that the underlying notion of authority cannot be understood as binary.

[8] Knop, n 3 above; S Toope and J Brunnée 'A Hesitant Embrace: The Application of International Law by Canadian Courts' (ch 14 of this volume).

between the majority and the dissent. *Baker* began as an application to review judicially a decision of an immigration officer who refused to allow Ms Baker to apply for permanent residence from within Canada. Ms Baker had lived in Canada illegally for many years and had four children in Canada. She asked to be exempted from the ordinary requirement that applications be made from outside the country. She argued that this would be justified because in her case there were 'humanitarian and compassionate reasons' as provided for in section 114(2) of the *Immigration Act*.[9] In particular, she pointed to the possible effect of her deportation on her children. The two lower courts rejected her application but the Supreme Court unanimously grated it.

Madam Justice L'Heureux-Dubé, writing for the entire court on all issues except the relevance of international law, found that the immigration officer who rejected Ms Baker's claim did not reasonably exercise his discretionary power when making the decision in question. Any reasonable exercise of his power must, among other things, be responsive to the needs and interests of children given how important those needs are in Canadian society. Because the decision contained no indication in it that it had been made in a manner which was 'alive, attentive or sensitive' to the interests of Ms Baker's children, it was unreasonable.[10]

The majority relies on a number of sources to derive the imperative that the decision-maker be alive to the interests of the children. The three primary sources are the purposes of the *Immigration Act*, international instruments and the guidelines that the Minister herself published for making humanitarian and compassionate decisions. However, international law appears to be the most important of these three sources of the obligation to attend to the needs of children. Not only are the *Act* and the guidelines discussed far more briefly than international law, but neither of those sources makes explicit reference to the importance of giving special weight to the interests of children. Instead, the Court must derive this point from more general references to family reunification and the importance of connections between family members. Of the sources the Court invokes, only the *Convention on the Rights of the Child* (the *Convention*)[11] specifically mandates the importance of the special needs of and therefore attentiveness to children.

However while the *Convention* may be the most on-point source for grounding a legal obligation to pay special attention to the interests of children, there is a difficulty with straightforward domestic recourse to it. This arises because although Canada signed and ratified the *Convention*, it had not been implemented by Parliament through legislation. Therefore, its

---

[9] RSC, 1985, c. I–2.
[10] *Baker*, n 3 above, para 75.
[11] *Convention on the Rights of the Child* Can TS 1992 No 3.

provisions have no direct application within Canadian law. It thus has, in the language that we have been using so far, no force. None the less, Madam Justice L'Heureux-Dubé continues, it may play a role in determining whether the decision-maker in question considered the proper factors and weighed them properly. But what exactly does this amount to and why would it be so? Looking to how *Baker* and related cases seem to respond to this and other cases may help to flesh out the idea of authority that Madam Justice L'Heureux-Dubé seems to invoke.

Effect Without Force

Madam Justice L'Heureux-Dubé begins her discussion of international law by stating that 'Another indication of the importance of considering the interests of children ... is the ratification by Canada of the *Convention*...'.[12] She also points to Canada's ratification of other international instruments that recognise the importance of children's rights. Both of these statements suggest that there is some domestic significance to the fact of Canada's ratification of these instruments, even though it will not be enough to give the documents domestic force. However, Madam Justice L'Heureux-Dubé's reasons are oblique on the exact role and relevance of the *Convention*. Thus, she also quotes *Driedger on the Construction of Statutes* for the proposition that 'the values reflected in international human rights law may help inform the contextual approach to statutory interpretation'.[13] The justification for this is that the legislature is presumed to respect the values and principles enshrined in international law. Similarly, she refers to the 'important role of international human rights law as an aid in interpreting domestic law' and its particular effect on the scope of rights contained in the *Charter*.[14] And she states that the rights in the *Convention* 'help to show the values that are central in determining whether this decision was a reasonable exercise of the [Humanitarian and Compassionate] power'.[15] Similarly, she says of all of the sources to which she refers, including the *Convention*, that they 'indicate that emphasis on the rights, interests, and needs of children and special attention to childhood are important values that should be considered in reasonably interpreting' the humanitarian and compassionate considerations that guide the exercise of discretion.[16]

---

[12] *Baker*, n 3 above, para 69.
[13] R Sullivan, *Driedger on the Construction of Statutes* 3rd edn, Markham, Butterworths, 1994 at 330 quoted in *Baker*, n 3 above, para 70.
[14] *Baker*, n 3 above, para 70.
[15] *Baker*, n 3 above, para 71.
[16] *Baker*, n 3 above, para 73.

Justice Iacobucci, speaking for himself and Cory J, dissented on this point alone. He points to the well-settled law that an international convention ratified by the executive is of no force or effect within domestic Canadian law until it has been implemented by the legislature. He notes the 'backdoor incorporation worry' when he states that the majority position undermines this domestic incorporation requirement by effectively enabling the appellant to achieve indirectly what she could not claim directly. The primacy accorded the rights of children in the *Convention*, he insists, is 'irrelevant' until domestic incorporation.[17]

Because Madam Justice L'Heureux-Dubé's justifications for invoking the *Convention* are so oblique, they are compatible with a number of possibilities, some of which have been addressed by commentators on international law.[18] But what I would like to suggest is that for all of this ambiguity, there is something to the idea that the fact of ratification gives the *Convention* a special status, but a status that is yet different than it would been have were it also incorporated. Indeed, it is the asserted impossibility of any such midpoint that the dissent in *Baker* responds to. And since *Baker*, very similar kinds of controversies can be seen working themselves out. Let us examine a few of them to see what illumination they may yield.

The idea that ratification is itself of some legal significance distinct from the question of force can also be seen at work in the opinion of L'Heureux-Dubé, Gonthier and Bastarache JJ in the Supreme Court of Canada decision in *Sharpe*. There, in considering whether the child pornography provisions of the *Criminal Code* could be justified under section 1 of the *Charter*, they refer to the relevance of Canada's ratification of the *Convention on the Rights of the Child*. The heading they use for this discussion is relevant, 'Actions Taken to Protect Children in Canada'. Ratification of the *Convention*, on their view, 'demonstrates this country's strong commitment to protecting children's rights'.[19] The view that ratification even without domestic implementation is an act with some domestic legal relevance for Canada is apparent in the fact that it is included in the discussion of the other actions taken by Canada to protect children. Thus, the ratified *Convention* is grouped with various provisions of the domestic *Criminal Code*, provincial child welfare legislation and various judicial decisions. In contrast, more purely persuasive authorities from international and comparative law are placed under a separate heading with the title 'Actions Taken Internationally to Protect Children'.[20] The sources in this section tend to be important internationally or in other countries but hold no special significance for Canada except to the extent that their existence

---

[17] *Baker*, n 3 above, para 81.
[18] See, eg, Brunnée and Toope 'A Hesitant Embrace', n 8 above.
[19] *Sharpe v AG Canada* [2001] 1 SCR 45, para 170.
[20] *Ibid*, para 175 ff.

and contents convince us of the importance of the objective. And it is here that they refer to the *Optional Protocol to the Convention on the Rights of the Child on the sale of children, child prostitution, and child pornography*.[21] The implication seems to be that since Canada has not signed the *Optional Protocol*, it is simply an 'international action' but not an 'action taken by Canada'. This, in contrast with the treatment of the *Convention*, points to the legal salience attributed to the Act of ratification alone.

A more explicit indication of the significance of ratified but unincorporated conventions can be found in *Thomas v Baptiste*, a decision of the Judicial Committee of the Privy Council.[22] That case involved an appellant, Thomas, who had been convicted of murder and sentenced to death in Trinidad and Tobago. Trinidad and Tobago had ratified the *International Covenant on Civil and Political Rights* (ICCPR)[23] and acceded to the Optional Protocol.[24] It had also ratified the *American Convention on Human Rights 1969* (ACHR). By ratifying the ACHR the state recognised the Inter-American Commission's competence to entertain petitions from individuals as well as the compulsory jurisdiction of the Inter-American Court to give binding rulings. Following his conviction, Thomas petitioned the Inter-American Commission alleging violations of his rights. The Inter-American Court issued an order requiring the government to refrain from carrying out the death sentence pending determination of the petitions. The government was prepared to defy this order and proceed with the death sentence. On appeal, the Privy Council accepted that Thomas could not enforce the terms of the ACHR since although it had been ratified, it had not been incorporated by legislation. However, the majority of the Privy Council went on to hold that the ratification none the less had some mandatory legal effect:

> By ratifying a treaty which provides for individual access to an international body, the Government made that process for the time being part of the domestic criminal justice system and thereby temporarily at least extended the scope of the due process clause in the Constitution.[25]

Their Lordships accordingly stayed the executions pending determination of the petitions by the Commission. Lord Goff and Lord Hobhouse dissented. In their opinion, the phrase 'due process of law' in the Constitution of Trinidad and Tobago simply referred to 'the law of the land'.[26] Since ratified

---

[21] A/RES/54/ 263 (2000) discussed at para 178, *ibid*.
[22] [1999] JCJ No 12.
[23] *International Covenant on Civil and Political Rights*, 19 December 1966, 999 *UNTS* 171 (entered into force 23 March 1976).
[24] *Optional Protocol to the International Covenant on Civil and Political Rights*, 16 December 1966, Can TS 1976 No 47 (entered into force 23 March 1976)
[25] *Thomas*, n 22 above, para 26.
[26] *Thomas*, n 22 above, para 61.

but unincorporated treaties are not part of the law of the land, rights contained therein cannot form the part of the due process guarantee within the domestic constitution.

A recent Ontario case provides a more detailed illustration of a similar dispute about the salience of ratified but unincorporated treaties. *Ahani v The Queen*[27] has a long and complicated history. However, the most relevant proceedings for our purposes concern the claim that the appellant, a Convention refugee who had been ordered deported for security reasons and had exhausted his domestic remedies, ought to be granted a stay of that deportation order until the United Nations Human Rights Committee (the 'Committee') considered his claim for relief under the Optional Protocol which Canada had ratified but not domestically incorporated. The Human Rights Committee made an 'interim measures' request that Canada stay his deportation order until it had considered the communication. Neither this interim request nor the Committee's final views on the matter were binding as a matter of international law. Canada refused to accede to the Committee's request. Ahani then sought an injunction restraining his deportation pending the Committee's consideration of his petition. He argued that the principles of fundamental justice under section 7 of the Canadian *Charter of Rights and Freedoms* gave him a right not to be deported until the Committee had considered and reported on his petition. The trial judge refused to issue a stay.[28]

A majority of the Ontario Court of Appeal dismissed Ahani's appeal. Laskin JA (Charron JA concurring) held that to give effect to Ahani's section 7 argument would have the untenable effect of converting a non-binding request in an unincorporated Protocol into a binding obligation in a domestic court. Speaking of the Covenant and the Protocol, Laskin JA pointed out that 'Absent implementing legislation, neither has any legal effect in Canada'.[29] Further neither the Covenant nor the Protocol were intended to be binding even as a matter of international law, much less of domestic law. Laskin JA distinguished *Thomas* by pointing to the binding nature of the Inter-American Court's orders and to the fact that the death penalty was involved. He also confessed to finding Lord Millett's reasoning in *Thomas* perplexing and to preferring the opinion of Lord Goff as more consistent with the principle that a ratified but unincorporated treaty is not part of domestic law. Rosenberg JA issued a powerful dissent. While he agreed that a ratified but unincorporated treaty did not give the appellant rights that could be enforced in a domestic court, here all that was claimed was the limited procedural right of reasonable access to the very Committee upon which the federal government has conferred jurisdiction. Since the

---

[27] [2002] OJ No 431.
[28] *Ahani v Canada (Minister of Citizenship and Immigration)* [2002] OJ No 90.
[29] *Ahani*, n 28 above, para 31.

federal government held out this right of review, limited though it might be, it was not entitled to render it practically illusory by deporting the appellant before the review was completed. Accordingly, Rosenberg JA would have stayed the deportation order pending the Committee's review.

These cases serve as but a sample of the on-going debate over the domestic significance of ratified but unincorporated treaties. None the less, they illustrate a move away from the automatic equation of the domestic force of a convention with its domestic effect. At the same time, however, they reveal anxiety about the implications of this for the rule that ratified but unincorporated conventions have no automatic force in domestic law. Thus we see judges seeking some alternative to the unpalatable extremes of the traditional position: on the one hand, that ratification makes no mandatory domestic difference until incorporation, or on the other, that ratification in and of itself effectively gives rise to rights in domestic law. The dissents in *Baker* and in *Thomas* both forcefully repudiate the idea that there is defensible terrain between the binding/non-binding extremes of the traditional position. But let us examine the attempts to articulate what that intermediate terrain might look like to see whether there is something in what the courts seek to articulate.

The Influential Authority of Ratified but Unincorporated Treaties

So, as we see, judges faced with international conventions that are ratified but not domestically incorporated often seem willing to hold that, notwithstanding the incorporation requirement, there is some domestic legal significance to the fact of ratification, even if does not give rise to substantive domestic rights. But how exactly do they put the nature of this salience? And how do they justify it? Often, judges suggest that there is some salience to these norms that doesn't amount to the conferral of the actual rights contained in the treaties. And perhaps because the significance they attach seems to operate in this sense at a different 'level' than the direct effect of the treaty would, they do not typically describe its effect in terms of the presumption of conformity. Instead, they point to something else, something that may have links to the presumption but is not reducible to it. In order to examine what the courts seem to be trying to get at in these cases, let us imagine the difference between the range of positions open to a state before and after ratification of the *Convention on the Rights of the Child,* for example.

Prior to signing and ratifying an instrument like the *Convention*[30] a whole range of possibilities are open to such a state (State A). Officials of A

---

[30] I am focusing here on the problem of ratified but unincorporated treaties since that is the issue that has most preoccupied courts. This analysis may, of course, hold distinct implications for signed, but unratified treaties as well.

could argue, were they so inclined, that children's rights do not matter in A at all. Such rights should be accorded, they might say, no special significance. But now suppose that A signs and ratifies the *Convention*. Its former position would no longer be open to A in the same way. This suggests that at a minimum ratifying the *Convention* affects the argumentative possibilities open to A. In part this happens because ratification changes what A would need to do in order to justify taking positions that might formerly have been perfectly open to it. Before ratifying, A could simply assert that children deserved no special consideration from the state and then try to defend that view on its merits. But after ratifying, what A would need to do to justify this position would change significantly. For now, not only would A have to defend its view on the merits, it would also have to try to give an account of how that view squares with the fact that it ratified a *Convention* that asserts values in direct opposition to those A claims it holds. A would have to, in other words, take account of the fact of ratification in any justification of a position it might take on issues that the *Convention* bears upon.

There are of course ways that A might do so. They range from relatively respectable arguments like pointing to the existence of strong countervailing values in the concrete case to 'bad faith' accounts that suggest that it might be in A's interest to hold itself out as caring about something that it does not actually care about. And one can imagine a whole range of positions in between. So there may well be arguments that State A could come up with to account for both the purported view and the fact of ratifying the *Convention*. But the fundamental point here is that there now exists the necessity of addressing and accounting for something that would not have exerted such an argumentative imperative, a demand for justification, before the *Convention* was ratified.

And in fact an illustration of just this kind of dynamic can be found in the various arguments in the Australian counterpart to *Baker*, *Teoh*.[31] It is somewhat striking that despite the similarity between *Baker* and *Teoh*, neither the majority nor the dissent in *Baker* specifically refers to *Teoh*. In part this is undoubtedly testimony to how controversial that case and its fallout have proved.[32] *Teoh* involved an application to review a refusal to grant Mr Teoh resident status because of his serious criminal record. Mr Teoh argued that the deportation would cause hardship for his wife and children. The Review Panel refused to review the decision although they acknowledged that deportation would cause serious hardship to Teoh's family. They justified this by pointing to his serious criminal record. Teoh applied for

---

[31] *Minister for Immigration and Ethnic Affairs v Teoh* (1995) 128 ALR 353.
[32] See for instance the discussion in Dyzenhaus, Hunt and Taggart, n 4 above 11–12 and the excellent discussion of *Teoh* in M Hunt, *Using Human Rights Law in English Courts* (Oxford, Hart Publishing, 1998) 242 ff. See also Allars, 'Of Cocoons and Small "c" Constitutionalism: The Principle of Legality and an Australian Perspective on *Baker*' (ch 12 of this volume).

judicial review and the Federal Court quashed the decision.[33] Two of the three judges held that the discretion had been exercised inconsistently with the *Convention on the Rights of the Child*, which Australia had ratified but had not incorporated into Australian law.

Particularly interesting to our exploration of how one might account for treating a ratified but unincorporated treaty as an influential source of legal authority is the opinion of Lee J. In Lee J's view, the legal salience of the *Convention* was a feature of the fact that its ratification was a statement to the national and international communities that Australia respected the rights contained therein. Consequently, the majority held that the fact of ratification, though it had no direct effect, none the less created a 'legitimate expectation' that the *Convention* rights would be respected by decision-makers. This expectation gave rise to a duty of procedural fairness to attend to the welfare of the children. The failure to do this meant that the power had not been exercised in conformity with the legitimate expectation that arose as a result of the ratification of the *Convention*.

Unsurprisingly, the Minister appealed to the High Court. The position of the Government turned on the argument that a ratified but unincorporated treaty could never give rise to rights in domestic law. Like the majority in *Baker*, the *Teoh* majority had no difficulty agreeing that a ratified but unincorporated treaty had no direct force domestically. However, this did not, in their view, mean that the ratified treaty was of no significance domestically. Instead, like Lee J in the Federal Court, Mason CJ, Deane J and Toohey J all invoke the idea that the ratification of the *Convention* was a kind of statement or undertaking both to the nation and to the larger international community that Australia cared about and intended to respect the rights contained in the *Convention*.[34] So the High Court majority found that for this reason ratification gave rise to a legitimate expectation of compliance with the ratified treaty. And the majority in *Teoh* is quite explicit about its disapproval of the 'bad faith' possibility—that is the hypocrisy of the state that ratified the *Convention* subsequently attempting to argue that that ratification should be ignored. Such a solemn act, they suggest, could not be dismissed as 'merely platitudinous or ineffectual' and of no legal effect whatsoever.[35] The High Court opinions in *Teoh* draw on the similar New Zealand case, *Tavita*. In *Tavita*, which also concerned the domestic impact of the ratified but unincorporated *Convention on the Rights of the Child*, the New Zealand Court of Appeal intimated that courts should be reluctant to accept an argument by the Government that implied that New Zealand's ratification of international instruments was 'at least partly window-dressing'.[36]

---

[33] (1994) 121 ALR 436.
[34] (1995) 183 CLR 273 (HCA) at 291 (per Mason CJ and Deane J) and at 301 (per Toohey J).
[35] *Ibid*, 291.
[36] *Tavita v Minister of Immigration*, [1994] 2 NZLR 257 at 266.

Indeed, in that case, Cooke P described the Government's position that it need not heed ratified conventions as 'unattractive'.[37] This all suggests that the act of ratification is itself of some domestic legal significance that does not amount to direct force, nor to the conferral of distinct rights, in domestic law. There are, however, difficulties we shall explore later associated with understanding the relevant obligation in terms of the doctrine of legitimate expectations.

A similar justification for the position that ratified but unincorporated treaties impose some legal imperatives is found in Rosenberg JA's powerful dissent in *Ahani*. Rosenberg JA's language is instructive when seen in light of *Teoh* and *Tavita*. He points out that, through the act of ratification, the federal government 'committed itself to these binding obligations' and that it 'held out' the right to communicate with the Committee.[38] Similarly, he repeatedly points out that the decision to ratify was 'voluntary',[39] that it was the federal government's decision to enable this recourse to the Committee, and that having done so, it could not frustrate the very right it established.[40] It is also instructive that Rosenberg JA quotes the dissenting speech of Lord Nicholls in *Briggs v Baptiste*[41] on the following point:

> By acceding to the Convention, Trinidad and Tobago intended to confer benefits on its citizens. The benefits were intended to be real, not illusory. The Inter-American system of human rights was not intended to be a hollow sham or, for those under sentence of death, a cruel charade.[42]

Thus, like the courts above, Rosenberg JA articulates a justification for treating ratification of a treaty as itself of some legal salience, a salience that is not limited to its actual application or force and that changes at least the kinds of arguments and justifications that the ratifying government can offer in support of its actions.

What these judgments suggest is that the exercise of public power must exhibit some degree of compatibility with publicly expressed values. Thus, it is not open to the government to 'hold out' internationally that it respects certain rights and then baldly state internally that it does not. Indeed, the justifications for the imposition of some kind of legal obligation are typically phrased in terms of holding out, creating expectations, and even the danger of bad faith. On this point, they echo the good faith requirement in *Vienna Convention*. And in fact in *Ahani* Rosenberg JA cites this very provision in the context of discussing the significance of Canada's external

---

[37] *Ibid*, 266.
[38] *Ahani*, n 28 above, para 73 and 93.
[39] *Ahani*, n 28 above, para 92.
[40] See for instance *Ahani*, n 28 above, para 86, 88, 92–93.
[41] [2000] AC 40 (JCPC).
[42] *Ahani*, n 28 above, para 98 quoting *Briggs ibid* para 47.

'undertakings' for its internal exercise of power.[43] The underlying notion is the 'simple principle of justice' that where there is a right there should be a remedy and that it should not be possible to claim the 'upside' of a certain position without also accepting the downside.[44] For this reason, the justifications for the legal salience of a ratified but unincorporated convention often seem to turn on an underlying commitment to a kind of integrity in the exercise of public power.[45] Public power must thus, at a minimum, exhibit some kind of fidelity to the values it has itself expressly adopted.

It is worth pausing to note the complexity of the source of this obligation. As discussed above, it does to some degree rest upon the values to which the officials have publicly committed themselves. But the fact of expressing values itself is not sufficient to generate an obligation. Instead, it also requires something less visible but equally crucial—underlying principles about the imperatives that govern the exercise of public power. So for instance at work in the background we can see common law principles based on conceptions of commitment and trust, integrity or consistency and the like. It is only when these underlying principles are brought to bear upon the fact of ratification that the obligation to respect the expressed values is generated. In this sense, then, the rationale at work in these cases weaves together certain assumptions about the nature of public power and attentiveness to exactly what it is that the state publicly expresses. Thus the authority for the obligation must be understood as inherently complex and multifaceted. But while this may help to account for the judicial refusal to accept that a solemn undertaking like signing and ratifying a convention is irrelevant to the domestic exercise of public power, lingering anxiety remains about ensuring a proper relation between the domestic legal order and international law.

The Demands of Influential Authority

What the above cases thus seem to point to is a norm or set of norms which, though explicitly not binding, none the less exerts a kind of imperative. But

---

[43] *Ahani*, n 28 above, para 70 citing *Vienna Convention on the Law of Treaties*, Can TS 1980 No 37, Arts 26–27.
[44] This source of obligation is by no means limited to this arena. Instead, two examples that might readily come to mind are the significance of the notion of 'holding oneself out' in a number of areas of law including tort law and corporate law. In both of those areas, someone who holds themselves out publicly as having certain skills or authority for instance will not easily be able to insist they should not be held to that standard.
[45] There are arguably many other examples of such justifications and accordingly the use of these cases is meant only to be illustrative, not exhaustive. For example, speaking of the justifications for the indirect effect of non-directly effective European Community law in UK courts, Murray Hunt rejects as superficial the 'traditional justifications' and notes that 'the courts recognised the impossibility of resisting the development consistently with the political reality of the UK's membership of the Community': *Using Human Rights Law in English Courts*, n 32 above, 122.

this imperative, our examples also suggest, operates somewhat differently than norms which have direct force and thus generate distinct rights. For rather than demanding that their actual terms be enforced, these influential sources instead insist that they be addressed, considered, weighed in the course of justifying a decision upon which they might rightly be thought to bear. They demand, one might say, respect as opposed to adherence with their terms. And these two features—the fact that the normative regime is itself not rights-generating[46] along with the fact that it none the less demands attention and justification—are characteristic of 'influential' authority.

In terms of exactly what it is that influential authority demands, it is worthwhile noting what significance Madam Justice L'Heureux-Dubé in *Baker* drew from the principles she cited, including prominently the *Convention*. The most relevant provision of the *Convention* is Article 3 which states that in all actions concerning children, 'the best interests of the child shall be the primary consideration'.[47] Interestingly, however the *Baker* majority held that what the relevant principles required was something slightly different: 'the decision-maker should consider children's best interests as an important factor, give them substantial weight, and be alert, alive and sensitive to them'.[48] But this does not mean that children's interests must always outweigh other considerations. Indeed, the majority in *Baker* states that the applicant is not entitled to a particular outcome nor does anything mandate a result consistent with the wording of the *Convention*.[49] This language suggests that while ratification of the *Convention* is not enough, in and of itself, to insist on conformity with its terms, it does rule out some courses of action. The way the majority puts the imperatives in *Baker* is illuminating:

> where the interests of children are minimised, in a manner inconsistent with Canada's humanitarian and compassionate tradition and the Minister's guidelines, the decision will be unreasonable.[50]

One way to describe the relationship between this demand and the fact of ratification would be to say that having ratified the *Convention*, it is not open to Canada to act in a manner which belies or makes a mockery of the act of ratification. As we have seen, this tracks the justifications invoked by various courts that have struggled with this question. Thus, while the *Convention* need not be complied with in all of its terms, its essential values,

---

[46] To say that the values do not themselves generate rights and obligations is not, however, to suggest their irrelevance to the articulation of such rights and obligations. In fact, because such values are an important element of the interpretive context, they are often crucial to the delineation and justification of specific rights and obligations.
[47] *Convention*, n 11 above.
[48] *Baker*, n 3 above, para 75.
[49] *Baker*, n 3 above, para 75.
[50] *Baker*, n 3 above, para 75.

its core principles, cannot be flouted by us once we have signed and ratified it. It now exerts influence and imposes some constraints on how we publicly exercise power in the sense at least that we must be able to justify that exercise as consistent with the core principles or values of the *Convention*.[51] Indeed, in a speech Madam Justice L'Heureux-Dubé herself points to this quality of ratified but unincorporated treaties when she states that 'the fact that Canada is a party to international human rights instruments certainly signals a commitment to abide by the terms of such documents and to the values they represent'.[52] The conclusion she draws is also significant: 'their existence cannot be ignored by the legal community'.[53] Thus, at a minimum judges and lawyers should be aware of any such treaty and should 'assess its relevance to the specific issues before them'.[54]

A similar approach to the distinctive demands of influential authority can be found in Rosenberg JA's dissent in *Ahani*. There, Rosenberg JA repeatedly points out that it would run counter to basic principles of justice to allow the executive that extended the right in the first place to turn around and frustrate that very right.[55] The effect of this principle, as Rosenberg JA articulates it, does not give rise to an absolute right of effective review. What the principle instead requires is that the government cannot deny the very right which it extended in the first place 'without some reasonable justification'.[56] Similarly, he says that the government cannot 'without reason' render the review illusory.[57] This leaves open the possibility, he notes, that the government could justify its decision by showing that the Committee process would result in 'intolerable delay'.[58] So for Rosenberg JA, ratifying the Covenant and the Protocol gives rise to the

---

[51] Interestingly, Brunnée and Toope criticise *Baker* on this ground for not giving full force to the obligations in the *Convention* but only to the 'values' and 'principles': 'A Hesitant Embrace', n 8 above. They argue that the presumption of conformity should have been sufficient to allow the Court to have recourse to the *provisions* of the *Convention* and not simply to its values and principles. However the argument in the text above is that the very feature which Brunnée and Toope identify as a weakness in the *Baker* majority may actually reveal the operation of a distinct form of authority—influential authority—that is not reducible to the traditional binding/non-binding distinction. It may also be that the presumption itself ultimately relies upon an underlying account that is hard to make sense of on the traditional model. Finally, on this view, it may be significant that although Brunnée and Toope describe the presumption as a presumption of conformity, the passage they cite from Driedger is slightly—and perhaps relevantly—more equivocal: 'In choosing among interpretations, therefore, the courts avoid interpretations that would put Canada in breach of any of its international obligations'. (see above n 13 at 330.) The role of the courts on the view outlined in the text may in cases of this kind of influential authority be better understood as ensuring some kind of baseline integrity by ruling out incoherent positions rather than as actually demanding full conformity.

[52] 'From Many Different Stones', n 3 above, 6.
[53] 'From Many Different Stones', n 3 above, 6.
[54] 'From Many Different Stones', n 3 above, 6.
[55] *Ahani*, n 28 above, para 86, 88.
[56] *Ahani*, n 28 above, 88.
[57] *Ahani*, n 28 above, 88.
[58] *Ahani*, n 28 above, para 110.

demand that the core values inherent in those regimes be respected or attended to, as they were in the majority decision in *Baker*. But, as there, this is not the same thing as requiring conformity with its terms nor does it therefore amount to extending the same rights to individuals that would be available under the Covenant. In fact Rosenberg JA explicitly affirms that the Covenant and the Protocol do not create 'rights in the appellant that can be enforced in a domestic court'.[59] They do however impose a justificatory burden—a demand for a reason why the government that ratified the treaty now wants to ignore its terms. So something more than raising the conventional argument that ratification does not give rise to domestic rights will be required to justify government inattentiveness in these cases. The demands of justification are accordingly more burdensome, even if the rights themselves are not by virtue of ratification alone automatically available.

In this regard, the majority decision of Laskin JA in *Ahani* is illuminating. For although he insists that absent implementing legislation, neither the Covenant nor the Protocol has 'any legal effect in Canada', he actually forwards the very kind of justification for the federal government's action that influential authority would seem to demand. Thus, he points out the non-binding nature of the Committee's final views, the fact that even under the terms of the Protocol Ahani has no right to remain in Canada until final determination, and Canada's potentially conflicting international obligations, including the obligation to fight terrorism.[60] Importantly this enables him to conclude that 'Canada is acting consistently with the terms under which it signed the Protocol'.[61] Similarly, he notes the worry about 'bad faith' but rejects the idea that judges are competent to assess this question.[62] To some extent then, the very arguments that Laskin JA invokes in *Ahani* cut against his insistence that the ratification is of no domestic effect. The conclusion, even for the majority, thus really seems to turn on the adequacy of the government justification rather than on the necessity for it, which even Laskin JA's own decision seems to assume.

Thus, although the majority decision in *Ahani* actually seems responsive to the demands of influential authority, it is clear that much of what drives it is the danger of 'backdoor incorporation'. And because of this concern, which is also apparent in the dissents in *Baker* and *Thomas*, it is worth paying a bit more attention to how this reading of *Baker* and *Ahani* differs from the High Court decision in *Teoh* and from the *Thomas* majority. In *Teoh*, the High Court found that the fact of ratification gave rise to a legitimate expectation on the part of Teoh that the decision about his deportation would be made with the best interests of his children as a primary consideration, as

---

[59] *Ahani*, n 28 above, para 93, 103
[60] *Ahani*, n 28 above, para 36–40, 42, 48.
[61] *Ahani*, n 28 above, at para 42.
[62] *Ahani*, n 28 above, para 45–49.

the *Convention* provides in Article 3. Because this expectation was objective in character, it did not matter that Mr Teoh had not subjectively relied on ratification. Instead, the doctrine bound the decision-maker who had in fact treated Mr Teoh's character as the primary consideration, not the well-being of his children.[63] McHugh J issued a strongly worded dissent on this very point. It was axiomatic in his view that undertakings in other states could not give rise to legitimate expectations domestically because conventions do not on their own have the force of law.[64] The effect of the majority decision, McHugh worried, was effectively to allow the 'backdoor incorporation' of the *Convention* into domestic law.[65] Significantly for our purposes, the majority responded by distinguishing legitimate expectations from 'binding rules of law'.

While there are undoubtedly affinities between the 'legitimate expectations' approach and the approach taken by the majority in *Baker* and the dissent in *Ahani*, there are also important contrasts. In both sets of cases, the decisions insist that they are respecting the difference between merely ratified and domestically incorporated conventions, but they do so in very different ways. *Baker* and the *Ahani* dissent do so by limiting the effect of the *Convention* to the insistence that core values of the ratified document must be respected rather than undermined. This remedy thus engages the ratified treaty only at the level of its general values or principles and imposes obligations of justification and respect, rather than conformity or compliance. In contrast, the majorities in *Teoh* and *Thomas* may seem to go much farther. Thus, in *Teoh* the majority invokes the doctrine of legitimate expectations which logically seems to give rise to the very rights enshrined in the *Convention*. It then attempts to avoid the indirect incorporation worry by pointing out that the rights are not as powerful as they seem in part because the relevant expectations can be defeated by announcing the intention to act inconsistently with the *Convention* and giving the affected parties notice and a chance to respond.

However, linking the significance of ratification to the doctrine of legitimate expectations seems to give rise to a number of problems that arise from treating the expectations of individuals as the rationale for the obligation.[66] First, because most individuals will actually not have any such expectations, the device seems fictional and creates additional justificatory obstacles. In order to respond to these difficulties, the idea of objective expectations is

---

[63] *Teoh*, n 31 above, 365–66; 374.
[64] *Teoh*, n 31 above, 385.
[65] *Teoh*, n 31 above, 385.
[66] See the excellent discussion of the difficulties with recourse to legitimate expectations in Hunt, *Using Human Rights Law*, n 32 above, 242–247 and in Dyzenhaus, Hunt and Taggart 'The Principle of Legality', n 4 above, 10–12. For a discussion of the subsequent executive efforts to defeat legitimate expectations see 'The Principle of Legality' at 11 and M Allars, 'Of Cocoons and Small "c" Constitutionalism: The Principle of Legality and an Australian Perspective on *Baker*' (ch 12 of this volume).

introduced. Beyond this though, the doctrine seems in one respect too strong for it seems to require fidelity to the specifics of the ratified convention, which thus gives rise to a more robust worry about 'back door incorporation'. But the obligation also seems in another way too weak for, as we saw in *Teoh*, it seems relatively easy to defeat these expectations and so to nullify the consequences of ratification. And, although the Privy Council decision in *Thomas* seems to avoid some of the difficulties with the doctrine of legitimate expectations, its reasoning is so cryptic that even sympathetic judges like Mr Justice Rosenberg find it 'strained'.[67] Undoubtedly part of the worry concerns the way that the Privy Council found that, notwithstanding the lack of domestic incorporation, the actual rights in the *Convention* became, even if only 'for the time being', 'part of the domestic criminal justice system' and hence relevant to the due process clause of the domestic constitution.[68] So, as in *Teoh*, the very rights contained in the *Convention* thereby come to have at least temporary domestic force notwithstanding the absence of domestic incorporation. But the consequence of this is that these decisions seem particularly difficult to square with the domestic incorporation requirement.

Baker followed *Teoh* by a number of years and the *Baker* court may well have had the benefit of assessing the fallout of that controversial decision. It is noteworthy that the *Baker* majority did not explicitly refer to *Teoh*. However, the majority in *Baker* did state that 'the doctrine of legitimate expectations did not mandate a result consistent with the wording of any international instruments ...'.[69] In fact, *Baker* can be read in conjunction with the *Ahani* dissent as pointing towards a rather different approach to the salience of ratified but unincorporated treaties—an approach that may be better captured in terms of influential authority. This understanding focuses on the integrity of public officials as the locus of concern, rather than on the expectations of individuals. And because the obligation attaches to the exercise of public office, it takes effect at the level of justifying the particular exercise of public power. The majorities in *Baker*, *Teoh*, *Thomas* and the dissent in *Ahani* all point to something that may seem curious or simply disingenuous from the point of view of the traditional model of the relationship between domestic and international law. The fact that a ratified but unincorporated convention has no domestic legal force, they insist, does not fully answer the question of its domestic effect. Because of this uncoupling of the orthodox equation of force and effect, the thrust of these cases sits uneasily with the fundamentally dualist underpinnings of the traditional account. Instead, these cases suggest that the effect that arises as a result of ratification is at once more and less demanding than

---

[67] *Ahani*, n 28 above, para 99.
[68] *Thomas*, n 22 above, para 26 (regarding the applicant's 'right').
[69] *Baker*, n 3 above, para 74.

either the presumption of conformity or the legitimate expectations approach, neither of which have much room for an understanding that does not equate effect with traditional binding force.[70]

In some respects, influential authority is more demanding than the legislative intention-based accounts. For instance, the effect of influential authority is more demanding than either a presumption of conformity or of legitimate expectations, the various decisions suggest, because absent withdrawal of ratification (as Trinidad and Tobago did during the *Thomas* litigation), it is not so clear that the influential effect of ratified treaties will be defeated by the simple expression of a contrary intention.[71] Indeed, the ineffectiveness of attempts by the executive in Australia to defeat the expectation that the *Convention* would be respected in the wake of *Teoh* may also point to the inaptness of understanding the obligation in terms of legislative intention. Thus, the fact that the obligation is not so easily defeated by a simple statement of counter intent suggests that legislative intention may not provide the best account of the foundations of the relevant obligation. The invocation of something like influential authority signals the possibility that there is a deeper and more complex picture of legal authority at work in these cases. In this picture, although legislative intention is certainly important, there are also underlying principles that shape and constrain the meaning of that intention in any particular case.[72] As the reactions to the expressions of contrary intention in Australia perhaps suggest, underlying presumptions of integrity or at least consistency may work against attempts

---

[70] The presumption of conformity and the doctrine of legitimate expectations are very closely linked and are probably best understood as simply two different perspectives on the same idea. The underlying content of the presumption is found in 'deemed' legislative intent. Legitimate expectations are the corollary of this view from the perspective of the citizen: the expectation is that the legislature will conform with international obligations, but these expectations are legitimate only until the legislature expresses a contrary intention. Thus the dualist, and essentially positivistic, commitments of both approaches are apparent in the fact that they locate the ultimate and exclusive account of legal obligation in the intention of the legislature.

[71] In contrast, '*unless there are unmistakable signals* pointing to the non-conformity of Canadian law with an international obligation, domestic law, including statutes and the *Charter*, should be interpreted to uphold Canada's treaty commitments': S Toope, 'The Uses of Metaphor: International Law and the Supreme Court of Canada' (2001) 80 *Canadian Bar Review* 534, 538. So the presumption, anchored as it is to legislative intention, seems open to the same weakness as legitimate expectations and could presumably be defeated in the same way. However, as noted, the aftermath of *Teoh* suggests that this may not be as simple as it seems.

[72] This suggests that there may well also be something to the decision of Gaudron J in *Teoh*, n 31 above, which located the source of the obligation to pay attention to children in the common law rather than the *Convention*. However, as the discussion in the text above suggests, developing a more integrative account of these various sets of norms may ultimately be more illuminating that locating the 'exclusive' source of the obligation in either domestic or international law. In this respect the judgment of Rosenberg JA in *Ahani*, n 28 above, seems more illuminating. There, he links the significance of ratification to the 'simple principle of justice' that where there is a right there must be a remedy (para 96). Similarly, his reasoning suggests that he is interpreting the significance of ratification in light of some idea of integrity which is implicit in fundamental justice under s 7 of the *Charter* (para 92/93, para 86/87).

by political officials to assert contradictory positions whenever they find it useful to do so. But this effect is difficult to fully explain with a presumption of conformity, legitimate expectations, or any other strictly intention-based accounts of obligation for it inevitably also draws on more general principles about the appropriate exercise of official power that do not find their source in the intention of the legislature or any other public body (though they may of course be expressed by them).

Ahani also illustrates another sense in which an influential authority approach may be more demanding than traditional intention-based conceptions of the obligations associated with ratified but unimplemented treaties. In *Ahani,* as discussed above, the relevant international procedure would never, because of its terms, give rise to a binding obligation either in international or in domestic law. The consequence of this lack of 'force', and of the traditional model's equation of force and effect, is that that model affords no basis for dispute with the majority in *Ahani*. If there is no force because no binding obligation will be generated, then any account that draws on the traditional model seems forced to the conclusion that the act of ratification is also devoid of any legal effect. Indeed, this impossibility of locating a binding obligation in an international process that could only ever issue advisory opinions was what drove the majority in *Ahani* to the conclusion that the ratification of that process exerted no effect whatsoever on the exercise of domestic political power. Similarly, commentators like Brunnée and Toope who have sought to explain the domestic significance of ratified but unimplemented treaties in terms of a presumption of conformity feel forced to reluctantly concur with the majority decision in *Ahani*.[73] If there is no binding force, on this model, then it is difficult to find any legal salience at all. But Rosenberg JA's dissent does not rest upon this dichotomous understanding of legal authority. Instead, he suggests that the 'principles of fundamental justice' demand that when the legislature itself establishes a right of review it is not open to it to 'unreasonably frustrate that right'.[74] The conception of influential authority that seems at work here thus holds open the possibility that non-binding norms and processes may also generate demands of respect that impose constraints and burdens, including justificatory ones, on political authorities.

At the same time however, because it functions primarily at the level of the basic values of the ratified treaty, influential authority also seems less demanding than intention-based accounts of these obligations. What it

---

[73] Thus Brunnée and Toope note that 'the majority decision is undoubtedly correct in so far as it is based on the non-binding nature of the [United Nations Human Rights] Committee process' n 8 above. Despite this, they confess to 'considerable sympathy' for Rosenberg JA's decision. However, as argued in the text, the *legal* significance of Rosenberg JA's decision can probably only be captured with a less bifurcated understanding of legal authority.
[74] *Ahani* at para 86.

demands from public officials is a justification of their exercise of power that does not mock or make a sham of the solemn undertaking of ratification. So, although the *Baker* majority has been criticised for the weakness of the obligation it found, arguably that 'weakness' signals something about influential authority. In this sense then, it and companion cases can be seen as part of an attempt to capture a more complex understanding of authority and to attend to the possibility, in that regard, that there may be norms that are best understood in terms of systemic values and underlying principles. And though these values and principles may not translate directly into discrete entitlements and obligations, they do none the less exert a mandatory influence on the way public power is exercised and, accordingly on the nature and justification of rights and obligations within the legal system.

To some degree the majorities in *Baker*, *Thomas* and *Teoh* and the dissent in *Ahani* seem to grasp for something just beyond their reach. And so, it may well be tempting to dismiss their efforts as either simply mistakes or as an attempt to dress up what they are really doing in fancier clothes. But what looks, under the traditional model, like 'confusion' or mistake in these decisions may actually reflect a different understanding of authority and judgment. Only within the realm of this alternative understanding can we make sense of the kind of 'influential authority' that is arguably illustrated by, though by no means limited to, the case of ratified but unincorporated treaties. Unlike the traditional view, this approach to legal authority is not sharply bifurcated. Indeed, this understanding of judgment and authority extends beyond the idea of persuasive authority per se, though it is also significantly indebted to it. For persuasive authority can yet be built into—indeed, in its 'purest' form it is perhaps dependent upon—the traditional picture. Everything that is not binding is, in this dichotomous world, optional or (more genially) 'persuasive'.

But noting, as we have in the cases above, the possibility of something like influential authority fatally complicates this neatly arranged world. For, as we have seen, influential authority cannot properly be placed into one category or the other. From the perspective of the traditional model, the temptation may well be to simply call this persuasive, thus shoring up the model. But influential authorities are 'demanding' in a way that distinguishes them from their purely persuasive counterparts. Yet their demands also differ in important ways from what the traditional model refers to as 'binding' authorities.[75] And beyond these difficulties, even were it possible

---

[75] I have purposely been somewhat circumspect about binding authority here because as numerous commentators have pointed out, this conception seems inapt to common law reasoning and indeed to much adjudication: S Perry, 'Judicial Obligation, Precedent and the Common Law' (1987) *Oxford Journal of Legal Studies* 215; AWB Simpson, 'The Common Law and Legal Theory' in Simpson (ed) *Oxford Essays in Jurisprudence* 2nd series (Oxford, Oxford University Press, 1973); Dyzenhaus, Hunt and Taggart, 'Principle of Legality', n 4 above. Indeed, outside of questions relating to the domestic effects of international treaty

to try to locate influential authority within the confines of the traditional picture, this does not seem the best way to understand what is at work in these cases.

Instead, the picture of judgement that seems to provide the background context for influential authority suggests that relevant sources may be many and their weight and significance may vary. Paying attention to the nature of influential authority also calls into question the very underpinning of the traditional picture—the positivist understanding that views legal authority as the exclusive province of the political authorities and thus as exhausted by their intentions, assumed or otherwise. For as we have seen, the kinds of obligations associated with influential authority seem to be more complex in derivation, owing something to the legal principles that have long been the province of the judiciary under the common law and something to the expressed intentions of political authorities. But this suggests that 'binding' authorities too may be multiple and may conflict with each other or with other authorities. In this way, the complexity of the account of judgment that makes sense of influential authority threatens to render almost nonsensical the idea of 'binding' law. Recognising that authorities may have no force and yet have effect, that sources with both force and effect may be multiple, conflicting and subject to the overarching demands of influential authorities seems to make the description of any particular authority as binding rather trite—one piece perhaps of an extremely complex puzzle. Thus, Trevor Allan seemed to capture something rather paradoxical about the explanatory power of the traditional model when he described sources as 'binding only in so far as they are persuasive'.[76]

Certainly, a decision-maker ultimately has to be persuaded and has to convince her audience that she has addressed the various sources with their various kinds of demands and claims in a meaningful way. To this extent, it seems correct that even a 'binding' source will ultimately only affect the decision in question if the decision-maker finds it 'persuasive' that it should. So particularly in the classic common law method, it does seem compelling to suggest that much that is of significance is captured in the question of the persuasiveness of the relevant authorities. For this reason, 'bindingness' and its positivist underpinnings, as many have noted, has always had great difficulty accounting for the common law.[77] Indeed, the fact that the doctrinal questions of the reception of international law rely on such a strong conception of bindingness may account to some degree for why the very salience of

---

obligations, commentators rarely suggest that the idea of bindingness itself has much explanatory or justificatory force in the adjudicative setting. I am grateful to David Dyzenhaus for reminding me of the implications of my argument for binding authority itself.

[76] Comment by Trevor Allan during 'The Unity of Public Law' 4 January 2003, Faculty of Law, University of Toronto.
[77] Perry, n 75 above; Simpson, n 75 above.

the traditional model seems especially implicated in the methodological debates in these cases.

Yet the invocation of the pure persuasiveness of the traditional common law method seems similarly unequal to the methodological puzzles illustrated by these complex 'boundary problem' cases. Authorities persuade or even compel attention for different kinds of reasons and accordingly demand different kinds of justifications. Any account of this process would therefore seem to require, if it is to take the process and its legitimacy seriously, more refined tools than persuasiveness alone offers to evaluate the nature of the relevant reasons and justifications. This seems particularly important when we remind ourselves that the common law method has been bedeviled by its own sometimes invidious conceptions of what seems persuasive. The history of the common law is replete with examples of the fact that courts all too often found persuasive arguments that rested upon the fundamental inhumanity of those who are disenfranchised or disadvantaged, for instance.[78] So the common law method and its reliance on a rather fluid conception of persuasiveness and values does not seem a particularly helpful alternative to the traditional model. This is particularly so because as *Baker*, *Teoh*, *Ahani*, and *Thomas* remind us, these cases will most often involve the claims of the disadvantaged.

Examining our next 'boundary problem' helps to respond at least in part to this worry. In fact, looking to the indirect effect of the *Charter* on the development of the common law provides a particularly apposite illustration of influential authority. Examining these cases more closely enables us to articulate some additional elements of influential authority. The indirect effect cases under the *Charter* also provide a further illustration of something we noted in the cases above, especially in Rosenberg's dissent in *Ahani*: this view of judgment inevitably contemplates a more integral link between the various relevant authorities including those authorities that are drawn from the common law itself. And beyond this, the *Charter*/common law cases also provide the beginning of a response to the problems inherent in the common law method itself. So the cases on the indirect effect of the *Charter* not only hold lessons for the issue of ratified but unincorporated treaties, they also illuminate some of the broader outlines of this alternative picture of authority and judgment.

THE CHARTER AND THE COMMON LAW

Although it has not been described as such, the clearest illustration of influential authority and its characteristic uncoupling of force and mandatory

---

[78] See M Moran, *Rethinking the Reasonable Person: An Egalitarian Reconstruction of the Objective Standard* (Oxford, Oxford University Press, 2003).

effect may be found in the jurisprudence that addresses the impact of the *Charter* outside the field of its direct application. Indeed, the growing appeal of the idea that an international law source could be effective, relevant, even insistent, without having any direct legal force, may well owe something to a judiciary that has worked to develop and understand a related idea in the context of the relationship between the *Charter* and the common law. Admittedly, it is as yet early days in the developing relationship between the *Charter*, the common law and private litigation.[79] And while there are many dimensions to this relationship, the discussion here will focus on its methodological significance and how it elaborates the idea of influential authority more broadly.

It is, since *Dolphin Delivery*, axiomatic that *Charter* guarantees do not apply directly to private litigation in the common law—they have in that sense no force. As McIntyre J states in *Dolphin Delivery*, although the *Charter* applies to the various branches of government whether their action is invoked in public or private litigation, it applies to the common law 'only in so far as the common law is the basis of some government action which, it is alleged, infringes a guaranteed right or freedom'.[80] In discussing this issue, McIntyre J draws a distinction that seems especially relevant to the idea of influential authority:

> Where, however, private party 'A' sues private party 'B' relying on the common law and where no act of government is relied upon to support the action, the *Charter* will not apply. I should make it clear, however, that this is a distinct issue from the question whether the judiciary ought to apply and develop the principles of the common law in a manner consistent with the fundamental values enshrined in the Constitution. The answer to this question must be in the affirmative. In this sense, then, the *Charter* is far from irrelevant to private litigants whose disputes fall to be decided at common law. But this is different from the proposition that one private party owes a constitutional duty to another .... [81]

So as this indicates, the legal salience of the *Charter* encompasses two distinct questions. First is the question of its direct application—does the *Charter* have direct force in any particular case in the sense that it can be the basis of a claim of obligation or entitlement? Second, and distinct, is the question of its effect or indirect application. And as McIntyre J importantly points out, although the *Charter* may not have force in any particular private dispute it may none the less continue to have effect.

---

[79] For an insightful discussion of the broader issues, see LE Weinrib and EJ Weinrib, 'Constitutional Values and Private Law in Canada' in D Friedmann and D Barak-Erez (eds) *Human Rights in Private Law* (Oxford, Hart Publishing, 2001) 43.
[80] [1986] 2 SCR 573, 598–99.
[81] *Ibid* 603.

In this sense then, the relationship of the *Charter* to the common law serves as an especially explicit instance of the disentanglement of the force of a legal norm and its effect. Thus, further exploration of how this distinct form of legal authority makes itself felt may assist us in developing a more precise picture of the idea of influential authority and its connection to an alternative conception of judgment. Since the argument here is that influential authority is in play when the mandatory legal effect of a source of law exceeds the sphere of its force or direct application, let us examine more closely exactly how courts have attempted to work with the implications of McIntyre J's passage in *Dolphin Delivery*.

There are a number of cases that address the question of how to understand what it might mean for the *Charter* to have an effect on the common law, even though it does not apply. However, most of the reasoning in these cases is quite limited and so they do not provide much insight into the nature of this kind of authority. But there are exceptions, the most useful of which for our purposes are *R v Salituro*,[82] *Hill v Church of Scientology*,[83] and *RWDSU v Pepsi-Cola*.[84] Let us briefly consider what these cases reveal about the nature of the influential authority that the *Charter* exerts on the common law.

Direct Application Versus Effect

One of the first cases that seriously considered the relationship between the *Charter* and the common law was *Salituro*. That case raised a question about the rule of evidence that provided that spouses were incompetent as witnesses for the prosecution. The question on appeal was whether there was a common law exception to this rule for spouses who were separated without any reasonable possibility of reconciliation. Since the rules at issue were common law rules of evidence, and since they seemed to rest upon an anachronistic view of the role of women and of the need to protect marital harmony at all costs, the case directly raised the question of the implications of McIntyre J's reasoning in *Dolphin Delivery*. Justice Iacobucci, speaking for the Court, carefully reviewed the changing judicial deference to past judicial decisions as well as the continuing limits on the power of the courts to change the common law. From this he drew the general conclusion that part of the judicial role involves adapting and developing common law rules to reflect changing circumstances in society at large. And, 'while complex changes' are best left to the legislature, 'the courts can and should make incremental changes to the common law to bring legal rules

---

[82] [1991] 3 SCR 654.
[83] [1995] 2 SCR 1130.
[84] 2002 SCC 8.

into step with a changing society'.⁸⁵ Applying this methodology to the common law rules regarding spousal incompetence, Iacobucci J found that the rule was incompatible with the *Charter* and an exception was accordingly warranted.

The question of how to understand the effect of the *Charter* on the common law was also central to the important Supreme Court of Canada decision in *Hill v Church of Scientology*. For our purposes, the most relevant aspect of that case concerned whether the common law of defamation complied with *Charter* values. The appellants, Morris Manning and the Church of Scientology, argued that it did not and that the common law of Canada ought to be modified to incorporate the 'actual malice' rule from the United States Supreme Court decision in *New York Times v Sullivan*.⁸⁶ The appellants had argued that the *Charter* applied directly because the respondent, Casey Hill, was an agent of the Crown. Cory J had no difficulty in dismissing the direct application argument and holding that 'the *Charter* cannot be applied directly to scrutinise the common law of defamation in the circumstances of this case'.⁸⁷ However, it still remained to be 'determined whether a change or modification in the law of defamation is required to make it comply with the underlying values upon which the *Charter* is founded'.⁸⁸ After undertaking an extensive analysis, Cory J found that the common law complied with the values of the *Charter*. So although the *Charter* had no direct application, it exerted an important influence on the common law.

In *RWDSU v Pepsi-Cola*, the Supreme Court of Canada considered the legality of secondary picketing and the relationship of the common law on that point to the *Charter*. The Court was particularly concerned with the *Hersees* approach which postulated that secondary picketing was unlawful *per se* and then crafted various exceptions. In *Pepsi-Cola* the Supreme Court measured this common law rule against the fundamental importance that the *Charter* places upon freedom of expression. Once again, the relationship of common law rules to *Charter* guarantees was a core issue in the case. Madam Justice McLachlin and Mr Justice LeBel delivered the opinion of the Court. They begin by considering the question of what relationship they ought to insist upon. They state:

> Although section 2(b) of the *Charter* is not directly implicated in this appeal, the right to free expression that it enshrines is a fundamental Canadian value. The development of the common law must therefore reflect this value. Indeed, quite apart from the *Charter*, the value of free expression informs the common law.⁸⁹

---

⁸⁵ *Salituro*, n 82 above, 666.
⁸⁶ 376 US 254 (1964).
⁸⁷ *Hill*, n 83 above, para 79.
⁸⁸ *Hill*, n 83 above, para 82.
⁸⁹ *Pepsi-Cola*, n 84 above, para 20.

And in *Pepsi-Cola*, the Supreme Court went on to hold that the common law as exemplified in the *Hersees* approach was inconsistent both with *Charter* methodology and with core *Charter* values. Accordingly, they fashioned a 'wrongful action' rule to ensure conformity between the core values of the *Charter* and the common law.

The Influence of the *Charter* on the Common Law

As these cases illustrate, courts have insisted that the fact that the *Charter* has no direct application to the common law does not answer the question of its effect. In fact, courts insist on the *mandatory* effect of the *Charter* notwithstanding its absence of force or direct application. But what is also noteworthy here, particularly in light of our discussion of ratified but unincorporated treaties, is how exactly the courts justify and articulate the nature of the *Charter's* influence on the common law.

Thus, for instance, in *Salituro* Iacobucci J found that the spousal incompetence rule reflected a view of women incompatible with the egalitarian values of the *Charter*. Further, the primacy that the spousal incompetence rule places upon the preservation of the marriage bond is inconsistent, in his view, with 'respect for the freedom of all individuals, which has become a central tenet of the legal and moral fabric of this country particularly since the adoption of the *Charter*'.[90] So what exerts mandatory influence on the common law is not the specific guarantees of the *Charter* but rather the central tenet, the 'basic theory underlying' the *Charter*. And rather than being located in a particular section or guarantee of the *Charter*, this central tenet 'finds expression in almost every right and freedom guaranteed in the *Charter*'.[91] Thus, Iacobucci J points to the right to choose one's own religion, philosophy of life, associations, expressions, location, and occupation as evincing the centrality of respect for individual choices within the *Charter's* framework. So the methodology seems to demand reading the various guarantees together in order to discern the central tenets, underlying and fundamental values of the *Charter*. And, it is these central values that are used to inform, develop and perhaps (as here) even reshape, the traditional rules of the common law.

The judgment of Cory J in *Hill* also helps to illuminate the operation of this form of influential authority. There, he points to important differences between how the *Charter* analysis proceeds where it applies directly and how it proceeds where it has mandatory effect but no direct force. Thus, he says of *Salituro* that the common law rule there did not infringe a specific right contained within the *Charter*. Rather, it was inconsistent with 'those

---

[90] *Salituro*, n 82 above, 673–74.
[91] *Salituro*, n 82 above, 673–74.

fundamental values that provide the foundation for the *Charter*'.[92] This suggests that the demands of this kind of authority are importantly different than where the *Charter* directly applies. The kind of conflict that triggers *Charter* modification of a common law rule is at once deeper and looser than the analysis that we find when the *Charter* applies directly. Because the guarantees do not apply per se, they cannot be infringed per se. So it is not the actual provisions or rights in the *Charter* that are engaged here, it is the substratum of the *Charter*—the fundamental values rather than the discrete rules and injunctions.[93] In this sense, *Hill* echoes and confirms *Salituro* in its suggestion that it is the foundational values of the *Charter*, rather than the concrete rights or guarantees, which are brought to bear on the rules of the common law.

And indeed, this insistence that it is the 'values' of the *Charter* not the 'rights' of the *Charter* that exert influence on the shape of the common law is also echoed in the approach that the courts in these cases take to section 1 analogue. In *Hill,* Cory J points out that the court in *Salituro* did not 'undertake an analysis similar to that which would be required under section 1 to determine if the *Charter* breach was justifiable'.[94] Instead, 'it proceeded to balance, in a broad and flexible manner, conflicting values'.[95] Thus, *Salituro* examined the justifications for the common law rule against the *Charter's* recognition of the equality of women and, more specifically, against the concept of human dignity which inspires the *Charter*. Since the *values* of the common law rule did not represent the values reflected in the provisions of the *Charter*, the common law rule had to be modified. Similarly, commenting on *R v Swain*,[96] Cory J points out one important reason why a section 1 analysis may be out of place in the common law context—in the case of the common law, the court is not limited to striking down the rule and remitting it to the legislature as in a traditional section 1 analysis because it is also open to the court to itself modify the rule to better reflect *Charter* values.

Cory J also attempts to get at the underlying reason why it is important to distinguish between cases in which the constitutionality of government

---

[92] *Hill*, n 83 above, para 86.
[93] There is a background question here about what relationship this approach contemplates between violations of discrete guarantees and inconsistency with fundamental or underlying values. Where a common law rule seriously compromises a core right of the *Charter*, presumably this would engage a worry about the fundamental or underlying values of the *Charter* even if only one right were engaged. It may be that the answer lies in the fact that, even where the *Charter* applies directly, the integrated nature of its guarantees means that more than one right or section will be in issue, though some will only be in the background. So perhaps in the cases to date, the fact that a common law rule engages several rights or guarantees simply reinforces the fact that it implicates the 'values' of the *Charter*, and not simply its discrete provisions.
[94] *Hill*, n 83 above, 86.
[95] *Hill*, n 83 above, 86.
[96] [1991] 1 SCR 933.

action is challenged and cases where there is no government action involved. Ordinary *Charter* analysis cannot be imported into private litigation because *Charter* rights do not exist in the absence of state action. Consequently, the most that a private litigant can do is to argue that 'the common law is inconsistent with *Charter* values'.[97] This distinction between *Charter* rights and *Charter* values is therefore crucial to maintaining the proper relationship between the *Charter* and the common law. So the *Charter* will demand modification of the common law only in so far as the common law is found inconsistent with *Charter* values. But given that the *Charter* also expresses our overarching mandatory values, courts also insist that the common law ought to positively develop in accordance with *Charter* values as well. And because the *Charter* analysis is operating at the level of conformity with systemic values, and does not involve discrete claims about *Charter* rights or duties, the balancing must be 'more flexible' than a traditional section 1 analysis.[98] The court should therefore weigh the principles underlying the common law against '*Charter* values, framed in general terms'.[99] And where the common law is at issue, Cory J states that the onus throughout remains on the party alleging inconsistency with the *Charter*. The reason seems to turn on a kind of reliance interest:

> One party will have brought the action on the basis of the prevailing common law which may have a long history of acceptance in the community. That party should be able to rely upon the law and should not be placed in the position of having to defend it.[100]

When Cory J actually undertakes the analysis of whether the common law of defamation measures up to *Charter* values, he stresses the integral relationship between the values of the common law and the values expressed in the *Charter*. Thus, he cites a number of important sources that predate the *Charter* as well as *Charter* cases for the proposition that while freedom of expression is central to democracy, it has never been understood as an unlimited right. In this regard, he specifically invokes the section 1 analysis in *Keegstra*[101] and *Butler*[102] along with other cases. And Cory J notes that the importance of reputation is recognised both at common law and under the *Charter*. Interestingly he points out 'although it is not specifically mentioned in the *Charter*, the good reputation of the individual represents and reflects the innate dignity of the individual, a concept which underlies all the *Charter* rights'.[103] And ultimately Cory J holds that the common law of

---

[97] *Hill*, n 83 above, para 95 (emphasis in original).
[98] *Hill*, n 83 above, para 97.
[99] *Hill*, n 83 above, para 97.
[100] *Hill*, n 83 above, para 98.
[101] [1990] 3 SCR 697.
[102] [1992] 1 SCR 452.
[103] *Hill*, n 83 above, para 120.

defamation complies with the underlying values of the *Charter* and hence need not be altered.

The more recent case of *Pepsi-Cola* also makes an important contribution to our understanding of how the influential authority of the *Charter* exerts its imperatives on the common law. After outlining the various different approaches available at common law and the significance of freedom of expression as a *Charter* value, the Court goes on to discuss what it means to 'conform' to *Charter* methodology. By stressing the methodological commitments of the *Charter*, the decision in *Pepsi-Cola* adds another element to our understanding of the requisite relationship between the *Charter* and the common law. Decisions like *Salituro* and *Hill* make it clear that the *Charter* imposes constraints upon the fundamental values that the common law can legitimately express. But according to the Court in *Pepsi-Cola*, the *Charter* also imposes methodological imperatives on the common law. The consequence is that being 'true' to *Charter* values means that 'our statement of the common law must start with the proposition that free expression is protected unless its curtailment is justified'.[104] This '*Charter*-mandated methodology' thus rules out any common law position that begins with the view that all secondary picketing is prima facie illegal and militates in favour of a rule that begins with the proposition that such picketing is legal, subject to justifiable limitations. In the opinion of the Court, the 'wrongful action' model, which permits secondary picketing except where it involves a tort or a crime, is therefore most consistent not only with *Charter* methodology but also with 'core' values of the *Charter*. And the Court briefly considers whether the rule though it 'respects the *Charter*' might be too permissive in the sense that it rules out justifications that would prevail under a traditional section 1 analysis.[105] Interestingly however the Court concludes that this will not be problematic, in part because the law of tort itself might be expected to develop in accordance with *Charter* values.[106]

Justifications for the Influential Authority of the *Charter*

As noted above, the influence of the *Charter* on the shape of the common law is more explicitly acknowledged and legitimated than is the influence

---

[104] *Pepsi-Cola*, n 84 above, para 67.
[105] *Pepsi-Cola*, n 84 above, para 102.
[106] *Pepsi-Cola*, n 84 above, para 106. This points to the fact, as does Cory J's decision in *Hill* along with numerous other cases, that the common law and the *Charter* ought not to be conceived as completely independent alternative sets of norms, nor ought we view the relationship as entirely unidirectional. Indeed an important part of the methodological challenge in these cases is to develop a non-reductionist understanding of the nature of the deep and mutual relation between constitutional rights and the common law. For this among other reasons, the standard conflicts model response to the existence of alternative sets of norms is methodologically inapt.

of ratified but unincorporated treaties in cases like *Baker*. Perhaps for this reason, it is possible to trace a greater evolution as the courts have slowly begun to explore the concrete ramifications of and justifications for such influential authority. Though we cannot explore this in detail, it is possible to outline the evolution of the more significant ideas at work here. Particularly important, perhaps, is the Supreme Court's gradual willingness to shift away from the traditional understanding of the role of the judiciary as adapting the common law to new facts and situations. Thus we see an increased acknowledgement that the fact that the *Charter* expresses mandatory values and constraints means that the judiciary is not simply keeping the common law up to date with changes to society. Instead, updating the common law in line with the imperatives of the *Charter* engages the courts in an enterprise that is more explicitly normative than its venerable role of keeping the common law in step with social changes.

The role of the judiciary in the common law has certainly always been more evaluative than many accounts give it credit for. None the less, it is still the case that where the judiciary undertakes (as it must always at least implicitly do) the *Charter*/common law exercise, it does not really capture the heart of that enterprise to describe it in terms of ensuring that the common law reflects social changes. There is an important normative and conceptual difference between updating rules to keep them in step with society, and allowing for the possibility that rules that are in fact quite consistent with social mores may none the less conflict with *Charter* values. This latter role that is confided to the judiciary under the *Charter* is undoubtedly closely related to the common law's 'ancient function of putting injustices right'. However because the relevant values are specified under the *Charter*, they do not pose quite the same interpretive challenge as the ancient jurisdiction tied simply to the identification of 'injustice'. Further, while the values authoritatively catalogued in the *Charter* are indebted in many respects to the judicially articulated rights of the common law, the *Charter* can also be seen as to some degree explicitly designed to correct for systematic difficulties with such articulations.[107] In these respects at least, coming to terms with the influence of the *Charter* on the common law places the judiciary in a more robustly evaluative and less straightforwardly 'reflective' review than has historically been its mainstay. In fact, even in the few cases discussed in detail here it is possible to trace a shift in the relevant judicial self-understanding along two dimensions: first, the shift from the idea of keeping up with social change to a more explicit recognition of the changing set of values that now exert their influence on the common law; and secondly, but

---

[107] Thus for instance the common law's record on putting right the injustice of discrimination is, to say the least, somewhat spotty: D Oliver, *Common Values and the Public-Private Divide* (London, Butterworths, 1999) at 104–05; JL Jowell, 'Is Equality a Constitutional Principle?' (1994) 47 *Current Legal Problems* 1.

not unrelated, an increasing willingness to describe the *Charter*'s influence on the common law in mandatory terms.

Thus, in an early case like *Salituro* we see the most modest rationale for the role of the courts in the *Charter*/common law relationship. There, Iacobucci J does note the evolving understanding of the judicial role with regard to the common law per se. Thus, he points out that courts no longer accept the traditional view that the courts simply discovered, rather than developed, the common law. With the demise of this view and its concomitant limitations on the power of judges to overrule precedents, as Iacobucci J indicates, it became accepted that courts had to adapt and develop common law rules to reflect changing social circumstances.[108] The conclusion that Iacobucci J draws from his review of the cases takes as its point of departure this refinement upon the traditional role of courts in the development of the common law. Thus, he notes that courts have and should take a flexible approach to the development of the common law, which is, after all, their province. They should accordingly 'adapt the common law to reflect the changing social, moral and economic fabric of the country'.[109] As this suggests, the traditional deferential stance towards the past is no longer appropriate. Judges must instead scrutinise common law rules and should 'not be quick to perpetuate rules whose social foundation has long since disappeared'.[110] And, although the legislature is the proper place for complex law reform initiatives, it is part of the proper role of the judiciary to advance 'incremental changes which are necessary to keep the common law in step with the dynamic and evolving fabric of our society'. But the fundamental justification that Justice Iacobucci invokes here is heavily dependent upon the fact that judges have traditionally developed the common law in order to adapt it to changing situations. The *Charter* under this approach is one extremely important part of that changing fabric. Although in his review of the spousal incompetence rule Iacobucci J undoubtedly does carefully scrutinise the *values* of the common law rules, in the justification which he forwards for the role that he assumes, he does not highlight this dimension of the analysis. Instead, he relies upon more general formulations which stress continuity with the traditional role such as keeping 'the common law in step with the dynamic and evolving fabric of our society'.[111]

In comparison with this rather modest understanding of the judicial role in the *Charter*/common law relationship, in *Hill* the Court is somewhat more explicit about the increasing distance between the traditional judicial role and the new dimension of that role mandated by the *Charter*. So unlike the justification for the judicial role in *Salituro*, in *Hill* the Court is more

---

[108] *Salituro*, n 82 above, 665.
[109] *Salituro*, n 82 above, 670.
[110] *Salituro*, n 82 above, 670.
[111] *Salituro*, n 82 above, 670.

straightforward about the evaluative nature of the new judicial role. So while in *Salituro* the justifications emphasise the continuity with the traditional role of ensuring the common law keeps pace with general changes to society, in *Hill* the Court explicitly acknowledges the significance of the role of *values*. So for instance Cory J describes the obligation of the courts to interpret the common law in a manner which is consistent with *Charter* principles as a 'manifestation of the inherent jurisdiction of the courts to modify or extend the common law in order to comply with prevailing social conditions and values'.[112] This flows from two features of the relationship: first, the courts are the custodians of the common law and as such are responsible for ensuring it reflects 'emerging needs and values';[113] second, the *Charter* represents a restatement of the fundamental values which guide and shape our democratic society and our legal system. From this it follows that courts should make incremental changes in the common law to ensure it complies with the values enunciated in the *Charter*. *Hill* is thus more explicit than *Salituro* in noting that judicial development may be more overtly evaluative than it traditionally was, now that courts have been given an authoritative statement of values in the *Charter*. *Hill* is also slightly more emphatic on the judicial role than *Salituro* on another dimension. Rather than emphasising that the common law ought to 'reflect' social changes, in *Hill* the Court puts it more strongly when it emphasises the idea of 'complying' with *Charter* values rather than simply 'reflecting' such values.

This trend towards describing in stronger and more evaluative terms the nature of the *Charter*'s influence on the common law is continued in *Pepsi-Cola*. This is apparent even in the description of the *Charter* itself. Thus, for instance, the Court points to the reason why the *Charter* would exert the influence it does on the common law when it notes:

> The *Charter* constitutionally enshrines essential values and principles widely recognised within Canada, and more generally, within Western democracies. *Charter* rights, based on a long process of historical and political development, constitute a fundamental element of the Canadian legal order upon patriation of the Constitution. The *Charter* must thus be viewed as one of the guiding instruments in the development of Canadian law.[114]

So in comparison with the cases before it, *Pepsi-Cola* puts the *Charter* front and centre. No longer is it captured within more general statements about Canadian society and values. Instead, it occupies a central place both because the values it expresses are the fundamental values of our legal order and because it expresses them in a mandatory way. And beyond this, the *Charter* also links us to a larger world of similarly shared values. So the

---

[112] *Hill*, n 83 above, para 91.
[113] *Hill*, n 83 above, para 91.
[114] *Pepsi-Cola*, n 84 above, para 18.

role of the *Charter* in the development of the common law here seems both more insistent and more crucial: it 'must' play a central role in the development even of the areas of law where it has no direct application because in addition to its rights-creating role, it both expresses and constitutes those essential values which knit together our entire legal system.

INFLUENCE AND INTEGRITY: SOME CONCLUDING THOUGHTS

Examining the cases that have had to consider in more detail just how to understand the relation between the ordinary cases of *Charter* application and the cases of *Charter* influence is revealing. Indeed, we see important continuities between this problematic and that of ratified but unincorporated treaties discussed above. In particular, in the case of the *Charter*, there is more explicit recognition of that which is only implicit in the international cases—that the influence or effect of a legal norm may extend well beyond its force, and that that influence or effect may be mandatory in a way that the traditional model typically associates with binding sources of law. But we can also trace another important analogy between cases like *Baker* and the *Charter*/common law cases. For while the effect or influence of these non-binding sources of law looks mandatory in a way that distinguishes them from pure persuasive authority, the nature of that influence also exerts itself in a very different way than in the 'force field' of direct application.

Particularly interesting here is the fact that courts discussing the influence of the *Charter* on the shape of the common law increasingly speak of the distinction between *Charter* rights which are engaged only in the direct application of the *Charter*, and *Charter* values which exert their pull on the common law. And part of the reason that this seems significant when poised against cases like *Baker* is that it looks like a more explicit example of what courts in cases like *Baker* strive towards. Thus, we see courts wanting to recognise that ratification has some legal significance without thereby undermining the incorporation requirement. And in this task they are increasingly moving away from the idea that the rights under the ratified treaty ought to be somehow attributed to the individual (as in the legitimate expectation model of *Teoh* and the time-limited rights model of *Thomas*). So although courts in cases like *Baker* have been criticised for weakening the rights content of the ratified treaty, the case law on the influence of the *Charter* on the common law suggests that there may be another way to understand what they are doing. For it seems arguable that both situations can instead be understood in terms of giving voice to the law's demand for some kind of foundational consistency in matters of expressed value (ratification on one hand, the commitment to the *Charter* on the other).

Undoubtedly, at one level there are and ought to be somewhat different rationales for why a ratified but unincorporated treaty would exert influence on the way public power could be exercised and why the *Charter* would be an influential source of authority for the development of the common law. But paying attention to the nature of this influential authority in both cases suggests that a similar imperative may in fact underlie both (and perhaps other) attempts to articulate the demands of influential authority. For an important part of what courts are striving for in these sets of cases is an understanding of what it means to decide individual cases in a system governed by broader imperatives expressed in various ways. What is the significance of the fact of deciding a case in a state which has ratified important international human rights treaties, for instance or of deciding common law cases in a regime that is now expressly committed to the overarching salience of the rights and values contained in the *Charter*? Those acts alter the way that power can be exercised and justified throughout that state and beyond.

The attempts to articulate what I have termed influential authority can be understood as part of an effort to think through more carefully how these normative commitments might exert broader demands on the exercise of public power. These demands are not aptly captured in terms of the rights contained in the *Charter* or in the discrete international convention and yet they make a profound difference to what we can justify in law's name and to how we can do so. Fundamentally therefore, the idea that underlies influential authority is that values as well as rights may be imperative, though by their very nature, they will be so in a different way. For what norms at this 'influential' level seem to demand is a certain kind of respect for the importance of the values they express. Because values operate at a higher level of generality, they do not translate directly into individual rights and obligations. None the less, they exert imperatives that inform how we extend and justify those discrete rights and obligations and so cannot be disregarded without raising concerns about the integrity of the exercise of public power. In this regard, the description of the dual function of the German constitution seems apposite. For though it does create rights that individuals can assert against the state, that does not exhaust its effect on the legal system. Instead, it also establishes 'an objective system of values' which center on the freedom of the human being to develop in society. And this system of values must 'direct and inform legislation, administration and judicial decision. It naturally influences private law as well'.[115] Like the constitutional values expressed in the *Charter*, these 'objective' values make themselves felt throughout the legal order.

---

[115] BS Markesinis, *The German Law of Obligations*, 3rd edn, (Oxford, Clarendon Press, 1997) at 355 quoted in 'Constitutional Values and Private Law', n 79 above, 51.

Finally, it is worth concluding this brief initial foray into thinking about influential authority with some reference to Dworkin's idea of 'law as integrity'. The word 'integrity' kept suggesting itself through the above discussion of the foundational imperatives and dynamics of influential authority. However, Dworkin's own conception of that ideal, particularly in *Law's Empire*, seems too indebted to the traditional model and too dependent upon the authority of the past to provide the underpinnings of an adequate account of influential authority. But while this question undoubtedly deserves far more substantial treatment than I can give it here, let me suggest that it may be possible to think about the power of Dworkin's central insight in a way that is more congenial to the alternative conception of judgment in which influential authority takes shape. Indeed, it may be that this account of judgment provides a more fertile ground for exploring what integrity in legal decision-making might be than Dworkin's own example of American constitutional law.

In *Law's Empire*, Ronald Dworkin argues that the idea of law as integrity provides the best account of adjudication, at least within the context of Anglo-American law. Dworkin's overarching ambition was to justify the decisions of the Supreme Court of the United States in *Brown v Board of Education* and in *Roe v Wade*. Law as integrity, he argued, could do this. Briefly stated, where law is understood as integrity, rights and responsibilities flow from past political decisions and so count as legal not just when they are explicit but also when they follow from the principles of political morality the explicit decisions presuppose by way of justification.[116] So this account identifies two primary sources of interpretive constraint that help to anchor the legitimacy of adjudication. These are commonly referred to by Dworkin and by his commentators as the dimension of 'fit' and the dimension of 'value'. Thus, in law as integrity, the judge faced with a claim of legal entitlement must come up with a coherent reading of past relevant decisions that is morally and politically attractive, that is, the interpretation must 'fit' past decisions and must be the most attractive possible reading of those decisions ('value').

But one difficulty this account faces, particularly given Dworkin's own explanatory ambitions, is the weight that it needs to give past judicial decisions. But the past may not anchor legitimacy in quite the way Dworkin assumes it does. To some degree this is because if the dimension of 'fit' with past decisions is not to be read so rigidly as to impede legal change (which clearly would not be Dworkin's preferred reading) then it may not actually serve as a terribly strong constraint. There is also, however, a deeper worry about uncritical acceptance of all past decisions as the touchstone for law as integrity. If, as seems likely, law as integrity depends heavily on the

---

[116] See, eg: *Law's Empire* (Cambridge, Mass, Harvard University Press, 1986) 95–96.

dimension of fit for its legitimacy, the account may have considerable difficulty with significant normative change over time.

Further, the uncritical attitude towards the past (in the sense that every past decision prima facie imposes the same explanatory demands) sits uneasily with the fact that it would actually seem wrong to try to render many pockets of the past coherent or consistent with our best account of current legal rights. Would we want, for instance, to give weight to the fugitive slave cases in developing our best understanding of the rules of evidence? It seems more likely that we would reject the idea that an account of the rules of evidence that justified such cases would on that ground be, even on the dimension of fit, a superior account. In fact, it even seems possible that it would count against a reading of the rules that its legitimacy was anchored in part on such an invidious set of cases. And this in turn raises the possibility that the past may not always be as attractive a constraint as Dworkin supposes. If the past is neither as constraining nor as attractive as Dworkin's account of law as integrity supposes, then substantive political morality inevitably ends up playing an extremely significant role in his account of law as integrity. This opens the account up to a strong version of the legitimacy worry. However, one possibility that the conception of judgment outlined in this paper suggests is the notion that there may be background *legal* sources of interpretive discipline—sources that have something in common with the substantive principles of political morality which Dworkin invoked and yet are not reducible to them.

Thus an account of adjudication (among other things) which locates the practice of justification within a larger matrix of legal values and influences may serve to shape and constrain our readings of the past in a much more disciplined and legitimate way than the straightforward role of political morality. Indeed, the influence of the *Charter* on the common law seems illustrative here. In *Salituro* for instance, paying attention to the values of the *Charter* which are, after all, legal values though not legal rights, enables Iacobucci J to effectively dispose of some aspects of the past which he need not struggle to reconcile with his best reading of the common law. Similarly, in *Pepsi-Cola* some common law rules can be set aside for their substantive values, no matter how well-entrenched they may be. The attitude to the past, in this sense, need not be as overtly uncritical or deferential as Dworkin suggests. And the principles and values that judges have recourse to in cases like these and in cases like *Baker* are importantly principles with some legal significance and weight not simply substantial political morality per se. This is not of course to say that there remains no role for substantial political morality. But to the extent that any particular decision is embedded in and justified by the kind of matrix of norms and values that this account of judgment presupposes, that role is correspondingly disciplined. The judge must give an account of value that makes sense of, respects, the values of the legal system as those values are expressed in, among other things, our solemn ratification of international treaties or in our commitment to an overarching constitutional set of values. And she must explicate the significance of those values in the exercise of public power and in the articulate of private rights, for example. Thus, unsurprisingly, the primacy of justification.[117]

Should this alternative view of judgment in which influential authority takes shape be understood as an instance of law as integrity? The divergences from Dworkin's own articulation of the idea are many and significant. Yet ironically the alternative view may actually more be a more robust expression of the relationship between legal decision-making and the demand for a certain kind of normative consistency that Dworkin's invocation of integrity pointed towards but imperfectly captured. In part this may be traced to his preoccupation with defending certain path-breaking American constitutional decisions in the terms of that system itself. Cases like *Baker* and the *Charter*/common law cases, however, are located in a significantly different legal context. To some degree, their very understanding of judgment takes shape in opposition to the tradition that Dworkin sought to defend. Critics inside and outside the American legal system have noted its 'closed' nature and resistance to influences which it perceives as external or non-binding.[118] In this it differs importantly from the family of post-war constitutional regimes that are distinguished in part by their openness to varying forms of authority and to the post-war international human rights regime.[119] Ironically, the ideal of integrity may actually be more apt for the post-war traditions that run counter to the dominant strains of American constitutionalism that gave rise to Dworkin's use of the term in the first place. Dworkin however, being no defender of authorial intention, ought not to mind.

---

[117] The account outlined here has obvious affinities to the idea that the rule of law expresses itself in terms of a culture of justification and that the very idea of law itself imposes some constraint on what can be done in its name. I am indebted to the work of David Dyzenhaus on this and broader matters. See, eg, 'The Justice of the Common Law: Judges, Democracy and the Limits of the Rule of Law', in C Saunders and K Le Roy (eds), *Perspectives on the Rule of Law*, (Sydney, Federation Press, forthcoming).
[118] Madam Justice L'Heureux-Dubé, 'The Importance of Dialogue: Globalisation and the International Impact of the Rehnquist Court' (1998) 34 *Tulsa Law Journal* 15; M Moran, 'An Uncivil Action', n 5 above; S Choudhry, 'Globalization in Search of Justification: Toward a Theory of Comparative Constitutional Interpretation' (1999) *Indiana Law Journal* 819; M Tushnet, 'The Possibilities of Comparative Constitutional Law' (1999) 108 *Yale Law Journal* 1225; K Knop, 'Here and There', n 3 above.
[119] LE Weinrib, 'The Supreme Court of Canada in the Age of Rights' (2000) 80 *Canadian Bar Review* 200.

16

The Common Law Constitution and Legal Cosmopolitanism

MARK D WALTERS

I

THE ENGLISH COURT of Appeal recently observed that people captured by the United States in Afghanistan and held without trial or access to counsel at Guantanamo Bay, Cuba, including several British nationals, appear to be in a 'legal black hole': their human rights are arguably being violated but neither domestic law (British or American) nor international law offer protection.[1] Immanuel Kant was concerned about such apparent holes or gaps between domestic and international law. In his 1795 essay entitled 'Toward Perpetual Peace', Kant asserts that relations within 'the community of nations of the earth' are so close that 'a violation of right on *one* place of the earth is felt in *all*', with the result that 'the idea of a cosmopolitan law is no fantastic and exaggerated way of representing right'; on the contrary, cosmopolitan law must form a 'supplement' to the 'unwritten code' of both state law and international law if the 'public rights of human beings' are to be secured.[2] This idea of a cosmopolitan law of global human rights that is distinct from both the internal laws of states and the international laws between states may be viewed today from both normative and historical perspectives. On the one hand, Kant's cosmopolitanism has inspired recent liberal-democratic theories of global justice by, among others, John Rawls and David Held.[3] On the other hand, Kant's cosmopolitanism was itself inspired by older traditions that Martha Nussbaum

---

[1] *R v Secretary of State for Foreign and Commonwealth Affairs, ex parte Abbasi* (6 November 2002, CA) at para 64. The Court observed that American courts had, at that point, refused to accept jurisdiction over claims made by non-American detainees (paras 12–14).
[2] 'Toward perpetual peace: A philosophical project' [1795] in I Kant, *Practical Philosophy*, MJ Gregor, ed and trans (Cambridge, Cambridge University Press, 1996), 8:360 and M Nussbaum, 'Kant and Cosmopolitanism' in J Bohman and M Lutz-Bachman (eds), *Perpetual Peace: Essays on Kant's Cosmopolitan Ideal* (Cambridge, MIT Press, 1997), 25 and endnote 1.
[3] J Rawls, *The Law of Peoples* (Cambridge, Mass, Harvard University Press, 1999), 10 and D Held, *Democracy and the Global Order: From the Modern State to Cosmopolitan Governance* (Cambridge, Polity Press, 1995), 227–34.

traces to Greek and Roman Stoicism.[4] In this chapter I argue that Kant's cosmopolitanism, considered in these normative and historical lights, may provide a compelling theoretical explanation for, or at least a useful theoretical insight into, the relationship between the common law constitution, judicial review and international law. I will also argue that this theoretical explanation or insight may have practical implications for the manner in which common law judges respond to arguments that governmental decisions must be informed by principles found in instruments of international law even when the relevant instrument has not been incorporated by statute into domestic law, and perhaps even when the relevant instrument has not been signed and ratified by the state. The practical implications of the theoretical acknowledgment of a cosmopolitan component to the common law constitution may not always be significant—there are obvious limits to what non-American courts can do in relation to the Guantanamo Bay detainees no matter how 'cosmopolitan' their inclinations—but under Kant's view of cosmopolitanism these limitations will be the result of failures in institutional design rather than 'black holes' in substantive legal principle.

My analysis is intended to be persuasive for lawyers and judges in common law jurisdictions generally, and it is premised upon the idea that there is a fundamental unity of reason and principle that binds constitutional, administrative and international law together in these jurisdictions. By 'common law constitution' I therefore have in mind the basic unwritten constitutional structures and principles that obtain in parliamentary/common law jurisdictions regardless of local constitutional differences relating to, for example, written constitutional provisions (or lack thereof), federal or unitary structures, or membership in regional economic unions or trade areas. My analysis will combine the normative claim for cosmopolitanism with the historical claim that it is firmly rooted within the legal heritage of the common law constitution. This historical footing, I argue, is found by exploring the connection between Kant's cosmopolitanism and the law of nations or *ius gentium* in its classical sense—ie, the *ius gentium* as a natural law of reason for humanity—and by identifying the relationship between this classical *ius gentium* and the common law. Before developing these aspects of the argument, however, I will begin by explaining the constitutional context of the argument in more detail. Why is there any need to refer to Kant or old theories of the *ius gentium* when identifying the relationship between the common law, judicial review and international law?

II

Of the various legal principles embraced by the common law constitution, AV Dicey emphasised two in particular: the rule of law and legislative

[4] Nussbaum above n 2, at 25–57.

(or parliamentary) sovereignty.[5] The rule of law is manifested today most clearly in the requirement that the discretionary powers of public officials be defined and supported by general laws and exercised in accordance with basic levels of procedural fairness and substantive rationality. The principle of legislative sovereignty ensures that Parliament has ultimate authority over making these 'general laws'; however, the judiciary has ultimate authority over constructing legislative meaning in specific cases and ensuring that when executive power affects individual interests it is supported by law and conforms to the relevant procedural and substantive standards. The interaction of the rule of law and legislative sovereignty within the common law constitution is, in other words, mediated by other constitutional principles securing the separation of powers and the independence of the judiciary. A statute may confer power upon a public official with very few explicit constraints, but judges will 'supplement' the statute by reading it against a 'background' of unwritten rules, principles and values, both procedural and substantive in nature, that derive their normative power from sources external to the statute.[6] These rules, principles and values include the basic structural principles of the common law constitution itself, like the rule of law[7] and the separation of powers,[8] as well as individual human rights[9] and (in some jurisdictions) cultural or linguistic minority rights.[10] Judges often say that Parliament *intends* to confer power subject to the constraints of this 'background', and some commentators assert that the legal normativity of the constraints derives ultimately from legislative will.[11] The better view, however, is to acknowledge, as Dicey did, that the principles and values within which statutes are judicially constructed are common law in character, and at least in some cases have normative power despite, not because of, legislative intention.[12] Their source lies, as

---

[5] AV Dicey, *Introduction To The Study Of The Law Of The Constitution* 7th edn (London, MacMillan & Co, 1908). The points made in this paragraph are explored in detail in TRS Allan, *Constitutional Justice: A Liberal Theory of the Rule of Law* (Oxford, Oxford University Press, 2001).

[6] *B (A Minor) v DPP* [2000] 2 AC 428 (HL), Lord Steyn at 470 (Parliament does not legislate on a 'blank sheet' but rather 'legislates against the background of the principle of legality' and it 'must be presumed to legislate on the assumption that the principle of legality will supplement the text').

[7] *R v Home Secretary, ex parte Pierson* [1998] AC 539 (HL).

[8] *R v Home Secretary, ex parte Fire Brigades Union* [1995] 2 AC 513 (HL).

[9] *R v Lord Chancellor, ex parte Witham* [1997] 2 All ER 779 (QB), Laws J at 784; *R v Minister of Defence, ex parte Smith* [1996] 1 All ER 257 (CA), Sir Thomas Bingham MR at 263.

[10] *Lalonde v Ontario* (2002) 56 OR (3d) 505 (CA).

[11] C Forsyth, 'Of Fig Leaves and Fairy Tales: The Ultra Vires Doctrine, the Sovereignty of Parliament and Judicial Review' [1996] *Cambridge Law Journal* 122; M Elliott, 'The Demise of Parliamentary Sovereignty' The Implications for Justifying Judicial Review' (1999) 115 *Law Quarterly Review* 119 and 'The Ultra Vires Doctrine in a Constitutional Setting: Still the Central Principle of Administrative Law' [1999] *Cambridge Law Journal* 129.

[12] Dicey above n 5, at 409. See also P Craig 'Ultra Vires and the Foundations of Judicial Review' [1998] *Cambridge Law Journal* 63 and 'Public Law, Political Theory and Legal Theory' [2000] *Public Law* 211; Allan above n 5, at 207–25.

Lord Steyn suggests, 'in our unwritten constitution' and in 'constitutional theory', or in the words of the Weiler and Sharpe JJA, in the 'unwritten principles of the Constitution', rather than in positive law.[13]

It is within this general constitutional context that the question can be asked: to what extent does international law provide a source of rules, principles or values within which the statutory delegation of discretionary power must be read by common law judges? The common law regards international law in two lights, depending upon whether it is conceived as a form of positive law found in treaties, conventions or customs or as a body of legal principles or values having force independent of such positive sources. In so far as international law is regarded as a form of positive law, the common law adopts a rule of dualism that secures a strict separation of domestic and international legal systems. As Lord Hoffmann recently explained, domestic-international dualism is necessitated by the principles of democracy and separation of powers: the Crown has the prerogative power to bind the state to international treaties 'without any participation on the part of the democratically elected organs of government', but the 'corollary' of this power is that Crown-ratified treaties have no effect in domestic law until incorporated into that law by the legislature.[14] The rule is, in other words, just one 'facet' of the general principle settled by 'the Civil War and the Glorious Revolution' that the Crown, or executive, cannot make law.[15] Parliament may implement a Crown-ratified treaty domestically or it may legislate contrary to it;[16] when legislative intent is ambiguous, however, judges presume a legislative intention to honour the state's treaty obligations. In short, dualism is a gate between international and domestic law that can be opened by legislative will alone.

In stark contrast to dualism, however, is the common law response to international law as conceived not as positive law but as a body of general or universal legal principles having force independently of positive sources.[17] International law in this sense has always been assumed to form an integral part of the common law. Blackstone's assertion that the law of nations is part of the law of England finds modern expression in Brennan CJ's assertion in *Mabo* that 'international law is a legitimate and important influence on the development of the common law'.[18] The two common law approaches

---

[13] *R v Home Secretary, ex parte Leech* [1994] QB 198, Steyn LJ at 210; *Pierson* above n 7, Lord Steyn (quoting N MacCormick) at 601; *Lalonde v Ontario* above n 10, Weiler and Sharpe JJA at 549.
[14] *Higgs v Minister of National Security* [2000] 2 AC 228 (PC) at 241.
[15] *Ibid.*
[16] *R v DPP, ex parte Kibilene* [2000] 2 AC 326 (HL), Lord Steyn at 367.
[17] A Brudner, 'The Domestic Enforcement of International Covenants on Human Rights: A Theoretical Framework' (1985) 35 *University of Toronto Law Journal* 219 at 222.
[18] W Blackstone, *Commentaries on the Laws of England* (Oxford, Clarendon Press; facsimile, University of Chicago Press, 1979), vol I, 43; *Mabo v Queensland (No 2)* (1992) 175 CLR 1 (HC) at 42. On the adoption of international customary law by the common law see M Hunt, *Using Human Rights Law in English Courts* (Oxford, Hart Publishing, 1997), 11–17.

to international law are no more in contradiction than the two general common law principles that Parliament alone can make law and that common law judges must, when deciding cases, develop the law incrementally.[19]

Arguments for and against the idea that executive decision-making is bound, in some fashion, by international law seem to have focused for the most part upon the first common law proposition about international law. The default position was articulated by the House of Lords in *Brind*: ratified but unincorporated treaties cannot bind public officials whose discretionary powers are defined by statute in unambiguous terms because the judicial imposition of a duty to comply with or even consider such a treaty would amount to incorporation of the treaty into domestic law through the 'backdoor'.[20] However, unincorporated treaties may have 'indirect effect'[21] in a number of ways. First, as stated in the Australian case of *Teoh*, the ratification of the treaty by the executive may in appropriate circumstances give rise to a legitimate expectation that government will adhere to the treaty when exercising powers, with the result that it cannot deviate from the treaty without first giving affected persons notice and an opportunity to make representations.[22] Secondly, as stated in *Launder*, where a public official does take the treaty into consideration as a relevant factor in making a decision, courts may review the decision to ensure that the treaty was applied in a rational manner.[23] In these first two examples the treaty is only a relevant and reviewable consideration in decision-making because the executive itself has, by its own conduct, made it so. But can unincorporated treaties ever constitute a *mandatory* consideration for decision-makers independently of their own conduct?[24] Three recent cases suggest that they can. In *Venables* Lord Browne-Wilkinson concluded that the welfare of children convicted of criminal offences is relevant to the exercise of the Home Secretary's discretionary power over the length of their incarceration, and that this conclusion is 'reinforced' by the unincorporated UN Convention on the Rights of the Child.[25] In *Baker* L'Heureux-Dubé J held

---

[19] Brudner above n 17, at 222.
[20] *R v Home Secretary, ex parte Brind* [1991] 1 AC 696 (HL), Lord Bridge at 747–48 and Lord Ackner at 760–62.
[21] *Higgs* above n 14, Lord Hoffmann at 241.
[22] *Ministry of State for Immigration and Ethnic Affairs v Teoh* (1995) 183 CLR 273 (HC). The *Teoh* principle is cited with approval at *R v Home Secretary, ex parte Ahmed and Patel* [1998] INLR 570 (CA), Lord Woolf MR at 583; *Thomas v Baptiste* [2000] 2 AC 1 (PC), Lord Millett at 25, Lords Goff and Hobhouse at 31–32; *Higgs* above n 14, Lord Hoffmann at 241; *Kibilene* above n 16, Lord Bingham at 338–39 and Laws LJ at 354–55. See generally M Allars, 'One Small Step for Legal Doctrine, One Giant Leap Towards Integrity in Government: Teoh's Case and the Internationalisation of Administrative Law' (1995) 17 *Sydney Law Review* 204.
[23] *R v Home Secretary, ex parte Launder* [1997] 1 WLR 839 (HL) at 866–69. See also *Kibilene* above n 16, Lord Steyn at 367.
[24] M Taggart, 'Legitimate Expectations and Treaties in the High Court of Australia' (1996) 112 *Law Quarterly Review* 50 at 54.
[25] *R v Home Secretary, ex parte Venables* [1998] AC 407 (HL) at 499–500.

that the same Convention, unincorporated in Canada as well, constitutes '[a]nother indicator' that the best interests of children are a relevant consideration in the exercise of the Immigration Minister's discretionary power to grant admission to the country on 'compassionate and humanitarian' grounds.[26] Lord Browne-Wilkinson's use of the Convention is arguably consistent with the rule in *Brind*, for he seems to refer to the Convention to resolve ambiguities about the Home Secretary's statutory powers.[27] However, L'Heureux-Dubé J goes a step further: although she describes the Minister's statutory power to make a decision on 'compassionate and humanitarian' grounds as 'relatively "open-textured"' she does not suggest that the statute is ambiguous; rather, the Convention is simply invoked as an 'indicator' of relevant humanitarian factors. Still, both Lord Browne-Wilkinson and L'Heureux-Dubé J insist that it is the *values* or *principles* reflected in the Convention, not the Convention itself, to which the decision-maker must have regard.[28] And both judges justify reference to the Convention as evidence of relevant values or principles despite its not forming part of domestic law on the ground that Parliament must have intended that the delegated powers be exercised in conformity with the state's international obligations under the Convention.[29] The somewhat broader approach in *Baker* was adopted again in *Spraytech* in which a bylaw regulating pesticide use was held to be within a town's statutory power to 'secure peace, order, good government, health and general welfare' for the local municipality.[30] Writing for a majority of the Court, L'Heureux-Dubé J stated that this conclusion is 'consistent with' international conventions and customary law that confirm a general environmental 'precautionary principle' necessary for sustainable development, and that these international sources and norms were, following *Baker*, an appropriate source of 'values' that legislatures, in this case the Quebec National Assembly, must be presumed to intend to respect when delegating executive or subordinate legislative power.[31]

The indirect effect of unincorporated treaties is therefore limited, though clear signs of flexibility are evident (especially in Canada). Problems may still arise, however, when states ratify but do not implement treaties that give or recognise individual or group rights. These individuals or groups will lack standing to enforce their rights at the international level, international law being a law between *states*, but may have, for the reasons given

---

[26] *Baker v Canada (Minister of Immigration and Citizenship)* [1999] 2 SCR 817 at para 69.
[27] Lord Browne-Wilkinson stated that it is 'legitimate in considering the nature of detention during Her Majesty's pleasure (as to which your Lordships are not in agreement)' to refer to the treaty: *Venables* above n 25, at 499.
[28] *Baker* above n 26, at para 70; *Venables* above n 25, at 499–500.
[29] *Baker, ibid; Venables, ibid.*
[30] *114957 Canada Ltée (Spraytech, Société d'arrosage) v Hudson (Town)* [2001] 2 SCR 241.
[31] *Ibid*, paras 30–33.

above, limited ability to enforce these rights domestically. Individuals or groups lacking domestic political power—for example, immigrants, refugees, children, people accused or convicted of crime, and minority groups such as indigenous peoples—are particularly vulnerable to such potential 'black holes' between positive sources of domestic and international law. The converse of the *Spraytech* situation is another potential problem: what if public officials or bodies refuse to honour international environmental commitments (eg, the Kyoto Protocol) by favouring powerful industrial lobbies over the health and environmental concerns of local communities? It has been argued that there is, or should be, a general exemption of treaties securing human rights or democratic values from the dualism principle. In a recent appeal from Trinidad and Tobago, Lord Millett, writing for a majority of the Judicial Committee of the Privy Council, acknowledged but decided not to address these arguments; instead, the majority found the human rights treaty at issue to have domestic legal effect through a written constitutional provision, an approach which is consistent with the Canadian rule that once a provision of the *written* constitution is at issue broad reference to international law, including ratified but unincorporated treaties, is warranted to guide constitutional interpretation.[32] In their dissenting reasons, however, Lords Goff and Hobhouse insisted that the dualism principle admitted of no human rights treaty exception: judges must articulate 'humane standards' for public officials but not by 'subverting the constitutions of states' or by the 'clear misuse of legal concepts and terminology'.[33] In *Baker* Iacobucci J objected to the use of values underlying unincorporated treaties for similar reasons: 'one should proceed with caution', he wrote, 'lest we adversely affect the balance maintained by our Parliamentary tradition', though he acknowledged that had that case involved a right secured by the Canadian *Charter of Rights and Freedoms*—ie, part of the *written* constitution—reference to international law, including unincorporated conventions, would have been appropriate as a guide for interpretation.[34]

If international law is regarded in a positivist light—as a distinct empirical thing—these various concerns are valid: so long as treaties may be ratified by Crown prerogative alone there are, and should be, only limited and indirect ways in which treaties affect domestic law without legislative implementation.

---

[32] *Thomas v Baptiste* [2000] 2 AC 1 (PC) at 23. For the Canadian approach, see, for example, *Slaight Communications Inc v Davidson* [1989] 1 SCR 1038 at para 23 and *Suresh v Canada (Minister of Immigration & Citizenship)* [2002] SCJ No 3 at paras 46, 60–75.
[33] *Thomas v Baptiste ibid*, at 33.
[34] *Baker* above n 26, at paras 80, 81 where Iacobucci J states that 'the result may well have been different' as to the application of international law had the claim been a *Charter* rights claim, in which case 'the Court would have had an opportunity to consider the application of the interpretive presumption, established by the Court's decision in *Slaight Communications* [see n 32 above]... that administrative discretion involving *Charter* rights be exercised in accordance with similar international human rights norms'.

Only the democratically-elected institution should let this alien 'thing' in. However, as Alan Brudner has argued, once international law is regarded in a non-positivist light the juridical boundary upon which dualism is premised loses its rigidity and the inquiry may legitimately turn from justifying the use of alien sources of law domestically to identifying points of substantive normative common ground amongst various layers of international and domestic law.[35] This process is, of course, already evident in the identification of underlying 'values' in international treaties in *Venables*, *Baker* and *Spraytech*. But the process remains trapped and therefore limited by its positivist premise that state and international law represent two isolated legal spheres and legislative will, even if only presumptive, represents the only potential point of connection. By adopting a different premise, that state and international law share common normative foundations and are therefore integrally connected for reasons that cannot be explained by reference to legislative will, the range of substantive legal and constitutional values that combine to determine the interpretative background for executive decision-making may be defined with far greater richness and subtlety, for that background can be said to include the critical reflections on rights and responsibilities provided by the global community. In the next two sections I will argue that this 'different premise' is actually the more traditional common law approach to international legal sources.[36] In addition I will argue that once this alternative approach is acknowledged and developed in earnest the assumption that law divides neatly into domestic and international categories is challenged and the possibility of what Kant called 'cosmopolitan law' emerges—or re-emerges. Building these arguments does, however, necessitate a historical detour.

III

In the late-eighteenth century, Jeremy Bentham invoked what he called a 'new' term to describe the law governing relations between nation-states, namely, 'international law'.[37] The new term was a welcome one, for the term previously used, the 'law of nations' or *ius gentium*, had conceptual origins that pre-dated the rise of the modern system of sovereign nation-states, and these origins, though very important to the articulation of a moral foundation for emerging ideas about the laws between states, remained a point of potential confusion. The appropriation of the *ius gentium* by Grotius and other seventeenth century theorists as the basis for modern international law was, wrote Sir Henry Maine, the result of a

---

[35] Brudner above n 17, at 225–26.
[36] Similar arguments are summarised at Hunt above n 18, at 2–3, 12–17 and Brudner above n 17.
[37] J Bentham, *Principles of Morals and Legislation* (1789), ch XVII, s 25, fn 1.

'misconception' of the classical context that informed the origins and meaning of the *ius gentium*.[38] By returning (briefly) to that classical context of the law of nations, however, valuable light is shed upon the connections between the common law, international law and legal cosmopolitanism.

The classical conception of the *ius gentium* as articulated in the Institutes of Gaius and Justinian is informed by a very broad understanding of the law of nature (*ius naturale*).[39] The Institutes define the law of nature as that law which governs all animals, both human and non-human. The *ius gentium* is then defined as the law which natural reason (*naturalis ratio*) appoints for people—it is, in other words, simply a subset of natural law applicable to humans. This human aspect of natural law is found in all nations and this is why, according to the Institutes, it is called the *ius gentium*. However *people*, not nations or states, are the relevant subjects of the *ius gentium*: it is the application of natural reason by and within humankind generally (*inter omnes homines*) rather than a law governing relations between nations or states (*civitates*). It follows, then, that the *ius gentium* must overlap the internal laws of nations or states. Thus, according to the Institutes, the people of every state are governed partly by the *ius gentium*, or the laws of reason or nature common to humankind, and partly by their own civil law (*ius civile*), or those laws suited only for local conditions and customs. According to Maine, the Roman *ius feciale*, a set of principles governing diplomacy between foreign peoples, was closer to what we would now call international law than was the classical *ius gentium*.[40]

This image of the classical *ius gentium* as merely natural reason for humankind is not wholly accurate, for it did have an important international (using that term very loosely) aspect.[41] Under Roman law, the *ius civile* extended to citizens only; Roman civil law governed only Roman citizens. However, because citizenship, and therefore Roman civil law, was denied to foreign peoples that were subsumed within the expanding Roman empire, some other body of law was required to govern relations between Romans and non-Romans, especially in the areas of trade and commerce. A foreign praetor (*praetor peregrinus*) was constituted in the second century BC to adjudicate disputes involving non-citizens, and thereby a body of law developed that was, in theory, based upon customs that appeared common to both Romans and non-Romans; it was this body of customary law that came to be called the *ius gentium*. It was only after Roman jurists embraced

---

[38] H Maine, *Ancient Law* (London, John Murray, 1905), 87.
[39] The discussion that follows is based upon *The Institutes of Gaius* F de Zulueta, trans (Oxford, Clarendon Press, 1946), bk I, s I and *The Institutes of Justinian*, TC Sandars, trans (London, Longmans, Green & Co, 1874), lib I, title II, ss 1–2.
[40] Maine above n 38, at 47.
[41] The discussion in this paragraph is based on: Maine above n 38, at 44–50; J MacKintosh, *Roman Law in Modern Practice* (Edinburgh, W Green & Son, 1934), 45–48; W Kunkel, *An Introduction to Roman Legal and Constitutional History* (Oxford, Clarendon Press, 1966), 72–73.

the natural law theories of Greek Stoicism that the *ius gentium* acquired the status (described in the Institutes) of ideal global law derived from natural reason. The classical *ius gentium* therefore combined both a pragmatic search for inter-cultural or inter-national (again, in the loose sense) custom and practice within the normative theoretical framework provided by the law of nature or reason.

To summarise, Roman law distinguished between three types of law: (1) the internal laws peculiar to a state and applicable to its citizens (*ius civile*), (2) a narrow set of principles governing diplomacy between states (*ius feciale*), and (3) the general laws of nature found within and across all peoples that formed the basis of a set of laws governing relations between citizens and aliens (*ius gentium*). Of course, the influence of this juridical framework lasted long after the Roman empire itself fell. Aquinas followed Gaius in describing natural law as a law governing human and non-human animals, and natural reason as the basis of the *ius gentium* that governed humans in particular.[42] For Aquinas, the *ius gentium* was that aspect of human or positive law that could be drawn by logical or scientific deduction from the first precepts of natural law, and which, as a result, owed its force partly to natural law and partly to human institution.[43] Like the Roman jurists, Aquinas distinguished the *ius gentium* from the *ius civile*, which he described as that part of positive law that is constructed from the general precepts of natural law in the way that particular shapes or styles are given by an architect to the general idea of a house; the content of *ius civile* therefore varied between peoples, and because it was not deduced directly from natural law its binding force was due to human institution alone.[44] For Aquinas, then, the *ius gentium* was a universal requirement of natural reason that was global in reach, whereas the *ius civile* was the distinct vision for natural law constructed by and for local communities.[45]

Aquinas, it is said, 'drew the great outlines [of law and state] for the following centuries',[46] and it was not until the Reformation and the emergence in the seventeenth century of the so-called 'Westphalian' international system based upon the sovereignty and equality of European nation-states that the uses of the term *ius gentium* changed. The middle ground occupied by the old *ius gentium* between the civil laws of particular nations and the rules of diplomacy between nations appeared to evaporate— and with it went the foundations for an overtly moral common law of humanity that transcended both (what may now be called) domestic and

---

[42] T Aquinas, *Summa Theologicae* (New York, Eyre & Spottiswoode and McGraw-Hill, 1964–75) II–II, q 57, Art 3.
[43] *Ibid* at I–II, q 95, Arts 2, 4.
[44] *Ibid*.
[45] *Ibid*.
[46] O Gierke, *Political Theories of the Middle Ages*, FW Maitland, trans (Boston, Beacon Hill Press, 1958), 74.

international law.⁴⁷ However, the label *ius gentium* and many of its substantive principles were appropriated and reworked by jurists to describe and explain the new idea of international law. In other words, the *ius gentium* was transformed from a rule of natural reason for *peoples* into a set of customary or conventional rules for *nation-states*. Grotius, for example, set out to identify a 'body of law which is maintained between states' based upon the 'laws of nature and of nations' distinct from the 'municipal law' of states, thus opting for a bi-polar juridical model and rejecting the old Roman tripartite model.⁴⁸ In his view, 'writers everywhere', including Gaius and Justinian, had proceeded upon erroneous and confusing grounds by equating the law of nations with the law of nature and applying it to people rather than states.⁴⁹ Grotius was eager to establish natural law as the relevant standard for states, but he insisted that human law arose from human volition alone and consisted of either 'municipal law' or the 'law of nations' between states.⁵⁰ Hobbes and Pufendorf would later deny the Grotian attempt to separate the law of nature from the law of nations, arguing instead that as between each other states were in a state of nature, and so the law of nations was no more than the law of nature applied to states; but they did not deny the Grotian assumption that the law of nations was, strictly speaking, the law between states as opposed to a common law of humanity.⁵¹ So while debate existed about whether the law of nations was conventional or natural (moral) in its derivation—a debate that continues today—there appeared little doubt from the seventeenth century on that the law of nations was the law of states, or international law, and the Roman/Thomist idea that the *ius gentium* was a common law general to all peoples was marginalised if not ignored. By the time Kant wrote at the end of the eighteenth century, the effect of the Grotian re-drawing of the conceptual map was complete. The result, however, was a significant gap in jurisprudential thought where the old *ius gentium* once was. By focusing upon municipal law on the one hand and the new law of nations, or the international law of states, on the other, jurists had left a jurisprudential 'black hole': no body of law appeared to address the unique problems that non-state beings (individuals or groups) might confront due to state conduct on the international stage. It was this gap that Kant filled by developing a theory of 'cosmopolitan law'.

---

⁴⁷ Maine above n 38, at 88–97.
⁴⁸ H Grotius, *De jure belli ac pacis libri tres* [1626] (Washington, Carnegie Institution of Washington, 1913–25), Prolegomena, ss 17–18, ss 39–41.
⁴⁹ *Ibid*, at Prolegomena, ss 39–40, 53.
⁵⁰ *Ibid*, at bk I, ch I, pt IX, s II; bk I, ch I, pt X, s I; bk I, ch I, pt XIV, s I.
⁵¹ S Pufendorf, *De Jure Naturae et Gentium Libri Octo* [1688], CH Oldfather and WA Oldfather, trans (Oxford, Clarendon Press, 1934), at bk II, ch III, s 23; he adopts here the view of Hobbes who equates *ius gentium* to the 'natural law of *commonwealths*' (*De Cive*, ch XIV, paras 4–5); Hobbes defines commonwealth as sovereign state or '*civitas*' (*De Cive*, ch V, para 9).

Before turning to Kant's cosmopolitanism, however, it is important to establish the common law position concerning the *ius gentium*. The leading constitutional decision of the early-seventeenth century, *Calvin's Case*, is illustrative. In *Calvin's Case* the English judges gathered in Exchequer Chamber to decide whether the Scottish subjects of King James VI of Scotland were naturalised in England upon James' accession to the English throne as James I of England. The case therefore involved the question of what we would now call *citizenship*. The question was not one of international law but one of English constitutional law with imperial and international dimensions. Sir Edward Sandes argued that there was 'no precedent' for the question in English law and so it was proper to consult 'the Law of Nations, which is called Jus gentium', for when both law and custom are deficient judges must resort to the 'ratio naturalis' or 'Law of Reason', also known as the 'Jus Gentium' or 'the Law of Nations'.[52] Here, then, was the invocation of the *ius gentium* in its classical form—not as international law as such but as a manifestation of natural reason in relation to a point of domestic constitutional law with imperial and international aspects. Moreover, it was an invocation of the classical *ius gentium* as an integral part of the *common law* constitution, a reference to the law of nations to determine the common law relationship between Crown and subject. In his reasons for judgment, Lord Ellesmere LC accepted the use of the *ius gentium* as natural reason to determine this point of English constitutional law, making very clear, however, that the basis for decision was indeed the *common law*: the 'common law of England is grounded upon the law of God, and extends itselfe to the originall lawe of nature, and the universall lawe of nations'.[53] In his reasons, Sir Edward Coke (then Chief Justice of the Common Pleas) preferred to emphasise the 'law of nature' as the basis for the reciprocal duties of allegiance and protection between sovereign and subject. Citing Bracton and St German's *Doctor and Student*, he concluded that 'jura naturalia sunt immutabilia' and even 'Parliament could not take away that protection which the law of nature giveth'.[54] But Coke's law of nature was not appreciably different from Ellesmere's *ius gentium*; indeed, the equation between the *ius gentium* and natural reason, or the law of reason, made in Sandes' argument was reflected in Coke's sources, Bracton and St German. Bracton's writings confirm that the common law had incorporated the *ius gentium* centuries *before* its reconfiguration as the conceptual basis of modern international law by Grotius; indeed, Bracton's description of English law was modeled squarely upon the discussion of natural law, *ius gentium*, and civil law found in

---

[52] *Le Case del Union d'Escose ove Angleterre* (1606) Moore 790 at 791–92; also at *Calvin's Case (The Case of the Postnati)* (1608) 2 St Tr 559 at 563.
[53] *Calvin's Case* (1608) 2 St Tr 559 at 669–70.
[54] *Calvin's Case* (1608) 7 Co Rep 1a at 13b–14a.

Justinian's Institutes.⁵⁵ In Coke's other source, *Doctor and Student*, St German argued that English law embraced the law of reason, a term that he equated with the law of nature ('lex naturalis'), natural reason ('ratio naturalis'), and the law of nations ('ius gentium'), emphasising its universal application to all *peoples* ('inter omnes homines'), Christian and non-Christian alike.⁵⁶

The proposition asserted by Bracton and St German and accepted in *Calvin's Case* that the common law incorporates a global law of reason for *humanity* or *peoples* known as the *ius gentium* was commonly acknowledged by seventeenth and early eighteenth century legal writers.⁵⁷ By the mid-eighteenth century, however, English legal literature began to reflect the conceptual and terminological shift evidenced in Grotius and Pufendorf, and the *ius gentium* was increasingly associated with that branch of the law of nature dealing with relations between *states*.⁵⁸ Still, judges continued to refer to the *ius gentium* as an integral part of the common law, both in cases having an international dimension⁵⁹ as well as cases involving wholly domestic issues.⁶⁰ In some cases the connection between the law of nations and the law of reason or nature was made explicit.⁶¹ In some cases the *ius gentium*

---

⁵⁵ H de Bracton, *De Legibus et Consuetudinibus Angliae*, SE Thorne, trans (Cambridge, Mass, Belknap Press, 1968), vol 2, 23–28.
⁵⁶ TFT Plucknett and JL Barton (eds), *St German's Doctor and Student* (London, Selden Society, 1974), 12. In subsequent English translations of the 1528 Latin edition of *Doctor and Student* the connection between the law of reason and the 'ius gentium' was de-emphasised, no doubt because St German, who argued that statutes against reason were void, did not wish to suggest that any custom practiced among all peoples qualified as one of the primary rules of reason that he thought were binding upon Parliament (see *Doctor and Student*, 13, 133–35).
⁵⁷ J Cowel, *The Institutes of the Lawes of England* (London, Tho Roycroft, 1651), 2–4; W Dugdale, *Origines Juridiciales, Or Historical Memorials Of The English Laws*, 2nd edn (Savoy, Tho Newcomb, 1671), 3; H Curson, *A Compendium Of The Laws and Government Ecclesiasitical, Civil and Military* (London, Asssigns of Rich & Edw Atkins for J Walthoe, 1699), 5; T Wood, *A New Institute of the Imperial or Civil Law* (London, WB for Richard Sare, 1712), 2.
⁵⁸ Blackstone above n 18 at vol I, 43; R Chambers, *A Course of Lectures on the English Law* [1767–1773] TM Curley, ed (Madison, University of Wisconsin Press, 1986), 91–94; J Mackintosh, *A Discourse on the Study of the Law of Nature and Nations* (London, J Debrett & W Clarke, 1799), 5.
⁵⁹ Admiralty cases: *The 'Fama'* (1804) 5 C Rob 106, *The 'Snipe'* (1812) Edw 381; rights of ambassadors and diplomats: *Barbuit's Case* (1735) Cases t Talb 28, *Heathfield v Chilton* (1767) 4 Burr 2015 at 2015; conflicts of law: *Scrimshire v Scrimshire* (1752), 2 Hag Con 395 at 417.
⁶⁰ Property: *Blundell v Catterall* (1821) 5 Barn & Ald 268; *Rex v Lord Yarborough* (1828) 2 Bligh NS PC 147; *Regina v Thurborn* (1848) 1 Den 387 at 390–91; law merchant: *Meggadow v Holt* (1692) 12 Mod 15 at 15–16; *Carter v Downish* (1690) 1 Shower KB 127 at 129; *Rowe v Young* (1820) 2 Bligh PC 391 at 518–19; wills and estates: *Hervey v Aston* (1738), West t Hard 350 at 384.
⁶¹ *Goss v Withers* (1758) 2 Keny 325 at 336 (whether a ship had been lost depended upon 'the law of nature and nations, or rather by the law of right reason, which becomes the law of nations'); *The King v Guerchy* (1765) 1 Bl W 545 at 546 (Blackstone, appearing for the defendant, sought and obtained a *noli prosequi* arguing that prosecution of an ambassador was 'a violation of the law of nations'; he said: 'The jus gentium arises from natural reason, interpreted by the practice of all civilized nations').

was used to define aspects of Crown authority, and (like *Calvin's Case*) are therefore particularly clear examples of the *ius gentium* as part of the common law constitution.[62] Missing from the cases, however, is any evidence of judicial concern that by invoking the law of nations courts were undermining the principle of domestic-international dualism and the principles of parliamentary sovereignty and separation of powers upon which dualism is based. To the extent that the *ius gentium* was invoked in its classical or Bractonian sense the concern was not the 'backdoor' incorporation of international law but the invasion of the common law's insularity by civilian traditions. It was argued that civil law, or Roman law, had no force in England except where it was derived from the *ius gentium* and adopted into common law through practice, and Bracton's word on practice was often (but not always) accepted as authoritative.[63] In one case Bracton's adoption of Justinian's position that by the natural law and *ius gentium* all rivers, riverbanks, ports and fisheries are public and may be enjoyed by all people (*omnium populorum*) or mankind (*hominum*) generally was argued to form the basis of the public's common law right to access the seashore for bathing.[64] In response to the counter-argument that Bracton's point could not be accepted as an accurate statement of the common law because it was taken from Roman civil law, it was said that the principle was derived from natural law and formed part of the law of nations and was, as a result, part of the common law.[65] Although Best J agreed with this submission, the majority simply concluded that, on this point, the common law did not agree with the civil law.[66] However, in another case the House of Lords upheld a decision in Chancery traversing a decision by commissioners that certain lands belonged to the Crown, ruling that lands formed by alluvion, or gradual deposits by the sea, belong to the owner of the adjoining land rather than the Crown.[67] Best LCJ delivered the opinion of the House, citing Bracton's conclusion that land created by alluvion belongs to the riparian landowner by the *ius gentium*, a conclusion that Bracton had taken almost

---

[62] *East India v Sandys* (1683–85) 10 St Tr 371 (in deciding whether the prerogative powers of the Crown extended over trade with 'infidel' nations, Jefferies CJ at 529 and 523 concluded that 'the common and statute laws of this realm are too strait and narrow' to govern, but that the courts may take notice of the 'law of nations' which having been 'received and used in England time out of mind, may be properly said to be laws of England'); *Rex v Lord Yarborough* (1828) 2 Bligh NS PC 147 (*ius gentium* was cited as basis for limiting Crown's right to lands formed by alluvion).
[63] *Hervey v Aston* (1738) West t Hard 350 at 384 and 435 (re: meaning of a testamentary condition). See also *Regina v Thurborn* (1848) 1 Den 387 at 390–91 (in a prosecution for theft of a bank note, Parke B cites Bracton's statement at 339 that found treasure belongs to the King by the *ius gentium*).
[64] *Blundell v Catterall* (1821), 5 Barn & Ald 268. References were to Bracton above n 55, at 39–40, which adopts Justinian above n 39, at bk II, title I, ss 1–4.
[65] *Blundell v Catterall* ibid, at 272–73.
[66] Ibid, at 278–81, 290–93.
[67] *Rex v Lord Yarborough* (1828) 2 Bligh NS PC 147.

verbatim from Justinian's Institutes.[68] There was some concern at bar about whether this principle formed part of the common law, not because as a rule of the *ius gentium* it was part of unimplemented international law, but because it was taken from the Institutes and was, therefore, a point of civil law; however, this concern was dismissed and Bracton's statement that the *ius gentium* forms part of the English common law was treated as authoritative.

Even in cases that involved more obviously 'international' dimensions, judges did not perceive any conflict between the common law's absorption of the law of nations and parliamentary sovereignty. In the *Emperor of Austria v Day* it was argued that 'the law of nations is founded on the broadest and purest principles of justice' and is therefore 'part of the common law of England'.[69] Sir John Stuart VC accepted this point and added that 'Acts of Parliament... made to enforce this universal law... are not considered as introductive of any new rule, but merely declaratory of the old fundamental constitution of the kingdom, without which it must cease to be part of the civilised world'.[70] This mid-nineteenth century assertion that the *ius gentium*, a universal rule of justice, is part of 'the old fundamental constitution'—part, that is, of the common law constitution—is not very different from more recent statements by common law judges. Says Lord Cooke of Thorndon, echoing sentiments of other judges, international conventions on human rights recognise rather than create rights that are 'inherent and fundamental to democratic civilised society' and that, as such, are already embedded in the 'common law'.[71]

IV

The effect (though perhaps not the intention) of Kant's development of cosmopolitan law is the resurrection of ideas formerly associated with the classical *ius gentium*. It may therefore be said that Rawls, Held and others who build upon Kant's cosmopolitanism are continuing this task. Of course, the connection is only a loose one. Kant's political and moral philosophy, not to mention that of his modern-day followers, is hardly a replication of ancient and medieval natural law traditions that supported the *ius gentium* of Justinian, Aquinas and Bracton. And, of course, cosmopolitan law and the classical *ius gentium* were informed by very different political-historical

---

[68] Bracton above n 55 at 44 and Justinian above n 39 at lib II, title I, s 20.
[69] *Emperor of Austria v Day* (1861) 2 Giff 628 at 670–671.
[70] *Ibid*, 678–79.
[71] *R v Home Secretary, ex parte Daly* [2001] 3 All ER 433 (HL) at 447. See also cases reviewed at *R v Home Secretary, ex parte Simms* [2000] 2 AC 115 (HL), Lord Steyn at 126 and Lord Hoffmann at 131–32. See also N Blake, 'Judicial Review of Expulsion Decisions: Reflections on the UK Experience', ch 9.

contexts, the latter being a response to diversity within an overarching imperial order, the former being associated with Kant's proposal for a federation of equal nation-states. Nevertheless, I think there are good reasons to draw connections between cosmopolitan law and the old *ius gentium*, for both represent the assertion that the law of reason establishes basic principles of justice for humanity on a global basis and that this law is both distinct from, but integrated with, the internal laws of states and international laws between states.

Martha Nussbaum argues that Kant's cosmopolitanism is 'saturated' with the ideas of the Greek and Roman Stoics, including their theories of a universal law of nature.[72] Kant was, of course, familiar with Roman law—he described the Roman *juris praecepta* as 'classical formulae' and used them to illustrate aspects of his doctrine of right.[73] And although Kant did not expressly connect his idea of cosmopolitan law with the classical *ius gentium*, his 'three divisions of public right'[74] representing the 'three possible forms of rightful condition',[75] correspond with the three-part division in Roman law between *ius civile*, *ius feciale* and *ius gentium*. In 'Toward Perpetual Peace', Kant wrote:

> [A]ny rightful constitution is, with regard to the persons within it,
>
> (1) one in accord with the *right of citizens of a state*, of individuals within a people (*ius civitatis*),
> (2) one in accord with the *right of nations*, of states in relation to one another (*ius gentium*),
> (3) one in accord with the *right of citizens of the world*, in so far as individuals and states standing in the relation of externally affecting one another, are to be regarded as citizens of a universal state of mankind (*ius cosmopoliticum*). This division is not made at will but is necessary with reference to the idea of perpetual peace.[76]

Kant's *ius civitatis* corresponds to Roman *ius civile* and, in modern terms, to the domestic or municipal laws of states; his *ius gentium* corresponds to Roman *ius feciale* and, in modern terms, to the (new) law of nations or international law between states; and, finally, his *ius cosmpoliticum* corresponds to Roman or classical *ius gentium* but—and this is significant—there seems to be no well-recognised modern equivalent for this cosmopolitan law. Kant's framework therefore confirms that he accepted the Grotian

---

[72] Nussbaum above n 2, at 28–29.
[73] *Metaphysics of Morals*, 6:237. References to Kant's *Metaphysics of Morals*, *Toward Perpetual Peace*, *Groundwork of The Metaphysics of Morals*, and *Theory and Practice* in the following notes are to the 1996 Gregor translations above n 2, and page citations are to the Berlin Academy Edition which are given in the margins of the Gregor translations.
[74] *Toward Perpetual Peace*, 8:377.
[75] *Metaphysics of Morals*, 6:311.
[76] *Toward Perpetual Peace*, 8:349.

appropriation of the ancient term '*ius gentium*', which had been a common law of humanity derived from natural reason, for the modern, but different, purpose of describing laws between nation-states. But Kant clearly thought that a common law of humanity was critically important.[77] He therefore (in effect) filled the terminological gap left by the appropriation by inventing a new term, *ius cosmopoliticum* or cosmopolitan law, to describe this—or at least a similar—body of global human rights. Like the old *ius gentium* this new cosmopolitan law is distinct from either internal state law and international law. And, like the old *ius gentium*, it is derived from a law of reason—albeit a peculiarly Kantian sort of reason.

Kant's cosmopolitan law is not just an afterthought but an essential component of his doctrine of right, which together with his doctrine of virtue forms his metaphysics of morality.[78] He went so far as to say that if the principle of right—ie, the reconciliation of individual freedoms—was 'lacking' at any of the state, inter-state, or cosmopolitan levels then the others would be 'undermined' and would 'finally collapse'.[79] Each of these levels of public right is premised upon the same 'a priori', 'pure', 'universal' principles that form the foundations of his general theory of law and morality; each finds its source within the individual's freedom of choice and practical reason, and can be identified by reason alone without reference to divine will or human nature, experience, conditions or customs.[80] Any theocratic, empirical or autocratic tendencies in the classical natural law version of the law of reason are stripped away by Kant to reveal a humanist, liberal, rationalist and secular law of reason—but one no less universal in scope and immutable in character.[81]

Kant's idea of morality and right is, simply put, that humans must each be treated as ends not means, and that consequently the articulation of moral or rightful norms involves securing that freedom for the individual that is consistent with everyone's freedom.[82] His doctrine of right states that 'right' represents 'the sum of the conditions under which the choice of one can be united with the choice of another in accordance with a universal law of freedom'.[83] Reason not only defines right but it imposes a duty upon people to leave the state of nature and form 'civil constitutions' or 'states' that create 'public laws' securing conditions of 'public right'; the doctrine

---

[77] See K Flikschuh, *Kant and Modern Political Philosophy* (Cambridge, Cambridge University Press, 2000) 151: 'Kant's highest level of public Right consists in global relations of justice between *individuals*, whereas Grotius restricts his account to relations of justice between *states*'. She discusses Kant's cosmopolitanism at 144–207.
[78] *Metaphysics of Morals*, 6: 205, 354.
[79] *Ibid* at 6: 311.
[80] *Ibid* at 6:216–17.
[81] *Ibid* at 6: 256.
[82] *Ibid* at 6:229–31, and generally *Groundwork of The Metaphysics of Morals* [hereinafter *Groundwork*], 4:402–36.
[83] *Metaphysics of Morals*, 6:229–31.

of right then provides the 'norm' for the 'internal constitution[s]' of these states.[84] In other words, the innate human right of equal freedom—the essence of Kant's doctrine of right—can only be secured by public right, or the creation of a civil constitution.[85]

The state, in Kant's theory, is simply a means to this end. The problem, of course, is that no matter how 'rightful' conditions are inside a state, so long as states remain in a lawless condition in relation to each other they are incapable of securing public right for their citizens in a meaningful sense.[86] Throughout his work Kant returns, in a prescient way, to the basic theme of global smallness and (hence) unity—the idea that human actions in one state will invariably affect people in other places.[87] In Kant's view, reason dictates that this global interconnectedness be matched by some mechanism of public right to secure individual freedom on a global basis—and so the need for a cosmopolitan law.[88] Reason, says Kant, requires entrance not only into a '*civil constitution*', or nation-state, but, in theory at least, entrance into a '*cosmopolitan constitution*' or worldwide state.[89] A worldwide state being impractical, however, Kant argues that states are under a duty to secure cosmopolitan right through treaties establishing a 'league of nations', a '*pacific league (foedus pacificum)*' or a 'federalism of various states'.[90] The point of this league would be to secure a cosmopolitan right—in particular the humane treatment of aliens in foreign states as a means of permitting global mobility and commerce—through an institutional mechanism based upon the law of nations in which internal state sovereignty would be acknowledged and protected.[91]

A number of important observations should be made about Kant's cosmopolitanism. First, it is clear that cosmopolitan law is not dependent upon states actually agreeing to either a cosmopolitan constitution or a less ambitious federal union. Like all of Kant's dictates of pure reason, its force as law is unaffected by human action or inaction, and he insists that people and states are obliged to behave as if its ends can be achieved, even if at a practical level those ends remain a long way off.[92] It is worth observing that he viewed the pact by which states enter into a federal union as analogous to the 'original social contract' that individuals enter upon leaving the

---

[84] *Ibid* at 6:242, 256, 264, 313.
[85] *Ibid* at 6:237.
[86] *Toward Perpetual Peace*, 8:349–50.
[87] *Metaphysics of Morals*, 6:311, 352; *Toward a Perpetual Peace*, 8:354, 358, 360. On this point see Flikschuh above n 77.
[88] Rawls above n 3 at 10.
[89] *On the Common Saying: That may be correct in theory, but it is of no use in practice* [hereinafter *Theory and Practice*], 8:310–11; also, *Toward Perpetual Peace*, 8:357.
[90] *Toward Perpetual Peace*, 8:355–56, 383; *Theory and Practice*, 8:312.
[91] *Theory and Practice*, 8:311; *Metaphysics of Morals*, 6:352; *Toward Perpetual Peace*, 8:356–58.
[92] *Theory and Practice*, 8:310–11; *Metaphysics of Morals*, 6:350; *Toward Perpetual Peace*, 8:377, 382–85.

state of nature.⁹³ If so, then perhaps it is fair to say that one of his purposes in developing the idea of such an international pact is not to refer to an actual event but, as is the case with his original social contract, only to construct '*an idea* of reason' that illustrates *a priori* rights and duties.⁹⁴ We may, then, follow the lead of Rawls and think of Kant's *foedus pacificum* as a model for a hypothetical second original position from which a 'law of peoples' can be identified independently of any actual institutional structure.⁹⁵

Secondly, it is clear that so long as a cosmopolitan constitution or worldwide state remains unattained, states and the international law that governs them will continue to exist. Nevertheless, since cosmopolitan law is an *a priori* dictate of reason, states are under an unconditional duty to secure, as best they can, its ends through treaties.⁹⁶ Cosmopolitan law is most clearly *not* the same as international law in Kant's view, but until a worldwide state is established, or because a worldwide state cannot be established, international law and internal state law are the only institutional means of securing cosmopolitan right. Cosmopolitan law is, as Kant says, 'a *supplement* to the unwritten code[s]' of state and international law 'necessary' for the 'public rights of human beings'.⁹⁷

The acknowledgment of cosmopolitan law's normative force as a supplement to unwritten state and international law has profound implications for the interpretation of both domestic and international law today. As David Held has argued, the proliferation of international organisations and institutions during the twentieth century (in some cases, like the European Union, surpassing Kant's idea of limited state union), with increasing emphasis on individuals and peoples rather than states, can be interpreted as the manifestation of cosmopolitan law, or a law of peoples, within international legal forms.⁹⁸ It may well be that for cosmopolitan law to be truly effective it must, as Habermas writes, go 'over the heads of the collective [state] subjects of international law to give legal status to the individual subjects ... [as] free and equal world citizens', and that this objective is inconsistent with Kant's defence of state sovereignty.⁹⁹ However, it must be said that Kant supports state sovereignty not in theory but only in practice, and even then he insists that states are, as always, under a duty to respect the doctrine of right. The 'statutory laws' within a civil constitution,

---

⁹³ *Metaphysics of Morals*, 6:344; *Toward Perpetual Peace*, 8:356.
⁹⁴ *Theory and Practice*, 8:297.
⁹⁵ Rawls above n 3 at 10.
⁹⁶ *Toward Perpetual Peace*, 8:382–85.
⁹⁷ *Ibid* at 8:360 [emphasis added].
⁹⁸ D Held, 'Law of States, Law of Peoples: Three Models of Sovereignty' (2002) 8 *Legal Theory* 1.
⁹⁹ J Habermas, 'Kant's Idea of Perpetual Peace, with the Benefit of Two Hundred Years' Hindsight' in *Perpetual Peace: Essays on Kant's Cosmopolitan Ideal* above n 2, at 128.

he says, 'cannot infringe upon *natural right*', ie, the *a priori* principles defining public right, including cosmopolitan right.[100]

Finally, it must be emphasised that the universalism inherent in Kant's cosmopolitanism need not be seen to threaten legitimate forms of cultural and political pluralism. On the contrary, Kant's ideas can be seen as an attempt to secure the 'maximum amount of pluralism consistent with social and global peace'[101]—though it may be necessary, as Rawls concludes, to modify Kant's model somewhat to accommodate at least some forms of non-liberal societies.[102]

V

Considerable work has been done to transform Kant's eighteenth century version of cosmopolitan law into a modern political theory of global justice. Rawls' 'reasonable law of peoples', Kuper's 'Cosmopolitan Law of Persons', Held's 'cosmopolitan democratic law', and Habermas' call for a 'positive law' of global human rights all take their inspiration from the Kantian insight that human rights cannot be secured fully by the internal laws that govern relations between individuals within states or by the international laws that govern relations between states.[103] It is beyond the scope of this chapter to consider these or other theories of cosmopolitanism in detail. Instead, in this last section I want to return to the common law constitution and consider its relationship to the general idea of legal cosmopolitanism that underlies these theories. The argument is a simple one. First, there is a persuasive normative claim for acknowledging some sort of 'cosmopolitan law' conceptually distinct from, but integrally related to, state and international law; conversely, there is a strong claim for denying the existence of 'legal black holes' between domestic and international law into which individuals or groups without standing or status in either may fall. Secondly, there is a very long—indeed ancient—tradition within the common law of acknowledging a juridical concept, the *ius gentium*, that in its classical form resembles in certain important respects this idea of legal cosmopolitanism, a tradition that is still evidenced, albeit obliquely, in the common law responses to international law today. Together, these two claims combine to form the basis of an argument for a cosmopolitan component to the common law constitution. This modern common law linkage

---

[100] *Metaphysics of Morals* 6:256.
[101] J Bohman and M Lutz-Bachmann, 'Introduction' in *Perpetual Peace: Essays on Kant's Cosmopolitan Ideal* above n 2 at 22 and fn 25.
[102] Rawls above n 3, at 44.
[103] Rawls above n 3; A Kuper, 'Rawlsian Global Justice: Beyond *The Law of Peoples* to a Cosmopolitan Law of Persons' (2000) 28 *Political Theory* 640; Held above n 3, at 227; Habermas above n 99, at 137–40.

of the classical and Kantian ideas of cosmopolitanism is not meant to involve the adoption of the specific content of either, but only the abstract notion of a universal law of reason capable of addressing the peculiar concerns of non-state beings, both individuals and groups, that cannot be adequately addressed by state or international law. By conceiving this cosmopolitan law as supplementing both state and international positive law it may go at least part way towards remedying their respective deficiencies, though the manner in which cosmopolitan law is manifested at state and international levels will no doubt vary. The gist of the argument, then, is to say in response to the concerns of Lords Goff, Hobhouse and Iacobucci J[104] that a vigorous approach by common law judges to the articulation of 'humane standards' for executive decision-making by more consistent and active reference to international legal sources need not be considered 'subverting the constitutions of states' or 'misuse of legal concepts and terminology' or upsetting 'the balance maintained by our Parliamentary tradition'. The principles of parliamentary sovereignty and separation of powers cannot be threatened by the 'backdoor' incorporation of international legal norms by this approach because the norms that qualify as cosmopolitan, as opposed to the positive legal sources in which they are evidenced, are not just parts of international law but are also part of the *ius cosmopoliticum* or *ius gentium* that forms an integral part of the common law constitution.[105] There seems to be no reason to conclude, as Iacobucci J in effect does in *Baker*, that the common law constitution is any less deserving of an 'international' interpretation than written constitutions.[106] It is this common law constitution that forms the web of unwritten rules, principles and values within which legislation delegating executive power is given full meaning and, therefore, within which executive power must be exercised. In so far as international law manifests legal norms properly associated with, or derived from, a rule of reason securing a common or global sense of humanity, judicial reference to it should not be contingent upon identifying legitimate expectations or finding ambiguity in the legislative provisions delegating executive power; these norms should, instead, be regarded as already part of the common law.

A few comments on the significance of legal cosmopolitanism may help to clarify its meaning. The result of acknowledging this theory of common law cosmopolitanism would be to affirm in slightly different theoretical

---

[104] See n 33 and n 34 above.
[105] As Mayo Moran argues in 'Authority, Influence and Persuasion: *Baker, Charter* Values and the Puzzle of Method' (ch 15), unincorporated international treaties have effect without force, or are an 'influential' rather than a 'binding' authority. This is a helpful way of thinking of sources of positive international law, but once the 'influence' of these sources has been measured and cosmopolitan norms underlying them identified, the norms themselves are, I think, binding common law principles.
[106] See n 32 and n 34 above.

terms what common law judges already acknowledge—that international law often confirms human rights or democratic values that are already embraced by the common law. It would provide, then, an alternative explanation for judicial reference to 'values' underlying international conventions in cases like *Venables*, *Baker* and *Spraytech*. However, it is more than a mere alternative for the legislative-intention-based arguments now used in such cases: it would require reference to international law and its underlying values even when statutory powers cannot be said to be ambiguous, or when legislative intent seems to suggest a contrary result. The default position in *Brind* would be reversed: cosmopolitan values underlying international treaties would always be a relevant factor to be considered by public officials exercising discretionary statutory powers. The practical effect would be a more robust judicial approach to the protection of interests of particularly vulnerable people or groups who would otherwise fall between domestic and international law. Furthermore, it would follow that even international instruments not ratified by the Crown could provide evidence of a common law cosmopolitan principle binding upon executive action, for the cosmopolitan component to the common law constitution would not be contingent on positive acts of either executive or legislative will.[107] Finally, it permits arguments to the effect that certain particularly fundamental cosmopolitan principles may bind Parliament itself and that particularly egregious violations by statute of cosmopolitan values could be held by common law judges to be void—at least in those common law jurisdictions in which unwritten constitutional norms have been held by courts to prevail over statute law.[108]

In response to the argument for legal cosmopolitanism it may be claimed that by letting go of the anchor provided by legislative intention and following an 'unwritten code' (to use Kant's phrase) of reason to derive normative standards from international legal sources, judges would be left drifting aimlessly. Appeals to laws of reason are always open to the Hobbesian claim that there are as many reasons as judges.[109] There are two related responses to these concerns. First, although Kant rejected inductive

[107] The approach therefore differs from that of J Brunnée and S Toope, 'A Hesitant Embrace: *Baker* and the Application of International Law by Canadian Courts' (ch 14), on a number of fronts. They focus upon the implications of ratification, and argue, in effect, that judges should give all ratified but unincorporated treaties concrete legal effect unless explicitly directed not to by statute, whereas I am suggesting that only sources of international law reflecting cosmopolitan values are deserving of this special judicial attention in absence of legislative implementation; in my view there may be good reasons why a treaty on trade giving multinational companies rights of access to local natural resources should not be given effect by judges until incorporated by some local democratic legislative process.
[108] This may be the case in Canada: Mark Walters, 'The Common Law Constitution in Canada: Return of *Lex Non Scripta* as Fundamental Law' (2001) 51 *University of Toronto Law Journal* 91.
[109] T Hobbes, *A Dialogue Between A Philosopher and A Student of The Common Laws of England* [1681], J Cropsey (ed) (Chicago, University of Chicago Press, 1971), 54–55.

reasoning in favour of 'pure' abstract reason,[110] cosmopolitanism can be given *common law* expression (if at all) only through the case-by-case development of reasoned responses to specific factual problems. In other words, we cannot and need not state the common law meaning of cosmopolitanism in advance. It will emerge (and indeed has been emerging) piecemeal. Of course, the idea of legal cosmopolitanism will not thrive unless judges adjust their interpretive methods somewhat. It requires, following Dworkin, that the ideal or Herculean judge aspire not simply to interpret his or her system as the best it can be as an isolated system, but to interpret it as the best it can be in light of its position within a global community of systems, institutions and peoples; answers to hard legal questions that show the system in isolation in its best light may not 'fit' as well if they must also show the system in its best light on a larger stage, for coherence and integrity would then have to be measured with reference to a much larger, diverse and richer historical legal record.[111] So long as this, or some similar, judicial perspective is adopted, the substantive elements of 'reason' that underlie cosmopolitanism will simply emerge as cases are decided, with as much precision and imprecision as any other set of common law rules and principles. It follows, then, that the basic substantive cosmopolitan principles that are reflected in both international and state law will likely be manifested at common law in unique forms that cohere with other parts of the particular common law system in question. A second but related response is to follow TRS Allan and articulate a rule of reason appropriate to liberal constitutionalism by reference to ideas of 'public reason' (Rawls) or a 'culture of justification' (Dyzenhaus).[112] Although these approaches differ in their details, they seem premised upon a common notion that rights are secured less by appeals to substantive visions of reason than by opportunities to compel public and reasoned justifications for state action. Judicial review of state action is a particularly effective forum in which the requirements of public reason can be articulated. The ultimate responsibility for sorting out how, in detail, treaties that appear to embrace cosmopolitan ideals should be applied must ultimately lie with government officials; judges can merely ensure that their efforts are publicly justifiable according to appropriate standards of rationality and constitutionalism. An unincorporated

---

[110] *Groundwork* 4:409–10.

[111] R Dworkin, *Law's Empire* (Cambridge, Mass, Belknap Press, 1986). For discussions on how orthodox legal theory might accommodate globalisation, see W Twining, *Globalisation and Legal Theory* (Evanston, Northwestern University Press, 2000) and KT Jackson, 'Global Rights and Regional Jurisprudence' (1993) 12 *Law & Philosophy* 157.

[112] Allan above n 5, at 25–29, 284–90, at which he discusses D Dyzenhaus, 'Form and Substance in the Rule of Law: A Democratic Justification for Judicial Review?' in C Forsyth (ed), *Judicial Review and the Constitution* (Oxford, Hart Publishing, 2000) and J Rawls, *Political Liberalism* (New York, 1993), chs 4 and 6. Kant's principle of 'publicity' is perhaps similar to these ideas. See J Bohman, 'The Public Spheres of the World Citizen' in *Perpetual Peace: Essays on Kant's Cosmopolitan Ideal* above n 2, at 182.

technical treaty on reducing emissions of greenhouse gases that cause global warming (eg, the Kyoto Protocol) could not form part of the common law; however, as *Spraytech* suggests, the requirement that ministerial decisions concerning industry, transportation and natural resources must take into consideration the harmful effects of those emissions on human health and dignity could be said to form a cosmopolitan common law principle evidenced by international conventions. It was, after all, harm caused by global unity and smallness that Kant sought to address through his idea of cosmopolitan law. This global unity is matched by a legal unity, a unity of reason and principle, that precludes any possibility of legal black holes between the various systems of positive law that exist at any given time. Indeed, it is this same unity of reason and principle that binds constitutional, administrative and international law together to secure a unity of public law in common law systems.

17
The Tub of Public Law

MICHAEL TAGGART*

Rub-a-dub-dub,
Three men in a tub,
And who do you think they be?
The butcher, the baker, and the candlestick maker,
They all jumped out of a rotten potato,
Turn 'em out, knaves all three.

THIS NURSERY RHYME has always intrigued me. As a child I learnt it and repeated it without ever understanding what it meant. During the conference that this book of essays sprung from, this rhyme kept coming into my head. No doubt, this was triggered by the reference to 'baker', and the centrality of the *Baker*[1] case to the gathering. Upon further reflection, it seemed also to capture the tripartite division of public law into the sub-disciplines of constitutional law, administrative law and international law, and the growing realisation that all these sub-disciplines are in the same boat, in the tub of public law so to speak.

I discovered after the event that the rhyme apparently refers to people being 'in a place where no respectable town-folk should be, watching a dubious sideshow at the local fair'.[2] While the Toronto gathering certainly could not be so characterised, there are many lawyers who disparage public law—'the rotten potato'?—as 'a diet of soft vagueness, conducing to intellectual flabbiness and other regrettable forms of degeneration'.[3] In this respect, all public lawyers are in the same boat!

---

* Thanks to Grant Huscroft and Paul Rishworth for comments at short notice, and to David Dyzenhaus for making it all happen.
[1] *Baker v Canada (Minister of Citizenship and Immigration)* [1999] 2 SCR 817; (1999) 174 DLR (4th) 193 (SCC)(hereafter referred to as *Baker*).
[2] WS Baring-Gould and C Baring-Gould (eds & compliers), *The Annotated Mother Goose: Nursery Rhymes Old and New, Arranged and Explained* (New York, Bramhall House, 1962) 106, quoting from I & P Opie (eds), *The Oxford Dictionary of Nursery Rhymes* (Oxford, Clarendon Press, 1951) 376.
[3] SA de Smith, *The Lawyers and the Constitution* (London, G Bell and Sons Ltd, 1960) 8 (published Inaugural Lecture at the University of London, London School of Economics, 10 May 1960).

My role at the end of the conference was to attempt to pull some of the threads in the papers and discussion together. Given the range and sophistication of the papers and the free-flowing discussion over two days, this was (and remains) a very tall order. In what follows I attempt something less.

RIGHTS, VALUES AND TRADITION

Many of the debates in modern day public law boil down to disagreements over the content and contours of the common law tradition(s). These are often expressed in the oppositional terms of antinomies or dichotomies—natural law versus positive law; positivists and anti-positivists; process versus substance; enactment versus interpretation; legislatures versus courts; fundamental constitutional values versus statute.[4] The truth seems to be that there is not one tradition, but several competing traditions or readings of the tradition, each of which contends—sometimes successfully, sometimes not—for the hearts and minds of the influential lawyers of the day.

One aspect of the common law tradition is the protection of rights, which often has been (and is still) swept up into the Rule of Law. But again the Rule of Law, being all things to all people, can be made to cohere with almost any reading of the common law tradition.[5] Be that as it may, rights-talk goes back a long way.[6] As Kenneth Pennington observed in his excellent book, *The Prince and the Law*:[7]

> a doctrine of individual and inalienable rights first surfaced in Western legal thought in the twelfth and thirteenth centuries. Political systems were not democratic, politics were not liberal, but jurists had a common set of norms to which they gave their consent. These norms were the building blocks upon which they constructed rights of property, obligations, marriage, defense, and due process. Today these rights are often protected against arbitrary magistrates of the sovereign state by constitutions.

Lawyers at that time drew on a remarkably wide range of material and sources for inspiration and guidance. To quote Pennington again,

> [b]efore the age of positivism ... law could be found in many cupboards: in nature, in the Bible (divine law), in customs of the people, in the law of nations (ius gentium), as well as in the positive law of the prince.[8]

---

[4] See D Dyzenhaus, 'Form and Substance in the Rule of Law: A Democratic Justification for Judicial Review' in C Forsyth (ed), *Judicial Review & the Constitution* (Oxford, Hart Publishing Ltd, 1999) 141.
[5] For discussion of the Rule of Law as an essentially contested concept, see J Waldron, 'Is the Rule of Law an Essentially Contested Concept (in Florida)' (2002) 21 *Law and Philosophy* 137.
[6] See generally: R Tuck, *Natural Rights Theories: Their Origin and Development* (Cambridge, Cambridge University Press, 1979).
[7] K Pennington, *The Prince and the Law, 1200–1600: Sovereignty and Rights in the Western Legal Tradition* (Berkeley, University of California Press, 1993) 288.
[8] *Ibid* 2.

This created over much of Europe a common body of law and legal thinking that is often referred to as the Western idea of law or *jus commune*. This was so in Britain as well, where some of these continental ideas were reflected in, and others reacted with, the 'ancient constitution' and the common law mindset(s).[9] The influence of Roman law, after its rediscovery in the eleventh century was critical to both the *jus commune* and the systemisation of the common law. Reason, often referred to in Coke's famous phrase as artificial or legal reason, also played a fundamental role; and this was often associated with natural law, which in turn was often closely connected to the law of nations.[10] This is the tradition that sustains common law constitutionalism, described as 'legal cosmopolitanism' in Mark Walters's chapter.

It is frequently remarked that the *jus commune* disappeared in the course of the nineteenth century.[11] Multiple causes and effects can be pointed to: nationalism, legal positivism, colonialism, the hardening of equity's arteries, laissez-faire dogma, the scientific turn in law, the Benthamite-inspired drive for legal certainty, the ascendancy of legal formalism and the rigidification of precedent.[12] What Michelle Graziadei calls 'the cosmopolitan attitude' of prominent lawyers was much less pronounced at the end of the nineteenth century than at the start.[13] The British legal system turned inward, becoming an insular national legal system. A system where custom and equity were subordinated to the positivist definition of law as a body of rules expressing the will of the State enforced by coercive sanctions.[14] National legislation became the norm, displacing custom, prerogative and local legislation. At much the same time, the range of legal argument in the courts narrowed and became more technical;[15] in other words, the legal shutters went up.

---

[9] See, eg, CC West, 'England: ancient constitution and common law' in JH Burns (ed), *The Cambridge History of Political Thought 1450–1700* (Cambridge, Cambridge University Press, 1991) 374: H Helmholz, 'Magna Carta and *Ius Commune*' (1999) 66 *University of Chicago Law Review* 297; JW Tubbs, *The Common Law Mind: Medieval and Early Modern Conceptions* (Baltimore, John Hopkins University Press, 2000) esp ch 9.
[10] Pennington, above at n 7, 122–23; DR Kelley, 'Law' in Burns, above at n 9, 66, 84–6.
[11] HJ Berman and CJ Reid, 'Roman Law in Europe and the *Jus Commune*: A Historical Overview with emphasis on the New Legal Science of the Sixteenth Century' (1994) 20 *Syracuse Journal of International Law and Commerce* 1, 26.
[12] See idem and M Taggart, *Private Property and Abuse of Rights in Victorian England: The Story of Edward Pickles and the Bradford Water Supply* (Oxford, Oxford University Press, 2002) ch 6.
[13] M Graziadei, 'Changing Images of the Law in XIX Century English Legal Thought (The Continental Impulse)' in M Reimann (ed), *The Reception of Continental Ideas in the Common Law World 1820–1920* (Berlin, Duncker & Humblot, 1993) 115, 121.
[14] Berman & Reid, above at n 11, 26.
[15] S Hedley, 'Words, Words, Words: Making Sense of Legal Judgments, 1875–1940' in C Stebbings (ed), *Law Reporting in Britain* (London, The Hambledon Press, 1995) 169, 171 & 182.

The liberties of Englishmen and women had been transported with them to over a quarter of the globe during the successive Empire-building phases. The British were both inordinately proud of their civil liberties record at home and distrustful of formal statements of rights. Hence, post-World War II the United Kingdom took a lead role in drafting and ratifying the European Convention of Human Rights, and used it as a model in the de-colonisation of the 'black' Commonwealth, but forbore to implement it domestically for nearly 50 years.[16] The UK acceded to the right of individual petition under the European Convention in 1966 and imperceptibly but surely the Convention seeped into domestic law and policy, eventually pulling the teeth of opposition to domesticating the Convention.[17] This exemplifies one of the defining characteristics of legal development in the second half of the twentieth century; namely, the creation and imbrication of international, regional and domestic human rights instruments throughout the world, including the common law world.

INTERNATIONAL LAW, GLOBALISATION, AND INFLUENCE

When Sir William Blackstone wrote his primer on English law for the aristocracy and landed gentry,[18] he treated the law of nations as part of the common law.[19] Within a century that view had been repudiated due to the rise of legal positivism.[20] As Mark Walters notes, the phrase 'international law' was first penned by Jeremy Bentham. But it was Bentham's disciple John Austin who denied it status as 'positive law', as it was not given by a 'sovereign to a person or persons in a state of subjugation to the [sovereign]'.[21] In the face of this onslaught of legal positivism, the prior Blackstonian notion that international law formed part of the law of the land came to find 'expression' in the interpretive principle that the common

---

[16] See RK Hahn, 'The British Influence on the Initiation and Introduction of Commonwealth Bill of Rights' (1988) 26 *Journal of Commonwealth Comparative Politics* 54 and generally AW Brian Simpson, *Human Rights and the End of Empire: Britain and the Genesis of the European Convention* (Oxford, Clarendon Press, 2001).
[17] See M Hunt, *Using Human Rights Law in English Courts* (Oxford, Hart Publishing, 1997).
[18] See, eg, CE Klater, 'The Americanization of Blackstone's *Commentaries*' in EA Cawthorn & DE Narrett (eds), *Essays on English Law and the American Experience* (Texas, Texas A & M University Press, 1994) 42, 45–47.
[19] W Blackstone, *Commentaries on the Laws of England* 9th edn ed by RI Burn 1783, vol 4, ch 5.
[20] A Anghie, 'Finding the Peripheries: Sovereignty and Colonialism in Nineteenth-Century International Law' (1999) 40 *Harvard International Law Journal* 1.
[21] J Austin, *The Province of Jurisprudence Determined* (London, Weidenfeld & Nicolson, 1954 ed by HLA Hart) 140–42. See MW Janis, 'Jeremy Bentham and the Fashioning of "International Law"' (1984) 78 *American Journal of International Law* 405 & M Koskenniemi, *The Gentle Civilizer of Nations: The Rise and Fall of International Law 1870–1960* (Cambridge, Cambridge University Press, 2002) 34.

law and statute should be interpreted in conformity with international law.[22] In other words, the principle was displaced into the sub-constitutional terrain of interpretation, which role Dicey had preserved for the judges, and these principles of interpretation instantiated Rule of Law values. These methods and the values they protected remained part of the common law—itself a source of law. This was the preserve of administrative law. Moreover, the particular interpretive principle shaped the development of the common law itself, most commonly through the portal of public policy.[23] There, use of the principle is justified by the Blackstonian notion of respect for the law of nations and the hospitality of the common law to all sorts of influences.[24]

The rise of legal positivism also explains the 'orthodox' account of the relationship of international law and domestic law in common law systems. The relationship has been described as 'dualist' because international law and domestic law are treated as inhabiting separate spheres.[25] In the orthodox account of the common law system, international legal obligations entered into by the executive do not become part of the domestic legal system unless 'incorporated' by the legislature. It is based on the premise that Parliament makes the law and the executive administers the law so made. If the executive, in the exercise of its extant prerogative power to enter into treaties and conduct foreign affairs, could thereby create obligations enforceable in domestic courts, that is thought to offend the separation of powers doctrine. This is closely allied to the doctrine of parliamentary supremacy, which in turn is based on the credo of classical legal positivism that all power must flow from (and be traceable back to) one authoritative source of power—namely, the legislature.[26] Under this dualist approach international obligations undertaken by the executive are binding on that country as a matter of international law only. Failure by that country to do what it has undertaken to other nations to do is not excused by the inability to change domestic law and the consequent incompatibility of domestic law with the international legal obligation. Nor does it

---

[22] H Lauterpacht, 'Is International Law a Part of the Law of England?' (1939) 25 *Transactions of the Grotius Society* 51, 57.
[23] See, eg, *Mabo v Queensland (No 2)* (1992) 177 CLR 1, 142 (Brennan J, with whom Mason CJ & McHugh J concurred)(HCA).
[24] See HP Glenn, 'Persuasive Authority' (1987) 32 *McGill LJ* 261 and the paper by Mayo Moran in this book.
[25] There is a large international law literature on the 'dualist' approach, often contrasting it with the so-called 'monist' approach that prevails in civil law countries. The point is often made that this dichotomy is a simplistic one created for the purpose of exposition. The reality is more of a spectrum between polar opposites, with most countries falling somewhere in between. There is no consistency in the terminology used in this area. Some writers describe the common law approach as one of 'transformation' and the civil law system as one of 'incorporation'. However, I prefer to speak of the 'incorporation' of treaties in the common law system.
[26] A Brudner, 'The Domestic Enforcement of International Covenants on Human Rights: A Theoretical Framework' (1985) 35 *University of Toronto Law Journal* 219, 224.

matter that the executive has changed, and so may the incumbent executive's attitude to the international obligations undertaken by its predecessors. The executive for the time being is the 'state' for this purpose and binds its successors (unless and until they take formal legal steps to change the international legal obligations).[27]

The dualist approach made most sense when the ambit of international law was the law of and between nations, based upon consent of the nations involved. Two phenomena have dramatically undermined this conception, however. First, dating from at least the end of the World War II, many international treaties have had the rights of individuals as their focus, and individuals as their intended beneficiaries. In respect of those treaties it has been difficult to justify keeping individuals (and domestic courts, as the right-bearer's most accessible forum) out of the frame of reference.[28] Secondly, the profound impact of what is called 'globalisation' is being felt here as everywhere else. The presupposition of positivism and the orthodox account of 'the existence of a single sovereign law-maker within a single sovereign nation-state' have been eroded by the enormous changes in the way nations, communities, corporations and individuals interact throughout the world.[29] The orthodox approach no longer is an accurate description of the distribution of power or of constitutional arrangements on the ground. But the orthodox view hangs on, as Felix Frankfurter once said, because '[o]ld pictures of a legal and political scene remain current long after it has been drastically modified'.[30]

Now that globalisation has brought the Cinderella subject of international law to the Ball, several 'domestic' disciplines have been trying on the glass slipper. Peter Spiro observes that there is evidence that 'other disciplines' now are interested in capturing the growing stature of international law for themselves.[31] As *Baker's* case illustrates, courts are increasingly using administrative law doctrines and techniques to give greater effect to international treaty obligations in domestic law.

In their contribution to this book, Jutta Brunnée and Stephen Toope argue that use of such administrative law techniques, as occurred in *Baker's*

---

[27] A Aust, *Modern Treaty Law and Practice* (Cambridge, Cambridge University Press, 2000) 145.
[28] Most of these treaties have established supranational bodies to enforce their terms or monitor performance, but these are not readily accessible or affordable as dispute resolution mechanisms. For example, an individual petitioning the United Nations Human Rights Committee alleging breach of the International Covenant of Civil and Political Rights is ineligible for legal aid in New Zealand: *Tangiora v Wellington District Legal Services Committee* [2000] 1 NZLR 17 (PC, New Zealand).
[29] See Hunt, above at n 17, ch 1.
[30] F Frankfurter, 'The Final Report of the Attorney-General's Committee on Administrative Procedure' (1942) 42 *Columbia Law Review* 585, 585.
[31] PJ Spiro, 'Globalization, International Law, and the Academy' (2000) 32 *New York University Journal of International Law and Politics* 567, 568.

case, runs the risk of diluting or marginalising international obligations. They contend that as ratified but unincorporated treaties are binding *on* Canada, not *in* Canada, they are (or should be) binding to the extent that Canadian law should be presumed to conform to international law. They fear that treating all international law as relevant or persuasive but not decisive or binding will 'water down' the potency and relevance of international law. On the face of it, they seem at odds with the approach advocated in Mayo Moran's chapter, which argues for the recognition of a middle category of 'influential' considerations, resting between binding and persuasive authority.

There are large questions raised by both approaches, which have more in common than the authors appear to think. Brunnée/Toope's approach is prescriptive rather than descriptive, but should it be adopted by the Canadian Courts international lawyers will be confronted with exactly the same issues the administrative lawyers have been in applying 'the strong interpretative principle' championed by Murray Hunt, that has caught on in English courts:[32] what is the difference between permissive and mandatory relevant considerations? Is 'ticking the box' sufficient? How does one ensure meaningful, sensitive consideration, and can this be done without assigning/enforcing particular weight? Can a mandatory relevant consideration become a decisive one, in effect a trump? How much deference, if any, should be paid to the reasoning and result reached by the decision-maker? And, with reference to Mayo Moran's chapter, would any of these issues be answered more easily if the word 'influential' were substituted for 'mandatory relevant'? Unpacking 'influence' may be every bit as hard as operationalising what Brunnée/Toope describe as 'mandatory consideration of binding international law'. In all this, one is reminded of Sir Henry Maine's insistence that, while the founders of international law may not have created a sanction, they did create 'a law-binding sentiment'.[33] Doctrinally speaking, how can effect be given to that sentiment?

THE *BAKER* CASE

Comparative Common Law

One of the unavoidable hazards of comparative common law conversations on public law topics—as occurs in this volume—is that the public law of each common law country can differ markedly because of the different

---

[32] See Hunt, above at n 17, and the cases referred to below in n 73.
[33] HS Maine, *International Law: A Series of Lectures Delivered Before the University of Cambridge, 1887* (New York, H Holt, 1888) 51, quoted in C Landauer, 'From Status to Treaty: Henry Summer Maine's *International Law*' (2002) 15 *Canadian Journal of Law and Jurisprudence* 219, 250.

conditions and doctrinal development in each country. We can take *Baker's* case to illustrate this.

To British lawyers, as Paul Craig and Nick Blake observed at the conference, *Baker* would have been an easy case to decide on the facts under English law. The Minister's guidelines reflecting the policy of considering any child's interest would create in English law a legitimate expectation that the courts would protect both procedurally and substantively. Canadian commentators pointed out, however, that the doctrine of legitimate expectations is less well developed in Canadian law, and this explains in part the Supreme Court of Canada's refusal in *Baker's* case to consider the High Court of Australia's decision in *Teoh*,[34] which had been the centre of attention in the court below. Furthermore, it is not immediately obvious to non-Canadian lawyers just how restrictive the Federal Court of Canada's jurisprudence was in this field. The law before *Baker* was that immigration officials were under no duty to give reasons and that there was in effect no duty to act fairly towards persons in Mavis Baker's position.[35]

To an administrative lawyer from the southern hemisphere, *Baker* looks like a straightforward statutory interpretation case. If, for simplicity's sake, everything is shorn away except the statutory phrase 'humanitarian and compassionate grounds', it seems axiomatic that on its own this would require the applicant's family situation to be considered. It surely would be an error of law for an official to interpret that phrase as excluding consideration of the family altogether. The Federal Court of Appeal in *Baker* appeared to agree, at least where the applicant brought the matter to the official's attention.[36] So the children's interests and that of the family are not irrelevant considerations. On the contrary, they are relevant, and indeed, given the tenor of the humanitarian and compassionate ground, must be mandatory relevant considerations (rather than simply permissive considerations). Generally speaking, once a mandatory relevant consideration is taken into account the courts will not examine on judicial review the weight given to any factor(s) by any decision-maker. That said, the courts in both Australia and New Zealand have said if an obviously important factor is given little weight or an unimportant one is given great weight the judges may infer

---

[34] *Minister for Immigration and Ethnic Affairs v Teoh* (1995) 183 CLR 273 (HCA) (hereafter referred to as *Teoh*).
[35] See *Shah v Canada (Minister of Employment and Immigration)* (1994) 170 NR 238 (Fed CA)(no hearing need be held and no reasons need be given).
[36] Strayer JA thought the children's interests were taken genuinely into account. He said it would not advance the appellant's cause 'to say that the welfare of the Canadian children of a deportee must be a factor, where raised by that deportee, in any determination as to the existence of adequate humanitarian grounds for exempting him or her from deportation. No one disputes that such is the case': *Baker* [1997] 2 FC 127, 136–37; (1997) 142 DLR (4th) 554, 560 (Fed CA).

unreasonableness.[37] Until *Baker*, Canadian law was otherwise.[38] On one interpretation of *Baker*, it can be seen as adopting that antipodean approach.

Indeed, the extraordinary thing about *Baker* is that an obviously relevant consideration—the interests of the family—which was intended to work to the advantage of the applicant, was actually used against Ms Baker! The Federal Court of Appeal accepted without demur the trial judge's finding that 'the situation of the children was a "significant factor in the decision-making process" by Officer Caden'.[39] But this is a perverse finding. The officer treated the interests of the children as a significantly negative factor. Convention or no Convention, as a matter of ordinary statutory interpretation the statutory phrase 'humanitarian and compassionate grounds' encompasses only positive factors pointing towards exercise of the discretion in favour of the applicant. By treating the interests of the child in a negative way the decision-maker committed an error of law by misunderstanding what the statutory test required. What should have been a positive factor in the 'humanitarian and compassionate' calculus was wrongly treated as a negative factor.

But *Baker* has been most commonly interpreted in Canada as holding the decision to be unreasonable for failing to give sufficient weight to the best interests of the child. This was viewed as the Supreme Court reassessing the weight that the decision-maker had given to a relevant factor. This is complicated a little by the presence of the Convention on the Rights of the Child (CRC), and the somewhat elusive role that the Convention played in the reasoning of L'Heureux-Dubé J. Article 3 of the CRC states that the 'best interests of the child' is to be 'a primary consideration' in any proceedings concerning children. The *travaux préparatoires* of the CRC disclose this was a compromise.[40] It is commonplace for judges considering

---

[37] *Minister for Aboriginal Affairs v Peko-Wallsend* (1986) 162 CLR 24, 40–42 (Mason J) (HCA); *New Zealand Fishing Industry Association Inc v Minister of Agriculture & Fisheries* [1988] 1 NZLR 544, 552 (Cooke P)(CA). Cf *Minister for Immigration and Multicultural Affairs v Eshetu* (1999) 197 CLR 611, 627–28 (HCA). See also P Craig, *Administrative Law*, 4th edn (Sweet & Maxwell, London 1999) 544.
[38] See, eg, *Douglas Aircraft Co. of Canada v McConnell* [1980] 1 SCR 245, 277, per Estey J.
[39] *Baker v Canada (Minister of Citizenship and Immigration)* [1997] 2 FC 127, 136; (1997) 142 DLR (4th) 554, 557 (Fed CA). The trial judge, Judge Sandra Simpson, said: 'The notes make it clear that Officer Lorenz emphasised the importance of the applicant's children. Mention of them in capital letters and, in the text of the notes, he records the CAS'.s [Children Aid Society's] concern that the children would suffer if their mother were to be returned to Jamaica. Accordingly, the evidence before me suggests that the children were a significant factor in the decision-making process' (*Baker v Canada (Minister of Citizenship and Immigration)* (1996) 31 Imm LR (2d) 150, 156 (Fed TD)).
[40] See S Detrick (comp & ed), *The United Nations Convention on the Rights of the Child: A Guide to the 'Travaux Préparatoires'* (Dordrecht, Martinus Nijhoff Publishers, 1992) 131–40. The initial drafting stated the best interests of the child as the 'paramount consideration'—repeating the phraseology of the *Declaration on the Rights of Children 1959*—but it was watered down to make it clear that decision-makers can take account of (and give decisive weight to) other equally important (ie, primary) considerations: D McGoldrick, 'The United Nations Convention on the Rights of the Child' (1991) 5 *International Journal of Law and the Family* 132, 135–36.

the CRC to point out it is 'a primary' consideration, and not 'the' primary one or the paramount one.[41] The assignment of weight to a human right, as the CRC does, is unusual in human rights treaties. Usually such instruments affirm a right followed by a limitations clause. Then the argument is that the discretionary power in question should be exercised in accordance with that right. This entails a 'balancing exercise', whereby the private right and public interests are weighed.

The fact that the CRC required 'primary' weight to be given to the best interests of the child incurred the wrath of the Federal Court of Appeal in *Baker*. The enforceability of the assignment by the CRC of 'primary' weight to the best interests of the children was seen as constitutionally objectionable on two grounds: (1) by 'limiting the discretionary authority granted by Act of Parliament'; and (2) giving legal effect to the executive Act of ratification.[42] This was thought to affront, in turn, the will and the power of Parliament. Because of the twists and turns the case took on appeal, the majority of the Supreme Court did not address these issues directly.

Perhaps this explains why the majority judgment in *Baker* deliberately avoids the phraseology of the CRC (ie, a 'primary consideration') preferring to talk of the 'centrality' and 'importance' of the children's interests, and insisting that they be given 'substantial weight' and requiring decision makers to be 'alert, alive and sensitive to them'.[43] It was emphasised that to give the interests substantial weight is not to say that the

> children's best interests must always outweigh other considerations, or that there will not be other reasons for denying an H & C claim even when the children's interests are given this consideration.[44]

But the spirit, if not the exact phraseology, of the CRC is manifest. The 'principles' of the CRC and 'other international instruments' placing 'special importance' on children 'help show the values that are central in determining whether [the] decision was a reasonable [one]…'.[45] In other words, they help illuminate the 'fundamental values of Canadian society', which the Court stressed limited the exercise of all discretionary power.[46]

Why Not a *Charter* Case?

One of several mysteries about *Baker* is why the Supreme Court elected to treat the case as raising administrative law issues, rather than invoking

---

[41] See, eg, *Puli'uvea v Removal Review Authority* (1996) 2 HRNZ 510, 517, per Keith J (CA).
[42] *Baker* (Fed CA), above at n 36, 141; 564.
[43] *Baker*, above at n 1, 864; 233.
[44] *Idem*.
[45] *Ibid* 862; 231.
[46] *Ibid* 855; 226.

the *Charter*. This is all the more puzzling as the case was argued by Baker's counsel and several of the intervenors (some of whom were in attendance at the conference) primarily on the basis of the *Charter*.[47] Madam Justice Claire L'Heureux-Dubé does not explain why the *Charter* was forsaken for administrative law. Several commentators in print and at the conference have speculated that the reason is because the *Charter* is an inhospitable environment for the protection of children's interests and family life.[48] Notwithstanding that Ms Baker's Canadian-born children were Canadian citizens and had the right to stay in Canada, the courts have said the decision to remove her Canadian-born children upon her deportation is a matter of 'private choice' for their mother and is not state action for the purposes of the *Charter*.[49] It should be pointed out that, in terms of the CRC, nationality of the children is irrelevant.

If the *Charter* had been implicated in the decision, and protected the non-citizen Ms Baker and/or the interests of her Canadian citizen children, any concerns as to the legitimacy of referring to the CRC would melt away. Justices Iacobucci and Cory dissented in *Baker* only to register their disapproval of the majority referring to 'the underlying values of an unincorporated international treaty in the course of the contextual approach to statutory interpretation and administrative law'.[50] According to this approach, for the values to operate at all in the domestic legal system they must be admitted by the hand of Parliament, not that of the executive. On this view, Canadian public law is cleaved into *Charter* rights[51] and the rest.

Cleavage, Continuum, Colander or Coordination?

One problem faced by public lawyers when a human rights instrument is injected into the legal system—whether it be entrenched (as in Canada and South Africa) or by way of an 'ordinary' statute (as in the UK and

---

[47] See S Aiken & S Scott, '*Baker v Canada (Minister of Citizenship and Immigration)* and the Rights of Children' (2000) 15 *Journal of Law and Society Policy* 211.
[48] The limited protections accorded the family and children under the Canadian *Charter* contrasts with the explicit recognition of 'family life' in the ECHR. In discussion Paul Craig pointed to this being another reason why *Baker* would cause less difficulty in the UK.
[49] *Langner v Canada (Minister of Employment and Immigration)* (1995) 184 NR 230 (Fed CA); *Naredo v Canada (Minister of Employment and Immigration)* (1995) 184 NR 352. See also *Schier v Removal Review Authority* [1999] 1 NZLR 703 (CA).
[50] *Baker*, above at n 1, 234.
[51] Highly ambiguous, not to say contradictory, dicta by Dickson CJ in *In the Matter of a Reference re Public Service Employee Relations Act* [1987] 1 SCR 313, 349–50 (SSC) suggests that the *Charter* is some sort of conduit for subsequent international human rights instruments to operate in Canadian law. This is touched on in Audrey Macklin's chapter and the unsatisfactory dicta explains in part Brunnée/Toope's insistence in their paper upon the need to identify binding international law. For further exploration, see G van Ert, *Using International Law in Canadian Courts* (The Hague, Kluwer Law International, 2002) 238–79.

New Zealand)[52]—is to know how to fit it in with existing administrative law.[53]

Those countries with entrenched human rights instruments are pulled in different directions. It is an established principle that the constitutionality of statutes is presumed, with the corollary that the constitutional sledgehammer of invalidation of legislation should not be used if the particular nut can be cracked by administrative law means. This points to pleading/arguing administrative law grounds first and only if that proves inadequate should the big constitutional guns be wheeled out. The countervailing principle is that the entrenched human rights instrument is superior in every respect to administrative law doctrine—more exacting, transparent and overt in its articulation of values, and hence more legitimate and direct—and should be used first. Why, it might be asked, should an applicant have to wander in the maze of administrative law when the motorway of the Constitution beckons?[54] Different legal systems place more weight on one approach or the other. Canada, for instance, has tended towards the second approach,[55] with some exceptions—*Baker's* case being a notable one.

The advantages of the Constitutional motorway (as David Mullan points out) is that *if* one can get on it, the protections are usually more secure, harder to dislodge and the remedies more robust. However, it is often more difficult to get on the motorway due to a narrow or inflexible conception of 'state action' and the satisfaction of a higher threshold to gain protection. Experience suggests that the fact that criteria are written down in such an instrument tends towards formalistic line drawing. It is for reasons like these that in those jurisdictions with entrenched human rights instruments the circle of Constitutional protection overlaps considerably but does not coincide exactly with the circle of administrative law. It is in the area of overlap—the area between the intersecting circles—that there is a choice of

---

[52] I am aware it is considered old-fashioned in some circles—indeed, almost politically incorrect—to use words like 'entrenched'. One can accept that the jobs of interpretation and application are identical under both entrenched and un-entrenched domestic human rights instruments, without disregarding the fact that at least in some cases in the absence of entrenchment the wall of sovereignty will be hit. Indeed, the Australian experience surveyed by Margaret Allars demonstrates this can even more easily occur in the absence of any domestic human rights instrument.

[53] Adding regional and/or international human rights instruments into the mix can complicate matters further. In the UK, as Paul Craig's chapter illustrates, it is possible for cases to raise points under EU law, Human Rights Act/European Convention, and administrative law. Audrey Macklin's chapter also deals with the impact of international law obligations on the *Charter*/administrative law relationship.

[54] The future Lord Diplock said the beauty of the common law is that 'it is a maze and not a motorway': *Morris v CW Martin & Sons Ltd* [1966] 1 QB 716, 730 (CA).

[55] See *Ross v New Brunswick School District No 15* [1996] 1 SCR 825; *Slaight Communications Inc v Davidson* [1989] 1 SCR 1038; *Blencoe v British Columbia (Human Rights Commission)* [2000] 2 SCR 307. Audrey Macklin and Geneviève Cartier discuss these cases in their chapters.

what law to use/argue first. Exactly the same choice pertains in countries where the domestic human rights instrument is not entrenched and the circles overlap but are not coincident. The only difference being that if arguments of interpretation and application hit the wall of sovereignty nothing can be done; whereas the courts can invalidate the statute where the human rights instrument is entrenched.

In the Canadian context, Geneviève Cartier, Audrey Macklin and David Mullan address the relationship between the *Charter* and administrative law. In *Baker's* case, David Mullan thinks the Supreme Court 'short changed' Ms Baker by not considering whether she had any *Charter* protection. If it had been determined that she did, then Ms Baker would likely have been entitled to an oral hearing (rather than one on the papers) and benefited from an even more intrusive standard of review (correctness rather than reasonableness *simpliciter*). This is because the Constitution is just that—it is a more powerful protection, without the legitimacy concerns that plague administrative law adjudication. Consequently, Mullan is blistering in his criticism of the post-*Baker* case of *Suresh*,[56] where the Supreme Court was much more deferential to Ministerial decision-making where *Charter* rights were implicated than in *Baker* where the *Charter* was not addressed. This is a 'serious anomaly', says Mullan, because the *Charter* in and of itself mandates greater vigilance as regards enumerated rights than administrative law does for unenumerated rights and interests.

Audrey Macklin illustrates the tension in the *Charter*/administrative law interrelationship by looking down the other end of the telescope. She points out that a permanent (unlawful) resident like Mr Chiarelli can be deported without crossing the *Charter's* section 7 threshold of 'life, liberty and security of the person' (the result in *Chiarelli v Canada (Minister of Employment and Immigration*[57]), whereas administrative law affords an unlawful migrant like Ms Baker greater procedural protection than the *Charter* gave Mr Chiarelli. She concludes that one or other of these decisions is going to have to give if the *Charter* and administrative law are sensibly to come into alignment.

The cleavage of public law into *Charter* rights on one side and everything non-*Charter* on the other is not attractive, and at the end of his chapter Mullan suggests 'a continuum of sorts'. But it is really a sliding scale, with the *Charter* at the top of the slide. This seems true also of Macklin's treatment of the *Charter*/administrative law relationship. The *Charter* seems to operate like a colander catching the Rights stuff while everything else trickles down to administrative law.

According to Geneviève Cartier, this is the 'hierarchical view' of the *Charter*/administrative law relationship that predominated prior to *Baker*.

[56] *Suresh v Minister of Citizenship and Immigration* (2002) 208 DLR (4th) 1.
[57] [1992] 1 SCR 283 (SCC).

The *Charter* operated like a giant sponge, absorbing all the values out of administrative law's treatment of discretion, rendering it desiccated and formalistic. Cartier suggests that *Baker* provides the foundation for a new kind of relationship, one of greater coordination, cross-fertilisation and ultimately unity.

Fundamental Values

There was discussion at the conference as to what 'fundamental values' means and exactly how they differ from the other items on the *Baker* shopping list, particularly the Rule of Law and the *Charter*. What might it entail? Does it, for example, include the protection of property? This 'right' was deliberately left out of the *Charter*,[58] although it has long been considered 'fundamental' in the common law tradition,[59] and Canada is no exception.[60] There is protection for the enjoyment of property in the earlier Canadian Bill of Rights 1960, which still operates at the Federal level. Moreover, property is specifically included in some of the international and regional rights instruments,[61] and has been included in almost all African and Caribbean Constitutions upon attaining independence from British colonial rule.[62] Is this a 'fundamental value' in the intended sense?

There is also a large body of administrative law that, through deployment of well-established techniques of statutory interpretation, protects property rights.[63] Which heading(s) on the *Baker* list do these principles fall within: the principles of administrative law, the Rule of Law, or fundamental values? An interpreter has a choice of interpretive principles in interpreting and applying discretionary powers,[64] and they offer choices between conflicting 'fundamental' values. The *Baker* list does not help in that endeavour.

---

[58] See A Alvaro, 'Why Property Rights Were Excluded from the Canadian Charter of Rights and Freedoms' (1991) 24 *Canadian Journal of Political Science* 309.

[59] See, eg, GW Gough, *Fundamental Law in English Constitutional History* (Oxford, Oxford University Press, 1955) 54 ('What ever rights were fundamental we may be sure they included the right to property').

[60] See RCB Risk and RC Pond, 'Rights Talk in Canada in the Late Nineteenth Century: The Good Sense and Right Feeling of the People' (1996) 14 *Law and History Review* 1.

[61] See, eg, the Universal Declaration of Human Rights (General Assembly Resolution 217A(III) of 10 December 1948), Art 17; American Convention on Human Rights 1969 (9 ILM 673), Art. 21; African Charter on Human and People's Rights 1981 (OAU Doc CAB/LEG/67/3, Rev. 5), Art 14.

[62] See generally T Allen, *The Right to Property in Commonwealth Constitutions* (Cambridge, Cambridge University Press, 2000).

[63] See generally M Taggart, 'Expropriation, Public Purpose and the Constitution' in C Forsyth & I Hare (eds), *The Golden Metwand and the Crooked Cord: Essays in Public Law in Honour of Sir William Wade QC* (Oxford, Clarendon Press, 1998) 91.

[64] See JM Evans, H Janisch, D Mullan and RCB Risk, *Administrative Law: Cases, Text, and Materials,* 4th edn (Toronto, Edmond Montgomery Publications Ltd, 1995) ch 9.

More generally, the issue raised by 'fundamental values' is who can legitimately divine and articulate them, and by what process?[65] Rights not enumerated in a Constitution, but read in, almost always pose a challenge to the legitimacy of the judges. It seems to me that one way to leap this legitimacy gap is to tell a compelling story about the way the legal system has responded over time to the issue or liberty at issue. Take the rights of children, for example. I find unconvincing Justice Gaudron's assertion in *Teoh's* case that reasonable people in a civilised society like Australia would expect the best interests of an Australian child to be taken into account as a primary consideration in any decision-making involving a family member.[66] There is no evidence proffered, or as I would say 'story' told, to back this up. A demonstration of how social attitudes towards children have changed over a considerable period in Australia and the reflection (with an inevitable lag) *both* in statute and common law, would have been more persuasive. And when that story is told any international influences—sometimes leading, sometimes following—are an important part of it. It is not irrelevant, to my mind, that the CRC is the most ratified treaty in the history of the world. History, tradition and international norms have important roles to play in the justification and legitimation of value inquiry. They assist in combating eclecticism and subjectivity in the identification of 'fundamental' rights.[67]

Bringing the Parts Together

One of the achievements of *Baker's* case was to bring together two parts of administrative law and to attempt to meld them into a coherent whole. The first, and much older, part was organised around the law of jurisdiction and centred on the interpretation of statutory language. The second, and more modern, part used the language of ultra vires (borrowed from nineteenth century corporations law) and encapsulated the earlier learning on control of discretionary power. The key to this amalgamation is the recognition that, both in interpreting particular words in statutes and divining the limits of broadly conferred discretionary powers, lawyers and judges are involved in the same interpretative exercise. Earlier attempts to say that words could be ambiguous, but broadly conferred statutory discretions could not, have been found to be unconvincing. The strongest support for

---

[65] See generally D Crump, 'How Do the Courts *Really* Discover Unenumerated Fundamental Rights? Cataloguing the Methods of Judicial Alchemy' (1996) 19 *Harvard Journal of Law and Public Policy* 795.
[66] *Teoh*, above at n 34, 304.
[67] At the conference several Canadians underscored this by reference to the importance of bi-culturalism and the recognition of the French language in Canada. See also the chapters by Mark Walters and David Mullan.

the separation of the interpretative and discretionary spheres, the House of Lords' decision in *Brind's* case, has been overrun in most jurisdictions, including the UK.[68]

But bringing these two parts of the doctrinal mosaic together highlights a tension in the fabric of administrative law. Outside North America, the common law courts had adopted a simplistic approach to the issue of who should have the final say as to what words in a statute mean. It was asserted all over the Commonwealth that the separation of powers doctrine required judges to have the final say on what statutory language means. The decision-maker at first instance must interpret its legislation but it is the right and responsibility of the court to review those interpretations, when challenged, and to correct them when wrong. This is, according to Lord Diplock, the fulfilment of the courts' constitutional role as interpreters of the written law.[69] It stands in the tradition of Dicey, and it was one of the tenets of faith of the Victorians that the 'ordinary' courts sat at the top of the heap fully competent to watch over (supervise) and administer the whole law.[70] At the theoretical level there is no whiff of deference. The closest to that view in this collection is in Trevor Allan's chapter, and the comment by Margaret Allars that deference has made little headway in Australia.[71]

It seems that three interrelated notions underpin this view that questions of statutory interpretation are ultimately for the courts to determine conclusively without overt deference to the initial interpreter or interpretation: (1) there is one right answer to questions of statutory interpretation; (2) that, as experienced and talented lawyers, the judiciary are the best placed persons to provide that answer; and (3) these questions of 'law' are separate and distinguishable from policy, discretion and fact-finding. Each of these notions is controversial, and together they have largely been rejected in the United States since the 1930s and in Canada since the late 1970s.

---

[68] *R v Secretary of State for the Home Department, ex parte Brind* [1991] 1 AC 696 (HL). This decision was ignored in *Baker's* case (above at n 1); it was leg-glanced in *Tavita v Minister of Immigration* [1994] 2 NZLR 257, 266, per Cooke P (CA) and criticised extra-judicially (R Cooke, 'The Quest for Administrative Justice' (1992) 18 *Commonwealth Law Bulletin* 1326, 1328); and it has been overtaken by the 'incorporation' of the European Convention by the Human Rights Act 1998 (UK). *Brind's* case was followed, however, by the High Court of Australia in *Teoh*, above at n 34.
[69] *In re Racal Communications Ltd* [1981] AC 374, 383.
[70] See S Wexler, 'The Forms of Action and Administrative Law' in *Proceedings of the Administrative Law Conference, Faculty of Law, University of British Columbia, Vancouver, BC, 18–19 October 1979* (1981) 292, 295 and generally H Arthurs, *'Without the Law': Administrative Justice and Legal Pluralism in Nineteenth Century England* (Toronto, University of Toronto Press, 1985).
[71] See generally M Aronson and B Dyer, *Judicial Review of Administrative Action* (Sydney, LBC Information Services, 2000) 12, 140, 151–92. My answer to those authors' question to me on p 191 n 244 is 'no'.

To cut long stories short, the justifications for deference to the 'reasonable' interpretations of administrative decision-makers included: the 'expertise' of the decision-maker; the inextricable linkage of interpretation with policy-making and the advancement of legislative objectives; legislative intent, as manifested by the delegation of administration to an expert body and sometimes by the inclusion of privative clauses; the thoroughness of the agencies' treatment of the issue and the persuasiveness of its reasoning; the consistency and longevity of its interpretation. Most of these justifications for deference boil down to the notions of legislative intent or expertise.

In contrast to the lack of deference shown to agency interpretation in most common law countries, there were oodles of deference shown in relation to discretionary power. The merits were taboo to judges; they were only for the decision-maker. The courts could only stand on the perimeter guarding the 'four corners' of jurisdiction but not interfere within the square unless perversity raised its head (aka *Wednesbury* unreasonableness). But once again things were not quite as simple as they seemed. In some jurisdictions decision-makers were found to have acted unreasonably where objectively it could not be said they had gone mad. This suggested strongly that the threshold for intervention was often lower and more flexible than the rhetoric allowed. Furthermore, first commentators and then judges demonstrated that the proper and principled basis of intervention for unreasonableness was the protection of rights, recognised in both the common law and affirmed in various regional and global treaties.[72] The adoption of regional and domestic human rights instruments in several of these countries in the last 20 years has accelerated this process. Most relevantly, in relation to discretionary power, there has been a powerful re-articulation of the principle of legality.[73]

As Lord Hoffmann explained, this 'principle of legality' is in effect a strong presumption that broadly expressed discretions are subject to the fundamental human rights recognised by the common law.[74]

> The principle of legality means that Parliament must squarely confront what it is doing and accept the political cost. Fundamental rights cannot be overridden by general or ambiguous words. This is because there is too great a risk that the full implications of their unqualified meaning may have passed unnoticed in the democratic process. In the absence of express language or

---

[72] See, eg, J Jowell and A Lester, 'Beyond *Wednesbury*: Substantive Principles of Administrative Law' [1987] *Public Law* 368.

[73] This principle is a very old one with a new label. It was labelled by Sir Rupert Cross in his text on *Statutory Interpretation*, 3rd edn (London, Butterworths, 1995) and was adopted by Lords Steyn and Hoffmann in *R v Secretary of State for the Home Department, ex parte Pierson* [1998] AC 539, 588 (HL), and by the House of Lords in *R v Secretary of State for the Home Department, ex parte Simms* [2000] 2 AC 115 and *R (Daly) v Secretary of State for the Home Department* [2001] 2 AC 532.

[74] *Ibid*, 131.

necessary implication to the contrary, the courts therefore presume that even the most general words were intended to be subject to the basic rights of the individual. In this way the courts of the United Kingdom, though acknowledging the sovereignty of Parliament, apply principles of constitutionality little different from those which exist in countries where the power of the legislature is expressly limited by a constitutional document.

The principle dovetails with that presuming conformity with international law, and merges in so far as domestic human rights instruments are identical to regional and global human rights instruments.

DUE DEFERENCE

Deference is a slippery word. As noted above, in the administrative law of common law countries (outside the United States) 'deference' was not used as a term of art until the late 1970s, when the Canadian Supreme Court imported the word and much of the learning surrounding its use from South of the border.[75] That does not mean, of course, that common law courts in those other jurisdictions knew nothing previously of deference.

For a start, many of the doctrines of administrative law were shaped by evolved understandings of separation of powers, institutional competence and deference. The ancient concept of jurisdiction, for example, operated as a saw cutting off those questions that the courts thought they were suited to decide the correctness of, from those that they thought were best left to be decided conclusively by the inferior court judges, tribunals, administrators and politicians. The modern realisation that the concept of jurisdiction was too blunt an instrument to properly 'saw off' or allocate interpretative authority between courts and administrative agencies, has lead to its abandonment in many parts of the common law world, and its replacement by the error of law standard.[76] Secondly, as Trevor Allan points out in his chapter, the principles that control the exercise of statutory discretion also have in-built deference. The famous or infamous (depending on your point of view) *Wednesbury* unreasonableness doctrine demanded deference unless the decision-maker had lost its rocker, or so the court said.[77]

Thirdly, the 'classic model' of administrative law that prevailed up until the 1960s in the UK and elsewhere in the Commonwealth was characterised

---

[75] See M Taggart, 'Outside Canadian Administrative Law' (1996) 46 *University of Toronto Law Journal* 649, 650.
[76] For a survey of Anglo-Commonwealth law on this topic, see M Taggart, 'The Contribution of Lord Cooke to Scope of Review Doctrine in Administrative Law: A Comparative Common Law Perspective' in P Rishworth (ed), *The Struggle for Simplicity in Law: Essays for Lord Cooke of Thorndon* (Wellington, Butterworths, 1997) 189.
[77] *Associated Provincial Picture Houses Ltd v Wednesbury Corporation* [1948] 1 KB 223 (CA) (hereafter referred to as *Wednesbury*).

by restricted grounds of review, a restrictive concept of locus standi, judicial restraint, and an emphasis on remedies over rights.[78] Moreover, as more fully explained later, this restrictive attitude to judicial review was manifested in terms of proof and the difficulty of discovering the reasons and motivation of the decision-makers. In these respects the classic model purported to keep the judges' noses out of the tent of politics—by restricting who could seek judicial review, avoiding 'policy' issues, ensuring the dispute was justiciable, restricting the proof and requiring the satisfaction of high thresholds for intervention, deferring to legitimate authority, and ensuring that the remedy matched the wrong. The *Wednesbury* case[79] became the emblem of the classic model of administrative law.

This is no place for a primer on developments in administrative law since the mid-twentieth century, but something must be said about the tremendous growth of the subject.[80] So rapid have been the developments in the UK since the mid-1960s that Lord Diplock felt able to say in the early 1980s that 'any judicial statements on public law if made before 1950 are likely to be a misleading guide to what the law is today'.[81] According to the orthodox account, in the mid-1960s the British judges awoke from their 'long sleep' and set about renovating the house of judicial review.[82] To list only a few developments: prerogative powers are no longer immune from judicial review; the concept of jurisdiction was first expanded and then collapsed into a flexible error of law standard; the administrative/judicial dichotomy has withered under the fairness sunlamp; the concept of legitimate expectation has emerged first as a procedural doctrine and latterly as a substantive one; some notion of estoppel in public law is emerging; evidential and factual review has sprung up. Some, but by no means all, of these developments occurred contemporaneously in Australia, New Zealand and Canada. There were different doctrinal emphases. As Geneviève

---

[78] C Harlow, 'A Special Relationship? American Influences on Judicial Review in England' in I Loveland (ed), *A Special Relationship? American Influences on Public Law in the UK* (Oxford, Clarendon Press, 1995) 79, 83.
[79] *Wednesbury*, above at n 77.
[80] For chapter and verse in the UK, see the trinity: P Craig, *Administrative Law*, 4th edn (Sweet & Maxwell, London, 1999); SA de Smith, H Woolf & J Jowell, *Judicial Review of Administrative Action*, 5th edn (London, Sweet & Maxwell, 1995); HWR Wade & C Forsyth, *Administrative Law*, 8th edn (Oxford, Oxford University Press, 2000). For Australia, see M Aronson & B Dyer, *Judicial Review of Administrative Action*, 2nd edn (Sydney, LBC Information Services, 2000) and M Allars, *Introduction to Australian Administrative Law* (Sydney, Butterworths, 1990). For Canada, see D Mullan, *Administrative Law* (Toronto, Irwin Law, 2001). For New Zealand, see GDS Taylor, *Judicial Review: A New Zealand Perspective* (Wellington, Butterworths, 1991) and P Joseph, *Constitutional and Administrative Law in New Zealand*, 2nd edn (Wellington, Brookers, 2002).
[81] *R v IRC, ex parte Federation of Self-Employed & Small Businesses Ltd* [1982] AC 617, 649.
[82] The quoted phrase is Stephen Sedley's ('Sounds of Silence: Constitutional Law Without A Constitution' (1994) 110 *Law Quarterly Review* 270, 279) but the sentiment is shared by all leading UK administrative textbook writers (see above at n 80). But see S Sterett, *Creating Constitutionalism? The Politics of Legal Expertise and Administrative Law in England and Wales* (Ann Arbor, The University of Michigan Press, 1997) ch 2.

Cartier and David Mullan point out in their chapters, *Wednesbury* unreasonableness proved much less popular in Canada than elsewhere in the Commonwealth.

Amid this expansion, paradoxically the *Wednesbury* formula not only survived but became a mantra, repeated literally thousands of times all over the common law world. In part, this is because the *dicta* have a protean quality; it is 'a legal formula, indiscriminately used to express different and sometimes contradictory ideas'.[83] As such, it is ideally suited to flexible application and, indeed, susceptible to reinvention.

This is no better exemplified than by Sir John Laws' extra-judicial description of the *Wednesbury* case as reflecting 'the rule of reason', whereby intrusions upon individual freedom by public authorities 'must be objectively justified'.[84] This stands the case on its head. The inscrutable Wednesbury Corporation never explained or justified its decision and the Court was complicit in this non-transparency by assuming the answer to the very question to be decided and inferring what the Corporation must have thought and done. *Wednesbury* is the antithesis of the rule of reason.[85] What are missing from *Wednesbury* to complete the desired reinvention are a rights-centred approach and the creation of the justificatory mechanisms to instantiate the Rule of Law. As we will see, recent developments have supplied those ingredients.

Many common lawyers are suspicious of deference. To some it brings to mind authoritarianism. As Joseph Vining observed, '[t]he very word *deference* calls up lowering the eyes, baring the covered head, laughing at jokes that are not funny'.[86] To others, such as Trevor Allan in his chapter, judges who unthinkingly defer forfeit their neutrality. Is deference compatible with the Rule of Law? In a piece that L'Heureux-Dubé J quoted with approval in *Baker*,[87] and which is relied on by several of the contributors to this volume, David Dyzenhaus has put forward the notion of deference as respect, rather than submission. The interpreter is thereby required to pay 'respectful attention to the reasons offered or which could be offered in support of the decision'.[88] The focus moves to the rationality and transparency of the justification for the outcome.

Trevor Allan welcomes this move to the particular, for he desires that the judges in each case explain why (or why not) the exercise of discretion satisfies

---

[83] The quotation is from Justice Felix Frankfurter in *Tiller v Atlantic Coast Railroad Co*, 318 US 54, 68 (1943).
[84] J Laws, 'Wednesbury' in Forsyth & Hare, above at n 63, 185, 186 & 191.
[85] See further M Taggart, 'Reinventing Administrative Law' in N Bamforth and P Leyland (eds), *Public Law in a Multi-Layered Constitution* (Oxford, Hart Publishing, 2003) 251.
[86] J Vining, 'Authority and Responsibility: The Jurisprudence of Deference' (1991) 43 *Administrative Law Review* 135.
[87] Above at n 1, 859; 229.
[88] D Dyzenhaus, 'The Politics of Deference: Judicial Review and Democracy' in M Taggart (ed), *The Province of Administrative Law* (Oxford, Hart Publishing, 1997) 279, 286.

due process and equality norms. Allan puts great store on the structuring of discretions by general rules and policies in order to ensure equal, consistent and fair administration, deserving of deference. There is more than a little of Dicey's (and Hayek's) distaste for discretionary power here, with the consequence that discretion is to be squeezed by rules. Other commentators, poles apart from Dicey, also favour particularism because they fear the blanket deference that immunises large areas from effective judicial review.[89] It remains to be seen whether particularism of the envisaged sort is workable in a heavy caseload judicial review system.

THE RIGHTS-CENTRED APPROACH

It has been argued elsewhere that administrative law is going through a process of constitutionalisation.[90] Briefly stated, this requires justification of alleged rights-infringing behaviour and the adoption of a constitutional methodology of proportionality, balancing of rights and interests, and reasoned elaboration. Internationalisation accentuates that development by reinforcing and in some instances adding to the rights that claim recognition from the courts. At least as regard 'rights' recognised by domestic human rights instruments or by the common law itself, the new constitutional methodology is firmly in place. In legal systems without a 'capital C' constitution, such as the UK and New Zealand, rights-based adjudication takes place, by default, through administrative law proceedings. Consequently, administrative law is in the throes of adjusting to that enhanced role. Elsewhere I have described that process as the reinvention of administrative law, because of the magnitude of the departure from the classic model of administrative law.[91] Consequently the emblem of the classic model—*Wednesbury* unreasonableness—is also in the process of being reinvented.

It appears that in the area of rights adjudication *Wednesbury* is to be replaced by the doctrine of proportionality.[92] As with rights-centred adjudication, the doctrine of proportionality has the potential to pull the elements of constitutional law, international law and administrative law into a coherent whole.

Proportionality is a European concept that took hold in the European Court of Human Rights and the European Court of Justice. It was exported

---

[89] See the paper by M Hunt, 'Sovereignty's Blight: Why Contemporary Public Law Needs the Concept of "Due Deference"' in Bamforth and Leyland, above at n 85, that was circulated before the Toronto conference and discussed there.
[90] See D Dyzenhaus, M Hunt and M Taggart, 'The Principle of Legality in Administrative Law: Internationalisation as Constitutionalisation' (2001) 1 *Oxford University Commonwealth Law Journal* 5.
[91] See Taggart, above at n 85.
[92] See *R (Daly) v Secretary of State for the Home Department*, above at n 73. There is already a large literature, which shows no sign of abating.

to Canada in the 1980s, when the courts there came to apply the balancing test laid down in section 1 of the *Charter of Rights and Freedoms*, which itself derived from the wording of the European Convention on Human Rights. The famous Canadian *Oakes* test incorporates all the features of Euro-proportionality. New Zealand followed both the wording of the *Charter* and the Canadian proportionality test.[93] The UK, which followed New Zealand's example by not entrenching the European Convention when it was domesticated in 1998, has adopted proportionality at the highest level.[94]

REASONS, RATIONALITY AND A CULTURE OF JUSTIFICATION

In at least one important respect administrative law never lived up to the Rule of Law rhetoric. The law presupposes that there are reasons for the decisions reached by decision-makers and that the administrative process is rational and not arbitrary, but it did not insist on the statement of findings of fact and reasons for decisions.[95] Indeed, the law of judicial review was positively curmudgeonly in relation to reasons in both the judicial and administrative spheres.[96] The bindingness of judicial decisions came from the fact of decision, rather than the reasons. It was more important that a dispute was resolved than it be explained. Even when reasons were volunteered these did not automatically become part of the 'record', that might be sent up to a superior court when demanded. The writ of certiorari meant literally to send up the record from the inferior body to the superior court to look at.[97] Only if the decision-maker both volunteered reasons and deliberately attached them to the record could the court receive and scrutinise the record. The Privy Council decision in a Canadian appeal, *R v Nat Bell Liquors Ltd*,[98] holding that deciding on 'no evidence' neither went to jurisdiction nor fell within review for non-jurisdictional error of law on the face of the record, accurately summarised the common law position and further entrenched it. The fact that *Nat Bell* is unheard of today, simply underlines how far the law has moved in the course of the last century.

---

[93] *Ministry of Transport v Noort* [1992] 3 NZLR 260, 283, per Richardson J (CA); *Moonen v Film & Literature Board of Review* [2000] 2 NZLR 9 (CA). See generally P Rishworth, G Huscroft, S Optican & R Mahoney, *The New Zealand Bill of Rights* (Melbourne, Oxford University Press, 2003).
[94] See above at n 92.
[95] See generally M Taggart, 'Should Canadian Judges Be Legally Required To Give Reasoned Decisions in Civil Cases' (1983) 33 *University of Toronto Law Journal* 1.
[96] In part, this goes back to the separation of Year-Book and record: JH Baker, 'Records, Reports and the Origins of Case-Law in England' in JH Baker (ed), *Judicial Records, Law Reports and the Growth of Case Law* (Berlin, Duncker & Humblot, 1989) 15, 34–6.
[97] See generally AS Abel, 'Materials Proper for Consideration in Certiorari to Tribunals: I' (1963–4) 15 *University of Toronto Law Journal* 102 (the anticipated second part of this article never appeared).
[98] [1922] 2 AC 128 (PC).

The initial advances in the area of reasoned elaboration were made by statute. The path-breaking general requirements to give reasons in the US Administrative Procedure Act 1946 and the UK Tribunal and Inquiries Act 1958, were emulated eventually all over the common law world, but with inevitable unevenness of both coverage and specificity.[99] Hence the gaps that have needed to be filled by common law developments have narrowed significantly over the second half of the twentieth century. It is only in the last decade or two that any progress has been made in changing the common law in this regard. Once again the progress has been uneven across the common law world, but the trend has been towards requiring reasoned elaboration.

The fact that historically judges have not been required to give reasoned judgments, until very recently, has retarded common law developments in the administrative law sphere. It is often overlooked that prior to the 1850s no judge of a superior court ever wrote a judgment at the end of a trial. The sphinx-like jury gave judgment in all trials, be they criminal or civil.[100] The first instance 'judgment' took the form of a jury direction, and this dictated its form, length and sophistication. With the emergence of judge-alone civil trials in the mid-nineteenth century comes the reasoned first instance judgment. This is one of the most important but least remarked upon changes in the last 200 years.[101] Today, a century and a half later, we view the non-reasoning jury as the exception rather than the norm that it was for the previous eight centuries or so.[102]

Twenty years ago only one common law country recognised in law what long since had become accepted practice in the common law world; namely, the giving of factually supported and reasoned decisions. That country is Australia, which insisted on judicial reasoned elaboration in all courts at whatever level since the early twentieth century.[103] Paradoxically, as Margaret Allars points out in her chapter, Australia's highest court has

---

[99] See M Shapiro, 'The Giving Reasons Requirement' [1992] *The University of Chicago Legal Forum* 179; S Shapiro and R Levy, 'Heightened Scrutiny of the Fourth Branch: Separation of Powers and the Requirement of Adequate Reasons for Agency Decisions' [1987] *Duke Law Journal* 387; AP Le Sueur, 'Legal Duties To Give Reasons' (1999) 52 *Current Legal Problems* 150; R MacDonald and D Lametti, 'Reasons for Decision in Administrative Law' (1990) 3 *Canadian Journal of Administrative Law & Practice* 123; M Taggart, 'The Rationalisation of Administrative Tribunal Procedure: The New Zealand Experience' in R Creyke (ed), *Administrative Tribunals: Taking Stock* (Canberra, Centre for International & Public Law, Australian National University, 1992) 91. For a summary of the Australian position see the chapter by Margaret Allars.
[100] P Devlin, *Trial by Jury* (London, Stevens, 1966) 130.
[101] See SFC Milsom, *Studies in the History of the Common Law* (London, The Hambledon Press, 1985) 218–19.
[102] For a recent treatment of the history of the jury, see JA Cairns & G Macleod (eds), *'The dearest birth right of the people of England': The jury in the history of the common law* (Oxford, Hart Publishing, 2002).
[103] See M Kirby, 'Reasons for Judgment: "Always Permissible, Usually Desirable and Often Obligatory"' (1994) 12 *Australian Bar Review* 121.

refused to extend that common law duty to administrative decision-makers.[104] In contrast, as explained fully in Mary Liston's chapter, the Supreme Court of Canada, first in *Baker*, announced a generally applicable common law duty to give reasons on administrative decision-makers,[105] and then more recently signalled the overturn of a long line of authority immunising criminal court judges from any duty to give reasons.[106] Elsewhere in the Commonwealth, the courts are heading towards recognition that both judges and administrators are required to justify their decisions.[107] The modus operandi in the administrative sphere has been to utilise procedural fairness to require reasons in ill-defined exceptional circumstances and then a gradual expansion of those exceptions, so they will eventually swallow the rule.

As Mary Liston makes clear in her chapter, the '*Baker* ethos' rests ultimately on creating and sustaining a culture of justification. Reason-giving is central to the whole enterprise. But, as Paul Craig pointed out at the conference, this new culture will require reforms of other adjectival rules and practices, in addition to requiring factually supported and reasoned decisions. Discovery once was non-existent and now is still limited in some jurisdictions.[108] Disclosure of error used to be restricted to what would appear on the face of the record or could be deposed to by way of affidavit. Judicial review proceeds on the papers. Permission to issue interrogatories or to cross-examine deponents is rarely granted.[109] There was and still is no duty on respondents to file an affidavit to explain why a decision was made.[110] Indeed, there is an obscure but strongly supported common law doctrine against permitting litigants 'to probe the mental processes of the administrator'.[111] The danger of not filing affidavits informing the court of

---

[104] *Public Service Board of New South Wales v Osmond* (1985–86) 159 CLR 656, 666–7 (HCA). For discussion see M Kirby, 'Accountability and the Right to Reasons' and M Taggart, '*Osmond* in the High Court of Australia: Opportunity Lost' in M Taggart (ed), *Judicial Review of Administrative Action in the 1980s: Problems and Prospects* (Auckland, Oxford University Press, 1986) 36 & 53.
[105] *Baker*, above at n 1.
[106] *R v Sheppard* (2002) 210 DLR (4th) 608. For further commentary, see C Boyle & M MacCrimmon, 'Reasons for Judgment: A Comment on Rv Sheppard and Rv Braich' (2002) 47 *Criminal Law Quarterly* 39 and MC Plaxton, 'Thinking about Appeals, Authority and Judicial Power after R v Sheppard' (2002) 47 *Criminal Law Quarterly* 59.
[107] For a recent survey, see HL Ho, 'The judicial duty to give reasons' (2000) 20 *Legal Studies* 42.
[108] See *O'Reilly v Mackman* [1983] 2 AC 237, 280, per Lord Diplock (HL).
[109] *George v Secretary of State for the Environment* (1979) 38 P & CR 609, 615, per Lord Denning MR (CA); *Minister of Energy v Petrocorp Exploration Ltd* [1989] 1 NZLR 348 (CA). In *O'Reilly v Mackman*, above at n 108, 282 Lord Diplock pointed out that since a 1977 Rule change cross-examination should be allowed whenever the justice of the case requires. There is little evidence of any subsequent liberalisation in UK practice.
[110] *New Zealand Fishing Industry Association Inc v Minister of Agriculture and Fisheries* [1988] 1 NZLR 544, 554, per Cooke P (CA).
[111] *United States v Morgan*, 313 US 409, 422 (1941), per Frankfurter J. See the cases referred to in Taggart, above at n 95, 37 n 148 & *Comalco New Zealand Ltd v Broadcasting Standards Authority* [1995] 3 NZLR 469 (HC), upheld on appeal: (1995) 9 PRNZ 153 (CA).

the basis of the decision is that the respondents may not discharge the evidential onus put upon them by the applicant's case. But where the threshold that the applicant must meet is very high—as the *Wednesbury* unreasonableness test was—in the past respondents have often got away with uninformative or otherwise self-serving affidavits.[112] So the information gathering and testing processes need to be renovated if the culture of justification is to become embedded in the common law.

CONCLUSION

It will be clear by now that the tub of public law is expanding. International human rights law has emerged as a sub-specialty, influencing all the other parts. The assertion of the primacy of human rights law in international law has far reaching consequences for international and domestic law.[113] In the same way the adoption of domestic human rights instruments has profound implications for administrative law and traditional constitutional law. The imbrication of international, regional and domestic human rights instruments reinforces the tub, strengthening and unifying it. This is just as well, for the choppy seas of globalisation threaten to capsize the tub into the sea of private law, non-State actors and the global market place. This is a replay on a broader front of what happened to administrative law in the face of privatisation.[114] Those that are knavish about working together in the tub should ponder the alternative.

---

[112] See, eg, JAG Griffith, 'Judicial Decision-Making in Public Law' [1985] *Public Law* 564.
[113] D Shelton, 'Hierarchy of Norms and Human Rights: Of Trumps and Winners' (2002) 65 *Saskatchewan Law Review* 301, 306.
[114] See generally M Taggart, 'The Nature of the State' in P Cane & M Tushnet (eds), *The Oxford Handbook of Legal Studies* (Oxford, Oxford University Press, 2003) ch 6. International lawyers were criticised for reacting too slowly to these changes. See P Alston, 'The Myopia of the Handmaidens: International Lawyers and Globalization' (1997) 3 *European Journal of International Law* 435, 445.

Bibliography

ABEL, AS (1963–4) 'Materials Proper for Consideration in Certiorari to Tribunals: I' 15 *University of Toronto Law Journal* 102.

AIKEN, S and SCOTT, S (2002) 'Baker v Canada (Minister of Citizenship and Immigration) and the Rights of Children' 14 *Journal of Law and Social Policy* 211.

ALLAN, TRS (1998) 'Procedural Fairness and the Duty of Respect' 18 *Oxford Journal of Legal Studies* 497.

——(1998) 'Fairness, Equality, Rationality: Constitutional Theory and Judicial Review' in C Forsyth and I Hare (eds), *The Golden Metwand and the Crooked Cord* (Oxford, Clarendon Press).

——(2001) *Constitutional Justice: A Liberal Theory of the Rule of Law* (Oxford, Oxford University Press).

ALLARS, M (1990) *Introduction to Australian Administrative Law* (Sydney, Butterworths).

——(1995) 'One Small Step for Legal Doctrine, One Giant Leap Towards Integrity in Government: Teoh's Case and the Internationalization of Administrative Law' 17 *Sydney Law Review* 204.

——(1999) 'Human Rights, Ukases and Merits Review Tribunals: The Impact of *Teoh's case* on the Administrative Appeals Tribunal in Australia' in M Harris and M Partington (eds), *Administrative Justice in the Twenty First Century* (Oxford, Hart Publishing).

ALLEN, T (2000) *The Right to Property in Commonwealth Constitutions* (Cambridge, Cambridge University Press).

ALSTON, P (1997) 'The Myopia of the Handmaidens: International Lawyers and Globalization' 3 *European Journal of International Law* 435.

——(ed) (1999) *The EU and Human Rights* (New York, Oxford University Press).

ALVARO, A (1991) 'Why Property Rights Were Excluded from the Canadian Charter of Rights and Freedoms' 24 *Canadian Journal of Political Science* 309.

ANGHIE, A (1999) 'Finding the Peripheries: Sovereignty and Colonialism in Nineteenth-Century International Law' 40 *Harvard International Law Journal* 1.

ARENDT, H (1977), *Between Past and Future: Eight Exercises in Political Thought* (New York, Penguin Books).

ARONSON, M and DYER, B (2000) *Judicial Review of Administrative Action* (Sydney, LBC Information Services).

ARTHURS, H (1985) *'Without the Law': Administrative Justice and Legal Pluralism in Nineteenth Century England* (Toronto, University of Toronto Press).

AQUINAS, T (1964–75) *Summa Theologicae* (New York, Eyre & Spottiswoode and McGraw-Hill).

AUST, A (2000) *Modern Treaty Law and Practice* (Cambridge, Cambridge University Press).

AUSTIN, J (1954) *The Province of Jurisprudence Determined* (London, Weidenfeld & Nicolson).

BAKER, JH (1989) 'Records, Reports and the Origins of Case-Law in England' in JH BAKER (ed), *Judicial Records, Law Reports and the Growth of Case Law* (Berlin, Duncker & Humblot).

BALDWIN, R and HOUGHTON, J (1985) 'Circular Arguments: The Status and Legitimacy of Administrative Rules' *Public Law* 239–84.

BALDWIN R and HAWKINS (1984) 'Discretionary Justice: David Reconsidered' *Public Law* 570.

BARING-GOULD, WS and BARING-GOULD, C (1962) (eds & compliers) *The Annotated Mother Goose: Nursery Rhymes Old and New, Arranged and Explained* (New York, Bramhall House).

BARNARD, K ST C (1999) 'Reflections on the Human Rights Role of the European Parliament', in P Alston (ed), *The EU and Human Rights* (New York, Oxford University Press).

BASTARACHE, M (2000) 'The Honourable GV La Forest's Use of Foreign Materials in the Supreme Court of Canada and His Influence on Foreign Courts' in R Johnson *et al* (eds), *Gérard V LaForest at the Supreme Court of Canada 1985–1997* (Winnipeg, Canadian Legal History Project).

BELLEY, J (1997) 'Law as *terra incognita*: Constructing Legal Pluralism' 12(2) *Canadian Journal of Law and Society* 17.

BENTHAM, J [1789] *An Introduction to the Principles of Morals and Legislation' JH Burns and HLA Hart (eds)* (London, Methuens, 1980)

BERMANN, HJ and REID, CJ 'Roman Law in Europe and the *Jus Commune*: A Historical Overview with emphasis on the New Legal Science of the Sixteenth Century' (1994) 20 *Syracuse Journal of International Law and Commerce*.

BERRYMAN, J (2000) *The Law of Equitable Remedies* (Toronto, Irwin Law).

BESSELINK, L (1998) 'Entrapped by the Maximum Standard: On Fundamental Rights, Pluralism and Subsidiarity in the European Union' 35 *Common Market Law Review* 629.

BLACHE, P and COMTOIS, S (1997) 'L'affaire *Ross*: Normes de contrôle judiciaire—Droits de la personne—Insuffisance de preuve. Rapport entre la norme de raisonnabilité de l'article 1 de la Charte et celle du droit administratif', *Revue du Barreau du Québec* 105.

BLACKSTONE, W [1765] *Commentaries on the Laws of England* (Oxford, Clarendon Press; facsimile, University of Chicago Press, 1979), Volume I.

BOHMAN, J (1997) 'The Public Spheres of the World Citizen' in J Bohman and M Lutz-Bachman (eds), *Perpetual Peace: Essays on Kant's Cosmopolitan Ideal* (Cambridge, Mass, MIT Press).

——and LUTZ-BACHMANN, M (1997) 'Introduction', in J Bohman and M Lutz-Bachmann (eds), *Perpetual Peace: Essays on Kant's Cosmopolitan Ideal* (Cambridge, Mass, MIT Press).

BOUCHARD, G and WAKE CARROL, B (2002) 'Policy-Making and Administrative Discretion: The Case of Immigration in Canada' 45 *Canadian Public Administration* 239.

BOYLE, C and MACCRIMMON, M (2002) 'Reasons for Judgment: A Comment on R v Sheppard and R v Braich' 47 *Criminal Law Quarterly* 39.

BRANDON, E (2002) 'Does international law mean anything in Canadian Courts?' 11 *Journal of Environmental Law and Practice*.

BRIDGES, L, MESZAROS, G and SUNKIN, M (1995) *Judicial Review in Perspective* (London, Cavendish).
BROWN, D and EVANS, J 'Discretionary Justice: Reasons and Reasonableness: Case Comment on Baker' www. brownandevans.com/case.
BRUDNER, A (1985) 'The Domestic Enforcement of International Covenants on Human Rights: A Theoretical Framework', 35 *University of Toronto Law Journal* 219.
BRUNNÉE, J (2002) 'A Long and Winding Road: Bringing International Environmental Law into Canadian Courts' in M Anderson and P Galizzi (eds), *International Environmental Law in National Courts* (London, British Institute of International and Comparative Law) 45.
BRUNNÉE J and TOOPE, SJ (2000) 'International Law and Constructivism: Elements of an Interactional Theory of International Law' 39 *Columbia Journal of Transnational Law* 19.
——(2002) *A Hesitant Embrace: The Application of International Law by Canadian Courts* 40 *Canadian Yearbook of International Law* 3.
——(2002) 'The Changing Nile Basin Regime: Does Law Matter?' 43 *Harvard International Law Journal* 105.
CALABRESI, G (1985) *Ideals, Beliefs and Attitudes: Private Law Perspectives on a Public Law Problem* (Syracuse, NY, Syracuse University Press).
CAIRNS, JA and MACLEOD, G (2002) (eds) *'The dearest birth right of the people of England': The jury in the history of the common law* (Oxford, Hart Publishing).
CAMPBELL, A and GLASS, KATHLEEN C (2001) 'The Legal Status of Clinical and Ethics Policies, Codes, and Guidelines in Medical Practice and Research' 46 *McGill Law Journal* 473–489.
CANON, B (2002) 'Studying Bureaucratic Implementation of Judicial Policies: Conceptual Approaches' paper presented to Tilburg Workshop on *Judicial Review and Bureaucratic Impact* (7 November 2002).
CANON, B and JOHNSON, C (1999) *Judicial Policies: Implementation and Impact*, 2nd edn. (Washington, CQ Press).
CARTIER, G (2001) 'La discrétion administrative: une occasion de dialogue entre citoyens et tribunaux?' in SG Coughlan and D Russell (eds), *Citizenship and Citizen Participation in the Administration of Justice* (Montreal, Éditions Thémis).
——(forthcoming, 2003) 'Administrative Law Twenty Years After the *Charter*', *Revue du Barreau du Québec, Numero Special* 197.
CASSESE, A CLAPHAM, A, and WEILER, J (eds) (1991) *Human Rights and the European Community* (Baden-Baden, Nomos).
CHAMBERS, R [1767–1773] *A Course of Lectures on the English Law: Delivered at the University of Oxford, 1767–1773* TM Curley (ed) (Madison, University of Wisconsin Press, 1986).
CHOUDRY, S (1999) 'Globalization in Search of Justification: Toward a Theory of Comparative Constitutional Interpretation' *Indiana Law Journal* 819.
CHINKIN, C (1989) 'The Challenge of Soft-Law: Development and Change in International Law' 38 *International and Comparative Law Quarterly* 850.
CHWIALKOWSKA, L 'Global law emerging, judge tells conference—Canada struggling to accommodate international treaties and tribunals' *The National Post* (13 April 2002) A6.
CITIZENSHIP AND IMMIGRATION CANADA, *The Ethical Compass* (March 1998), at http://www.cic.gc.ca/english/pub/values%2De.html#case4.

CLAPHAM, A (1990) 'A Human Rights Policy for the European Community' 10 *Yearbook of European Law* 309.
COOKE, R (1992) 'The Quest for Administrative Justice' 18 *Commonwealth Law Bulletin* 1326.
COPPEL, J and O'NEILL, A (1992) 'The European Court of Justice: Taking Rights Seriously?' *Legal Studies: The Journal of the Society of Public Teachers of Law* 227.
COWEL, J (1651) *The Institutes of the Lawes of England* (London, Tho Roycroft).
CRAIG, P (1994) 'The Common Law, Reasons and Administrative Justice' 53 *Cambridge Law Journal* 282.
——(1997) 'Formal and Substantive Conceptions of the Rule of Law: An Analytical Framework' [1997] *Public Law* 467
——(1998) 'Ultra Vires and the Foundations of Judicial Review' *Cambridge Law Journal* 63.
——(1999) 'Competing Models of Judicial Review' *Public Law* 428
——(1999) *Administrative Law* 4th edn (Sweet & Maxwell, London).
——[2000] 'Public Law, Political Theory and Legal Theory' *Public Law* 211.
——(2001) 'The Courts, the Human Rights Act and Judicial Review' 117 *Law Quarterly Review* 589.
CRAIG and DE BÚRCA (2002) *EU Law, Text, Cases and Materials* 3rd edn, (Oxford, Oxford University Press).
CREYKE, R and MACMILLAN, J (2002) 'The External Review Project' 9 *Australian Journal of Administrative Law* 163.
CRUMP, D (1996) 'How Do the Courts *Really* Discover Unenumerated Fundamental Rights? Cataloguing the Methods of Judicial Alchemy' 19 *Harvard Journal of Law and Public Policy* 795.
CROSS, SIR RUPERT (1995) *Statutory Interpretation* 3rd edn, (London, Butterworths).
CURRIE, JH (2001) *Public International Law* (Toronto, Irwin Law).
CURSON, H (1699) *A Compendium Of The Laws and Government Ecclesiasitical, Civil and Military* (London, Asssigns of Rich & Edw Atkins for J Walthoe).
DANIELS, RJ, MACKLIN, P, and ROACH, K (eds) (2001) *The Security of Freedom: Essays on Canada's Anti-Terrorism Bill* (Toronto, University of Toronto Press).
DAVIS, KC (1969) *Discretionary Justice: A Preliminary Inquiry* (Baton Rouge, Louisiana State University)
DAUSES, M (1985) 'The Protection of Fundamental Rights in the Community Legal Order' *European Law Review* 398.
DE BRACTON, H (1968) *De Legibus et Consuetudinibus Angliae*, SE Thorne (tr) (Cambridge, Mass, Belknap Press).
DE BÚRCA, G (1993) 'The Principle of Proportionality and its Application in EC Law' 13 *Yearbook of European Law* 105.
——(1993) 'Fundamental Human Rights and the Reach of EC law' 13 *Oxford Journal of Legal Studies* 283.
——(1997) 'The Role of Equality in European Community Law' in S O'Leary and A Dashwood (eds), *The Principle of Equal Treatment in EC Law* (London, Sweet & Maxwell).
DE SMITH, SA (1960) *The Lawyers and the Constitution* (London, G Bell and Sons Ltd) 8 (published Inaugural Lecture at the University of London, London School of Economics, 10 May 1960).

DE SMITH (1995) in Woolf and Jowell, *Judicial Review of Administrative Action* 4th edn, (London, Sweet & Maxwell).
DE WITTE, B (1997). 'The Past and Future Role of the European Court of Justice in the Protection of Human Rights' in P Alston (ed), *The EU and Human Rights* (New York, Oxford University Press).
DE ZULUETA, F (tr) (1946) *The Institutes of Gauis* (Oxford, Clarendon Press).
DES ROSIERS N and FELDTHUSSEN, B (1992) 'Discretion in Social Assistance Legislation' *Journal of Law & Social Policy* 204.
DETRICK, S (comp & ed) (1992) *The United Nations Convention on the Rights of the Child: A Guide to the 'Travaux Préparatoires'* (Dordrecht, Martinus Nijhoff Publishers).
DEVLIN, P (1966) *Trial by Jury* (London, Stevens).
DICEY, AV (1908) *Introduction to the Study of the Law of the Constitution* 7th edn (London, MacMillan & Co).
DOYLE, HON J (1999) 'Accountability: Parliament, the Executive and the Judiciary' in S Kneebone (ed), *Administrative Law and the Rule of Law: Still Part of the Same Package? 1998 Administrative Law Forum* (Canberra, AIAL).
DUGDALE, W (1671) *Origines Juridiciales, Or Historical Memorials Of The English Laws*, 2nd edn (Savoy, Tho Newcomb).
DWORKIN, R (1978) *Taking Rights* Seriously (Cambridge, Mass, Harvard University Press).
——(1986) *Law's Empire* (Cambridge, Mass, Belknap Press).
DYZENHAUS, D (1997) 'The Politics of Deference: Judicial Review and Democracy' in M Taggart (ed), *The Province of Administrative Law* (Oxford, Hart Publishing).
——(1998) 'Law as Justification: Etienne Mureinik's Conception of Legal Culture' 14 *South African Journal on Human Rights* 11.
——(1998) 'Reuniting the Brain: The Democratic Basis of Judicial Review' 9 *Public Law Review* 98.
——(1999) (ed) *Recrafting the Rule of Law* (Oxford, Hart Publishing).
——(2000) 'Form and Substance in the Rule of Law: A Democratic Justification for Judicial Review?' in C FORSYTH (ed), *Judicial Review and the Constitution* (Oxford, Hart Publishing).
DYZENHAUS D and FOX-DECENT, E (2001) 'Rethinking the Process/Substance Distinction: *Baker v Canada*' 51 *University of Toronto Law Journal* 193.
DYZENHAUS D and TAGGART, M and HUNT, M (2001) 'The Principle of Legality in Administrative Law: Internationalization as Constitutionalization' 1 *Oxford University Commonwealth Law Journal* 5.
DYZENHAUS, D (2002) 'Constituting the Rule of Law: Fundamental Values in Administrative Law' 27 *Queen's Law Journal* 445.
——(forthcoming) 'Humpty Dumpty Rules or the Rule of Law: Legal Theory and the Adjudication of National Security' *Australian Journal of Legal Philosophy.*
——(forthcoming) 'The Justice of the Common Law: Judges, Democracy and the Limits of the Rule of Law' in C SAUNDERS and K LE ROY (eds), *Perspectives on the Rule of Law*, (Sydney, Federation Press).
ELLIOT, M (1999) 'The Demise of Parliamentary Sovereignty: The Implications for Justifying Judicial Review', 115 *Law Quarterly Review* 119.
——[1999] 'The Ultra Vires Doctrine in a Constitutional Setting: Still the Central Principle of Administrative Law' *Cambridge Law Journal* 129.

——(2001) *The Constitutional Foundations of Judicial Review* (Oxford, Hart Publishing).
ELLIS, E (ed) (1999) *The Principle of Proportionality in the Laws of Europe* (Oxford, Hart Publishing).
EVANS, JM (1991) 'The Principles of Fundamental Justice: The Constitution and The Common Law' 29 *Osgoode Hall Law Journal* 51.
EVANS, JM and JANISCH, H, MULLAN, D, RISK, RCB (1995) *Administrative Law: Cases, Text, and Materials* 4th edn, (Toronto, Edmond Montgomery Publications Ltd).
EWING, K (1999) 'The Human Rights Act 1998' 62 *Modern Law Review* 79.
EWING, K and GEARTY, C (1997) 'Rocky Foundations for Labour's New Rights' *European Human Rights Law Review* 146.
FINN, P (1995) 'The Forgotten "Trust": The People and the State' in M Cope (ed) *Equity Issues and Trends, 1995* (The Foundation Press).
FLIKSCHUH, K (2000) *Kant and Modern Political Philosophy* (Cambridge, Cambridge University Press).
FLYNN, L (1999) 'The Implications of Article 13—After Amsterdam Will Some Forms of Discrimination be More Equal than Others?' 36 *Common Market Law Review* 1127.
FORSYTH, C [1996] 'Of Fig Leaves and Fairy Tales: The Ultra Vires Doctrine, the Sovereignty of Parliament and Judicial Review' *Cambridge Law Journal* 122.
FOX-DECENT, E (2003) 'Sovereignty's Promise: The State as Fiduciary' (PhD thesis, Department of Philosophy, University of Toronto).
FRANKFURTER, F (1942) 'The Final Report of the Attorney-General's Committee on Administrative Procedure' 42 *Col LR* 585.
FULLER, L (1969) *The Morality of Law* (New Haven, Yale University Press).
——(1958) 'Human Purpose and Natural Law' 3 *Natural Law Forum* 68.
GALLIGAN, D (1986) *Discretionary Powers: A Legal Study of Official Discretion* (Oxford, Clarendon Press).
——(1996) *Due Process and Fair Procedures: A Study of Administrative Procedures* (Oxford, Clarendon Press)
GANZ, G (1987) *Quasi-Legislation: Recent Developments in Secondary Legislation* (London, Sweet & Maxwell).
GEARTY, C (2002) 'Reconciling Parliamentary Democracy and Human Rights' 118 *Law Quarterly Review* 248.
GIERKE, O (1958) *Political Theories of the Middle Ages*, FW Maitland (tr) (Boston, Beacon Hill Press).
GILLIS, C 'Mother in battle over deportation legally a resident', *National Post* 22 December 2001.
GLEESON, HON M (2000) *The Rule of Law and the Constitution* Boyer Lectures 2000 (Sydney, ABC Books).
GLENN, P (1987) 'Persuasive Authority' 32 *McGill Law Journal* 262.
GOUGH, GW (1955) *Fundamental Law in English Constitutional History* (Oxford, Oxford University Press).
GRAHAM, CB and HAYS, SW (1986) 'Citizen Access and the Control of Administrative Discretion' in DH Shumavon and HK Hibbeln (ed), *Administrative Discretion and Public Policy Implementation* (New York, Praeger Publishing).

GRAZIADEI, M (1993) 'Changing Images of the Law in XIX Century English Legal Thought (The Continental Impulse)' in M Reimann (ed), *The Reception of Continental Ideas in the Common Law World 1820–1920* (Berlin, Duncker & Humblot).
GRIFFITHS, JAG (1977) *The Politics of the Judiciary* (London, Penguin Books).
——(1985) 'Judicial Decision-Making in Public Law' *Public Law* 564.
GROTIUS, H [1646] *De jure belli ac pacis libri tres* 2 Volumes, Volume II: FW Kelsey (trs) (Washington, Carnegie Institution of Washington, 1913 (Volume I) 1925 (Volume II)).
HABERMAS, J (1997) 'Kant's Idea of Perpetual Peace, with the Benefit of Two Hundred Years' Hindsight' in J Bohman and M Lutz- Bachman (eds), *Perpetual Peace: Essays on Kant's Cosmopolitan Ideal* (Cambridge, Mass, MIT Press).
HAHN, RK (1988) 'The British Influence on the Initiation and Introduction of Commonwealth Bill of Rights' 26 *Journal of Commonwealth Comparative Politics* 54.
HALLIDAY, S (2000) 'The Influence of Judicial Review on Bureaucratic Decision-Making' *Public Law* 110.
HAMMOND (1998) 'Judicial Review: the continuing interplay between law and policy' *Public Law* 34.
HANDLER, J (1988) 'Dependent People, the State and the Modern/Postmodern Search for the Dialogic Community' 35 *UCLA Law Review* 999.
HARLOW, C (1995) 'A Special Relationship? American Influences on Judicial Review in England' in I Loveland (ed), *A Special Relationship? American Influences on Public Law in the UK* (Oxford, Clarendon Press).
HARRINGTON, J (2002) 'The Year in Review: Developments in International Law and Its Application in Canada' (Presentation to the Canadian Bar Association Conference on Directions in International Law and Practice, Ottawa, 30 March 2002) at 8 [unpublished, on file with authors].
HARVEY, C (2000) *Seeking Asylum in the UK: Problems and Prospects* (London, Butterworths).
HAWKINS, K (1992) 'The Uses of Legal Discretion: Perspectives from Law and Social Science' in K Hawkins (ed), *The Uses of Discretion* (Oxford, Clarendon Press).
HAWKINS, RE (1983) 'Making Section 1 Work' in The Law Society of Upper Canada, *Charter of Rights and Administrative Law 1983–1984* (Toronto, Carswell).
HEDLEY, S (1995) 'Words, Words, Words: Making Sense of Legal Judgments, 1875–1940' in C Stebbings (ed), *Law Reporting in Britain* (London, The Hambledon Press 169.
HELD, D (1995) *Democracy and the Global Order: From the Modern State to Cosmopolitan Governance* (Cambridge, Polity Press).
——(2002) 'Law of States, Law of Peoples: Three Models of Sovereignty' 8 *Legal Theory* 1.
HELMHOLZ, H (1999) 'Magna Carta and *Ius Commune*' 66 *University of Chicago Law Review* 297.
HEYDON, HON JD (2003) 'Judicial Activism and the Death of the Rule of Law' 47 *Quadrant* 9.
HIEBERT, J (1991) *Determining the Limits of Charter Rights: How Much Discretion do Governments Retain* (Toronto, Ph.D. Dissertation).
HO, HL (2000) 'The judicial duty to give reasons' 20 *Legal Studies* 42.

HOBBES, T [1681] *A Dialogue Between A Philosopher and A Student of The Common Laws of England*, J Cropsey (ed) (Chicago, University of Chicago Press, 1971).

HOGG, P and BUSHELL, A (1997) 'The *Charter* Dialogue Between Courts and Legislatures (Or Perhaps the *Charter of Rights* Isn't Such a Bad Thing After All)' 35 *Osgoode Hall Law Journal* 75.

HOULE, F (2001) 'La zone fictive de l'infra-droit: l'integration des regles administratives dans la categorie des texts reglementaires' (2001) 47 *McGill Law Journal* 161.

——(2002) 'L'arrêt Baker: Le rôle des règles administratives dans la réception du droit international des droits de la personne en droit interne' 28 *Queen's Law Journal* 511.

HUNT M (1998) *Using Human Rights Law in English Courts* (Oxford, Hart Publishing).

—— (forthcoming) 'Sovereignty's Blight: Why Contemporary Public Law Needs the Concept of "Due Deference"' in N Bamforth and P Leyland (eds), *Public Law in a Multi-Layered Constitution* (Oxford, Hart Publishing).

JACKSON, KT (1993) 'Global Rights and Regional Jurisprudence' 12 *Law & Philosophy* 157.

JACOBS, F and WHITE, R (1996) *The European Convention on Human Rights* 2nd edn (Oxford, Oxford University Press).

JANIS, MW (1984) 'Jeremy Bentham and the Fashioning of "International Law"' 78 *American Journal of International Law* 405.

JANISCH, HN (1992) 'The Choice of Decision-Making Method: Adjudication, Policies, and Rule-Making' in Administrative Law: Principles, Practices, and Pluralism, Special Lectures of the Law Society of Upper Canada (Scarborough, Carswell)

JANISCH, HN and MULLAN DJ and RISK, RCB (1995) *Administrative Law—Cases, Text and Materials*, 4th edn (Toronto, Emond Montgomery Publications).

JANISCH, HN and SMITH, E (1995) *Administrative Law Supplement*, a supplement to *Administrative Law—Cases, Text and Materials*, 4th edn (Toronto, Emond Montgomery Publications)

JOSEPH, P (2002) *Constitutional and Administrative Law in New Zealand* 2nd edn (Wellington, Brookers).

JOWELL, JL 'Is Equality a Constitutional Principle?' (1994) 47 *Current Legal Problems* 1.

——(1999) 'Of Vires and Vacuums: The Constitutional Context of Judicial Review' *Public Law* 448.

JOWELL, JL and LESTER, A (1987) 'Beyond *Wednesbury*: Substantive Principles of Administrative Law' *Public Law* 368.

KANT, I [1795] 'Toward Perpetual Peace: A Philosophical Project' in MJ Gregor (tr and ed), *Practical Philosophy* (Cambridge, Cambridge University Press, 1996).

——*The Metaphysics of Morals*, in MJ Gregor (tr and ed) *Practical Philosophy* (Cambridge, Cambridge University Press, 1996).

——*Groundwork of The Metaphysics of Morals*, in MJ Gregor (tr and ed) *Practical Philosophy* (Cambridge, Cambridge University Press, 1996).

——*Theory and Practice*, in MJ Gregor (tr and ed*) Practical Philosophy* (Cambridge, Cambridge University Press, 1996).

KELLEY, K and TREBILCOCK, M (1998) *The Making of the Mosaic: A History of Canadian Immigration Policy* (Toronto, University of Toronto Press).
KELLY, J (1999) 'Bureaucratic Activism and the *Charter* of Rights: The Department of Justice and its entry into the Centre of Government' 42 *Canadian Public Administration* 476.
KERANS, RP (1994) *Standards of Review Employed by Appellate Courts* (Edmonton, Juriliber).
KINDRED, HM (2002) 'The Use of Unimplemented Treaties in Canada: Practice and Prospects in the Supreme Court' in C Carmody *et al* (eds), *Trilateral Perspectives on International Legal Issues: Conflict and Coherence* [forthcoming in 2002] [manuscript on file with the authors; page references to manuscript].
KIRBY, M (1986) 'Accountability and the Right to Reasons' in M Taggart (ed), *Judicial Review of Administrative Action in the 1980s: Problem and Prospects* (Auckland, Oxford University Press).
——(1994) 'Reasons for Judgment: "Always Permissible, Usually Desirable and Often Obligatory"' 12 *Australian Bar Review* 121.
KLATER, CE (1994) 'The Americanization of Blackstone's *Commentaries*' in EA Cawthorn & DE Narrett (eds), *Essays on English Law and the American Experience* (Texas, Texas A & M University Press).
KNOP, K (2000) 'Here and There: International Law in Domestic Courts' 32 *New York University Journal of International Law & Politics* 507.
KOH, HH (1988) 'Bringing International Law Home' 35 *Houston Law Review* 623.
——(1997) 'Why Do Nations Obey International Law?' 106 *Yale Law Journal* 2599.
KOSKENNIEMI, M (2002) *The Gentle Civilizer of Nations: The Rise and Fall of International Law 1870–1960* (Cambridge, Cambridge University Press).
KUNKEL, W (1966) *An Introduction to Roman Legal and Constitutional History* (Oxford, Clarendon Press).
KUPER, A (2000) 'Rawlsian Global Justice: Beyond *The Law of Peoples* to a Cosmopolitan Law of Persons' 28 *Political Theory* 640.
LAFOREST, GV (1988) 'The Use of International and Foreign Materials in the Supreme Court of Canada' 17 *Canadian Council of International Lawyers Proceedings* 230.
——(1996) 'The Expanding Role of the Supreme Court of Canada in International Law Issues' 34 *Canadian Yeabook of International Law* 89.
LANDAUER, C (2002) 'From Status to Treaty: Henry Summer Maine's *International Law*' 15 *Canadian Journal of Law and Jurisprudence* 219.
LAUTERPACHT, H (1939) 'Is International Law a Part of the Law of England?' 25 *Transactions of the Grotius Society* 51.
LAWS, J (1998) '*Wednesbury*', in C Forsyth and I Hare, *The Golden Metwand and the Crooked Cord: Essays on Public Law in Honour of Sir William Wade* (Oxford, Clarendon Press).
LEBEL, L and CHAO, G (2002) 'The Rise of International Law in Canadian Constitutional Litigation: Fugue or Fusion? Recent Developments and Challenges in Internalizing International Law' (Fifth Annual Analysis of the Constitutional Decisions of the Supreme Court of Canada, Osgoode Hall Law School, 12 April 2002) at 6 [unpublished, on file with authors].
LEIGH, I (2002) 'Taking Rights Proportionately: Judicial Review, the Human Rights Act and Strasbourg' *Public Law* 265.

LENAERTS, K (1991) 'Fundamental Rights to be Included in a Community Catalogue' 16 *European Law Review* 367.
LE SUEUR, AP (1999) 'Legal Duties To Give Reasons' 52 *Current Legal Problems* 150.
L'HEUREUX-DUBÉ (1998) 'The Importance of Dialogue: Globalisation and the International Impact of the Rehnquist Court' 34 *Tulsa Law Journal* 15.
——(2001) 'From Many Different Stones: A House of Justice', Notes for an Address to the International Association of Women Judges, Montreal 10 Nov 2001.
LIPSKY, M (1980) *Street Level Bureaucracy: Dilemmas of the Individual in Public Services* (New York, Russell Sage Foundation).
LOWE, V (2000) 'The Politics of Law-Making: Are the Method and Character of Norm Creation Changing?' in M Byers (ed), *The Role of Law in International Politics: Essays in International Relations and International Law* (New York, Oxford University Press).
MACDONALD, RA (1980) 'Judicial Review and Procedural Fairness in Administrative Law: I' *McGill Law Journal* 520.
MACDONALD, RA and LAMETTI, D (1990) 'Reasons for Decisions in Administrative Law' 3 *Canadian Journal of Law and Administrative Practice* 123.
MACDONALD, RA (1998) 'Metaphors of Multiplicity: Civil Society, Regimes and Legal Pluralism' (1998) 15 *Arizona Journal of Comparative and International Law* 69.
MACDONALD, R St J (1974) 'The Relationship between International Law and Domestic Law in Canada' in R St J Macdonald, G Morris and DM Johnston (eds), *Canadian Perspectives on International Law and Organization* (Toronto, University of Toronto Press).
MACKINTOSH, J (1934) *Roman Law in Modern Practice* (Edinburgh, W Green & Son).
MACKINTOSH, J (1799) *A Discourse on the Study of the Law of Nature and Nations* (London, J Debrett & W Clarke).
MAINE, HS (1888) *International Law: A Series of Lectures Delivered Before the University of Cambridge, 1887* (New York, H Holt).
——(1905) *Ancient Law* (London, John Murray).
MARKESINIS, BS (1997) *The German Law of Obligations* 3rd edn (Oxford, Clarendon Press).
MASHAW, J (1985) *Due Process in the Administrative State* (New Haven, Conn, Yale University Press).
MASON, K (1995) 'The Rule of Law' in P Finn (ed), *Essays on Law and Government Vol 1 Principles and Values* (Sydney, Law Book Co).
MCGOLDRICK, D (1991) 'The United Nations Convention on the Rights of the Child' 5 *International Journal of Law and the Family* 132.
MCLACHLIN, B (1999) 'The Role of Administrative Tribunals and Courts in Maintaining the Rule of Law' 12 *Canadian Journal of Administrative Law and Practice* 171.
MILSOM, SFC (1985) *Studies in the History of the Common Law* (London, The Hambledon Press).
MORAN, M (2001) 'An Uncivil Action: The Tort of Torture and Cosmopolitan Private Law' in C Scott (ed), *The Tort of Torture* (Oxford, Hart Publishing).
——(2003) *Rethinking the Reasonable Person: An Egalitarian Reconstruction of the Objective Standard* (Oxford, Oxford University Press).

MORRIS, MH (1998) 'Administrative Decision-makers and the Duty to Give Reasons: An Emerging Debate' 11 *Canadian Journal of Law and Administrative Practice* 155.
MULLAN, D (1999) 'Baker v Canada (Minister of Citizenship and Immigration)—A Defining Moment in Canadian Immigration Law' 7 *Reid's Administrative Law* 145;
——(2000) 'The Role of the Judiciary in the Review of Administrative Policy Decisions: Issues of Legality' Mossman and Otis (eds), *The Judiciary as Third Branch of Government: Manifestations and Challenges to Legitimacy* (Montréal, Les Éditions Thémis).
——(2001) 'The Supreme Court of Canada and Tribunals—Deference to the Administrative Process: A Recent Phenomenon or a Return to Basics?' 80 *Canadian Bar Review* 399.
——(2001) *Administrative Law* (Toronto, Irwin Law).
NANDA, VP (2001) 'Self-Determination and Secession Under International Law' 29 *Denver Journal of International Law and Policy* 305.
NEUWAHL, N and ROSAS, R (eds) (1995) *The European Union and Human Rights* (Martinus Nijhoff Publishers; The Hague, Kluwer Law International).
NEDELSKY, J (1997) 'Embodied Diversity and the Challenges to Law' 42 *McGill Law Journal* 91.
NUSSBAUM, M (1997) 'Kant and Cosmopolitanism', in J Bohman and M Lutz-Bachman (eds), *Perpetual Peace: Essays on Kant's Cosmopolitan Ideal* (Cambridge, Mass, MIT Press).
O'LEARY, S (1995) 'The Relationship between Community Citizenship and the Protection of Fundamental Rights in Community Law' 32 *Common Market Law Review* 519.
O'LEARY, S and DASHWOOD, A (ed) (1977), *The Principle of Equal Treatment in EC Law* (London, Sweet & Maxwell).
OLIVER, D (1987) 'Is the Ultra Vires Rule the Basis of Judicial Review?' *Public Law* 543.
——(1999) *Common Values and the Public-Private Divide* (London, Butterworths).
OPIE, I and P (eds) (1951) *The Oxford Dictionary of Nursery Rhymes* (Oxford, Clarendon Press).
PEERS, S (2002) 'The New Regulation on Access to Documents: A Critical Analysis' 21 *Yearbook of European Law*.
PENNINGTON, K (1993) *The Prince and the Law, 1200–1600: Sovereignty and Rights in the Western Legal Tradition* (Berkeley, University of California Press).
PERRY, S (1987) 'Judicial Obligation, Precedent and the Common Law' *Oxford Journal of Legal Studies* 215.
PHELAN, D (1992) 'Right to Life of the Unborn v Promotion of Trade in Services: The European Court of Justice and the Normative Shaping of the European Union' 55 *Modern Law Review* 670.
PLAXTON, MC (2002) 'Thinking about Appeals, Authority, and Judicial Power after R v Sheppard' 47 *Criminal Law Quarterly* 59.
PLUCKNETT, TFT and BARTON, JL (eds) (1974) *St. German's Doctor and Student* (London, Selden Society)
PUFENDORF, S [1688] *De Jure Naturae et Gentium Libri Octo*, 2 Volumes, Volume II: CH Oldfather and WA Oldfather (trs) (Oxford, Clarendon Press, 1934).

RAWLS, J (1993) *Political Liberalism* (New York, Columbia University Press).
——(1999) *The Law of Peoples* (Cambridge, Mass, Harvard University Press).
RAZ, J (1977) 'The Rule of Law and its Virtues' 93 *Law Quarterly Review* 195.
——(1979) *The Authority of Law: Essays on Law and Morality* (Oxford, Clarendon Press).
——(1990) 'The Politics of the Rule of Law' 3 *Ratio Juris* 331.
RICHARDSON, G and MACHIN, D (2000) 'Judicial Review and Tribunal Decision-Making: A Study of the Mental Health Review Tribunal' *Public Law* 494.
RICHARDSON, H (1999) 'Administrative Policy-Making: Rule of Law or Bureaucracy?' in D Dyzenhaus (ed), *Recrafting the Rule of Law* (Oxford, Hart Publishing).
RISHWORTH, P, HUSCROFT, G, OPTICAN, S, and MAHONEY, R (2003) *The New Zealand Bill of Rights* (Melbourne, Oxford University Press).
RISK, RCB and POND, RC (1996) 'Rights Talk in Canada in the Late Nineteenth Century: The Good Sense and Right Feeling of the People' 14 *Law and History Review* 1.
ROACH, K (2001) 'Constitutional and Common Law Dialogues Between the Supreme Court and Canadian Legislatures' 80 *Canadian Bar Review* 481.
——(2001) *The Supreme Court on Trial: Judicial Activism and Democratic Dialogue* (Toronto, Irwin Law).
ROBSON, P (1998) 'Judicial Review and Social Security' in T Buck (ed), *Judicial Review and Social Welfare* (London, Pinter).
SANDARS, TC (tr) (1874) *The Institutes of Justinian* (London, Longmans, Green & Co).
SANTOS, B (1995) *Toward a New Common Sense: Law, Science and Politics in the Paradigmatic Transition* (London, Routledge).
SCHABAS, WA (2000) 'Twenty-five Years of Public International Law at the Supreme Court of Canada' 79 *Canadian Bar Review* 174.
SCHEININ, M (unpublished 2002) 'The Human Rights Committee's Pronouncements on the Right to an Effective Remedy—an Illustration of the Legal Nature of the Committee's Work under the Optional Protocol'
SCHWARZE, J (1992) *European Administrative Law* (London, Sweet & Maxwell).
SEDLEY, S (1995) 'Human Rights: a Twenty-Frist Century Agenda', *Public Law* 386.
——(1994) 'Sounds of Silence: Constitutional Law Without A Constitution' 110 *Law Quarterly Review* 270.
SHAPIRO, M (1992) 'The Giving Reasons Requirement' *The University of Chicago Legal Forum* 179.
SHAPIRO, S and LEVY, R (1987) 'Heightened Scrutiny of the Fourth Branch: Separation of Powers and the Requirement of Adequate Reasons for Agency Decisions' *Duke Law Journal* 387.
SHARPE, RJ (1995) *The Law of Habeas Corpus* 2nd edn (Oxford, Clarendon Press).
——(2001) review of D Clark and G McCoy, *The Most Fundamental Legal Right: Habeas Corpus and the Commonwealth*, 1 *Oxford University Commonwealth Law Journal* 287.
SHELTON, D (2002) 'Hierarchy of Norms and Human Rights: Of Trumps and Winners' 65 *Saskatchewan Law Review* 301.
SHILTON, E (1993) 'Charter Litigation and the Policy Processes of Government: A Public Interest Account' in P Monahan and M Finkelstein (eds), *The Impact of the Charter on the Public Policy Process* (North York, On, York University Centre for Public Law and Public Policy).

SIMON, W 'Legality, Bureaucracy and Class in the Welfare System' 92 *Yale Law Journal* 1198.
SIMPSON, AWB (1973) 'The Common Law and Legal Theory' in Simpson (ed) *Oxford Essays in Jurisprudence* 2nd series, (Oxford, Oxford University Press).
——(2001) *Human Rights and the End of Empire: Britain and the Genesis of the European Convention* (Oxford, Oxford University Press).
——(1992) *In the Highest Degree Odious: Detention Without Trial in Wartime Britain* (Oxford, Clarendon Press).
SOSSIN, L (1992) 'The Politics of Discretion: Toward a Critical Theory of Public Administration' 36 *Canadian Public Administration* 364.
——(1994) 'Redistributing Democracy: Authority, Discretion and the Possibility of Engagement in the Welfare State' 26 *Ottawa Law Review* 1.
——(2000) 'Developments in Administrative Law: The 1997–98 and 1998–99 Terms', 11 *Supreme Court Law Review* (2d) 37.
——(2001) 'Regulating Virtue: A Purposive Approach to the Administration of Charities in Canada' in J Phillips, *et al* (eds), *Charities: Between State and Market* (Kingston, McGill-Queen's Press).
——(2002) 'An Intimate Approach to Fairness, Impartiality and Reasonableness in Administrative Law' 27 *Queen's Law Journal* 809.
——(2002) 'Law and Intimacy in the Bureaucrat-Citizen Relationship' in N des Rosiers (ed), *No Person is an Island: Personal Relationships of Dependence and Independence* (Vancouver, University of British Columbia Press).
——(2002) 'The Politics of Soft Law: How Judicial Decisions Influence Bureaucratic Discretion in Canada' paper presented to the Tilburg Workshop on *Judicial Review and Bureaucratic Impact*.
——(2003) 'Public Fiduciary Obligations, Political Trusts and the Evolving Duty of Reasonableness in Administrative Law' 66 *Saskatchewan Law Review* 101.
——'Discretion Unbound: Reconciling Soft Law and the *Charter*' (2002) 45 Canadian Public Administration (forthcoming).
SOSSIN L and BRYANT, M (2002) *Public Law* (Toronto, Carswell).
SOSSIN L and SMITH, C (2003) 'Hard Choices and Soft Law: Ethical Codes, Policy Guidelines and the Role of the Courts in Regulating Government' 40 *Alberta Law Review* (forthcoming).
SPIELMANN, D (1999) 'Human Rights Case Law in the Strasbourg and Luxembourg Courts: Conflicts, Inconsistencies and Complementarities' in P Alston (ed), *The EU and Human Rights* (New York, Oxford University Press).
SPIRO, PJ (2000) 'Globalization, International Law, and the Academy' 32 *New York University Journal of International Law & Politics* 567.
SPRAGUE, JLH (1999) 'Another View of Baker', 7 *Reid's Administrative Law* 163.
——(2000) 'Remedies for the Failure to Provide Reasons' 13 *Canadian Journal of Administrative Law and Practice* 209.
STERETT, S (1997) *Creating Constitutionalism? The Politics of Legal Expertise and Administrative Law in England and Wales* (Ann Arbor, The University of Michigan Press).
STUART, MACKENZIE LORD. (1977) *The European Communities and the Rule of Law* (London, Stevens).
SULLIVAN, R (1994) *Driedger on the Construction of Statutes* 3rd edn (Markham, Butterworths).

SUNKIN, M (2002) 'Methodological and Conceptual Issues in Researching the Impact of Judicial Review on Government Bureaucracies' (paper presented to Tilburg Workshop on Judicial Review and Bureaucratic Impact).

SUNKIN, M and PICK, K (2001) 'The Changing Impact of Judicial Review' *Public Law* 736.

TAGGART, M (1983) 'Should Canadian Judges Be Legally Required To Give Reasoned Decisions in Civil Cases' 33 *University of Toronto Law Journal* 1.

——(1986) (ed) *Judicial Review of Administrative Action in the 1980s: Problems and Prospects* (Auckland, Oxford University Press).

——(1988) 'Expropriation, Public Purpose and the Constitution' in C Forsyth and I Hare (eds), *The Golden Metwand and the Crooked Cord: Essays in Public Law in Honour of Sir William Wade QC* (Oxford, Clarendon Press).

——(1992) 'The Rationalisation of Administrative Tribunal Procedure: The New Zealand Experience' in R Creyke (ed), *Administrative Tribunals: Taking Stock* (Australian National University, Canberra, Centre for International & Public Law).

——(1996) 'Outside Canadian Administrative Law' 46 *University of Toronto Law Journal* 649.

——(1996) 'Legitimate Expectations and Treaties in the High Court of Australia' 112 *Law Quarterly Review* 50.

——(1997) 'The Contribution of Lord Cooke to Scope of Review Doctrine in Administrative Law: A Comparative Common Law Perspective' in P Rishworth (ed), *The Struggle for Simplicity in Law: Essays for Lord Cooke of Thorndon* (Wellington, Butterworths).

——(2002) *Private Property and Abuse of Rights in Victorian England: The Story of Edward Pickles and the Bradford Water Supply* (Oxford, Oxford University Press).

——(2003) 'The Nature of the State' in P Cane and M Tushnet (eds), *The Oxford Handbook of Legal Studies* (Oxford, Oxford University Press).

——(2003) 'Reinventing Administrative Law' in N Bamforth and P Leyland (eds), *Public Law in a Multi-Layered Constitution* (Oxford, Hart Publishing).

TAYLOR, C (1985) 'What's wrong with negative liberty' in *Philosophy and the Human Sciences: Philosophical Papers* 2 211.

TAYLOR, GDS (1991) *Judicial Review: A New Zealand Perspective* (Wellington, Butterworths).

TOOHEY (1993) 'A Government of Laws, Not Men?' 4 *Public Law Review* 159.

TOOPE, S (1998) 'Canada and International Law' 27 *Canadian Council of International Lawyers Proceedings* 33.

——(1999) Case Comment on *Quebec Secession Reference* 93 *American Journal of International Law* 519.

——(2001) 'The Uses of Metaphor: International Law and the Supreme Court of Canada' 80 *Canadian Bar Review* 534.

——(2001) 'Inside and Out: The Stories of International Law and Domestic Law' 50 *University of Brunswick Law Journal* 11

TREMBLAY, LB (1984) 'Section 7 of the *Charter*: Substantive Due Process?' 18 *University of British Columbia Law Review* 201.

TRIDIMAS, T (1999) The General Principles of EC Law (Oxford, Oxford University Press).

TROUWBORST, A (2002) *Evolution and Status of the Precautionary Principle in International Law* (Boston, Kluwer Law International).
TUBBS, JW (2000) *The Common Law Mind: Medieval and Early Modern Conceptions* (Baltimore, John Hopkins University Press).
TUCK, R (1979) *Natural Rights Theories: Their Origin and Development* (Cambridge, Cambridge University Press).
TULLY, J (2000) 'The Unattained Yet Attainable Democracy: Canada and Quebec Face the New Century' (Montreal, Programme d'études sur le Québec de L'Université McGill).
TUSHNET, M (1999) 'The Possibilities of Comparative Constitutional Law' 108 *Yale Law Journal* 1225.
TWINING, W (2000) *Globalization and Legal Theory* (Evanston, Northwestern University Press).
TWOMEY, P (1994) 'The European Union: Three Pillars without a Human Rights Foundation' in D O'Keeffe and P Twomey (eds), *Legal Issues of the Maastricht Treaty* (London, Chancery Law).
VAJDA, C (1979) 'Some Aspects of Judicial Review within the Common Agricultural Policy—Part II' 4 *European Law Review* 341.
VAN DIJK, P and VAN HOOF, G (1998) *Theory and Practice of the European Convention on Human Rights*, 3rd edn (Netherlands, Kluwer).
VAN ERT, G (2000) 'Using Treaties in Canadian Courts' 38 *Canadian Yearbook of International Law* 3.
——(2002) *Using International Law in Canadian Courts* (The Hague, Kluwer Law International).
VINING, J (1986) *The Authoritative and the Authoritarian* (Chicago, University of Chicago Press).
——(1991) 'Authority and Responsibility: The Jurisprudence of Deference' 43 *Admin Law Review* 135.
VITORINO, A (2001) *The Charter of Fundamental Rights as a Foundation for the Area of Freedom, Justice and Security* (Centre for European Legal Studies, Exeter Paper in European Law, No 4).
VON BOGDANY (2000) 'The European Union as a Human Rights Organization? Human Rights and the Core of the European Union' 37 *Common Market Law Review* 1307.
WADE, HWR and FORSYTH, C (2000) *Administrative Law* 8th edn (Oxford, Oxford University Press).
WADHAM, J (2001) 'The Human Rights Act: One Year On' *European Human Rights Law Review* 620.
WALDRON, J (2002) 'Is the Rule of Law an Essentially Contested Concept (in Florida)' 21 *Law and Philosophy* 137.
WALTERS, M (2001) 'The Common Law Constitution in Canada: Return of *Lex Non Scripta* as Fundamental Law' 51 *University of Toronto Law Journal* 91.
WEILER, J (1992)? 'Thou Shalt not Oppress a Stranger: On the Judicial Protection of the Human Rights of Non-Community Nationals—a Critique' *European Journal of International* 65.
WEILER J and LOCKHART, N (1995) '"Taking Rights Seriously" Seriously: The European Court and its Fundamental Rights Jurisprudence' 32 *Common Market Law Review* 51.

WEILER J and FRIES, S (1999) 'A Human Rights Policy for the European Community and Union: The Question of Competences' in P Alston (ed), *The EU and Human Rights* (New York, Oxford University Press).

WEINRIB, LE (2000) 'The Supreme Court of Canada in the Age of Rights' 80 *Canadian Bar Review* 200.

WEINRIB LE and WEINRIB, EJ (2001) 'Constitutional Values and Private Law in Canada' in D Friedmann and D Barak-Erez (eds), *Human Rights in Private Law* (Oxford, Hart Publishing).

WEISER, I (1998) 'Effect in Domestic Law of International Human Rights Treaties Ratified Without Implementing Legislation' 27 *Canadian Council of International Lawyers Proceedings* 132.

—— (2002) 'Undressing the Window: A Proposal for Making International Human Rights Law Meaningful in the Canadian Commonwealth System' (September 2002; on file with authors).

WEST, CC (1991) 'England: ancient constitution and common law' in JH Burns (ed), *The Cambridge History of Political Thought 1450–1700* (Cambridge, Cambridge University Press).

WEXLER, S (1981) 'The Forms of Action and Administrative Law' in *Proceedings of the Administrative Law Conference, Faculty of Law, University of British Columbia, Vancouver, BC, 18–19 October 1979* 292.

WOOD, T (1712) A New Institute of the Imperial or Civil Law (London, WB for Richard Sare).